GOD AND ENCHANTMENT OF PLACE

GOD AND ENCHANTMENT OF PLACE

Reclaiming Human Experience

DAVID BROWN

OXFORD
UNIVERSITY PRESS

OXFORD
UNIVERSITY PRESS

Great Clarendon Street, Oxford OX2 6DP

Oxford University Press is a department of the University of Oxford.
It furthers the University's objective of excellence in research, scholarship,
and education by publishing worldwide in

Oxford New York

Auckland Bangkok Buenos Aires Cape Town Chennai
Dar es Salaam Delhi Hong Kong Istanbul Karachi Kolkata
Kuala Lumpur Madrid Melbourne Mexico City Mumbai Nairobi
São Paulo Shanghai Taipei Tokyo Toronto

Oxford is a registered trade mark of Oxford University Press
in the UK and in certain other countries

Published in the United States
by Oxford University Press Inc., New York

First published 2004
First Pulished in paperback 2006

British Library Cataloguing in Publication Data

Data available

Library of Congress Cataloging-in-Publication Data

Brown, David, 1948 July 1–
God and enchantment of place : reclaiming human experience/David Brown.
p. cm.
1. Sacred space. 2. Religion and geography. 3. Natural religion. I. Title.
BL580.B78 2004
263'.042–dc22   2004018349

Typeset by SPI Publisher Services, Pondicherry, India
Printed in Great Britain
on acid-free paper by
Biddles Ltd., King's Lynn, Norfolk

ISBN 0–19–927198–4   978–0–19–927198–6
ISBN 0–19–928876–3 (pbk.)   978–0–19–928876–2 (pbk.)

1 3 5 7 9 10 8 6 4 2

To Ann
sine qua non

PREFACE

THIS work and its sequel have been a long time in gestation. In 1993 to mark the nine hundredth anniversary of the foundation of the Norman cathedral at Durham, Ann Loades and I organized a series of sixteen public lectures and fourteen seminars on the theme of sacramental spirituality, with contributions not only from theologians of the stature of Wolfhart Pannenberg, Stephen Sykes, Rowan Williams, and Nicholas Wolterstorff but also from the literary critic George Steiner, the composer John Tavener, and the then Astronomer Royal, Arnold Wolfendale. Thereafter we taught a joint graduate course on 'Reconceiving the sacramental', in which we experimented with various ways of approaching the subject. Inevitably there were some wrong moves, and we had at times to crave the patience of the participants. But our thoughts were honed in this way, as our respective skills and interests mutually complemented one another. It was, for instance, Ann who first encouraged me towards noting the relevance of ballet and dance, Ann who first alerted me to the need for sacramental penance and reconciliation to take account of the fact that 'guilt' is sometimes felt most profoundly not by the guilty party but by the innocent, an issue explored at length in her *Feminist Theology: Voices from the Past* (Oxford: Polity, 2001), 140–65. At one time it looked as though we might produce a joint work, but in the end this proved impossible; different writing styles, a different, though overlapping, range of interests, and Ann's impending retirement all played their part. None the less, it is true that without her help and encouragement this book would never have been written. She was unstintingly generous in devoting time to reading and commenting on whatever I wrote, energetic in directing me to new reading and potential new avenues of thought, and always encouraging when I seemed weighed down by the proposed range of the project. That is why this book is dedicated to her.

Others, however, have also made important contributions. Quite a number of papers and notes were already in existence by the time the opportunity arose to apply for nine months' research leave in 2002 (funded in part by the Arts and Humanities Research Board). Normally, such extended leave would have been impossible for me, given my other role as a canon of the cathedral. None the less, my clerical colleagues were insistent that I should apply, even though vacancies in the cathedral chapter were likely to impose additional burdens on them. Ann volunteered to take on my research students for the duration, while the temporary lecturer appointed in my place, Paul Murray, showed his mettle and is now a permanent member of the department. I am thus deeply grateful to cathedral and departmental colleagues alike, as well to the AHRB, for making the completion of at least this first volume possible.

Friends and colleagues have also been generous in giving their time and expertise to read and comment on particular chapters. Particular mention should be made of David Kennedy, David Hunt, David Fuller, Sheridan Gilley, Margaret Harvey, Paul Harvey, Martin Kitchen, Stephen Laird, Andrew Louth, Anthony Meredith, Stephen Pedley, Geoffrey Rowell, Clemence Schultze, and Kenneth Stevenson. It is good to know individuals of such widely diverse talents and perspectives. In enriching my world, they have also, I hope, helped to enrich the reader's. I am also grateful to the three OUP manuscript readers for their encouraging comments and helpful suggestions.

D.W.B.
University of Durham
St Cuthbert's Day, 2004

CONTENTS

LIST OF PLATES

Although every effort has been made to trace and contact copyright holders before publication, the publishers will be pleased to rectify errors or omissions at the earliest opportunity, if they are notified of any.

The plates appear after page 404.

1. Jacob van Ruisdael's *View of Egmond aan Zee* (1648). Reproduced by permission of the Currier Museum of Art, New Hampshire
2. John Constable's *Salisbury Cathedral from the Meadows*. Private Collection. Bridgeman Art Library
3. Vincent van Gogh's *The Sower* (November 1888). Reproduced by permission of Van Gogh Museum, Amsterdam (Vincent Van Gogh Foundation)
4. Vincent van Gogh's *The Raising of Lazarus* (May 1890). Reproduced by permission of Van Gogh Museum, Amsterdam (Vincent Van Gogh Foundation)
5. Piet Mondrian's *New York City 1942*. Oil on canvas, 119.3 × 114.2 cm. © 2004 Mondrian/Holtzman Trust c/o hcr@hcrinternational.com; Photo Bridgeman Art Library
6. Vassily Kandinsky's *On Points* (1928). Bridgeman Art Library, © ADAGP, Paris and DACS, London 2004
7. English *Psalter World Map* (*c.*1265). Reproduced by permission of the British Library, MS Add. 28681, fo. 9
8. The Labyrinth of Chartres Cathedral (dedicated 1260). Sonia Halliday Photos
9. Antoni Gaudí's Guell Colony Crypt (1898–1917). Bridgeman Art Library
10. Le Corbusier's Notre-Dame-du-Haut at Ronchamp (1955). Bridgeman Art Library/Paul Maeyaert. © FLC/ADAGP, Paris DACS, London 2004
11. Tadao Ando's Church of the Light, Osaka (1989). © Richard Pare 2004

Introduction

ALTHOUGH what follows can be read entirely independently, readers familiar with my two earlier volumes on *Tradition and Imagination* and *Discipleship and Imagination* may find it helpful if the present project is located more precisely within some overall scheme.[1] In those two earlier works my aim was to widen the perspective of theology by insisting that greater attention should be given to the history of the Church as a focus of divine revelation. So far from contrasting biblical revelation and subsequent ecclesiastical tradition, I wanted to suggest that an evolving tradition is itself the motor that under God guides biblical and post-biblical community alike. The community tradition, instead of being conservative or reactionary, has in fact a dynamic of change inherent within it that entails that biblical stories are read in new ways in each generation, and this applies as much to the biblical period as subsequently. What happens, I suggested, was that triggers in the wider society encourage an imaginative re-engagement with the story that can lead to significant new emphases and insights. Over the course of the two works I offered a wealth of studied examples where I believed this to be so, using art no less than the written word to illustrate the nature and means of change.

Here the emphasis is different, but not unrelated. Once more I am concerned to widen the range of material that is thought relevant to constructive theology. Once more also I take seriously what most modern academic work on the subject tends to place on the periphery, if reckoned with at all. In the West the passing of the centuries has marked an increasing marginalization of religion till today it is often seen by many as just one more possible leisure

---

[1] *Tradition and Imagination: Revelation and Change* (Oxford: Oxford University Press, 1999); *Discipleship and Imagination: Christian Tradition and Truth* (Oxford: Oxford University Press, 2000).

activity, with its own distinctive compensations. Some sociologists (and indeed some theologians) have seen this as an inevitable consequence of modern life.[2] I am unconvinced, and would indeed wish to lay much of the blame for the development on the Church itself and its theologians. There is too much of a mismatch between what the Church takes to be significant and the actual experience of the wider population.[3] God is found in nature and gardens, in buildings and place, in music and bodies, in ways to which much attention was once given but is now largely lost. Contemporary Christian theology seems willing to concede at most only an instrumental or utilitarian value. Buildings, for instance, are discussed wholly in terms of their usefulness for worship; gardens, as though exercise or relaxation were the only issues. That seems to me quite wrong. A God active outside the control of the Church needs to be acknowledged, and the implications heeded. That entails a careful listening exercise, the final result of which cannot be predetermined in advance. So, for example, I fail to see why the Christian should not concede genuine experience of God to be mediated through the structures of mosques and temples. What further consequences such an admission might have I do not discuss in this volume. Here my aim is more limited, simply to secure recognition of the fact of such experiences and how they are achieved.

This is the first of two volumes. The contents of the second are indicated in the course of Chapter 1, as also why sacramentality is used as the principal medium for this exploration. Sacraments are often treated as though they were quintessentially 'churchy'. My view is quite different. As in my two earlier works, I am concerned to argue for a God engaged with the whole of life, the entire history of the Church certainly (the theme of the two earlier volumes) but also with all human experience (its cultural dimension is the topic of the present volumes). Culture needs to return as a Christian concern, but one where as much time is spent listening as in trying to contribute. This has, I believe, implications for the philosophy of

---

[2] Bonhoeffer is the obvious theological example of someone who takes this view. Cf. *Letters and Papers from Prison* (London: SCM, 1953), e.g. 122, 153, 162–3.

[3] Supported by the recent British census that found 76% of the population espoused religious belief (72% of them Christian). It is not that most of the population are covert Christians after all, but rather that they have used the nearest cultural equivalent to express their own experience of the transcendent.

religion no less than for theology. The so-called argument from religious experience has in my view been altogether too narrowly conceived.

One final remark. On the whole reviewers have been remarkably generous and kind in assessing *Tradition and Imagination* and *Discipleship and Imagination*. The only criticism repeated more than once was the desire that I should have said more about the criteria under which I was operating. In response I could direct attention to a whole section entirely devoted to questions of authority and criteria and also to the various ways in which these were indicated implicitly during the course of the discussion of specific topics.[4] But I take the point that more could have been said. None the less, there remains the question of when best to do it. British thought is often contrasted with Continental as more naturally empirical in approach. I believe that to be not only true but also right. Criteria set in advance can all too easily read like alien impositions that have failed to grapple sufficiently with the way the world is. In this work and its successor *God and Grace of Body* I am still exploring that reality, and trying to learn from it. One day, though, I do intend to return to the issue. Inevitably, it will be a very much drier book than this one. In the meantime I hope that the reader enjoys the record of discovery that follows as much as I did in experiencing it. It is my earnest wish that others more gifted than myself will now try to make those areas explored their special concern, and so encourage their fellow Christians and, indeed, society generally to a broader vision.

No bibliography is provided. Instead, complete bibliographical details are to be found at the first mention *within* a chapter of the particular work concerned. To include even a representative number of illustrations for the large number of works of art and buildings that I discuss would have been prohibitively expensive. So, as a compromise, in addition to the few plates provided there is an Appendix that lists some useful sites on the Internet where colour illustrations or virtual reality tours can be found.

---

[4] For the relevant section, *Discipleship and Imagination*, 289–406.

I

Sacrament and Enchantment

Reconceiving the Sacramental

IN this first chapter, I want to stake out my claim that the Church has made a number of serious errors in withdrawing from theological engagement with large areas of human experience that were once religion's concern. That development which accelerated in the West from the sixteenth century onwards is sometimes called 'the disenchantment of the world'. The phrase was popularized by Weber, and to Weber I shall return in due course. My own view is that one way to recover enchantment and so a holistic view of how God relates to human experience in its totality is through a reinvigorated sense of the sacramental.[1] As my usage of the term is not the most conventional, I conclude the chapter with a discussion of how that term has been used over the centuries. However, I want to begin by offering some more general reflections on what has led me to approach the subject in this way.

Divine Generosity and Natural Religion

The sequel to this volume culminates in a discussion of the eucharist, supremely for the Christian 'the means of grace' that mediates divine generosity, a generosity that is seen as manifest more generally in the 'sacramental'. Yet even so, few readers would, I suspect, anticipate finding topics such as landscape art, town planning, sport, and gardening set alongside the traditional sacraments (as I do in what follows), whether these sacraments be thought of as limited to the standard two of Protestantism or Roman Catholicism's further

---

[1] The Catechism's definition of sacrament as 'an outward and visible sign of an inward and spiritual grace' will do as a working definition until the more detailed consideration at the end of the chapter.

five.[2] The fact that in the companion volume discussion of the eucharist is preceded by chapters on body and food, music and dance might well add to the puzzlement. Nor will that puzzlement necessarily be confined to those in the pews. Although, as we shall see, there are some signs of change, it is still true that for the most part the sacraments are treated as the most 'churchy' or ecclesiastical part of a theology course. Left to the end, the sacramental is thus treated as an issue for the inner circle, as it were, those most committed to the specifics of Christian belief.

Professional theologians and those more widely read will of course already be familiar with a wider usage, and it is that wider usage to which I shall appeal by way of justification at the end of this chapter. In outline, my argument will be that the first millennium legitimated a much more general application of the term, to which much twentieth-century theology, including the Second Vatican Council (1962–5), has in my view rightly returned. Even so, my aim is rather broader than simply the endorsement of what has already happened. Rather, it is to suggest that this process should be carried still further, and, so far from the sacramental being seen as essentially ecclesiastical or narrowly Christian, it should instead be viewed as a major, and perhaps even the primary, way of exploring God's relationship to our world. Here too, as we shall see, others have anticipated me, but not, so far as I am aware, in the range of data considered.

Before we proceed to detail, however, it may help the reader if I first reveal something of my underlying motivations. Basic to Christian conviction is belief in a generous God. In his life, death, and resurrection Jesus Christ revealed a loving and merciful God who, while calling human beings back from sin, none the less fully endorsed our material world by himself becoming part of it. Little wonder, then, that, though the phraseology as such was not used at the Second Vatican Council the incarnation has increasingly since then been spoken of as the 'primordial sacrament', the one in terms of which all others must be understood.[3] Even so, I continue to doubt whether the implications of that divine generosity are as yet

---

[2] To baptism and eucharist are added confirmation, confession, marriage, orders, and unction.

[3] The first use of the term was in 1934 in German (*Ursakrament*) by Carl Feckes: so H. Vorgrimler, *Sacramental Theology* (Collegeville, Minn.: Liturgical Press, 1992), 30–2 esp. 32.

generally taken with sufficient seriousness. For, if on the one hand there are some signs of this in a major twentieth-century Protestant theologian such as Paul Tillich or a comparable Roman Catholic figure such as Karl Rahner, on the other the second millennium ended with two theologians more prominent in influence, both strong in emphasis on divine generosity but yet surprisingly weak in conceding that the Church might have anything to learn from outside its frontiers. Although Barth's later theology is undoubtedly much more positive about the work of God outside the biblical revelation, the extent of the change seems to me often exaggerated and his earlier negative comments on 'religion' in effect largely stand.[4] Balthasar as the equivalent figure in Roman Catholic thought might initially seem to be in a quite different category. His magnum opus could be viewed as a sustained attempt to do precisely this, to take seriously the activity of God outside the Church, particularly in the world of the arts.[5] But what one finds in Balthasar no less than in Barth is that it is the Christian revelation that constantly sets the criteria of assessment. So there is little sense of learning or of discovery, and more a feeling of the imposition of predetermined judgements.[6]

None of this is intended to be dismissive of Barth and Balthasar. In fact, on many issues my views would be closer to one or other of them than to Rahner or Tillich. Rather, my point is that such talk of divine generosity in Barth and Balthasar is inadequately worked through; otherwise, the paradoxical nature of their assertions could

---

[4] A work such as *The Humanity of God* (London: Collins, 1961) or his positive comments elsewhere on Mozart are sometimes quoted as indicating a profound change of mind: *Church Dogmatics* (Edinburgh: T & T Clark, 1961), iii. 3, 297; *Wolfgang Amadeus Mozart* (Grand Rapids: Eerdmans, 1986). But his view remained that covenant is the internal basis of creation, and so without clear reference to the Trinity (cf. *Church Dogmatics*, iii. 4) a perverted understanding is the inevitable result.

[5] *Herrlichkeit* has lots of studies of specific gifted individuals; *Theodramatik* detailed consideration of the nature of dramatic action. There is much to learn, but there could, I believe, have been much more, had Balthasar allowed those with whom he dialogues more often to have an independent voice that could sometimes call into question his own.

[6] Balthasar's attitude to other religions is a case in point: cf. J. O'Donnell, *Hans Urs von Balthasar* (London: Geoffrey Chapman, 1992), 10–17. Polytheism and pagan myth do not seem to me to require, as it did for Balthasar, the conviction that all we are dealing with is human projection. Rather, like the results of all experience, including Christian, these can be seen as a mixture of both divine initiative and fallible human interpretation.

scarcely be sustained. On the one hand, we have God portrayed as marvellously generous in the way he has disclosed himself through the biblical revelation and in the Church; on the other, he speaks outside that revelation faintly and only then in a manner that acquires proper legitimacy and intelligibility when set in the context of Christian faith. But if God is truly generous, would we not expect to find him at work everywhere and in such a way that all human beings could not only respond to him, however implicitly, but also develop insights from which even Christians could learn? Many theologians resist the logic of such a case because they believe that its implications will inevitably lead to a diminution of Christian conviction. But this is hardly inevitable.

It would only be so were biblical criteria always clear on the sorts of contexts and issues I am about to discuss. But this is seldom so. Principles of architecture, for example, can be extracted only with difficulty.[7] In other cases, such as sport, the Bible has no comment at all to offer.[8] Yet that did not mean that in the past religion in general or Christian theology in particular thought that it had nothing to say. Instead, often a quite highly specific understanding was 'read off' the nature of the world as God's handiwork. The divine was seen as vouchsafing human beings certain key experiences that could then be codified and even aided by subsequent human action taking care to clarify and perhaps even create the most suitable settings for such experience. Christian theories of music and architecture, for example, once reflected such beliefs. Even where no such overall rationale was sought, actual practice might now seem to demand just such a resolution. Despite initial opposition within several major religions, pilgrimage became virtually universal, and so might plausibly be viewed as entailing something about how God may be experienced.

Those familiar with the history of theology will have guessed by now that the exercise upon which I am engaged is in effect a form of what used to be called natural religion. For some the work of such people as David Hume and James Frazer may well seem to have exploded any potential for such a project, but I hope by the

---

[7] Principles derived from both Old and New Testaments are discussed in Ch. 5.

[8] 1 Corinthians 9: 24–7 can scarcely be used to build support for the religious significance of running and boxing, any more than the repeated biblical analogy with kingship entails that this is the only legitimate form of government for human beings.

time the reader has finished these two volumes it will be conceded that my endeavour here is in fact quite different.[9] Nor should this be seen as simply another exercise in natural theology as currently conceived. Philosophy of religion, particularly in its analytic form, is currently flourishing, and I would not wish to decry its concerns. But from my perspective its present conventions and practice are symptomatic of a malaise that affects theology in general, and that is the assumption of very limited horizons as its domain which are in fact the product merely of the Western world's more recent history.[10] Whereas it was once inconceivable for human beings to think religion irrelevant to their lives, now more often than not it functions (at least in the developed world) more like an optional extra, almost like just yet one more competing leisure activity. The response of theologians has been to try to point to various ways in which Christian doctrines might still be pertinent to personal and/ or political concerns, while philosophers have presented various arguments to establish the credibility of belief in God's existence. But even if we accept the plausibility of such presentations, something important still seems lacking, and that is any sense of relevance to those large tracts of human experience where a religious view was once seen to be essential. Sport, drama, humour, dance, architecture, place and home, the natural world are all part of a long list of activities and forms of experience that have been relegated to the periphery of religious reflection, but which once made invaluable contributions to a human perception that this world is where God can be encountered, and encountered often. The reduction of the relevance of such areas to the moral, political, or philosophical is what I want to resist as I seek to expand and transform what used to be called 'natural religion'. In such areas to discern and meet God through grace was once what was meant, and could be again; hence the subtitle to this volume, *Reclaiming Human Experience*. If the objection is made that such experience is clearly of limited value because culturally conditioned, I respond that this is true of all

<hr/>

[9] David Hume's *Natural History of Religion* dates from 1757, J. G. Frazer's *The Golden Bough: A Study in Magic and Religion* from 1890.

[10] Analytic studies of religious experience, for example, typically exclude from consideration most of what follows in subsequent chapters. There is also the question of the extent to which the discipline has in fact been largely shaped in response to the perceived threat of atheism: cf. M. J. Buckley, *At the Origins of Modern Atheism* (New Haven: Yale University Press, 1987).

experience, religious or otherwise, and so the key issue is not the conditioning but what is given none the less through it.[11]

Many of the examples that follow are visual. Wherever possible, I have always tried to give sufficient description to enable the reader unfamiliar with the particular example still to have a clear conception of what is in mind. Even so, some might have preferred that more of my examples had been drawn from literary contexts. There are good and bad reasons for such preferences. The bad is where it is supposed that the verbal is inherently less problematic. As I shall argue in my second volume, words can be the occasion for idolatry no less than images. Spoken or written metaphor can be just as seductive and limiting as visual symbol, indeed more so, since so often listener or reader is unaware of what is occurring just beneath the surface. Therein lies one major advantage of the visual. The issue of engagement is to the fore, and so what is at stake can be more quickly identified.

None the less, on the positive side the numerous parallels between written metaphor and visual symbol do make me want to insist that words too can act sacramentally. That precise issue awaits my companion volume. In the meantime before examining the history of the concept to demonstrate how my own usage represents a return to the wider understanding of sacramentality that was once common before the second millennium, I want to introduce gently that question of the potential re-enchantment of the world, of taking such experience seriously, by first considering what has been lost. I illustrate this with two possibly controversial examples, attitudes to success in sport in the ancient Greek world and the current popularity of house and garden arrangements proposed by Chinese Feng Shui. I take such apparently marginal cases precisely in order to illustrate the range of what is at stake. As we shall see, both relate to a sense of place.

Vanished Sacramentality: Sport and Feng Shui

Sport is seldom now a topic where potential religious implications are either contemplated or discussed.[12] At most, clergy comment

---

[11] Conditioning, I take it, is different from cultural determination, that is, there remains some freedom within an underlying and often unseen influence.
[12] A few examples are given later, in Ch. 7.

regretfully on how sport has become, like art, an alternative religion, but little more seems meant than that footballers and other sportsmen and women are occasionally idolized. How much significance one might appropriately attach to the fact that even in this secular age more continue to go to church each week than to football matches, it is hard to say. In any case sports-stars are sometimes themselves their own best critics of too materialistic an image and lifestyle. In the part of England where I live two obvious examples would be the Olympic athlete Jonathan Edwards and Niall Quinn, the Sunderland football star.[13] It remains true, though, that apart from religion sport is the only major reason in the modern world why people gather together in a specific place. If now the only obvious sign of some connection with religion is the occasional singing of hymns at rugby and football matches, there was once an intimate and profound link. It seems appropriate, therefore, at least to note what has been lost.

The Olympic Games themselves amply illustrate what has occurred. Revived in 1896, their present lack of involvement with religion is perhaps the most obvious point of contrast with an earlier tradition that lasted from 776 BC until AD 426.[14] So I shall first characterize those connections before making explicit the sacramental dimension. Although confined for most of that history to the Greek-speaking world, a cosmopolitan character was given to them not only by the spread of Greek cities throughout the Mediterranean but also by a religiously guaranteed truce that required safe conduct to be observed for all who intended to participate, even where states were at war.[15] Contestants usually arrived a month early for training at nearby Elis, and then on the day before the five-day celebration a solemn pilgrimage procession took place

---

[13] The former, a graduate of Durham and living in Newcastle, has often spoken publicly about the relation between his faith and sport, while the latter donated all the proceeds of his farewell, testimonial match in 2002 (approx. £1,000,000) to local children's charities.

[14] The date of the final festival is uncertain. In the text I have opted for the year in which Zeus' temple was burnt down, but Theodosius I's banning of all pagan cults in 393 might well have been enough to stop any version, however muted allusion to Zeus now was.

[15] Three heralds, known as *spondopheroi* and decked in olive leaves, were sent out to all Greek states well in advance, to announce that the time for the Olympic Truce had now come.

from Elis to Olympia, a distance of fifty-eight kilometres.[16] At Olympia itself there was a famous grove, the Altis, which was dedicated to Zeus, but still better known was his temple with its massive statue by Pheidias. At thirteen metres high, this filled the interior. Although there were viewing platforms to allow closer inspection, tourism was very far from being the primary point, and indeed various aids were employed to increase the overall sense of awe, among them a large oil pool at the statue's base which produced a mystical, glowing reflection of the god.[17] Upon arrival oaths were sworn to Zeus to abide by the games' rules, while to symbolize the involvement of the god in the competition itself, the finishing line for athletic events was placed close to an outside altar in the Altis. Indeed, even when this track was subsequently moved, care was taken to ensure some continuing connection with the sacred grove, for it was from leaves from its sacred olives that the athletes' crowns were made. Again, the celebratory feast that concluded proceedings on the fifth day used meat from the hundred oxen that had been sacrificed to Zeus on the third.[18] Other gods, though, also played their part, most notably Poseidon to whom individual sacrifices were made prior to the chariot races. Yet even here Zeus' principal role was not forgotten, for a splendidly dramatic representation of Zeus was employed to start the race: a mechanical contraption pulled open the stalls by degrees, as Zeus' carved eagle was seen at the same time rising symbolically into the air.[19] Other gods were by no means neglected. Two out of the three other major games that took place in intervening years were dedicated to gods other than Zeus, while even at Olympia, though women were forbidden to compete in the four-yearly festival, they

---

[16] For details, J. Swaddling, *The Ancient Olympic Games* (London: British Museum Press, 2nd edn., 1999), 50–2.

[17] That this was the overall effect is in no way lessened by the fact that the original purpose of the oil had been practical, to prevent the ivory with which the statue was covered from drying out.

[18] For the oath-taking, Pausanias, *Description of Greece*, v. 24. 9–10; for the position of the track, Swaddling, *Ancient Olympic Games*, 29–31; for sacrifices and feasting, ibid. 53–5 esp. 55.

[19] Described by Pausanias, vi. 20. 10–13. At the same time as the bronze eagle rose, a dolphin plunged, the latter presumably being intended to allude to Poseidon's role.

did have their own games, and on that occasion the goddess Hera was patron.[20]

All this religion was by no means incidental, as though just a matter of conventional piety or even caution money, as it were, in case the gods were hostile. Something much deeper was seen as being at stake, and this was the sense that the athlete could reflect something of the glory that the god enjoyed. The beauty of the athletes' bodies and the skill of their actions were not just made possible by the gods, they were also seen as borrowing some of the gods' own lustre.[21] So, significantly, the language of 'grace' is by no means absent, and that is what makes me want to speak here of a sacramental attitude. Something of the god becomes, as it were, embodied. Sport offered a heavenly vision, some sense of the beauty, perfection, and grace of the gods, and so it is no accident that the graced body emerges in the context of a sacred place.

Poetry written to celebrate victory in such contexts can still give us some sense of how the audience responded, of the intimacy of the perceived connection between victory on the one hand and divine favour and presence on the other. Although, perhaps inevitably because of his Theban birth, the piety of Pindar (c. 518–438 BC) is at its most obvious when he is celebrating victories at nearby Delphi, his *Olympian Odes* can be used almost as effectively to illustrate this sacramental sense of divine engagement.[22] Pindar is throughout concerned to defend the morality of the gods;[23] so excluded is any interpretation that presupposes that he saw prayer as merely a wise precaution beforehand.[24] Instead, for him the games are 'holy' and so their intimacy with religious concerns, both mythical and practical, must be highlighted.[25] It is against this background that Pindar's depiction of the god himself taking a role in equipping the athlete should therefore be set. 'It is by the

---

[20] Swaddling, *Ancient Olympic Games*, 43. Although at Nemea patronage was once more under Zeus, for Delphi (the Pythian Games) it was Apollo, and at Corinth (the Isthmian) it was Poseidon.

[21] An athlete's lustre was aided by anointing with oil as was the chryselephantine statue of Zeus with its oil pool below.

[22] Half the *Pythian Odes* (for Delphi) celebrate charioteers. For a human gleam or radiance reflecting a divine: VIII. 95–8.

[23] e.g. *Olympians*, I. 35, 52; IX. 37.

[24] Though he does offer prayers, e.g. VI. 102–5; VII. 87–90 (for a boxer).

[25] For 'holy games': e.g. XIII. 15; for the finish being close to the altar: X. 101.

god's gift that a man flowers,' he writes.[26] Something of the divine is transferred to the athlete himself, whether this be found in the skill of the boxer and charioteer or more directly in the graceful limbs of the runner. Thus of a charioteer he can write: 'God glorified him and gave him a golden chariot and horses with untired wings,' or of a runner: 'Let the son of Sostratus know that in this sandal he has a foot blessed by heaven.'[27] Indeed, those who think that they can achieve results by their own prowess alone are duly reprimanded, while, if the overall result is not always beauty (boxing could produce some very bad injuries), the language of grace is seldom other than to the fore.[28] It is in his celebration of a victory other than at Olympia, though, that Pindar makes the parallel most explicit: 'Single is the race of men and of gods; from one mother we both draw breath, but a wholly sundered power keeps us apart... Yet we can approach the immortal gods in greatness of mind or of body.'[29]

Some of my fellow Christians may be inclined to dismiss all of this as no more than crude anthropomorphism, with the athlete presented as now possessing a little of the god's own material body. I discuss this issue at more length in the relevant chapter on body in my second volume, but suffice it to say here that, however the Greeks regarded their gods, they possessed no ordinary bodies. Their food is no ordinary food (a sacrifice's fragrance is sufficient sustenance).[30] They can appear and disappear at will, and are bilocational at the very least. If their blood can flow, it is not ever subject to haemorrhage and so they never die. Christians who believe that their Lord retains his body in heaven ought therefore to hesitate before they dismiss too summarily the Greek attitude as absurdly literalistic. The athlete's success comes from a communicated grace of body but it in no way becomes the same body as that of the gods. Certainly, the gods give something of themselves, but what is communicated is not exactly the same as what they already possess: rather, it is a distinctive and analogous bodily lustre that speaks of the athletes being graced by, not made identical with, the

---

[26] *Olympians* XI. 10 (my trans.)   [27] I. 86–7; VI. 9 (my trans.).

[28] For the reprimand: IX. 100–4; for two examples of grace and beauty: X. 99–105; XIV. 1–13.

[29] *Nemean Odes*, VI. 1–5 (my trans.).

[30] For 'ambrosia' and 'nectar', e.g. *Iliad*, 19. 38–9; *Odyssey*, 4. 445–6. For further detailed references and discussion, see my second volume.

divine. Even so, were a sacramental understanding of sport to be revived in our own day, it would almost certainly need to take a quite different form. Direct physical imagery for God is still altogether too remote from the Christian tradition to be easily acceptable.[31] Yet there are, I believe, some hints of a viable sacramental approach in sport even today, and so I want to return to this issue in the final chapter.

The previous paragraph's rejection of physical imagery may seem to fly in the face of much contemporary thought, not least the Gaia movement and its attempt to represent the world itself as God's body, Mother Earth.[32] It is intriguing that the suggestion first arose in a scientific context, and that the current popularity of Feng Shui arrangements reflects a similar desire for a setting in our environment that is at one and the same time 'scientific' and 'spiritual'. The notion has its roots in the Taoist Chinese tradition, and seeks to produce arrangements of office, house, and garden such that the totality of forces, material and otherwise, combine to work for the good. In Hong Kong even major banks have agreed to have the designs of their skyscrapers modified to conform to such principles, while in Europe and the United States numerous guides are available to aid the individual in improving his or her environment in this way.[33] The fact that some elements in the advice are simply sound common sense probably aids acceptance of the more controversial elements.[34] The harnessing of *chi* and the balance of *yin* and *yang* quickly expands into a complex astrological system,

---

[31] Yet there are some parallels, perhaps most notably on the question of whether the incarnate Christ would have been beautiful or not. If Isa. 53: 2 pulls in one direction, there is no shortage of others expressing a contrary view, e.g. Hopkins in his sermon for 23 November 1879: W. H. Gardner (ed.), *Gerard Manley Hopkins: A Selection of his Poetry and Prose* (Harmondsworth: Penguin, 1953), 137–9.

[32] The notion originated in the 1970s with the British scientist James Lovelock's suggestion that in view of the world's delicate balance the earth should be treated as a self-regulating, living organism. For a critique of some of its applications, C. Deane-Drummond, 'God and Gaia; Myth or Reality?' in *Theology* 95 (1992), 277–85.

[33] For modifications to Sir Norman Foster's design for the Hong Kong and Shanghai Bank and the Bank of China's response, G. Hale, *The Practical Encyclopedia of Feng Shui* (London: Select Editions, 2001 edn.), 195.

[34] For examples of common sense, note the advice on the positioning of desks and layout of garden paths, Hale, *Encyclopedia of Feng Shui*, 122, 156, 231.

where, for instance, it matters deeply that my own birth sign is the earth rat.[35]

My point in raising the strategy here is not to endorse it, but to suggest that it well illustrates what happens when more conventional religions retreat from the areas that I will discuss over the course of subsequent chapters. A vacuum is left, and in its place come alternative spiritualities, but because there is no longer any established tradition of what is appropriate religious discourse in such contexts, these are modelled superficially on the science of the day. Sadly, it is in effect a retreat to magic, if we understand by magic the attempt to control the spiritual influences on one's life by formal rule and regulation. Sacrament, by contrast, because it includes an element of divine initiative, is more open to mystery and unpredictability: God may promise his presence but how that will work out in practice is yet to be seen, and so faith must await in hope what will happen. The varied character of plants also ensures an element of unpredictability in how gardens are, as a matter of fact, experienced by their owners. So a sacramental understanding of gardens could possibly be argued to be nearer to their true character than even the most careful or cautious application of Feng Shui.[36] Certainly, historically gardens were once seen in just such a way. Whether that can still be so or not, I likewise leave for consideration to the final chapter.

My two examples have been introduced to make two simple points. First, with sport, I observe that sacramentality was once a way of addressing areas where theology now seems to have nothing much to say; secondly, with Feng Shui, that the rise of so much pseudo-spirituality in our own day cannot be blamed entirely on others when it comes from a vacuum caused by religion itself. To the nature of that retreat and its causes, I now turn.

Recovering Enchantment

Theologians tend to know only one fact about the German sociologist Max Weber and that is his authorship of the influential

---

[35] *Chi* is the total energy force present; *yin* and *yang* the complementary elements that need to be balanced within it.

[36] For Feng Shui at its most astrological in respect of gardens, J. Dee, *Feng Shui for the Garden* (London: Caxton, 2000).

account of the origins of capitalism, *The Protestant Ethic and the Spirit of Capitalism*, first published as a two-part article in 1904–5. His much-criticized thesis of an intimate connection between the pursuit of wealth and Calvinist theology is not our concern here.[37] In passing, though, he does make a number of disparaging references to sacramentality.[38] For him medieval understandings of sacrament were intimately intertwined with magic, from which the Reformation in both its major forms successfully extricated itself. Lutheranism on his view retreated into a private mysticism, while Calvinism went one stage further into a purely instrumental rationality.[39] What is less widely known is that Weber sees all this as part of a more general pattern about the way the world is going, the continuing advance of rationality into all areas of life and the resultant retreat of religion. Taking up a phrase of Schiller's, he described the process in a number of places as 'the disenchantment of the world', and it is that contention which I would like to examine in a little more detail here.[40]

Enchantment can, of course, very easily suggest spells and magic, and so his linking of the rise of rationality with the decline in focus on sacrament is no doubt not accidental. The claim to a priestly control not amenable to independent assessment is one aspect that troubled him, but so too, and more profoundly, did the notion of a mysterious externality not subject to rational analysis.[41] Science, he

---

[37] In outline his argument was that, though Calvinism condemned the direct pursuit of wealth, indirectly it greatly fostered it, for the believer now sought reassurance of divine grace in prosperity and the ability this gave to perform good works. For the current state of the argument, H. Lehmann and G. Roth (eds.), *Weber's Protestant Ethic: Origins, Evidence, Contexts* (Cambridge: Cambridge University Press, 1993).

[38] Discussions of the Protestant response to medieval understandings of sacrament are often cursorily summarized by phrases such as 'the elimination of magic from the world' and 'the rationalization of the world', or even both together: e.g. M. Weber, *The Protestant Ethic and the Spirit of Capitalism* (London: Unwin, 1984), 104–5, 116–17.

[39] *Protestant Ethic*, 84–6, 106–8. 'Instrumental', with everything measured as a means either to God's glory or to human salvation.

[40] The most important occurrence of the phrase is in his essay, 'Science as a Vocation': H. H. Gerth and C. Wright Mills (eds.), *From Max Weber* (London: Routledge & Kegan Paul, 1948), 129–56 esp. 155; cf. 148. The editors attribute first use to Schiller: 51.

[41] Once magic has failed, mystic experience is seen as one of religion's last retreats: cf. Gerth and Mills, *From Max Weber*, 282, cf. 155.

held, was concerned with the elimination of mystery and its substitution by explanation, and his own pursuit of sociology was one stage further in that process. Yet, although he thought such developments virtually inevitable, he did not regard them as historically determined or ineluctable. Indeed, he seems to have viewed them with some degree of pessimism, for he talks of human beings as a consequence being confined, as it were, in 'an iron cage'.[42] His mother had been a devout Lutheran.[43] He himself had no religious belief, but he does seem to have felt that something was missing, for he described himself as 'religiously absolutely "unmusical"' and yet in this 'a cripple, a deformed human being'.[44] Perhaps in this he was like Thomas Hardy: knowing otherwise, but yet 'hoping it might be so', or the contemporary poet P. J. Kavanagh who knows that 'tomorrow will be brown | with disappointment' but yet wants to risk a 'Yes',

> As when we sense a presence in a room
> We thought was empty, and we ask, uncertain.[45]

A number of contemporary sociologists have tried to respond by seeing if there are ways in which enchantment might indeed either survive or be restored. One such suggests that the whole notion is still very much alive and kicking in contemporary academic thought. He considers two examples in some detail (the work of Clifford Geertz and of Claude Lévi-Strauss), but also extends his argument to other major twentieth-century figures, such as Foucault, to maintain that in much social science characterization remains preferred to testable explanation.[46] He himself appears to want more 'maturity', but he doubts whether this will easily be achieved, so well disposed are human beings to appeal to mystery at the heart of human endeavour. Another uses some remarks of

---

[42] *Protestant Ethic*, 181.

[43] Her anxieties over Max's failure to perceive deeper spiritual issues behind confirmation are described in Gerth and Mills, *From Max Weber*, 5–6.

[44] In a letter to Tönnies, 19 February 1909; quoted in L. A. Scaff, *Fleeing the Iron Cage* (Berkeley, Calif.: University of California Press, 1989), 225–6.

[45] From his poem *Whitsun*, of particular interest in this connection as it is part of a collection entitled *An Enchantment* (London: Carcanet, 1991), 33–4. The quotation from Hardy is the last line of his poem *The Oxen* which describes the legend told to him in his childhood of oxen kneeling each year anew on Christmas Day.

[46] M. A. Schneider, *Culture and Enchantment* (Chicago: University of Chicago Press, 1993). For Geertz: 55–82; for Lévi-Strauss: 83–113; for Foucault: 187–91; for 'maturity': 169–76.

Habermas on aesthetics to suggest that at the intersection between culture and system there is hope for a 'transformation' that will find a place for both rationality and enchantment.[47] If that writer's discussion is conducted entirely within the frame of modernity, yet a third sees in postmodernism an escape from the cage. In one of his books, films such as *The Exorcist* and *The Omen* are used to explore how in postmodernity no one particular perspective is allowed to dominate, while another from the following year opens with the declaration: 'postmodernity can be seen as restoring to the world what modernity presumptuously had taken away: as a re-enchantment of the world that modernity tried hard to disenchant'.[48] I doubt if matters are quite that simple. Insecurity within pluralism can all too easily lead to a resurgence of dogmatism rather than its elimination, while that same pluralism entails that there are no easy guides to where enchantment might most profitably be sought.[49] Still, the possibility is there.

From the perspective of this book, though, more interesting are the attempts of another sociologist, Kieran Flanagan, to argue that the Church has been its own worst enemy and that what is needed is the resacralization of liturgy in order to bring enchantment once more. In blaming theology he is in continuity with Weber's own views,[50] but in this case the claim is set against the changes introduced by the Second Vatican Council, where function is seen as replacing mystery. The argument is in my view spoilt by a relentless conservatism that sees all change as bad.[51] Where its strength lies is

[47] The argument of the final chapter of Scaff's *Fleeing the Iron Cage*, 223–41 esp. 235, 239.

[48] For the significance of the two films, the final chapter on 'Postmodernity' in Z. Bauman, *Modernity and Ambivalence* (Ithaca, NY: Cornell University Press, 1991), 231–79 esp. 238–45; for the quotation, *Intimations of Postmodernity* (London: Routledge, 1992), p. x.

[49] In other words, I suspect that the truth may well exist at the opposite extreme to Bauman's claim that 'emancipated from modern hubris, the postmodern mind has less need for cruelty and humiliating the Other' (*Modernity and Ambivalence*, 257).

[50] For Weber's view, cf. Gerth and Mills, *From Max Weber*, 357: 'the more systematic the thinking about the "meaning" of the universe becomes, the more . . . the conscious experience of the world's irrational content is sublimated', in other words, the more it is moved into a very narrow area.

[51] K. Flanagan, *The Enchantment of Sociology* (London: Macmillan, 1996), e.g. pp. xi–xii, 10, 85, 221. His earlier work *Sociology and Liturgy* (London: Macmillan, 1991) had also appealed to notions of enchantment: e.g. 210.

in identifying the danger in too simplified a theory of meaning, of supposing that symbols work only if they are fully comprehended and endorsed.[52] There needs to be a richness in language and action that allows the worshipper to explore and be explored by a Being who is beyond all possible containment.[53]

Flanagan is right to attack the reduction of worship to function and instrumentality. In the language of Weber escape from disenchantment (*Entzauberung*) is likely to occur only if the attempt is made to go beyond mere purposive or instrumental rationality (*Zweckrationalität*). Worship has therefore to be seen as more than just a matter of strengthening the community for mission and service. At its heart lies the adoration of God, basking in his presence in and for its own sake. Failing to acknowledge that deeper dimension to liturgy, though, is part of a very much wider malaise that Flanagan fails to address, and that is the general retreat of theology under similar pressures from numerous other areas of human life. Take the two examples considered in the previous section. Feng Shui attempts to introduce an element of enchantment into home and garden under the guise of a piece of pseudo-rationality: do this and well-being will ensue. But the more ambitious course would surely be to attack the need for instrumental value at all. Gardens need not be cultivated for health or produce. They could be regarded as simply exercises in the creation of beauty in and for its own sake, or even, as Christianity once understood them, as reflections of the Great Gardener himself.[54] Again, the kind of attitude evinced in the ancient Olympic Games refused to concede that exercise was always instrumental to some further goal such as efficiency in war; instead its glory could lie simply in a graced body, the perfection of the human body reflecting that of the gods' greater lustre.

There are a number of reasons why present-day Christianity lies at so great a distance from such attitudes. Factors internal to Chris-

---

[52] Cf. *Sociology and Liturgy*, 52.

[53] Flanagan has little to say on language, presumably because he still longs for the days of the Latin mass. By contrast he is very perceptive on the role of the body: e.g. *Sociology and Liturgy*, 186–206.

[54] Considered in the final chapter, but an image not entirely alien even to modern times. In 1940 Emile Nolde produced a magnificent painting of God as *Der große Gärtner*. M. Reuther (ed.), *Emile Nolde: Die religiösen Bilder* (Cologne: DuMont, 2000), 157.

tianity itself need to be acknowledged before Weber's *Zweckrationalität* is brought into play once more. Body and garden came under suspicion partly because showing interest in such seemed to place too high a value on this world and partly because they seemed to allow the possibility that human beings might themselves set the conditions under which God could be experienced.[55] If the former worry is now no longer common, the latter is still very much with us, but it is hard to comprehend why. After all, the traditional sacraments already set a framework within which God is seen as having promised to act. Extending this to other areas thus amounts to no more than acknowledging the fact that God might speak not only through the biblical revelation but also through implicit promises given in the way the world has been made. Subsequent chapters will examine how such promises were in the past read off from the nature of creation and applied to great tracts of human experience, from town planning to sacred architecture, from music to food. If major Catholic theologians seldom assigned real importance to such reflections, one's suspicion is that this was because to do so would have undermined the Church's complete control over sacramentality. Equally destructive, though, were Protestant worries, even if these were of a quite different kind: recognition would exclude the Bible from always having an exclusive, determining say.[56] In both cases there was a preoccupation with power that ironically circumscribed divine freedom of action far more severely than any of the notions that were seen as a potential threat.

Fortunately over the centuries, at some times more vociferously than at others, a countercurrent of protest continued. What, though, caused further retreat (and here Weber's analysis is pertinent) was Western adoption of a particular model of rationality that seemed to suggest that once something was 'explained' there was no further need to address religious questions to that specific area. So, for example, if the natural world is treated as an arena for 'proving' God's existence, then once such proofs are undermined, retreat would seem inevitable. But the question remains why proof should be seen as the only way of experiencing the divine impact

---

[55] Intriguingly, the first worry already displays instrumentalist elements: body and garden were not seen as aiding the path to an other-worldly salvation.

[56] Despite these restrictions Protestant and Catholic reflection did, of course, occur, but it seldom came from theologians, more often from Christians whose primary discipline, as we shall see, lay elsewhere.

on our world. Instead of always functioning as an inference, there was the possibility that a divine structure is already implicit in certain forms of experience of the natural world, whether these be of majesty, beauty, or whatever.[57] In other words, it would be a matter of an immanent given rather than of certain neutral features pointing instrumentally beyond themselves. Again, church architecture is often seen merely as one particular means of facilitating some general strategy such as communication of the faith, and of course if that is all it is doing, the response might well be to relegate it to an issue of minor importance because other means are so often more effective.[58] But suppose the aim is not means but expression. Then something quite different comes to be at stake, whether the architecture aids an experience of God or not. Again, to take a quite different example, saying grace at meals can be made a matter of ethics, of fulfilling one's obligation of thankfulness to God, but it can also be part of a religious experience, of all life coming as a generous, divine gift.

Given the current revival of interest in the relation between theology and the arts, attitudes might seem to be changing, but I am far from sanguine about how far this is really so. For so deep does instrumental rationality run in our culture that the practice of theology also often reflects that same approach, valuing the arts not in their own right but only in so far as they 'preach the gospel'. Put like that, it might seem as though a Christian could scarcely but agree with such an aim, but not only is there frequently too much certainty about what God might be requiring but also a further reduction in the conviction that unless what is being asserted is translatable into ethics or politics it cannot be of importance. The fact that in what follows I almost entirely ignore both types of question is not because I think the issues unimportant but precisely because their instrumentality is so often allowed to substitute for other valid concerns. Enchantment, I suggest, lies in the discovery of God under such forms, whether or not any further practical consequences follow.

---

[57] The full range of possibilities is considered in Ch. 3.

[58] For an influential example of such stress on instrumentality (in this case circular churches reinforcing a communal liturgy), cf. P. Hammond, *Liturgy and Architecture* (London: Barrie & Rockliff, 1960), esp. 42–3.

All academic writing is addressed to specific contexts, and in that this work is no exception. There is far more of exposition and analysis than there is of critique, not because I could not think of appropriate objections or wished to reject them in their entirety. Rather, it is because I detect a need to hear at the present time some more basic assertions: in particular, the way in which God can be mediated through nature and culture in experiences that have their own intrinsic value. That means that they must first be heard in their own right before any critical assessment is offered, and that is what at present seems to me to be largely lacking. I have therefore written sympathetically about, for example, the emperor Augustus' planning of imperial Rome or the elaborate sculptural programmes in Hindu temples.[59] Of course, there was a negative side, but that was not all that there was (or is). In any case, Christians need to recognize the complexities of their own world before pronouncing unqualified judgement on the situation of others. The exclusion of 'untouchables' from Hindu temples was a great tragedy, but so too was the treatment of women in the medieval cathedral at Durham.[60] But that did not mean in either case that all mediation of the divine through such buildings was therefore excluded, even in respect of the groups in question. It is only by listening carefully to perspectives other than one's own, allowing them their own distinctive voice, that more balanced judgements will ensue. It is precisely with that thought in mind that Chapter 2 takes the form it does. Here there is an extended critique, but again it is addressed to our present context. The present ecclesiastical fashion in the West is to praise icons and denigrate Renaissance art. I offer the case on the other side. Even here, though, I do not allow critique the final word, because later in my discussion I note how the trend in icons that I criticize is countered by other aspects of Orthodox culture.

[59] In Chs. 4 and 7 respectively.
[60] In Norman England a black line was introduced at the back of the nave beyond which women were not allowed to pass. The concentration of women pilgrims at nearby Finchale was one consequence, but there is no reason to think that this precluded women from all experience of the divine at the cathedral. The exterior and the Galilee at the west end could still have an impact, just as such limited experience of temples remained possible for 'untouchables' but was also supplemented by alternative priesthoods. For Finchale and Durham compared: R. Finucane, *Miracles and Pilgrims* (London: Dent, 1977), 126–7. The situation in India is now also changing, with increasing resistance to the view that only higher castes can function in the temples as priests.

In this volume a unifying theme will be the enchantment of place, how situatedness might help in engendering a sense of divine presence. In a suggestive work Martin Heidegger, following hints in the poet Hölderlin, has suggested that being is intimately linked with dwelling, and that dwelling in turns carries a sense of us poised between heaven and earth, between gods and men.[61] Although not himself a believer, what Heidegger seems to have had in mind is the way in which the sky seems to be pregnant with the notion of something transcendent against which we feel the need to measure ourselves.[62] Many others have detected a range of natural symbols of this kind: mountains trees, caves, and standing stones, for example.[63] Certainly, the pattern is widely disseminated, but to treat such phenomena as the most important because the most primitive and 'natural' would be like supposing that a religion's scriptures cannot be revelatory at the deepest level because already embedded within human reflection. A stone stood on its end presumably has just as much potential to be revelatory as one found pointing heavenwards naturally, and that is no doubt one reason why both have been found in contexts of worship. Similarly then, with religiously inspired landscape painting or architecture: they merely carry that insight one stage further, in bringing to consciousness more complex experienced relations of divine presence. Not that this is always so. Such presentations are no doubt at times no more than a matter of inference or even of rote. My point is that they are none the less quite often so much more: a direct expression of experience, of the enchantment that comes from perceiving particular ways of God relating to human beings and their world.

One recent survey of the morphology of religious architecture across the religions uses the notion of 'allurement' as a unifying concept.[64] Although nothing is made of this, the term ultimately

---

[61] M. Heidegger, *Poetry, Language, Thought* (New York: Harper & Row, 1971), esp. 145–61, 213–29. His attempt to argue from a linguistic connection between *bin* and *bauen*, though, seems to me somewhat problematic: 146–7.

[62] e.g. 221–2. For the religious element in Heidegger's thinking, see my *Continental Philosophy and Modern Theology* (Oxford: Blackwell, 1987), 95–6.

[63] A repeated theme in Mircea Eliade: e.g. *Patterns in Comparative Religion* (London: Sheed & Ward, 1958); *The Sacred and the Profane* (San Diego: Harcourt Brace Jovanovich, 1959), esp. 116–213.

[64] L. Jones, *The Hermeneutics of Sacred Architecture*, 2 vols. (Cambridge, Mass.: Harvard University Press, 2000).

comes from the falconer's art in which the hawk is enticed into more than it realizes; so the connection with enchantment would seem more than merely superficial.[65] Allurement, the author notes, comes in a great variety of forms, and in a way that means Gothic architecture may share more in common with Tibetan mandalas than it does with the Renaissance designs that follow it.[66] But what all share is the desire to draw in the worshipper. At times the method employed relies on obviously human impositions, but that is by no means always so.[67] It is the allure of the non-human that I want to explore in what follows. One way of putting that is to talk of the sacramental, of the presence of God being mediated in and through the material, whether that material be naturally occurring or humanly structured to reflect perceived divine givens. Why it is not an abuse of language to apply such terminology well beyond the range of the Christian sacraments is the final issue to which I now turn in this introductory chapter.

Sacrament: Changing Usage

For some the mention of the possibility of 'sacraments' in other religions may well have already been enough for them to reject my whole approach. If so, it will be salutary for them to recall that the term 'sacrament' is itself a borrowing from the wider classical world, as is its nearest Greek equivalent in the New Testament world, *musterion*. Although *musterion* is not used in the New Testament directly of the conventional sacraments, it is not hard to see how such an application came to develop. It was because the eucharist and baptism were viewed as the Church's supreme mysteries or 'secrets'.[68] It seems likely that it was in this sense also that

[65] The 'lure' was a device in which the bird found its food at the same time as having its training reinforced.

[66] For Jones's morphology summarized: *Hermeneutics*, ii. 3; for the specific example: ii. 17.

[67] For some examples across the religions: ibid. ii. 79 (Maya); ii. 130 (Christian); ii. 137–8 (Sikh).

[68] Even in Eph. 5: 31–2 *musterion* probably refers not to the sacrament of marriage as such, but rather to prophecy of the future relations between Christ and the Church which the author believes lie 'hidden' in Gen. 2: 24. That hidden, eschatological meaning is the New Testament usage elsewhere: e.g. Mark 4:

sacramentum was first used rather than in its alternative meaning of an oath of allegiance.[69] If the latter is also given application, especially in relation to baptism, the extent to which the former idea shaped understanding is particularly evident by the fourth century, in eucharistic practice where the communication of 'secrets' had now become a major theme.[70]

Even so, the way in which *sacramentum* and *musterion* eventually became virtually interchangeable helped to broaden the sense attaching to the former. The word eventually came to be used to cover a far wider range of significance than the traditional sacraments might ever have led us to expect.[71] That process was greatly helped by the African translation of the Greek Scriptures where *sacramentum* is employed to translate *musterion* in passages where Jerome's Vulgate would decide simply to transliterate (as *mysterium*).[72] Typological and other forms of participation in hidden realities thus became the order of the day. In effect 'sacrament' had come to mean any mysterious indwelling that anticipates or points to some greater reality. Throughout the first millennium the Greek and Latin word ranged over such a varied spectrum of objects and rites that even the most stubborn critic would, I contend, be hard put to it to explain why it is not essentially the same concept being deployed both within and beyond Christian practice. Indeed, Augustine explicitly observes that 'within no religious bond, whether true or false, can human beings be united, except they are bound together through some little sign or visible sacrament'.[73] So it

11–12; 1 Cor. 2: 7. Commentators who deny any parallels with the mystery religions are therefore, I believe, mistaken, as 'secrets' is precisely what Christian and pagan use most obviously share in common.

[69] Though inevitably hard to prove, as both meanings are put to use. For a scriptural example of *sacramentum* as 'secret', cf. the Vulgate version of Tobit 12: 7.

[70] Tertullian (d. 225) represents the first known application of *sacramentum* to baptism and the eucharist: *De baptismo* 1; *De corona* 3; *Adversus Marcionem* 5. 8. For how close the parallels with the mystery religions had become by the 4th c., E. Yarnold, *The Awe Inspiring Rites of Initiation* (Slough: St Paul, 1972), e.g. 52.

[71] Contrast e.g. Tertullian's use to mean religious rite in general (*Apologia*, 15. 8) with Jerome's to talk of the mystical meaning of Scripture (*Letters*, 52. 2, 3).

[72] As in 1 Cor. 4: 1 and 13: 2. Contrast Eph. 5: 31–2, where Jerome also has *sacramentum*.

[73] *Contra Faustum*, 19. 11 (my trans.): 'in nullum autem nomen religionis, seu verum, seu falsum, coagulari homines possunt, nisi aliquo signaculorum vel sacramentorum visibilium consortio conligentur.'

is perhaps no surprise that he includes among his 'sacraments' the Lord's Prayer, the Creed, the sign of the cross, ashes of penitence, oil of anointing, and even the Easter liturgy itself.[74] That last example is a particularly interesting instance as Pope Leo the Great takes him up on that specific point, to widen usage still further. Augustine had contrasted Easter with Christmas which he called a mere *memoria*.[75] Not so for Leo, who insists that Christmas worship is also equally participation in the mystery of salvation: a *sacramentum salutis*.[76]

Not that all theologians at this time admitted an equally wide usage. Chrysostom, for example, uses *musterion* almost exclusively of the eucharist, but that contrasts markedly with the more characteristic Ambrose who applies *mysterium* and *sacramentum* widely to numerous biblical incidents as they anticipate or reflect 'the sacrament of the cross'.[77] Admittedly, such usage was to become the exception as the more precise definitions of the high Middle Ages began to gain dominance, and the number of the sacraments came to be limited to seven, with clearly articulated requirements.[78] Even so, the older usage never entirely died out. An intriguing example comes from Luther who in *The Babylonian Captivity* speaks of 'one sacrament and three sacramental signs'.[79] Although part of his intention is probably polemical, he is clearly using 'sacrament' in its older meaning to refer to Christ as the foundational divine 'mystery.' Still, that is very much the exception rather than the rule, and one must await the twentieth century before conventions

[74] Mainly because of the principal role he assigns to the role of sacraments as 'signs': cf. e.g. *Contra Faustum*, 2. 1.

[75] Augustine's argument (to be found in *Letter* 55) is that only Easter involves a renewal of one's participation in the mystery of baptism. Christmas is by contrast a simple anniversary celebration.

[76] Reparatur enim nobis salutis nostrae annua revolutione sacramentum (Sermon 22. 1); nativitatis dominicae sacramento clarius coruscante (Sermon 28. 1).

[77] e.g. in commenting on Exod. 15: 22–5 and Judg. 7: 6. For John Chrysostom's narrower usage, E. Mazza, *Mystagogy* (New York: Pueblo, 1989), 131–4.

[78] If for Peter Damian (d. 1072) there were still twelve, the *Sentences* of Peter Lombard (d. 1160) effectively fixed them at seven (endorsed by the Council of Lyons in 1274).

[79] *Luther's Works* (Philadelphia: Fortress, 1967), xxxvi. 18; cf. 94–5 for anti-Roman thrust. Luther may be thinking of the *Vulgate* at 1 Tim. 3: 16: Et manifeste magnum est pietatis sacramentum, quod manifestatum est in carne.

in general change once more, due to factors both internal and external.

Internal change was generated as a result of growing conviction that there was too much focus on the specific sacraments and not enough on their underlying rationale. One sees this reflected early in the century in a number of individual theologians: within Anglicanism Charles Gore, Oliver Quick, and William Temple are three names that spring to mind.[80] If Rome moved rather more slowly, the change was all the more profound when it finally came. In effect, since the Second Vatican Council most Catholic theology has set its discussion of specific sacraments within the wider frame of Christ as 'the primordial sacrament' and the Church as 'the fundamental sacrament'.[81] Although such a frame may still seem essentially Christian, it is worth observing that to explicate it requires some independent form of identification of how sacrament is understood before Christ can be claimed as its primordial form, and this is sometimes explicitly acknowledged.[82] Earlier definitions had by contrast presumed more specific Christian contingencies, as for example that sacraments had been instituted by Christ or mediated certain specific Christian goods.

At the same time as this development was occurring those with a Christian education were also broadening the word's use for other purposes. Anthropologists and students of other religions found 'sacrament' helpful as a term with which to describe some of the rites and rituals that they had encountered in their work. The result is that these days it is not uncommon to find the practices of the adherents of some of the other major religions described as 'sacramental', and indeed for this also to be said of some long-defunct

---

[80] Quick is discussed later. For Temple the universe is 'the fundamental sacrament' and the incarnation 'the perfect sacrament intensively': *Christus Veritas* (London: Macmillan, 1949), 234. Gore has a key chapter on 'the sacramental principle' in his *Body of Christ* (London: John Murray, 1901), 36–47, esp. 39–40. For a rather later, Presbyterian example of talk of a sacramental universe, D. Baillie, *Theology of the Sacraments* (London: Faber, 1957).

[81] In this Karl Rahner played a leading role. Some (e.g. Vorgrimler, *Sacramental Theology*, 31) have appealed to Aquinas in *Summa contra Gentiles* IV. 41. 10, but he seems to mean no more than that the incarnation is a 'mystery'.

[82] e.g. in P. E. Fink (ed.), *The New Dictionary of Sacramental Worship* (Dublin: Gill & Macmillan, 1990), Bernard Cooke's entry on 'Sacraments' opens with the declaration that 'sacramentality is not monopolised by Christianity; it extends to all human experience': 1116–23 esp. 1116.

religion.[83] Indeed, within Hinduism so deep are the parallels perceived to be that 'sacrament' is now the most common translation
used for *samskara*, the name for the sixteen rituals that mark the
chief phases of a Hindu's life. So English schoolchildren having
their first introduction to Hinduism will also find themselves being
inducted into the use of this word.[84]

In a similar way literary scholars have sometimes found this the
most useful way of describing the poets they study.[85] Contemporary Christian discussion also reflects that wider range of meaning by
applying the concept to areas even further removed from the usual
historical perimeters. One recent book, for example, applies the
notion to the modern cinema,[86] while another discussion contends
that this is a helpful way of exploring gay people's vulnerability in
the Church of today.[87] More Protestant Christians may lament the
lack of focus on the two principal biblical sacraments as a major
source of the Christian's faith and life, but the underlying question
is whether their significance is reduced or enhanced by such a more
inclusive approach. Some modern Catholic theologians observe
that for many, perhaps most, Catholics before the Council it was
the so-called 'sacramentals' or minor sacraments that actually fulfilled the greater role in Catholic life. That is to say, the rosary,

[83] For application to ancient religions generally, E. O. James, *Sacrifice and
Sacrament* (London: Thames & Hudson, 1962), esp. 232–51; to ancient Egyptian
religion, A. M. Blackman, *Gods, Priests and Men: Studies in the Religion of Pharaonic
Egypt* (London: Kegan Paul, 1998), 183–96. The last example is particularly
interesting as, although the chapter is headed 'Sacramental ideas and usages in
ancient Egypt' (1918), the term itself is never actually used in the body of the
article, so obvious are the parallels thought to be: e.g. 'water not only cleansed
those who washed in it of their impurities, but also imbued them with life' (185).

[84] e.g. V. P. Kanitkar, *Hinduism* (Cheltenham: Stanley Thornes & Hulton,
1989), 18–29 esp. 20; V. Voiels, *Hinduism: A New Approach* (London: Hodder &
Stoughton, 1998), 92–8 esp. 92.

[85] e.g. W. V. Spanos, *The Christian Tradition in Modern British Verse Drama: The
Poetics of Sacramental Time* (Princeton: Princeton University Press, 1967).

[86] P. Fraser, *Images of the Passion: The Sacramental Mode in Film* (Trowbridge:
Flick Books, 1998). Some plausible parallels are drawn between earlier attempts to
draw us into the redemptive power of the Passion narrative (e.g. Ignatian spirituality and Tolstoy's stories) and modern cinematic techniques: cf. 1–12.

[87] C. Glaser, *Coming out as Sacrament* (Louisville, Ky.: Westminster John Knox
Press, 1998). The point seems to be that the greater vulnerability that is made
inevitable by suspicion or condemnation helps open up the individual to the
action of divine grace, and so to sacramental encounters: esp. 7–15.

litanies to the saints, pilgrimages, and other such devotional practices had the greater sacramental impact on people's life of faith.[88]
That can of course be seen as a corruption, but the fault in part arose
because there was no such wider consideration of what it was for
God to act sacramentally. A dogma was proclaimed, but judged by
the most obvious tests its promised effects seemed most clearly
achieved elsewhere.

But if all this argues for a conceptualization that precludes automatic narrowing to within Christianity's own borders, it is not easy
to produce an acceptable definition for such a range. Some suggest
that the attempt should in any case be abandoned.[89] Additional
support for such a view would seem to be afforded by the further
historical complexities introduced through the influence of philosophy. For even more variety was created not only through the
impact of Platonism during the patristic period but also by the
introduction of Aristotelian ideas in the Middle Ages. In order,
therefore, to avoid prejudging too many issues, perhaps a loose,
intuitive notion will do as a working definition for the moment,
something like 'the symbolic mediation of the divine in and
through the material'. In a sense such a description must apply to
all God's actions since all his communication with us must be
mediated in one way or another, given that God and human beings
are so clearly two utterly different sorts of reality. But if sufficient
stress is placed on 'symbol' and on the two prepositions, then one
can perhaps see why divine 'action' in the world or 'answers'
to prayer would not normally fall under such a definition. In a
proper sense of the sacramental, the mediation is not purely
instrumental; instead the material symbol says something about
God in its own right, and so it is an indispensable element in
assessing both the immediate experience and any further significance it may have.[90]

Oliver Quick suggested that a major distinction should be drawn
between what he calls aesthetic and ethical sacramentalism. For the
former the stress is on the beauty of expression, whereas for

[88] So J. Martos, *Doors to the Sacred* (London: SCM, 1981), 124–7.

[89] Vorgrimler, *Sacramental Theology*, 43.

[90] 'Symbol' is a slippery word. For some of the complexities, see my entry
under 'symbolism' in A. Hastings (ed.), *The Oxford Companion to Christian Thought*
(Oxford: Oxford University Press, 2000), 690–2.

the latter it is a matter of instrumental goodness.[91] Although he does not put it like this, his contrast does correspond remarkably well to what motivates Platonic approaches to sacramentality (the 'aesthetic') and the new Aristotelian ideas that began to gain ascendancy in the second millennium (the 'ethical').[92] In rough, the difference can be highlighted by observing that whereas what matters under the Platonic scheme is participated presence, for the Aristotelian it is a matter of achieved effects. At first sight the contention may seem patently false to anyone who recalls the great stress laid on eucharistic presence in the Middle Ages, in the development of which the Aristotelian Aquinas played such a leading role.[93] But the point is not that one group ignored presence and the other effects, but rather where the weight of the thinking of each lay. First-millennium Christianity was on the whole content with the mystery of a participated presence, whereas the more rigorous Aristotelian sought to identify and define impact. The consequence was increasing recognition of a gap to be bridged, replacing the earlier sense of a dependency already there: either already acknowledged or only waiting to be made explicit.

In an important book Henri de Lubac has drawn attention to the way in which the whole notion of mystery changed between the first and second millennium. In former times all three 'bodies' (incarnational, eucharistic, and ecclesiastical) had been viewed as tightly bound together in a single related unity, but with the eucharistic body taken as the primary referent of the term *corpus mysticum*. However, the eucharistic controversies that followed Berengar's challenges in the eleventh century led to the Church being described primarily in this way and the eucharistic body now treated as the 'real' body, in theory a clarification but in practice de Lubac suggests a demotion.[94] For the net result was that, whereas once the sacrament had been conceived as a matter of the transformation of human beings into the Church as the body of Christ,

---

[91] O. C. Quick, *The Christian Sacraments* (London: Nisbet, 1932 edn.), 19–54 esp. 25.

[92] There are perhaps too many subordinate contrasts. Plato is mentioned (35–7), but not Aristotle.

[93] Aquinas wrote the liturgy for the newly established Feast of Corpus Christi.

[94] H. de Lubac, *Corpus mysticum: l'eucharistie et l'église au moyen âge* (Paris: Aubier, 1949). The trend begins with Berengar (d. 1088) and culminates in William of St Thierry (d. 1148): 18, 95.

instead came an undervaluing of the holistic character of symbolism in general. In effect the codifying of the sacramental body as having its own unique terminology entailed that questions could now be asked and answered of it without any wider reference.[95] Although living earlier than the main revival of his thought, Berengar had used Aristotelian logic to argue for a 'real' but spiritual presence in the eucharist. The response that eventually came was a threefold distinction between 'the sign only' (*sacramentum tantum*), 'both sign and reality' (*sacramentum et res*) and 'the reality by itself' (*res tantum*), with the *res*, the grace we receive, effectively subordinated to what was seen as the central, contentious middle term. Fruits in the life of the believer, therefore, almost inevitably were made subordinate to consideration of immediate cause and effect, and so the focus of interest moved almost entirely to sacramental change in the symbol itself. Even the most ardent Aristotelian could scarcely deny that not all the technical distinctions that emerged were of benefit to the sacramental life of the Church.[96]

My point in rehearsing this history is not to try to arbitrate between the two approaches. Aristotelianism is in many ways more in tune with contemporary secular ways of thinking, as also with some keys aspects of historical Christianity. Set, for example, against such a frame it becomes much easier to assert the radical independence of God over against the world. The frame, though, also carries with it a greater burden in bridging the gap, whether it be in the need for arguments for God's existence (philosophy of religion) or in the requirement for a radical intervention on God's part (an exclusively revelation-orientated theology). To make English analytic philosophy of religion and Barthian revelation bedfellows may seem odd at first, but my point is that both presuppose the disenchantment of the world. It is seen as a secular reality to which more has to be added by one means or another, if God is to assume centre stage once more. The means are of course hugely different, but against both can be placed the fundamental question that both Platonism and postmodernism (again, two strange bedfellows) alike suggest: whether it is not possible to view our world with God as

[95] Cf. 98, 274. Abelard, for example, never uses the word 'mystery' of the eucharist: 275.
[96] Martos laments the way in which canon law eventually took over, and sacramental practice degenerated into 'sacramental magic': *Doors*, 85–96 esp. 96.

already given in the individual's experience of it. In rejecting foundationalism postmodernism of course only raises the possibility, whereas Platonism has the dynamics of the interconnections presupposed throughout. Whether one thinks of our world imitating or participating in other-worldly Forms (as in Plato) or of emanation from an overflowing divine richness (as in Plotinus), Platonic terminology appears to suggest intrinsic and not extrinsic connections. For some that may be precisely what it is wrong with Platonism, that it inevitably concludes in some form of pantheism. But the same thought can of course be expressed without the philosophical apparatus. Christianity has had a long history of seeing the world as God's 'second book'. It also asserts that human beings are made in the divine image. Both claims can be read in very general terms. But the more generously they are interpreted, the more it becomes possible to see specifics in nature and in human creativity as a reflection of the divine, there to be experienced as such even in advance of any specific revelation.

Light is one such element much stressed in Christian Neoplatonic writings, but, as noted earlier, anthropologists have alerted us to many other examples besides. Whether key Christian material signs such as water, bread, and blood might share such a transcultural status as 'natural' symbols is an issue that can be more suitably treated in this volume's successor.[97] What, however, must even now be conceded is that the natural seldom acts apart from the cultural: apart, that is, from particular traditions of interpretation. Yet even these should not be confused with the purely human: God can also be active within particular traditions and patterns of interpretation.[98] Indeed it is arguable that, because all human experience occurs within specific contexts, even God cannot be experienced without being interpreted in the light of what is already understood or known. Crude contrasts between the 'specific' and the 'general' or 'universal' need therefore to be avoided. Potentially, all may function as experiences of God.

---

[97] In *Natural Symbols* (Harmondsworth: Penguin, 1973), Mary Douglas stresses the social contribution. Cf. also my 'God and symbolic action' in B. Hebblethwaite and E. Henderson (eds.), *Divine Action* (Edinburgh: T & T Clark, 1990), 103–22, esp. 113 ff.

[98] A major part of the argument of my two recent volumes, *Tradition and Imagination: Revelation and Change* and *Discipleship and Imagination: Christian Tradition and Truth* (both Oxford: Oxford University Press, 1999 and 2000).

Looking Ahead

I want, therefore, in the chapters that follow, to take seriously this mixture of nature and culture, of human artefact no less than creation reflecting experience of the divine. So Chapter 3 explores some of the various ways in which nature has been seen to communicate the divine, but it does so by examining landscape painting and the abstract art that derived from it. One obvious advantage paintings afford is conciseness; their general thrust is far more quickly deduced than is the case from many pages of prose. Another is that the human contribution is usually much more to the fore. Descriptions of experience of nature can sound deceptively neutral, whereas often readily identifiable are the various ways in which an artist has modified the scene before him in order to induce viewers to share in some particular perspective. Yet the fact that certain contexts and periods encourage artists to bring one feature to prominence and others another should not be taken to imply the absence of such features in nature itself, far less the absence of an underlying divine presence. Different contexts open up different possibilities. In a similar way the chapter that follows it, in considering the sacramentality of specific locations, will need to reckon with a complex dialectic of place that has found God not only in the given of nature (mountains, caves, and so on) but also both in chosen forms of permanence (such as particular types of home and town plans) and in flight from these (in pilgrimage). Thereafter, the notion of choice becomes even more conspicuous as the human imaginative contribution in architecture is considered. To the uninitiated, architecture (the topic of the two subsequent chapters) may well seem an entirely human, purely cultural product, but this is certainly not how it has been commonly regarded for most of human history. Just as music was once seen to imitate simple harmonies that were both divine gift and human product, so architecture was held to embody, at its best, principles that reflected the divine architect behind the world's own making. A 'natural' element was thus postulated, even if that natural element was in each case significantly modified through interaction with other religious and cultural assumptions, the specificities of time and place.

If only to render the project manageable, most of the illustrations in what follows of necessity come from within my own Christian tradition. The argument, however, is intended to apply more generally. So occasional examples from other traditions are offered throughout, while the final chapter deliberately ends by looking more widely, at mosques and temples, gardens and sport venues. However, the chapter that immediately follows this one uses a debate within Christianity to focus two quite different ways of conceiving God's relationship with place, the transcendence of icons and the immanence of Renaissance art. As we shall see, the tension between transcendence and immanence is a topic to which I shall need to return more than once. Initially, the contrast may seem clear and unproblematic, but, as our discussion proceeds, complexities will emerge, not least in the commonly felt need to find both in human experience of God.

Before going further, however, it might be helpful to the reader if I attempted to characterize in a little more detail the type of project on which I conceive myself to be engaged. These days subdivisions within theology departments are often closely guarded, with scholars disliking the idea that their own particular patch might be invaded by someone in another field. That seems to me a great pity as much can be learnt by mutual fertilization. So, although I have already delineated this project in brief as an exercise in natural religion, I hope it also contributes to breaking down some of the artificial barriers that exist between philosophical, historical, and doctrinal theology. Sacrament in my view can only be kept to the doctrinal or revealed side of the line by highly artificial strategies, while again I would question whether the experience of revelation that led to our present Scriptures should ever be treated as wholly distinct from experience of God within the natural order. So inevitably traditional subject divisions are treated lightly, and the dominant stress varies from chapter to chapter. If my discussion of pilgrimage, for example, verges sharply towards the historical, the treatment of landscape painting in Chapter 3 raises some conventional questions (such as the problem of evil) that are usually associated with the philosophy of religion. Again, if Chapter 2 uses Platonism to illustrate how even philosophers are culturally conditioned, the final chapter does not hesitate to enter the field of other religions to demonstrate that conditioning is not the same thing as complete cultural determination, with no room for manœuvre or free response.

Not that the differing emphases are just a matter of whim. They are all part of my wider aim of trying to engage the reader in a form of perception that has largely been lost in our utilitarian age, experiencing the natural world and human imitations of it not just as means to some further end but as themselves the vehicle that makes possible an encounter with God, discovering an enchantment, an absorption that like worship requires no further justification. Some of the types I discuss require no background education; some much. But education is not in the end what makes the difference; it is openness to the possibility of such experience.

2
The Place of Encounter
Icons of Transcendence and Renaissance Immanence

In the chapters that follow this one I shall examine the sacramentality of 'place' in a more obvious sense of the term, in places such as the natural world, sites of pilgrimage and specific buildings, 'secular' no less than 'sacred'. Here, however, I want to focus on what kind of mediation the material offers in that encounter between God and ourselves. To presuppose a point of contact is far from entailing that 'the place of encounter' will necessarily always be understood in the same way. Certainly, two worlds interconnect, but is the force of the interconnection to give us some sense of another, divine reality that draws us beyond our own, or is the experience rather one of the divine invading the material order and transforming it? One way of highlighting such a contrast is to talk of transcendence on the one hand and of immanence on the other. In the final analysis both words are only metaphors: God is neither quite 'beyond' the world nor 'in' it. More is really being said about how God is consequently perceived, and what that means for our relationship with him. It is my conviction that both perspectives are in fact essential for any adequate theology. But before explaining why, I want to pursue in some detail the contrast and its potential implications, particularly if either way of thinking is left to itself. It will enable us to examine various tensions in how our experience is read, and thus the need to weigh such aspects against other elements if a balanced overall assessment is to be produced of what experience as a whole communicates. A useful way of pursuing such questions will be to contrast the most common form of theology applied to icons and the quite different way in which Renaissance art has been defended.

Orthodox theologians are often dismissive of Western art, particularly as it has developed since the Renaissance. The 'compliment' was returned by the Renaissance. Nowadays, however, in so far as Western theologians discuss the issue at all, they tend to treat icons on their own terms, and so offer a purely positive evaluation. Indeed, they are often found endorsing the view that icons preserve a sense of the holy in a way that was already lacking in the late Middle Ages and still more so by the time of the Renaissance.[1] This seems to me unfortunate, not because icons have no merits; far from it. But because faults are not debated, it means that each side learns little from the other, and so there is little comprehension of what is at stake between the underlying theologies. In order to rectify that problem, I plan here to look at Eastern art first and then at its Renaissance counterpart. As we shall see, the East is less uniform than might initially be supposed. Likewise, I shall contend that the Renaissance is not always correctly understood, even in the West. It is more deeply based in the Christian religion than is usually admitted. One reason why this is not always fully understood is because the influence of Platonism on the movement is presumed to have been in a purely pagan direction. It is precisely in order to counter such an assumption that, before examining Renaissance art in its own right, I shall consider first the history of Platonism. In drawing attention to how it might be used to reinforce incarnational and sacramental belief, I note the great variety of forms that Platonism has taken over its history, and in particular how it has influenced Orthodoxy in a quite different direction from the impact it had on the Renaissance. One added advantage that such an analysis will give is the way in which it can illustrate the wider conditioning of perception, in philosophical thought no less than elsewhere. This does not mean that we cannot lessen its impact (conditioning is not determination), but forearmed is forewarned.

Icons and Eastern Sacramentality

Those whose understanding of icons has been most shaped by icons of the Mother of God in loving interaction with her young Son could easily be forgiven for supposing that the difference between

---

[1] e.g. D. W. Hardy (quoting others), 'Calvinism and the Visual Arts: A Theological Introduction', in P. C. Corby, *Seeing Beyond the Word* (Grand Rapids: Eerdmans, 1999), 1–16 esp. 3–4, 7–8.

East and West is not all that great.[2] Such icons came to prominence at the very time when the influence of East on West was likely to be most marked thanks to the Crusades and eventual conquest of Byzantium. But thereafter Orthodoxy refused to go any further in the direction that the West now plotted. Instead the earlier iconography of the centuries immediately following the defeat of the iconoclasts was held up as the ideal, and that meant endorsing various devices that limited immanence and so countered the iconoclasts' charge that icons had become more like relics than vehicles towards engagement with the existence of another, transcendent world. One such feature is the hieratic frontal pose that is often employed even in images of Virgin and Child, but is of course much more prominent elsewhere.[3] In endorsing that kind of approach, Platonism, as we shall see, played a significant role.

So in focusing on the kind of theology that emerged and the defence that it continues to be given to this day, it is important to note that that I am not denying the complexities of Orthodox history nor the existence of icons that might seem to pull in a rather different direction. But a broad sweep will at least enable me to highlight the contrast with the Renaissance, and also some of the strengths and weaknesses of such an approach. Attacks on the Renaissance are so common that it is a pity that note is so seldom taken of the limitations of the Orthodox approach. East and West will only enter into mature dialogue when mutual faults and pitfalls are fully acknowledged. In any case, as I shall suggest towards the end of my discussion of icons, not only are other possible approaches available (however muted) within Orthodoxy itself, they are also surprisingly resilient in some of the smaller churches of the East. Attitudes in these non-Chalcedonian churches in some ways share more in common with the sacramentality of the Renaissance than they do with the standard theology of the icon.

---

[2] Most obvious in the image of the Mother of God as 'compassionate', known in Greek as *Eleusa* and in Russian as *Umilenie* and common from the 12th c. onwards. For an example of a Westerner attempting to use Marian icons to combine nearness and otherness, R. Williams, *Ponder These Things: Praying with Icons of the Virgin* (Norwich: Canterbury Press, 2002).

[3] In the *Hodegetria* image Virgin and Child are commonly portrayed looking directly at the worshipper; the Virgin points to her Son, and the Son, mature beyond his years, gives a blessing.

Finally, three qualifications of the discussion that follows need emphasizing. The first is that I only discuss the most common way of approaching the issue known in the West; there are others.[4] Secondly, the theology addressed is that applied to individual icons. The question takes on a rather different hue when a total ensemble is being considered, such as those set within the architecture of a typical Orthodox church.[5] Finally and most importantly, transcendence does not mean absence; it is one of two ways of mediating presence. The difference is primarily directional, in how that presence makes itself felt, and thus, secondarily, on the valuation attached to the world as such. Transcendence stresses the otherness of God, immanence the closeness, but both embody a relationship, transcendence for example in the implied power to effect change. One question that will concern us throughout this chapter is whether the one does not in the end require some of the other, if transcendence is not to slip over into absence, or immanence into endorsement of this world and nothing more. Sometimes such qualifications can come in the art itself, as in those icons of Virgin and Child I have already mentioned; sometimes, and perhaps more commonly, through the totality of what is presented in a church.

Orthodox Transcendence

'In a nutshell, *the icon is a sacrament* for the Christian East; more precisely it is the vehicle of a personal presence.'[6] That might seem self-evidently so, given the degree of veneration accorded icons, but it is worth observing that one consequence of the iconoclastic controversy in the eighth and ninth centuries was the need to distinguish icons from the way in which Christ was thought to be present in the eucharist: the icon is not consubstantial with what it represents in the way the bread and wine are with Christ's presence.[7] The result has been in the East great insistence that the divine presence should not be confused with what appears on the

---

[4] In forming Western perceptions, the Russian émigré school of Paris has been most influential. Somewhat different emphases are found in Pavel Florensky and Sergeii Bulgakov.

[5] Discussed near the beginning of Ch. 5.

[6] P. Evdokimov, *The Art of the Icon: A Theology of Beauty* (Redondo Beach, Calif.: Oakwood, 1990), 178 (italics, Evdokimov's own).

[7] cf. Evdokimov, *Art of the Icon*, 193–6.

board itself, but rather be viewed as a vehicle for participation in what remains essentially a transcendent reality.[8] It is thus holy by participation rather than holy in itself, a 'sacrament of Light where history is already drawn up into eternity'.[9] One contemporary Russian scholar describes the role of the domestic shrine thus: 'the main corner of a Russian peasant house was the "High Jerusalem," "the window to heaven," "the image of the other world."'[10] It is to achieve this effect that a certain style is employed, one that forces the viewer to halt at the surface of the board and look beyond.

So the argument is that icons should not be concerned with representation or imitation of this world, nor make any appeal to natural emotion, but rather engage with transfiguration, and thus with how the viewer might be pulled into viewing and appreciating an alternative reality.[11] To do this, the figures should be free of the weight of flesh and their faces exude a light that can speak of supernatural grace.[12] Likewise background buildings or landscape should not be portrayed realistically, but rather reduced to relative insignificance, in order to reflect the fact that the beauty of the supernatural is of an altogether different kind and status from human artefact or even natural beauty.[13] But perhaps most important of all is what is held to justify inverse perspective, with the size of the figures determined by importance and not receding view; so, whenever deemed appropriate, those at a greater distance can be made the same size or even larger than those closer to our vision.[14] It is that very lack of realism which, it is held, will enable us to acknowledge an immaterial world beyond our own.[15]

[8] Cf. ibid. 200.
[9] The words quoted are by Olivier Clément in his Foreword to Evdokimov, ibid. p. vi; cf. also 201.
[10] O. Tarasov, *Icon and Devotion: Sacred Spaces in Imperial Russia* (London: Reaktion, 2002), 39.
[11] So L. Ouspensky, *Theology of the Icon* (Crestwood, NY: St Vladimir's Seminary, 1992), i. 181; ii. 348. Cf. also L. Ouspensky annd V. Lossky, *The Meaning of Icons* (Crestwood, NY: St Vladimir's Seminary, 1982 edn.), 35.
[12] Ouspensky and Lossky, *Meaning of Icons*, 109, 127.
[13] Ibid. 40, 132; Evdokimov, *Art of the Icon*, 41.
[14] Ouspensky and Lossky, *Meaning of Icons*, 41: 'inverse perspective does not draw in the eye of the spectator... it concentrates the attention on the image itself'. Cf. ibid. 207.
[15] Evdokimov, *Art of the Icon*, 220–1.

It is into this way of understanding the art of icons that we must therefore fit attacks from Orthodox theologians on Western art. Renaissance art is condemned not just for its sentimentality but also for its realism. Even what is now commonly regarded in the West as one of the world's most moving religious paintings, Grünewald's Isenheim Altarpiece, is summarily dismissed as conjuring up merely a 'tragic feeling of absence'.[16] If Romanesque is given qualified praise, even Fra Angelico is already seen as compromised by a false intellectualism of a type that reaches its nadir in Raphael.[17] Nor have modern painters from the East such as Kandinsky or Kupka been able to halt the deleterious results of all such trends towards realism; the reaction of modern Western art to realism has only been fresh errors in its turn.[18] If by the time of Raphael the corruption was too deep-seated to be capable of correction, even long before the high period of Romanesque art, it is suggested, things were already going badly wrong. For, unlike the response in the East, Charlemagne and the Franks' reaction to the iconoclastic controversy was to put a purely utilitarian value on religious art.[19] Not that the Orthodox world has been without its problems, but these are seen to stem largely from corrupting Western influences that councils such as Trullo and Stoglav did much to put under restraint.[20] That there is some element of truth in these criticisms can scarcely be denied, but there is also, I think, much on the other side to be noted.

The main problem is that transcendence seems to be claimed as the only legitimate element and immanence downplayed or even

---

[16] Ibid. 171. For a similar critique with 'emotion' seen as replacing 'royal majesty': C. Kalokyris, 'The Content of Eastern Iconography', in L. Macdonald and D. Power (eds.), *Symbol and Art in Worship* (Edinburgh: T & T Clark, 1980), 9–17 esp. 15–17.

[17] Ouspensky, *Theology of the Icon*, ii. 228, 493; Evdokimov, *Art of the Icon*, 74, 264.

[18] Evdokimov, *Art of the Icon*, 81–3.

[19] It was simply to decorate, or else to educate; cf. Ouspensky, *Theology of the Icon*, i. 142–3. The subordination of image to word in the Carolingian period did sometimes go to extraordinary lengths, including paintings overwritten with words: for examples, W. J. Diebold, *Word and Image* (Boulder, Colo.: Westview, 2000), 110–12.

[20] Trullo took place in 692, as the name implies in a 'chamber' in the imperial palace; Stoglav ('the hundred chapters council') in Moscow in 1551. For further details, Ouspensky, *Theology of the Icon*, i. 91–100; ii. 287–323.

ignored altogether. Under such a scheme it is no longer the worle. as such that reveals God, but only that world when transformed under divine grace. The claim may seem innocent enough, but of course it entails a world that always needs some further action upon it over and above creation itself, that is to say some further act of divine grace, in order to point to its creator. So it seems more than an accident that in icons not only do such characteristic Western images as the labours of the months and celebration of crafts find no place but also even the blue sky is made to yield to divine gold.[21] In respect of Christ himself that same pattern is repeated. The stress lies on Christ transfigured as the clue, and significantly it is the icon of the same name that is most commonly used as the principal inter-pretative guide in comprehending the intention behind icons. Other events in Christ's life are thus meted out similar treatment, and it is the timeless quality of the events that is stressed rather than the engagement of God with history as such.[22] So it comes as no surprise that in marked contrast to Western treatments the apostles are not given any distinctive signs of martyrdom but rather por-trayed as they are now, in a timeless realm of joy.[23] Dostoevsky once claimed that a saint cannot be portrayed in terms of this world. He was himself of course Orthodox, but it is intriguing to note his view fully endorsed by Orthodox theologians.[24] For it looks as though the whole movement of the icon is seen as decisively in one direction, not towards the world but rather drawing us out of that world and into another. This is not to deny the icon's sacra-mental character, but it is to observe that its mediation of the divine is very much of a participatory pull elsewhere rather than an endorsement of what is already before one's eyes (and so, for example, quite different from the ancient Greek attitude to sports-men that I considered in the previous chapter).

One way in which one might justify such attitudes would be to stress the fallenness of our world, that in the presence of sin divine glory cannot be seen except where transmogrified under the impact of divine grace. The role of icons, it might then be said, is not to encourage flight from the world but rather to transfigure that world

---

[21] Both are found in the medieval glass of Chartres. For the point expanded, C. Mango, *Byzantium* (London: Weidenfeld & Nicolson, 1980), 270–1.

[22] Cf. Evdokimov on the nativity and last supper, *Art of the Icon*, 133.

[23] Ouspensky and Lossky, *Meaning of Icons*, 125.

[24] Evdokimov, *Art of the Icon*, 42.

s diaphanous to the glory of God. Certainly that is
)rthodox thinking, but as an approach to icons it
/o disadvantages. In the first place, such meaning
n the painting itself but externally through church
ne cannot claim that this is what the icon 'means', or
how .. .tself experienced. Secondly, in common with other
branches of Christianity (such as Calvinism) that stress a fallen
world, such an emphasis seems artificially to separate creation and
revelation, as though creation was not already a sphere of divine
grace simply in virtue of God being its source. The result is
considerable temptation to downgrade natural beauty.[25] So, despite
the undoubted power of so many icons, their limitations do also,
I think, need to be acknowledged. The stress on transcendence can
sometimes be so great as to make the divine world seem totally set
apart from this world rather than integrating with it and so transforming it.

Resistance to Change

A not unrelated difficulty is the suspicion of change that also tends
to results from such views. In order to preserve the timeless,
supernatural imprint, the inclination is to claim certain inviolable
conventions about what can or cannot be depicted, and in what
manner, and these are held not to be subject to any further revision.
Indeed, to minimize any sense of change, continuity is claimed
with the New Testament itself through the form of various famous
icons having been instituted from the very beginning, even if the
original is now no longer with us.[26] Apart from the evidential
problems inherent in any such claims, there is a deeper issue, and
that is that this prevents the Church from engaging with the actual
fact of change and continuing development. The Council of
Stoglav even went so far as to instruct that 'painters are in no way
to use their imagination'.[27] So, if difficulties in the Western approach must be conceded, the same applies no less to what has
happened in the East. A few remarks on change would therefore

---

[25] Largely true of icons, but not of Calvinism, as we shall see in the next
chapter.
[26] So Ouspensky, *Theology of the Icon*, i. 51, 58.
[27] Stoglav, ibid. ch. 41; quoted with approval, ibid. ii. 291, cf. 299.

seem apposite at this stage: first on its actual existence in the Eastern iconographical tradition despite such claims; then, secondly and more directly pertinent to my theme, why such lack of engagement on this point might bode ill for sacramental effectiveness.

Although conceding that sometimes a strong impression of unbroken continuity across the centuries is successfully conveyed, in surveying the history of Eastern Christianity one Western art historian none the less observes more than once that that sense of an unbroken tradition is 'a fiction'.[28] In this he is supported by many other scholars. In one major work, for instance, a number of external influences are detected, moving the art now in one direction, now in another: both classical and Egyptian, for instance, at the beginning, and then classical once more in the ninth to eleventh centuries. Even the influence of the West is to be observed in some of Byzantium's finest creations not long before the city finally fell to the Ottoman advance in 1453.[29] Islam is also seen to have had its own characteristic impact.[30] If classical realism is still to be found in the early icons of the monastery of St Catherine at Sinai, and is revived in as famous a work as the Khludov Psalter,[31] even the flat surface forms that are now thought of as so characteristic of the spirituality of the icon need to be handled with care, since initially at least even secular rulers were accorded similar treatment.[32] Indeed, it looks as though the religious justification may well have followed adoption of the practice rather than initiated it. Then again the later Byzantine tension between a more intense emotionalism or else stress on immateriality may possibly be more the result of competing responses to the insecurities of the age than

---

[28] J. Lowden, *Early Christian and Byzantine Art* (London: Phaidon, 1997), e.g. 187, 391.

[29] K. Onasch and A. Schnieper, *Icons: The Fascination and the Reality* (New York: Riverside, 1997), for early influences: 9–10, 16; for later classical influence: 45; for Western influence: 33, 46, 72.

[30] J. Durand, *Byzantine Art* (Paris: Terrail, 1999), 139–40. Durand notes in particular the influence on textiles and pottery, helped by the fact that up till the 11th c. there was a functioning mosque within the city.

[31] Ibid. 43, 121. The Khludov Psalter (late-9th c.) has over two hundred paintings that 'reveal a remarkable familiarity with antique models which it draws upon indiscriminately'.

[32] Ibid. 55–7. For another example and commentary, Lowden, *Early Christian and Byzantine Art*, 219–20.

initiatives generated internally from within the iconographic tradition alone.[33]

None of this is to deny the undoubted power of icons to suggest
another world. Rather, it is to challenge whether they are all
uniform in objective, or intending quite the same kind of message.
For, as I noted earlier, some precedents for a more Western approach were already implicit in some artists' work, available in due
course to have their impact as so many of these artefacts moved
Westwards, especially from the time of the Crusades onwards.
Mention might be made here of presentations of the beauty of
nature in manuscripts,[34] but relevant too was the emotional dynamic in icons themselves, between Virgin and Child or between
Christ crucified and those at the foot of the cross, that were of
course eventually to become more marked features of Western
art.[35] But those signs of change also went with much resistance in
approach, and it is that resistance which, I believe, sometimes
undermines the sacramental potential of icons.

Perhaps a few representative examples may be allowed to make
the point. Consider first how the Annunciation is treated. Even in
modern times Mary is still to be found with the spindle that had
long since been abandoned by Western art in favour of a book.[36]
What is lost in the East is engagement with a changing society. In
the West what had originally been an allusion to Isaiah's prophecy
quickly became transformed into an argument for female piety and

[33] Although the city regained its independence from Latin rule in 1261, external threat was a constant reality until its fall in 1453. Durand contrasts the emotive
power in works at the famous church at Chora (in modern Istanbul) with the stress
on immateriality that is so characteristic of the icons of Theophanes the Greek:
ibid. 180, 188–93.

[34] For illustrations of engagement with the beauty of nature, in the 10th-c. *Paris
Psalter*, Durand, ibid. 114, 118–19; and in the 11th-c. *Psalter of Basil*.

[35] For some examples (12th c. and later), M. Vassilaki (ed.), *Mother of God:
Representations of the Virgin in Byzantine Art* (Milan: Skira, 2000), 464–92. In their
accompanying article (452–63) M. Vassilaki and N. Tsironis, while acknowledging
development, tend to want to see the main influence as coming from sermons
rather than any impact from the West. Whatever the explanation, the contrast is
certainly marked compared with icons of earlier centuries.

[36] For a 17th-c. example from the Tretyakov Gallery in Moscow, S. Kutschinki
and J. Poetter, *Russische Ikonen und Kulturgerät* (Cologne: DuMont, 1991), illus. 20.
That was also still the view in the 18th c. when Dionysius of Fourna produced his
Painter's Manual (trans. P. Hetherington, Torrance, Calif.: Oakwood, 1989), 32,
para. 85. The practice continues to this day.

literacy, the right of women to have access to prayer manuals and still more generally their entitlement to some form of education. The developing trend even led to pictures of Mary as a child being taught to read by her mother, St Anne.[37] Of course, one might reply that the East was in any case changing more slowly, but the irony is that, so far from the icon representing a timeless reality, such representations now draw attention to a world that is gone, and so place Mary firmly in the past rather than as part of our world. Yet at the same time other developments were occurring that could have offered more of a suggestion of the event being part of our world. For some icon painters do toy with giving a greater sense of movement to the angel as he advances towards Mary. Yet in the end such possibilities do not seem to have been pursued.[38] Again, if the positive side of Eastern portrayals of Mary's Dormition is role-reversal and so Christ now caring for his mother as she once cared for him (Mary's soul is portrayed as like a baby held in the adult Christ's arms), the negative side is the implicit suggestion that somehow it is only an immaterial reality, her soul, that is carried beyond our world, not her humanity as a whole, body and soul.[39] By contrast, the equivalent Western image of the Assumption, whatever other difficulties it may encounter, certainly cannot be accused of undervaluing the material world. El Greco well illustrates the point, as he produced paintings of the Assumption according to both patterns, and there seems little doubt as to which is the more effective. As a matter of fact, Orthodoxy does also believe in the assumption of Mary, body and soul, into heaven.

[37] A touching example occurs in a Burgundy Breviary of 1415: Harley MS 2897, British Library.

[38] For how different the portrayal can be as a result, note two good examples illustrated in A. Trivonova, *The Russian Icon of the Novgorod Museum Collection* (St Petersburg: Madoc, 1992), 115, 129 (both from the 16th c.). One might contrast them with the tiny hints of movement that are permitted in a 6th-c. icon from Sinai (Onasch and Schnieper, *Icons*, 18–19), or again with the static but unusual format adopted in an icon of the 12th c.: K. Onasch, *Russian Icons* (Oxford: Phaidon, 1977), illus. 10 (the unusual element is the inclusion of the Child Jesus already within Mary).

[39] The symmetry of the relationship is stressed in those churches that have Mother and Child in the eastern apse and the Dormition on the western wall. The same theme is found in a poem by the emperor Leo VI: 'Because you held God when he was invested with flesh, you are held in the hands of God when you are divested of flesh' (J. P. Migne (ed.), *Patrologia Graeca* (PG), 107. 164A).

My point is that, because a particular way of representation is followed unthinkingly, it carries the misleading impression than something less than the complete reality is now with God.[40]

In many cases the problem seems to be simply one of tradition for tradition's sake, even where the deleterious consequences seem clear. Images of Christ as a child inside Mary's body, or again on the paten at the eucharist can, for instance, all too easily reduce to a manipulative relationship, with Mary's intercessions or the priest's power seen as exercising decisive control.[41] Yet the Western lamb on the altar, precisely because it looks so unnatural, cannot possibly be made subject to the same kind of critique. Admittedly, occasionally there are hints of an internal debate on just such questions. So, for instance, those Pentecost icons that culminate at the head of the table in an empty space for divine action seem much more powerful than others where this gap is filled with Mary herself.[42] Again, great care has at times been taken to circumvent any suggestion of a possible pagan parallel, as in those icons that deliberately distort Jesus' manner of feeding at Mary's breasts to make the act look as unnatural as possible, precisely in order to ensure that the viewer is not reminded of any pagan goddess such as Isis in a similar role.[43] Mary, we are being told, is a very special, indeed unique, mother.

But for the most part patterns seem simply to be repeated without further thought. A notable instance of this is the mysterious figure commonly portrayed in the arcade at the foot of Pentecost

---

[40] Implicitly acknowledged in some icons where Mary is represented growing in scale as she moves heavenwards: e.g. Kutschinski and Poetter, *Russische Ikonen*, no. 35 (16th c.) For the El Greco contrast D. Davies (ed.), *El Greco* (London: National Gallery, 2003), 75, 201 (where immaculate conception themes are also present).

[41] The latter became common from 1200 onwards. For two examples, Onasch and Schnieper, *Icons* 137. Ironically, though known as the *Amnos*, any symbolic representation of Christ as Lamb had been prohibited at Trullo, and so no actual 'lamb' occurs: Ouspensky, *Theology of the Icon*, i. 92.

[42] Contrast e.g. two icons from the 15th c. in Trivonova, *The Russian Icon*, 53, 109.

[43] So Onasch and Schnieper, *Icons*, 173. Contrast, though, the development of Mother and Child as a life-giving spring, to counter pre-Christian sacred springs dedicated to Asclepius where, whatever the intention, the impact is more likely to have been one of endorsement. For illustration, ibid. 175.

icons.[44] It is hard to credit that the figure is suppos͜
humanity, still less that his crown is the crown of sı͠
confusion exists over the icon in which St Christophe͞
dog's head.[45] Even where the reasons for some strange prac͜
widely known, their continuing value can certainly be calle͜
question. So, despite the original intention being clear, it is ha͠   ͜
see any deepening of engagement in the continuing practice of
giving Mary three hands,[46] or in placing mythological figures in the
river Jordan.[47] I say all of this not to ridicule Orthodoxy, but out of
a desire for greater acknowledgement of faults on both sides.
Despite the undoubted power of so many of its images, when we
turn to detail, the East still has just as many problems to confront in
respect of its individual images as does the West. What is experienced is thus not necessarily more powerful than what is on offer in
the West. Alienation from modern life, muddle, or confusion can
sometimes be part of an icon's impact, and so inhibit a sense of
divine presence. Of course, comparative faults can also be identified
in Renaissance art; the difference is that these are commonly
acknowledged.

One objection that could be raised against what I have said thus
far is that it ignores how Orthodox theologians in fact treat the
world, where instead of us being drawn into another world the talk
is of God's Spirit infusing all things. Indeed, one could quote many
a modern or ancient theologian apparently to precisely that effect,

[44] There is little attempt at clear or meaningful iconography. Contrast the royal
figure described by Ouspensky and Lossky (*Meaning of Icons*, 206–8) with the two
figures in strange clothing on a possibly 6th-c. icon, illustrated in Onasch and
Schnieper (*Icons*, 29). The crown of sin is a 17th-c. explanation supported by
Ouspensky and Lossky, ibid. 208.

[45] Conflicting explanations of the origin of the dog-head are given. Contrast
the later explanation that the aim was to avoid tempting local girls (Onasch and
Schnieper, *Icons*, 283) with the more likely source in the legend of the *cynocephali*, a
race with such heads: J. Taylor, *Icon Painting* (Oxford: Phaidon, 1979), 65.

[46] For the legend of Mary's three hands, with its allusion to her cure of John of
Damascus' severed hand, Onasch and Schnieper, *Icons*, 58, 63, 162. The practice
is sometimes defended on the grounds that only two of the hands look as though
they belong to Mary, but this is not always true: contrast ibid. 63 with 58 and
162.

[47] For such figures, representing the defeat of the river's pagan powers, ibid.
107. Perhaps the most extraordinary example is on the dome of the Arian
Baptistery at Ravenna where the figure is as big as Christ and apparently given a
positive connotation.

with, for instance, Schmemann from our times or Denys the Areopagite from the more distant past.[48] Indeed, one recent exhibition of Orthodox art might seem to provide the decisive counter-blast to my interpretation, for it was even hosted under the title 'Heaven on Earth'.[49] But caution is necessary in interpreting such language. Significantly, the commentary accompanying the exhibition expounded the theology of the artefacts presented in exactly the way I have just indicated, that is, as a drawing up rather than as a downward thrust, in short as deification.[50] And therein lies the problem. If this approach is carried too far, what is offered is an alternative world hovering, as it were, alongside our present reality rather than actually engaged with it. The eventual triumph of Hesychast theology in the fourteenth century and its advocates' special liking for the image of the transfiguration does, therefore, seem to me a matter of no small moment.[51] It is a special theophany

---

[48] Although Schmemann talks of the eucharist as 'cosmic in that it embraces all creation', the stress he lays on its eschatological side ends up by pulling him in a quite different direction; for the quotation, A. Schmemann, *The Eucharist* (Crestwood, NY: St Vladimir's Seminary, 1988), 34. Similarly, although in his *Divine Names* Dionysius talks of God's presence in all things, in the end a much greater emphasis is to be found in his claim that God radically transcends everything: cf. e.g. I. 5; VII. 3.

[49] The title alludes to the perhaps legendary comments of the Russian ambassadors who in the 10th c. attended the liturgy at Hagia Sophia in Constantinople and which supposedly led to the conversion of Russia: L. Safran (ed.), *Heaven on Earth: Art and the Church in Byzantium* (University Park, Pa.: Pennsylvania State University Press, 1998), 54, 56 n. 39.

[50] Stressed by Safran in her Introduction, 5, and still more so by E. Perl in his article, 'That Man Might become God', *Heaven on Earth*, 38–57. Perl observes that this is why it was so important to represent deified humanity on the cross, and for even 'King of Glory' to be substituted for 'King of the Jews' as the cross's superscription: ibid. 43–4.

[51] Hesychasm (from the Greek for 'quietness') was a movement particularly associated with the monks of Mt. Athos. A quiet, receptive posture and constant repetition of the Jesus Prayer was held eventually to bring a vision of the divine light that had been experienced at the transfiguration. Although Gregory Palamas (1296–1359) moderated its theology somewhat, the assumption remained that God needed to perform some act additional to the way the world now is, in order to make his presence known: cf. Onasch and Schnieper, *Icons*, 49, 108, 261. God vouchsafed his own light as individuals were themselves transformed in prayer before icons such as those of the Transfiguration or the Hodegetria (Mary pointing the way): cf. e.g. Dionysius of Fourna, *Painter's Manual*, trans. Hetherington, 4, para. 5.

that casts the three disciples to the ground, not an alternative way of perceiving the world as it already is, with the divine implicitly there all around them.[52]

Had all the above been offered as a universal judgement on icons, it would certainly have been altogether too sweeping. As I mentioned earlier, a different estimate of the role of icons becomes possible once a church context is taken into account. But much the same is true had the focus been on periods in the history of icons other than the time immediately subsequent to the iconoclastic controversy, now commonly held up as the ideal. Not all that much later, patterns of much deeper human engagement were to emerge that gave the impetus for the characteristic styles of Western medieval art, despite initial hostility in the West and indeed critique of the East for producing what was seen as too human, too this-worldly.[53] Some wonderful examples continue to be endorsed, but in the main it was restraint that won through. Again, although few icons have survived from the period before the controversy, it is now often suggested that the iconoclasts had a point.[54] In those early centuries icons were in effect treated more like relics, and so more like representatives of an immanent rather than transcendent spirituality.[55] It was precisely in order to counter the iconoclast objections to a 'relic defined by contact' that Orthodoxy moved to a transcendent 'icon defined by relation'.[56] So there are already resources within Orthodoxy for a different sort of emphasis. But this is also no less true of the smaller, oriental churches that have continued to maintain their own distinctive approach.

---

[52] Orthodoxy has greatly developed a verse unique to Matthew's account of the incident: 'The disciples . . . fell on their faces, and were filled with awe' (17: 6 RSV).

[53] As in the papal legate's complaints in 1054 over Greek painting of dead Christs: J. P. Migne (ed.), *Patrologia Latina* (*PL*), 143. 986–7. Discussed in H. Belting, *Likeness and Presence: A History of the Image before the Era of Art* (Chicago: University of Chicago Press, 1994), 270.

[54] For an excellent presentation of the iconoclast case, C. Barber, *Figure and Likeness: On the Limits of Representation in Byzantine Iconoclasm* (Princeton: Princeton University Press, 2002), esp. 83–105.

[55] Ibid. 29–37; Belting, *Likeness and Presence*, 60–2, 77, 106–7, 172–3.

[56] Barber's terminology: *Figure and Likeness*, 139.

Iconography in Non-Chalcedonian Churches

Given the kind of stress we have found in Orthodoxy, it is often assumed that the other smaller churches of the East must inevitably have followed suit. But, while there are numerous points of contact, there are also some illuminating differences of stress. These are worth highlighting here, not least because it will help undermine any simplistic posing of opposition between East and West. What I will eventually identify as characteristically Renaissance attitudes can be seen to have some surprising and unexpected antecedents. Just as the crisis of the iconoclastic controversy generated a more transcendent emphasis within Orthodoxy, so other factors were to pull in a quite different direction in the oriental churches. Assessing the meaning and implications of religious experience can thus never be safely divorced from careful consideration of contexts.

These churches' origins stem from the failure of the Council of Chalcedon in AD 451 to produce universal agreement about how the nature of Christ should be understood. Although among them the Nestorian church was once strong in the Middle East,[57] its theology is quite different, and so it will suffice here to look at the four principal churches now found in Armenia, Egypt, Ethiopia, and Syria, the so-called monophysites or, as they themselves prefer to be known, the miaphysites.[58] Such 'one-nature' Christologies were condemned by the wider Church for failing to treat Christ's humanity with sufficient seriousness. That might in turn suggest an undervaluing of the world, but in fact very much the reverse is seen to be the case. There is, if anything, a stronger sense of the divine presence in our world, even if this is in general worked out through symbolic representations other than icons as such. This might seem to raise the possibility that their art in some ways represents a compensation for their Christology, but matters, as we shall see, are not quite that simple.

---

[57] The Nestorians were particularly supportive of the Mongols when they conquered Bagdad in the 13th c. At first this worked to their advantage, but when the Mongols converted to Islam, the Church experienced a marked decline.

[58] Following the terminology of Cyril of Alexandria, 'one nature' rather than 'single' or 'solitary' nature, as though one of Christ's two natures (divine and human) had been abandoned.

Three out of these four churches in fact spent many centuries under Muslim rule, and if the fourth (the Ethiopian) faced the threat only for a short while, even here the closeness of the Muslim world can be seen also to have exercised a marked effect.[59] What one observes is a far greater interest in ornament than is noticeable in the Christian East generally. Whether we assign early hesitations over representation as also a sign of Muslim influence is a contentious question, but certainly figures, when they do appear, are quite often to be found in Muslim dress of the time, and occasionally patterns from even further afield are to be detected, with Mongol-, Indian-, or Buddhist-influenced imagery.[60] As with the monophysite Christology, Muslim influence might have been expected to generate an increased sense of divine transcendence. Yet, whether through conscious reaction or not, there is in fact much evidence of strong counter-pulls the other way. So Muslim borrowings and Muslim influence need carefully to be distinguished. Indeed, a likely explanation for so much immanent art is that it was used to compensate for the ideology of the transcendent religion that would otherwise dominate their environment, with Muslim borrowings thus subtly subverted. Whether it is also an unconscious compensation for a monophysite Christology is a more complex issue. While that might seem a natural perspective to adopt from outside, internally the churches in question saw themselves as securing the humanity (no less than the divinity) more effectively than Chalcedon, and thus also greater divine involvement in the world.[61] Divinity suffused the humanity of Christ in a 'single nature', and so, it was held, brought God closer, not more remote. How this was expressed may be examined by looking at each nation in turn.

The Armenian may be considered first, because it was the first to declare itself a Christian nation. The story goes that King Tiridates

---

[59] Considerable destruction took place in Ethiopia during the Adalite invasion (1527–43).

[60] If an Ottoman style in a Nestorian Gospel book of 1499 is not unexpected, more remarkable is the Buddhist influence on work from 18th-c. Ethiopia; for illustrations, M. Zibawi, *Eastern Christian Worlds* (Collegeville, Minn.: Liturgical Press, 1995), 93, 260. Zibawi talks of how 'osmosis between styles gives birth to an Islamic-Christian art having integrity and homogeneity' (27).

[61] Later advocates of the position such as Severus of Antioch saw Chalcedon as yielding ground to Nestorius, and so failing to secure a full incarnation.

IV (Trdat) was converted by Gregory the Illuminator in 314, and that he took his subjects with him.[62] In the main Armenian churches even to this day are much plainer than the average Orthodox church. That there were groups of the population, including monks, who supported iconoclasm is agreed by all, but there is much less unanimity as to how deep such opposition ran.[63] Certainly, there is a rich manuscript tradition of representational art.[64] Certainly too, there are a number of intriguing, distinctive elements in the Armenian painting tradition, such as the ram hanging from the tree in representations of the sacrifice of Isaac, the presence of Eve's skull in Nativity scenes, or a lion placed at the foot of the Cross.[65] But what is, I think, the most fascinating feature of Armenian symbolism is the prominent and unusual treatment given to Christ's cross, which has in effect become a great symbol of blessing and fruitfulness. This is most obvious in the tradition of *katchk'ars* or stone crosses where fruit symbols such as grapes or pomegranates abound on, in, or about the empty cross; it is also reflected in some powerful manuscript paintings.[66] This approach finds echoes in Armenian worship where such an important evocation as the Trisagion (used in all Eastern liturgies) is transferred from the Trinity to the crucified Christ.[67] Again, while it shares with the

[62] The earlier date of 301 is now commonly rejected, and so Trdat is seen as following Roman changes of policy rather than initiating his own distinctive line. For some necessary qualifications regarding the completeness of the country's conversion, A. E. Redgate, *The Armenians* (Oxford: Blackwell, 1998), 113–39 esp. 116–19.

[63] Iconoclasm certainly lasted much longer in Armenia than elsewhere in the East, with one group, the T'ondrakians, still active in the 10th and 11th c.: V. Nersessian, *Treasures from the Ark: 1700 Years of Armenian Christian Art* (London: British Library, 2001), 84–7.

[64] Discussed in the chapter on 'word' in this work's companion volume.

[65] My first example depends on a variant translation of the relevant biblical passage, the second on similar reasons to what inspired the West to place Adam's skull at the foot of the cross, while the presence of the lion is thanks to the ancient belief that lion cubs are born dead and revive after three days: for further details, Nersessian, *Treasures* 67, 69, 71.

[66] For some examples of such stone crosses, ibid. 110–13. For examples of similar treatment in manuscripts, Zibawi, *Eastern Christian Worlds*, 128, illus. 32 (from the *Gospel Book of Vaspurakan*, 1450), Nersessian, *Treasures*, 15 (from 1655).

[67] A practice it shares with other Oriental churches. Orthodoxy ascribes to the Trinity the petition, 'Holy God, Holy Strong, Holy Immortal, have mercy on us.' By inserting 'who was crucified for us' the Armenians transfer the address to Christ.

Byzantine Orthodox the practice of dramatically plunging a cross into the baptismal waters on the feast of Christ's baptism, it is not only baptism and crucifixion that are thus effectively linked but also crucifixion and nativity, since among the Armenians the same day is used to mark both Christ's natural birth and his second birth at his baptism, so important is that connection held to be.[68] At certain times of the year the cross is also prominent in Orthodoxy, most notably perhaps in the liturgy for Holy Thursday and Holy Friday but also in its weekly remembrance on Wednesdays and Fridays. None the less, such symbolism is considerably more prominent among the Armenians: almost wherever one looks, one sees not only the form of the cross but also often that form blossoming with nature. This suggests to me a lively engagement with its impact on our present world, whereas with Orthodoxy the orientation is much more towards the aid it offers in securing our eventual destiny with Christ.[69] That would seem confirmed by Orthodoxy's treatment of the resurrection. Instead of the characteristic image of the resurrection that one finds in the West, the descent into hell is substituted. That suggests an essentially transcendent benefit, and so the use of natural imagery finds little, if any, place.[70]

Further support for this contrast comes from the quite different treatment accorded the transfiguration, for in marked contrast to Orthodoxy Luke is followed and not Matthew; the result is that the disciples come to the experience waking gently from sleep, rather than being immediately cast down by the force of what has happened and overwhelmed with awe.[71] What this suggests, as do those flowering crosses, is God coming towards us and our world, endorsing it, rather than overwhelming us with his otherness and so pulling us out of it. The strong emphasis on a physical resurrection, as evidenced by the inclusion of 3 Corinthians in the Armenian

---

[68] Zibawi, *Eastern Christian Worlds*, 152; Nersessian, *Treasures*, 40, 176, 221.

[69] Theodore the Studite even calls into question whether the cross on its own can ever be seen as a life-giving image: *PG* 99. 457B–C. The passage is quoted in Barber, *Figure and Likeness*, 95–6.

[70] 'Transcendent,' because the primary impact of the resurrection is portrayed as taking place in another world, in releasing the already dead into a new form of life.

[71] Nersessian, *Treasures*, 198–9.

canon, seems to point in the same direction,[72] as does the Armenian version of the Dormition where it is not Mary's child-like soul that is taken up but a smaller version of herself as an adult, and so clearly Mary in her totality.[73]

How far similar conclusions should be drawn for Syria it is not altogether easy to determine. Certainly, as with Armenia, there is some distinctive imagery, such as Mary being placed alongside Abraham with both bearing the faithful in their bosom.[74] Two complications, though, preclude any simple judgement. With Antioch being the third largest city in the Roman Empire, not surprisingly there was extensive interaction with the wider world in the earlier period, while later after the Muslim conquest most of the relevant evidence was inevitably subject to destruction, whether deliberately or otherwise. However, one recent study does argue strongly for a vibrant native tradition that in many ways confirms the pattern that I am suggesting existed elsewhere on the edges of the Byzantine world.[75] Thus churches took on a distinctive form. On the exterior, arch, oculus, and ornament were given major roles, while internally triumphal arches took the place of an iconostasis.[76] More relevant to note here is the extensive use made of carved crosses with life-giving, affirmative roles not only for churches but also for homes.[77] It is also to Syria that we owe one of the oldest surviving representations of the crucifixion, in the Rabbula Gospels, where significantly Christ has his eyes set firmly open unlike the two thieves on either side of him.[78] Intriguingly,

---

[72] For the appeal to 3 Corinthians to endorse a strongly physical resurrection, see another book by Nersessian, *The Bible in the Armenian Tradition* (London: British Library, 2001), 29, cf. 20. For what 3 Corinthians (part of *The Acts of Paul*) actually says on the subject, see W. Schneemelcher (ed.), *New Testament Apocrypha* (Cambridge: James Clarke, 1992), ii. 256.

[73] A 1311 MS provides a good example. Mary is presented as a smaller, awake version of her sleeping body: Nersessian, *The Bible in the Armenian Tradition*, 69.

[74] Zibawi, *Eastern Christian Worlds*, 78, illus. 14a.

[75] I. Peña, *The Christian Art of Byzantine Syria* (London: Garnet, 1997). Note his comment that 'we cannot categorize it [i.e. Syrian art] as a sub-division of Byzantine art' (48).

[76] For symbolism in the arch: ibid 72–3; for the triumphal arch: 76. Apart from baptisteries, domes are given no role.

[77] Ibid. 51, 172–3. Circle and star were often used to reinforce its positive meaning.

[78] From AD 586, now in Laurentian Library, Florence. Illustrated in Peña, *Christian Art*, 131.

what the face is intended to convey has been the subject of diametrically opposed interpretations.[79] What can be said is that its crucifixion is meant to qualify, as well as lead into, the absolute confidence of the resurrection portrayed below. So, as with Syria's own version of the flowering cross, it would seem that there is more evidence for immanence, of God invading every aspect of our world, than parallel Byzantine representations might have led us to expect. If so, Syrian and Armenian art would not after all stand that far apart.

At least with Egypt and Ethiopia there is no such comparable shortage of evidence. If in Egypt instead of the iconostasis metal church screens are beautiful but abstract, once again crosses flower, while images accompanying texts are sometimes substantially modified to drive home essentially the same message: John the Baptist's axe, for example, is turned into a tree already bearing fruit.[80] However, there are also differences, and one of the most interesting is the strong sense of sacramentality assigned to both lands. The name for the Christian Church in Egypt, 'Copt', is the Arabic abbreviation for the Greek name for the land, *Aegyptos*. It is no accident that the Church is so named, for numerous legends have helped to bond land and biblical witness. So, for example, tradition has it that the Holy Family lived here for three years, and many legends have accrued to the period as a result, among them that the penitent thief who had hung on one side of Christ's cross was identical with a brigand who had tried to rob them during this time.[81] Indeed, one place where the Holy Family is believed to have rested now attracts some three to four million pilgrims annually.[82] That sense of presence in the land is, if anything, intensified when it comes to entering a church. Shoes are removed before one enters, and the high value attached to the relics that are normally present accentuates the sense of a heavenly community present with the faithful.[83] Icons are not kissed directly but rather the hands that have touched the sacred object.[84] It is their way of

[79] Zibawi describes the figure as 'impassive' (*Eastern Christian Worlds*, 52), Peña as displaying 'suffering and physical torment in all its realism' (*Christian Art*, 234).

[80] For aniconic screens, Zibawi, *Eastern Christian Worlds*, 202–3; for flowering crosses: 165; for the axe of Matt. 3: 10 turned into an almond tree: 172–4.

[81] Ibid. 155.

[82] Durunka, near Asyut: J. Kamil, *Christianity in the Land of the Pharaohs* (London: Routledge, 2002), 12.

[83] Ibid. 208–9.

[84] Ibid. 218.

transferring blessing from icon to worshipper, so characteristic of Coptic practice in general that one author uses the term 'palpability' to encapsulate their understanding of presence.[85] It may well be the case that Orthodox icons displaying Mary in intimate relation with her Son first came west from Egypt.[86] Certainly, other images of this kind are also now to be found, such as one of their best-loved saints, Menas, portrayed in loving embrace with Christ. Currently the church is enjoying a revival, and in its artwork there is freedom, naturalism, and richness of colour that would look strange in a more narrowly Orthodox context.[87]

But it is to Ethiopia that one must turn to see this way of thinking in full flood. The biblical story of the visit of the Queen of Sheba to King Solomon is well known.[88] Sheba as a place is usually located on the opposite bank of the Red Sea from Ethiopia, in nearby Arabia.[89] However, whatever its historical location, legend has it that it was not long after her meeting with Solomon that the Ark of the Covenant itself moved to Ethiopia,[90] and this is part of a string of stories and places sacralizing the land. The strength of historical associations with Judaism is still a matter of dispute, not least because of the number of key aspects of Judaism retained even to this day within the Christian Church in that land.[91] What, however, is certain is that Christianity arrived in the fourth century, and that its capital, Aksum, claimed to house the Ark of the Covenant

---

[85] G. Gabra, *Coptic Monasteries* (Cairo: American University in Cairo Press, 2002), 32.

[86] So Onasch and Schnieper, *Icons*, 170; for the connection made back to Isis and Horus, with illus., Kamil, *Christianity in the Land of the Pharaohs*, 15.

[87] Christ is commonly portrayed with his arms on or round the shoulders of Menas, a 4th-c. soldier-martyr. For freedom, Kamil, ibid. 256–7; for Egypt's best-known contemporary icon painter, A. and B. Sadek, *L'Incarnation de la lumière: le renouveau iconographique copte à travers d'Isaac Fanous* (Limoges: Association le Monde Copte, 2000).

[88] 1 Kings 10: 1–13; 2 Chr. 9: 1–12.

[89] Also written as Saba and Seba, the country is now usually identified with south-west Arabia, and so with Yemen. It is possible that Ethiopia was initially colonized from here, and certainly the process was reversed in the 4th c. AD.

[90] The story of how their son, Menelik I, succeeded in abducting the ark is told in the Ethiopian national epic *Kebra Negast*.

[91] Jewish practices that are continued within the Christian church include circumcision, distinguishing between clean and unclean animals, observing the Sabbath, and levirate marriage. In addition, one notes the presence of the Falasha ('the exiles') or Black Jews, whose origins are disputed.

from at least the sixth century. Moreover, when under the Zagwe dynasty the capital moved to Lalibela in the twelfth century, the new city was laid out as a whole to reflect the Jerusalem of the biblical past.[92] Indeed, each individual church throughout the land is now modelled on similar symbolism, with a special shrine constructed to hold a replica of the ark,[93] and each part or aspect of the church and its furniture given either a symbolic geography or else some other appropriate theological reference.[94]

Perhaps precisely because of the strength of this presupposed connection with the Holy Land, Old Testament prohibitions are treated with great seriousness. So, for example, although the work known as *The Miracles of Mary* has been adopted as one of the church's most holy texts, all positive references to sculpture have been excised from it, while the evidence (or rather lack of it) may possibly suggest that it took until the fifteenth century before an iconic tradition could develop.[95] This was greatly aided by Jesuit influence in the seventeenth century, but it would be wrong to see the resultant art as wholly a foreign import.[96] On the contrary, if there is only one painter who is widely known outside Ethiopia (Fere Seyon), and much is indeed rather poor imitation of Western painting, there is also much that is highly distinctive, and indeed occasionally almost disturbingly modern. Some angel figures remind me of the haunting work of Paul Klee on the same theme, while match-stick figures in a crucifixion scene even conjure up parallels with the French artist, Jean Dubuffet, or the still more recent techniques of the American, Jean-Michel Basquiat.[97] Perhaps one

---

[92] Individual hills were identified with various events in Christ's life, while a church called Bethlelem was placed almost the same distance from the capital as the present town is in reality from Jerusalem: R. Griegson (ed.), *African Zion: The Sacred Art of Ethiopia* (New Haven: Yale University Press, 1993), 12–13.

[93] Known as a *manbara tabot*. For examples and use, Griegson, ibid. 136–9.

[94] Each part of a censer, for example, has a symbolic referent: Zibawi, *Eastern Christian Worlds*, 217.

[95] For changes in *The Miracles of Mary* (originally a Latin work of the 12th c.), Zibawi, ibid. 257–8. For the introduction of icons possibly dating from as late as the 15th c., Griegson, *African Zion*, 16.

[96] In the early 17th c. three kings in a row subscribed to Rome: Zibawi, *Eastern Christian Worlds*, 227.

[97] For 15th-c. crucifixions, ibid. 222, illus. 173, 174; for 19th-c. angels: 254–5, illus. 94, 95. For Klee, S. Frey and J. Helfenstein, *The Private Klee* (Edinburgh: National Galleries of Scotland, 2000), 173–5; for Dubuffet, L. Peiry, *Art Brut*

might speak of an easy familiarity with a spirit-filled world, with the figures made engagingly close but also intriguingly different.[98]

In drawing this contrast between the non-Chalcedonian churches and the East more generally I do not pretend that there are no exceptions. It is a matter of degree rather than any absolute difference. Even so, despite the long and sustained resistance of the non-Chalcedonian churches to representational art, there is a world-affirming character in the symbolism of stone cross, flowering abstract art, and attitude to the land that makes one feel that God is invading our space, as it were, rather than attempting to pull us out of it, as with the characteristic thrust of Orthodoxy's icon painting. That is not to condemn one or the other, and certainly I would not wish to follow a typical Renaissance figure such as Vasari in his contemptuous dismissal of icons.[99] This would merely be to repeat the East's mistake, for both East and West have their own distinctive rationale. But it is to suggest that, if my contrast is anywhere near accurate, the direction in which Western art and sacramentality moved decisively with the Renaissance is not without precedents even in some surprising quarters. If this was in any sense a compensation for Islamic transcendence (and perhaps monophysite Christology), there may also be parallels with the way in which Gothic transcendence acted as compensation for the extreme immanence of the eucharistic theology of the time.

That question, however, must await another chapter.[100] What I want to do next is approach the Renaissance and its own alternative sacramental vision. I shall do so, though, indirectly through an exploration of the history of Platonism and its influence. The advantage of proceeding thus is that it will help illuminate how an apparently unvarying philosophy such as Platonism could still

(Paris: Flammarion, 2001), 36, 37; for Basquiat, R. Marshall, *Jean-Michel Basquiat* (New York: Whitney Museum, 1993), 90, 170, 212, 231. There is a good film about Basquiat's meteoric rise to fame in the early 1980s, simply entitled *Basquiat* (1996) and directed by Julian Schnabel. Despite being directed by a fellow artist, it is much stronger on how insecurity affected his life than as an analysis of his graffiti art.

[98] This seems confirmed by Ethiopian attitudes to medicine, discussed in the chapter on the body in my accompanying volume.

[99] For relevant quotations, H. Maguire in Safran (ed.), *Heaven on Earth*, 121, 151 n. 1.

[100] A later chapter on architecture explores how the immanence of transubstantiation and soaring Gothic spires act as counterpoise to one other.

influence decisively two quite different, indeed almost opposed, approaches, in affecting both icons and Renaissance art. The practice and influence of philosophy operates in particular cultural contexts, no less than religious experience in general. Readers uninterested in the history of philosophy may wish to proceed immediately to my discussion of Renaissance art,[101] but what follows is by no means an irrelevant detour. Philosophers have for too long believed themselves immune from such cultural conditioning. Christian theology has always been shaped by its wider intellectual context, and it is as well to make such debts explicit.

Varieties of Platonism, Icons, and the Renaissance

As already indicated, I intend to approach the Renaissance indirectly through the history of Platonism. It is all too easy to assume that the latter's influence on Christianity went only one way, towards at worst a world-denying focus or at best an other-worldly one. But, as with most long-standing traditions, including Christianity itself, its initial foundations gave the possibility for development in quite a number of different directions. What I want to suggest here, therefore, is that not only did it aid the type of theology that we have seen came to be associated with the icon, but also quite a few centuries later made a decisive contribution to the quite different perspective of the Renaissance. To understand why two such different sacramental theologies could be generated from the same beginnings, it will be necessary to trace the history of Platonism through its various transformations. An additional advantage in tracing this history is that it will make occasional brief allusions in subsequent chapters to the continuing influence of Platonism easier to comprehend.

Changes within Pagan Platonism

Among contemporary theologians hostility to Plato is common.[102] His influence in the past is blamed for making the Church too

---

[101] To the section entitled, 'Platonism and Renaissance Art' pp. 73 ff.

[102] It is not that trends in Plato are incorrectly identified, but that they are assumed to be the whole picture, and so it is conveniently forgotten that much the

world-denying, with Platonic dualism of body and mind seen as diverting Christianity from its real roots in the Jewish view of human beings as psychosomatic unities. His attack on art is then viewed as just yet another part of that complex, with religious belief presented as a purely mental construct uninterested in the material world. But that is, in my view, to offer altogether too simple an account. Plato was in any case mediated to Christianity through his subsequent pagan interpreters. These will engage our attention in a moment, but first something needs to be said about another complicating factor, and that is Plato himself. Because of the varying character of his opponents Plato's dialogues as a whole are by no means consistent in their emphasis. So by too narrow a focus it is very easy to make Plato appear more unqualifiedly hostile to the arts than he really was. Thus, if in the *Republic* art is placed at a lower level of reality than the work of the humblest artisan, by contrast in the *Symposium* the beauty of the human body is posited as a natural medium in the ascent towards more divine concerns.[103] Again, if in the *Gorgias* concern with style and persuasion is seen as the corrupting concern of the sophist, in another dialogue, in the *Phaedrus*, the poet is actually ceded divine inspiration.[104] If there remains to the end a continuing element of critique that would subordinate art to moral concerns, I would still side with those who see a real struggle within Plato himself, based on the recognized need to address aspects of the personality other than the rational not only in others but also even in himself.[105]

same sort of attack could be mounted against Scripture itself, again with similar selective highlighting (e.g. Mark 8: 34–6; John 18: 36; Phil. 3: 20). For two examples at random of what I have in mind: J. Moltmann, *God in Creation* (London: SCM, 1985), 248–50; C. Gunton, *The One, the Three and the Many* (Cambridge: Cambridge University Press, 1993), 2–3, 46–51.

[103] For art at a third remove from reality, with art imitating the craftsman's work, and the craftsman nature, and nature the Forms, *Republic*, x. 595–608. In the *Symposium* the body is, in effect, treated as itself a work of art.

[104] For the four types of divinely inspired madness in the *Phaedrus*, 244–5. What Plato explicitly rejects is the reliance on 'technique alone' (245a).

[105] For someone who emphasizes the continuity, C. Janaway, *Images of Excellence: Plato's Critique of the Arts* ((Oxford: Clarendon Press, 1995), esp. 158–81. For a more nuanced view, R. B. Rutherford, *The Art of Plato* (London: Duckworth, 1995), 228–39 esp. 234; 251–60 esp. 255–6. For the claim that even some of his apparently more narrowly conceived philosophical dialogues should be acknowledged to have an indispensable literary dimension, M. Warner, *Philosophical Finesse* (Oxford: Clarendon Press, 1989), 67–104 (on the *Phaedo*).

For there is no doubt that he is himself one of the world's great artists both as a stylist and as a creator of new myths.[106] In addition, due note should also be taken of the fact that, so far from despising the world, he can at times offer us marvellously evocative descriptions of its beauty and in describing its creation he does not hesitate to call it 'most beautiful'.[107] Indeed, it would not be difficult to be convinced that one was listening to someone like Traherne or Wordsworth and not Plato when he evokes the following scene: 'a beautiful resting place' by streams 'suitable for young girls to play by' with 'a high, overshadowing plane tree' and 'a tall, fragrant willow in full bloom', an 'exceedingly pleasant and lovely place with a gentle breeze' that 'echoes with a shrill summer chorus of cicadas'.[108] Certainly the world and art were for him means to an end (in invoking love for the transcendent Forms that give our world intelligibility and meaning), but that should not be interpreted as entailing that as means they were therefore automatically demoted as of no positive worth. Subordination and contempt are two quite different attitudes.

It was that very complexity in Plato's position that allowed different aspects of his thought to be stressed by different elements in the subsequent tradition of interpretation. Plato's use of myth, for example, made variant readings of his account of the world's origins in the *Timaeus* perhaps inevitable.[109] The result was that some of the pagan writers associated with the period we now know as Middle Platonism came close to Christianity's own understanding of creation, and so strengthened patristic inclinations to use some of their terminology and ideas. If the three descending levels of divinity in Plotinus (d. 270) as the founder of new or Neo-Platonism suited the doctrine less well, it still helped with making sense of the doctrine of the Trinity. The Christian use of Logos suggested analogies between the Son and Plotinus' intermediate principle of the Divine Mind, while the third principle of the

---

[106] 'The most obvious paradox . . . is that Plato is a great artist': I. Murdoch, *The Fire and the Sun: Why Plato Banished Artists* (Oxford: Oxford University Press, 1977), 87.

[107] For the creation as *kallistos*, *Timaeus*, 29a5; 92c8 (in the latter case, the very last words of the dialogue).

[108] *Phaedrus*, 229a–230e; my trans.

[109] Among pagans both Plutarch and Numenius take his talk of 'creation' literally; cf. J. Dillon, *The Middle Platonists* (London: Duckworth, 1977), 206–8, 366–72.

World Soul activating the world yielded some obvious parallels
with the immanent role of the Holy Spirit.[110] More problematic
might seem the original first principle beyond thought and action,
the One, but, rightly or wrongly, that too was taken to speak in a
trinitarian fashion, of the Father not only as origin of the other two
persons but also as in some sense, if not impersonal, at least beyond
adequate conceptualization. The fact that Plotinus derived this
conception from a dialogue of Plato, the *Parmenides*, which almost
no modern commentator thinks means any such thing (and which
even some in the ancient world contested),[111] again demonstrates
how dangerous it is to suppose that Platonism must always mean
exactly the same thing.[112] Platonism subsequent to Plotinus was to
adopt a more extreme version of this emanationist understanding of
the divine. How this affected Orthodoxy I shall consider in a
moment.

But first another feature of Plotinus relevant to our theme needs
to be noted, and that is the fact that he also adopted a quite different
view on art from Plato.[113] Not only are Gnostics attacked for
denying the value of this world, but also in a key passage the

---

[110] The fact that the *Timaeus* already supplied those two elements in the
Demiurge (or Creator) and World Soul is no doubt why this became the most
popular Platonic dialogue in the Middle Ages. The fact that the Demiurge looked
to a transcendent world of ideas rather than to another particular divine being
could easily be remedied (at least so long as the *Republic* continued to be known)
by noting that such ideas were united in the Form of the Good in the *Republic*
(508e1–509b10) in language reminiscent of Plotinus' understanding of the *Parmenides*' One.

[111] This seems to be the position of Alcinous (2nd c.), who treats the *Parmenides*' syllogisms as purely hypothetical in his *Didascalos*, 6. 6.

[112] The way in which Plotinus' interpretation of the *Parmenides* affects not just
that dialogue but also his reading of all the others is stressed by J.-M. Charrue,
Plotin: lecteur de Platon (Paris: Société d'édition: Les Belles Lettres, 1987), 131:
'Pour Plotin, c'est le *Parménide* en effet qui commande toute interprétation
ultérieure.' For the standard modern view, that the dialogue is 'aporetic', setting
out a number of unresolved logical dilemmas, R. E. Allen, *Plato's Parmenides* (New
Haven: Yale University Press, 1997); for the classic earlier exposition of a similar
view, F. M. Cornford, *Plato and Parmenides* (London: Routledge & Kegan Paul,
1939); for a more controversial suggestion that it represents a staging post on the
way to the metaphysics adopted in the *Philebus* (still quite different from Plotinus),
K. M. Sayre, *Plato's Late Ontology* (Princeton: Princeton University Press, 1983).

[113] For a helpful analysis, L. P. Gerson, *Plotinus* (London: Routledge & Kegan
Paul, 1994), 212–18.

artist is seen as adding to that value by making more explicit the connection of the natural (for example, a stone) with a higher intelligible world (for example, through giving it a particular sculpted form).[114] As with Plato, though, there are passages that could easily be read as evincing hostility to, or even contempt for, the world. His editor, Porphyry, adds to the problem by recording that Plotinus felt 'ashamed of being in the body'.[115] Some have suggested that, unlike Plato who saw bodily love as a means to his end, Plotinus at most favoured human love as a suitable analogy for the higher intellectual pursuits.[116] Whether so or not, what does seem clear is that Plotinus' vision of his quest is much more introverted than Plato's. Beauty has no simple, easily accessible principles, and it is on oneself that one must primarily work, not through deep engagement with a wider world.[117] Thus, although in theory his emanationist view of divinity should have brought the divine closer to the world than was the case with Plato, on the whole the reverse seems to be the case. That, as we shall see, was to have implications for Orthodoxy.

Platonism and Icons

Platonism by no means stood still with Plotinus. If much has perished of the writings of Porphyry and Iamblichus, and on the whole they were not particularly influential on subsequent history, the surviving corpus of another, Proclus (d. 485), is great, and it is his writings that help set the context for the defence and

[114] For the Gnostics, *Enneads* II. 9; for his different theory of beauty, ibid. V. 8. The example in the text is Plotinus' own opening illustration.
[115] Used as her opening example in M. R. Miles's defence of Plotinus' attitudes in her *Plotinus on Body and Beauty* (Oxford: Blackwell, 1999). She notes how lack of context and misleading translations all add to misunderstanding: e.g. 31, 40–1, 91–2, 97–8.
[116] P. Hadot, *Plotinus or the Simplicity of Vision* (Chicago: University of Chicago Press, 1993), 48–57 esp. 54–5. He suggests that Plotinus uses Plato's *Symposium* in the way Christian mystics have traditionally used the Song of Songs.
[117] Rather surprisingly, proportion and harmony are rejected as universal principles at *Enneads*, I. 6. I. Again, at I. 6. 9 Plato's image of working on the statue of one's beloved is transformed, significantly, into one of working on one's own statue: cf. A. H. Armstrong's comments in 'Platonic *Eros* and Christian *Agape*' in *Plotinian and Christian Studies* (London: Variorum, 1970), ix. 112.

interpretation of icons during the iconoclastic controversy.[118] Proclus had a profound influence on the anonymous writer variously known as Dionysius the Areopagite or Pseudo-Denys. Denys had a marked impact on Maximus the Confessor who in turn was a major influence on the thought of John of Damascus, writer of the definitive defence of icons at the time. Proclus introduces a whole range of additional ranks in between the One and our world, and this is reflected in Denys' own writings.[119] Indeed, so deep runs the influence that, in the days when Denys was still thought of as a contemporary of St Paul, it was often postulated that the influence in fact ran the other way, with Proclus merely a pagan imitator of Denys.[120] If all the intermediate levels of divinity seem to increase dramatically the sense of divine transcendence and so set even further back Plotinus' limited optimism about the possibility of communion with the divine,[121] there was a countervailing tendency in the notion of theurgy, religious ritualistic actions which it was believed could help bridge the gap.[122] In modern discussions these are often portrayed as narrowly mechanistic or magical, and so contrasted with the Christian liturgy to which Denys appeals. But the difference is not so marked as is often claimed. Certainly, there is no doubt that Proclus was deeply religious, and that notions of divine grace would by no means have been unintelligible to him.[123]

[118] Although opinions are divided over the value and even the authorship of Iamblichus' *De mysteriis*, it is useful in indicating possible connections between Christian sacramentality and theurgy.

[119] For the introduction of 'henads' in Proclus and his motivation, E. R. Dodds, *Proclus: The Elements of Theology*, 2nd edn. (Oxford: Clarendon Press, 1963), 100–45, 257–60; for some examples of influence on Denys, 190, 253, 276.

[120] This is the view taken in the 11th c. both by the famous Greek encyclopedist, Suidas (s.v. Dionysius) and by the philosopher and historian, Michael Psellus (*De omnifara doctrina*, 74). The writer gets his name from the person who heard Paul in Acts 17: 34.

[121] Here I follow Dodds (p. xx) rather than J. M. Rist, 'Mysticism and Transcendence in Later Neoplatonism', in *Platonism and its Christian Heritage* (London: Variorum, 1985), XV. 213–25.

[122] For a short (but unsympathetic) account, E. R. Dodds, *The Greeks and the Irrational* (Berkeley: University of California Press, 1968), 283–311.

[123] Dodds in his *Proclus* focuses on his 'weather magic' (p. xxiii), but in Marinus' *Life of Proclus* this is given only a passing mention, and in fact much more attention is devoted to his interaction with the gods, including hymns at his death, visions, and a prayer to Asclepius that results in the cure of a child (20, 29).

So far as the subsequent influence of Denys is concerned, this was mostly exercised positively in terms of adding to a sense of the mystery and majesty of God rather than in any way undermining the nature of the Christian revelation.[124] In large part this was because his surviving corpus was interpreted as the kind of thing that a follower of Paul might well have written. But it remains a moot question whether the author himself has not ventured too far down one particular Neoplatonic avenue in stressing the distance between human beings and God. Some have sought to interpret him as thoroughly liturgical in his orientation, with even his hierarchy of graded divine attributes and nine ranks of angels there to stress the divine glory rather than its distance from ourselves.[125] But the problem is that, if this was his intention, there is little in his surviving writings to give us complete confidence that this was so. The language of emanation is preferred to creation, with even Christ himself in his earthly life made wholly dependent on angels, while in our own present world membership of the Church is also seen in rigorously hierarchical terms.[126] More important for icons, the unlikeness of symbols to their originals is emphasized, and, if in his discussion of sacraments this qualification is not restated, it would still seem reasonable to assume it presupposed, not least because no contrast or correction is issued.[127] Indeed, despite his use of the term 'theurgy', its actual employment hints at a more spiritualized understanding than was true of later Neoplatonism, for the second half of the eucharist is described as the more, and not the less, otherwordly part of the service.[128] Thus, while the downward

---

[124] In his study of the work and its influence, Paul Rorem sees it transformed by the way in which Bonaventure and others 'read into it not only the cardinal Christian concepts of grace, faith, and especially love, but also Christ himself': *Pseudo–Dionysius* (New York: Oxford University Press, 1993), 240.

[125] Notably, A. Louth, *Denys the Areopagite* (London: Chapman, 1989), esp. 29–31, 105–9.

[126] For emanation, *Divine Names*, v. 1–2; xii. 4; for even Jesus not having direct communion with God, *Celestial Hierarchy*, 4; for hierarchy in church, *Ecclesiastical Hierarchy*, 5–6; for salvation mediated hierarchically, *Cel. Hier.*, 8.

[127] *Eccles. Hier.* 2; for a different view, Louth, *Denys the Areopagite* 56.

[128] For the use of 'theurgy', *Eccles. Hier.* 3, 7 (PG 436C); cf. 'not of this world' at 3. 7. At 3. 3 (PG 427C) in addressing the sacrament, significantly he asks: 'uncovering the symbolic garments of the mysteries that surround you, fill our mental vision with a single and unveiled light' (my trans.). 'Mental' seems to pick up his earlier stress on the 'immaterial' (e.g. 1. 4).

thrust of the divine is undoubtedly stressed, the value of the material remains purely mediatorial, to pull us beyond its own particular reality.[129]

While the classic defence of icons during the iconoclastic controversy of the eighth century lacks the same heavy reliance on metaphysics that is to be found in Denys, the echoes are undoubtedly there. Admittedly, if one reads John of Damascus' three defences on their own, one is likely to be struck most by their moderation and the limited extent of his objective. Image and prototype are carefully distinguished, and it is a theology of respect by association that is inculcated rather than any strong sense of sacramental identity. Thus it is veneration that is recommended, and not adoration, and indeed parallels are repeatedly drawn with how such marks of respect are also appropriate in purely human contexts.[130] But, as soon as one turns to the role of icons, the same Platonic echo is there; their purpose is to 'lead us through matter to the invisible God'.[131] Turn to his more formal expositions of faith and I think one sees why.[132] As in Maximus' exposition of the symbolism of church architecture, God's act of grace draws us through the material to his transcendent world rather than endorsing that world as it is. This is not of course to suggest that icon painters were constantly resorting to such writings. In a largely illiterate society their influence would have been far more indirect, and in any case there were precedents elsewhere in the ancient world for the flat technique employed by the icon painter.[133] But what Denys and his followers did offer was a theological justification for such a technique, with images hard up against the frame

---

[129] 'it is quite impossible for the mind in us to rise up to the immaterial in the imitation and contemplation of heavenly hierarchies without the guiding hand of things material' (*Cel. Hier.* 1. 3; *PG* 122C–D, my trans.).

[130] e.g. *First Apology*, 14.

[131] *Second Apology*, 23 (my trans.). So a contrast is repeatedly drawn between representing the Son as God incarnate (a legitimate aim) and representing God in any other form (which would be sinful): e.g. 5.

[132] Although there are some signs of John modifying Platonism to give a more positive estimate of the world: A. Louth, *St John Damascene* (Oxford: Oxford University Press, 2002), 45–6, 217–18. Maximus' views on architecture are presented in the context of the liturgy in his *Mystagogia*.

[133] Egyptian art had avoided depth for religious reasons, while from the third century on, though not for the same reasons, the practice seems to have been gathering momentum more generally. For further discussion, A. Grabar, 'Plotin et

and without significant depth: as in Plotinus' view of art, they pull us into a transcendent world far more effectively than the natural world itself.

Platonism at the Renaissance

Apart for John Scotus Eriugena, Denys was to have little influence in the West until the twelfth century.[134] Significantly, that was the century which also saw the birth of Gothic in the architecture of the abbey church of St-Denis. As a subsequent chapter will observe, whatever the extent of the direct influence of Denys himself, Gothic was to find its rationale in a similar theology to that of the icon. But meantime I jump the centuries and consider why the Renaissance, in witnessing a return to Platonism, none the less discovered something quite different within it, so that the result was not really otherworldly at all but much more an endorsement and exploration of God immanent within this world. One qualification, though, is necessary before I do so, and that is to note that contrasts between periods of Platonic and Aristotelian influence are sometimes overdrawn. For there is a sense in which Platonism in the West never really died out, just as in the East Aristotelianism remained much stronger than is usually recognized.[135] A salutary reminder of that more complex reality is given by Giovanni Pisano's statue (from 1290) of Plato joining Habakkuk in Siena Cathedral as one of the prophets of Christ, despite the revival of Aristotelianism earlier that century, in Aquinas among others.

However, that said, the Medicis' Academy in Florence did bring Platonism to a prominence in the fifteenth century that it had not

les origines de l'esthétique médiévale', in *Cahiers archéologiques*, i. *Fin de l'antiquité et moyen âge* (Paris: Van Oest, 1945), 15–34; E. Alliez and M. Feher, 'Reflections of a Soul' in M. Feher, R. Naddaff, and N. Tazi, *Fragments for a History of the Human Body* (New York: Zone, 1989), ii. 47–84.

[134] The Irish philosopher, John Scotus Eriugena (d. 877), as well as being heavily influenced by them, also translated Denys's works into Latin.

[135] The continuing influence of Platonism on Aquinas through Augustine and Denys would now be widely acknowledged; for an extreme statement of the case, W. Hankey, *God in Himself* (Oxford: Oxford University Press, 1987). In the case of the East, it is often forgotten that study of the Neoplatonists themselves was only renewed under Psellus in the 11th c., while even as late as the 15th c. both Pletho and George of Trebizond, in comparing Plato and Aristotle, could write knowledgeably about both.

enjoyed for some time, not least through the extensive translation work of its head, Marsilio Ficino (d. 1499).[136] Aristotle was no longer 'the philosopher', as he had been for Aquinas; in his place came Plato. So it will be useful to focus on Ficino's understanding of what was entailed by Platonism, and the kind of impact it could have on art, and often did. In this connection it is worth drawing attention to three key features of Ficino's version of Platonism. First, one observes that, though his ontology is a little more complex than that of Plotinus, it has nothing like the complexity of Proclus, or of Denys for that matter. Indeed, it is possible that he chose to entitle his principal work *Platonic Theology* precisely in order to show that he was offering a corrective to Proclus.[137] For, although there are five principal layers or levels of reality, human beings are now significantly placed in the middle (with soul), and commentators seem agreed that the intention (and net result) is thus to bring the divine much nearer to our own world.[138] Again, while the language of the One is still employed, it is clear that his conception of the One is much more like the Christian creator God than any of his predecessors.[139] His most famous pupil, Pico della Mirandola, may have been reprimanded for treating the *Parmenides* as merely a piece of syllogistic reasoning,[140] but Ficino himself did not hesitate to identify the One with the Demiurge of the *Timaeus*, interpreted as containing the forms or ideas in himself

[136] By 1464 he had completed ten dialogues of Plato, the rest by 1484. His translations of Plotinus and Denys were completed in 1492.

[137] Itself the title of Proclus' longest work. The suggestion is made in their introduction by the editors of the 5 vol. Latin/English edition currently being produced: M. J. Allen and J. Hankins (eds.), *Platonic Theology* (Cambridge, Mass.: Harvard University Press, 2001), i. p. xii.

[138] A leading theme in P. O. Kristeller, *The Philosophy of Marsilio Ficino* (Gloucester, Mass.: Peter Smith, 1964), esp. 74–91, 399–401. The five are God, angel, soul, quality, body. The soul has unmediated access to God, and 'links and unites all the levels above it and below it' (*Platonic Theology*, III. 1–2; Allen and Hankins, i. esp. 231). As a *creatio ex nihilo* it could only come directly from God (v. 13; Allen and Hankins, ii. 279).

[139] Cf. C. H. Lohr, 'Metaphysics', in C. B. Schmitt and Q. Skinner, *The Cambridge History of Renaissance Philosophy* (Cambridge: Cambridge University Press, 1988), 538–84 esp. 572. Lohr also notes the way in which Ficino's undermining of hierarchy had been anticipated by Nicholas of Cusa; ibid. 552.

[140] The story is told in R. Klibansky, *Plato's Parmenides in the Middle Ages and the Renaissance* (Munich: Kraus International, 1981), 312–25.

rather than above and external to him.[141] The incarnation then also becomes the natural bridge between God and all creation.[142] And for Pico too the incarnation is that bridge,[143] with Pico, if anything, making humanity even more central to his conception than it was to Ficino's. Thus the world is described as a 'superb temple of divinity', with human beings as the microcosm placed at its mid-point.[144]

Secondly, if some of the thinking behind theurgy continues as an influence from Proclus, it is in the process transformed from being in any sense the manipulation of knowledge of the supernatural into a question of free human response to a wider patterning that reflects the indwelling of the divine in all aspects of reality. God is seen as moving all things from within but in a way that does not threaten human freedom.[145] However, because this means that all things are related in an overall harmony, each part is seen as having a potential effect on any other, and so what to our minds appears most strange becomes entirely natural in Ficino's system and that is that astrology is taken with the utmost seriousness. It is worth recalling, though, that Ficino had read medicine at university, and astrology was still at this time part of its teaching course.[146] As Ficino expanded on these aspects of his thought, his attitude to the material world emerges with great clarity. It is far from being contemptuous. I will consider his interpretation of Plato on art in a moment, where a more unqualifiedly positive interpretation is countenanced than Plato deserves. Ficino's reinterpretation

[141] e.g. *The Letters of Marsilio Ficino*, I. 43 (English trans. (London: Shepheard-Walwyn, 1975), i. 85–8).

[142] So Kristeller, *Philosophy of Marsilio Ficino*, 405–6. This view is elaborated in his *De religione christiana*.

[143] Seen most clearly in the *Heptaplus*, e.g. 5. 7; 6. 7; 7. 7: C. G. Wallis, P. Miller, and D. Carmichael (trans.), *On the Dignity of Man*, etc. ((Indianapolis: Hackett, 1965), 137–8, 145–6, 169).

[144] For microcosm, *Heptaplus*, 5. 6 (135); for temple and midpoint, opening of *On the Dignity of Man* (4).

[145] God, we are told, makes the universe as like himself as possible and moves everything from within, but without every impinging on our freedom: *Platonic Theology* I. 5, II. 13 (Allen and Hankins, i. 77, 199, 209).

[146] For two helpful articles on the subject, Pearce and Da Costa in M. Shepherd (ed.), *Friend to Mankind: Marsilio Ficino* (London: Shepheard-Walwyn, 1999), 88–100, 167–80. For reflection on his own attitude to illness, cf. *Letters*, I. 80, 81, 92 (Eng. trans. i. 125–30, 141–4).

entailed also a more positive estimate of body, with desire fully recognized as capable of being intrinsically good in itself.[147] Indeed, precisely because of interaction between body and soul in which 'the form of the body, as best it can, represents the form of the soul', physical and spiritual graces should in his view be seen as one in reflecting divine beauty.[148]

Some of the elements behind this thinking are to be laid at the door of our third key factor, and that is the influence of the Hermetic tradition. At the request of Cosimo de' Medici Ficino interrupted his programme of translating Plato's dialogues in 1463 to do the same for the *Corpus Hermeticum*, the writings ascribed to the Egyptian mythical figure, Hermes Trismegistus.[149] Although there is evidence of the collection existing in Greek only from the eleventh century, its contents are certainly very much older.[150] Some postulate a gradual growth from as early as the fourth century BC, but in their present form the texts are unlikely to be much earlier than the third century AD, given some obvious parallels with Neoplatonic and Gnostic thinking. As presently constituted, the collection exhibits little of the magical side of hermeticism that was once so familiar to the classical world and which is still prominent in some other independently surviving texts.[151] These display a number of parallels with the theurgy of later Neoplatonism, and indeed were used by Iamblichus to bolster his defence of such an approach against Porphyry.[152] It has been suggested that it was

---

[147] Cf. M. J. B. Allen, *The Platonism of Marsilio Ficino: A Study of his Phaedrus Commentary* (Berkeley: University of California Press, 1984), 185–203 esp. 191, 199–200.

[148] *Letters*, v. 51 (Eng. trans. iv. 66–7).

[149] 'Thrice-greatest', used perhaps to distinguish the Egyptian Thoth from the Greek Hermes, though in fact they shared much in common and were often identified: for stress on difference, W. Scott (ed.), *Hermetica* (Boston: Shambhala, 1993), 4–5; for commonality, G. Fowden, *The Egyptian Hermes* (Princeton: Princeton University Press, 1983), 23–4.

[150] For 11th-c. reference, Fowden, *Egyptian Hermes*, 7–8; for some as early as the 4th c. BC, B. P. Copenhaver (ed.), *Hermetica* (Cambridge: Cambridge University Press, 1992), p. xvi.

[151] See esp. the first volume of A. D. Nock and A. J. Festugière, *Corpus Hermeticum* (Paris: Budé, 1946–54), i–iv. It is important to note that Ficino's text stopped at the 14th discourse, and so that even Copenhaver's edition is larger (English only) and Scott's still more so (Greek also).

[152] In his *De mysteriis*. For a helpful discussion that suggests also some involvement even from Plotinus, see Fowden, *Egyptian Hermes*, 126–41.

probably Byzantine editors who purged the *Corpus*, and that such magic was once regarded simply as the lower stage on the way to more intellectual forms of intimacy with God.[153] But, whatever the reason, it meant that the texts were mediated in a relatively pure form of reflection in and through Ficino's translation. For Ficino this had two consequences. The first was that it was not difficult for either him or the wider society to believe that they were part of an earlier divine revelation that predated the divisions between the religions and so provided some sort of universal revelation. Indeed, within a decade or so such a notion was being enshrined in the pavement of Siena Cathedral.[154] Secondly, their content could function as reinforcement for his view that God has come close to our world, and is inherent throughout. For, although the various discourses are not entirely consistent and sometimes have negative allusions to the world,[155] on the whole these could easily be subordinated to the more common assumption of God 'pregnant with all things', creating an eternal cosmos that deserves our unstinted praise.[156] Thus, though our destiny is spiritual, the material order can be seen to play an indispensable part, and so reflect what is for the Christian the pre-eminent divine disclosure in the incarnation.

Platonism and Renaissance Art

Given this general approach, the culture of Florence at the time and the philosopher Ficino's friendships with some notable artists, it is initially somewhat surprising to discover that his appeals to art are relatively rare.[157] He himself was an accomplished musician, and

[153] For alteration of text, Fowden, ibid. e.g. 9, 117; for part of single strategy, e.g. 79–87, 116–26.

[154] A succession of transmission running down to Plato was given in the preface to Ficino's translation, Scott, *Hermetica*, 31; for the Siena pavement, with Hermes and Moses in dialogue, frontispiece, 32 n. 1. The antiquity of the work was not challenged till Casaubon's refutation, published in 1614.

[155] e.g. in Discourse X, the world is declared to be 'beautiful, but not good'.

[156] In Discourse V God is 'ungrudging', 'seen through the entire cosmos', and 'pregnant with all things'. Towards the end of Discourse XIII there is a fine hymn to the 'Lord of creation', praising its variety and providential character.

[157] His friends included the architect Alberti and the painter Pollaiuolo: *Letters*, VI. 26. For one of those rare examples, note his comparison of the intricacy and balance of the world to a finely crafted cabinet that he had seen recently in Florence and which was full of fascinating details such as mechanically operated animals: *Platonic Theology*, II. 13 (Allen and Hankins, i. 201–5).

that presumably explains why allusions to music and its potential for beauty are more frequent.[158] None the less, it is clear from his writings that he is concerned to offer a re-evaluation of Plato according to which, so far from viewing the arts with suspicion, they are in fact seen as indispensable. Thus it is noted that not only was Plato a poet in his youth, but also his later prose style continued to be poetic in form, with him truly a painter in words.[159] Then, again, any element of irony in dialogues such as the *Ion, Phaedrus*, and *Symposium* is seen as wholly directed against misuse, and so even the *Republic* itself comes to be viewed as concerned with misdirected creativity, not human creativity as such.[160] Art and nature can therefore, without any sense of embarrassment, be directly compared as both alike exhibiting the rational principles of order, proportion, and harmony. Although also (wrongly) seen as Plato's own position, the importance of such a view lies in the freedom these notions gave the Renaissance to see art as emulating God's own handiwork, both alike immanent in our world.

In academic as well as popular presentations of the Renaissance it has for long been common to present the period as marking the liberation of humanity in general, and art in particular, from religion. In the nineteenth century, for instance, Jacob Burckhardt spoke of a 'general spirit of doubt' in which the new subjectivity was 'conscious of no sin' and so acted as 'the leader of new ages',[161] while Walter Pater, though trying to be fair to underlying religious convictions, none the less insists that what the artists expressed constituted in effect a marked shift away from religion and towards a more open future.[162] Perhaps most significant for my argument

---

[158] For references to his own performances, Kristeller, *Philosophy of Marsilio Ficino*, 307; for self-interrogation of the motives behind his own lyre-playing: *Letters* V. 11 (Eng. trans. iv. 16–17).

[159] *Letters* I. 18; III. 3, 4, 19 (Eng. trans. i. 57; ii. 9–10; iii, 34, 39).

[160] In *Letters* I. 130 the *Ion* is used to argue that true poetry is always a refection of the divine: 'vera poesis a Deo ad Deum'.

[161] In his classic *The Civilisation of the Renaissance in Italy* of 1860, 3rd edn. (London: Phaidon, 1995). The final part (Part 6) focuses on 'Morality and Religion', with a concluding section on a 'General Spirit of Doubt' which is taken to mark transition to 'new ages': 357–65 esp. 364. Subjectivity and the absence of sin are noted earlier: 322–3.

[162] Seen e.g. in his essays on Pico and Michelangelo in *The Renaissance: Studies in Art and Poetry* of 1873 (London: Senate, 1998). Pico, it is suggested, was not satisfied by his own theories: 30–49 esp. 48; the Michelangelo of the Medici tombs

here is the contention in the twentieth century from Hans Blumenberg that secularization is the inevitable product of Christianity's response to its own internal dilemmas at this time and subsequently.[163] In particular he stresses Christianity's attempt to solve the problem of evil by producing an increasingly more transcendent god who would then in due course inevitably be shuffled off the scene. I contend precisely the opposite, that the Renaissance was in fact a move in a quite different direction, towards a more immanent and involved God, and that this is what one finds in the art of the time. Certainly it was a time when more stress came to be placed on the individual, but this subjective orientation actually generated more religious fervour rather than less. This can be seen, for example, in the extent to which lay fraternities now demanded their own services and rites,[164] and if their penitential form might be taken to suggest suspicion of the body, on the other side one needs to note not only the limited, instrumental character of such action but also the way in which their practices were combined with material values such as a love of theatre and spectacle as an essential part of religion.[165] It is even possible that Ficino's own Platonic Academy was modelled on such guilds.[166] So it should occasion no surprise that in the earlier

'so ignorant of the spiritual world . . . that he does not surely know whether the consecrated Host may not be the body of Christ': 73–97 esp. 95.

[163] H. Blumenberg, *The Legitimacy of the Modern Age* (Cambridge, Mass.: MIT Press, 1985), esp. 125–226. Blumenberg identified two major times of crisis, during the lifetime of Augustine and again at the end of the Middle Ages, with Descartes taken as symptomatic of what was entailed by the latter crisis. The almost exclusive focus on philosophy in my view distorts his interpretation of what was really happening.

[164] For special services at Florence, and their character, J. Henderson, 'Penitence and the Laity in Fifteenth Century Florence', in T. Verdun and J. Henderson (eds.), *Christianity and the Renaissance* (Syracuse, NY: Syracuse University Press, 1990), 229–49 esp. 232, 235, 240–1. For sermons at the Academy and Pico's support for special prayer and hymns, R. Weissman, 'Sacred Eloquence', ibid. 250–71 esp. 252, 266.

[165] N. Newbigin, 'The Word Made Flesh: The *Rappresentazioni* of Mysteries and Miracles in Fifteenth Century Florence', in Verdun and Henderson, *Christianity and the Renaissance*, 361–75. Flagellation had been largely confined to the clergy until the 13th c.: 230.

[166] Explored in P. O. Kristeller, *Studies in Renaissance Thought and Letters* (Rome: Edizioni di storia el letteratura, 1956), 99–122. It is often forgotten that Ficino was himself a priest (109).

Renaissance we already find devout artists delighting in empirical detail in a way that was not found in any previous generation, so firmly were their predecessors still under Byzantine influence.[167]

So far as Ficino's own times and later are concerned, it is fortunate that the extent of that influence has been thoroughly investigated by a number of distinguished art historians, among them Ernst Gombrich, Erwin Panofsky, and Edgar Wind. There is no need to repeat all their conclusions here. It will suffice to note a few of the examples they detect of the influence of Ficino's Platonism on art, adding, where appropriate, what did not concern them: how this might represent a more incarnational version of Plato. That matter is of particular importance, not least because, although these distinguished scholars of Renaissance art were fully cognizant of differences between Plato and Plotinus, their assumption still seems to be that Ficino simply read Plato through the eyes of Plotinus rather than producing his own distinctive system: different, that is, not only from pagan Neoplatonism but also from earlier Christian readings of Neoplatonism such as those of Denys.[168]

One much-discussed example of the influence of Platonism on Renaissance art is the work of the earlier Botticelli, especially his *Primavera* (1482) but also to some extent his *Birth of Venus* (1485).[169] Although the details are disputed, the influence of the Platonic notion of two types of love seems not to be in doubt.[170] Much

---

[167] In answering Blumenberg, S. A. McKnight contrasts Duccio's hierarchical work with Giotto's incarnationalism, the latter delighting in incidentals such as stubborn camels: *The Modern Age and the Recovery of Ancient Wisdom* (Columbia, Miss.: University of Missouri Press, 1991), 60–90 esp. 60–1, 68. For another analysis which also focuses on the incarnation, D. Kent, *Cosimo de'Medici and the Florentine Renaissance* (New Haven: Yale University Press, 2000), 95–106 esp. 103, 106.

[168] Cf. E. Wind, *Pagan Mysteries in the Renaissance*, 2nd edn. (London: Faber & Faber, 1967), 23–4. It is a mistake to take the actual words of Ficino at face value because essential to his purpose of elucidating a universal theology was the minimizing of difference.

[169] E. H. Gombrich, *Symbolic Images*, 3rd edn. (Oxford: Phaidon, 1985), 31–81; E. Panofsky, *Renaissance and Renascences* (New York: Harper & Row, 1969), 191–200; Wind, *Pagan Mysteries*, 113–40.

[170] Wind severely criticizes Gombrich for not getting to the heart of the matter: 114 n. 6. For the two types of love, Plato, *Symposium* 180d–e, Ficino, *De amore* 11. vii; Pico, *Commento*, 11. 7. For Pico's insistence that this should not lead to the disparagement of earthly love, Wind, *Pagan Mysteries*, 138–9; cf. *Commento*, II. 24.

the same could also be said for Titian's later *Sacred and Profane Love*.[171] For those inclined to parody Christian and Platonic attitudes to the body it comes as a salutary warning to learn that Botticelli's gentle sensualism is part of a Christian and Platonic vision, still more so that in Titian's painting sacred love is the naked woman and profane love the clothed. The key role of sensual beauty is thus fully acknowledged. Although we know Ficino to have commissioned a number of paintings, none has survived.[172] But, if in his case that kind of direct connection is now lacking, it is provided for his pupil, Pico, who had the related theme of the three Graces inscribed on a medallion of his, with inscriptions reflecting the Neoplatonic notion of processions, conversion, and return.[173] If in itself the imagery could have occurred at any point in the history of Neoplatonism, what is new is the context, where the beauty that inspires the whole movement is now much more explicitly identified with what is to be found in this world. Sight rather than purely intellectual vision is, in the end, the key.[174]

However, it is works from the century following Botticelli that provide the clearest evidence of strong links between Platonism and art. Throughout the œuvre of Michelangelo, in works as varied as the Medici Chapel, the tomb of Julius II, and the Sibyls on the ceiling of the Sistine Chapel, the influence of Platonism can be seen.[175] Indeed, various connections back to Ficino himself are sometimes postulated.[176] If some find in Michelangelo's later

[171] Wind, *Pagan Mysteries*, 141–51; E. Panofsky, *Studies in Iconology* (New York: Harper & Row: 1972), 150–3. The original is in the Galleria Borghese in Rome.

[172] For the Villa Careggi, where the Platonic Academy met; cf. Gombrich, *Symbolic Images*, 77.

[173] Wind, *Pagan Mysteries*, 36–52 esp. 43–4. The divine beauty (*Pulchritudo*) generates pleasure (*Voluptas*) which results in love (*Amor*); the specific terminology is found in Ficino.

[174] 'One cannot describe how much more easily the sight of beauty inspires love than words can do'; for this quotation from Ficino in context, Gombrich, *Symbolic Images*, 44–5.

[175] Panofksy, *Iconology*, 171–230; E. Wind, 'Michelangelo's Prophets and Sybils', in G. Holmes (ed.), *Art and Politics in Renaissance Italy* (Oxford: Oxford University Press, 1993), 263–300. Panofsky notes the important mediating role of the commentary on Dante by Landino, himself a member of the Platonic Academy: 179.

[176] Apart from the influence of Landino, Kristeller suggests that Michelangelo probably met Ficino in his youth and also could well have read the vernacular works of Ficino's principal successor, Francesco da Diacceto: *Studies*, 287–336 esp. 324–6.

work a cooling of that wider vision and restriction to a more
narrowly Christian conception, it remains possible to read even
the late poetry with its reference to 'fables of this world' which take
from him 'the time given for contemplating God' as constituting
not a rejection of Platonism as such but rather a move away from
the positive evaluation of the world in Ficino's Platonism to something closer to Plato's own views.[177] A similar negative move, it is
suggested, also marked Botticelli's later work as he came under the
influence of Savonarola. But even if parallels can be drawn between
Botticelli's Fogg *Crucifixion* and Michelangelo's *Last Judgement*, it
would seem to be quite wrong to say that the more negative vision
also pervades Botticelli's *Mystical Nativity*.[178] In any case Savonarola's views were not quite so negative as they are commonly
portrayed. He himself was a man of considerable culture, and his
reforms appear to have been motivated more by the desire that art
have a clear message than by any hostility to Platonism as such.[179] In
a sense he anticipates the Counter-Reformation's similar desire for
clarity of perspective and so simplicity of message.

The Counter-Reformation in due course yielded place to the
more complicated dynamic of Baroque in the seventeenth century.
Even here, though, its own distinctive version of incarnational
theology was aided by Platonism. At the turn of the century
works on art theory were already preparing the ground. In his
two treatises of 1584 and 1590 the acknowledged Platonist, Giovanni Lomazzo, uses Ficino's general theory of beauty to argue that
the role of art is to bring out the underlying reality of the world and

---

[177] For the negative estimate, Panofsky, *Iconology*, 229; for the 1555 sonnet in
full, from which these quotations are taken, C. Ryan (trans.), *Michelangelo: The
Poems* (London: Dent, 1996), 233 n. 288.

[178] Both the Boticelli pictures were painted around 1500, a time when many
expected the end of the world. However, while in the *Crucifixion* Mary Magdalene
is used to plead on behalf of the city of Florence, the apocalyptic references in the
Mystical Nativity are much more subdued.

[179] M. C. Hall is careful to make such points, which is why I find it all the more
surprising that she perceives the joyful side of his *Mystical Nativity* undermined by
'another premonitory homily': 'Savonarola's Preaching and the Patronage of Art',
in Verdun and Henderson, *Christianity and the Renaissance*, 494–522 esp. 503.
Certainly there is a warning inscription and devils hiding in the details of the
painting, but the mood of the larger, dancing angels is surely still overwhelmingly
joyful. Is the situation really much different from the frequent allusions in Renaissance Nativities (with thistles etc.) to the forthcoming crucifixion?

so also make theological abstractions such as Christ's divinity or Mary's virginity visible to us. Then again, at the beginning of the following century in 1607 Federico Zuccaro, though nominally an Aristotelian, reaches not dissimilar conclusions that the artist's *disegno* is really a sign of God (*segno di Dio*).[180] It is during the same period that we also find the poet Torquato Tasso using Ficino as a dialogue partner to argue that God was himself a poet, and so that the role of poetry is to create a miniature world that allows the reader to see the underlying harmony of the world given to it by God.[181] One brief example of how such Platonic affirmations of art worked themselves out in baroque architecture will suffice. Angels and representations of abstract ideas such as the virtues now appear realistically as part of our world in the ceilings of churches and palaces.[182] Through *trompe-l'œil* flat ceilings come to resemble the vault of heaven itself. In short, heaven now enters the viewer's space, and in part that way of seeing things is a consequence of Platonism, yet a Platonism utterly different in directional feel from what had inspired icons, where the primary pull was actually in the opposite direction, not to draw heaven down to share our world but to raise us into its.

None of this is to suggest that Renaissance art and what followed it were exclusively products of a different way of approaching Platonism, any more than a particular conception of icons was, centuries earlier, of another. It was only one element, though a crucial one, among several in a total package of cultural shaping. My point is simply that the theological concept of sacramentality does not work in isolation, nor with one single self-understanding. Philosophy also plays its part, conditioned and conditioning in its turn, and so in assessing any experience the influence of philosophy for good or for bad also needs to be weighed in the balance.

[180] For Lomazzo, R. Williams, *Art, Theory, and Culture in Sixteenth-Century Italy* (Cambridge: Cambridge University Press, 1997), 123–35 esp. 133; for Zuccaro, ibid. 135–50 esp. 148. Although Zuccaro is an Aristotelian on sensation and universals, he uses Plato to argue that *disegno* in painting can give us access to underlying invisible realities: 144–5.

[181] Ibid., 150–62 esp. 156–7, 161. Tasso's *Discorsi del poemo eroico* appeared in 1594, a year before his death.

[182] For their effect, Gombrich, *Symbolic Images*, 155–7. While agreeing that symbols were treated as more than mere metaphor, I find it harder to assess Gombrich's claim that the abstract ideas were actually sometimes thought of as Platonic Forms: 123–6.

Conflict and Complementarity

Given how critical I was of some aspects of the theology of icons and their supporters, it may seem surprising that I have so far devoted little attention to the limitations of Renaissance art. That was partly because I wanted to keep the main focus on the impact of Platonism, so often misunderstood as it is, but also because the alleged defects of Renaissance art are in any case well known: an excessive humanism that supposedly deprives the biblical scenes of an appropriately religious dimension. That this sometimes happens can scarcely be denied, but I would suggest that it does so more commonly in our day than at the actual time of composition simply because our contemporaries come with a different set of assumptions to what would have inspired Renaissance artists and their audience. Indeed, Platonic sacramentalism of the kind indicated above, suitably popularized, would have been part of that inheritance. By contrast in our own day we lack the education to attend to the signs that speak of divine immanence, and so instead see only humanism. Think, for instance, of how often the symbolic dimension is misidentified as simply a pretty detail. A goldfinch in a painting of Madonna and Child, for instance, would once have been seen immediately as alluding to the crucifixion (because such birds are often seen amid thistles and thistles suggest thorns).[183] Nowadays, however, the artist concerned is more likely to be accused of sentimentality, when in fact there is none. Icons then become more appealing, in part because their obvious otherness demands less work of us, and so can quickly be equated with transcendence, even if we have no natural inclinations that way.

Yet, as I observed at the beginning of this chapter, what an adequate theology really needs to derive from such experiences is a stress on both immanence and transcendence. God is omnipresent; so is literally neither 'in' or 'beyond' the world, but everywhere or nowhere equally. None the less, these metaphors are indispensable because they indicate our struggling attempts to explore how an essentially different kind of reality such as God relates to ourselves and the material world that is the setting for our lives.

---

[183] Goldfinches like to eat the seeds of various thistles. The presence of fruit, birds, or plants more often than not has such symbolic resonances.

Transcendence speaks of that otherness which is a non-physical, immaterial reality; immanence of its involvement in the material. The danger in heeding only the transcendence is that an unbridgeable gap is created between ourselves and God; the danger in accepting only immanence is that the divine is reduced to something like ourselves, his reality in effect treated as equivalent to the totality of the world. So both are needed to complement each other. That is why advocates of icons and of the Renaissance each have their proper place.

Suitably expressed, so far from simply creating a gap, transcendence can actually remind us that human beings too have a transcendent, immaterial dimension. This is surely one of the great strengths of icons: they draw us into that heavenly reality, while still retaining the essential otherness of God in their strict rules about representation of the divine.[184] This is not the place to enter into detailed discussion of the nature of human beings, whether we should think of them as dual entities consisting of both soul and body or as psychosomatic unities or whatever. Suffice it to say that it is one undoubted great merit in Platonism that it recognized that without the postulation of some shared immaterial element, human survival of death or of any relationship with the divine seems meaningless.[185] My own view is that this need not be expressed in conventional dualist terms, but the point about theology of the type of icons upon which I have chosen to focus is that they are premised on that shared element, and so on the ability of God to draw us into his own world. Yet human beings are more than souls or minds; they are also profoundly shaped by material reality, and indeed nothing can happen in this world without having some effect on matter, even if it is only the firing of neurones in our brains. So for God to impact on every aspect of us immanence must also be claimed: God involved with matter. Christians believe that this happened at the deepest and most profound level in the incarnation, but if there is to be a continuing effect this cannot have

---

[184] Only God the Son can be represented, in virtue of his incarnation. The uniform transcendence of God the Father is thus maintained, in sharp contrast to the symbolic images that occur in Western art.

[185] This is not to deny resurrection of the body, but it is to assert that such resurrection makes sense only if there is something immaterial in us (if not a soul, then at the very least information-bearing patterns) that could then relate to a re-established form of material existence.

happened just once, but must relate to all material existence. It is this insight that the Renaissance takes up and defends in its art.

Yet the contrast cannot be left quite so stark, as though Renaissance art were all about immanence and icons all about transcendence. What I have been trying to get at is the most likely form of religious experience generated by one or the other, but historical reality is seldom quite that simple. In order to convey divine immanence, that something more than the purely human is present, Renaissance artists had to include an element of idealization in their religious figures, and that, of course, could of itself suggest transcendence, a moving beyond the world as well as an invasion of it. One of the many factors that makes Michelangelo a great artist is the ability his figures have to conjure both notions together: they are 'larger than life' in more ways than one. Again, Raphael in his Nativities does more than just offer us naturalism; no imperfection is allowed in the mother while a triangular structure is often given to the holy grouping to suggest a more than human stability and purpose. In his Crucifixions real suffering is qualified by beauty of body and a participating nature.[186]

Likewise, even the most apparently transcendent of icons can at times hint at immanence. For example, one recent study has proposed that the insubstantiality of monks and bishops in some icons is deliberately contrived to act as a contrast to the corporeality of the apostles and Virgin Mary, made so precisely in order to underline their association with the immanent reality of the incarnation.[187] Yet another has detected a continuing 'dialectic' between 'transcendental dematerialization' and a Hellenistic realistic naturalism that runs across the centuries.[188] Yet while important and legitimate qualifications, a fundamental contrast between most icons and most Renaissance art must, it seems to me, still be allowed to stand, and so the question remains with us of how people's experience might

---

[186] As with sun and moon in London's National Gallery version.

[187] H. Maguire, *The Icons of their Bodies: Saints and their Images in Byzantium* (Princeton: Princeton University Press, 1996), 48–99.

[188] E. Kitzinger, *Byzantine Art in the Making* (Cambridge, Mass.: Harvard University Press, 1977). For the terminology, e.g. 4, 62, 74, 80, 106. Sinai's bias in the former direction is, e.g. contrasted with the earlier return to more naturalistic forms at S. Vitale and with what happened subsequently at S. Maria Antiqua: 82–4, 99–100, 113–15.

be helped in the right direction if both aspects are indeed an implication of how the divine reality relates to us.

As an implicit recognition of the need for both affirmations, what one now sometimes finds in Western churches is the presence of icons alongside late-medieval or modern art. Sometimes this works; sometimes in my view the only result is rather confused messages.[189] What such practices ignore, however, is the extent to which in the past other complementary aids have in fact been put to use, such as liturgy and architecture. It would take too long to explain at this point how and to what degree this has proved successful in either Orthodox or Renaissance churches. Instead, let me offer an example that can be sketched in a single sentence, what happened in the late Middle Ages in the West: greater natur-alism in painting and sculpture went hand in hand with pointed arches and soaring spires, immanence and transcendence affirmed at one and the same time.

How that complementarity has been deliberately sought through much of the history of Christianity is an issue I shall examine in Chapters 5 and 6, as I explore architecture, including that of Orthodox churches. Meanwhile, however, I want to move beyond the point of encounter that we have been discussing here and towards place as such. Experience of nature as the Creator's work has always been held to tell us much about the character of God. In the next chapter I shall attempt to survey some of the main types of experiential response, among them reactions to the evil inherent within nature.

---

[189] The series in Winchester Cathedral integrates perfectly with the building; those in Westminster Abbey seem more problematic.

3
The Natural World
Mediated Experience and Truth

IN the previous chapter I explored the place of encounter, and noted how religious experience can pull in two quite different directions, towards transcendence or towards immanence. Both, I suggested, needed to be affirmed when thinking of God. In a later chapter which deals with architecture I shall argue that the most successful forms of religiously adequate architecture are those that try to balance precisely those two aspects in the overall expression that the building seeks to achieve. However, in the two intervening chapters (this one and its successor) it may seem from their titles that the focus will be entirely on immanence. That is not so. In Chapter 4 (on place) an element of transcendence is introduced by the way in which any absolute value for a particular place is seen to be undermined by tactics such as symbolic geography and pilgrimage, while in this chapter (on the natural world) experiences of transcendence through nature will also be found to have a clear role. Indeed, one might argue that such experiences, where they occur, are even more strongly transcendent than is the case with the icon (discussed in the previous chapter). For, while the latter draws us into another world which its iconography indicates we can one day expect to share, often experience and representations of transcendence through nature propose something quite different: God as an unqualifiedly different kind of reality from what we are. So care will be needed as we explore the range of sacramentality available through nature.

This is, of course, an investigation that could have been conducted in numerous ways other than the one I have chosen. I might, for instance, have focused on the experiential accounts of ordinary believers, literary reflections of poets and others, or on the wonder generated through scientific explanation. Landscape painting and the abstract art that developed out of it have been selected instead for a number of reasons, not least because their religious dimension is so often undervalued or misunderstood. It may be objected, though, that in choosing this method I am in effect committing myself to examining experience at its least pure. After all, it will be said, the artist works slowly in recording his or her response to nature, and so there is more opportunity to introduce elements extraneous to what is being taught by nature itself.[1] I am far from sure, though, if this is so. Certainly, few would fall into the trap of supposing that landscape painting is merely a matter of copying the view. As Ernst Gombrich has observed, 'the innocent eye is a myth... all perceiving relates to expectations and therefore to comparisons'.[2] But no less true is the fact that poet and prose writer alike usually record their impressions of God at work in the countryside in reflective tranquillity (after, for example, having returned from a walk).

On the other hand, consideration of the issues through art provides a number of clear, positive advantages. Landscape art can be just as expressive as prose, but it is always concise in a way other media seldom are. There is thus less danger of the point being lost amid a wealth of detail. That very conciseness also ensures that there is brought to prominence what is often thought to be the most decisive objection to religious experience, its historically conditioned character. Ranging over a number of literary accounts, it may not always be clear which features are conspicuous in which generations, but with art there is little doubt.[3] Some ways of perceiving nature have undoubtedly come more to the fore in one generation rather than in another. So, for example, although it is possible to point to some earlier anticipations of the kind of approach that finds God in the grandeur of mountainous terrain, in such places as the Scottish Highlands or the American Rockies,[4] it is really only with the Romantic movement of the late eighteenth and early nineteenth centuries that the finding of the divine in nature at its most majestic or awesome was to become commonplace. To earlier generations Switzerland or the Lake District were

---

[1] Such as purely aesthetic considerations. Slowness is of course not necessarily an enemy to purity of record. It is only that there are then more opportunities for reflection to take off in fresh directions.

[2] E. H. Gombrich, *Art and Illusion* (London: Phaidon Press, 1960), 254.

[3] Although poetry, unlike prose, might be said to have some of the advantages I claim here for art.

[4] Such as in the paintings of Salvator Rosa (d. 1673), discussed below.

most likely to conjure up purely negative images, of forbidding threat or fear, and indeed to retreat into such places was often seen as the northern equivalent of moving into the desert, a place where demons had to be fought and overcome. From the admission of such variety it is then but a short step to the conclusion that all such responses to nature are really entirely determined by historical and cultural setting, and therefore can provide no independent access to truth about God.

The fallacious character of such an inference, however, becomes immediately obvious as soon as note is taken of how easily comparable arguments could be generated for whole areas of human experience where we are less tempted to draw such conclusions. Landscape paintings may, for instance, embody conservative or radical political claims, but to make these explicit is hardly in and of itself to rob such contentions of all validity.[5] Although independent assessment is still required, complete success in such a task is scarcely achievable without reference to the artistic works themselves. For it is not just that the paintings make a truth claim about politics, but that this truth is believed to be closely related to the way in which the landscape presents itself to our eyes. Similarly, then with religion. Radically different ways of experiencing the natural world have come to particular prominence at various points in history, and there are cultural explanations as to why this might be so. But the truth claims embodied in the paintings still require an assessment that goes beyond recognition of such conditioning into engagement with the dynamics of both how the painter experienced his world and what he has deduced from it.

Above all, what needs to be guarded against is a model that presupposes that the only form of truth is where the individual stands apart in independent assessment over against what is being assessed rather than as engaged actively within it. This is disenchantment at its worst. That it is the model advocated in the modern world for many areas of life is perhaps scarcely surprising,

---

[5] For hidden political claims in art generally, cf. J. Berger, *Ways of Seeing* (London: Penguin, 1972), esp. 83–112. Berger considers his point least applicable to landscape, but he uses Gainsborough's *Mr and Mrs Andrews* as a counterexample: 104–8. For a contrary view that explores Constable's political claims and their impact on the society of today, P. Bishop, *An Archetypal Constable: National Identity and the Geography of Nostalgia* (Madison: Fairleigh Dickinson University Press, 1995).

but, ironically, it is also often endorsed even by Christians for Scripture itself. The conservative sees the postulation of an unconditioned text as the only way of preserving integrity for God's word; the liberal the objectivity of historical and literal analysis as requiring a similar standing apart, though for quite different reasons: those who wrote the text were conditioned, but the scholar must not be. But to my mind because such conditioning is inevitable, engagement and the search for objectivity need to be pursued in tandem, and not in opposition to one another. We are affected by our context whether we like it or not. But this does not mean truth cannot be ascertained; only that its pursuit is more difficult.

In trying to move towards such truth, it needs to be stressed that the various types of experience identified below should not necessarily be seen as in conflict with one another. Rather, it is the case that some sets of historical circumstance make it easier to experience God in one way rather than another, and the task of the reflective theologian is therefore to see how such insights can be combined in an intelligible whole. Not that such integration will always be possible. Some types of experience (such as what is labelled below as a 'symbolic reminder' experience) do indeed appear more like a projection from antecedent assumptions than anything else. That is no doubt one reason why the specific instance quoted now seldom functions in the modern world. But considerable care will need to be exercised before any form is dismissed, because it may well be that such dismissal is really just a case of the tail wagging the dog, of not considering first the experience in its own right but rather antecedent theological assumptions determining evaluation. Some examples of this will be given in due course.

Although arguably we are now moving once more to a more visually based society, the temptation for any written culture is still there, to suppose the natural superiority of the verbal over the visual. That assumption I want to challenge in what follows. I begin to do so by attempting to draw some parallels between art and theology, and in particular the way in which changes in the wider culture have had comparable impacts on both their more recent histories. Thereafter I consider seven types of experience of the natural world and their implications, culminating in a final section that considers how some artists of the twentieth century sought to explore the issue of evil through an abstract art that had itself developed out of their interest in the natural world. That last element is of particular interest as, if my account is accepted, it shows that alternative approaches to the issue can be pursued visually no less than conceptually, in words. In all of this, though, my overarching theme should not be forgotten, the way in which God can come sacramentally close to his world and vouchsafe experiences of himself through the material.

Theology and Art Compared

The visual arts and philosophy of religion are often thought to be at opposite extremes from one another, the latter a model of analytic rigour, the former appealing to vague emotional and aesthetic values. Some elements in this contrast are legitimate, but by no means all of them. Today it has become a commonplace to remark that in many ways art has now taken over the role once exercised by religion. Art galleries are described as the new churches where contemplation and spiritual enrichment are sought, and as if in confirmation one might note the Rothko Chapel at Houston in Texas, where surrounding a room with abstract panels by this artist is deemed sufficient on its own to carry the appropriate religious dimension, in this case a highly apophatic one.[6]

Admittedly, such comparisons are often quite superficial, but it is, I think, possible to draw a more extended analogy that could prove helpful to the understanding of both art and theology. Indeed, what I want to suggest is that some of the key issues raised by philosophical theology, including its most frequently discussed problem of evil, can be just as easily mediated through art, and that this sometimes provides insights seldom noted by professional theologians and philosophers. To see why the comparison is not as implausible as it may initially sound, let me offer a sketch of the way in which the history of art and that of Christian theology have in fact closely paralleled one another across the centuries.

---

[6] Although commissioned by Roman Catholic patrons, and having the traditional eight-sided form of a Christian baptistery, it was dedicated at an inter-faith service in 1971 that anticipated its future use outside any specific religious tradition.

Prior to the Reformation the pattern followed in reading Scripture allowed it four senses, only one of which was literal, the others to varying degrees symbolic, and for large tracts of the Bible, though the literal was never entirely discounted, the symbolic clearly took precedence in the Church's self-understanding.[7] Art, though, was similarly conceived. Here too there were elements of the literal, but the elongated figures of Romanesque or the positions of angels' wings, to take two examples at random, were made so not because there was ignorance of anatomy—though there was that—but because symbolic considerations were likewise held to take precedence. However, with the Renaissance's emphasis on perspective came increasingly a move towards naturalism and a corresponding literalism in representation, but that of course finds its exact parallel in Reformation and Counter-Reformation, in the decline in acceptance of the other three senses of Scripture and an almost exclusive focus upon the literal. There are in fact numerous parallels between the growth of biblical literalism on the one hand and artistic naturalism on the other.[8] One sees, for example, the way in which attacks within theology (Catholic as well as Protestant) on the composite figure of Mary Magdalene find their analogue in art in Carvaggio's insistence on introducing torn clothes and dirty feet into his religious scenes.[9] Theology and art alike now held up literal correspondence as their ideal for truth.

Over the past two centuries, however, both theology and art have had to face radical challenges to their identity, and so needed

[7] In the classic four senses of Scripture, apart from the literal meaning attention was also given to the moral or tropological, the allegorical, and the anagogic (as a pointer to future earthly or heavenly realities). This is not to deny that the literal did of course sometimes take clear precedence, e.g. in the events of Christ's life, or that the patristic period had a more nuanced version of these four meanings: see further F. Young, *Biblical Exegesis and Christian Culture* (Cambridge: Cambridge University Press, 1997).

[8] They both could, for example, be interpreted in terms of a search for new, less contested forms of authority, in what, superficially at least, appears self-authenticating.

[9] For torn clothes, his *Supper at Emmaus* (National Gallery, London); for dirty feet, his *Madonna of Loreto* (Sant'Agostino, Rome); illustrated in A. Moir, *Caravaggio* (London: Thames & Hudson, 1989), 83, 99. Ironically, though, Caravaggio remains a traditionalist in his treatment of Mary Magdalene; cf. his *Penitent Magdalene*: ibid. 61. In this last case his patron might, of course, be to blame.

to adopt fresh approaches if they were to retain plausibility as conveyers of meaning and truth. In the case of theology the challenge came through the rise of the historical-critical method, in the case of art with the invention of the camera.[10] Both undermined any simple claim to realism. However conservative the biblical scholar, he could scarcely claim that the Bible offered a one-to-one mapping of reality; whatever the evangelists were seen to offer, it could not be regarded as purely descriptive or historical; even before the Gospel of John is taken into account, the variants between the synoptics demonstrated that much. But, equally, as techniques improved, the camera could claim to catch better than the artist not merely physical resemblance but mood and character as well. It looked as though there were alternative mediums that could do their respective jobs better, the camera in literally recording what we see, science and historical research in enabling us better to comprehend our world.

Ever since, theology and art have been trying to secure a satisfactory response to those challenges. To avoid conflict, in theology various attempts at redefinition have been made, such as Schleiermacher's focus on experience, Ritschl's on morality, Bultmann's on existential meaning or, most recently, in the postmodernist underpinning of Barth, so popular in contemporary theology, that is held to make any final resolution of competing perspectives unnecessary (theology, it is claimed, has its own internal and independent criteria).[11] Art also tried various strategies in its competition with the camera, the most obvious in the nineteenth century being Impressionism and its attempt to capture the immediate moment of perception before an image had been resolved by either the organizing mind or the long-exposure camera. Current postmodernist retreat in theology is also paralleled in art, by those who continue to insist that art be viewed in purely aesthetic terms, an

[10] The rivalry between the two is already there right at the beginning, as the camera's inventor, Daguerre, working in Paris in 1839, was a scene painter who had already experimented with dioramas.

[11] In effect, Barth is portrayed as the theologian who best anticipates the collapse of the Enlightenment and modernist consensus on the necessity for shared values, by insisting that these can only be generated internally from within particular communities and their own distinctive narratives of discourse.

early influential instance of the approach in the twentieth century being the writings of Roger Fry (d. 1934), or Walter Pater in the previous century.[12]

In these dilemmas English philosophy has not been particularly helpful, operating as it has been for much of the twentieth century with an exceedingly narrow correspondence theory of truth. Russell's blunt declaration in respect of *Hamlet* is well known, that 'the propositions in the play are false because there was no such man', while Frege is scarcely any more helpful with his view that such propositions were neither true nor false.[13] Such attitudes fail to take seriously the way in which fiction, art, and the Bible itself all offer a symbolic mapping of reality that does indeed make truth claims but not in a way that is easily reducible to a one-to-one correspondence with literal fact. In two recent volumes I sought to explore how biblical stories and their later developments could be said to be true without necessarily being historically true.[14] Here in this chapter I wish to pursue that same issue from the side of art, to explore how various types of painting, both landscape and abstract, might be said to embody truth claims about God's relationship with the world without, however, there being any simple one-to-one correspondence in terms of how this is done. What for me makes such an exploration especially interesting is some of the radical solutions adopted in the art of the twentieth century, where not only is any pretence of one-to-one correspondence abandoned but it is also asserted that such abandonment constitutes the best way of presenting metaphysical or religious claims. What in effect we discover is religious art moving away from the use of explicit Christian symbols and towards an alternative, more neutral set of metaphors—based predominantly or exclusively on form and colour alone—where the artists' intention has in effect become to offer a

---

[12] For Fry's approach, *Vision and Design* (Mineola, NY: Dover, 1981). Bullen in his Introduction stresses a resultant 'radical distinction between art and nature' in which, as with Whistler, it is proposed that 'nature is very rarely right': p. xiii.

[13] B. Russell, *An Inquiry into Meaning and Truth* (London: Routledge, 1962), 277. John Urmson applies Frege's view to the opening sentence of *Persuasion* to conclude that 'Jane Austen writes a sentence which has the form of a assertion beginning with a reference, but is in fact neither asserting nor referring': 'Fiction', *American Philosophical Quarterly* 13 (1976), 153–7 esp. 155.

[14] *Tradition and Imagination* (Oxford: Oxford University Press, 1999); *Discipleship and Imagination* (Oxford: Oxford University Press, 2000).

new version of natural theology, with truth claims made about the existence of God and his relation to the world by means of these new metaphors. But, though the means are new, the artistic claims are not, and what we see is such exploration at work throughout the history of the representation of nature in art. The result is in my view the need to acknowledge the presence in art and theology alike of symbolic worlds where the relation between symbol and literal fact is at last acknowledged to be a highly complex one. That complexity is underscored by a much canvassed modern analogy, the far from simple relation between music and representation, itself the favoured analogy of all three of the modern artists with whom this chapter will end: Kandinsky, Klee, and Mondrian.

However, I want to begin elsewhere with a survey of some of the range of experiences of God that have been claimed through artistic representations of the world, at the same time examining what kind of divine being is thought to lie behind the experience. The order is roughly historical but, as will be seen, the sort of experience that generates a painting is by no means necessarily confined exclusively to just that one particular epoch. Consideration will be given in turn to what I have chosen to label, respectively, sacramental placing, symbolic reminder, ordered cosmos, transcendent awe, mystic immanence, vibrant colour, and deep form, seven types in all. Some will be found to have their own distinctive character; others to be the experiential and artistic equivalents of some traditional arguments in the philosophy of religion, such as the cosmological and teleological arguments for God's existence. Ending with abstract art is not as strange as it may at first appear. Not only did it emerge, in the case of the artists I discuss, out of their earlier work on nature but it also provided an opportunity, through their own wrestling with the issue of how to represent nature, to face what is often regarded as the decisive objection against thinking of God as sacramentally at work in nature, namely, that already mentioned problem of the fact of evil.

Sacramental Placing: Dream Painting

Even as late as the nineteenth century the supposition about primitive art was that it was just an early stage on the way to something more significant, its earliest forms like childen's doodlings.[15] So it was hardly surprising that the Aboriginal art of Australia was dismissed, at most valued as a curiosity or souvenir.[16] That went with similar attitudes to the people themselves. It was only in the 1970s that the native population began at last to recover their land rights. The first exhibition of Aboriginal art was somewhat earlier, in 1929, but it was as late as 1984 that a separate department was established in the National Gallery in the capital at Canberra.[17] Now of course one must not go to the other extreme and romanticize, but the Aborigines are an especially interesting case of a 'primitive' culture, as theirs is believed to be at least 40,000 years old, with some rock painting surviving from 18,000 years ago.[18] If the European invasion of their lands meant that their culture did not entirely stand still, and the new desire of Western collectors for their art has entailed further change, there is still sufficient continuity to speak of a living tradition.

Modern works are now done mostly on acrylic, and sometimes engage with contemporary issues, but for the most part they continue to reflect certain key themes, in particular that the role of painting is to give meaning to one's placement within a certain environment.[19] Called dream painting, the objective is to recall how the artist's present situation relates to the rocks, streams, pathways, waterholes, and animals about him. Dream-time refers not to dreams, but to the foundational age at which such patterns were established, and in particular the present relation of the spirit world to the artist's own location, tribe, and identity.[20] One reason for the popularity of such paintings among the general public is their vibrant colours and designs, but it is as well to remember that the primary motivation for these is not aesthetic but religious.

[15] P. Jones, 'Perceptions of Aboriginal Art: A History' in P. Sutton (ed.), *Dreamings: The Art of Aboriginal Australia* (London: Viking, 1989), 143–79 esp. 157–64; Tylor as quoted making the comparison with children's art: 163.

[16] Jones speaks of 'trophies': Sutton, *Dreamings*, 151.

[17] In Melbourne: ibid. 165. For the separate department at Canberra, A. Quaill, *Marking Our Times* (Canberra: National Gallery of Australia, 1996), 6.

[18] Sutton, *Dreamings*, 5; W. Caruana, *Aboriginal Art* (London: Thames & Hudson, 1993), 22.

[19] For examples of some more contemporary themes, Caruana, *Aboriginal Art*, 45 (on the Second World War); Quaill, *Marking Our Times*, 34, 66 (for interactions both positive and negative with Christianity).

[20] For definition, Caruana, *Aboriginal Art*, 10.

Lustre is seen as giving an added sense of spiritual presence, whether it be on rock, bark, or body, or the more recent form of acrylic.[21] The concentric circles of the waterholes and the pathways leading to and from them help to unify the landscape. By refusing to indicate one starting point or a single perspective from which the painting should be viewed, the artists see themselves as yielding power to the spiritual presences in nature rather than asserting human conquest of it. Indeed, sometimes it is quite obvious that it is a spirit's perception that has been granted to the viewer, not the artist's own.[22] It thus becomes impossible to think of the land except as a divinely sanctioned dwelling-place, in terms of which even one's movements across it come to take on sacramental associations.[23]

A similar pattern emerges among the Indians of North America. One writer who has been investigating the petroglyphs and pictograms of the land for the past twenty years observes that they too are used to intensify a sense of presence.[24] Fortunate in having an elderly shaman to induct him, he came to see how the landscape is viewed quite differently by native Americans. It is not that there is a series of discrete locations where communication with the spiritual world is possible, but that the landscape is everywhere marked by such contacts, sometimes through already existing natural features, sometimes by these designs on the rocks that bring to prominence their otherwise subdued significance, and sometimes by the stories that connect them with one another.[25]

Modern environmental art such as the work of Richard Long in England, Robert Smithson in the States, or Joseph Beuys in Germany may seem far removed from such notions, but significantly the tendency among such artists is to speak of spiritual values.

---

[21] Stressed by Caruana, ibid. 59–60.

[22] For a good example, ibid. 143, 145 (illus. 125). In Ada Bird Petyarre's *Sacred Grasses* (1989) our world is viewed from below, the perspective of the supernatural beings who sustain its life.

[23] There is apparently only a single word for land and home, while the dream imagery can even be applied to modern sneakers: Sutton, *Dreamings*, 17, 38.

[24] T. Conway, *Painted Dreams: Native American Rock Art* (Minocqua, Wisc.: NorthWord, 1993). Pictographs are paintings, petroglyphs are carvings: 21. Iron hematite and sturgeon oil are used to produce the red ochre: 39–41.

[25] Ibid. 83–101 esp. 83–4. In view of the key role played by concentric circles in Aboriginal art, it is interesting to find them used here as 'spirals of coiled energy': 47.

The work of Andy Goldsworthy may be treated as representative. As well as stones or rocks gathered in interesting patterns to deepen our appreciation of similar forms already existing in nature, he has also made much of tracks created by slates, poppy petals, or beech leaves, and so a parallel with Aboriginal art could be drawn.[26] Although he is not a member of any church, yet he does speak reverentially of nature and is very insistent upon his art being generated by respect for specific natural contexts.[27] Also worth noting is his observation that the mystery and beauty of the world often lies in what appears most common and obvious, in the colours of magpie or sycamore, for instance.[28] The German Anselm Kiefer is a rare contemporary example of someone with environmental aspects to his art who engages directly with religious themes.[29] Sometimes pessimistic, sometimes optimistic,[30] he has recently spoken of his desire to use more immanent language of the divine than would have found favour in the Catholicism of his youth.[31] The question remains for Goldsworthy (and others like him) whether to speak of human inventiveness is adequate to mark the full significance of what he elaborates from nature, a value and worth that he himself sees as independent of his own actions.

Despite the labour invested, particularly where numerous dots are involved, the Aborigines have tended until recently to treat their own work as ephemeral, not least because of their nomadic lifestyle, and so the need for fresh dreams in new contexts is always present. Their attitude was thus in marked contrast to the first white

---

[26] For some examples of such pathways, T. Friedman and A. Goldsworthy, *Hand to Earth: Andy Goldsworthy Sculpture 1976–90* (Leeds: Henry Moore Centre, 1990), 39, 55, 59, 69.

[27] Ibid. 127, 161, 167. Cf. 164: 'it is also an intensely spiritual affair that I have with nature'.

[28] Ibid. 18, 99

[29] The environmental aspect shows itself in use of additional materials in his paintings (e.g. straw or wood shavings) rather than in installations of the sort Goldsworthy and others produce.

[30] His *To the Supreme Being* has been interpreted as signifying the death of God, but contrast his Neoplatonic *Emanation* of two years later (1985): J. C. Gilmour, *Fire on the Earth: Anselm Kiefer and the Postmodern World* (Philadelphia: Temple University Press, 1990), 23–4, 103, fig. 1, pl. X. A negative reading of the latter is implausible.

[31] 'Horizontally, so that heaven is always mixed in the earth': part of a 1997 interview quoted in commentary on a fairly conventional *Descent of the Spirit* of 1974: N. Rosenthal, *Anselm Kiefer* (New York: Abrams, 1998), 36.

settlers who, as the name implies, longed for permanence, and indeed used the imagery of the ancient settlement of Israel to justify their own acquisition of the land.[32] More recently, though, Australians have tried to stand back and see whether they might after all have something to learn from the more positive side of the culture they supplanted. Some of the results can be seen in novels such as Peter Carey's *Oscar and Lucinda* (1988) and Patrick White's *Fringe of Leaves* (1976).[33] In the latter case White tries to shock us into the recognition of something new and worthwhile by observing how an abducted white woman taking part in a cannibalist rite in the desert none the less feels 'tempted to believe that she had partaken of a sacrament': the land and context seemed to demand it.[34]

Whether White succeeds or not, the point is that it just will not do to suppose right wholly on one side; even 'the Other's barbarities' can hint at something more. Christianity may or may not be to blame for our current ecological crisis, but it is certainly the case that the biblical revolt against nature cults encouraged society in directions where the sense of the mystery of the world was undermined.[35] Yet, if God is nature's creator, is such presence not exactly what one would expect to find? 'Turn but a stone and start a wing!' urged the poet Francis Thompson.[36] It may be that while the Hebrew prophets were right in their day, the Church now pays too high a price, conditioning its followers to expect only a disenchanted world. If it is objected that the stories associated with Aboriginal and American Indian sacred sites can scarcely be described as true, I respond by observing that mythical and literal truth are not the same thing; even Christians would not want every case

---

[32] Explored in V. Brady, *Can These Bones Live?* (Sydney: Federation Press, 1996), 20–45 esp. 25, 31.

[33] In Carey's novel the native population consistently behaves better than the white immigrants, and the two principal characters grow as they acquire some of their values, not least attachment to the land.

[34] P. White, *A Fringe of Leaves* (London: Cape, 1976), 272.

[35] For the article that began the debate about Christianity's role, Lynn White, 'The Historical Roots of our Ecological Crisis', *Science* 155 (1967), 1203–7.

[36] In his poem on the way in which the unseen world may impinge on our own, *The Kingdom of God*: D. Davie (ed.), *The New Oxford Book of Christian Verse* (Oxford: Oxford University Press, 1981), 256–7. Cf. Newman: 'Every breath of air and ray of light and heat, every beautiful prospect, is, as it were, the skirts of their garments, the waving of the robes of those whose faces see God in heaven': *Parochial and Plain Sermons* (San Francisco: Ignatius, 1987), ii. 29 (453).

of angel apparition understood literally, whether within Scripture or beyond.[37] Again, Christianity is a faith that quite happily lives with two versions of the creation myth in Genesis, and sometimes even with eight complementary models of how atonement was realized through Christ.[38]

Clearly, fully to establish my point I would need to examine some of these myths in detail, and consider the extent of their compatibility or otherwise with a religion such as my own. There is not the space to do so here, but I concede that almost certainly some conflicts would emerge, but of course that can also happen even within Christianity itself. The cult of some saint or angel appearance becomes absolutized in a way not dissimilar to what sometimes happens with some particular spirit within these ancient cultures. So limited conflict should not be confused with complete incompatibility. The time is surely past for supposing that 'primitive' necessarily entails less profound. More problematic is when the stories are treated as no more than human projections, simply as a way of human beings making themselves at home in their world.[39] Thereby, I believe, something vital and important is lost, for those early cultures have, unlike our own, maintained throughout a deep sense of the divine continually mapping itself out onto the surrounding empirical realities. European barbarism (both deliberately, and accidentally through disease) destroyed such peoples in their millions. None the less, their myths remain as a witness to that earlier enchantment of the world, and so could be heard again

---

[37] There is now a considerable contemporary literature claiming such appearances: e.g. J. M. Howard, *Commune with Angels* (Virginia Beach, Va.: A.R.E. Press, 1992). For them performing a major role in contemporary literature, cf. Paulo Coelho's bestseller, *The Valkyries* (London: HarperCollins, 1995), e.g. 153, 199, 215, 227. For a more historical perspective, R. E. Guiley, *Encyclopedia of Angels* (New York: Facts on File, 1996); for a French philosopher attempting to draw parallels with modern communication issues, M. Serres, *Angels: A Modern Myth* (Paris: Flammarion, 1995).

[38] For the two versions in Genesis: Gen. 1: 1–2: 4a, 2: 4b–25. The former is conventionally assigned to P and the latter to J. For eight complementary stories of atonement, Doctrine Commission of the Church of England, *The Mystery of Salvation* (London: Church House Publishing, 1995), 102–19.

[39] In Bruce Chatwin's *Songlines* (London: Vintage, 1998), there is a marvellous evocation of the way in which the manner of telling the myths echoes the contours of the land, but surprising little about how this might lead to certain types of spiritual attitude, and that despite his own upbringing in a vicarage. For the Aboriginal version of Genesis: 11–15, 72–3.

in a more healthy interaction this time between conquering and native cultures.

Symbolic Reminder: Animals

Here I want to examine a quite different view of the relationship between the divine and the natural world, an approach especially characteristic of medieval attitudes, though towards the end of the section I shall give some examples from much earlier in history. Given its belief in a creator God one might have thought that Christianity would have shown great enthusiasm for the natural world, but, at least so far as art is concerned, there is in fact a marked diminution of interest compared with the ancient world generally. Although this can no doubt in part be explained by the prohibitions of Exodus 20, landscape was of such absorbing interest in Hellenistic painting that it comes as a shock to discover quite how far it was demoted within the Byzantine tradition. Examples do still occur, not least in manuscripts, but with icons one might even talk of its almost complete disappearance. That would seem all part of the underlying desire, noted in the previous chapter, of drawing the viewer beyond this world and not more deeply into it. If Western attitudes were a little more sympathetic, it is still not possible to speak of an interest in the natural world in its own right. Rather, what fascinates is its symbolic resonance, the way in which each item in one's field of vision can function as a symbolic reminder of God's overall plan for human salvation. It is for this reason that both theologians and art historians have come to speak of a 'symbolist mentality'.[40] Rocks and mountains, for instance, were seen less in terms of their specific form as rocks or mountains and more as symbolic of obstacle and difficulty.[41]

Again, although in his *Canticle of the Sun* St Francis goes on to list the principal features of our world and how they illustrate God's

[40]   The term comes originally from M.-D. Chenu, *Nature, Man and Society in the Twelfth Century* (Chicago: University of Chicago Press, 1957), 99–145. Significantly, the opening chapter on medieval art of Kenneth Clark's classic *Landscape into Art* (London: John Murray, 1979; first pub. 1949) is entitled 'The Landscape of Symbols': 1–31.

[41]   London's National Gallery painting by Giovanni di Paolo of *The young Saint John going into the Wilderness* is a commonly used example.

care for his creatures, significantly he begins by declaring that the most powerful of them, the sun, should be seen primarily as a symbol of God's own glory: 'Praise be to you, my Lord, together with all your creatures, above all, Sir, for Brother Sun, who is the day, and you give us light through him. He is beautiful and radiant with great splendour and of you, most high Lord, he conveys meaning.'[42] Similar observations might also be made in respect of attitudes to animals. Natural theology, as in Aquinas' classic five arguments for God's existence, already presupposed a world that points to God, but this was reinforced by seeing specific creatures as themselves offering us moral and religious lessons, sermons if you will, rather than as simply there to be directly experienced in their own right. Although the illustrated books known as Bestiaries are common only in England, there seems no reason to doubt that their contents reflect attitudes prevalent throughout the Europe of the time.[43] The individual items in the world, plants and flowers as well as animals, were believed to be polyvalent in meaning. As well as their familiar role, there were also various moral and doctrinal lessons that they carried with them as part of their overall significance in the scheme of things. It is still often asserted that in consequence the zoology was poor, but this has been challenged of late.[44] Yet, even if so, the mythological beasts that appeared on church walls were inevitably intended to play a quite different role.

Even today some of these stories survive in the corporate memory, as, for instance, the parallels between Christ feeding us in the eucharist and the pelican reviving its chicks with its own blood.[45] So too do some of the associations, such as the snake or the

[42] My trans. For the Italian original, R. D. Sorrell, *St Francis of Assisi and Nature* (New York: Oxford University Press, 1988), 100–1.

[43] For one such Bestiary reproduced (the 13th-c. Oxford MS, Bodley 764), R. Barber (ed.), *Bestiary* (Woodbridge: Boydell Press, 1999): 'a peculiarly English phenomenon': 11.

[44] The challenge comes from two zoologists, W. George and B. Yapp, *The Naming of the Beasts: Natural History in the Medieval Bestiary* (London: Duckworth, 1991), e.g. 28, 66–7 (on weasels), 79 (on deer). Even the unicorn is seen to have plausible origins in the oryx: 87–8. Contrast Barber, *Bestiary*, 7.

[45] The cathedral at Durham provides an interesting variant. During the Middle Ages, possibly at the instigation of Bishop Richard Fox, there was a pyx with a pelican on it suspended before the high altar. The pix having been destroyed at the Reformation, the 19th-c. authorities transferred the imagery to the Word by having a brass lectern made in similar style.

ape with evil, the hare and rabbit with lust and fertility or the dog with faithfulness.[46] On the other hand, even those well versed in Scripture might have difficulty conceiving how particular biblical verses were expanded to make the eagle a symbol of renewal,[47] the stag of perseverance, or the lion of resurrection,[48] far less of the lessons without biblical underpinning as in the association of the beaver with chastity, the hydrus with salvation, or the peacock with resurrection.[49] Although in the latter cases ultimately derived from paganism, it would be a mistake to dismiss such borrowings as no more than that, for in the process of adoption they have usually also been thoroughly Christianized. This is true even of the widely disseminated image of the so-called Green Man,[50] so popular today in non-Christian circles, for the vegetation that emerges from his mouth, eyes, and ears could easily be adapted to speak of the Christian theme of renewal. Likewise the strange hybrid creatures that are depicted quite commonly in romanesque art were far from being cultivated as mere 'freaks' but more as object lessons or even as themselves worthy of salvation.[51] Occasionally also experience seems to have pulled in a different direction from that suggested by Scripture.[52]

Nor must we think Christianity alone in generating such attitudes. Although on the Indian subcontinent quite a few centuries

---

[46] For books that usefully link images from English churches with the range of associated meanings: M. W. Tisdall, *God's Beasts* (Plymouth: Charlesfort Press, 1998); J. R. Allen, *Norman Sculpture and the Medieval Bestiaries* (London: Whiting, 1887), 334–95.

[47] Isa. 40: 31; for legends of the eagle flying into the sun (and thus the presence of God), Tisdall, *God's Beasts*, 75–8.

[48] For the stag, Ps. 42: 1 and Tisdall, ibid. 119–22; for the lion, Rev. 5: 5 and Tisdall, ibid. 158–62. In respect of the latter, note especially the legend that cubs born dead are then restored to life three days later through their parents licking them.

[49] Tisdall, ibid. 32–3, 134–8, 193–4. The hydrus is a water snake that was allegedly able to slip down a crocodile's throat and then destroy it from the inside. It thus provided a useful analogy for Christ's descent into hell.

[50] The term is in fact of recent origin, having been coined by Lady Raglan only in 1939.

[51] In the Romanesque tympanum at Vézelay among those streaming towards Christ for salvation are to be found pygmies, *cynocephali* (men with dogs' heads), and Scythians with huge ears.

[52] So, e.g. the goat on the high hills is seen as an image of Christ even in contexts where Matt. 25: 35 is quoted: Barber, *Bestiary*, 54–5

seem to have elapsed during which there was no animal or figurative art, since at least the third century BC there has been a continuous tradition, with animals frequently represented on the façades of
temples and elsewhere, and by no means only for purely decorative
purposes.[53] Indeed, most Indian gods have one particular animal
associated with them, known as their vehicle or *vahana*. This is
much more than just a mode of transport, with Brahma, for
instance, riding on a goose or swan and Shiva on a bull. In reality
it also tells us something about the nature of the god concerned.
Thus, to take a different example, Ganesha, the god of enterprise,
has the rat as his *vahana* precisely because the rat is viewed as
rivalling the god in his ability to get past any obstacle. Again, Shiva's
bull, Nadi, is seen as there to emphasize not only the god's virility
(one of Shiva's characteristic emblems is the phallic *linga*) but also,
paradoxically, his ability to control such forces as an ascetic. But if
there are points of comparison, there are also differences. So, for
instance, dogs are viewed negatively but that very lowliness does in
fact allow them sometimes to become an image of reversal.[54]
Snakes might seem another point of contrast inasmuch as in India
they are taken as tokens of rebirth, but in fact the Bestiaries, rather
than following Scripture, also apply the image of the snake
sloughing its skin to resurrection and renewal.[55]

There has always been a temptation in religion to maximize the
contrast between one's own religion and 'false' alternatives, but too
often this victory is a cheap and shallow one. So in this case it is
important that the language of idolatry be not too quickly invoked.
If in India the animals in question function as rather more than just
reminders, it does not necessarily follow that they are therefore
being worshipped in themselves. Perhaps the point can be made
most clearly by considering a specific example from yet another part
of the world, the alleged worship of the cat in ancient Egypt. Egypt
was almost certainly the first place to domesticate this animal, and

---

[53] For the revival in the Maurya period, George Mitchell, in S. Snead with
W. Doniger and G. Mitchell, *Animals in Four Worlds: Sculptures from India*
(Chicago: University of Chicago Press, 1989), 27.

[54] Snead, ibid. 14, 18. Dogs are viewed just as negatively in the Bible; if one
excludes the apocryphal book of Tobit, there are in fact no positive references. For
the biblical attitude, cf. Deut. 23: 18; Ps. 59: 6–7; Prov. 26: 11; Matt. 7: 6; Rev. 22:
15.

[55] e.g. Barber, *Bestiary*, 196; Snead, *Animals in Four Worlds*, 15.

from there it was eventually to spread to western Europe and beyond, replacing an earlier tendency to use the weasel as the favoured form of domesticated pest control.[56] From around 1000 BC cats begin to appear in religious contexts. The sun-god Amun, for instance, is sometimes represented as a cat, but it was with the Plotemaic period (332–330 BC) and the worship of one particular goddess, Bastet, that the cat is especially associated. Herodotus reports huge numbers of people already attending her festival.[57] Christians were quick to dismiss such worship, not least as it had spread elsewhere in the empire through the identification of Bastet with Artemis/Diana.[58] But, as Celsus and modern writers alike stress, it was not the cats themselves that were being worshipped but the idea behind them.[59] In Amun's case it was the triumph over his enemy the snake, and more generally the cat symbolized fertility, cunning, and an ordered universe.[60] It thus just will not do to talk without qualification of the idolatrous worship of cats. Bastet symbolized something more, a particular way of perceiving the realities of the divine in relation to human existence: something like order and fulfilment through the cunningly mysterious. Ironically, it is highly likely that the Christian adoption of an alternative symbolic range that equated the cat with witchcraft was a significant contributing factor to the Black Death that so devastated medieval Europe: instead of being a figure of mystery the black cat became identified with evil, and so was persecuted rather than encouraged as a weapon against the rat.[61]

It may well have been that feeling of mystery or otherness that induced ancient peoples to think of animals as manifestations of the divine.[62] As one famous example of such attitudes continuing

[56] For a general history, J. Malek, *The Cat in Ancient Egypt* (London: British Museum, 1993). For rough dates: 56–7.

[57] A figure of 700,000: *Histories* 2. 59–60.

[58] For the image of Diana with cats, D. Engels, *Classical Cats* (London: Routledge, 1999), 120–1.

[59] For Celsus, Origen, *Contra Celsum*, 3. 19. Supported by Malek, *The Cat in Ancient Egypt*, 76; Engels, *Classical Cats*, 25–6.

[60] For Amun and the snake, Malek, *The Cat in Ancient Egypt*, 82–4; for fertility, Engels, *Classical Cats*, 8, 29–31; Malek, *The Cat in Ancient Egypt*, 57, 61. Cats also had an indispensable role in securing order in the home and in storehouses (eliminating rats, snakes, etc.).

[61] Engels, *Classical Cats*, 160–2, 183–8.

[62] Suggested by H. Frankfort in his *Ancient Egyptian Religion* (Mineola, NY: Dover, 2000 edn.), 12–14.

within Christianity mention should certainly be made of the work of the eighteenth-century Anglican poet Christopher Smart. Even in his earliest writing there are indications of him reading items in the world in a hermetic or sacramental way as ciphers for God,[63] but only in his incomplete work *Jubilate Agno* is this carried through to full effect. Not only are many biblical figures identified with specific animals,[64] but also in a probable reference back to Egypt the bull is made to represent the word of God and his own cat Jeoffrey given a very special role.[65] If at times Smart sentimentalizes the cat, it is clear that Jeoffrey does provide him with mediated experience of God. Earlier he had attacked Newton for depriving colours of their divine imprint, and here of Jeoffrey it is also clear he is concerned to assert that 'the divine spirit comes about his body to sustain it in complete cat'.[66] It was into something of that spirit that Benjamin Britten was to enter in his twentieth-century setting of Smart's poem.[67] Of course, what is mediated is not exactly the same as what occurred in the ancient world, but what that tells us, I suggest, is not the absence of mediation but rather that different aspects will come to prominence in accordance with changing needs and expectations.[68]

Despite Smart, it is a way of looking at the world that has been almost wholly lost in modern Western society. The underlying presumption across many civilizations was the assumption that individual animals were granted to us as a form of divine code by

[63] Cf. his *On the Eternity of the Supreme Being*, 1–5, 40–2, in *Christopher Smart: Selected Poems*, ed. K. Williamson and M. Walsh (London: Penguin, 1990), 17, 18. The editors speak of this as 'the earliest intimation . . . of his sacramental conception of nature': 334. He was well read in Hermetic and kabbalistic literature: 340.

[64] Old Testament figures in Fragment A, New Testament in Fragment B. It should be noted that in this he is often picking up hints in the Bible itself: e.g. among the patriarchs Judah is identified with the lion (Gen. 49: 9), Issachar with the ass (49: 14), Dan with the snake (49: 17), and Benjamin with the wolf (49: 27).

[65] For Jeoffrey, Fragment C, 695–768 (105–7). The bull immediately precedes the cat, and there is a direct reference to Egypt at 756.

[66] B, 742. For Newton, 648. For an exploration of why these 'Orphic' ideas lead him to join Plato in opposition to the mimetic arts, F. Easton, ' "Mary's Key" and the Poet's Conception', in C. Hawes (ed.), *Christopher Smart and the Enlightenment* (New York: St Martin's Press, 1999), 153–75.

[67] Under the title *Rejoice in the Lamb*. A treble solo is given to Jeoffrey, and an alto solo to the Mouse.

[68] In Smart fertility has gone and peacefulness arrived, but much else remains unchanged; e.g. the cat as a force against evil: 717–20.

which we might interpret our setting in the world and the spiritual and moral demands made on us by the divine. Apart from being premised on wrong interpretations of animal behaviour, there is now the added problem that evolution makes us doubt such detailed programming no less than the various moral interconnections that were proposed. My own view is that experience based on this way of viewing the world is no longer easily recoverable. What it reflects is how the overlay of belief can sometimes swamp experience. But that this sometimes happens scarcely proves that the same holds in all cases. Although the dangers of sentimentality are great, for some pet owners their dog or cat can still fulfil something of this mediating role. If this tempts us to a more positive interpretation, so then also should the cult of animals in more distant times in ancient religions. The idea that God only cares for, and interacts with, human beings and leaves the rest of creation bereft seems little short of an appalling piece of human arrogance.

Cosmic Order

Some writers suggest that landscape as a genre could only flourish once the power of Christianity had declined. By way of support it is observed that not only did landscape flourish in China under Taoism centuries before it did in Europe, but also it flourished in pagan Hellenistic and Roman artwork long before the rise of Christianity, only to decline as that religion advanced.[69] According to this view Christianity prevented interest in landscape primarily because of its low estimate of the natural order. To my mind, though, the explanation seems somewhat more complex, more a matter of alternative ways of conceiving the relation between the divine and the natural emerging from within Christianity itself. Slowly artists and theologians alike moved towards new ways of conceptualizing and interpreting their experience, and, largely as an incidental consequence of this, landscape painting without any intended religious meaning gradually emerged. The more careful

[69] The view of K. Bazarov in *Landscape Painting* (London: Octopus, 1981), 6–23 esp. 14. Pliny the Elder in his *Natural History* ascribes to Studius in the 1st c. BC the introduction of landscape wall paintings into Roman art: so E. Langmuir, *Landscape* (London: National Gallery, 1997), 9.

depiction of nature to be found in artists such as Dürer and Leonardo da Vinci of course helped, but it is not in fact till the Netherlands of the seventeenth century that a full flowering occurs. Even then, as we shall see shortly, a strong religious dimension remained. First, though, a brief comment about the Renaissance itself.

Perception and experience help shape one another, and so it is not really surprising that, as nature came to be more closely observed, so this generated new types of experience that themselves came to be reflected in painting. Notable significant moments in that history might include the scientific observations of Albert the Great, Aquinas' teacher, in the thirteenth century, or in the fourteenth Petrarch's famous climbing of Mount Ventoux to take in the view, or the growth of paintings with the *Hortus conclusus* as their theme.[70] If Konrad Witz's *Christ Walking on the Water* of 1444 is often labelled the first specifically identifiable landscape in Western art, it still remains fully religious in content, as both its title and still more so any detailed examination indicate.[71] What was abandoned at the Renaissance was not religious content as such or even the earlier symbolist mentality but rather its precise form. In effect the Renaissance sought to naturalize nature's symbols. One moves, as it were, from divine hieroglyphs to concealed or disguised symbols, with the elements in the landscape still having a meaning but also simultaneously, so far as possible, functioning as natural products of the environment.[72] In Titian's *Noli Me Tangere*, for instance, the tree at the painting's centre looks entirely natural, but there is little doubt that it is also intended to speak of the resurrection, positioned as it is between Christ and Mary Magdalene, with the angle of Mary's back continued in the tree and so naturally leading our vision heavenwards.[73] For two centuries after Witz such a

---

[70] The Petrarch incident took place in 1335, and is described in a letter of 1336 to Fra Diongi de'Roberto de San Sepolcro. The presentation of Mary in an 'enclosed garden' to represent her virginity begins with a few examples before 1400 and grows exponentially thereafter: so Clark, *Landscape*, 15.

[71] The scene is Lake Geneva, and the painting celebrates the elevation of the lay Duke of Savoy as the anti-pope Felix V, one of many attempted reforms in the Church of the time. For details, R.-M. and R. Hagen, *What Great Paintings Say* (Cologne: Taschen, 1997), iii. 12–17.

[72] For a concise discussion of the issue, E. Panovsky, *Early Netherlandish Painting* (Cambridge, Mass.: Harvard University Press, 1966), 141–3.

[73] The painting is in the National Gallery, London: illustrated e.g. M. Kaminski (ed.), *Titian* (Cologne: Könemann, 1998), 24.

symbolic, or else purely decorative, function was to remain for the most part landscape's role. It was a subordination reinforced by the conviction that landscape could not in any case offer the artist sufficiently high themes for his art: these should be sought in religion, history, or myth.[74] All that changed, though, in the seventeenth century. One result was 'secular' landscape art; another the mediation of new forms of religious experience. Without in any way discounting the value of the former, it is on the latter that I wish to focus here, particularly as manifested in two different contexts, Rome and the Netherlands.

Nicolas Poussin (d. 1665) and Claude Lorrain (d. 1682) were Frenchmen who spent most of their working lives living in Rome. That the intellectual climate of the city was now more sympathetic to landscape is suggested not only by the fact of their ecclesiastical patrons but also by the way in which even someone of the piety of Federico Borromeo could make landscape art one of his major concerns. Although in his writings there are remnants of the earlier symbolist attitudes, the primary focus is now on the contemplative power of nature, in evoking a sense of God's goodness and design.[75] Poussin's use of wax models for his figures and Claude's transfer of buildings to unfamiliar contexts, may suggest purely artificial creations without relevance to religious experience.[76] Certainly, their paintings are compositions, essentially composite in character, with items drawn indifferently from record, imagination, and memory.[77] But that should not force on us the conclusion that the paintings are therefore essentially a matter of theory and not experience. Poussin

---

[74] Clark notes a few Italian examples later than Witz, but still similarly characterizes the period from c.1475 to c.1650: *Landscape*, 53; for the key role of Michelangelo: 54.

[75] P. M. Jones, 'Federico Borromeo as a Patron of Landscapes and Still Lifes', *Art Bulletin* 70 (1988), 261–72. His youth was spent in Rome, partly under the influence of St Philip Neri. In 1618 he founded the Pinacoteca Ambrosiana in Milan with his own collection of such paintings. For contemplation, 264; for symbolic mentality, 266.

[76] For Poussin's wax models, A. Blunt, *Poussin* (London: Pallas Athene, 1995 edn.), 242–4. For the Capitol, and Constantine's Arch and the Colosseum, transposed to new contexts, H. Langdon, *Claude Lorrain* (Oxford: Phaidon, 1989), illus. 24, 64 (in both cases by water).

[77] For some of Claude's sketches from nature, J. J. L. Whiteley, *Claude Lorrain: Drawings from the Collections of the British Museum and the Ashmolean Museum* (London: British Museum, 1998). For some comments on his methods: 23–35.

once declared that 'the idea of beauty does not descend into matter unless it has been prepared as much as possible'.[78] It is this ability of himself and Claude to make such preparations and so draw us into their own experience of how they have understood nature that gives their landscape paintings their evocative power.[79] Nor should this be seen as simply a matter of confirming what the viewer already knows. Certainly, art often reflects already existing human experience of the world, but it can also on occasion initiate this by enabling us to look at our world in a new way.[80] Recall Browning's familiar lines:

> For don't you mark? We're made so that we love
> First when we see them painted, things we have passed
> Perhaps a hundred times nor cared to see;
> And so they are better, painted—better to us,
> Which is the same thing. Art was given for that.[81]

In Poussin's case his attempts to offer this extra perspective appear to have been premised on quite wide reading, with his paintings reflecting a Christianized version of Stoicism,[82] as well as a good knowledge of the ancient world.[83] If that explains the prominence of certain moral themes,[84] in his landscapes from the late 1630s onwards there is to be found great emphasis on the ordered nature of the world. Matthew writing his gospel and Paul

---

[78] Quoted in Blunt, *Poussin*, 364. Order, mode, and form are mentioned as Poussin's three desiderata.

[79] Sometimes aided in Claude's case by the perspective requiring the viewer to step down into the painting, and in Poussin's by the participants looking towards us: cf. M. R. Lagerlöf, *Ideal Landscape* (New Haven: Yale University Press, 1990), 139, 160.

[80] Ernst Gombrich quotes a number of examples, including Aretino discovering the beauty of Venetian sunsets through looking first at Titian's work: *Norm and Form*, 4th edn. (Oxford: Phaidon, 1985), 117–18.

[81] From Robert Browning's *Fra Lippi Lippi* where this is one of the poem's principal themes: W. E. Williams (ed.), *Browning* (Harmondsworth: Penguin, 1954), 194–206 esp. 203.

[82] He was known as *Pictor philosophus*: Blunt, *Poussin*, 3. For the combination of Stoicism and Christianity: 157–207.

[83] In his two series on the Sacraments great care is taken with historical accuracy.

[84] As in the *Continence of Scipio*, *Landscape with Diogenes*, and his two paintings on the theme of Phocion.

in ecstasy alike find divine endorsement in nature.[85] But if in both these cases the major key remains the human beings involved, with a painting such as the *Landscape with the Ashes of Phocion* the action is almost invisible, so subordinate is it to the perfect balance and proportion of the world in which it is set.[86] Indeed, so great is Poussin's desire to present such order that sometimes it leads him to forget how nature behaves, and so for balance in his *Orpheus and Eurydice* smoke is made to billow in one direction and clouds move the opposite way, as though the wind could be blowing in both directions at once.[87] In the early 1650s there are two paintings that display the power and ferocity of nature without any further accompanying comment,[88] but in his last paintings he once again returns to the theme of order. *Landscape with Orion* has perhaps been subject to over-interpretation,[89] but *Apollo and Daphne* does seem to speak of the balance of opposites, while his *Four Seasons* fully integrates biblical themes and the natural world to offer a powerful, final testament of nature in its ordered succession witnessing to the Christian theme of death and resurrection.[90] That may suggest only some vague generalities, whereas what in fact one finds is not only each picture reinforcing our sense of order but also numerous hints that it is through the Church's sacraments that the individual can become fully incorporated into the same pattern, perhaps not surprising as a theme from someone who twice painted series on the theme of the seven sacraments.[91]

[85] The Berlin *Landscape with Matthew and Angel* sets them amid classical ruins in the foreground, with a river leading to a rebuilt landscape in the background, while in the Louvre's *Ecstasy of Paul* the angle of Paul's sword is echoed no less than three times in the distant landscape: P. Rosenberg and V. Damian, *Nicolas Poussin: Masterpieces 1594–1665* (London: Cassell, 1995), 74–7, 104–5.

[86] Ibid. 98–101. Blunt comments: 'Never has the order and harmony of nature been more impressively depicted' (*Poussin*, 294).

[87] Lagerlöf, *Ideal Landscape*, 118, 210.

[88] Rosenberg and Danian, *Nicolas Poussin*, 110–13. Blunt, *Poussin*, 297–9.

[89] Blunt, *Poussin*, 315–31. For a critique of his similar treatment of the *Birth of Bacchus*, Lagerlöf, *Ideal Landscape*, 126–8. For *Apollo and Daphne*, Blunt, *Poussin*, 347–8.

[90] Rosenberg and Damian, *Nicolas Poussin*, 122–33. *Spring* uses Gen. 2; *Summer*, Ruth 2; *Autumn*, Num. 13; *Winter*, Gen. 8.

[91] For the frieze-like character of *Summer*, Blunt, *Poussin*, 335. In *Summer* bread and wine are being prepared for distribution on the left, in *Autumn* grapes are being brought back to the Israelites, while in both *Winter* and *Spring* water plays a prominent role.

One commentator describes how in a work such as *Summer* 'the mood of the *Georgics* is raised to a kind of sacramental gravity',[92] but, if the sacramentality is certainly there, it is to Claude that one must turn to discover the full impact of Vergil. Dostoevsky's intuitions were right when he misremembered one of Claude's paintings as having the title *The Golden Age*.[93] There is a marvellous atmospheric luminosity that Poussin cannot rival.[94] Claude's biographer once described him as 'good-hearted and pious', but he had none of the learning of Poussin.[95] Yet we should not deduce from this an unreflective art. As one art historian puts it, 'For Claude paintings were not sections of nature; they were not views but symbols for vision.'[96] Order and proportion are thus still there, as, for instance, in his *Landscape with Apollo and the Muses* with its suggestion that it is nature that will inspire,[97] in the more complex harmony of *Landscape with Adoration of the Golden Calf* where clearly the rugged severity of Sinai is made to balance the golden calf and his dancers,[98] or again in *Landscape with Abraham expelling Hagar and Ishmael* where the evening warmth on the right towards which the pair is being expelled speaks of God's continuing care after all.[99] But, as his inspiration of Constable makes clear,[100] we are in some ways already moving towards a quite different conception, with a

[92] So Clark, *Landscape*, 135.

[93] The Dresden *Acis and Galatea* is so described in Dostoevsky's novel, *The Possessed*. Langdon repeatedly refers to Vergil.

[94] Although it is sometimes suggested that he learnt to copy it in later life: M. Kitson, 'The Relationship between Claude and Poussin in Landscape', *Zeitschrift für Kunstgeschichte* 24 (1961), 142–62 esp. 156–8.

[95] Sandrart, quoted in Langdon, *Claude Lorrain*, 17.

[96] L. Gowring, 'Nature and the Ideal in the Art of Claude', *Art Quarterly* 37 (1974), 91–6 esp. 93. He notes that the paintings are deliberate 'simplifications' of his original drawings, with human figures mainly introduced 'to interpret the speechless drama of nature'.

[97] National Gallery, Edinburgh; Langdon, *Claude Lorrain*, illus. 82. Apollo reflecting alone on the right is balanced by his temple on the left, with singers and dancers enjoying the fruits of his reflections.

[98] Karlsruhe; Langdon, *Claude Lorrain*, illus. 86. The complementing harmonies suggest to me the thought that, though Sinai must modify what is going on to its left, it cannot ultimately destroy altogether the value of what is taking place.

[99] Munich; ibid. illus. 107. Lagerlöf, *Ideal Landscape*, 84, says that it speaks of Abraham's love, but this can scarcely be right, since he, unlike God, has no power over the weather.

[100] Through Sir George Beaumont's *Hagar and the Angel*: J. Walker, *Constable* (London: Thames & Hudson, 1991 edn.), 7–9.

more mysterious, more immanent god. Unlike Poussin, many of Claude's compositions focus on the changing effect of various times of day, and so the sun often plays a leading role. Yet the sun can be used to suggest transcendence as well as immanence, and all within an ordered world.[101] Some caution is thus necessary lest too sharp a contrast is drawn with Poussin. The question is more a matter of where the greater emphasis falls.

Some Dutch painting of the time also suggests a primary emphasis on immanence rather than order, but given the influence of Calvinism in that part of Europe it is scarcely surprising that it is order that continues to carry the greater weight. In the *Institutes* Calvin had waxed lyrical on God's majestic ordering of creation, on how nothing happens by chance.[102] Although he prohibited all representation of God, it is often forgotten that he spoke well of historical painting and so might also have responded positively to landscape, had opportunity and instruction as to its potential been available to him.[103] Some scholars want to speak of Dutch landscape as simply a faithful record; others detect religion everywhere:[104] the truth probably lies somewhere in between.[105] The varied treatments of Bentheim Castle provide a useful, purely secular example to illustrate that usually something rather more than simple representation was at stake.[106] Some Dutch artists were influenced by Claude,

[101] His various seaport scenes provide good examples of the two themes combined. In her detailed analysis of *Seaport with Ulysses returning Chryseis* Lagerlöf strangely insists that 'no "beyond" is suggested here' *Ideal Landscape*, 224–31 esp. 231. Yet there is no sun itself, only its glow.

[102] *Institutes of the Christian Religion*, I. 16. csp. 2.

[103] *Institutes*, I. 11. 12. Paintings of 'histories and events . . . have some use in teaching and admonition': ibid. ed. J. T. McNeill (Philadelphia: Westminster Press, 1960), i. 112.

[104] For allegorical readings, note J. Bruyn, 'Towards a Scriptural Reading of Seventeenth Century Dutch Landscape Paintings', in *Masters of 17th-Century Dutch Landscape Painting* (Boston: Museum of Fine Arts, 1988), 84–103. For an attack on religious interpretations generally, R. L. Falkenburg, 'Calvinism and the Emergence of Dutch Seventeenth Century Landscape Art—a Critical Evaluation', in P. C. Finney (ed.), *Seeing Beyond the Word: Visual Arts and the Calvinist Tradition* (Grand Rapids: Eerdmans, 1999), 343–68.

[105] Some of Bruyn's suggestions do seem altogether too specific, such as a bridge as Christ or Bentheim Castle as Mount Zion: 'Towards a Scriptural Reading', 97–9.

[106] Both Ruisdael and Berchem radically alter the reality, to achieve quite different effects: C. Brown, *Dutch Painting*, 2nd edn. (London: Phaidon, 1993), 54.

among them Nicholaes Berchem and J. B. Weenix through their stay in Rome (1642–5), and Aelbert Cuyp subsequently. The resultant play of light in their paintings could bespeak just an interest in its effects. But the fact that the light remains Italian in its strength and not Dutch even in portrayals of their own native land surely suggests something different, not least in the case of Cuyp who was an elder of his church and did paint some incontestably religious pictures, such as *Orpheus*.[107] But even an ordinary country scene with sleek, fat cows bathed in light seems to denote more: 'a blessed landscape, in effect a kind of divine light suggesting a country on which God had bestowed his blessing'.[108]

It is the more characteristically Dutch work of Jacob van Ruisdael (d. 1682) and his pupil, Meindert Hobbema (d. 1709), though, that best illustrates our theme of cosmic order. The Dutch landscape in itself is of course too little differentiated to allow trees and hills on their own to speak of order. Ruisdael solved the problem by using churches and windmills,[109] for it can scarcely be an accident that they are generally viewed from a low vantage point, and complemented by effective use of sun or clouds.[110] In his *Jewish Cemetery* the contours of the land are altered for a different purpose, to emphasize both the transience of life (a rushing stream, dead trees) and hope of something more (a rainbow with sun breaking through).[111] Intriguingly, however, in the most recent work to appear on the artist the large number of contributors

---

[107] Temperamentally incompatible animals surround Orpheus, suggesting Eden restored. He may have had in mind the traditional equation of Orpheus with King David.

[108] Rebecca Lyons' words accompanying the National Gallery video, *Aelbert Cuyp*.

[109] Only some types of mill are depicted, those that can most easily be used to stress the prosperity that comes through divine order: L. O. Goedde, 'Naturalism as Convention', in W. Franits (ed.), *Looking at Seventeenth-Century Dutch Art: Realism Reconsidered* (Cambridge: Cambridge University Press, 1997), 129–43 esp. 131–2.

[110] Note, for instance, his brilliantly lit church in the far distance in his early *View of Naarden*, the centrally placed church in his *View of Haarlem with Bleaching Fields*, and the windmill given greater prominence in *Windmill at Wijk bij Duurstede* by removal of an inconvenient gate: J. Kiers and F. Tissink (eds.), *The Golden Age of Dutch Art* (London: Thames & Hudson, 2000), 132, 224–5. In the second case, the clouds that enhance the church are actually the sort that disappear at sunset despite this being the alleged time at which the scene is set: 221.

[111] Ibid. 226–7; S. Slive, *Jacob van Ruisdael* (New York: Abbeville, 1982), 67–77.

appear united in detecting religious themes also in his more ordinary landscapes. Gone, though, is detailed allegory, and in its place comes either an already existing harmony or else one still being worked towards, as human transience faces the stability of divine order.[112]

Transience is a frequent theme in another common form in Dutch art of the time, the still life. Again, there is a danger in seeing it all as religious, when much was not. Yet the *vanitas* theme apparently became very popular after the Thirty Years War,[113] while there seems no shortage of other religious ideas as well. Eucharistic symbolism, for instance, finds itself placed in some unusual contexts.[114] An overflowing basket of fruit or flowers conjures up notions of God's bounty and generosity, but the way in which these were arranged or the use of material from different seasons could easily also be employed to suggest divine providence or order. Yet in some ways the Spanish approach to this is more impressive: utter simplicity of contents as well as arrangement being utilized to convey precisely the same message.[115]

Still lifes are sometimes portrayed as under threat of disease and decay, and Poussin and Claude likewise, as noted above, sometimes allude to evil. But for neither group was it a major concern. I think it is possible to see why. The artists concerned invite us to see the world in its primary reality first, as rendered ordered and beautiful by God, for that in itself could already be read as indicating providential care, even if that care remains at times hidden in how exactly it might work out in practice.[116] If such a separation is thought odd, it is salutary to recall that it is common not only in theology but also in the philosophy of religion, where the argument from order (or design) is usually treated quite separately from theodicy, and likewise given prior treatment. Intriguingly, though, what has already emerged from some of our examples is the need

---

[112] M. Sitt et al. (eds.), *Jacob van Ruisdael: Die Revolution der Landschaft* (Hamburg: Hamburger Kunsthalle, 2002). For harmony: e.g. 62–3, 82–3, 118–19; for unresolved contrasts: 90–1, 116–17, 120–1. Bentheim Castle is placed in the latter category: 108–9 (transient human power before the might of nature).

[113] N. Schneider, *Still Life* (Cologne: Taschen, 1994), 77–87 esp. 79–80.

[114] If the German Georg Flegel uses sugar to support eucharistic theory, the Calvinist Lubin Baugin sets bread and wine in opposition to music and cards: ibid. 71, 73, 88–9.

[115] Seen in the work of Zurburan and Cotán: ibid. 123–5.

[116] A theme common in Calvin, e.g. *Institutes*, I. 16. 9.

felt by artists to probe more deeply, in order to find that order and design; hence the reason why canvases so often do not simply depict reality as it is. Of course aesthetic considerations for this are sometimes primary, and it is not always easy to establish conclusively what influence is operating when. As we shall see, when the two themes of order and evil return in twentieth-century art, the artists in question no longer have any doubt that truth cannot lie on the surface of things but is only ascertainable by getting underneath appearances. For the moment, though, our investigation turns next to how experiences of divine transcendence have been communicated through landscape art.

Transcendent Awe

Here I want to focus on the work of Caspar David Friedrich (d. 1841) in Germany and of Thomas Cole (d. 1848), Frederic Church (d. 1900), J. F. Cropsey (d. 1900), and others associated with the Hudson River School in the United States. Although there is no direct influence of the former on the latter, and much of the work of Cole, Cropsey, and Church is distinctively American, there is none the less sufficient overlap in landscape themes for it to be entirely appropriate that they should be treated together. Not that those themes emerged first only in the nineteenth century. Salvator Rosa (d. 1673) was a contemporary of Poussin and Claude. His landscapes, though, are quite different.[117] Already one finds in some of them the religious fascination with the awesome grandeur of nature that was to so delight Friedrich and Cole:

> What'er Lorrain light-touched with softening hue,
> Or savage Rosa dash'd, or learned Poussin drew.[118]

He himself spoke of the 'terrible beauty' of 'the sight of a river hurling itself off a precipice', and in his landscapes he strives to intensify such effects by having the viewer step up into the canvas, and not down as with Claude.[119] Although he himself accepted

---

[117] For examples of the transcendent dimension, *L'opera completa di Salvator Rosa* (Milan: Rizzoli, 1975), illus. 19, 42–8, 52, 60.

[118] From James Thompson's *The Castle of Indolence*: quoted in J. Scott, *Salvator Rosa: His Life and Times* (New Haven: Yale University Press, 1995), 225.

[119] For the quotation, ibid. 139; for two examples of the upward move: 202–3.

current evaluations of such art as of inferior worth to religious and historical painting, in due course the Romantic movement was to see in him one of its own great heroes and precursors.[120]

It is into that context that Friedrich should be set. He was born in Greifswald in what is now north-eastern Germany, and a key influence on him was a local pastor, poet, and theologian, G. L. T. Kosegarten. Kosegarten's *Uferpredikten* ('Shore-Sermons') envisage liturgy and sermon taking place on the nearby island of Rügen, subsequently used in some of Friedrich's own works.[121] Kosegarten also mediated aspects of Neoplatonism, while a not unrelated variant in the writings of the early seventeenth-century German mystic Jacob Böhme (1575–1624) was a great favourite with Friedrich's fellow Pomeranian and fellow artist, Philipp Runge (d. 1810).[122] Like Rosa, Böhme is an interesting example of continuities. Dating from the early seventeenth century his ideas were revived during the Romantic movement, and these bear some comparison with both late-Platonic theurgy and the symbolical mentality of the Middle Ages, though they were now largely used to argue for a more immanent understanding of God.[123] But if that was one side of the Romantic movement, another was a sense of divine transcendence also derived from nature. For, whatever the underlying reason, even where Friedrich seems to intend immanence, on the whole it is transcendence that emerges.[124] This is of course unqualifiedly so in his most famous paintings, where huge mountains, thick forests, or great sea vistas are the characteristic theme. In many cases this is aided by explicit Christian symbolism, such as cross or crucifix, anchor or cathedral. Friedrich's response to such symbolism is not always consistent. He seems, for instance, to

---

[120] He was portrayed as an anti-religious rebel, whereas in fact his morals and religion were fairly conventional: ibid. 5, 64, 81, 88, 145–6, 229.

[121] J. L. Koerner, *Caspar David Friedrich and the Subject of Landscape* (London: Reaktion, 1990), 77–8. Cf. I. Becker, *Caspar David Friedrich: Leben und Werk* (Stuttgart: Belser, 1983), 36: 'das Erlebnis der Natur und der Schönheit sei damit einem Gottesdienst vergleichbar'.

[122] W. Vaughan, *German Romantic Painting* (New Haven: Yale University Press, 1980), 41–63 esp. 43, 51–2, 58.

[123] See particularly his *Signature of All Things* (Cambridge: James Clarke, 1969). For a helpful table of the proposed correspondences, R. Waterfield: *Jacob Boehme: Essential Readings* (Wellingborough: Crucible, 1989), 208.

[124] In *Swans in the Rushes*, despite his own comments, God seems to lie in the light beyond, not in the reeds themselves: Koerner, *Caspar David Friedrich*, 16–17.

have changed his mind on Gothic, and it is certainly true that he thought the Christian religion in need of reform.[125] Yet commentators go altogether too far when they deduce from the paintings a sense of divine absence.[126] Indeed, the hint of a presence in a far beyond is precisely what one might expect from the type of strongly Protestant piety in which he had been reared. Friedrich knew Schleiermacher, and this might be thought to argue for a strongly subjectivist reference.[127] But again I think this wrong. His familiar figures with their backs to us (*Rückenfiguren*) are there to invite us into his perception of the world.[128] Certainly, they also suggest that of its essence the experience will be solitary and isolated, but this emphatically does not entail that it cannot be communicated or endorsed. The art is there, precisely to offer just such an opportunity. Whether the use of the cross necessarily helps, though, is a moot point.[129] Certainly, the Americans to whom we now turn only occasionally utilized such additional supports.[130]

It is only quite recently that the Hudson River School has begun to return to prominence even in its own native land.[131] There are quite a number of instances where works once acquired by public galleries were then disposed of, only now once more to be regarded as significant. The school's founder was an immigrant Englishman from Bolton, Thomas Cole (d. 1848), while also important are his friend J. F. Cropsey (d. 1900) and pupil, Frederick Church (d. 1900). Cole was a conservative, suspicious of Jackson's purely pragmatic

[125] He had none of the nostalgia for the Middle Ages that the Nazarene painters exhibited, and Gothic ruins seem initially to have represented for him a rejected past: J. C. Jensen, *Caspar David Friedrich: Leben und Werk* (Cologne: DuMont, 1983 edn.), 157–69 esp. 162–4.

[126] R. Cardinal, *German Romantics in Context* (London: Studio Vista, 1975), 74–8; Koerner, *Caspar David Friedrich*, 27–8, 148, 194.

[127] Koerner, *Caspar David Friedrich*, 59.

[128] Though once in a more twisted way, to suggest his wife hemming him in: C. Sommerhage, *Deutsche Romantik* (Cologne: Taschen, 1988), 88–90.

[129] Some landscapes, if anything, seem more effective on their own: e.g. Koerner, *Caspar David Friedrich*, illus. 16 (38), 73 (151), 77 (155), and even 81 (*Easter Morning*, 161).

[130] Occasionally, even with unnecessary learning, as in Church's *Oxbrow* where Noah and Shaddai appear in Hebrew: M. Baigell (ed.), *Thomas Cole* (New York: Watson-Guptill, 1985), 54.

[131] Helped in Britain by a major recent exhibition at the Tate in the spring of 2002.

approach to American expansion, and so in some cases the message even of landscape is primarily or exclusively political, particularly where people also play a part.[132] More commonly, though, what we are afforded by these painters is the landscape in its own right, usually characterized by deep vistas and/or radiant skies. Again and again one's eyes are drawn through and up, and indeed even where the pressure initially seems downwards the final resolution is once again an ascent.[133] Such landscapes could of course be read in purely subjectivist terms in the manner of Burke and Kant, as pointing to human beings overwhelmed by sheer scale in their experience of the sublime.[134] But another option is to identify what is occurring as one experiential variant on what philosophers call the cosmological argument, of the fragile dependence of everything in one's vision on something beyond (just as the paintings of cosmic order discussed in the previous section might be taken to recall the argument from design). In favour of the latter option is the fact that almost always the experience is portrayed as of something only partially revealed, whether it be the rays of the sun, a cloud formation, or a mountain range, compared with the painting itself a great 'Beyond', cosmic in scale. It is perhaps no accident that *What Dreams May Come*, a film depicting heaven, is replete with images drawn from the Hudson River School.[135]

The paintings should, of course, be allowed to speak for themselves, but they can be usefully supplemented by the sentiments expressed in Cole's poetry and by the work of another member of the group, Asher Durand and his 'Letters on Landscape Painting' that appeared in the art journal *The Crayon*. All were Protestants, Church in particular a good friend of his parish minister, the

[132] For his attitude to Jackson, A. Wilton and T. Barringer, *American Sublime: Landscape Painting in the United States 1820–80* (London: Tate, 2002), 51–4; for his *Expulsion from Eden* and *Course of Empire* as a critique, 91–109; for the contrast with Cropsey and the latter's ability to integrate progress into landscape, especially in his *Starrucca Viaduct*, 140–1.

[133] As when one is pulled through the gloom below into the opening of the red sky in Cole's *Mountain Sunrise*, or from the redness of the river to still more powerful colours in the sky above in Church's *Twilight in the Wilderness*: illustrated in Wilton and Barringer, ibid. 73, 131.

[134] Kant, *The Critique of Judgement* (Oxford: Clarendon Press, 1928), e.g. 103, 130 (quoting Burke).

[135] Dating from 1998 and starring Robin Williams; Cole, Church, and Durand are all mentioned in the screen credits.

influential theologian Horace Bushnell. Durand observes that 'the true province of landscape art is the representation of the work of God',[136] and Cole finds this pre-eminently in a sense of the infinite:

> Cloudless the ether—deeper and more deep
> It grows—The piercing eye is lost
> And life itself will not suffice to sound
> Depths that are infinite.[137]

Some commentators have sought to identify in all of this a distinctively Calvinist approach to art, both in terms of doctrine and antecedents. In respect of the latter it is true that America's best-known early theologian, the Calvinist Jonathan Edwards, spoke of nature's capacity to reflect God, and that Bushnell endorsed this view.[138] Ruskin, who had had a Calvinist upbringing, also wrote of infinity in art as one of the key pointers to God.[139] Antecedents for this are easy to find in the writings of Calvin himself, with his great stress on divine transcendence. So clearly there is some truth to the contention.

None the less, it would be a great pity if such authors were also followed in their supposition that appreciation of the religious dimension of this art of itself required endorsement of a Calvinist position or for that matter that it need be exclusive to the detriment of other forms of expression.[140] The sad thing is that the commentators seem less broad-minded than the artists themselves. Both Cole and Durand eventually sought something rather different from Calvinism, and it could be argued that this is already implicit in some of the paintings of Cropsey and Church.[141] My intention

[136] *The Crayon* (1855), 354; quoted in J. F. Cooper, *Knights of the Brush: The Hudson River School and the Moral Landscape* (New York: Hudson Hill Press, 1999), 42.

[137] M. B. Tymn (ed.), *Thomas Cole's Poetry* (York, Pa.: Liberty Cap, 1972), 166.

[138] For relevant quotations from both, G. E. Veith, *Painters of Faith: The Spiritual Landscape in Nineteenth Century America* (Washington, DC: Regnery, 2001), 37–46. Bushnell describes the world as 'a vast temple of being' (41).

[139] The 'expression of infinity of distance' is 'the most typical of the nature of God, the most suggestive of the glory of his dwelling place': *Modern Painters* (London: George Allen, 1906), ii. 44–5. The point is developed throughout Part III, Section V as a whole (41–53).

[140] Both Cooper and Veith take this line. For Veith, *Painters of Faith*, e.g. 56–8, 82–3; for Cooper see below.

[141] Cole became an Episcopalian in 1844, Durand gradually abandoned his strict Calvinism. For examples of more immanent paintings by the other two, Wilton and Barringer, *American Sublime*, 141, 169.

in saying this is not to attack Calvinism as one specific form of Christian belief. Rather, it is to draw attention to the danger of imposing patterns of belief simply because they sit well with a particular theology. The complicating factor in the case of the Americans is that there was some influence on them from Calvinism, but the work of Friedrich (or for that matter Rosa in an earlier century) demonstrates that the experience is not quite the same thing as the theology. Theologians are perhaps by temperament inclined to believe that art can only illustrate theology, not make its own distinctive contribution. The range of these artists proves otherwise. They are not using art to illustrate a dogmatic position. Rather, they are telling us how they experienced God, and the fact that they could also produce paintings of a quite different character shows that they experienced the divine through nature in more than one way.

Nor were they alone in this. For, intriguingly, what happened in the United States was that, partly under the influence of the Unitarian thinker and minister, Ralph Waldo Emerson, there was a definite move towards decidedly more immanent images in the second half of the century. Although some speak of an inevitable decline towards purely secular landscape art, I fail to see why, for the implicit religious symbolism can sometimes be just as powerful.[142] There is a nice irony, though, in the fact that Emerson's movement is known as Transcendentalism despite its essentially immanent approach, as in Emerson's often quoted words: 'the currents of the Universal Being circulate through me; I am part or parcel of God'.[143] The impact can be seen in painters such as John Kensett, S. R. Gifford, and, though at more of a remove, in George Inness also.[144] Sometimes there is even the fascinating possibility of observing how differently the same natural features were treated.[145] Grandeur of scale is not always abandoned, but it is

---

[142] For the suggestion of decline, Cooper, *Knights of the Brush*, 60–1.

[143] Quoted in Wilton and Barringer, *American Sublime*, 57; Baigell, *Thomas Cole*, 25.

[144] For an intriguing case where the landscape is doing all the work, see *Christmas Eve* in A. Werner (ed.), *Inness: Landscapes* (New York: Watson-Guptill, 1977), 38–9; cf. also 32–3.

[145] Kensett's and Cole's treatment of the White Mountains can be compared in Wilton and Barringer, *American Sublime*, 78, 81. Notice how the reflection of the mountain in the river transforms Kensett's composition.

a grandeur where the sky suffuses the earth below, however massive the rock formations.[146] It is to such experiences of mystic immanence that I now turn.

Mystic Immanence

Although I shall include in this section some twentieth-century painters, other, key, representatives of this tradition will be excluded, as I want to deal with them separately in the next section, where the use of colour to express this theme is considered. Colour is, of course, only one possible medium. Others include diffused light, atmospheric conditions such as clouds, mist, rainbows, and dew, and luxuriant vegetation. By 'mystic' I intend to convey the notion of a spreading presence, and it is in this sense, I think, that art historians sometimes speak of this form of art as sacramental in a way that the more transcendent focus of the previous section is not.[147] Even at the dawn of modern landscape painting, one can see something of this kind of effect, in the work of Albrecht Aldorfer (d. 1538). Sometimes claimed as the author of 'the first independent landscapes in the history of European art',[148] his approach in this context is in many ways less interesting than some of his religious works, where luxuriant vegetation can take over, enveloping the Madonna and Child or saint, and indeed where even architecture sometimes turns itself into a living, growing form.[149] Although interpretable as a form of paganism, much more likely, in view of his continuing involvement in Christian practice, is that such a style represents a lively sense of God being mediated through the richness and dynamism of nature.[150]

---

[146] One might contrast Gifford's *October in the Catskills* of 1880 with Cole's *Mountain Sunrise, Catskill* of 1826: ibid. 73, 149. Note the continuity of colours in the Gifford painting.

[147] As do Wilton and Barringer when they speak of 'sacramental calm' in the works of the mature Kensett: ibid. 197. Note, though, the argument of my previous chapter that it is more a matter of two quite different types of sacramentality.

[148] C. S. Wood, *Albrecht Altdorfer and the Origins of Landscape* (London: Reaktion, 1993), 9.

[149] For this effect on Mary and St George, ibid. 89, 132; for architecture in *Susanna and the Elders*, 94; for an immanent, pure landscape, 140.

[150] For Wood's paganism argument, ibid. 177–92, 281–2; for Altdorfer's continuing practice of Catholicism, 234–5, 251, 281.

Aldorfer influenced Elsheimer who in turn had a marked impact on Rubens (d. 1640), especially in his own atmospheric land-scapes.[151] Rubens in the main painted landscapes for his own private pleasure. Occasionally even here his devout Catholicism shows through, but his two most famous works in this genre indicate a more general kind of piety.[152] One is of the country estate that he acquired for himself and his new, young wife at Het Steen, and the other of a related landscape with a rainbow.[153] The rainbow is of course a biblical sign of divine promise, and the two paintings, apparently intended as a pair, celebrate the richness of God's blessing both on him and on the Flanders of the time.

In nineteenth-century England Constable was effusive in his praise of Rubens's landscapes.[154] Nowadays Constable's popularity among the general public has worked to his detriment, and he is often seen as simply a realist painter of picturesque scenes. So it might be thought better for me to turn to Turner at this point. But Constable, though the lesser painter, was a devout Anglican and this did, I believe, enable him to express powerfully the impact of God on his environment in ways that are now seldom acknowledged, and so do need to be better known. In any case, there is the added difficulty with Turner that one can scarcely engage with the painter without also engaging with the central role he plays in John Ruskin's classic *Modern Painters*, and that could scarcely have been done briefly.[155]

Poetry appears to have exercised some influence on Constable, but it was more the poetry of the eighteenth than of the nineteenth

---

[151] For two examples, C. Brown, *Rubens's Landscapes* (London: National Gallery, 1996), 76–7.

[152] The *Farm at Laeken* in the Royal Collection looks initially like a simple scene of fat cows and milkmaids, but the famous pilgrimage church in the background transforms it into a celebration of 'a prosperity which flourishes under the protection of the Virgin': Brown, ibid. 42–7 esp. 47. Rubens was a daily communicant.

[153] For illustrations and details of the relation between the two, ibid. 59–70.

[154] See e.g. his comments on Rubens's rainbows in C. R. Leslie, *Memoirs of the Life of John Constable*, 3rd edn. (London: Phaidon, 1995), 268.

[155] Note particularly Ruskin's comments on 'Turnerian mystery' in *Modern Painters*, iv. 4–5. Not that Turner always agreed with Ruskin's analyses: cf. A. Bailey, *Standing in the Sun: A Life of J. M. W. Turner* (London: Sinclair-Stevenson, 1997), 348–9.

century, far less his contemporary Coleridge.[156] So one is not able, as in the case of Coleridge, to point to the other side of Neoplatonism to what Friedrich experienced with Kosegarten.[157] The immanent perspective, though, is still there. If his sallies into explicitly religious painting were little short of disastrous, Constable was very much concerned to use at least some of his paintings as a means of advancing religious and moral sentiment.[158] In his earlier work this is done primarily through focus on the individual tones of sky and leaves, though in the *Cornfield* a church is added to indicate divine blessing.[159] Notoriously, the Bishop of Salisbury objected to a cloud hanging over his cathedral, but Constable himself was not averse to adding a rainbow in a later painting to express his own thankfulness to God for escape from the perceived threat to the Church in the run-up to the great Reform Bill of 1832.[160] That might suggest a rather superficial use of symbolism, but the painting is in fact one of Constable's best, and powerfully conjures up a sense of church and nature alike arising with a new freshness after a troubling storm. It is perhaps, though, his last paintings such as *Hadleigh* and *Stonehenge* that most conjure up a panentheistic world, one in which God is suffused throughout his creation but never reduced to identity with it. Some see only despair at the death of his wife, but to my mind those scholars are right who find instead a sorrow transfused with joy and raised to a cosmic scale.[161]

---

[156] M. Rosenthal offers numerous parallels in his *Constable: The Painter and his Landscape* (New Haven: Yale University Press, 1993). The influence of Cowper, Thomson's *Seasons* and the rather later Bloomfield's *Farmer's Boy* are all noted: 48–55, 71–8. The more transcendent side of Wordsworth's response to the Lake District, however, did not appeal: 41.

[157] The reason for the different stress in Coleridge can be explained by its different mediation. See further, T. McFarland, *Coleridge and the Pantheist Tradition* (Oxford: Clarendon Press, 1969); D. Hedley, *Coleridge, Philosophy and Religion* (Cambridge: Cambridge University Press, 2000), esp. 33–45.

[158] For two indifferent paintings of Christ, J. Walker, *Constable* (London: Thames & Hudson, 1991), 13.

[159] For sky as 'the chief organ of sentiment': Leslie, *Memoirs*, 73; for leaves: 233–4; Walker, *Constable*, 58; for addition of church: 94.

[160] For the two paintings, Walker, ibid. 88–9, 108–9.

[161] For illustrations of the two paintings and of *Hampstead Heath with Rainbow* (also relevant), ibid. 103, 123, 124. For Rosenthal's pessimistic verdict, *Constable: The Painter*, 218, 235. Walker speaks of a 'serene . . . transcendent pantheism': *Constable*, 46.

Constable's allusions to religion are quite subtle and indirect compared with those of another committed Anglican, Samuel Palmer, whose key work at Shoreham overlaps with Constable's later years, though he did not in fact die till 1881.[162] In his *Newton*, William Blake, one of Palmer's heroes, had portrayed the dreadful consequences that follow from a narrowly scientific approach to nature.[163] Palmer therefore seeks to renew his public's vision in drawings such as *Valley Thick with Corn*, where the message of the corn resonant of divine blessing is reinforced with a quotation from Psalm 65 placed on the original mount by the artist himself: 'Thou crownest the year with thy goodness . . . the valleys also shall stand so thick with corn that they shall laugh and sing.'[164] One of his favourite symbols is the moon, sometimes full, sometimes crescent. Palmer talks of one such scene of the full moon (*Shepherds under the Full Moon*) as offering 'such a mystic and dreamy glimmer as penetrates and kindles the inmost soul',[165] while of *Harvest under a Crescent Moon* his biographer comments: 'the golden seas of corn seem sacramental, and the crescent moon holds its darker area of earthshine like a monstrance holding a Host.'[166] But such verbal comments are scarcely necessary. Even an unbeliever can hardly fail to be aware of the intention to convey a sense of sacramental presence infusing the natural world and uniting humanity and nature as one.[167] There is no shortage of other artists both from the time of the Romantic movement and later who expressed themselves in related ways. One from France may be taken to illustrate a recurring problem, the confusion between such a religion of nature and nostalgia. For if the devout Camille Corot offers us canvases where 'everything is misty, everything shivers at the

---

[162] His father was a Particular Baptist, whereas Palmer himself became 'a Church of England fanatic': so R. Lister, *Samuel Palmer: His Life and Art* (Cambridge: Cambridge University Press, 1987), 59. His key years at Shoreham in Kent were from 1825 to 1835.

[163] From 1795 and in Tate Britain, London; illus. in K. Raine, *William Blake* (London: Thames & Hudson, 1970), 84 (illus. 61). Newton is so absorbed in his calculations that he fails to notice the beautiful rock encrustations behind him.

[164] Ps. 65: 12a, 14b (*Book of Common Prayer*); C. Harrison, *Samuel Palmer* (Oxford; Ashmolean Museum, 1997), illus. 9.

[165] From the 1824 *Notebooks*; Harrison, *Samuel Palmer*, illus. 15.

[166] Lister, *Samuel Palmer*, 38, with illus.

[167] Note the shepherd sleeping on top of the sheep in *Late Twilight*: Harrison, *Samuel Palmer*, illus. 10.

fresh breath of the dawn',[168] it is not without significance that whereas Monet painted the railway bridge at Argenteuil, Corot deliberately chose to move the medieval bridge at nearby Mantes into a still more rural setting.[169]

Nor did such problems cease with the nineteenth century. English art saw the revival of a sense of mystic communion with the divine through nature in the group of artists known as the Neo-Romantic movement (dating to the mid-years of the twentieth century, roughly between 1935 and 1955). As this was the period of the rise of the dictators, a world war, and post-war austerity, it is perhaps hardly surprising that the movement had a strongly pessimistic streak, but it was also combined with the nostalgia that seemed to infect much of the rest of the nation. Opinion polls during the Second World War soon discovered that people thought that they were fighting to defend an image of British life that had for most of them only ever lived in their imaginations—'village life, country churches and thatched cottages'. It was therefore particularly appropriate that a 1987 retrospective exhibition of these artists' work should be entitled *A Paradise Lost*.[170]

Among the most pessimistic was Graham Sutherland, a convert to Roman Catholicism, so pessimistic indeed that one commentator feels compelled to speak of his 'Catholic miserabilism'.[171] But on the other side it is worth observing that the year in which Sutherland painted his agonizing *Crucifixion* for St Matthew's Church in Northampton (1946) was also the same year that saw his series on the *Thorn Tree*, and to me there seems little doubt that such hope as is allowed to emerge in the former painting is conveyed through the thorns seemingly coming to life, with even the rope altar rail at Christ's feet taking on something of the same appearance.[172] David Jones, another devout Roman Catholic, is now very much better known for his poetry than for

---

[168] For the quotation, M. Clarke, *Corot and the Art of Landscape* (London: British Museum, 1991), 89; cf. 121; for his piety: 105.

[169] Clarke, *Landscape*, 98, 100–1.

[170] At the Barbican Art Gallery, London. For the comment, N. Aldred, 'A Canterbury Tale', in D. Mellor (ed.), *A Paradise Lost* (London: Lund Humphries, 1987), 118.

[171] Mellor's own phrase in *A Paradise Lost*, 72.

[172] This is to run counter to Sutherland's own view of the matter, for whom the thorn was 'the essence of cruelty'. But they do seem to take over and suggest in

his paintings, but in both alike there is a close integration of his religious faith, a strong attachment to nature and the wider Celtic tradition. As his essay *Art and Sacrament* (1955) makes clear, for him such use of nature was no accident, but integral to what it is to be human: 'Angels only: no sacrament. Beasts only: no sacrament. Man: sacrament at every turn and all levels.'[173] Sometimes nature functions simply as symbolic reminder of the Christian story.[174] At other times, though, something more seems at stake: in *Farm Door* the animals function virtually as an alternative gaze or perspective, as signs of a deeper overarching reality than the narrowly human.[175]

Most quintessentially English of them all, and perhaps also the most nostalgic were the couple John and Myfanwy Piper who were confirmed as Anglicans in 1938.[176] Colour played an increasingly important role in the works of John from the 1950s onwards.[177] If his Shell Guides to Britain often evoke a nostalgia for the past, so too can his paintings where churches and other ancient buildings were set against an increasingly rich range of colours. For, if the warmth of the colours was primarily intended to suggest immanence, their very strength can sometimes hint at a blessing on the buildings in the frame now no longer generally available. That is no doubt one reason why his paintings and prints continue to command high prices to this day. Yet more typical of the group is perhaps the more mystical bent to be found in Cecil Collins, Paul

their own way life and hope, helped no doubt in part by the colours used. For quotation and illustration, M. Fréchuret et al., *Sutherland: une rétrospective* (Paris: Réunion des musées nationaux, 1998), 41–2.

[173] For the essay, D. Jones, *Epoch and Artist: Selected Writings* (London: Faber & Faber, 1959), 143–79 esp. 167.

[174] In the 1930 *Nativity* the beasts echo the concerns of the Virgin: P. Hills (ed.), *David Jones* (London: Tate, 1981), 75–6 (no. 14). In *Tywysog Cariad* the crucified Christ merges into the branches of a tree, while in *Vexilla Regis* (1947) this is carried one stage further, with three growing trees themselves representing the crucifixion: 91 (no. 62), 113–15 (no. 122).

[175] For illustration, Hills, *David Jones*, 41 (no. 102); for comment, P. Hills, 'Making and Dwelling Among Signs', in P. Hills (ed.), *David Jones: Artist and Poet* (Aldershot: Scolar, 1997), 78–88.

[176] John was art adviser to the avant-garde quarterly *Axis* which Myfanwy edited.

[177] Although some find the effect contrived, his prints and gouaches of the 1970s and 1980s have a much wider and richer colour range than those of the 1950s and 1960s.

Nash, and Ceri Richards.[178] Richards was responsible for the Blessed Sacrament Chapel in Liverpool's Roman Catholic Cathedral, but it for his use of sexual symbolism in what is perhaps his most famous painting, *Cycle of Nature*, that he is best known. Grapes, leafy bodies, vine tendrils, and galloping cyclops' feet all combine to suggest the luxuriousness of nature, and so God's generosity in creation. Paul Nash offers what is in many ways a more easily accessible form of symbolism, to link the built world and the natural. Thus in *Pillar and Moon* each is seen to take up the other, while in his most famous painting *Totes Meer* ('Dead Sea') a dumping ground in Oxfordshire for enemy aircraft is transformed into the waves of the sea lapping against the shore. But, if that suggests some form of nature mysticism, it is to Collins that we must turn for a more obviously Christian form.[179] In *A Marriage in Paradise* of 1938, in addition to the carefully chosen natural setting, also to be observed is the presence of a symbolic Egyptian ankh, a goblet that looks suspiciously like a chalice, and even a rubbish burner in the garden that bears a remarkable resemblance to a chasuble.[180] Yet, though Collins insisted that his art was just as sacramental as Jones's work, he wanted it to be more open, not least because he believed that the conventional symbolism of Christianity was now either counterproductive or else exhausted.[181]

The element of nostalgia in this type of painting has now been noted several times. It is a problem that continues to this day in much popular landscape painting, wherever artists depict misty or sentimental scenes that reflect not so much a vanished age as an idealized one. The danger of the overlay of belief is thereby once more highlighted, the basic experience being given a particular

[178] Some, though, would take a quite different view. Malcom Yorke in *The Spirit of Place: Nine Neo-Romantic Artists and their Times* (London: Constable, 1988) includes only Nash, Sutherland, and John Piper of those discussed here. For his reasons for excluding the others: 24.

[179] His work is now likely to become much better known thanks to his widow's bequest in 2000 of about 275 paintings and drawings to be distributed around galleries throughout the country: *Art Fund Quarterly* (Summer 2001), 26–31.

[180] For *Cycle of Nature*, Mellor, *A Paradise Lost*, 29; for Nash's most famous painting: 91; for the Collins painting: 17, 20.

[181] For his art as 'sacramental': C. Collins, *The Vision of the Fool* (Ipswich: Golgonooza Press, 1994), 131–3; for the problems with Christian symbolism, including 'the obscene image of Christ hanging and bleeding on the cross': 19, 62, 131. For role of natural images, including clouds: 104–5.

slant that is not in any sense inherent within it. Yet, as Constable himself may be used to illustrate, the trouble does not necessarily stem from any accompanying religious belief. For, as the examples I gave earlier indicate, those canvases most evocative of mystic immanence are not the reproductions most commonly found in so many homes. Even in the case of Salisbury Cathedral, it was a less familiar view that has most mystic impact. So misty nostalgia and mystic immanence are by no means the same thing. It is only with the latter that we have the detection and representation of eternal value in what is none the less transient and impermanent.

How this works out in respect of the use of colour by two famous artists of the nineteenth century will be considered in a moment. It seems appropriate, therefore, to delay till then consideration of the objection that pantheism now substitutes for Christianity in this form of landscape art. Certainly, Collins's negative verdict on Christian symbolism has been a common judgement in the art of modern times. It should not be confused, though, with abandonment of the attempt to express religious experience through art nor with rejection of a continuing quest for truth. Admittedly, one could go further and present the modern preoccupation with form and colour as purely a matter of aesthetics. But as a universal judgement that would be grossly unfair because, as we shall see, there is no doubt that in reality both have also sometimes functioned as alternative ways of exploring the divine's relationship with our world. The fact that from a Christian perspective such expressions are almost always necessarily partial should not be used to belittle the attempts, for not everything can be said at once. Colour is considered first and then form.

Vibrant Colour: Van Gogh and Cézanne

So accustomed are viewers to expecting explicit symbolism to be the principal means whereby art is enhanced with a religious dimension that more often than not the artist's more obvious potential tools of form and colour have been wholly or largely neglected, whether one thinks of the twentieth century or of the more distant past. While the contribution form and colour make is often purely aesthetic in terms of balance and harmony, issues of meaning and truth have for long also made their presence felt. So, for example, in my view it would be a mistake to suppose that purely aesthetic factors have determined the triadic structure of so many of Raphael's *Madonnas and Child*, where the central figures are so often encased in an isosceles or equilateral triangle.[182] Of course such a formal pattern adds to the pleasure of the composition, but it surely also asserts the solidity of the divine–human bond enclosed therein and even its ability to triumph over suffering, once account is taken of the symbolic allusions to the cross also often present in such compositions.

Much the same can be said about the use of colour. I want therefore to make some remarks in general about that before focusing more narrowly on the role of colour in landscape, and in particular in the works of van Gogh and Cézanne. Admittedly, despite consistent attempts to establish universal meanings for specific colours, studies of the history of their use do appear to have established conclusively that this is not so.[183] Such apparent arbitrariness seems reinforced by the fact that not only do other animals experience the colour spectrum quite differently, but also time and place can have markedly different results on human perception.[184] Yet it would be folly to jump from that conclusion to the supposition that colour therefore bears no meaning at all. Not only can particular cultures impose meanings, but also some element of objectivity can be seen to remain, once we take into account the way in which judgements are affected both by intensity of hue and by the presence of other colours in the neighbourhood.[185]

[182] e.g. his *Madonna of the Goldfinch*, now in the Uffizi, where the Christchild strokes a goldfinch held by John the Baptist, or his *Garvagh Madonna*, now in the National Gallery, London.

[183] A definitive survey is provided by John Gage in his *Colour and Culture* (London: Thames & Hudson, 1993).

[184] These points are stressed by articles in A. Portmann et al., *Colour Symbolism* (Dallas: Spring, 1977). Portmann himself offers a detailed comparison with bees (1–22); Rowe notes that the ancient classical world was more interested in lustre than colour as such (23–54); Zahan the positive estimate of black in Africa, even if modified by white for heaven (55–80).

[185] On first hearing, the views of Kandinsky and van Gogh may seem utterly incompatible when we learn that the former associated blue with the divine and yellow with aggression, whereas for van Gogh yellow was the colour of the divine. But depending on precise shade blue can so easily move from suggesting calm to depression, while yellow can glow or 'shout', depending on context.

A couple of examples may help. Tempting though it is to find an explanation for the use of ultramarine and vermilion in the Virgin Mary's robes solely in the symbolic potential of these colours (blue to indicate heaven and red the blood of suffering), we are reliably informed that the main reason almost certainly lies elsewhere, in the costly character of the paints involved, just as gold featured earlier on icons for similar pragmatic reasons.[186] Even so, this of itself cannot be used to preclude the possibility of deeper meanings. The very richness of these two colours could always be used to identify where the main focus of the painting must lie. This is so even where the figure in question was placed in shade, as Piero della Francesca's Montefeltro altarpiece well indicates: a particularly fine example, as the resultant contrast of the shaded figure with light elsewhere also allows the artist to make his nativity scene speak simultaneously of cross and resurrection. Mary's dark blue robes draw us into the dark, deathlike panelling behind and so up to the hanging white ostrich egg that speaks of the resurrection. Again, to give a quite different example, Giotto can use a yellow glare not only to speak of the nature of Judas' betrayal but also by paralleling Peter's robe in softer lines and hue to indicate that he too betrays Christ in striking at Malchus' ear, even if at a less severe level.[187] In the past sharp contrasts have been drawn between Florentine concern with *disegno* and Venetian with *colore*, but as the recent cleaning of the Sistine Chapel indicates, the Florentine Michelangelo was not after all simply a sculptor missing his favourite medium, but in fact used colour extensively to suggest movement and tension. Raphael's *Saint Cecilia* altarpiece may then be used to illustrate a different application, where colour and dark shade are employed to balance one another and so argue that word (Paul in bright colours) and action (Mary Magdalene, partly in deep shade) perfectly combine to produce sacred music. Even rape can be given a positive evaluation when suitable colour combinations are utilized, as Titian so startlingly indicates in a number of his mythological compositions.[188]

[186] Explored in D. Janes, *God and Gold in Late Antiquity* (Cambridge: Cambridge University Press, 1998).

[187] Both paintings are illustrated and discussed in M. Hall, *Colour and Meaning: Practice and Theory in Renaissance Art* (Cambridge: Cambridge University Press, 1992), 79–84, 36–41.

[188] Well argued by Hall in respect of Titian's *Rape of Europa*, ibid. 204–6. The point is that the raped Europa is made to blend in with the landscape (through

Even so, it is only with the invention of the camera that meanings associated with colour and form began to assume centre stage. If the response of the Pre-Raphaelites in England and the Symbolists on the Continent was to resort to increased use of images and symbols, the Impressionists offered an alternative form of realism, one that claimed to capture the immediate moment of perception before the richness of colour had been resolved and codified by our mental ordering processes.[189] The considerable lengths to which they were prepared to go in order to ensure accuracy of portrayal are well known.[190] Perhaps less familiar are the modifications to those aims introduced by Post-Impressionists such as van Gogh and Cézanne, and the way in which they set the pattern for the future of art. Cézanne, for instance, forced recognition of the fact that lines and contours as perceived are not necessarily as the mind orders them, and so he can be said to have prepared the way for Cubism and its refusal to give priority to any one particular perspective.[191] The fullest or truest account ceased to be accurate correspondence with one particular vantage point. Again, both he and van Gogh insisted that colour was more than simply a matter of representation and so prepared the way for the Fauvists and Expressionists in the following century for whom colour was something rich in potential meaning, even if, especially in the latter case, seen as pre-eminently affective or emotional. What, though, from a theological perspective is particularly fascinating about these two decisive precursors of twentieth-century art is the way in which both, even where their motivation for a specific canvas was religious, finally decided against

the use of echoing colours and lines), not fight against it, and so the underlying rationale behind the story is endorsed: that the continent of Europe is in effect a divine creation.

[189] Rather surprisingly, Clark in discussing Monet's Cathedral series talks of the result as 'the arbitrary colour of cathedrals': *Landscape*, 177.

[190] Monet's famous Cathedral series took six months concentrated work, the artist operating from a rented room opposite the cathedral in Rouen, as he sought to capture the effect of light at different times of day: D. Mannering, *Monet* (Bristol: Parragon, 1997), 196. Again, on one occasion in 1885 while painting a seascape, he and his canvas were carried by a huge wave out to sea: P. H. Tucker, *Claude Monet* (New Haven: Yale University Press, 1995), 115.

[191] In his *Still Life with Plaster Cupid* of 1895 the lines of the table in the painting do not continue in a straight line where broken by the statues. Yet this is apparently often how our eyes see matters before our mind automatically corrects the perception: P. Smith, *Interpreting Cézanne* (London: Tate, 1996), 42–4.

explicit Christian symbolism. Instead they opted for colour as their principal medium for conveying a sense of divine presence in our world. How this works out in practice I shall now illustrate by looking briefly at the work of each artist in turn.

It is largely because he took his own life in 1890 that van Gogh, unlike Cézanne, must be fitted exclusively within a nineteenth-century context. His earlier spiritual life admits of certainties: that he was the son of a Dutch Reformed clergyman and that in early adulthood his commitment to religion intensified, even to the extent of going to serve as a missionary among miners in Belgium, where, apparently, he was a good pastor but poor preacher. Thereafter, though, commentators disagree. Some see the result of his loss of faith in 1880 as the blossoming of a purely natural mysticism,[192] but to my mind reading his surviving letters very much suggests continuing religious concerns.[193] One recent work argues that the contrast between the two stages of his life was in fact much less marked than is commonly supposed. The reason is because his father belonged to the more liberal branch of the Dutch church which was already seeking for new ways of negotiating a sense of divine presence, partly under the influence of Schleiermacher's writings.[194] Certainly he rebelled against his father, but from his own perspective what he now sought was not the total rejection of Christianity but rather its transmutation into a more immanent and more tolerant form of religion.

Art was to be his own personal contribution to that process, and in this colour was to play a leading role, in evoking a sense of the presence of the divine within the natural order. His friend, Emile Barnard, reported that 'he was passionately fond of yellow, the colour of divine clarity',[195] and that is what one finds reflected in a large number of his later paintings. One notes, for instance, how alive his sunflowers seem to be in comparison with those of

---

[192] The view of T. Kodera in *Vincent van Gogh* (Amsterdam: Benjamins, 1990) and of I. F. Walther and R. Metzger in *Van Gogh: The Complete Paintings* (Cologne: Taschen, 1997), 607–31 esp. 631.

[193] For example, M. Roskill (ed.), *The Letters of Vincent van Gogh* (London: HarperCollins, 1983), 141–2, 275–6.

[194] So K. P. Erickson in *At Eternity's Gate: The Spiritual Vision of Vincent van Gogh* (Grand Rapids: Eerdmans, 1998), esp. 9–60.

[195] Quoted without reference in Portmann, *Colour Symbolism*, 162. One might also note his remark in one of his letters that 'I am absorbed in colour' (Roskill, *Letters*, 167).

Monet,[196] and indeed he himself underlined their religious dimension by drawing a parallel with the stained glass of churches in the interaction between background and theme.[197] Again, not only does the sun transform all it touches in his paintings but sometimes it appears even to give a halo to the peasant toiling in the field.[198] Late in life he produced modified versions of some famous works by others. One of the most intriguing is his extraordinary adaptation of Rembrandt's *Raising of Lazarus*, where the figure of Christ himself disappears to be replaced by a glowing sun.[199] Blue can also sometimes perform the role of suggesting divine presence. Most notable perhaps is his *Starry Night* of June, 1889, where the sky appears to have become alive in a kind of swirling intensity, as if to compensate for the threatening tree below.[200] In a letter from the previous year he had already confessed his need of religion and that this now took the form of 'going out at night to paint the stars'.[201] One notes too from the same year his use of blue in a portrait to suggest ' infinity', 'like a star in the depths of an azure sky'.[202] Also worthy of remark is the inclusion of a northern spire in this southern landscape, as it gives added poignancy to the painting's religious dimension. It is almost as though, like Friedrich, he is trying to retain some general validity for the specifics of Christian symbolism. Admittedly, such explorations were all to end on a profoundly pessimistic note in works such as his *Wheatfield with Crows* of 1890. But while the painter may have allowed despair to

[196] Contrast his *Still-life: Vase with twelve sunflowers* of 1888 (illus. Walther and Metzger, *Van Gogh*, 409) with Monet's *Sunflowers* of 1881, now in the Metropolitan Museum, New York.

[197] J. van Gogh-Bonger and C. de Dood (eds.), *Complete Letters of Vincent van Gogh* (Greenwich, Conn.: New York Graphic Society, 1959), 3, 511.

[198] One might note the contrast between *The Sower* of June 1888 with two paintings of the same title, completed in November of that year, where the sun moves to encompass the sower: illustrated in Walther and Metzger, *Van Gogh*, 452, 453.

[199] From May, 1890: illus. ibid. 626.

[200] Now in the Museum of Modern Art, New York; illus. ibid. 520–1. Note also how the church spire has also been made unnaturally tall.

[201] Letter of 29 September 1888.

[202] Roskill, *Letters*, 278. In this *Portrait of Eugène Bloch* (Walther and Metzger, *Van Gogh*, 420) van Gogh wanted to create 'a mysterious effect' but by juxtaposing the blue 'infinity' of the background with his sitter, the net effect seems to me rather to increase our sense of human fragility.

have the last word, there is no reason why we should follow suit, and so give a negative value to his earlier efforts.[203]

Indeed, it seems to me entirely appropriate to speak of a thoroughly sacramental employment of colour to express the relation of the divine to our own world. It is not simply nature mysticism because the divine is presented as more than just the surface appearances of the world, and indeed van Gogh appears to have continued to believe in an afterlife even after he abandoned the practice of Christianity.[204] It is, however, a different sort of sacramentality from that with which he had begun his artistic career. Many speak of his *Potato Eaters* of 1884 as sacramental in character, and indeed as evoking the spirit of the Supper at Emmaus.[205] That seems right, but the sanctity of ordinary toil is also reflected in a number of his other earlier paintings, sometimes mediated through light striking figures bent in the field or else in the great care with which even defective produce is portrayed.[206] His own personal isolation, though, seems increasingly to have led him to abandon such human mediation for the direct contribution of nature itself. It is only then that colour could achieve a sacramental value in its own right. Despite what I said earlier though, this does not mean just a simple equation of yellow or blue with God. Rather, what we have in any particular canvas is a dynamic interaction between the relevant colour and other colours or objects that then give the yellow or blue its precise resonance. So, just as in purely secular works the juxtaposition of two conflicting colours can speak of violent emotions,[207] so

[203] The painting is now in the Rijksmuseum, Amsterdam. It was only the previous year that he had painted *Starry Night*.

[204] Used as an element in N. M. Maurer's argument that van Gogh's suicide was really altruistic, motivated by the desire to resolve his brother Theo's continuing financial crisis in supporting him: *The Pursuit of Spiritual Wisdom: The Thought and Art of Vincent van Gogh and Paul Gauguin* (Cranbury, NJ: Associated University Presses, 1998), 112–13.

[205] e.g. M. Shapiro, *Vincent van Gogh* (New York: Abrams, 1950), 40.

[206] For an example of the former, *Farmers planting potatoes*: Maurer, *Pursuit of Spiritual Wisdom*, illus. 43; for the latter, Maurer's own comment: 'By . . . depicting their "defects" with respectful care, the artist imparts a sacramental quality to his lowly subjects' (48).

[207] Cf. van Gogh's own comments on his *Night Cafe*, quoted in Maurer, ibid. 72, and for a similar application note van Gogh's suggestive treatment of *Gauguin's Armchair*, implying a man subject to strong emotions. For illustrations, ibid. illus. 124, 136.

cypresses and olives where placed in relation to blue sky or yellow cornfield can acquire a quite different meaning, in affirming that suffering can be overcome and a divine hope be realized.[208]

Quite a few of Cézanne's earliest canvases were religious.[209] Yet, even after his return to religious practice in 1891, there was no comparable return to explicitly religious topics. It is possible to downplay that religious commitment, especially as quite a few of his comments on religious faith have a cynical edge to them,[210] but the truth seems to be that he found God in the landscape and used colour and (to a lesser degree) form to express that vision. In a letter of 1904 he speaks of 'the spectacle which the *Pater Omnipotens Aeterne Deus* spreads out before our eyes',[211] and by that he may have meant not simply that God was its creator but that a deeper mystical correspondence exists between our perceptions and the way God ultimately makes himself present in our world. At all events a theory to that effect had been elaborated by Baudelaire in his *Salon* of 1859, and would fit well with Cézanne's general approach.[212] He himself remarked: 'How can one look at nature without thinking of its author? The artist must look upon the world as his catechism.'[213] Certainly, unlike the Impressionists' concern with the fleeting moment, his interest was in the permanence of nature.[214] That might help explain too his continual fascination with Mont Sainte-Victoire, the landscape that he was painting

---

[208] For olives suggesting 'the tortuous process of weathering and ageing' and dark cypresses alluding to suffering and death, ibid. 90–3. For some applications: illus. 150–1, 153–5.

[209] These appear to reflect his involvement in Provençal religious culture with its Corpus Christi traditions and Easter plays and the revival of the Magdalen pilgrimage to Sainte-Baume: so M. T. Lewis, *Cézanne's Early Imagery* (Berkeley, Calif.: University of California Press, 1989), esp. 25–62.

[210] 'I think that to be a Catholic one must be devoid of all sense of justice, but have a good eye for one's own interests': letter to his son, 12 August 1906. For some other strange religious attitudes, P. Callow, *Lost Earth: A Life of Cézanne* (London: Allison & Busby, 1995), 294, 321.

[211] Letter to Emile Barnard, 15 April 1904; quoted at length in N. Wadley, *Cézanne and his Art* (London: Hamlyn, 1975), 106.

[212] The connection is noted briefly in Smith, *Interpreting Cézanne*, 39.

[213] R. Kendall (ed.), *Cézanne by Himself* (London: Little, Brown, 2001 edn.), 293.

[214] 'Nature is always the same, but nothing remains, nothing of what appears before us. Our art must provide some fleeting sense of her permanence': ibid. 302.

when he had his final collapse during a rainstorm in 1906,[215] and to which he had repeatedly returned during the last four years of his life. In this connection it is fascinating to contrast his own use of blue in such paintings to suggest the stability and order of nature, even in contexts where individual forms appear to dissolve, with Monet's startling painting of the death of his companion of fourteen years where dissolution and the impermanence of human existence are so clearly the message.[216] Also worthy of note is the way in which Cézanne uses blue to effect dominance for the mountain in his repeated paintings of the scene, despite the way in which blue normally gives to our vision a sense of something receding. Often Mont Sainte-Victoire was more than eleven miles off from where he was painting.[217] Even so, Cézanne uses his palette to make it wholly dominate our vision.[218] Blue might suggest an entirely heavenly or transcendent vision, but what we are in fact offered in each of the canvases is emphatically not this but rather something mighty drawing near. If in his paintings from 1896–8 there is little sense of engagement between the mountain and what lies at its feet and the mountain is bluey-grey rather than grey-blue, in the later landscapes one finds not only much stronger blues but also the invasion of the countryside below by similar blues and even some of the countryside green affecting the mountain and its sky in turn.[219] It is thus possible to talk about an interplay between transcendence

[215] For the centrality of Mont Sainte-Victoire to him, U. Becks-Malorny, *Cézanne* (Cologne: Taschen, 1995), 67–79.

[216] In Monet's *Camille on her death-bed* of 1879, not only does her bouquet of flowers virtually vanish, there is also little to indicate individual personality: illus. in Mannering, *Monet*, 134.

[217] One can see the difference clearly in the contrast between Cézanne's and Renoir's painting of the same scene, as also in the difference between photograph and actual painting: E. Loran, *Cézanne's Composition*, 3rd edn. (Los Angeles: University of California Press, 1963) 100, 104–5. The point repeatedly emerges in the photographic comparisons in P. Machotka, *Cézanne: Landscape into Art* (New Haven: Yale University Press, 1996), e.g. 98–9, 108–9, 116–17, 136, 144–6.

[218] Achieved partly by the strength of colours employed and partly by what he allows to fill the intervening area. A good example of a purely aesthetic change in visual perception is what he does in *Landscape at la Roche-Guyon* where the house is brought closer, the intervening valley eliminated, and the distant hill raised: Loran, *Cézanne's Composition*, 46–7.

[219] Becks-Malorny, *Cézanne*, offers one example from before 1894 (79) one from 1896–8 (73) and five from 1904–6 (69, 74, 75, 76, 77). For some more examples, M.-T. Benedetti, *Cézanne* (New York: Crescent, 1995), 226, 228, 247,

and immanence, with the distinctions between divine and earthly certainly not abolished but none the less considerably softened.

Such qualifications may tempt some critics to speak of pantheism and still more so with van Gogh, given his abandonment of the Christian faith. A two-stage response may be offered. First, care needs to be exercised in assessing the validity of an experience and its doctrinal implications. The danger is that the theologian will start from doctrine and declare a particular experience invalid, whereas what needs to be noted first is the precise character of the experience, whether or not it appears to support a particular faith or otherwise. The fact that some artists' work reflects a largely or wholly immanent God could be argued to imply the limitations of their experience rather than either the truth or the falsity of pantheism as such. Secondly, even in the case of the two artists discussed here, one may note how a more complicated dynamic is in fact occurring. In the case of Cézanne I found myself speaking of an interplay between transcendence and immanence. If some of van Gogh's canvases such as his sunflower series seem exclusively immanent in tone, others also hint at transcendence. The introduction in *Starry Night* of the unnaturally elongated spire echoing the twisted tree would be a case in point. Perhaps influence from van Gogh's earlier experiences within the Christian fold lived on, despite his own explicit disavowal.[220] Whatever the explanation, the import of these artists' strongly pantheistic works, it seems to me, should not be rejected but rather balanced by some of their other works, as also by how God was experienced among artists with quite different starting points such as those belonging to the Hudson River School.

Cézanne is now undoubtedly better known for the way in which his use of form anticipates Cubism, and there are certainly many of his paintings where it is form that is central to his

256–60 (five more). Intriguingly, the one from before 1894 anticipates some of the later themes. There is an excellent site on the Internet (with ten illustrations and commentary) in the Web Museum, Paris, at www.ibiblio.org/wm/paint, accessed 24 Jan. 2004.

[220] T. S. Eliot offers a fascinating parallel in literature with his argument that James Joyce, unlike D. H. Lawrence, continued to evince a Christian sensibility even after loss of faith: *After Strange Gods* (London: Faber & Faber, 1934), esp. 35–9.

intentions.[221] Even so, this should not be allowed to detract from his powerful use of colour in the kind of contexts we have just been discussing. Although he employs colour to convey other religious meanings,[222] undoubtedly in these paintings he is wrestling with how best to convey God's sacramental relationship with our world. But it is to form that we now turn.

Deep Form and the Problem of Evil

The move towards abstraction seen in Cézanne was to advance apace in the twentieth century. So too was the decline of the Church, particularly after the First World War. Since abstraction inevitably sounded the death-knell for high value continuing to be accorded to landscape painting, it might seem that my analysis should therefore end historically at this point. But there are two reasons against this. The first is that, though organized religion declined, engagement with spiritual issues through art was much less severely affected.[223] The second reason is that this is particularly true of the three artists on whom I shall focus here, Mondrian, Kandinsky, and Klee, all of whom began their careers in an engagement with landscape even if, Klee excepted, this was subsequently abandoned. In its place comes a preoccupation with form and colour as means of highlighting the underlying divine reality of the world. As this also marks a sustained attempt to comment on the role of evil or tragedy in human existence, the following will also provide an appropriate conclusion to our discussion of visual art as a

[221] The Philadelphia *Women Bathers* is a good example, where three triangles dominate the composition, and add to the forbidding and inaccessible character of the women.

[222] For a fascinating example, note his *Uncle Dominic as a Monk* of 1866. The strong colours of the face are made to contrast with the white of his habit, to suggest a determined character subdued, a motif reinforced by the angle of the eyes and the nature of the folded hands. The result is thus more than an individual portrait; the artist is insisting that there can be no monastic vocation without considerable self-denial. For illustration and some further comments, M. Schapiro, *Cézanne* (London: Thames & Hudson, 1988 edn.), 48–9.

[223] For a general survey of the extent of 20-c. art's engagement with spiritual issues, R. Lipsey, *An Art of Our Own: The Spiritual in Twentieth Century Art* (Boston: Shambhala, 1997). Ironically, more explicit Christian art such as Dalí, Rouault, or Spencer is excluded.

means of exploring issues in natural religion. What is different now, though, is that these artists move well beyond simply reflecting their experience of the divine as mediated through nature. Instead, major initiatives are taken in interpreting that experience, in trying to integrate it into some overall grid of meaning. There is nothing wrong in this. Indeed, the prospect is exciting. It is just that abstract art is less a matter of raw data, and more, as its name implies, a conceptual exercise, and so to be assessed accordingly, though with this concession that its roots remain (in the case of these three artists) thoroughly experiential.

American Abstract Expressionism might of course have been considered instead. Unlike its European counterpart, though, it does not seem to have emerged out of interest in nature as such, while its form of theology is also significantly different. That difference can perhaps best be seen if we consider for a moment the work of Barnett Newman and Mark Rothko, both of whom died in 1970, the latter by suicide. Although both keen to insist upon content and not just form, their aim seems to have been to evoke through sustained reflection on the canvas a hint of the transcendent rather than any particular view of the divine's relation to our world. Rothko, for example, describes how, in order to create 'transcendent experience', 'the familiar identity of things has to be pulverised in order to destroy the finite associations with which our society increasingly enshrouds every aspect of our environment'.[224] That, inevitably, leaves little that can be said. Some have drawn parallels between his work and that of Friedrich, but, while there is certainly a strong sense of transcendence also in Rothko it is seldom as reassuring as in Friedrich.[225] His compositions for the Houston Chapel are a rare exception, and in most of his implicitly religious canvases one senses more a tragic longing for transcendence rather than some fixed belief.[226] Such hints are sometimes allowed to emerge out of the juxtaposition of closely

[224] N. Serota (ed.), *Mark Rothko, 1903–70*, rev. edn. (London: Tate, 1996), 84.
[225] Friedrich's *Monk by the Sea* (1809) and Rothko's *Green on Blue* (1956) are compared in the opening pages of R. Rosenblum, *Modern Painting and the Northern Romantic Tradition: Friedrich to Rothko* (London: Thames & Hudson, 1975), 10–11.
[226] The contrast between a tragic Rothko and optimistic Newman is a repeated theme in J. Golding's analysis of the two: *Paths to the Absolute* (London: Thames & Hudson, 2000), 153–232 esp. 157–9, 187, 220; cf. also his own expectation of tears, Lipsey, *An Art of Our Own*, 316.

related hues.[227] Newman by contrast is in general much more optimistic. His placement of zips (narrow bands of colour in a larger canvas) allows the suggestion of the divine invading our world, as in his *Adam* or in *Onement*.[228] Yet, when he sought to say more, as in his *Stations of the Cross*, the attempt is often deemed unsuccessful.[229]

How much such attitudes were a function of the Jewish roots of the two artists concerned it is hard to say, but what can be noted is how far distant such claims would remain from traditional, orthodox Christianity, unless further qualified: it is hard, for instance, to see any place for divine involvement in the world of the kind postulated by the incarnation. In actual practice within Christianity assertions of a *via negativa* have almost always been studiously balanced by more positive assertions. Newman and Rothko might, of course, be right, that no more can in fact be said, but even Jewish theologians would usually wish to go further than their co-religionists, and so it is worth exploring the quite different use to which abstract art was put on the opposite side of the Atlantic. In rough, the view of Kandinsky, Klee, and Mondrian was that art offered an alternative access to the nature of reality, quite different from what is conveyed perceptually, however much the images they employed might be ultimately derived from perceptual experience. To postulate an alternative way of accessing reality might initially sound implausible, but all three drew the parallel with music and that seems helpful, for a piece of music can evoke scenes or attitudes without necessarily using any sounds commonly associated with them, far less specific visual images. At all events, it is to their work and an estimate of its significance that I now turn, particularly as this affects the issue of how the problem of evil is to be approached. As we shall see, three radically different 'solutions' are proposed.

---

[227] Such as *Number 10* or *Black on Maroon*, both of 1958: illus. Serota, *Mark Rothko*, 150, 151.

[228] For illustrations and helpful discussion, Golding, *Paths*, 195–203.

[229] Fourteen paintings produced between 1958 and 1966 and executed entirely in black and white, now in the National Gallery, Washington. How difficult the task he set himself was is well indicated by another minimalist composition to which he also gave a tragic interpretation, but which could so easily be read as a sign of hope: *Untitled Etching 1* (1969): G. Schor, *The Prints of Barnett Newman* (Stuttgart: Hatje, 1996), 113 cf. 34.

All three artists represent a common phenomenon in modern art, a sitting loose to the specific doctrines of Christianity but continued real engagement with spiritual issues. What, however, makes them different is the degree to which such concerns were at the forefront of what they produced. Christian imagery is occasionally employed, but more commonly they sought new forms of symbolism in form and colour in order to highlight what they saw as the underlying religious character of the world. Another shared factor is their reliance, to varying degrees, upon a rather exotic form of syncretistic religion known as Theosophy that took its origins in part from comparative religion and partly from Neoplatonism as mediated through certain aspects of the Western mystical tradition such as the Jewish Kabbalah and the writings of Jacob Böhme. Founded by Madame Blavatsky in 1875, its writings were later reinforced by the work of Annie Besant and Charles Leadbeater, but given a more Christian focus when Rudolf Steiner founded the Anthroposophical Society in 1913. Despite the strangeness of some of its proposals, the reasons for the popularity of the movement are not difficult to comprehend.[230] Not only did it try to take the plurality of religions seriously, it also offered the individual the possibility of direct access to an underlying spiritual reality unmediated by the dogmatism of the churches. Of special interest to the artist was what was said about colour and form. Plato was often quoted to the effect that 'God geometrizes', while colour was assigned specific meanings, and even held to produce a special aura attaching to different character types.[231] Much was made of the notion of development occurring through the reconciliation of opposites, and this was found to be reflected in the significance given to verticals and horizontals, as well as to the various geometric figures.

[230] The wide extent of its popularity among artists is explored by the contributors to M. Tuchman (ed.), *The Spiritual in Art: Abstract Painting 1890–1985* (New York: Abbeville, 1986); for Kandinsky, Klee, and Mondrian in particular, esp. 82–5, 131–53, 201–17.

[231] In Plato's *Timaeus* geometrical forms are treated as foundational to the construction of material reality. A number of colour charts with putative meanings are provided in Leadbeater's *Man Visible and Invisible* (1902) and in Beasant and Leadbeater's *Thought Forms* (1905). For some examples, Tuchman, *The Spiritual in Art*, 135, 137.

All this might suggest a necessary incompatibility with Christianity, as also its basic idea of all reality deriving from a single divine source by pantheistic emanation. Certainly, there is much that stands at a far remove from traditional Christian approaches. Even so, it would be a mistake to suppose that the meaning implicit in the art that drew its inspiration in part from this source must necessarily fall foul of a similar critique. Of the three artists we shall consider, only Mondrian seems to have remained committed to the movement throughout his life, but even in his case there is only an occasional painting that can be related to the specifics of theosophical belief. It is more a case of the movement acting as a spur towards various experiments in natural religion, in trying to convey through abstract means alone, through form and to a lesser extent colour, a religious understanding of the world. What I therefore want to consider is what kind of truth claims the three artists were concerned to assert, and in particular what were their various approaches to the question of the existence of suffering in the world.

All three assert that the underlying reality of the world is spiritual, not purely material. This they do by using the harmony of line and colour to indicate a deeper formal, intellectual unity than that merely perceived by the senses. Various changes of style are to be observed as their art develops. Mondrian, for instance, displaces his earlier classical rhythms for those of jazz, while with Kandinsky at least four phases can be observed: concern with the interaction of colours gradually displaces an early interest in more traditional symbolism; this in turn yields to a new interest in formal shapes, before finally this too is displaced by the biomorphic patterns that assume central place in the last stages of his life. How significant any of these changes are, it is not always easy to determine. Kandinsky's biomorphic paintings might, for instance, be taken to indicate a new interest in movement and change, but in fact such an interest is already detectable in early canvases that use the symbolism of rider and rower. Similarly, Mondrian's earlier apparently closed formal paintings are found to have an open-ended structure at their peripheries that could well be read as anticipating the dynamism of his later jazz paintings. So it might well be appropriate sometimes to talk more about a change of emphasis rather than any complete alteration of perspective. It is a matter that we shall need to consider as we examine the work of each individual artist. Of the three, I shall end with Klee. It is Mondrian, however, who remained the most committed to Theosophy throughout his life; so I shall begin there.[232]

Mondrian was the son of a teacher who was a committed member of the *Hervormd* (Reformed) church, and Mondrian himself seems to have been active in that church until about 1895.[233] Certainly, many of his earliest paintings reveal a Christian commitment, and indeed even after he had abandoned Christianity one finds him using the symbol of the cross to represent permanence and transcendence.[234] Yet he came eventually to see it as a problematic image, at once too particular in its reference and, somewhat ironically in view of his earlier theories, too resolved in its implications.[235] In 1909 he finally joined the Theosophical movement, and although he was not always treated well by his fellow members, he never abandoned their underlying ideas.[236] One notion that remained central throughout his subsequent artistic career was his conviction that abstract art could express better than the copying of nature its underlying unity and perfection.[237] In the earliest phase of

[232] Though it would be a mistake to suppose that in Mondrian's case identification meant literal copying, or that with the other two later standing at a critical distance entailed no further influence from Theosophy.

[233] For the family position, H. Henkels, 'Mondrian in Winterswijk', in H. Overduin (ed.), *Mondrian: From Figuration to Abstraction* (The Hague: Gemeentemuseum, 1988), 145–64 esp. 146–8.

[234] As in *Windmill*: illus. in H. L. C. Jaffé, *Mondrian* (New York: Abrams, 1985 edn.), 57. For the connection with the cross, Henkels in Overduin, *Mondrian*, 176.

[235] Analysing a mill painting a decade later, he now finds its cross problematic, and puts the emphasis instead on colour complementarity: Y.-A. Bois et al., *Piet Mondrian* (Boston: Bulfinch, 1995), 119. For his critique of the cross as too swift a resolution of vertical and horizontal: 339.

[236] In 1914 he had an important article rejected by their main journal: letter to L. Schelfhout, 12 June 1914. His *Evolution triptych* of 1911 is often treated as the best example of his commitment, but, though this is true in respect of its use of theosophical symbols, in my opinion it has little of the challenge of his more abstract works: for illustration, S. Deicher, *Mondrian* (Cologne: Taschen, 1995), 29. For a more interesting candidate, see *Woods near Oele*, where the repeated horizontals balancing the trees may reflect theosophical notions: so Welsh in Tuchman, *The Spiritual in Art*, 82–3. As well as foreign theosophists, an important Dutch influence on him was the work of M. H. J. Schoenmaekers.

[237] 'Relationship is precisely more alive when it is *not* veiled by the natural but manifests itself in the flat and the straight': *Natural Reality and Abstract Reality* (New York: Braziller, 1995), 21–2; cf. 35 and 39, where he describes his aim as being 'to see nature more perfectly'.

his work this aim was largely pursued through the identification of form, as can be seen in the way in which he gradually dissolves trees into abstract forms, as also buildings such as the church at Domburg or the Paris skyline.[238] If his subsequent use of human artefacts in his abstract paintings occasions surprise, it should be noted that for Mondrian 'the destruction of the natural' was essential to discovering its underlying spirituality; in other words, any preoccupation with the immediate appearance of nature or human constructions from nature such as buildings or roads could on his view only mislead by drawing too much attention to the particular.[239] Colour only gradually emerged as a major preoccupation, as he sought to express the world's underlying harmony through a harmony of simple forms and primary colours.[240]

How simple those forms had to be in Mondrian's view is well indicated by his conflict with his fellow artist, Theo van Doesburg, over the latter's use of diagonals.[241] The meeting of horizontal and vertical, with rectangles of varying colours, was quite enough. Yet, if that suggests tedious patterns, this is far from being the case. Mondrian procures a balance that is delicately qualitative rather than strictly quantitative, as can easily be seen from the fact that not only does the amount of space devoted to each colour vary, but also the forms are open-ended at the edges (perhaps as a way of more directly engaging the viewer).[242] The late 1920s and early 1930s, however, found him experimenting not only with further reduction of colour range but also introducing a double line to give a more explicit sense of dynamism and movement to his canvases. In one of his later writings he talks about 'the fundamental law of dynamic equilibrium',[243] and this

[238] For the gradual resolution of trees into their constituent forms, note the progressive character of illustrations in Jaffé, *Mondrian*, 67, 83, 85, 87. For the church at Domburg, note contrast in Deicher, *Mondrian*, 26, 40. For a good example of his treatment of the Paris skyline, Bois, *Piet Mondrian*, 152.

[239] For some development of these views, Bois, *Piet Mondrian*, 190.

[240] Focus on the three primary colours of blue, yellow, and red, together with the contrast between light and dark may have been derived ultimately from Goethe's *Zur Farbenlehre* via some lectures of Steiner: ibid. 319–20.

[241] For Mondrian's response, Jaffé, *Mondrian*, 110–11.

[242] Cf. ibid. 106–9. For engagement of viewer and open-ended character, particularly helpful is M. Schapiro, *Mondrian: On the Humanity of Abstract Painting* (New York: Braziller, 1995), esp. 28 ff.

[243] In 'Figurative and Non-figurative Art' of 1937; repr. in Overduin, *Mondrian*, 15–23 esp. 19.

is of course exactly what one finds most reflected in his final work, where he borrows from jazz and from the streets of London and New York to suggest in his now much more complex patterns a more syncopated rhythm to the nature of the underlying unity of all reality that he was concerned to bring to human consciousness.[244]

Put like that, it suggests a pantheistic aspect to his thought, and this seems correct. As I tried to indicate in the previous section, though, this need not entail an automatic conflict between his painting and Christianity. Christian doctrine in any case shares the artist's belief in the underlying unity of all reality, at least to the degree that all is seen as stemming from a single source in the one God, and what appears on the canvas does not necessarily differentiate between the two positions. A more plausible source of conflict would be his insistence that art should not represent the tragic. His grounds were that something is only tragic from a particular perspective and not in relation to the larger whole.[245] Even the invention of poison gas could not dampen his optimism.[246] Mondrian's art is thus essentially of its very nature celebratory. It is instructive in this connection to note the horror with which he met Kandinsky's enjoyment of a particular piece of natural beauty, as itself a temptation away from the universal.[247] Thus even with his later move to a jazz analogy there is little sense in Mondrian of his paintings indicating some sense of direction to the movement he depicts. It is almost as though what we are offered is a celebration of the present moment or, rather, of everything caught up in that moment rather than any notion of a real enmeshment in a history that has some purposive direction to it. The latter would have brought him nearer to a benevolent doctrine of providential guidance, but perhaps his Calvinist upbringing in the end proved too strong, and so God's hand in history had to remain hidden.

---

[244] As in well-known paintings such as *New York City* or *Broadway Boogie Woogie*: illus. in Bois, *Piet Mondrian*, 290, 292.

[245] 'The lack of balance between the individual and the universal creates tragedy . . . art, being abstract and the opposite of natural tangibility, heralds the gradual disappearance of tragedy': his views as reported in a newspaper interview, reproduced in Overduin, *Mondrian*, 29.

[246] Cf. his comments in Bois, *Piet Mondrian*, 327.

[247] Their 1934 meeting is described in M. Lacoste, *Kandinsky* (Näfels: Bonfini, 1979), 81.

Instead, the harmony can already be found, he believed, in the present moment. For, though, as we have seen, it is important for Mondrian that the existence of creative tensions should be acknowledged and accepted, nothing, it appears, is allowed to be wholly evil. Instead, any such assumption is presumed to indicate the partiality of a more local and particular perspective. Because such claims are embodied in art, they can only remain implicit, but that does not mean that their symbolic representation is any less a truth claim than is, for instance, the case with the more famous poetic declaration of a very similar view in Pope's *Essay on Man*:

> All nature is but art unknown to thee;
> All chance, direction which thou canst not see;
> All discord, harmony not understood;
> All partial evil, universal good.

Such serene optimism is unlikely to be shared by many, and so, despite the undoubted beauty of his work it is perhaps with a measure of relief that one turns to Kandinsky. Kandinsky was resident for most of his artistic life in Germany, and there are some fine country portraits surviving from his early career. It is to his Russian Orthodox upbringing, though, that we must turn to explain his early image of the rider (via St George) and thus the sense of dynamic movement and direction that this helped give to his own use of form and colour. In fact, quite a number of Kandinsky's earliest paintings are explicitly Christian in their imagery,[248] and, though this no longer remains the case in his more developed work, apart from a brief period in his youth he was to remain in some kind of connection with the Orthodox church right up until his death.[249] Indeed, the battling St George is to be found even in what are otherwise almost wholly non-representational paintings, as is also sometimes so with his oarsmen. If *Lyrical* admits fairly easily of a reading that speaks of the triumph of the spiritual over the material, one has to work harder to detect

---

[248] 'A large number of religious and biblical themes': so Lacoste, ibid. 40. For a couple of early, more conventional examples, 26, 27. For the connection between All Saints paintings and the Apocalypse (including the horse), U. Becks-Malorny, *Kandinsky* (Cologne: Taschen, 1994), 84–5.

[249] His widow declared that 'he was a believer, but did not attend church regularly'; for this comment and other pieces of evidence, J. Hahl-Koch, *Kandinsky* (New York: Rizzoli, 1993), esp. 25–32, 26; cf. also 126–8, 258.

George's lance at work defeating the strange beast on the left in *Painting with White Border*, or the oarsmen carrying us towards the heavenly blue in *Improvisation 26*.[250] As with Mondrian, though, the point is not that the viewer should continue to recognize the concrete amidst the abstract. Rather, the concrete is held to dissolve naturally into colour and/or simple forms as its underlying reality.

In the works he was doing just before the outbreak of the First World War there is a marked contrast with Mondrian. For form in general gradually begins to disappear, with colour taking on the main burden of meaning. Indeed, so much is this so, that one can easily come away from such paintings thinking that only disorder is present, and there is thus a striking contrast with what Mondrian was attempting to achieve at roughly the same time. It is important, therefore, to understand Kandinsky's intentions. Like Mondrian, he came to the view that naturalism was a distraction, and that, like music (which he saw as well in advance of the visual arts), art should aim to use its own distinctive methods to reveal the underlying spiritual character of the world.[251] In this connection he particularly welcomed the arrival of atomic theory which he saw as undermining the primacy of immediate perception and so of a naturalistic or materialistic view of the world.[252] Where he differed, though, from Mondrian was in the conviction that, just as his friend Schoenberg could generate music out of apparent dissonance, so also could art identify a similar identity to reality as a whole.[253] A good example of this would be *Composition VI* of 1913, where an original painting of the Flood is transformed into a colourful assertion of the possibility of a new creation.[254]

---

[250] Illustrated in T. M. Messer, *Kandinsky* (London: Thames & Hudson, 1997), 73, 89, 81. Even where titles give a clue, as in *St George II* (75), one still has to work hard, which of course was part of Kandinsky's intention. For the interpretation of *Lyrical*, Becks-Malorny, *Kandinsky*, 67; for another example of this role for blue: 74.

[251] Music is held up as the ideal in his *Concerning the Spiritual in Art* of 1911 (New York: Dover, 1977), 19–20. He also urges that ballet should move beyond the representational: 50–1.

[252] F. Whitford, *Kandinsky: Watercolours and Other Works on Paper* (London: Royal Academy of Arts, 1999), 21. Golding, *Paths to the Absolute*, 81, is misleading at this point.

[253] With apparent dissonance of form concealing an underlying music and harmony: ibid. 17–18.

[254] Hahl-Koch, *Kandinsky*, 203, 205 for illustration and comment. The less successful *Composition V* had had resurrection as its theme.

How much all this was due to the influence of Theosophy is a complex question which we need not pursue here.[255] Certainly, other influences also played their part, as seems likely in his subsequent move to making form his primary medium, for here the influence of his time in Russia and meeting with Kasimir Malevich cannot be discounted.[256] Yet if colour contrasts begin eventually to give place entirely to tension between triangle and circle or acute and obtuse angle, even here religious considerations were not absent, as in his claim that 'the meeting between the acute angle of a triangle and a circle has no less an impact than Michelangelo's finger of God touching that of Adam'.[257] However, it would be unwise to take his written comments on either the various colours or on forms entirely at face value, since he provides no shortage of exceptions to his own rules. The truth seems to be that the dynamic interaction within each painting is worked out in isolation, and so only sometimes do we find his specific shapes and colours conforming to his own rules.

That, however, does not mean that they fail to sustain a truth claim, only that it takes time and contemplation to discover what this might be (precisely Kandinsky's intention). Where its character differs from that in Mondrian would seem to be in two key respects. The first is Kandinsky's willingness to go beyond a purely present dynamic equilibrium or creative tension into some continuing movement towards resolution. It is almost as though the painting forces its story to be concluded beyond the actual confines of the canvas. Then, secondly, one observes—rather than the presence of what is presented as merely a complementary opposite—some sense of an actual evil needing to be faced. So there is certainly full acknowledgement of the extent of human

[255] A detailed study of possible influences is provided by S. Ringbom, *The Sounding Cosmos: A Study in the Spiritualism of Kandinsky* (Turku: Academia Aboensis, Åbo, 1970).

[256] Also an abstract painter and a believer, if a somewhat unorthodox one: Golding, *Paths to the Absolute*, 78.

[257] My trans.: *Cahiers d'art* 6 (1931), 352. For Kandinsky's own declaration that the circle was intended to fulfil a similar role to the horseman, Becks-Malorny, *Kandinsky*, 157. For his detailed reflections on geometric symbolism, *Point and Line to Plane* (New York: Dover, 1979). The acute angle he relates to the aggressiveness of yellow, the obtuse to blue on the way to becoming a circle: e.g. 73. For the tension between triangle and circle at its simplest, *Green and Red* (Lacoste, *Kandinsky*, 69); for a more complicated dynamic, *Composition VIII* (Messer, *Kandinsky*, 107).

suffering that may ensue before any potential resolution. Even so, it is unclear how lasting such a recognition really was, inasmuch as in the end Kandinsky appears to want to exclude any sad or ultimately tragic element. Even his most famous painting to speak of chaos, *Composition VII*, offers only a subdued threat, and on closer inspection appears to guarantee its resolution.[258]

Indeed, in general there is a sublime optimism that intensifies in the final stage of his artistic career.[259] Writing the year before he died (in 1943), he could even speak of the year 2000 as the time when he expected to see 'the great results of all the terrible suffering that we have been enduring for almost 150 years'.[260] In that last stage the inherent tension that he saw in the line develops into the wavy movements of primitive biomorphic forms, almost all of which suggest not only confidence in the future but also joy.[261] Despite his later distancing of himself from Theosophy, it is perhaps not implausible therefore to detect in such attitudes its continuing influence, since such canvases are most naturally read as the portrayal of necessary antitheses that need to be worked through or complemented by the other rather than confrontation with the wholly negative. So, of his four main periods (the semi-representational; colour in the ascendant; the primacy of form; and the biomorphic), it is only the middle two that seem to have retained not only a directional quality to reality but also the possibility that evil is both deep-seated and not easily conquered.

This is perhaps the most obvious difference between Klee and the other two painters, inasmuch as we are left in no doubt by some of his canvases that not only is sadness, suffering, or evil present but also that they admit of no obvious resolution.[262] Much of this was

[258] For a similar interpretation of *Composition VII*, Messer, ibid. 92–3.

[259] *Sky Blue* of 1940 is a good example: illustrated in H. Düchting, *Kandinksy* (Cologne: Taschen, 1991), 78.

[260] Quoted in Whitford, *Kandinsky: Watercolours*, 86.

[261] For the suggestion that this later development along with Arp's similar interest comes via Boehme, cf. H. Watts, 'Arp, Kandinsky and the Legacy of Jacob Böhme', in Tuchman, *The Spiritual in Art*, 239–55.

[262] If *Sad Flowers* and *Cross and Spiral Blossoms* leave little room for hope, the vegetation against which *Tropical Twilight with the Owl* is set perhaps offers a more optimistic image: for illustrations, E.-G. Güse (ed.), *Paul Klee: Dialogue with Nature* (Munich: Prestel, 1991), 63, 103, 81. For an example of evil, *Walpurgis Night*, intensified of course by its use of the normally heavenly blue: illustrated in D. Hall, *Klee*, 2nd edn. (London: Phaidon, 1992), 107.

only achieved through anthropomorphizing nature, and so one might complain of the *naïveté* of some of the results. But it is important to note that this was deliberate on Klee's part.[263] Almost 10 per cent of his work consists of studies of nature, and, while he was perfectly capable of careful, realistic studies, his aim was to highlight both the close interrelationship of humanity and nature and the inevitability of suffering also in the non-human world. At the other extreme lie his paintings of unity in colour and form. More elaborately patterned than those of Mondrian, they found their inspiration in Klee's delight in gardens and in the landscape and light of southern Europe and north Africa.[264] At one point Klee was even led to declare: 'colour and I are one'.[265] The religious content of such work is well indicated by one commentator who speaks of the 'animistic power' of his botanical images and of 'an almost sacramental magic' to be found in his portrayal of nature as a whole.[266]

Of the extent of Klee's religious commitment there can in fact be no doubt. While he describes himself as disbelieving in God as a child, there are quite a number of indicators in the *Diaries* of him wrestling towards a real religious faith, including trying to pray for his adopted country's enemy, England.[267] There are also various references to the impact of religion on his art.[268] At one point in their lives, while both were teaching at the Bauhaus, he lived next door to Kandinsky, and Kandinsky is clearly someone whose art he admired. Nevertheless, unlike Kandinsky, he seemed soon to have become completely disenchanted with the details of Theosophy.[269]

[263] Hall speaks of 'a childlike simplicity that often deceives the unwary into thinking Klee a lightweight artist': ibid. 13.

[264] A visit to Tunisia in 1914 was quite decisive, and this was reinforced by visits later to Sicily and Egypt. For some examples of their impact, note illustrations in Hall, ibid. 83, 85, and 103. The first two typify Klee's practice of doubling or halving layers of colour either side of a vertical.

[265] *Diaries of Paul Klee, 1898–1918* (Berkeley, Calif.: University of California Press, 1964), no. 9260.

[266] Rosenblum, *Modern Painting*, 155, 152.

[267] For childhood disbelief, no. 11; for struggle, nos. 99, 176; for praying for enemies, no. 1098.

[268] He describes the aim of the artist as being to 'try to relate myself to God': *Diaries*, no. 1008. Also significant are the words used as an epitaph on his tombstone: 'I am as much at home with the dead as with those beings not yet born. A little closer to the heart of creation than is usual. And yet not as close as I would wish' (quoted in *Diaries*, p. 419).

[269] Note e.g. his dismissive comments in the *Diaries*, nos. 1088, 1105.

That, however, does not mean that he did not continue to share many of its presuppositions, including its holistic vision. The question, therefore, arises whether he succeeded any better at integrating acceptance of the reality of evil and suffering.

What in general we appear to find is two types of painting offering quite different messages, one his acceptance of the inevitability of suffering and the other his confidence in the ultimate integration of everything that takes place within a unifying divine purpose. The achievement of Kandinsky was to indicate tension with evil and suffering and its potential resolution within the same canvas, whereas only occasionally does this happen with Klee in his earlier work.[270] However, the concluding years of his life were marked by personal suffering, as he slowly died of an incurable illness (the rare condition of scleroderma) and, although the result is often simply an increased reference to the more negative side of creation, some of his paintings do indeed succeed in focusing on just such an integration.[271] From this period his angel paintings are particularly poignant. Not only do angels cease to be immune from suffering, but also Jacob wrestling with the angel becomes one of his last images.[272] In its original biblical context that wrestling marked an encounter with God, and for Klee at the end it seems that suffering was part of the way towards just such an encounter. So, of the three artists whom we have discussed, it can perhaps be claimed that it is Klee who is closest to a view of reality that allows suffering its full weight before making any attempt at integration in his art, though it would also be important to note that much of his art seems concerned to refuse any such integration: the tragic is thus presented as having carried the day.[273]

---

[270] This might be the implication of the luxuriant growth in *Botanical Theatre*, despite the cactus hands held up in horror: Hall, *Klee*, 67. Elsewhere, otherwise lyrical pictures are sometimes punctuated by hints of negativity, such as a door leading elsewhere or a human being facing ambiguously both towards joy and sorrow: for examples, ibid. 71, 75.

[271] Will Grohmann offers just such an interpretation of one of his very last paintings *Captive*, where blue and the symbolism of the cross may well have been used to refuse finality to death: *Klee* (New York: Abrams, 1985 edn.), 126–7.

[272] For three illustrations and some commentary, J.-L. Ferrier, *Paul Klee* (Paris: Terrail, 1998), 194–7.

[273] For Walter Benjamin's change of mind (from negative to positive in interpreting one of Klee's angels, the *Angelus Novus* of 1920), M. Roskill, *Klee,*

Mondrian, Kandinsky, and Klee can thus all rightly be regarded as religious painters, despite their common rejection of explicit Christian symbolism in their mature work. Not only that, they can also be seen to be wrestling with one of the major issues of natural theology, and each offering his own characteristic 'solution' or 'solutions', since much would seem to depend on what period of their artistic output one is considering. Mondrian seeks solace in an underlying balance of opposites that becomes a more creative or dynamic tension as he grows older. Kandinsky is more aware of the reality of evil, but he is still reluctant to concede to evil any final or definitive status, and so this is why his canvases are so often full of movement, and of a movement that can even stretch beyond the picture frame itself. Finally, with Klee one encounters someone much more willing to concede the tragic dimension of suffering, and it is by no means always integrated into some overall victory for the good. Some readers will prefer one approach, others another. I do not intend to arbitrate here. My aim has been a more limited one, to illustrate how even complex theological issues can be pursued through the visual and not just in words. God engages humanity in the issues that affect them most deeply in mediated, reflective visual experience, no less than in story or in situations totally divorced from sacramental presence, such as the philosopher's study.

Conclusion

I began this chapter by drawing attention to some of the parallels that exist between the history of theology and the history of art. Both in the twentieth century experienced a crisis in the use of their symbols. Like theology itself, art was faced with a challenge that made the more literal, representational theories of the past impossible. But unlike much theology, art saw this as a liberation. So, for instance, Klee could declare that 'photography was invented at the right moment as a warning against materialistic vision'.[274] The result was a new interest in the potential of colour and form, now

Kandinsky, and the Thought of their Time (Chicago: University of Illinois Press, 1992), 162.

[274] *Diaries*, no. 677.

acting on their own, to make a religious point. Not only did the two most important precursors of modern art, Cézanne and van Gogh, go down this path, three of the best-known European artists of the twentieth century followed a similar direction. So, in considering the nature of twentieth-century art, it is important not to be dismissive of its spiritual content.

What in effect they sought was a new form of natural theology, where claims about the spiritual nature of the world could be made through form and colour. As a matter of historical fact, such an approach was adopted partly as a consequence of disillusion with Christianity and partly through enthusiasm for the potential offered by a new and somewhat bizarre version of Neoplatonism. But such a genesis should not mislead us into supposing that the truth claims embodied in such art must necessarily be closely tied either to Theosophy or indeed to some other objectionable form of Neo-platonism.[275] On the contrary, they are, as I have tried to show, in fact quite amenable to independent assessment. New and powerful forms of natural theology have been developing throughout the twentieth century without either philosophers or theologians having given them the attention they deserve.[276]

But also present in earlier centuries, as we noted, was a more straightforward exploration in art of how God is experienced sacramentally through nature. In the course of the earlier part of this chapter I tried to indicate how the various forms of such experience might be assessed and their possible interrelations with one another, as well as the degree to which antecedent belief might sometimes have helped to shape the experience. No one can deny

[275] In *The Rhetoric of Purity* (Cambridge: Cambridge University Press, 1991), M. A. Cheetman presents Mondrian and Kandinsky as engaging directly with the Platonic challenge to the arts, and in consequence producing a new totalitarian form of absolutism, with Klee offering an appropriate subjectivist, non-transcendent alternative. I disagree with his analysis of Klee, but more importantly what Cheetham ignores is that, however objectionable some of their views may be have been (e.g. Mondrian on women), subjectivist positions can be potentially no less dogmatic and destructive in their pragmatism. Are comparisons with Hitler really fair or appropriate? e.g. 130, 135, 137.

[276] Nor should it be forgotten that some of these issues could also be explored through the ordinary 'secular' literature of our time. For an intriguing detailed description from a contemporary novelist of an immanent experience of God mediated through nature: S. Faulks, *Birdsong* (London: Vintage, 1994), 363, cf. 390.

the complicated character of the last issue, but, as I warned, in numerous other areas of human life there is the same mix, and yet no temptation to say that it is all just a matter of projection. In the chapter that follows (on the sanctity of place) that mixture becomes so prominent that some theologians are tempted to retreat altogether, and say that in such contexts only people and not places can be viewed as sacramental. That seems to me a mistake. What people say and do exhibits no less complexity. The excitement of place, as with the natural world, is of a God valuing more than the simply human, and instead using the material, even where decisively shaped by human beings, to tell us something of himself and thereby draw us more deeply into his presence.

4

Placement and Pilgrimage

Dislocation and Relocation

IN the previous chapter I used landscape painting as a way of illustrating how the natural world can function sacramentally. It is not that God speaks only in one way through the natural order but that significantly different types of experience tend to come to prominence in different epochs. In this, though, religion is no different from the rest of human thought. Some conditioning of expectation is inevitable, but that does not mean that there is no objective correlate any more than is the case in our experience of one another, in the workings of science, or in the perception of moral values. Here, however, as I turn to place, it might be thought that the parallel can no longer be sustained. At least with the landscape, it may be suggested, the focus was still on what could plausibly be seen as a divine creation whereas in this case, and even more so in the subsequent discussion of buildings, what we have are purely human artefacts. One possible response would be to appeal once more to the landscape, and note the way in which religious placement or building has traditionally identified with certain natural features such as mountains, rivers, and caves. But that would be to sidetrack us from the larger issue, the question of what happens when human imprints are imposed irrespective of unusual natural features.

Places can of course be given value for a multitude of different reasons. Sometimes the grounds are domestic (key family events), sometimes national (historical landmarks), and sometimes explicitly religious (where a couple were married, the hermitage of a great saint, the site of Christ's tomb, and so forth). Once again the temptation is, perhaps inevitably, to narrow the focus almost immediately onto the most obviously religious instances. But in my view that would be a serious mistake, for thereby no account can be taken of the possibility that any and every place that has a human imprint on it may actually have the potential to function sacramentally.

What makes the difference, though, is not the human being as such but whether God can be experienced in speaking either through the place as found or else as it has now been contexualized.[1] To speak thus, though, will be for some already to go in quite the wrong direction. To value place in its own right, it will be said, entails losing Christian theology's own distinctive voice and perhaps even coming close to idolatry: giving unconditional value to something other than God. So far from offering veridical experience of God, it is then seen as essentially blasphemous to view place in this way. With the stakes so high, it is impossible to proceed further without attempting some answer to this objection.

Cherishing Place, and Idolatry

The worry is a common one, particularly in Protestant theology. At most it is people who make places sacred, we are told, not the sites themselves.[2] In effect the previous chapter challenged that view by talking of landscape as itself already potentially sacramental. The situation envisaged here, however, might be thought to be essentially different, inasmuch as human beings are now directly involved, and so to prioritize place above the people who live or work there might well be held to violate a proper scheme of value. I want to attempt a two-stage answer, first by considering biblical attitudes in their own right and then the more nuanced position that I believe can be justified not only from Scripture but also from the wider empirical realities that confront us.

There is no shortage of biblical scholars willing to contrast New Testament attitudes with Old. We are told, for example, that in Paul's theology 'the people of Israel living in the land had been

[1] In the latter case human beings have, of course, made a contribution, but this does not necessarily entail that it is how they envisaged the place that now matters. The construction may have had one end in view, and its experienced impact be of quite a different order.

[2] For a strong presentation of such a point of view, S. White, 'The Theology of Sacred Space', in D. Brown and A. Loades (eds.), *The Sense of the Sacramental* (London: SPCK, 1995), 31–43. She is supported by Rowan Williams in *Open to Judgement* (London: Darton, Longman & Todd, 1994), 101–4. Too recent to be discussed here, a more moderate version of the same position is to be found in J. Inge, *A Christian Theology of Place* (London: Ashgate, 2003).

replaced by a universal community which has no special attachment',[3] while in respect of the Gospels it could be argued that their various geographical reference points are offered simply as indicators of historicity rather than as indispensable constituent elements in the significance of what occurred. Certainly, there is much in the New Testament to suggest a new orientation. The book of Revelation provides an image of the new Jerusalem that makes no attempt to relate it to the city's present earthly location and reality. While it would be going too far to talk of it as now a purely spiritualized concept, the city has in effect acquired a material existence that encompasses all reality rather than one tied to any specifics of time and place. Again, although Paul not only shows concern for his fellow Christians in Jerusalem but also continues to give a unique and privileged role to Jews in the Christian dispensation,[4] significantly nowhere in his surviving corpus does this extend to valuing the land of Israel or the city of Jerusalem as such. So there would seem to be much to be said for taking St John as our cue, and thus Christ's words in that Gospel to the woman of Samaria: 'Woman, believe me, the hour is coming when neither on this mountain nor in Jerusalem will you worship the Father . . . But the hour is coming, and now is, when the true worshippers will worship the Father in spirit and truth.'[5] It is thus possible to present the strong focus on land and city in the Old Testament as merely transitional to a wider vision, indeed as now an inhibiter to peace and mutual tolerance.[6]

But there is something to be said on the other side. For a start, what needs to be questioned in respect of the Hebrew Scriptures is how far identification with land and city are really merely incidental

[3] W. D. Davies, *The Gospel and the Land: Early Christianity and Jewish Territorial Doctrine* (Berkeley: University of California Press, 1974), 182. Elsewhere he speaks of the gospel demanding 'a breaking out of its territorial chrysalis' (336). For a fuller treatment of Old Testament attitudes by the same author, *The Territorial Dimension of Judaism* (Minneapolis: Fortress Press, 1991).

[4] 1 Cor. 16: 1–4; Rom. 9–11. In the latter passage, Gentiles are compared to a wild olive shoot grafted onto the original tree (11: 17–18).

[5] John 4: 21, 23 (RSV). For a discussion of the passage and a critique of John's attitude to place, T. D. Swanson, 'To Prepare a Place: Johannine Christianity and the Collapse of Ethnic Territory', *Journal of the American Academy of Religion* 62 (1994), 241–63.

[6] One thinks here of the biblical justification so often given for the 'settlements' in the occupied territories of Palestine.

to more fundamental theological concerns that could legitimately sweep away such identification once it had fulfilled its interim purpose. On that way of thinking geography becomes purely instrumental as an aid in providing a specific forum for divine action in shaping the community's consciousness. But, as a number of Old Testament scholars have observed, the image of land and city is much more important than that. Deep attachment is encouraged, with possession of the land seen as a proper aim both in the Exodus and in the longing for return from Exile. Indeed, some of the best-known phrases in the Bible display the same affectionate but exaggerated description of the homeland that so often characterizes such love among other peoples: 'a land flowing with milk and honey', for example, or the numerous eulogies of Mount Zion despite its relatively small size.[7] What is important in all of this is the way in which the biblical writers are wrestling with the question of how God's blessing will be realized within the specificity of a particular time and place. That is one reason why the Hebrew notion of peace refuses to confine the word to purely internal or interpersonal relations but also insists on the totality of a changed environment.[8] One recent rich study of the issue concludes that to put the main Old Testament emphasis on divine action in history or on emancipation is radically to misrepresent biblical categories: 'the central problem is not emancipation but *rootage*, not meaning but *belonging*, not separation from community but *location* within it, not isolation from others but *placement*'.[9]

With the New Testament there is certainly a change of emphasis but there is a danger of interpretations being skewed if insufficient attention is given to the Gospels' witness. The incarnation of course occurred in a specific time and place, but since for it to occur at all this was essential, perhaps less can be made of this fact than

[7] For former, e.g. Exod. 3: 8; Deut. 8: 7–9. The image is probably intended to suggest more than enough of basics (milk) and of luxuries (honey). For the latter, e.g. Ps. 132: 13 or the rather strange Ps. 133: 3 where it is associated with a very large mountain roughly eight times its height (Mt. Hermon).

[8] *Shalom* includes material well-being and good relations with animals (Lev. 26: 6). Inevitably, this wider conception helped to broaden the rather narrower sense implicit in its Greek equivalent, *eirene*. So, for instance, in the Septuagint doctors are portrayed as aiming at 'peace' (Ecclus. 38: 8).

[9] W. Brueggemann, *The Land: Place as Gift, Promise, and Challenge in Biblical Faith*, 2nd edn. (Minneapolis: Fortress, 2002), 197–201 esp. 199–200 (italics in original).

theologians sometimes suppose. But what is interesting is that the historical Jesus clearly did have a vision that took land and city seriously. Choosing twelve disciples shows a real engagement with the traditions of Jacob and his twelve sons who were the eponymous founders of the twelve tribes of Israel, each of whom (with the exception of Levi) were of course identified with specific areas of the land.[10] Again, all the Gospels are agreed not only about Jesus' observation of the Jerusalem feasts but also that his own sense of his mission called him to make it culminate in that city. It is surely also significant that it is the city that is apostrophized when he weeps over Jerusalem, and thus only indirectly its people.[11]

If the passage from John already quoted represents one type of response to the new significance now found in Jesus' life, death, and resurrection, it is important to note that it is not the only one. Though rather irritating for the historian, one major reason why the various accounts of the resurrection appearances cannot easily be reconciled is precisely because Matthew and Luke subordinate historical fact to an engagement with symbolic geography. Luke appears to place the first appearances in Jerusalem in order to stress continuity of the old faith and its values with the new, while Matthew provides a Galilean setting not to discount Jerusalem but in order to pick up on the resonances of this more mixed area as 'Galilee of the Gentiles'.[12] None of this is to deny that the great bulk of New Testament thought pulls in a rather different direction, but it is to challenge whether it all does so. Moreover, given that it is an inheritance written against the backdrop of expectation of the imminent end of the world, it is also to question whether the same indifference would have been continued into a quite different situation.

---

[10] Gen. 49; Matt. 19: 28. To keep the number in possession of the land at twelve, the tribe of Joseph was conventionally divided into two: Ephraim and Mannaseh. In actual fact the number of tribes probably varied. The list in Deut. 33 has eleven and that in Judg. 5 only ten. That the ideal, however, remained twelve is suggested by passages such as Ezek. 48.

[11] Matt. 23: 37–9.

[12] For a brief statement of Matthew's designs, J. C. Fenton, *Saint Matthew* (Harmonsdworth: Penguin, 1963), 452. In my view he deduces non-historicity too quickly since theological motives behind Luke's geography also raises such questions: cf. H. Conzelmann, *The Theology of Saint Luke* (London: Faber & Faber, 1969), 73–94. Perhaps there were appearances in both places, the precise location of which can no longer be determined.

Some willing to concede this much may, though, still have profound reservations. Valuing place in its own right will still be seen as a form of idolatry that inevitably undercuts the sharpness of any possible theological critique of this world's forms and institutions. A number of recent publications in England may be used to illustrate this worry and also a methodology quite different from my own. One highly influential discussion that wants to lay claim to the inheritance of Augustine draws a stark contrast between the corrupt *polis* of Aristotle and actual cities and their sociologies with the Christian idea of the *civitas* and its sociology.[13] Another that seems initially to engage with the factual realities of city life in modern Britain quickly turns to presentation of a contrasted ideal that is worked out on the basis of eucharistic theology.[14] The third and most biblically based succeeds best at integrating empirical realities and its own searing critique, but even here what one misses amidst all the compassion is any sense that what the Christian says might have to be significantly modified in the light of what is encountered.[15] That is to say, although there is much in these writers that I would gladly endorse, what is missing, I believe, is full recognition of the fact that the two realities confronting one another are really alike, in being at one and the same time both divine and flawed. So it is not that sacred and secular need to be sharply juxtaposed as 'revelation' on the one hand and as 'sin' on the other, but rather that each (though to different degrees) alike to be acknowledged as existing on both sides of the equation.

Take the 'secular' side first. It is surely worth asking whether the embodied character given in creation to human beings by God does not make attachment to place in some sense natural to them, and

[13] J. Milbank, *Theology and Social Theory* (Oxford: Blackwell, 1990), e.g. 335–6, 380–2.

[14] G. Ward, *Cities of God* (London: Routledge, 2000). In theory Ward's position should have come close to my own since he ends Part I by declaring that 'an adequate Christian response . . . risks encounter, knowing that its own voice is never pure, never innocent' (70). But he never returns to specifics in the way one might have anticipated.

[15] T. J. Gorringe, *A Theology of the Built Environment* (Cambridge: Cambridge University Press, 2002). There is one key chapter, 'But is it art?' (193–221), which seeks to address the kind of issues I am concerned with in this chapter. Otherwise, however, the focus is almost entirely ethical and political (for occasional exceptions, e.g. 31, 39–40, 83–4).

indeed one might use the notion of 'home' in support. Admittedly, it is possible for some human beings to remain rootless throughout their lives. More often than not, however, this state appears to have been forced upon them rather than deliberately chosen, as can be seen from the way in which in so many such cases it turns out to be in reaction against the ugliness or unpleasantness of the environment in which they have grown up (poor housing, dysfunctional families, and so forth). The exceptions might then be argued not to disprove the key role of place in providing adequate human and religious identity but rather there to alert us to the need for caution in explicating how this works out. For example, a sparkling new council estate can sometimes prove far more destructive of human identity than any street of run-down slum tenements,[16] or again what appears like a soulless setting when traversed on foot could well be viewed quite differently if the related buildings that give identity are easily accessible by car.[17] Even the most monotonous of terrain can become familiar and loved, as Kathleen Norris has attempted to demonstrate in one of her books on Dakota.[18] So in asking questions about the sacramentality of place we must take care not to project our own prejudices. Much will depend on specific contexts, and the religious issue must not be confused with the aesthetic.[19]

None the less, they may be connected. One recent study of how the built environment might engage us moves directly from landscape to architecture. Some landscape painters, unlike others, attempt to draw us into the scene depicted, and this is offered as a model for the potentially 'participatory environment' of the

[16] One of the discoveries of post-war reconstruction was the realization that social problems were sometimes actually worsened as people moved out from close-knit, inner-city slums in cities such as Liverpool and Glasgow to outlying new council estates (e.g. Kirkby in Liverpool, Castlemilk in Glasgow).

[17] Certainly true of Los Angeles. For the point developed, Y.-F. Tuan, *Topophilia* (New York: Columbia University Press, 1990), 150–244 esp. 214.

[18] K. Norris, *Dakota: A Spiritual Geography* (Boston: Houghton Mifflin, 1993). Quoting St Hilary that 'everything that seems empty is full of the angels of God', she goes on to remark: 'The magnificent sky above the Plains sometimes seems to sing this truth; angels seem possible in the wind-filled expanse' (11). All depends, she suggests, on accepting the landscape on its own terms: cf. 145–53.

[19] Obviously there is sometimes overlap, but that means the need for great care in analysing how the experience is described.

architect.[20] While the power of the rectilinear is accepted, more weight is in the end given to the anticipatory prospect implied in the curve. A similar position is taken by another art-historian who wants to argue for 'natural symbolism' in landscape painting.[21] The use of 'prospect' and 'refuge' reflect our basic biological origins. If so, the religious believer might also see in this the hand of God, since it means that certain ways of mediating a relationship will come naturally to humanity: refuge suggesting presence and care, the distant prospect the possibility of a 'beyond' that invites further exploration.

The very character of such experiences would seem to suggest a more than purely instrumental value, in creating community for example. For it is through the valuing of place in and for itself that such a drawing closer to God becomes possible, whether this be detected in a sense of divine immanence or in a pulling beyond the specific context, into transcendence. Some specific examples will be given in due course, but first one potential source of confusion needs to be addressed, and that is the false assumption that such valuing, if for its own sake, is necessarily absolute and unconditional and therefore a form of idolatry. The issue is well illustrated by what seems to me the false opposition often drawn between sinful human constructions of place and the religious and ethical communitarian values that allegedly exist alongside but completely independent of them. Matters are just not that simple. Splendid churches, great palaces and their gardens, even whole cities that may well turn out to have been largely built on the backs of the poor can still speak to us of God and of positive social values, just as the reverse is also sometimes so: the slum or shanty town fills us only with horror, even though the generosity and resilience of its inhabitants warm our hearts. The temptation is to try to resolve the conflict by refusing any value to the constructed place except in so far as it

---

[20] A. Berleant, *Art and Engagement* (Philadelphia: Temple University Press, 1991). Cole is given as an example of an artist who adopts 'contemplative disinterestedness' with 'no effort to extend the landscape beyond the painting to the space of the observer' (65). For the application of the contrast to architecture: 76–104.

[21] J. Appleton, *The Symbolism of Habitat* (Seattle: University of Washington Press, 1990). Despite his talk of 'mechanisms of survival behaviour' (22) he accepts that these can be experienced religiously, for example when the refuge is a church (88–92), or the horizon behind a crucifixion (37).

contributes to predetermined ethical criteria. But human experience does not work quite like that. The poor can come to love their city and its public buildings, and even find God in them, even when they are fully aware of the mixed or wholly corrupt motives that lay behind the desire of their rulers to erect them. The political and the aesthetic slide into the religious, and are no worse for that. This is not to discount the ethical, and certainly not to suggest that it can never overrule such considerations. It is merely to observe that other values also come into play, and need to be given due weight, even where the 'sinful' source of such constructions seems self-evident. That is precisely why in what follows I take imperial Rome as one of my examples.

Scripture itself in any case exhibits similar ambiguities. Consider the very words employed. If metaphors such as 'king' and 'husband' can break free of the negative overtones they already bore in the culture of the time to speak to us of God, so surely too can places and buildings with their equally ambiguous history.[22] Meaning is thus not just a function of what human beings have done but also of the symbolic potential inherent in the artefacts themselves. Taking place seriously, therefore, must mean conceding that places too, like words, can have independent revelatory power despite all the ambiguities both share. As the history of some famous works of literature can remind us, words are often at their most powerful when they cease to be closely aligned with the original intentions of specific authors.[23] Much the same applies to Scripture. Part of its power lies precisely in the ability it has to acquire new meanings for guiding the community of faith, as fresh challenges arise over the course of the centuries.[24]

[22] In the Hebrew Scriptures both terms are used positively of God (e.g. Ps. 47: 7, Jer. 31: 32), and yet the history of the monarchy during the same period is overwhelmingly negative, while the term 'husband' (*baal*) has unpleasant overtones of lordship.

[23] This is not to deny the legitimacy of questions of authorial intention, only to observe that literature and literary figures can at times acquire a life of their own. Think, for instance, of the transformations undergone by Ulysses, or the way in which Vergil's *Fourth Eclogue* was for long read as a messianic prophecy fulfilled in Christ.

[24] How this happens is considered in detail in my two volumes: *Tradition and Imagination: Revelation and Change* (Oxford: Oxford University Press, 1999) and *Discipleship and Imagination: Christian Tradition and Truth* (Oxford: Oxford University Press, 2000).

So potentially then also with places. It is their capacity to develop a symbolic and imaginative reality that is larger than the construction of specific individuals that keeps their power alive. Theoretically, such power could lead to the idolatry of place, but there is no necessity that this should be so. It is not the valuing of place in its own right that is in itself the problem but how this is balanced against other potentially competing values. Nor, more importantly, is it a problem simply for the 'secular' city, it is equally one for Scripture itself. As a subsequent chapter will explore in more detail, the Book of Deuteronomy is so worried by the identification of God with the Temple that it develops an alternative, more transcendent theology. But, despite this, it is no less at fault in its exclusiveness towards the land. Although, fortunately, unlikely ever to have been what historically happened, it does envisage God requiring the Israelites to exterminate the whole of the native population.[25] Again, narrow vindictiveness is displayed against some of the lands that have mistreated Israel, such as Edom and Nineveh, while even Isaiah's vision of all peoples finding their good in Jerusalem is spoiled by stress on their subservient role.[26] So we need to reckon with a flawed and divine view of place in the Bible not less than in ordinary human experience.

Fortunately, previous generations of Christians were fully alive to such dangers. While valuing place in its own right, two major devices were commonly employed to undermine any unqualified absolute claim, in particular for where they now lived: setting it against a place elsewhere which was treated as a symbolic standard, and actually travelling to another place to see for themselves an alternative and better reality. The first notion involves the idea of symbolic geography, the second pilgrimage. Both, I believe, still have much to teach us. So in the penultimate part of this chapter I shall examine how Jerusalem was once accorded just such a symbolic role, while the chapter will end by considering how pilgrimage also functioned as a critique against absolutizing place. But I want to begin nearer to where so many of us now are, not in

[25] Deut. 20: 10–18 esp. 16–18; unlikely to be true, because Deuteronomy is commonly thought to be an 'idealized' vision of commitment that was written centuries later towards the end of the 7th c. BC during the reign of King Josiah. For absurd territorial pretensions from a writer in the same school, Josh. 1: 4.

[26] For hostility to Edom, Obadiah; to Nineveh, Nahum; but contrast Jonah. For Isaiah, e.g. 60: 10–16.

the idolatry of place but in the secularized home and city. Our own world is so different from the past that it is important to note how far we stand from the sacramental understanding that once prevailed. What I want to suggest is that, so far from decrying such past attitudes, there is much of value worth retrieving. Seeing God in our midst in home and city need not imply idolatry but rather the complex mix of divine presence and human sin that is the reality of our world. For most readers this may seem to take us rather far from the world of pilgrimage, but, as I shall indicate in due course, there are more overlaps than one might initially suppose.

Estrangement and Belonging: The City as Place of Encounter

Nowadays it is the idealized city of the prophets and still more so of the book of Revelation that is most likely to spring to the mind of contemporary Christians, if asked to reflect on biblical attitudes to the city.[27] After all, this is pictured in readings frequently heard in church, and also reflected in familiar hymns. As such the images provide a neat contrast to the dysfunctional city as it is now so often encountered. But a moment's reflection would, of course, remind us that the latter image is also not absent from the Scriptures. If the Tower of Babel is the most familiar version, the hostility of the opening chapters of Genesis in fact runs very much deeper. After murdering his brother Abel, it is Cain who builds the first city, while Abraham seems deliberately called out of a city in order to lead an alternative, itinerant life, and that seems confirmed by the implicit condemnation of Lot for returning once more to such a city lifestyle.[28] As the details of the story of Babel indicate, what worried the biblical writers was human arrogance and the way in which self-reliance was being substituted for dependence on God. The ideal city was, therefore, by contrast just such a city of faithful trust.

The trouble with applying that type of theology in the modern world is that it is too absolute, too unwilling to take account of more complex realities. Take the city of Jerusalem itself. Its present

---

[27] e.g. Isa. 60–2; Rev. 21.
[28] Gen. 4: 17; 11: 1–9; 12:1; 13: 8–13; cf. 2 Pet. 2: 6–10.

tragedies are not caused by a shortage of those willing to acknowledge dependence on God, but by that dependence inadequately contextualized. The different faith communities (even the different Christian denominations) live in isolation from one another, and so fail to appreciate the degree to which that divine dependence works through specific historical contexts and thus implicitly through their dependence on one other. So, for example, Jews treat the Wailing Wall as their most holy site, but often conveniently forget that it is a survival from the final and most splendid version of the Temple complex created by someone who was racially a non-Jew, Herod the Great.[29] Again, above is Islam's holiest site outside Arabia, but it only initially became so because of the value Muhammad himself placed on early Jewish traditions of what had occurred there.[30] Finally, Christians need to recall that their ancestors actually inhibited preservation of the Temple site while their own most holy building was to need help from Muslims, a fact that continues to this day.[31] While, therefore, in the following section attention will be given to Jerusalem as symbolic ideal, here I want to focus on the presence of the divine in more ambiguous situations, and that I believe means taking seriously how expression of this has been sought in religions other than Christianity. So in what immediately follows consideration will be given first to contemporary experiences of estrangement and then to that earlier, wider theological tradition, before finally seeing to what extent it might be recoverable in our own day.

Dislocation and the Modern City

One reason why I want to begin here rather than with the more obvious theological instances which I shall consider later in the

[29] It is unfortunate that the Greek version of the name for his race is commonly used (Idumaean), for that disguises his origins in the hated Edomites: cf. e.g. Obadiah, Jer. 49: 7–22; Ps. 137: 7.

[30] It is valued now, of course, because of it being the location of the Prophet's Night Journey, but one needs to ask the prior question of why Muhammad valued the site in the first place. For early developments, F. E. Peters, *Jerusalem* (Princeton: Princeton University Press, 1985), 176–214.

[31] Christians had treated the Temple area as a rubbish dump. Umar on conquering Jerusalem in 638 saved the Church of the Holy Sepulchre. To this day a Muslim holds its key, to prevent squabbling among rival Christian sects.

chapter is because this chimes well with my general strategy in this work of insisting that religion and theology have wrongly retreated from areas that were once also their domain. Looking at our contemporary context, though, the task of recovery may well seem an impossible one. Any potential for the built environment to speak of God, it will be said, has long since vanished amidst the noisy rush and fumes of traffic and buildings thrown up without any apparent regard for their relation to one another. London is itself a case in point. Post-war reconstruction was clearly necessary after the Blitz, and it is not that there is anything necessarily wrong with tall buildings or skyscrapers in themselves, but so often they lacked character and no attempt was made to integrate them into the wider site. Indeed the view from across the river at the new Tate Modern still leaves Wren's masterpiece, St Paul's Cathedral, set against soulless blocks in desperate need of demolition.[32] However, it is across the Atlantic that one can see such problems at their most acute.

This issue has recently been analysed in a best-seller that significantly bears the title, *The Geography of Nowhere*. The author identifies one key underlying cause of the problem in the long history of American individualism. Initially few towns imposed any regulations at all. Grids for subsequent development were arbitrarily divided into equal plots, irrespective of terrain or suitability of their use for one purpose rather than another.[33] Massive expansion therefore occurred without any thought of how parts related to the whole.[34] The introduction of the motor car then exacerbated the problem as such units now became arbitrarily related to one other solely on the basis of this mode of communication, with the death of public transport actually actively encouraged.[35] As might be expected, in answering such blight the need for a community

---

[32] The overshadowing of St Paul's by taller buildings was perhaps inevitable, but at least they might have had the character of some of the more interesting skyscrapers in cities such as New York or Chicago. Not all cities engaged in post-war reconstruction made the same mistake; contrast Leningrad, as it then was.

[33] J. H. Kunstler, *The Geography of Nowhere* (New York: Simon & Schuster, 1994), 29–37.

[34] Chicago is given as an example: ibid. 54–6. Between 1850 and 1900 the population grew from approx. 30,000 to 1,700, 000.

[35] Kunstler records the way in which the motor car was subsidized and the destruction of public transport actively sought: 85–112 esp. 90, 97, 99; 190–3.

focus (such as a proper city centre) is fully acknowledged, as is the
requirement that buildings need to be integrated into their streets,
private buildings no less than public.[36] Yet how far we have come
from past attitudes is well indicated by the fact that at no point does
the author see religion as making a potential contribution. Indeed,
his only theological reference is to the way in which the imagery of
the Garden of Eden actually intensified the problem, as individuals
sought their ideal home away from the city in country estates.[37]
Ironically, though, his final words echo a need for some sanctity to
place: 'we want to feel that we truly belong to a specific part of the
world'.[38]

The sense of rootlessness and isolation that modern cities can so
often evoke is perhaps nowhere expressed more powerfully than in
one of America's best-known painters of the twentieth century,
Edward Hopper (d. 1967). Hopper was, it seems, naturally inclined
to pessimism in any case, but, whatever the cause, his paintings do
allow the viewer to absorb to the full the terrible sense of loneliness
and desolation in much of America's street life.[39] Sometimes this is
achieved by setting a solitary human figure against a backdrop of
unyielding buildings, or else the latter threateningly on their own;
sometimes, as happens in some of his most famous works, by putting
several figures in the same scene, each failing to communicate with
the other.[40] Even the countryside is sometimes subjected to the same
treatment; gas stations become lonely, soulless places despite abut-
ting that potential hive of activity, the roadway. Hopper even treats a
country cottage in exactly the same way.[41] Perhaps, however, his
most memorable image is his Gothic mansion set on a hill now
cut off by a railway line, a home that once related but does so no

[36] Ibid. 249–50. For Portland's success in this respect, 200–2.

[37] An initial reference to Eden as the first colonists' ideal (ibid. 17–18) is
subsequently used as a linking theme to explore suburbia (39–57).

[38] Ibid. 275.

[39] Already 6 ft. tall at 12, his eventual height of 6 ft. 5 in. seems to have added to
his sense of isolation, and indeed is reflected in his portrayal of one tall building to
which he initially gave the title *Self-Portrait*: for illustration, G. Levin, *Hopper's
Places*, 2nd edn. (Berkeley: University of California Press, 1998), pp. vii–viii.

[40] For examples of the former (*Sunday* and *Early Sunday Morning*), Levin,
Hopper (Vaduz: Bonfini, 1994), 42, 43; for examples of the latter (*Summer Evening*
and *Nighthawks*), 66, 74, 81.

[41] For gas stations, ibid. 70–1; for the country cottage looking out of place on
the lonely road, *Solitude*, 85.

more.[42] Hopper had been brought up in a devout Baptist home, but, though he did sometimes paint churches, there are seldom any more signs of hope in them than in any other building about him.[43] Although Hopper's balance may be wrong, there is no denying that the contribution of churches is sometimes also negative, adding to, rather than diminishing, this sense of isolation.[44]

So it will not do for theologians to suggest that all that is required is a return to Christian notions of community. Congregations can be just as much shut in on themselves, and their buildings proclaim as much. Nor should we over-romanticize the role churches played in the past. Certainly, it can scarcely be denied that parish churches did eventually become a much-loved part of the landscape. None the less, this should not blind us to the reasons why some sites were chosen, and how the accompanying associations may well for many have corrupted attitudes to both building and Church. So, for example, in the north-east of England St Cuthbert (d. 687) is often represented as having purely spiritual motives for retreating to the island of Lindisfarne and subsequently to the still more remote, inner Farne, but the Northumbrian royal capital of Bambrough in fact lay nearby, and so it is impossible to discount the desire for political influence in the first move, if not in the second. Likewise, in the later Middle Ages the frequent closeness of the parish church to the local manor would seem to speak volumes.[45] Sometimes it was a case of the secular power seeking control, perhaps most conspicuously so in the case of the so-called family monasteries, but on other occasions there can no doubt that the desire came from the clergy themselves.[46] A somewhat different

[42] *House by the Railroad*, ibid. 36, 49. The image now strikes us as even more desolate thanks to Alfred Hitchcock's use of a related image in his 1960 film *Psycho*.

[43] For Baptist background, ibid. 7, 13. Only Mexican churches seem to have elicited a positive response: *Places*, nos. 39, 40. With Paris and North America matters were quite otherwise, *Places*, no. 45; ibid. 50–1.

[44] In Kunstler's home town churches blocked their walls off from the main thoroughfare which 'had become too abominable to connect with': ibid. 139.

[45] R. Morris, *Churches in the Landscape* (London: Phoenix, 1989), 248–52, cf. 232. The type of stone used in building England's most complete Saxon church at Brixworth has recently been used to argue for a royal connection: M. Aston, *Monasteries in the Landscape* (London: Tempus, 2000), 51.

[46] For an attempt to place such family-owned monasteries in a more positive light, reflecting the religious commitment of the nobility, P. Wormald, 'Bede, Beowulf and the Conversion of the Anglo-Saxon Aristocracy', in R. T. Farrell (ed.), *Bede and Anglo-Saxon England: British Archaeological Reports* 46 (1978), 32–95 esp. 57.

form of the pursuit of power was the utilization of the already existing authority of pagan cult, as evidenced by wells or groves, or through juxtaposition with the burial sites of Christian saints, their legends sometimes suitably expanded.[47] Again, in towns it is not always clear whether the presence of markets beside churches is largely coincidental or was positively fostered by the church to its own profit.[48]

Nor do monasteries exhibit a less ambiguous history. If to begin with the model of the desert was pursued and isolated places often chosen, and that pattern renewed by the Cistercians once earlier enthusiasms had waned, it is still the case that this often involved the displacement of peasantry and an excessive growth of wealth that needs to be balanced against the clearing of marshland and the increased productivity of the land that also resulted.[49] Again, the invention of the cloister may now suggest to us a marvellous haven of quiet and reflection, but by contrast with an earlier situation where monasteries were sometimes the nearest equivalent to towns in the area, and indeed called 'cities', this new idea must initially have suggested much more a turning in on themselves of the community without particular regard or concern for what lay beyond.[50] In saying all this my point is not to discount the positive value of the church or monastery as a focus, still less to suggest that 'only people count', but rather to reinforce in the mind of the reader a point I have already made, that ambiguity is inherent in all symbolism. If modern cities so often present images of estrangement and alienation, so too must at times the churches and monasteries of the past. The valuing of place has thus to be pursued in the face of ambiguity, not in retreat from it.

[47] For former, Morris, *Churches*, 46–92. One instance of the latter is the element in Welsh place-names *Merther* which came to mean 'place with remains of a saint'; so ibid. 103.

[48] Morris, though conceding the connection and also the existence of Sunday markets, doubts whether churches were actually responsible for their founding: ibid. 212–13.

[49] The founding of Witham Priory in Somerset in 1179, for example, involved the displacement of 150 peasants: Aston, *Monasteries*, 23, cf. 88. For Gerald of Wales's comment on the success of the Cistercians: 134; for urban speculation (by Reading Abbey): 107.

[50] Synods at Aachan in the early 9th c. encouraged the use of cloister, as did the widely disseminated St Gall plan: ibid. 64–6. For earlier use of the language of 'cities' (*civitates*), 54.

That such complexity was sometimes taken seriously in the past is well illustrated by eighteenth-century arguments over land 'improvement'. The tendency was for the country house to migrate into its own separate parkland carefully designed by the likes of Capability Brown, and for agricultural improvements and other changes to be imposed elsewhere on the estate.[51] Nowadays we tend to see the arguments on either side as purely practical, but they were in fact deeply theological and also in some ways even sacramental. Among those arguing for improvement was that familiar exponent of the argument from design, Archdeacon Paley, who, like Adam Smith, saw the possibility of a trickle-down effect, with apparent harm still producing overall good.[52] On the other side were ranged those who insisted that God had created a delicate and complex world of reciprocal balance and compensation that entailed corresponding duties on both sides. Elements of the latter argument can be found in Bishops Butler and Berkeley, many of the poets of the time including Wordsworth and Coleridge, and the novelist Jane Austen, not least in her *Mansfield Park*.[53] As William Cowper put it:

> Improvement too, the idol of the age,
> Is fed with many a victim. Lo! He comes,—
> The omnipotent magician, Brown appears.

But it is not just the poor who suffer, it is also the countryside itself:

> the grace
> Of hedge-row beauties numberless, square tower,
> Tall spire.[54]

It may be an unfashionable Tory argument, but the appeal to the unity of nature and society with house, church, and nature speaking as one is scarcely less a religious argument for all that. Not that it was just an argument, for many a writer, including Cowper, tried to

[51] For examples of the degree of destruction involved, including the new impractical church at Nuneham Courtenay, N. Everett, *The Tory View of Landscape* (New Haven: Yale University Press, 1994), 39–45, 53–8.

[52] Paley's famous argument from design was in effect political, given his contention that 'temporary distress' could generally be seen to yield great benefits: Everett, ibid. 34–5.

[53] For a key quotation from Butler, ibid. 13–15; for Jane Austen: 188–202.

[54] From *The Task*, Bks. III and I: W. M. Rossetti (ed.), *The Poetical Works of William Cowper* (London: Ward, Lock, n.d.), 120, 163.

illustrate how it also functioned as part of their experience of God within the world. Yet it is often thought that such experience is no longer recoverable in the changed conditions of modern living, and indeed Wordsworth portrays the London and Paris of his day as antithetical to such possibilities.[55] I am not so convinced. But before looking at the modern city, I want first to go back to the ancient world, and remind the reader of the extent to which homes and cities were once conceived of in essentially religious terms, and so as vehicles for opening human beings up to the possibility of experiencing the divine through them.

Home and City as Sacramental Realities

As noted earlier, the Bible exhibits a constant dualism in its attitude to home and city. For if on the one hand the first founder of a city is also presented as the first murderer and that suspicion intensified by the story of the Tower of Babel,[56] love of Jerusalem indicates a quite different attitude, as do the various formal rules for the city's foundation and land's holiness laid down elsewhere.[57] The square grid recommended for Jerusalem was in fact adopted in nineteenth-century Mormon planning.[58] In such detailed sacred regulations Jerusalem was by no means alone in the ancient world. There were similar expectations for Hindu towns based on mandalas prescribed in texts such as the *Mansara*,[59] while in China Confucianism sought to give value to the city in the face of Taoism's more negative attitudes. However, here I want to use attitudes in ancient Rome as my studied example. Roman religion is often caricatured as the most superficial in the ancient world. So, if it can be shown to have had deeply sacramental attitudes to home and city, a fortiori we might expect similar attitudes more generally in the ancient world.

[55] In the *Prelude*, Bks. 7–10, e.g. 8. 598–664.

[56] Gen. 4: 17; 11: 1–9. Oppression in Egypt is also linked to city building: Exod. 1: 8–14; 5: 5–21.

[57] For Jerusalem loved by God, e.g. Ps. 46: 4–5; 48: 8. For areas of increasing holiness as the Temple area is approached, Ezek. 42: 15–20; 45: 1–6.

[58] J. W. Reps, *Town Planning in Frontier America* (Columbia: University of Missouri Press, 1980), 282–90. As well as the influence of Ezekiel, that of Num. 35: 1–5 and Lev. 25: 29–34 should also be noted.

[59] Part of the 1st-c. BC *Silpa Shastra*. Pagan in Burma and Anghor Thom in Cambodia would be examples from the Middle Ages, and Jaipur in India from the 18th c.

Consider first its attitude to home. Although new possibilities opened by wealth on the one hand and pressures on space on the other began to force changes at the turn of the Christian era, the earlier design of the Roman house certainly constituted a powerful combination of rituals of power and religion. Entering through a narrow entrance, the *fauces* (literally, 'the jaws'), one passed through an open courtyard to enter the main room, the *tablinum*, where the head of the house would be waiting, already visible from the entrance in the distance. But the intervening courtyard (the *atrium*) was also normally the place of religious observance, with an altar to the domestic gods placed there. Secular power and religious piety were thus simultaneously on view, without any sharp distinction being drawn between them. It was also where in addition to daily offerings major rites of passage took place, such as the boy's assumption of the *toga virilis* or the girl's abandonment of her dolls on marriage.[60] The mixing of power and piety of course witnesses to the potential for corruption, but it also suggests with equal force that divine presence was seen as central to how the home was conceived. Hinduism perhaps provides the nearest modern equivalent to such dissolution of the boundaries between sacred and secular. Either a cupboard or a whole room is dedicated to the deities of the household.

Ancient Israel was by origin a nomadic community, and it tried in various ways to keep such traditions alive. It is therefore interesting to observe how far the home is treated as a locus of divine activity among nomadic communities of today. Native North Americans can still be found praying thus, as a new tepee is set up: 'Today is the day I put up my home. I leave you to the care of the four winds . . . You, our Maker, direct us whether it be good or bad; it is your will. Help us to think of you every day we live in this lodge; guard us in our sleep; wake us in the morning with clear minds for the day, and keep harm from us.'[61] Further north, and we find the Inuit treating their igloos as a sort of microcosm of the larger world. The domed roof is treated as the sky, the ice window

---

[60] For more detail and discussion of the role art also played, J. R. Clarke, *The Houses of Roman Italy, 100 BC–AD 250: Ritual, Space and Decoration* (Berkeley, Calif.: University of California Press, 1991), esp. 1–29.

[61] Part of a Plains Cree prayer, quoted in D. Pearson, *Earth to Spirit: In Search of Natural Architecture* (London: Gala, 2000), 48.

as the sun, and the door as the moon,[62] and similar notions are to be found spread throughout the world.[63] Presumably, by implication the imagery is intended to evoke a blessing from the Creator on a world that is seen as deliberately modelled on his own creation. Again, to note one last variant on the same idea, the traditional Hejazi house in Arabia is expected to parallel the perfection of the highest summit of God's creation and so the home's constituent parts are identified as corresponding to parts of the human body and therefore named accordingly.[64]

Returning once more to Rome, one finds the people's attitude to their city not dissimilar, which is all the more surprising given the fact that by the beginning of the Christian era it had come to rival the size of many a modern conurbation, at approximately one million inhabitants. Acceptance of a sacramental character is well evidenced by the Roman notion of each city having its own characteristic *pomerium*. This was used to defined the sacred bounds of Rome, as of other towns. It was, however, by no means equivalent to any city's actual size or even to what was contained by its walls. However strongly an original mythical ploughing of those limits by Romulus was postulated for Rome itself, the way in which the extent of *pomerium* was periodically adjusted during historical times does suggest something rather more: a religious concept in practice and not just in theory.[65] Only within those bounds could certain functions be performed such as auguries or formal political discussion, while, significantly given Rome's reputation, questions of war were banished to the other side of the divide, the one exception being the actual day of a victor's triumph.[66] Elements of cosmic symbolism were also present in the

[62] So C. Humphrey and P. Vitebsky, *Sacred Architecture* (Boston: Little, Brown, 1997), 41. Intriguingly, also to be found is the variant I mention later, with the igloo as a whole treated as a womb and its entrance as the vagina.

[63] For some native American and Guinea examples, A. Lawlor, *The Temple in the House* (New York: Putman, 1994), 46–7.

[64] Further details in H. A. S. Jomah, 'The Traditional Hejazi House as a Macrocosm', in E. Lyle's *Sacred Architecture* (Edinburgh: Edinburgh University Press, 1992), 151–68.

[65] By Vespasian's reign the area was more than double what it had been at the beginning of the century (from 325 hectares to 745): M. Beard, J. North, and S. Price, *Religions of Rome* (Cambridge: Cambridge University Press, 1998), i. 177–81.

[66] Ibid. i. 179.

arrangements, and in this it parallels the often-forgotten earlier meanings of 'temple' that link heaven and earth, the word originally meaning both an area of the heavens and a corresponding place on earth.[67]

There thus seems little doubt that for the ancient Roman religion lay at the heart of communal dwelling, and indeed one commentator plays with the possibility that the nearest parallel to the Church was in fact the city itself.[68] Even so this is still quite different from supposing that even the complete *pomerium* was experienced in religious terms, far less the city as a whole. Much more likely is a series of distinct points, including the home at one extreme and the acropolis or its equivalent at the other. So, for example, although Aristotle found aesthetic pleasure in the regular streets of planned Greek colonies, the way in which houses generally in the Greek world turned in on themselves must have made them essentially uninviting to the population at large, while in a city as large of Republican Rome with its noisy, narrow, unpaved thoroughfares there must inevitably have been a certain trepidation before setting forth.[69] Indeed, it appears that by the first century BC many of its temples were shabby through neglect, while ostentatious private wealth was also visible at the other extreme.[70] Although some attempt at improvement had been made under Sulla and Julius Caesar, the city remained basically a number of islands of significant buildings without any overall sense of unity, and so perhaps not hugely different from the modern city and its besetting problems.[71]

It was the achievement of Augustus that he changed all that. Caesar had already banned traffic during the day. Augustus reorganized the fire-brigade and made it more of a local, district

[67] Ibid. ii. 86–7, 94. As well as a building, *templum* could indicate both an area of the heavens where signs of the gods were present and a place suitable for taking auguries (not necessarily the same as the building's sacred enclosure).

[68] C. Sourvinou-Inwood, 'What is *Polis* Religion?' in O. Murray and S. Price (eds.), *The Greek City from Homer to Alexander* (Oxford: Clarendon Press, 1990), 295–322 esp. 302.

[69] For Aristotle, *Politics*, VII. 10. 4. For a general discussion of planned Greek cities and the privacy of the home, M. Jameson, 'Private Space and the Greek City', in Murray and Price, *The Greek City*, 171–95 esp. 176–7, 195.

[70] Diane Favro in her book *The Urban Image of Augustan Rome* (Cambridge: Cambridge University Press, 1996) talks of a lack of moral match: 49.

[71] Ibid. 55–78 esp. 68.

responsibility.[72] Roman houses each had its own altar (in the atrium). To this Augustus added altars for each district, and if aspects of his reorganization of the Forum again suggest an imperial cult, this remained subordinate to a wider respect for the gods.[73] His own home on the Palatine hill, though visible from afar, was in fact relatively modest and certainly so when compared with his new temple to Apollo nearby.[74] On the Capitol the principal temple of Jupiter Optimus Maximus remained the most significant building in the city. Augustus added, though, a small temple to Jupiter Tonans, where its jingling bells no doubt contributed to the sense of divine presence as one climbed the hill to reach these temples.[75] Myth had enabled some sense of unity to be given even to the Republican city, but now vistas, paved streets, and more obviously planned fora provided a real overall unity in which imperial pride and religious commitment marched hand in hand.[76] Before the reader rushes too quickly to condemn such an alliance, it is worth recalling that the same mix between religious conviction and national pride continues to this day for many Jews and not a few Christians in respect of Jerusalem. Of course, the Augustan era had its negative side, but the fact that Augustus' motives were no doubt mixed in giving Rome this new vision can scarcely of itself result in condemnation, without leading also in turn to the condemnation of most church building.

In a culture of increasing ignorance about the ancient world it would be all too easy for modern Christians to draw a sharp contrast between the birth of Jesus and the empire in which it was set. Of course, it contained much evil, but good features need surely also to be acknowledged. As one modern German scholar observes, Octavian, now secure in his triumph in the civil war, did move from 'self-glorification' to a policy of 'religious devotion' that demoted

---

[72] For fire-brigade arrangements: ibid. 138; for new public baths: 115, 161.

[73] For an illustration of an altar of the Lares Compitales (of the crossroads) with Augustus symbolically present: ibid. 125. The temple of the Divine Julius formed the visual terminus of one end of the Forum.

[74] For the story of its origin, ibid. 100.

[75] ibid. 201. The 'Thunderer' was given bells like those carried by night-watchmen.

[76] For how incidents from the supposed life of Romulus linked different bits of the city, ibid. 10. Her two descriptive walks through the city before and afterwards (in ch. 2 and 7) marvellously evoke the contrast Augustus must have effected.

earlier extremes of personality cult.[77] Instead of Caesar's plan for a rigorously rectilinear city, in its place came one which respected traditional sites of piety and affection, with new public buildings going hand in hand with the restoration of the old and hallowed, including eighty-two temples.[78] If the extremes of wealth and poverty remained, with the bulk of the population continuing to live in tenements or *insulae* that were both unsanitary and a fire-hazard, Augustus himself lived modestly and where possible encouraged others also to devote their wealth to public works.[79] Some of the great mansions were in fact demolished and public buildings and gardens put in their stead. The result was that, for example, citizens in the poor Subura district 'could leave behind their dark houses and the chaos of the narrow little alleys to enjoy the glorious colonnades, filled with works of art, the light and fresh air, fountains and grape arbours'.[80] My point is not that Augustus was after all a saint; far from it. But his building programme did ensure that Rome was experienced not simply as a city of rich and poor but also as a city with a public social consciousness in which divine presence was also mediated through its buildings. Certainly Christians would not want to endorse every aspect of that sense, but I fail to see why it should be necessary to speak of an all-or-nothing affair. Augustus himself encouraged some approaches and discouraged others, and so Christians too can surely make similar kinds of discrimination.[81] To say that God was never experienced through such a built city precisely because he was never acknowledged but spoken of only in relation to a plurality of gods is surely to inhibit unnecessarily the activity of God. The omnipresent majesty of God must mean that his activity is more comprehensive than the attempts of any religion, including my own, to limit and so possess him.

[77] P. Zanker, *The Power of Images in the Age of Augustus* (Ann Arbor: University of Michigan Press, 1990), esp. 79–166. For the change, including removal of images of himself from temples, 85–6, 141.

[78] For Caesar's different vision, ibid. 154. The number of temples is Augustus' own: *Res Gestae*, 20.

[79] Including a change of policy from his friend and adviser, Agrippa, who established the first public baths: ibid. 139–43.

[80] Ibid. 139.

[81] Augustus discouraged the cults of Isis and Cybele on the grounds that they were too individualistic, for example rebuilding the latter's temple in cheaper materials (tufa instead of marble) when it was burnt down in AD 3: ibid. 109.

The negative attitude of so much early Christianity to the city is no doubt in part explained by the fact that under the Empire cities were so often sites of persecution. Augustine famously draws a sharp distinction between the earthly and the heavenly city in his *City of God*, and that attitude was also reflected in actual practice, as imperial buildings were allowed to decay, and churches often became the only significant buildings in provincial towns.[82] The Carolingian revival of the idea of the Roman empire produced some change in attitude, but even as late as the beginning of the nineteenth century we still find deep-seated suspicion of the city of Rome as distinct from its cultural inheritance. As if in confirmation, Napoleon sought to clear the Forum solely in order to justify his own view of Paris as the new Rome.[83] Yet by contrast some found in the ruins themselves religious meaning, among them Turner who seems to have experimented with a number of possibilities.[84] But by the later nineteenth century the focus had moved to the impact of ancient Rome on the ordinary populace, and it is to that kind of impact, of the city in general on people, but in the quite different context of nineteenth-century town planning, that I now turn. Augustus in his city planning had helped facilitate religious experience, but was this still possible so many centuries later, especially given that the direct aim was no longer in any obvious sense religious?

Recovering the City as Place of Encounter

It is a commonplace in modern theology to find discussions of God being encountered through people. Such talk is eminently sensible and correct, but it does err in my view when the claim becomes an exclusive one. Cities are more than just the sum of the individuals

[82] For analyses of the change, J. Rich (ed.), *The City in Late Antiquity* (London: Routledge, 1992), esp. chs. by J. Harries and C. La Rocca, 77–98, 161–80. Ambrose spoke of *semirutarum urbium cadavera* ('corpses of half-ruined cities'): Letter 39.

[83] When he occupied Rome in 1812. After his departure, though, the area returned to its traditional usage as cow pasture: the Campo Vaccino.

[84] For the three key paintings and their interpretation, M. Liversidge and C. Edwards (eds.), *Imagining Rome: British Artists and Rome in the Nineteenth Century* (London: Merrell Holberton, 1996), 76–8, 81–2, nos. 5, 6, 9. The book as a whole traces the move away from suspicion and use of *exempla virtutis* to concern with ordinary citizens, particularly from the 1860s onwards.

who happen to live there. Buildings and the layout of cities can also help initiate experience of God, and that is an insight which the contemporary Church has largely lost. Admittedly, few of the experiences I am about to mention have the explicit character that would have once been a person's experience of city life, but they do at least draw individuals out of themselves and so, potentially at least, into that larger reality that is God. Where this might occur is best pursued by examining some aspects of the city's more recent history. I shall take planning, mediated social interaction, and a sense of history each in turn.

In an important general survey of the history of the city, the author suggests that the city began in pilgrimage and continued with a strong religious dimension until the end of the medieval period. 'The first germ of the city is in the ceremonial meeting place that serves as a goal for pilgrimage', while the role of the Church in the medieval town in effect 'universalised the monastery', giving the towns a similar ideology and practice especially with the arrival of the friars.[85] It was only really with baroque grandeur that planning came largely to support strategies of control, with great avenues built to manage the populace and speed the activities of the privileged, only to dissipate in modern times into our own characteristically unfocused conurbations.[86] The nineteenth century, though, remained a period of tight controls. Attitudes to urban parks provide an interesting illustration of this. Although tenacity of historical precedent may have played its part (with planners continuing to impose a uniform, unvarying grid wherever possible),[87] financial savings and ease of policing were probably more pertinent in explaining the sustained opposition that the creation of parks met with in many large industrialized cities of the nineteenth century. There was considerable resistance, for example, early in that century to a facility such as New York's Central Park, as also a little later to anything comparable in industrial Middlesbrough. Yet, had the planners been more open, they

---

[85] L. Mumford, *The City in History* (London: Secker & Warburg, 1961), 10 (cf. 36–7), 268.

[86] For baroque control: ibid. 356–71.

[87] As well as New York and Middlesbrough, grids are found imposed in cities as varied as 4th c. BC Priene and 13th c. AD Aigues-Mortes: S. Kostof, *The City Shaped* (London: Thames & Hudson, 1991), 95–157 esp. 109, 121–4, 125, 149.

might have found in those same parks the potential for better workers, through improved health and recreation facilities.

That suggests, though, still purely utilitarian considerations. Alternatives to the grid at least indicate something rather different. So, for example, the most obvious advantage the use of a circular plan had was in creating a natural centre as focus. Though occasionally found in the West, the most famous example is that of Muslim Baghdad, possibly itself modelled on an earlier Persian example at nearby Ecbatana.[88] The Romans had tried to solve the problem in a different way. A sense of direction was given to their streets by including a vista at one end, wherever possible, such as an arch. Modern parallels can be found throughout Europe as, for instance, in Berlin's Brandenburg Gate and Siegessäule or at Versailles.[89] The disadvantage in a single focus, though, was that it might well fall on some aspect of past or present community life with which not all could agree.[90] So, in some ways a better option was the solution proposed as long ago as the fifteenth century by Alberti who had argued in favour of curves rather than straight lines, and thus the prospect of new vistas being created all the time as one gradually traversed some particular road.[91] Regent Street in London would be one such example, the Ringstrasse in Vienna another, but it has also been adopted with varying degrees of success in many a suburban estate.

Occasionally, explicit religious symbolism is to be found in the town plans of more recent centuries, most obviously perhaps in the Rome of Pope Sixtus V, though there is no shortage of less prestigious examples, among which is even a backwater such as Sherpenheuvel, near Louvain.[92] Although one may laud the inten-

[88] Ibid. 183–5; for religious influence: 164. For an early Western example in 16th-c. Palmanova: 160–1.

[89] ibid. 236–8, 271–3. In the case of Versailles a trivium was employed, which enabled the hinterland to be both private and secure (cf. 189).

[90] In 1830s Paris Ignace Hittorff attempted to defuse political tensions by placing an Egyptian obelisk as a neutral focus at the centre of the Place de la Concorde.

[91] L. B. Alberti, *Ten Books of Architecture* (New York: Dover, 1986), 75 (IV. 5).

[92] For details, Kostof, *The City Shaped* 173–4, 221–2. Not that the approach of Sixtus (1585–90) was necessarily typical of the papacy. Pursuit of glory and power in continuity with ancient Rome was a major determining factor behind Renaissance reorganization of the Capitol, though the Counter-Reformation did bring a change of emphasis; cf. C. L. Stinger, *The Renaissance in Rome* (Bloomington: Indiana University Press, 1985), 254–64 esp. 262.

tions, it is hard to contest their artificiality. Even square or circular plans in such contexts are unlikely of themselves to make one think of divine reason; more likely perhaps of a rather narrow human rationalism. Yet vistas and surprise prospects do seem a rather different category. Le Corbusier once contemptuously dismissed winding streets as the product of the meandering pack-donkey that goal-directed human beings should ignore, following instead the straight and rational course.[93] But it is precisely those turns that often add to the interest and excitement of walking city streets, as new horizons emerge and perhaps even fresh ways of seeing the same thing now that it is set at a different angle or in a new context. Although such experience is clearly not necessarily religious, that dimension can enter through the sheer newness of the vista drawing one out beyond oneself. The security of the street as known now becomes a platform to invite the individual into new and unexpected prospects. Again, a street that seems to sit especially well in its natural setting can also generate religious emotions. Although one side of Princes Street in Edinburgh was badly damaged by 1960s development, its openness on the other side to the valley below and the huge rock-face above create not only a superb romantic setting (especially when the castle is shrouded in mist) but also a sense of humanity at one with the natural world that God has made.

Earlier I contrasted the Emperor Augustus' respect for the natural development of Rome with his great-uncle Julius Caesar's desire for a strictly ordered city. It is a pattern that has repeated itself throughout history. One of the best-known Renaissance plans for an ideal city (Filarete's) actually built in a ten-storey house of 'Vice and Virtue' complete with lecture rooms and brothel, while Ebenezer Howard's Garden Cities had eventually to be modified in a more organic and less structured direction.[94] On the other hand, living in a city that is unplanned and without any significant focus can itself be a devastating experience, and indeed something else on the distant landscape may actually be adopted in an attempt to give some kind of substitute meaning.[95] So there is a delicate balance to

[93] Le Corbusier, *The City of Tomorrow* (London: Rodker, 1929), 5–6.
[94] R. Eaton, *Ideal Cities: Utopianism and the (Un)Built Environment* (London: Thames & Hudson, 2002), 50–3, 147–50.
[95] A point made about Jersey City in relation to the New York skyline by K. Lynch, *The Image of the City* (Cambridge, Mass.: MIT Press, 1960), 25–32 esp. 29.

be sought here, and that balance is not unconnected with religion. One needs both a sense of the city as an appropriate presence in the landscape and a sense that it does not constrain, that there is more to be said. In more theological terms, one aspect speaks of immanence and of a reassuring security, and the other of transcendence and of the freedom to transgress existing limits. The potential for experience in the modern city to move in a more explicitly religious direction cannot be discounted.[96] Sacramental urban geography is thus by no means a nonsensical notion.[97]

The nature of the cityscape can also help mediate or otherwise various types of social interaction. The next question that therefore arises is whether, if at all, this might facilitate religious experience on a more explicitly social level. Certainly, to point in such a direction, it is by no means always necessary that the buildings in question should themselves be especially prominent. Many a city council has worried about this issue, and so insisted that no erections in the area of the Town Hall should surpass in height their own symbol of communal identity.[98] But New York provides an excellent illustration to the contrary. Until 1875 Trinity Church was the city's highest building, but the great tranche of skyscrapers since do not, to my mind at least, undermine the city's desire to stress social values precisely because, despite the real-estate values involved, all its main communal buildings remain firmly lateral and so easily accessible, whether these be churches, libraries, or galleries. As such one may contrast the situation with post-war Frankfurt, where the little historical enclave is so completely overwhelmed by the financial skyscrapers surrounding it that it feels like an irrelevance.

Earlier I mentioned Greek houses turned in on themselves. In the modern world the most obvious parallels are in the fortress

---

[96] Mumford also draws such a conclusion in his concluding paragraphs. 'The city first took form as the home of a god' and its 'final mission' remains 'to further man's conscious participation in the cosmic and the historical process': *The City in History*, 575–6.

[97] For discussion of a Canadian poet applying just such a notion, D. Bowen, 'John Terpstra and the Sacramental in Urban Geography', *Literature and Theology* 16 (2002), 188–200.

[98] This was one reason why American state capitals were often deliberately located other than in the largest town. For the principle applied to city halls, note the arguments in respect of Chicago and Los Angeles: Kostof, *The City Shaped*, 311, 321.

homes and estates of the rich, in places such as Beverly Hills, but the segregation of the social classes in London and other large English cities is merely a variant on the same theme. As such it contrasts markedly with seventeenth-century Edinburgh or nineteenth-century Vienna.[99] It is even different from an earlier London, for it is worth observing that, though the contrast is now less marked than it once was, England from the nineteenth century onwards became very much a land of single dwellings in a way that the continent of Europe never has been.[100] Even in posh Viennese suburbs so ingrained was the practice of lateral dwelling that villas had to be split and offered as single-floor dwellings.[101] It is also a contrast that was once also accentuated within, with each room in the modern English house usually having a single, distinctive function whereas it has been quite normal on the Continent until fairly recently to have a bedroom, for instance, serving multiple purposes.[102] Retreat to a more private lifestyle certainly has its positive side, and could even be defended on theological grounds.[103] But the self-centred dwelling and room can also act as a considerable inhibitor to religion's social dimension. Any feeling for communal identity may well be lost, and thus any sense of sharing in the history of that particular street.[104] In war-ravaged continental Europe in flattened towns street plans were preserved, and often not just in areas of great cultural significance. The people valued the history of their interactions. So we should not think only of

[99] If in Edinburgh the pattern was for different floors to represent different classes, the more common Continental practice was for a different sort of accommodation to be available nearby.

[100] Hackney and Westminster, for example, were both once very mixed areas. While on the Continent the great majority of housing in towns consisted of flats, in the England of 1911 only 3% did so.

[101] D. J. Olsen, *The City as Work of Art* (New Haven: Yale University Press, 1986), 176. English dislike of association with trade may also have been a factor; contrast this with Vienna where the wealthy frequently live above shops and even the city's archbishop above a Pizza parlour: 65, 190.

[102] As study and extension of entertainment rooms: ibid. 124–5. The contrast is explored in detail: 101–31.

[103] Privacy is obviously more conducive to contemplation, while Muslim protection of family life also comes to mind.

[104] The connecting rooms of Continental flats suggest accessibility, while often much is made architecturally of communal entries: for a splendid example: Olsen, *The City as Work of Art*, 99.

the restoration of major landmarks such as the recent work with the Frauenkirche in Dresden or now with the Stadtschloss in Berlin.[105]

Significantly, it has been claimed that the English invented the home and the French the street.[106] Britain in the past had an advantage over some parts of Europe in having a more homogeneous population. Now, however, with that changed it may well be that there is less to fall back on than there is elsewhere. Certainly, the story of the street can only truly be part of one's identity if one actually knows something about how both buildings and people have developed within it. Nor is this purely a sociological point. It is a matter of relating to people through how they express themselves, in, for example, the colour of their front doors, the way they lay out their gardens, and so, ultimately, through the values embodied therein. Aquinas argued long ago that it is communal living that is most likely to lead us to God.[107] If the shape of streets and appropriate vistas can raise our vision beyond the narrowly mundane, involvement with the history of the street or neighbourhood in which we live can draw us out of ourselves into a greater sense of interdependency on each other and thus perhaps towards some sense of dependence on the ultimate source of all in God.

In Fritz Lang's classic 1927 film *Metropolis* alienation between workers and their masters is symbolized by two different cities, the former's underground and the latter's a series of skyscrapers that culminate in a new Tower of Babel.[108] The film is, in fact, full of religious symbolism, and ends architecturally as it had begun, with the city's old cathedral's steps now the place of reconciliation. Lang's message (the 'epigram' of the film) is a simple one: 'the mediator between head and hands must be the heart'. But I doubt

---

[105] In July 2002 the German government took the decision to rebuild the Kaiser's Palace, the ruins of which had been blown up by the Communist government to make way for its own parliament building, the so-called People's Palace.

[106] P. G. Hamerton, *Paris in Old and in Present Times* (London: Seeley, 1892), 308.

[107] In *De regimine principum*, I. 1, Aristotle's familiar formula is modified to man as *animal sociale et politicum*; more commonly he simply drops *politicum* and so subtly changes the emphasis.

[108] Although more than a quarter of the film is now lost, what survives has recently been digitally remastered. Other elements in the religious symbolism include the machine that turns into a consuming Moloch, and Maria as the female figure who inspires the saviour, Freder, to act.

whether this is adequate. Cathedrals no less than towers can have ambiguous histories. I myself live beside one (Durham Cathedral) that Sir Walter Scott labelled 'half church of God, half castle' gainst the Scot'. The heart can also be very selfish and inward looking. So it is not that the heart or the cathedral can of itself give us the answer. Rather, there needs to be a whole range of different factors at work. Not least of these, I believe, will be the types of building style that encourage interaction between different individuals and different social groups. Thereby there can come a turning away from self and thus potentially also a movement towards something larger than any one self, namely God, and thus the potential to experience that being as always present within one's environment.

Finally, I said I would mention something about the role of a sense of history. This is particularly pertinent, given what is currently happening architecturally within Postmodernism. In contrast to Modernism quotation from past styles has now become quite acceptable, as well as, increasingly, the desire to preserve rather than demolish the past. Yet there remains a downside. A number of commentators have observed that in contemporary culture what dominates is the quickly flashing image, with superficial repetition valued over deep memory.[109] One writer who has examined the matter at length notes how both the modern theatre and museum tend to put us in the position of being purely passive observers. In the era before artificial lighting the theatre would have demanded of spectators much more imagination, and of course what is now in the museum would commonly have been elsewhere and expected our participation.[110] While these criticisms are true of earlier twentieth-century theatre, with such dramatists as Brecht and Beckett, and in modern theatre design, there has been a sustained attempt to produce greater audience involvement.[111] Even so, it is not clear that the change is sufficiently deep-seated to have affected society in

[109] Umberto Eco talks of 'the aesthetics of seriality' with our electronic world placing the emphasis on the repeatable and expected: 'Innovation and Repetition: Between Modern and Postmodern Aesthetics', *Daedalus* 114 (1985), 161–84.

[110] M. C. Boyer, *The City of Collective Memory* (Cambridge, Mass.: MIT Press, 1994). For a gradually increasing emphasis on realistic illusion in the theatre: 74–127.

[111] Usefully explored in E. Bentley, *The Theory of the Modern Stage* (Harmondsworth: Penguin, 1980). A good example of the modern, open stage is the Olivier auditorium at the National Theatre in London.

general. Thus, so far as architecture is concerned, her point seems to me still largely to hold. Historical districts are more likely to be observed, rather than experienced as part of people's own lived identity, even by those who make their home there.

Much pride is taken in how tolerant our own generation has become at preserving the past, but it can be seriously questioned whether there is really all that much tolerance at large. For we tend to take the past on *our* terms rather than letting earlier cultures and contexts speak for themselves. So, for instance, museums seldom encourage visitors to put themselves in anything like the position of an early viewer of the artefact concerned.[112] Again, though Viollet-le-Duc and Gilbert Scott are now widely condemned for restoring buildings to a purity they probably never had, there is still resistance to allowing the past to continue to develop in so-called historical areas.[113] It is almost as though we are frightened of granting them any independent vitality that would allow them to interact with their environment and thus, of course, also with ourselves.[114]

Here too I would suggest there is a religious dimension, because for believers their identity is given not as individuals but as part of a particular human story and, if that is so, then some ways of experiencing that story can surely, like the memory required in the eucharist, communicate God. The past can help give us an identity but it can also challenge us to see our present in a new light. Heritage that is allowed its own distinctive voice may thus have a very important role to play in enabling us to escape from the narrowness of our present perspectives. The new fashion of having audio guides where the compère actually speaks with the mindset of the time is therefore particularly to be welcomed. It is now possible to hear Christian monks or Aztec warriors as they would have perceived their world, and not as we would interpret it. Nor need that kind of approach be confined only to areas of great

[112] Contrast a rare exception in the walk-about tape available to accompany visits to the National Gallery in Edinburgh, where at one point the visitor is even recommended to kneel to experience the glittering gold of a religious painting as a worshipper might once have experienced it.

[113] It is often forgotten how much destruction was involved in the 19th-c. re-creation of classical Athens (most of the city's churches, for instance): Boyer, *City of Collective Memory*, 152–75.

[114] Contrast Patrick Geddes' great book of 1914, *Cities in Evolution*, which insisted on the need for town planners to consider a city's 'collective soul'.

architectural significance. Urban history has gone through various transformations in the twentieth century.[115] One of the most encouraging recently has been attention to the history of the marginalized. Establishing a black heritage trail in Boston's fashionable Beacon Hill district or the battle to preserve a building in Los Angeles that had been the site of Latino garment workers' protests are matters of no small moment.[116] They give a placed identity for those who might otherwise see themselves as alien and alienated. In and of itself this is unlikely to make them think of God, but without removing the source of alienation not even the first steps can be made.

Yet for some all this must seem to be the pursuit of little more than a will-o'-the-wisp. After all, it will be said, at least two huge forces now conspire against any and every attempt to experience the city in the way that was once possible: its cosmopolitan, pluralist character and the transience of its inhabitants. Let us then end this section by examining the impact of each of these two factors in turn.

In considering pluralism and its multiple meanings for the city, it is salutary to reflect on what were allegedly more closed societies. For modern reluctance to participate in shared social events may well indicate a less engaged society in more senses than one. To see why, an intriguing eighteenth-century diary may help. A certain individual, Pierre Barthès by name, has left us in his diary a record of all the main public events in the city of Toulouse from 1738 to 1780. What emerges is a city punctuated by ritual enactments of various kinds, thanks in particular to monarchy, courts of justice, and the Church's liturgical year. It is a world hugely different from our own, and it is easy to suppose it closed in the way our social setting is not. Yet, as one recent study observes, ritual in such contexts can function not only as a reinforcer of how things are but also as an indicator of how they might be, and this emerges with special clarity in the various tensions that are implicitly described: confessions on the scaffold, for instance, or religious processions contrasting with the essentially static celebration of monarchy and

---

[115] For a survey, P. Clark, 'The City', in P. Burke (ed.), *History and Historians in the Twentieth Century* (Oxford: Oxford University Press, 2002), 37–54.

[116] Two of the examples given in D. Hayden, *The Power of Place: Urban Landscapes as Public History* (Cambridge, Mass.: MIT Press, 1995), esp. 188–209.

with the otherwise violent character of the streets.[117] Barthès always participates, but does not always agree. Sometimes he does so enthusiastically, only to find his views changed in the process. Nowadays so many of us stand apart when we have doubts. Such studied indifference, though, is surely not at all the same thing as an open tolerance, for that would surely involve a lively engagement with what is 'alien' so that it might be better understood.[118] It is often only through radical reinterpretation of aspects of the Christian liturgy that the contemporary believer can claim to be wholly endorsing what is being said and done. Yet, if such conduct is acceptable in church, might not greater openness also be more sensible elsewhere? Sharing in the Hindu festival of Divali surely does not require prior endorsement of every aspect of Hindu belief,[119] nor celebration of the golden jubilee of a monarch the conviction that monarchy must for the foreseeable future remain the only acceptable form of government for Britain. My point is a simple one. The extensive retreat from public celebration in modern society means that there is in fact now less exposure to 'the other' and thus to the transcendent than there was in what were apparently very closed societies.

And yet civil religion is by no means dead. A recent study has explored in detail how this works out in practice in present-day Washington. Using the two categories of 'archaeology' and 'pilgrimage' the author makes a plausible case for deep-seated religious elements in current American attitudes to that city.[120] Masonic and

---

[117] For the challenge to Maurice Bloch's view that ritual is essentially conservative and ossifying, R. A. Schneider, *The Ceremonial City: Toulouse Observed 1738–80* (Princeton: Princeton University Press, 1995), esp. 10–11, 141. For public execution experienced in quite a different way from Foucault's presentation of them as exercises in free speech, 93–102; for the tensions generated by religious processions and the contrast with the essentially passive celebration of monarchy, 139–47, 179–84.

[118] I have argued elsewhere that the meaning of 'tolerance' has changed from an earlier, more active understanding: 'Tolerance: Virtue or Vice?' in D. R. Bromham et al. (eds.), *Ethics in Reproductive Medicine* (London: Springer-Verlag, 1992), 201–9.

[119] Divali is the Hindu festival of lights held in October/November and especially associated with the goddess Laksmi, wife of Vishnu and bringer of good luck and plenty (her Sanskrit name literally means 'riches').

[120] J. F. Meyer, *Myths in Stone: Religious Dimensions of Washington, D. C.* (Berkeley: University of California Press, 2001), 5. Civil religion, Meyer insists, at least in the American context, does not entail an uninvolved god and certainly not deism.

Calvinist beliefs are found reflected in the city's layout,[121] while respect for the Declaration of Independence and the Constitution resemble those towards Scripture or a 'sacramental sign'.[122] If all this sounds too much like an endorsement of the status quo, it is important to note how much attention is given to the way in which the city has been used to change attitudes (for example, over discrimination) and is still doing so, with the Smithsonian Institute right at the heart of the city acting in the role of critical theologian.[123]

Transience is certainly also a problem. The typical American, for example, moves home every four years. Some historians of thought put the blame firmly on Christian theology, observing that the ancient assumption of the absolute priority of place was gradually and progressively eliminated in favour of infinite space, largely because of Christian belief in an infinite and universal God.[124] For Plato and Aristotle the world's coming into existence was a matter of the ordering of things in particular places, whereas by the time we get to Newton God's infinity and the infinity of space are effectively equated, with place simply a way of affirming God's omnipresence: 'completely present in each place'.[125] Place was now merely a matter of point or position rather than one of deep relation. As one further factor for inclusion, mention might also be made of New Testament insistence on transience, with its emphatic declaration that the believer has 'no continuing city'.[126]

---

[121] Congress is orientated east like Solomon's Temple: ibid. 39. Capitol and White House are on different axes, reflecting Calvinist suspicions of human corruptibility: 63–7.

[122] Meyer, ibid. 76–98. For scriptures, 84; for 'sacramental sign', 95; for shrine photo, 97.

[123] For Lincoln Monument used to endorse and then reject discrimination, ibid. 217, 221–2. For the Smithsonian used to challenge conventional attitudes on Columbus and Hiroshima, 235–43.

[124] The argument of E. S. Casey, *The Fate of Place: A Philosophical History* (Berkeley: University of California Press, 1997), e.g. pp. x, 77–8, 106–8. Although I agree, his argument is greatly weakened by the decision to give no detailed consideration to Christian writers earlier than Philoponus in the 6th c.

[125] For Newton, ibid. 142–50 esp. 149. Not that there was complete uniformity of perspective; see e.g. Nicholas of Cusa's distinction, 118–19.

[126] Heb. 13: 14 (AV). For a book that takes the biblical suspicion of the city seriously, J. Ellul, *The Meaning of the City* (Carlisle: Paternoster Press, 1997). The 'parasite' human creation is contrasted with the future transcendent Jerusalem that owes nothing to humanity (e.g. 148–63). While undoubtedly capturing the biblical rhetoric, there is no attempt to set that in the context of a small, oppressed people.

Against such a backdrop frequent dislocation might seem to be essentially a good thing, and indeed the erstwhile Jesuit, the philosopher Michel de Certeau, has argued dissatisfaction with place is essentially the right attitude since the God of the empty tomb is to be found, if at all, in the absence, in knowing 'of every place and object that it is *not that*, one cannot stay *there* nor be content with *that*'.[127] But, intriguingly, the general direction of philosophical thought on the matter in the twentieth century has tended to move in the opposite direction, in lamenting what has been lost. As part of his attempt to soften the contrast between science and art Gaston Bachelard, for example, devotes much attention to the symbolism of the home, while even Michel Foucault admits the continuing 'hidden presence of the sacred' in various contrasts that resist the desanctification of place that he believes has been advancing since at least the seventeenth century.[128] Luce Irigiray goes further and finds female bodily placement as a continuing means of access to the divine.[129] It is perhaps Martin Heidegger, though, who has reflected on the issue most deeply, a tendency that increased markedly over the course of his long life and which one finds particularly prominent in his 1951 essay 'Building, Dwelling, Thinking'.[130] One small sign of how his reflections seem to pick up on a common longing in present-day society is the way in which sales of local history guides continue to soar.

Pluralism and transience with its accompanying lack of engagement with locality are thus undoubtedly two major inhibitors of history and story functioning as a means of mediating the divine in the modern city. It is thus perhaps here rather than in modern town planning or the limited possibilities of social interaction which it offers that the issue is at its most acute. It is to be noted, though, that the point is not that God is absent but that human decision-making

[127] M. de Certeau, *The Mystic Fable* (Chicago: University of Chicago Press, 1999), 299 (italics in original); cf. also G. Ward (ed.), *The Certeau Reader* (Oxford: Blackwell, 2000), 235–7. Also helpful is Ward, 'Michel de Certeau's "Spiritual Spaces"', *New Blackfriars* 79 (1998), 428–42.

[128] For Bachelard, *The Poetics of Space* (New York: Orion, 1964), chs. 1–2. For Foucault, 'Of Other Spaces', *Diacritics* 16 (1986), 22–7 esp. 23.

[129] Of special importance in this context are her two essays, 'Place, Interval: A Reading of Aristotle, *Physics* IV', and 'The Envelope: A Reading of Spinoza, *Ethics*', in *An Ethics of Sexual Difference* (Ithaca: Cornell University Press, 1993).

[130] In *Poetry, Language, Thought* (New York: Harper & Row, 1971).

makes it more difficult to provide stimulants towards such experiences. I want to end this chapter by considering whether the attractiveness of pilgrimage does not lie in part in the way in which it offers both a critique of the idolatry of place and, contra Certeau, some limited reassurance of rootedness.[131] But first my intention is to pursue Heidegger's thought a little further. In his discussion of place he repeatedly emphasizes how limit is necessary to identity. Yet he does not think that such limits need necessarily be physically close.[132] Place can thus be a matter of relating to what geographically is some distance off. Although Heidegger does not allude to the fact, this is actually a theme as old as Christianity itself. Jerusalem was not only placed at the centre of the Christian universe but also brought imaginatively close, so that it could shape fully the believer's identity. It may not be an attitude any more recoverable for the modern Christian and so no answer to the problems that I have raised in this section, but to pursue the issue will at least help explain why geography did once give the believing Christian an identity that he or she now often lacks.

Jerusalem and Symbolic Geography

Here I want to consider one major way in which religious geography differs markedly from the purely secular, and that is in the desire to bring distant parts of the world close, so that in effect the pattern of experience that was granted elsewhere by God can also be reflected in the community's own immediate environment. Attitudes to Jerusalem are for the Christian an obvious case in point.[133] It was there that Christ's sacrifice took place, there too

---

[131] One recent engagement with Certeau is P. Sheldrake, *Spaces for the Sacred* (London: SCM, 2001). Although he attempts to qualify Certeau through appeal to Christian understandings of the eucharist (64–89), in my view he fails to go far enough, because the notion of place he derives from the eucharist is an undifferentiated one spatially (though not morally).

[132] Cf. Heidegger, *Being and Time* (Oxford: Blackwell, 1962), 135: 'Every entity that is "to hand" has a different closeness, which is not be ascertained by measuring distances.'

[133] Parts of what follows in this section were originally delivered as a lecture at a conference in Jerusalem in 2000. These are used by permission of Thomas Hummel, the editor of the conference proceedings; they will eventually appear as a Melisende publication (London).

that a divinely instituted practice of worship was once celebrated. Christian believers sought to make experience of the sacramental presence of the divine in their midst a reality by in effect doing all they could through building work, art, and other means to draw Jerusalem close symbolically, if not in fact. Such acts of course also ensured that for those who behaved in this way their own particular place never became absolutized as an idol, for there was the standing reprimand of a higher status achieved elsewhere.

In the history of Western Christianity it is undoubtedly the image of the new Jerusalem rather than the historical city as such that has exercised the greater influence. One notes, for instance, the frequency of the former's appearance in well-known hymns,[134] as also the major role it has exercised in the writings of some English poets, such as Blake or Spenser.[135] In this section, however, it is upon representation of the historical city that I want to focus. Initially, that might be thought to introduce quite different issues from the symbolic, but this is far from being so. For in actual practice the historical city, no less than the new Jerusalem, was employed in a largely ideal or representational way, and so it is symbolic and not purely historical questions that continue to be addressed in what follows. So, for instance, even as a more detailed understanding of the history of the Temple was becoming better known, Renaissance artists did not hesitate to bypass history in order to offer instead what they saw as the ideal expression of the presence of the divine in architecture, just as in the twentieth century even where King David is the nominal subject and the artist Jewish as is the case with Marc Chagall, it is to Europe that he looks for an appropriate image and not to David's own city.[136]

There are of course not dissimilar tensions in Scripture itself, long before the new Jerusalem becomes essentially a heavenly one, as the city promised to the returning exiles well indicates.[137] Again,

[134] Note e.g. the half-dozen or so in *Hymns Ancient and Modern: New Standard* (Bungay: Chaucer Press, 1983), nos. 184–91, among which Bernard of Cluny's 'Jerusalem the Golden' is perhaps the most famous.

[135] Blake's 'And did those feet?' (*Hymns*, 294) comes from his *Milton*. There is also his epic and difficult poem *Jerusalem* where Jerusalem is treated as both city and woman, with an opposite Vala, identified with Babylon. The heavenly Jerusalem is also given a significant role in Spenser's *Fairie Queen* e.g. Bk. I, canto 10, stanza 50 ff.

[136] Both examples are discussed below.

[137] In Isa. 62, for example, Jerusalem is already the ideal city of the 'new Jerusalem'.

it could scarcely be claimed that Mount Zion deserves the kind of eulogies it receives by any objective criteria that took proper account of its relative status as a mountain—it is, in fact, quite an insignificant, little hill. How that tension is worked out in the history of post-biblical Christianity will be my theme. It is most conveniently explored under three subheadings. I shall end by noting continuing tensions between realism and relevance in modern times. The middle section will explore the search for continuity, as this was reflected in the desire that the church near at hand should reflect the distant Temple, a matter, as we shall see, of much more than purely historical concern. Both of these sections will be in part illustrated from art. I begin, though, with an expertise no longer considered part of the artist's domain, though it was so at the time, and that is the whole question of medieval maps. Jerusalem was brought near by being placed firmly at the world's centre.

Medieval Maps: Jerusalem at the World's Centre

The practice of some medieval cartographers in making Jerusalem the centre of the world is often misunderstood.[138] For it is easy to assume from such conventions that the medieval world must therefore not only have thought Jerusalem literally at the centre of the world but also, as a consequence of this, the world flat. But nothing could be further from the truth.[139] The earth was in fact commonly envisaged as a sphere, and, as other features of such maps make clear, Jerusalem was in fact being thus identified as the spiritual centre of the world, not its actual centre.[140] One might compare the way in which in so much medieval painting the size of a human figure indicates relative importance, not something physical;

---

[138] Inevitably, most medieval maps had more limited objectives than presentation of the known world, but even many of this kind show no such interest: e.g. the Munich, Sawley, and Vercelli maps.

[139] Even if occasionally more literal readings are to be found. So e.g. in the early Middle Ages pilgrims at Jerusalem were sometimes shown the alleged navel of the world: J. Wilkinson (ed.), *Jerusalem Pilgrimage 1099–1185* (London: Hakluyt Society, 1988), 160.

[140] The learned 7th-c. Spanish saint, Isidore of Seville, notes that the most we can speak of is Jerusalem as the centre of its region (*umbilicus regionis totius*), not of the whole world: *Etymologiae* XIV, iii. 21.

patrons, for example, are often minuscule in relation to the saints in whose honour they have commissioned the painting. Again, one might note the way in which Dante also places Jerusalem at the centre, but in his case leaves no doubt that he believes the world spherical, since the Purgatory Mount is placed on the opposite side of the globe with its earthly paradise on top and thus firmly out of reach of sinful humanity on this side of the globe.[141]

To understand such maps, we need in any case to allow our minds to enter into quite a different way of using world maps and the geography that went with them. In the Middle Ages when people wanted to get to a particular destination they would have relied on personal guides and itineraries. World maps (of which relatively large numbers have survived)[142] combined history and geography in a single format in order to convey in effect the meaning of our world, and that is why artistic representation is often an integral element in their composition. The reconfiguring of the geography of the world began early, as can be seen in the work of the fourth-century *Bordeaux Itinerary*,[143] or perhaps still more clearly in the fine sixth-century mosaic map found at Madaba, which places Jerusalem at its centre.[144] But for what are to the modern eye the most extraordinary transformations we must await the high Middle Ages. So, for instance, Christ's body in seen as encompassing the entire world in a thirteenth-century Psalter map, now in the British Library,[145] a pattern that is also to be found, though less prominently, in the more famous Ebstorf world map, once the world's largest but destroyed during an air-raid in 1943, though copies fortunately survive: in this case Christ's head, feet,

[141] Note e.g. the direct comparison drawn at the opening of Canto 2 in *Il Purgatorio*, with dusk settling over Jerusalem as dawn rises for Mount Purgatory.

[142] The probable number is thought to be over a thousand.

[143] For discussion of this aspect of the *Bordeaux Itinerary*, J. Elsner, 'The Itinerarium Burdigalense: Politics and Salvation in the Geography of Constantine's Empire', *Journal of Roman Studies* 90 (2000), 181–95. Elsner describes the guidebook as 'a work of remarkable ideological innovation' in which the author intends to 'present Jerusalem as the centre of its world and yet as the spiritual and scriptural Other to the administrative and secular norms of its world' (194, 195).

[144] Though, since it is a regional map with much lost, this inference could be challenged.

[145] Front and back illustrated in E. Edson, *Mapping Time and Space* (London: British Library, 1997), pl. VI (after116) and fig. 7.1 (136).

and hands are actually made part of the map.[146] If such forms are relatively infrequent, visual reference to biblical story and classical legend most certainly is not, though this did not necessarily imply agreement as to positioning or degree of prominence. So, for instance, in the case of the Psalter map just mentioned, the Garden of Eden, with the heads of Adam and Eve enclosed within a little frame, is placed at the top in mainland Asia, whereas in what is now the largest and most elaborate map to have survived from before the fifteenth century, the *Mappa Mundi* at Hereford, we find the Garden placed beneath a depiction of the Last Judgement, but clearly an island.[147] Again, though mythical creatures abound, which ones are selected for inclusion varies greatly. The Psalter map has a whole stream of examples in continuous succession at one corner, while the Hereford map, as well as placing the landing of the Ark in Armenia, records this also as the dwelling-place of the 'tigolopes', a semi-human creature with webbed feet and a tail.[148] The creature is represented as holding what looks like a thyrsus, a staff with a sort of pine-cone at the top. If that is a correct identification, then the intention may be to imply that here is where worshippers of the god Bacchus (the Greek Dionysus) once dwelt, or perhaps still dwell.

Considering that all this is mixed up with the locating of contemporary European cities, the temptation might well be to dismiss the entire exercise as symptomatic of a bygone conceptual world. Admittedly, such geography in the modern sense as there is (shapes of continents and so forth) seems to date back to Roman times.[149] Even so, there is a real attempt to integrate three worlds into one: the classical, the Christian, and the contemporary. So, for instance, many towns that post-date the fall of the Roman empire do make an appearance on the Hereford map, among them Bremen,

[146] Illustrated in P. D. A. Harvey, *Mappa Mundi: The Hereford World Map* ((London: British Library, 1996), 31. At 10 sq. ft., it would have been the largest surviving medieval map, though an even larger (at 20 sq. ft.) in Chalivoy-Milon, near Bourges, had been destroyed only in 1885.

[147] Although now owned by Hereford Cathedral and probably copied there, the map was originally designed at Lincoln in the late 13th c. For a general view and the position of Eden: ibid. 1.

[148] For Psalter map creatures, Edson, *Mapping*, pl. II; for Armenia on the Hereford map: 40, lower illus.

[149] Although this is at best an inference since so little of relevance has survived from Roman times: so ibid. 10–11.

Compostela, Dublin, and Venice. That attempt at integration can also be seen in the way the mythical creatures of the classical world are treated. For contrary to what might perhaps have been expected, the semi-human among them are generally given sympathetic treatment. As on the tympanum at Vézelay, they are seen as open to the possibility of salvation, and indeed in one case a dog-head became a Christian saint, namely Christopher, among the Cynocephales.[150] Similarly, on the Hereford map the Cicones (a bird-like people) are placed in close association with a pelican acting in a Christlike manner in feeding its young with blood from its own breast.[151]

It is therefore against this larger vision that the placing of Jerusalem in the centre of such maps should be considered. Just as the figure of Christ either encloses or heads the map, and all are therefore seen as potentially open to his salvation or judgement, including the strange creatures that inhabit our world, so the real centre of that world must be seen as the place from which all such historical and theological understanding flows: Jerusalem as the site of Christ's death and resurrection. That is a case of history affecting geography, but it is possible also to locate the symbolic argument in reverse, with geography affecting history. Thus, where in paintings a skull is observable placed at the foot of Christ's cross, it is clear that more was intended than simply to allude to the name of the place as Golgotha, 'place of the skull', and so presumably an erstwhile cemetery. Instead, the skull was taken to allude to 'history', to the sinful first Adam, who is thus made to die in precisely the same place as where later the new Adam brings life.[152]

Sometimes on the maps the point is made in a highly abstract way, as in a chart from Thorny Abbey where Jerusalem is simply written across almost its entire horizontal length with only a tiny

[150] For his story, J. B. Friedman, *Monstrous Races in Medieval Art and Thought* (Cambridge, Mass., 1981), 72–4; for illustration, J. Taylor, *Icon Painting* (Oxford: Phaidon, 1979), 65. In Russia the tale has been rationalized into an association with the more famous St Christopher; he asked for a dog's head so as not to tempt local girls: so K. Onasch and A.-M. Schnieper, *Icons* (New York: Riverside, 1995), 283.

[151] Illustrated Harvey, *Mappa Mundi*, 4, bottom.

[152] As, for instance, in the Fogg Art museum Crucifixion by Fra Angelico where there is a skull beneath the cross, while above one finds the cross already blooming into a tree where a pelican feeds her young: C. Lloyd, *Fra Angelico* (London: Phaidon, 1992 edn.), 126–7.

space left for Jericho at one side.[153] More commonly, though, there is some symbolism accompanying the name. So, for instance, the Hereford map, apart from a central compass point and surrounding walls, also has what is now a rather faded portrayal of the crucifixion immediately above.[154] Again, the Ebstorf map has a fine depiction of Christ rising from the dead in the centre of a city, only the square walls of which are shown.[155] Although the British Library Psalter map is plainer than either of these, with Jerusalem simply placed at the centre within a circle, it perhaps makes the point just as effectively. What in effect we are being told is that it is only if we understand the significance of Jerusalem that we will then understand the world's history and geography as a whole, and in particular God's purposes for that world. Although in maps that do not place Jerusalem at the centre such considerations are scarcely as explicit, it by no means follows that symbolism did not continue to take precedence over geography in the narrow sense. Indeed, one German scholar has argued recently that the use of triangle, circle, and cross as a framework for such maps' structures were intended to evoke the Trinity, perfection, and redemption, in other words a world ordered by God.[156] While the application of her analysis is almost certainly extended too widely, such a pattern would at least help to explain why knowledge inherited from the ancient world became distorted so quickly.[157]

If the modern secularist is inclined to scoff, one possible response might be to note that our modern maps are not quite so far removed from such attitudes as may initially appear. One need only think of the way in which British maps used to be so structured as to emphasize the scale of the British empire (usually painted red, and with Britain at the centre), or even today the arbitrary

[153] Illustrated Edson, *Mapping*, 88.

[154] Illustrated, Harvey, *Mappa Mundi*, frontispiece.

[155] Ibid. 33.

[156] B. Englisch, *Ordo orbis terrae: Die Weltsicht in den Mappa mundi des frühen und hohen Mittelalters* (Berlin: Akademie Verlag, 2002). She argues that following a pattern established in the 8th-c. Isidore world map (now in the Vatican) was widely copied elsewhere, even sometimes where Jerusalem was placed at the centre.

[157] Her analysis is at its most plausible with the Isodore map itself, which she argues is constructed out of an equilateral triangle (the Trinity) and three concentric circles (divine perfection): note especially the illustrations at 570–1. The theological background is well handled: 67–122.

convention that places the northern hemisphere at the top of our maps, as though places like Europe and the United States were necessarily more important than Africa or South America. Such practices aided particular political perceptions of the world, and indeed for some may have made them almost intuitive or second-nature. That does not make them automatically correct, but equally it does not of itself invalidate the experience; similarly, then, with Jerusalem experienced sacramentally. God may be the objective correlate in one case, as are forms of political power and influence in the other. A measure was given which required one to interpret one's local context against the canon of the central image. Of course it 'slanted' how experience was then read, but so too did the modern secular analogue of painting the map red. The ultimate objectivity of the referent of either experience cannot thus of itself be undermined by acknowledgment of this fact.

Locating the Temple There and Here

While medieval maps may be used to illustrate the way in which Jerusalem functioned as the spiritual centre for understanding both the world's history and its geography, consideration of the perceived relation between Jewish Temple and Christian church suggests the existence of a more complex understanding in the medieval and later Christian Church. What I want to do now is examine that history in some detail. What I suggest was sought was some way of bringing into the present the existence of a building that was thought once to have vouchsafed deep and profound experiences of God. As we shall see, this did not result in one single method of attempting to secure the result.

Certainly, initially Christianity ignored the site. It even appears to have been used as a rubbish dump, while such associations as survived were moved to the Church of the Holy Sepulchre.[158] But the astonishing achievements of the Muslim architects after the seventh-century conquest, combined with the reflection that in some way the biblical dispensation must have provided a perman-

---

[158] The Muslim sources for the conquest of 638 actually use the term 'dung-heap': Peters, *Jerusalem*, 187. Even if this is regarded as Muslim propaganda, neglect can certainly be substantiated. Egeria mentions that Solomon's ring was displayed in the Holy Sepulchre church.

ent model for all subsequent ecclesiastical building, did lead to a rethink. Even then, though, imitation and claims to continuity are often complicated by misunderstandings about what the past was in fact like, while also found is the conviction that present ideal must in reality have existed in that ideal past. The sacramental drawing near of the Temple thus sometimes produces the honour of imitation while perhaps more often it generates the accolade of the present projected into the past.

Given the detailed descriptions of Solomon's Temple that are available in Scripture,[159] it is surprising what little impact they had on how churches were constructed, or on how the building is portrayed in the history of art, at least until modern times. Thus in respect of the latter there appear in general to be no obvious parallels even when an appropriate Old Testament story is in view, while of the former at most what one can say is that eventually interest arose in Christian churches imitating the same proportions as the original building, with the relation between nave and chancel paralleling that between Holy Place and Holy of Holies. One possible explanation might lie in the Temple's subsequent two reconstructions, since it would of course have been Herod's Temple rather than Solomon's that would have been of primary concern to a Christian trying to envisage the city of Jerusalem in Jesus' day. Given that building's subsequent destruction and the lack of any description in the New Testament, one might think that at last the reason was clear: there was simply no available evidence upon which to rely. But this is quite untrue. Josephus offers a detailed description, and his writings were widely available throughout Christian history.[160] So we must look for an explanation elsewhere.

In fact some historical interest is shown. So, for instance, the seventh-century *Codex Amiatinus*, now in the Laurentian Library at Florence but generally thought to have been produced at Jarrow in Northumbria, contains a plan of the Temple precincts, while in the twelfth century Richard of St Victor produced a diagram of Ezekiel's vision of the Temple as he imagined it, as well as a literal

[159] 1 Kgs. 5–6; 2 Chr. 3–4.
[160] Especially *Antiquities of the Jews*, 15. xi. For a series of visual reconstructions of how this Temple looked, A. Edersheim, *The Temple* (Aylesbury: Candle Books, 1997), e.g. 36–7, 43, 118–19, 188–9, 229, 234–5.

commentary on Solomon's Temple.[161] Reconstructions of aspects of its furniture also occur, most notably perhaps the two pillars labelled *Iachim* and *Booz* in Würzburg Cathedral and the magnificent menorah in Essen Minster.[162] Such interest, though, is rare and more common patterns are of a quite different kind. The borrowing of models immediately to hand in the design of contemporary churches may delay us least. Sometimes, no doubt, such representations are rightly taken to imply a lack of imagination on the artist's part, with convenience taking the place of any real engagement with the story. But this will not always have been so, for sometimes this will have been seen as precisely the right means to encourage the viewer to see the events portrayed as pertinent to their own life and times.

More interesting, though, are other types of approach. Among them is what happens on the fifth-century triumphal arch to be viewed in Rome's Santa Maria Maggiore, where Jerusalem is portrayed as a walled city but Solomon's Temple within modelled on a pagan temple, in this case probably the Temple of Venus and Rome (a joint dedication).[163] If so, the choice was no accident. For that temple, built by the Emperor Hadrian close to the Forum and the largest temple ever built in the city, was intended to celebrate by means of its two cellae the close relationship between divinity and Rome.[164] A few centuries later, and the Church was in effect now making a similar claim through the story of one who, having triumphed over the Temple authorities in Jerusalem, could now unite Church and city once more.

Such implicit claims are seldom recoverable elsewhere, but the phenomenon of borrowing from anything save the Jewish Temple

[161] *Codex Amiatinus*, I. fos. 2^v–3. For Richard of St Victor's challenge to the way in which Gregory the Great had ignored the literal sense of such passages, B. Smalley, *The Study of the Bible in the Middle Ages* (Indiana: University of Notre Dame Press, 1964), 107–9.

[162] Although the former were moved inside in 1644 and placed in front of the baptismal chapel, their original role had been to serve as guardians of the western portal when they were first set there in the mid-13th c.; cf. 2 Chr. 3: 15–17. The Essen menorah dates from *c.* AD 1000; a large one with a statue of Mary on top survives from the early 16th c. in Tallinn.

[163] So A. Grabar, *L'Empereur dans l'art byzantine* (Paris: Les Belles Lettres, 1936), 216 ff.

[164] For a recent account of the importance of this temple, Beard, North, and Price, *Religions of Rome* i. 257–9.

itself seems ubiquitous.[165] Indeed, so much is this so that one commentator has suggested that what we actually find instead is three quite different patterns, the imitation of structures from the classical world, a Temple derived from more recent Eastern models (no less true of art in western Europe than of its natural home), and finally the direct copying of contemporary Western churches.[166] The first and last we have already briefly noted. The use of the Greek ciborium, however, needs a little more explanation. This is a simple structure that has four supports or columns on which rests a roof that can assume various forms. In actual use its significance lay in what happened to be venerated beneath the canopy. From an artistic perspective its obvious advantage was to be found both in the relative simplicity of the structure and in the way in which it could be used to highlight the events occurring beneath it. A fairly simple version can be seen in the mosaic of Christ cleansing the Temple at Monreale in Sicily,[167] while more complicated versions are to be noted in Giotto's Scrovegni Chapel at Padua. In the latter case some look more obviously Western than others.[168] Giotto's lack of consistency perhaps tells us much. As with classical or contemporary models, what really mattered was effect rather than literal truth. An added sense of awe, a feeling of relevance to the viewer's own place and time, a contrast with earlier history might all play their part. Similar motivations can also be observed within Islam. In treatments of Muhammad's Night Journey Jerusalem is

[165] As also of course the copying of patterns already established. Stanley Ferber, for instance, detects a similar pattern to that employed at Santa Maria Maggiore in the Old Testament manuscript known as the *Quedlinburg Itala* and in the *Milan Iliad*: 'The temple of Solomon in early Christian and Byzantine art' in J. Gutmann (ed.), *The Temple of Solomon* (Missoula, Mont.: Scholars Press, 1976), 21–43 esp. 24–7.

[166] The taxonomy is that of C. H. Krinsky, 'Representations of the Temple of Jerusalem before 1500', *Journal of the Warburg & Courtauld Institutes* 33 (1970), 1–19. He found only two realistic depictions prior to 1500, one in the 11th-c. Roda Bible from Ripoll, the other accompanying a 14th-c. manuscript of the *Speculum humanae salvationis* (19).

[167] Although presumably there is no intention to imply that the scene is also that of the Temple, a similar ciborium is used in the portrayal of Paul being baptized by Ananias.

[168] Ciboria are to be seen e.g. in the Presentation of the Virgin in the Temple and also in the Suitors' Prayer before the Rods: illustrated in B. Cole, *Giotto: The Scrovegni Chapel, Padua* (New York: George Braziller, 1993), 56, 60. The cleansing of the Temple is more Western: ibid. 90.

often made to resemble an already existing Muslim city.[169] None of these approaches were of themselves intended to imply the inferiority of the Old Covenant. Even the use of classical buildings could be a compliment, since these were often assumed to be the nearest comparable achievements now easily available for copying.

Yet an element of competition was sometimes present. Thus there is little doubt that major churches were sometimes deliberately conceived as architectural rivals to the Temple. So, for instance, the poet-bishop, Corippus, declares of Sancta Sophia in Constantinople: 'Let discussion of Solomon's Temple now fall into silence, and let the wonders of the world yield place.' Although he goes on to concede the divine founding of the Temple, he adds that the new church is 'the new shrine of Wisdom. Here is the royal house, here is the House of God.'[170] The same kind of claim was also to be repeated in respect of a some key buildings in western Europe. So, for example, the way in which the Frankish kings were anointed from Pepin onwards was apparently intended to imply that the mantle of David now rested with them, just as the ornamentation of the church at Aachen by Charlemagne proclaimed a new Temple.[171] It has also been suggested that a similar motivation underlies the extensive ecclesiastical building programme undertaken by the early Norman Kings of Sicily. This is a dynasty that not only had themselves anointed but also were to play a key role in the history of Jerusalem, not least in the person of Frederick II.[172] It is with their earlier history, though, that we should be concerned here, and in particular the dynasty's three principal churches on the island. Certainly, not only was Roger II's church at Cefalù decreed a cathedral in 1131 on a day particularly associated with Jerusalem (Holy Cross day),[173] but also the group of Augustinian regulars to whose care he entrusted the

[169] P. Soucek, 'The Temple of Solomon in Islamic Legend and Art', in Gutmann, *Temple of Solomon*, 73–123 esp. 99–111. She also suggests that mosaics of trees and fruit on the Dome of the Rock were meant to assert continuity with Solomon's Temple via Jewish legends about Solomon's golden garden: ibid. 95–9.

[170] *In Praise of Justinian*, iv. 283. Translated and quoted in R. Milburn, *Early Christian Art and Architecture* (Aldershot: Scolar, 1988), 188.

[171] In 751 Pepin was anointed but it was only in 814 with Louis the Pious that anointing and coronation were combined into a single ceremony.

[172] He seized the throne of Jerusalem in 1228.

[173] The day traditionally identified as the one on which Helena, Constantine's mother, discovered the remains of the true cross.

building were canons of the Church of the Holy Sepulchre, currently being rebuilt.[174] However, in the view of recent scholarship it is neither Cefalù nor the Palatine Chapel in Palermo that best expresses the dynasty's new ideology, but rather Monreale, built by Roger's grandson, William II. Like the Temple of Solomon the church is set on a hill. Within we find William portrayed as crowned by Christ himself, with a psalm quoted that specifically allows him to be seen as the new David, while the lions at the foot of his throne (immediately beneath this mosaic) are most naturally taken as an explicit allusion to Solomon's throne.[175]

In the following century Louis IX built Sainte-Chapelle (1244–8) to house the holy relic of Christ's Crown of Thorns, ransacked from Constantinople and bought by the saint for an astonishing 135,000 livres, equivalent to more than half the annual income of the French monarchy at this time.[176] By contrast, the cost of building Sainte-Chapelle itself seems minuscule, a mere 40,000. Even so, no expense was spared. Louis had already been to the Holy Land, and was to go on crusade in due course. That, though, apparently did not mean that he deemed Jerusalem more important than his own kingdom, for in fact he saw God as now adopting his own monarchy as his special concern in much the same way as the Davidic had once been. Jerusalem deserved respect for its past history, not for its present status. So in the chapel the reliquary, the *grande châsse*, is deliberately so designed to recall for the perceptive viewer Solomon's throne. To the uninitiated observer, it looks altogether different. None the less, the connection is a plausible one, even if at times irritatingly complex.[177]

To understand properly the symbolism of this famous chapel, one needs first to recall the developments that occurred as a result of Solomon being treated as a type or anticipation of Christ. Solomon is the Old Testament image of wisdom, and 'behold a greater than

---

[174] Holy Cross day celebrates Constantine's dedication of the Church of the Holy Sepulchre on the site where his mother, Helena, is alleged to have found the true cross. For relevant details on Cefalù, E. Borsook, *Messages in Mosaic: The Royal Programmes of Norman Sicily 1130–87* (Woodbridge: Boydell, 1990), 6–16.

[175] For Monreale: ibid. 51–79 esp. 67–8. For a description of Solomon's throne: 1 Kgs. 10: 18–20.

[176] The figures are given in D. H. Weiss, *Art and Crusade in the Age of Saint Louis* (Cambridge: Cambridge University Press, 1998), 16.

[177] For the story: ibid. 53–74.

Solomon is here'.[178] As Solomon pronounces from his throne, so also, it was observed, Christ even in his earthly life had a 'throne', his mother's lap. The analogy is as early as Athanasius, but it took to the eleventh century before such images become commonplace. Mary is then regularly portrayed as the *Sedes Sapientiae* or Seat of Wisdom, not of course strictly in the sense of herself as wisdom but as that on which Wisdom sits, though no doubt the precise relationship was sometimes confused. One can see such iconography in easily recognizable form—with the Christchild on Mary's lap and a throne accompanied by the requisite number of lions—on the central portal of the west façade of Strasbourg Cathedral,[179] but unfortunately such obvious simplicity of reference became complicated by alternative forms of representation that derive ultimately from a brief allusion in Scripture to the façade of Solomon's hall of justice.[180] In the case of Sainte-Chapelle it is the use of similar arcading that is employed to allude to Solomon. In effect, we are being told, a greater wisdom is now enthroned in the King's chapel than was ever present in the hall of the palace where Solomon once displayed his wisdom.[181]

Ironically, similar modifications were incorporated even into the façade of the El-Aqsa mosque in Jerusalem, when it passed into the possession of the Templars, and indeed it is not impossible that this is the ultimate source for Louis's version of the *Sedes Sapientiae*.[182] The reason why they gave the building that form is probably because some of them at least were convinced that, so far from it being an entirely Muslim structure from the eighth century, it was actually continuous with Solomon's own palace. The builder would thus have seen himself engaged, not, as we do, in introducing the new Gothic style but rather as restoring the building to what it had once looked like. In fact, from the eleventh century

[178]　Cf. Matt. 12: 42.

[179]　There is a simplified version on the right portal of the west front of Chartres Cathedral. There is also an unusual version with four lions (against Strasbourg's $2 + 6 \times 2$) in a painting by Jan Van Eyck, now in Frankfurt. The normal pattern is derived from 1 Kgs. 10: 18–20.

[180]　1 Kgs. 7: 2–5. Of particular importance is v. 4 with its reference to 'window frames in three rows' (RSV).

[181]　Meanwhile in England Henry III used the imagery of Solomon not only for his throne but also for the royal beds (following Song of Songs 3: 7–10): N. Coldstream, *The Decorated Style* (London: British Museum, 1994), 123.

[182]　So Weiss (following Davis), *Art and Crusade*, 65.

onwards it was a common belief that the Temple and palace of Solomon had actually survived. For the two mosques on the site, the Dome on the Rock and the El-Aqsa, came to be identified as respectively the 'Temple of the Lord' (*Templum Domini*) and the Palace of Solomon (*Templum* or *Palatium Salomonis*).[183] Many at the time tried to point out the error, but the desire for pilgrims to see something from the past seems to have kept the belief alive.

That being so, it is perhaps therefore not surprising that the evidence is somewhat confused as to how far the Templars in their building programme outside the Holy Land were influenced by these buildings and how far by the Church of the Holy Sepulchre. It is often stated that the few round churches that survive in western Europe derive directly from the latter, but documentary confirmation is seldom available. So, for instance, it seems a plausible contention in the case of the Round Church in Cambridge,[184] but with the more impressive Temple Church in London matters are much less clear.[185] The common practice of the Templars seems in fact to have been to model their buildings on the Palace of Solomon, after which their order was named and which in its heyday held as many as three hundred knights, and thus combine a square building with a round tower as in the El Aqsa mosque,[186] but it is not impossible that even the Dome of the Rock itself exercised some influence, as its dominating dome could easily create the impression of a round building, despite its octagonal base. To find Christians so deeply affected by Muslim building work may seem surprising enough, but there are also illustrations that indicate that even Jews also identified the Dome of the Rock with their own historical Temple, as in one impressive fifteenth-century Hebrew manuscript

[183] For a brief account of these developments, Krinsky, 'Representations of the Temple', 2–7. For a 12th-c. map of Jerusalem with such labelling, S. Kochav, *Israel* (London: Thames & Hudson, 1995), 116.

[184] Known as Holy Sepulchre, the church dates from 1130, and appears actually to have been commissioned by a particular group known as 'the fraternity of the Holy Sepulchre'.

[185] Still being asserted in the most recent history of the church, but without documentary evidence: D. Lewer and R. Dark, *The Temple Church in London* (London: Historical Publications, 1997), 18.

[186] C. C. Addison, *The Temple Church* (London: Longman, 1843), 79. Addison had also produced a detailed and fully documented history of the order in the previous year: *The Knights Templars* (Longman, 1842). The full title of the order was *Pauperes Commilitones Christi et Templi Salomonis*.

of Maimonides' *Book of Worship*.[187] The problem of determining what influenced what in respect of church building is in fact not dissimilar to the question of how far the influence of the internal structure of the Church of the Holy Sepulchre extended. The edicule over where Christ was believed to have been buried seems once to have been a typical ciborium in structure. The temptation then is to suppose influence where the Temple is so represented in art, but this seems unlikely,[188] and so the actual number of specific imitations turns out to be relatively few.[189]

So it looks as though, despite the brief return of the city of Jerusalem to Christian control during the Crusades, this did not bring any comparable desire for more realistic depictions of the city and its principal buildings in Western art. With the Renaissance, though, one might have thought that things would be quite different. After all, this movement brought not only a new concern with historical scholarship but also a desire for more naturalistic painting. Even so, there were significant factors pulling the other way, and in fact it was not until well into the nineteenth century that accuracy became a major concern in art. In part there remained the continuing commendable desire to present Christ's world as the viewer's own. Sometimes this is readily intelligible, as when Pieter Bruegel applies the Parable of the Sower to what could only be a northern European landscape.[190] But the desire for greater naturalism actually pulled away from allowing Jerusalem itself to appear in realistic form, principally because the artist's local landscape was now seen as itself capable of giving added meaning to the canvas. One can see this, for instance, in the Galitzin Triptych by Raphael's teacher, Perugino, where Florence's Arno valley is employed to draw us in towards identification with the crucified Christ.[191] But if the new

[187] Illustrated in D. Bahat and S. Sabar (eds.), *Jerusalem: Stone and Spirit* (New York: Rizzoli, 1998), 101.

[188] Ciboria were already in use in quite a number of different contexts.

[189] For some illustrations, M. Biddle, *The Tomb of Christ* (Stroud: Sutton, 1999), e.g. 22, 25, 35. Perhaps most interesting of all are the occasional attempts at a complete rebuilding, as at Eichstätt in *c.*1160 (29).

[190] From 1552 and now in San Diego; illus. in C. Vöhringer, *Pieter Bruegel* (Cologne: Könemann, 1999), 30.

[191] Illustrated in J. A. Becherer (ed.), *Pietro Perugino* (New York: Rizzoli, 1997), 261. There are paths on both side panels that encourage our ascent under the leadership of penitent saints (Mary Magdalene and Jerome) towards Christ. The painting could be as early as 1483.

factor of naturalism acted in a way that might not have been expected, so too did another, much more distinctive feature of the Renaissance, its conception of what the Temple ought to have looked like. For it was felt that the Temple, built as it was by divine order, must have been perfect in its design and the popular Platonic theory of the time deduced that this therefore must mean that it had been a circular building.[192] The actual facts of the case of course colluded with such a view, since both the Church of the Holy Sepulchre and the Dome of the Rock (in part) bore that shape, but in fact there is little attempt to copy these actual buildings.[193] Instead, one is much more likely to find idealized versions of what the perfect ecclesiastical building should look like. One highly unusual variant on this is the Jesuit Villalpando's design for Philip II's Escorial Palace, where Ezekiel's vision of the temple is in theory taken as his model but a classical building the result.[194]

One can see the net impact of such assumptions if one contrasts the work of a northern artist such as Gerard David with that of Raphael. Whereas the former paints Christ's resurrection in 1505 against a backdrop of a round church that could possibly come from medieval Jerusalem,[195] Raphael leaves us in no doubt that it is the Renaissance ideal that concerns him. A good example would be his *Marriage of the Virgin* from 1504, where the Temple in the background is circular but in a way without parallel in Jerusalem, or again his thoroughly Renaissance interior for his *Expulsion of Heliodorus from the Temple* of 1512.[196] Rather than the relevant events

[192] For a detailed analysis of the background theory, R. Wittkower, *Architectural Principles in the Age of Humanism*, 5th edn. (Chichester: Academic Editions, 1998).

[193] Still, they could be quoted as precedent, along with a number of other significant Christian and pagan religious buildings (not always correctly interpreted): A. Bruschi, 'Religious Architecture in Renaissance Italy', in H. A. Millon (ed.), *Italian Renaissance Architecture* (London: Thames & Hudson, 1996 edn.), 123–81 esp. 126.

[194] For design and discussion, J. Bennett and S. Mandelbrote (eds.), *The Garden, The Ark, The Tower, The Temple* (Oxford: Museum of History of Science, 1998), 135–42.

[195] In the Metropolitan Museum of Art, New York; illus. in M. W. Ainsworth, *Gerard David* (New York: Abrams, 1998), 137.

[196] Both illustrated in J. B. Beck, *Raphael* (New York: Abrams, 1976), 86–7, 138–9. The former may have been influenced by Perugino's *Delivery of the Keys to St Peter* of 1480, in the Sistine Chapel.

from Christ's life it is incidents from the apocryphal life of the Virgin, though, which are most likely to yield such portrayals of the Temple. Their absence elsewhere, however, was not the consequence of some new-found artistic respect for history, but presumably because architectural features placed behind the cleansing of the Temple or the crucifixion could so very easily have distracted attention from such paintings' central message. By contrast, the legend of the Virgin's dedication to the Temple at a young age offered the possibility of a dramatic approach by her to the building, while her marriage was also often envisaged as taking place in front of the building itself. One can see the result in Ghirlandaio's splendid depiction of the two scenes in the church of Santa Maria Novella in Florence, while Titian working in Venice brilliantly exploits the splendours of Renaissance architecture to highlight the assurance of the 3-year-old girl despite her awesome surroundings.[197]

Some of the potential difficulties in making the Temple's architecture prominent in other contexts can be observed in the work of a number of painters. In Cornelisz's *Temptations of Christ*, for example, our eye more readily takes in the architecture than Christ's trials, and indeed even the artist himself seems undecided whether to follow his inclinations and make the Temple a purely Renaissance building or include some allusion to context.[198] Even major artists can exhibit similar tensions and difficulties. In Botticelli's work on the same theme in the Sistine Chapel he chose to please his papal patron by making the Temple a copy of the latter's San Spirito Hospital, but again at the cost of distracting the viewer with irrelevant details.[199] Titian was therefore no doubt wise in his famous depiction of Christ's appearance to Mary Magdalene to reduce Jerusalem to an insignificant hill town.[200] Yet there are

[197] For illustrations of Ghirlandaio's two paintings, A. Quermann, *Ghirlandaio* (Cologne: Könemann, 1998), 76, 79. For the *Dedication* Ghirlandaio chooses to portray Mary as a young girl rather than as a child. For an illustration of Titian's version, M. Kaminski, *Titian* (Cologne: Könemann, 1998), 66–7.

[198] The painting is now in the Suermondt Museum, Aachen. An Eastern onion is added to what otherwise looks like a Renaissance Temple. For another example of an illegitimate orientalizing of the Dome of the Rock from the 15th c., see the splendid manuscript illustrated in Kochav, *Israel*, 117.

[199] The relevant pope was Sixtus IV.

[200] His *Noli me tangere*, now in the National Gallery, London. Illustrated in Kaminski, *Titian*, 24.

exceptions. If Grünewald's famous Isenheim altarpiece lacks any architectural allusion, the same cannot be said for his *Christ Carrying the Cross*, but significantly the references are plain: a crossbeam quoting Isaiah 53 in German, and a simple round temple behind that could conceivably have come from Jesus' own day.[201] Perhaps the most intriguing, though, is Mantenga's *Agony in the Garden*, where included in the canvas is a city that appears to include the Roman Colosseum, an imperial equestrian statue and the Muslim crescent crowning some buildings.[202] On this occasion at least the architecture reinforces the principal message of the work. Christ struggles to fulfil the divine will for the sake of a humanity (the city) that has not only been drawn deep into rebellion against God but also adopted conventions of power quite different from Christ's own.

What this brief survey of the treatment of the Temple in architecture and art implies, I suggest, is no single way of relating to the building but rather a general desire to bring it imaginatively close to one's own world, so that once profound experiences of worship in the Temple could be renewed in the fresh and quite different context of western Europe. In modern Christianity many, perhaps most, of these ways are no longer commonly known or, if known, understood. That to my mind is a great pity, because it was not indifference to history or geography that led to such attitudes (though this no doubt sometimes played its part) but rather the conviction that what had once mediated divine presence could do so again. Place and building were thus seen to have the capacity for an impact no less powerful than word. More Protestant readers, though, may object that what I have ignored in all this is the New Testament critique of the Temple. Certainly, the argument of Hebrews is that Christ's sacrifice on the cross has made its rites redundant, but both Jesus and the early Church allowed themselves to be shaped by its worship which suggests something other than total rejection.[203] So, even if continuity of rites is rejected, it might still be possible to speak of the re-creation of the building functioning as a reminder of the divine shaping of Jesus and thus also of

[201] The painting now hangs in the Staatliche Kunsthalle in Karlsruhe.

[202] Now in the National Gallery, London.

[203] Despite the prominence he gives to the Cleansing of the Temple (2: 13–22), John structures his Gospel round Jesus' attendance at the principal Temple feasts, while Acts records the disciples' continuing worship in the Temple: e.g. 3: 1.

subsequent generations of believers. More pertinent to our concern here, though, is the undoubted fact of what such practices reveal: the decision to try to draw the Temple sacramentally close to the experience of Christians in their own day. The danger in realism is that it leaves only a distance not easily bridged.

Realism and Relevance: The Modern Dilemma

I ended the previous section with examples drawn from Renaissance art. No significant new developments are then to be observed in the intervening period until the nineteenth century, when a fresh approach begins to assert itself, demonstrating in particular a new concern for historical accuracy. A number of factors combined to induce such a change of perspective, not least among them the rise of a new professionalism in historical research as well as, perhaps more importantly, a public now eager to learn about foreign lands and their culture. The invention of the camera in any case meant greater awareness of what Palestine really looked like.[204] Visits to the Middle East also became more feasible, if still treacherous particularly in the first part of the century. Even so, such visits did not necessarily produce the type of painting that we might expect. As we shall see, the new desire for realism had to be tempered by continuing demands for spiritual significance and relevance, and indeed this even affected the new science of photography.[205]

Perhaps of all the artists whose work was inspired by personal observation the best known today is the Scot, David Roberts. He visited the country in 1839 and his sketches were subsequently published to great critical acclaim. Undoubtedly, part of the reason for that success was the way in which his depictions chimed in with the Romantic assumptions of the time. Although never exactly falsifying, there is in fact extensive use of artistic licence, particularly in order to make the scene in question more awe-inspiring. Com-

---

[204] Usually attributed to Daguerre, and dated to 1839.

[205] Although patrons spoke of 'facsimiles of nature,' in practice what they wanted was for the land to look as they envisaged it would at the time of Jesus, and so this meant selectivity not only in respect of buildings but also with regard to which elements of the native population figure in the photographs. See further, R. V. Hummel, 'Reality, Imagination and Belief: Jerusalem in 19th and early 20th Century Photographs', in S. Auld and R. Hillenbrand (eds.), *Ottoman Jerusalem* (London: Melisende Press, 2000), i. 235–78.

parison with photographs taken from the same vantage point well illustrate this fact.[206] For instance, the towers of the city's citadel seem to be given a greater height, and in particular the one known as the Tower of David is made to appear more impressive than it really is. Again, the area in front of the Church of the Holy Sepulchre is made markedly more spacious than its cramped conditions really allow, and with the cupolas easily visible, while a number of distant views of the city, including that from the Mount of Olives, become more dramatic, especially in terms of the landscape or the visibility of the city's monuments.[207]

Fifteen years later Holman Hunt made the first of several visits to the Holy Land. On that first occasion in 1854 he was accompanied by another Pre-Raphaelite, Thomas Seddon. Their two approaches form an interesting contrast with one another. Both were concerned with historical authenticity, and indeed the considerable efforts and dangers to which Hunt exposed himself in order to paint his famous *Scapegoat* are well known.[208] Even a painting such as his *Finding of the Saviour in the Temple* that appears to lack verisimilitude reveals on closer inspection the great care to which Hunt has gone to achieve precisely that effect.[209] Yet, even so, his attitudes remained fundamentally different from those of Seddon, as can be seen from his response to the latter's *Valley of Jehoshaphat*.[210] Seddon had deliberately rejected the more impressive view of the city from the north in order that he might highlight the actual place of Christ's agony in Gethsemane. As his brother subsequently explained, 'he wished to present to those who could not visit it themselves an accurate record, not a fancy view, of the very ground our Saviour so often trod'.[211] With that sentiment Hunt would not have disagreed, but he feels that art required more than literal representation. As he wrote, 'in conventional art the demand

---

[206] Usefully provided in D. Roberts, *The Holy Land* (London: Terra Sancta, 1989 edn.).

[207] Ibid. I–17, I–21, I–45.

[208] For an account A. C. Amor, *William Holman Hunt* (London: Constable, 1989), 125–32.

[209] To the modern eye the Islamic architecture is disconcerting, but apparently he thought its forms derived from more ancient sources, while the marbled floor and pineapple column both do in fact derive from ancient sources: L. Parris (ed.), *The Pre-Raphaelites* (London: Tate, 1984), 158–9.

[210] Illustrated with commentary, ibid. 151–3.

[211] *Athenaeum*: 22 March 1879, 386.

for variety of tones is satisfied by exaggeration and tricks', and this helps explain the extent to which colour and other forms of symbolism play a crucial role even in his apparently purely descriptive paintings.[212]

If Roberts, Seddon, and Hunt represent one form of a suitably modified pursuit of realism in the portrayal of the city's buildings and ruins, Sir Edward Poynter and Henry Ossawa Tanner may be used to present two other versions, the former the new preoccupation with the interior of buildings and the latter interest in the landscape of the Holy Land as such. The former in fact earned his reputation and eventual knighthood (in 1896) for his large and carefully researched historical tableaux. One of the most famous in its day was *The Visit of the Queen of Sheba to King Solomon.*[213] What makes it particularly interesting from the perspective of our present discussion is the way in which, unlike the *Sedes Sapentiae* tradition to which it gave rise, Solomon's throne now carefully conforms to its biblical description, while the pillars of the palace are deliberately non-classical in construction. Tanner is quite a contrast. The son of an African-American Methodist-Episcopal minister, he trained under Thomas Eakins at the Pennsylvania Academy of Fine Arts, but lived most of his life in France, declaring that he could not fight prejudice in America and paint at the same time. From his father he learnt to see the land of Israel as a 'fifth Gospel', and so he visited the country a number of times.[214] His religious painting is mostly of high quality, with some biblical scenes presented in a remarkably original way.[215] What is surprising is that it is entirely the landscape as such that has an impact on him and not buildings, far less the city of Jerusalem. The area around Jerusalem he described as a 'barren, broken-cisterned, sterile' landscape, which may suggest an entirely negative attitude, but elsewhere he also observes that 'those barren hills that can blossom like

---

[212] Hence the contrast not only with the Manchester version of *The Scapegoat* (Parris, *Pre-Raphaelites*, 155), but also even with his *Jerusalem by Moonlight* (271–2), where, for example, a symbolic woman is introduced.

[213] Now in the Art Gallery of New South Wales, Sydney.

[214] His father quotes Renan's famous declaration that 'seeing Palestine is the fifth gospel' in his *Theological Lectures*: quoted in D. F. Mosby, *Henry Ossawa Tanner* (New York: Rizzoli, 1991), 166.

[215] One of the best known is his *Annunciation* from 1898, where the angel is presented simply as a blaze of light: ibid. 162–3.

a rose, with irrigation, were to me a natural setting, a fitting setting, to a great tragedy. The country, sad and desolate, is big and majestic.'[216] The net consequence of such attitudes is that in his depiction of the annunciation to the shepherds, Bethlehem is duly subordinated and only just visible through the harsh landscape in which the angels take on a mystic blue, ethereal form, almost merging with the darker blue of the mountains behind that dwarf the shepherds. Much the same could be said of his fine painting, *Return from the Crucifixion* where Jerusalem is only just visible on the horizon as a distant white smudge, with the great expanse between a rather oppressive dirty greyish-brown.[217] Although without clear landmarks, even so the city was probably intended to carry a symbolic role: as indicator of hope, however hard one has to search for it. If so, the city would then function jointly with a much more obvious sign in the painting, the way in which the penitent thief's cross seems already to be taking off out of the picture and heaven-wards.[218]

Tanner's reputation was already firmly established by the late nineteenth century. *Return from the Crucifixion*, however, dates from the year before his death in 1937. So with equal appropriateness he might have been compared with the work of twentieth-century artists, where we observe a marked retreat from nineteenth-century concerns with realism and a return to the exploration of symbolic alternatives to the actual city. One major exception, however, should be noted, and that is Oskar Kokoschka's well-know depiction of Jerusalem from 1929. How far it is an exception could, though, be contested, inasmuch as it is essentially a romantic view, something the painting shares with some of his other city-scapes, among them his view of London, where St Paul's is given a prominence to which it is not in fact entitled.[219] The work, though, lacks the details of any specific action, and that perhaps explains why it remains so untypical of the twentieth century. For,

---

[216] Quoted ibid. 160, 166. The accompanying landscapes illustrate the point: 161, 167.

[217] Illustrated ibid. 225, 289.

[218] It is placed at a very curious angle at the edge of the painting, and like the other two crosses is not immediately noticeable. Clearly for Tanner the viewer was meant to work at comprehending his meaning.

[219] Both illus. in R. Calvocoressi, *Kokoschka* (London: Academic Editions, 1992), nos. 61, 103.

overwhelmingly, in seeking to establish the relevance of Christ's life to their own day, Christian artists have returned to earlier practice and set the events of the Saviour's life in their own immediate environment. This is, for instance, what happens with Salvador Dalí's use of Port Lligat, or Stanley Spencer's repeated use of his home village of Cookham in Berkshire. It is a practice also that continues with contemporary artists, such as Mark Cazalet's placing of Jesus' trial amid his own local London industrial skyline.[220]

What is perhaps more surprising is that even Jewish artists show similar tendencies. Thus the nearest the greatest Jewish artist of the twentieth century ever comes to a realistic depiction of Jerusalem is in his rather oppressive portrayal of the *Wailing Wall* (1932).[221] More often it is his native Vitebsk that Chagall uses as his image of the holy city, as in his 1945 painting *Around Her* which laments the recent loss of his wife, Bella.[222] Even his *King David* of 1962, which seeks to link earthly and heavenly love, uses Vitebsk for the former, while it is his new home of Vence in the south of France that symbolizes the latter, not Jerusalem.[223] Indeed, even when working in Jerusalem itself, the city is seldom, and then only somewhat vaguely, represented. This could of course be because the principal monuments of the city are no longer Jewish.[224] But even the Orthodox Jewish painter, Shalom of Safed, who lived all his life in Palestine, in his *Levites Playing Music in the Holy Temple* gives us a wholly imaginative and not historical reconstruction of the Temple.[225]

It looks, therefore, as though the nineteenth-century pursuit of realism was a brief hiccup in the history of Western art. The

---

[220] An illus. of *Christ Sentenced* (1999) by Cazalet (b. 1964) can be found in *Stations* (Bury St Edmunds: Art Gallery Publications, 2000), 6; cf. also 32–5.

[221] Illustrated in J. Baal-Teshuva, *Chagall* (Cologne: Taschen, 1998), 137. One might contrast his 1917 *Jewish Gates*, so marvellously evocative of resurrection: ibid. 80.

[222] Ibid. 167.

[223] Illustrated in W. Haftmann, *Chagall* (New York: Abrams, 1998), 143.

[224] Note his tapestry for the state reception hall of the new Knesset, *Entry into Jerusalem* (illus. in Baal-Teshuva, *Chagall*, 232). The only significant feature is a tower, which could be intended to allude to the Tower of David. Although much rebuilt over the centuries, this is the only structure visible from a distance which has Jewish origins (as a Maccabean fort).

[225] He was born in Galilee in 1885, and this painting, now in the Jewish Museum in New York, dates from 1972.

twentieth century witnessed a return to the more conventional pattern of offering symbolic analogues, and, to judge by younger artists such as Mark Cazalet, that pattern will continue into the twenty-first century and perhaps beyond.[226] Thus, whether one takes the 'realism' of modern art, the specifics of Renaissance symbolism and earlier, or medieval map-making, the same conclusion emerges. Jerusalem has, as it were, become universalized. But, far from this entailing an identity that is now taken to exist indifferently anywhere and so a demotion of place, what it suggests to me rather is a high doctrine of the possibility of the city's relocation. If the analogy does not sound too forced, like Christ himself, the city is no longer confined to Palestine, but living (as in the eucharist) wherever the same significance is sought through a re-enactment that brings a different place and a different time into one's own place and time. Symbolic geography is thus used to negotiate the transfer of one place to another, with the specifics of both not only retained but also enhanced. For how else could it be, if Jerusalem is to retain its own specific story, and the believer's hers or his? Factual record is thus not enough. A famous location for experience of the divine is not allowed to remain simply in the past. Indeed, the attempt is made to bring it into one's own time and place so that God can be experienced anew. That of course does not automatically establish the validity of the experience, but it does at least raise the issue as a serious possibility.

Movement, though, has often gone the other way, not in drawing Jerusalem close but in pilgrimage to that holy city, as also to other such places. It is to how such pilgrimage should be understood that I therefore finally turn in this chapter. Pilgrimage is often treated by hostile critics as an overvaluing of the particular. What I want to suggest instead is that its symbolism exercises a dual critique, both of the place from which pilgrims have come and also, perhaps more surprisingly, of the goal towards which they travel, for even that place is now also seen as provisional in the divine dispensation. Yet at the same time all this does nothing to lessen the increased sacramentality given to both places, for it is precisely through place that such discoveries are made and God more fully known.

[226] A young British artist who sets the major incidents of Christ's life against modern city and industrial backdrops.

Journey and Goal in Pilgrimage, and the Transformation of Place

It has been a recurrent protest throughout the history of all the major faiths that to value place in its own right is to underplay the real heart of religion, which lies in internal dispositions. Pilgrimage is then seen as the worst form of such valuing of externals, precisely because on this scenario place is doubly valued, both in itself and in the effort and process of getting there. Indeed, it is possible to argue that this was one key respect in which Christianity sought to reform Judaism, with the notion of pilgrimage to Jerusalem for the three annual feasts and the great stress on a chosen land replaced by the notion that the Christian has 'no continuing city'.[227] If that view is taken, a more fundamental Protestant critique of medieval practices then becomes possible in addition to where most of the complaints actually centred, on pilgrimage's implicit works ethic and the shrines' acquisition of wealth through indulgences and superstition.[228]

But on the other side needs to be set the apparent depth not only of the human instinct to identify, as we have seen, with particular places (most obviously in the notion of 'home') but also of the urge to uproot oneself and seek solace from particular places. What is fascinating about the latter is that it is a phenomenon that seems to emerge at some point in almost every religion, irrespective of the wider presupposition on which that religion is apparently based. This is certainly true of Christianity despite the New Testament's apparent indifference, but it is also the case with some other major religions where indifference to such notions might otherwise have

[227] The three main Jewish festivals were Passover (celebrating the Exodus), Pentecost or Weeks (celebrating the end of the barley harvest), and Tabernacles or Booths (celebrating the autumn harvest). Note that it was only with King Josiah's reform in 621 that their celebration was moved from local, tribal shrines to Jerusalem. Note also that for many Tabernacles or *Sukkoth* surpassed Passover or *Pesach* in importance: R. De Vaux, *Ancient Israel*, 2nd edn. (London: Darton, Longman & Todd, 1965), 495. For New Testament attitudes, Heb. 13: 14 (AV); cf. Phil. 3: 20.

[228] The critique, though, did not just come from Protestants. Erasmus is scathing in his *Colloquies*, while medieval attacks can also be quoted: for some examples of the latter, D. J. Birch, *Pilgrimage to Rome in the Middle Ages* (Woodbridge: Boydell, 1998), 5, 67.

been presumed. Islam is arguably the most transcendent of the major three monotheistic religions; yet the hajj is one of the five pillars of Islam. Again, Buddhism's stress on mental meditation and on the impermanence of all material things might have led to the exclusion of such ideas; yet modern times have seen, if anything, an intensification of Buddhist pilgrimage rather than its diminution. I shall consider first, therefore, why pilgrimage should thus be virtually universal, before turning specifically to Christianity. In the Christian case I shall use the image of the labyrinth to try to comprehend the significance attaching to the journey as such and then a number of pilgrimage destinations, including in particular Rome, to indicate how understandings of place are also changed in the process.

Pilgrimage Universal across Religions

The factors that have encouraged pilgrimage across the centuries are of course legion. Some are clearly secular. If nowadays it might be joy in walking or tourism, in the medieval world there was trade and curiosity. Even when the motives are religious, they can be of questionable worth; for example, the attempt to establish a high positive status before God or one's fellow human beings. But such factors have always gone with more profound motives, which are the ones I want to explore here, particularly the desire to enter into a new reality, the crossing of a threshold that dislocates but also makes possible a new relation with God.

In considering how deep-seated notions of pilgrimage are, one might observe that it is a phenomenon by no means confined to 'advanced' religions, or to those that have survived into our own day. Even in the remote past such practices are to be found.[229] The religion of ancient Greece affords one such example. Thus, despite their remoteness or distance it was oracles such as Delphi that were favoured for consultation,[230] while the sick frequently travelled

[229] Archaeologists have labelled a charming rock carving at Capo di Ponte from the 9th c. BC 'the two pilgrims'; for illus., P. C. von Saucken (ed.), *Pèlegrinage* (Paris: Zodiaque, 1999), 19.

[230] Delphi was normally approached by sea, which was why the shrine was closed for three months in the winter. In evoking the right atmosphere, its location must also have helped. Similarly, at Cumae in southern Italy the necessity for the pilgrim to traverse an extended tunnel before consultation must have added to the impact.

long distances in search of a cure at the temples of Asculapius.[231] It is also worth noting that, as we saw in an earlier chapter, the four major games (Isthmian, Nemean, Olympian, and Pythian) were all treated as sacred events that entitled those attending to the same rights of safe passage as other pilgrims enjoyed.[232] One could of course say that in such instances the motivations were always pragmatic, the desire to get cured, the fame of the oracle, and so forth, but I doubt if that provides the entire answer. The reorientation provided by the pilgrimage may, for example, have been seen as part of the cure, as indeed was to be the case in medieval Europe.

If little by way of critique emerged in Greece, it was quite otherwise in ancient India. Yet what is fascinating to observe in this connection is how religions initially hostile eventually conceded to pilgrimage its point and purpose. Thus it was to become an integral part of Buddhism and (much later) of Sikhism, and that despite the fact that in both religions it began in a climate of hostility. Thus, although the Buddha had scornfully dismissed traditional Hindu pilgrimage with the declaration that 'if the waters of the Ganges could truly wash away sin, then all fishes would go straight to heaven', his concession of stupas as markers for lay devotion quickly expanded into their endorsement among the *sangha* or monastic community as well.[233] Again, among Sikhs the first Guru (Nanak, 1469–1539) opposed pilgrimage as without religious worth, whereas by the time of the fourth, Ram Das, the famous shrine at Amritsar was already being built.[234] The change in modern Buddhism is especially marked, as sites neglected for centuries once more assume a major place in devotion. From its high

[231] The three main sites were Epidauros on the mainland, Kos in the Aegean, and Pergamon in Asia Minor. Although the type of healing involved (overnight incubation accompanied by a dream) was clearly a form of faith healing, doctors seem to have worked alongside rather than in competition, as Kos in fact became Greece's principal medical centre: M. Dillon, *Pilgrims and Pilgrimage in Ancient Greece* (London: Routledge, 1997), 74–80 esp. 76. Incubation continued to be practised within Christianity; for the Church of the Holy Sepulchre, von Saucken, *Pèlegrinage*, 77.

[232] Sacred truces were organized, and there were special officials to welcome those bringing news of festivals (*theorodokoi*) as well as others who went as official representatives (*theoroi*): Dillon, *Pilgrims and Pilgrimage* 1–59 esp. 1–18, 59.

[233] M. Boord, 'Buddhism', in J. Holm with J. Bowker, *Sacred Place* (London: Pinter, 1994), 8–32 esp. 9, 15, 18.

[234] B. Dhanjal, 'Sikhism', ibid. 149–73 esp. 150–1, 155–6.

point under the emperor Asoka (*c.*274–232 BC) Buddhism gradually declined in India to virtual non-existence by the ninth century,[235] but British rule gave opportunity for the restoration of places associated with Siddhārtha's life, and these now evoke the full range of responses that are to be found elsewhere in other religions.[236] Again, though Buddhism experienced a similar fate in Indonesia, the great shrine at Borobodur with its marvellous symbolism is once again attracting pilgrims.[237]

In trying to find some common denominator across the religions some anthropologists have sought to treat the phenomenon in entirely secular terms,[238] but Edith and Victor Turner are surely right to suggest an intimate connection with van Gennep's notion of liminality, the attempt to move or initiate oneself into a new sphere.[239] The search for health or through an oracle to establish a new relationship with the divine, as in the examples discussed above, surely suggests as much. In support of such a view one could also note the strong connection within Hinduism with rivers. The old Sanskrit word for a pilgrim, *thirthayatrika*, apparently literally means 'one who wanders about, seeking river crossings'.[240] So the connection with crossing boundaries is an intimate one, and for the Christian at least the implied parallel with baptism illuminating.

[235] The historical Asoka is very difficult to disentangle from the legend. In Santosh Sivan's recent film of the same name (2001), for example, the plot is a rousing tale, movingly told, but one learns little from it of his relation to Buddhism.

[236] Well illustrated by the collection of pilgrim literature in M. E. Aitken, *Meeting the Buddha: On Pilgrimage in Buddhist India* (New York: Riverhead, 1995). For some positive responses verging on the sacramental, 30, 37, 68, 346; for negative reactions, 28, 65, 128, 222, 241, 340. For opposing views in quick succession, 83–8; for extreme reverence towards leaves taken from the tree of enlightenment at Bodh Gaya, 101–2, 111.

[237] For a brief exposition of that symbolism, N. C. Brockman, *Encyclopedia of Sacred Places* (Santa Barbara, Calif.: ABC-CLIO, 1997), 28–30.

[238] Conspicuous among the contributors to J. Eade and M. J. Sallnow (eds.), *Contesting the Sacred: The Anthropology of Christian Pilgrimage* (London: Routledge, 1991). Pilgrimage is in that book 'almost dissolved into its social, cultural and political contexts' according to S. Coleman and J. Elsner, *Pilgrimage: Past and Present in the World's Religions* (London: British Museum, 1995), 196–213 esp. 199.

[239] V. Turner and E. Turner, *Image and Pilgrimage in Christian Culture* (Oxford: Blackwell, 1978), esp. 1–39. Arnold van Gennep's influential *Rites of Passage* appeared in 1908.

[240] *Thirtha* or *tirtha* is the word for a ford; *yatrika* means a wanderer.

Yet, within Christianity the search for radical change of this kind is perhaps less immediately clear, especially if we consider major pilgrimage sites such as Rome or Compostela and the rituals associated with them in isolation. It is only if we look at the practice as a whole that underlying parallels become clearer. One notes, for instance, the stress that was once placed on the breaking of old bonds before one could go on pilgrimage in the first place. In the case of international sites a purely practical explanation might of course be given, inasmuch as pilgrims could be absent for months or even years (especially if Jerusalem was the goal), and so needed to set their affairs in order.[241] But that rather more was at stake is surely indicated by the mixture of practical and devotional redirection that was commonly adopted in the Middle Ages. For instance, in Scotland under a law dating back to David I (1124–53) pilgrims abroad were required to put their property under royal protection, while to secure a welcome overseas and guaranteed safe passage also needed as official documents were not only letters of commendation from the Church but also others from the English monarch as well, through whose territory they would probably need to pass.[242] However, if at first sight that continues to suggest the purely practical, given the dangers of travel at the time pilgrims were in effect forced by these measures to take seriously this real break with their past, and that would in any case have been reinforced by the religious ceremonies that were also involved. For, before they departed, pilgrims were formally blessed in church, this being the point at which they received their badge of identification, a staff, and a scrip (or satchel). If such rituals have long ceased to be features of modern Christian pilgrimage, parallels remain in the Muslim world. While women have some freedom in what they wear on the hajj, a uniform dress is imposed upon all men, the *ihram* (two pieces of seamless white cloth intended to indicate a purified state). Equally, at the end of their pilgrimage to Mecca the continuance of a distinct identity is maintained, through use of a deferential way of addressing pilgrims thereafter as *hajji* (man) or *hajja* (woman).

[241] The earliest account that we possess of a Christian pilgrimage to Jerusalem, that by the so-called Bordeaux Pilgrim, implies that he took a year to complete the task, averaging twenty miles a day, with three months spent in the Holy Land itself (Coleman and Elsner, *Pilgrimage*, 88).

[242] For further details, P. Yeoman, *Pilgrimage in Medieval Scotland* (London: Batsford, 1999), 110–12.

Against such shared commonality one might, though, point to the way in which, within Christianity, pilgrimage became for a time at least almost wholly equated with the attempt to obtain remission of penalty for sins in the next life. Yet, on the other side needs to be set the fact that many forms of Christian pilgrimage involve no particular consciousness of sin; even where they do, the desire to give concrete expression to one's sorrow for past sins can still plausibly be viewed as one aspect of this notion of liminality or search for reorientation. Leaving familiar contexts was taken as expressing the desire to break past bondage, while the inevitable burdens of travel could offer specific signs of a willing penitence; so it was not just the conclusion of the journey that was held to have significance. This can be seen, for example, in James IV of Scotland's repeated pilgrimages throughout his reign. His aim was to atone for guilt in participation in the rebellion that led to his father's death, but he did so by walking to the requisite destinations where the symbolism of the shrine affirmed his new status as forgiven.[243]

If in 1300 it looked as though the connection between penitence and pilgrimage was made indissoluble when Boniface VIII declared the first Jubilee Year with its promise of a plenary indulgence on fulfilment of a pilgrimage to Rome,[244] it remains the case that today probably only a minority of the twenty million or so who travelled to Rome for the Jubilee in 2000 had similar thoughts, with liberation from the penalties for sin as their primary motivation. Indeed, so great is the difference that a new objection might well be raised to a common underlying theme for pilgrimage across the religions: that liminality or transformation is no longer the primary motive for Christian pilgrimage, but rather identification, whether this be in the desire for closer communion with God, or the particular saints in question, or else simply on the purely human level with those who happen to share the same outlook on life. That was of course

---

[243] Ibid. 101–9 esp. 101. St Ninian's at Whithorn took pilgrims underground before releasing them into the light. It has to be admitted, though, that James was not above trying to have it both ways; sometimes his mistress was placed conveniently en route: 105.

[244] Such indulgences had hitherto been promised to those who went on crusade to Jerusalem; so in effect this decree marks the attempt to transfer from Jerusalem to Rome the true centre of Christian consciousness. Less creditable motives must also be acknowledged, most obviously perhaps financial opportunism on the part of the pope.

already one factor in the past, as in the common badge of identity once worn by Christian pilgrims, but it is by no means a feature unique to Christianity. The presence of two million Muslims or so all at the same time in Mecca, all wearing the same garments irrespective of race or place of origin, must have a remarkable effect on the participants.[245] What Christianity now offers is on a much smaller scale, but there would still seem some analogy in the shared chants that take place at Christian shrines or in the co-operative spirit that develops in helping the sick at such places as Lourdes.

None the less, I think it important to challenge the view that identification necessarily offers an alternative analysis to transform-ation. For, often identification is presented in the form of trans-formation, particularly where communion with the divine is offered in the form of a revelatory element at the shrine in question. In the classical world this was most obviously the case where oracular utterance was given or a dream expected, as with those seeking cures, or in the various mystery cults. Although given its proximity to Athens Eleusis could have continued to function as a purely local cult, in the end such was its reputation that even some Roman emperors sought initiation.[246] Yet, surprisingly, despite some modern detective work, its secrets have never been satisfac-torily unravelled. Perhaps it may have been nothing more compli-cated than the vision of a new sheaf of corn against the dawning light of a new day.[247] That may seem trivial but anticipation could well have conspired to enable participants to perceive their world in a new light. In a similar way in the pilgrim experience in Jerusalem and the Holy Land as evoked by Egeria, there is both the common-ality of the shared participation in devotion and worship around the *loca sancta*, and also the transformation of entering, as it were, into

---

[245] Some Christian shrines accumulate as large numbers but only over the year as a whole. Even with Islam this is a fairly new phenomenon (thanks largely to the new possibilities created by air flight). In 1934 there were only 20,500 pilgrims to Mecca. Also new is the large number of female participants, currently estimated at a third of the total: A. Parker and A. Neal, *Hajj Painting* (Washington: Smith-sonian, 1995), 6.

[246] Hadrian, Marcus Aurelius, and Julian were among those initiated.

[247] The view of the Christian Hippolytus (*Refutatio* 5. 8, 39–40). Tertullian, no doubt to discredit the rite, says that the revelation was of a phallus: *adversus Valentinianos*, 1.

the pages of Scripture as they are brought to life before the pilgrims' very eyes.[248]

Nor are parallels absent from past practice at more local shrines, where the custom of placing the saint's burial-place underground seems to have been used to similar effect. Thus, if one thinks of the shrines to Wilfrid at Hexham and Ripon or of the now lost shrine to Ninian at Whithorn, the required journey beneath the earth seemed to hint at a symbolic death and rising once more to life as one returned to the main body of the church. Not that all shrines would have had this effect; sadly at Durham the raising of the tester over Cuthbert's tomb was likely to have induced a more worldly awe, as the wealth with which his tomb was encrusted became exposed. My point is simply that, whatever religion one takes, and whatever period, although transformation and identification could be opposed, my suspicion is that, more often than not, they worked together rather than in opposition.

Another threat to acknowledged commonality would be if too much attention is paid to the specific objects of the pilgrimage rather than underlying objectives. For the form they take is of course hugely varied, and it would be a pity if revulsion against the content of another religion's pilgrimage prevented recognition of an underlying shared form. Because of the Reformation's attack on the idolatrous character of shrines, it is tempting, for instance, to assume some intrinsic link between pilgrimage and images, but any such supposition would be quite unfair. The sheaf of corn at Eleusis is scarcely the same thing as the image of a god, while, as we have already noted, it is in Islam, perhaps the most aniconic of the world's religions, that the practice of pilgrimage is growing the fastest, now that Muslims can at last afford to perform the fifth pillar of their faith, the hajj.

Extensive though the rituals are, none involve images. Extending over several days, the ceremonies begin with circulation of the Ka'ba, the sacred stone building at the heart of the Great Mosque in Mecca, and end with a long prayer from noon to sunset at the foot of Mt. Arafat. For the latter no supporting imagery is

[248] J. Wilkinson, *Egeria's Travels to the Holy Land*, rev. edn. (Jerusalem: Ariel, 1981). For the importance of visible objectives in antiquity, G. Frank, *The Memory of the Eyes: Pilgrims to Living Saints in Late Antiquity* (Berkeley: University of California Press, 2000).

supplied, while the former is simply a plain piece of rock with no paintings inside or out. But there is certainly a sustained attempt at symbolic identification not only with the life of Muhammad but also with other great figures from the past, among them Abraham, Hagar, and Ishmael. If the Ka'ba allows association with Adam and Abraham,[249] the ritual of Zamzam is of particular interest, as it requires all Muslims, male no less than female, to imitate a woman, Hagar, in her desperate running back and forth in search of water for her son Ishmael. Ishmael's near-sacrifice is recorded in the slaughter of an unblemished animal, a practice that takes place annually whether a Muslim is on pilgrimage or not.[250] There is thus a sense of unity with all Islam at this point, whether physically present or not. Without the need for any strong visual imagery the various rituals therefore all combine to reinforce a sense of identification with the foundational events of faith that are believed all to have once occurred in this area.

But, as in other cases, the issue is not entirely one of identification. A number of clues are available to help us understand the deeper significance of what is taking place. One notes, for instance, that, particularly among the poor because of the expense involved, the hajj is commonly undertaken only late in life and then used as a way of orientating oneself to old age and eventual death. Through the dislocation of the journey, a new identity is sought for the remainder of one's earthly life. But that is far from the whole story. One notes continuities as well, and in particular the key role that continues to be played by the body. For, although Islam is largely a non-visual religion, it would be a mistake to infer from this that it is therefore exclusively aural, for one place where sacramentality seems to assert itself is in the way in which the body is used to express underlying attitudes and commitments. So integral is bowing to the ground, for example, as part of the ritual of prayer that the devout sometimes proudly display calluses on their forehead (called a *maahrab*). If in the fast of Ramadan the attempt is

---

[249] There is already the association with Abraham and Ishmael in the Qur'an; the connection with Adam is made later. For details and a history of practice across the centuries, F. E. Peters, *The Hajj* (Princeton: Princeton University Press, 1994), esp. 5–7.

[250] It is called Id al-Adha, and is one of Islam's major festival days. In Islam, the elder son Ishmael is almost always associated with Abraham's call to sacrifice, rather than Isaac.

made to curb bodily powers and subjugate them to wise use, one way of reading the rituals of the hajj is to see them as a means of using bodily gestures as a vehicle towards acquiring fresh spiritual potential. Postures and actions are in effect being used to deepen existing religious commitments or else re-establish them in a new central role.

One way of ascertaining what the hajj has meant to participants is to note what happens in Egypt, where houses in the Upper Nile are frequently painted with scenes recalling individual incidents. As one might expect, competing or conflicting interpretations do occur, for instance on how willing Ishmael is portrayed to offer his own life in sacrifice.[251] But all seem agreed on the importance of the Ka'ba, which is the most frequently recurring image. When its black form is set against the myriads of white-clad pilgrims surrounding it, the sense of a single corporate identity is overwhelming, while at other times the context and colours are made so surreal that there seems little doubt that the intention is to convey a powerful sense of divine presence and immanence.[252] That might be challenged by those who wish to portray the God of Islam as essentially transcendent, but on the other side needs to be set not only pictures such as these but also the extensive cult of saints that has grown up in Islam, whose shrines can often attract very large numbers.[253]

Hitherto our discussion has treated pilgrimage exclusively as a religious notion, but of course, as Chaucer's *Canterbury Tales* reminds us, motives have always been mixed.[254] Less familiar is the converse, that modern tourism may be less wholly secular than is commonly supposed.[255] Certainly, such tourism began as a religious exercise, in that the oldest English travel firm Thomas Cook in fact began with a Baptist evangelist of the same name

[251] For some examples, Parker and Neal, *Hajj Painting*, 73, 76, 78, 80.

[252] For the former: ibid. 52–3; for the latter: 54.

[253] For a powerful description of devotion at one shrine (at Shiraz in Iran) and the contrast with the failed attempt to create similar attitudes at Ayatollah Khomeini's tomb, A. Dowling, *Godless Pilgrim* (London: Fusion, 1999), 42–6, 54–7.

[254] For some examples of the way in which trade could also play its part, M. Harvey, *The English in Rome 1362–1420* (Cambridge: Cambridge University Press, 1999), 23–9, 128–30.

[255] For an amusing attempt to recapture the mixture of motives in ancient Roman tourism, T. Perrottet, *Route 66AD* (London: Random House, 2002).

organizing a special temperance excursion by train between Leicester and Loughborough in 1841.[256] But even the most blatantly
secular modern beach holiday can offer some analogies, in particular with the desire to break a routine pattern, so that the regularities
of normal life may be pursued with fresh vigour. Where as part of
the holiday insight and understanding are sought into a different
time or culture, arguably the similarities become closer still, with in
some sense the new context perhaps being used to provide a fresh
evaluation and measurement of one's home environment. Of
course, in the modern world this may progress no further than an
acceptance of difference but where some challenge is accepted then
the parallels can be seen.[257]

Among differences, one deserves special mention. Whereas in
the past the ambiguities of life (both good and bad) were likely to
be encountered at the same site, as with the massacring of non-
Christians in Jerusalem, or the presence of hawkers and prostitutes
at more local shrines, nowadays sites of evil can often be the specific
goal, as with Auschwitz or the Holocaust Museum in Jerusalem.
Indeed, there may even be a claim that no adequate understanding
is possible without such an explicit encounter, as in the argument
over whether the then British Foreign Secretary, Robin Cook,
when on an official state visit, should attend the latter, despite
having visited the place on a previous occasion. Where the aim in
such cases is dislocation and the undermining of entrenched prejudices, that would seem again to offer parallels with pilgrimage in its
more positive sense, but sometimes it is hard to resist the conclusion
that the main motive has now become instead justification for
present attitudes and policies, and if so, however appropriate, that
then makes such practices more a matter of politics than religion.

In the course of identifying an underlying commonality that
extends at times even to secular pilgrimage, various sacramental
connections have emerged. Apart from the valuing of place, the
rituals associated both with the journey itself and the acts performed

---

[256] For further details, W. F. Rae, *The Business of Travel* (London: Thomas
Cook, 1891), esp. 12–42. By the 1880s pilgrimages to Mecca were also being
organized: 208–15. For a modern assessment, J. Pudney, *The Thomas Cook Story*
(London: Michael Joseph, 1953), esp. 30–9 (for the first journeys), 181–92 (for the
Holy Land).

[257] Some of these thoughts are pursued in P. Cousineau, *The Art of Pilgrimage:
The Seeker's Guide to Making Travel Sacred* (Shaftesbury: Element, 1998).

at the shrines suggest the attempt to use one's body as a means of allowing the divine to draw closer to the participants' lives and so effect some level of transformation, however limited. As we noted, a sense of sacramental immanence seems in such contexts to overwhelm even Islam, that most transcendent of religions.[258] But it is to Christianity that I now turn specifically, in order to clarify the sacramental issue. Before examining how the destination is itself viewed, I consider first the route, and here I want to pursue the idea of the labyrinth as a helpful clue.

The Journey: Maze and Labyrinth

Here I want to consider how the journey itself opened up the possibility of certain forms of experience of God drawing sacramentally close. Why I find the image of the labyrinth the most helpful in exploring that possibility will emerge in due course.

Imagine some such scene as the following in one of the world's great cathedrals: round its dean the canons dance in a large circular movement that gradually and progressively narrows in a complex pattern towards the centre, as the dean all the while weaves in and out, passing a ball now to one canon, now to another, all singing antiphonally as they move.[259] A natural temptation is to suppose this a pleasing fiction, but to doubt that it ever happened. But happen it did, and apparently in quite a number of French medieval cathedrals. The precise meaning of the symbolism is no longer available to us, but what makes the dance fascinating is that it illustrates one usage to which labyrinths inscribed on church floors were once put. In this case, as the antiphons sung were those for Easter,[260] the dean probably represented the Risen Christ either delivering souls from hell or else, more generally, leading the worshippers towards a share in his resurrection. The presence of the ball may have had no deeper reason

---

[258] For other examples of such sacramental immanence with Islam, see Ch. 7.
[259] Our most detailed description comes from Auxerre, where the practice lasted from the 14th to the 17th century. For further information, H. Kern, *Through the Labyrinth* (New York: Prestel, 2000; rev. version of 1983 German 2nd edn.), 146–7; P. R. Doob, *The Idea of the Labyrinth* (Ithaca: Cornell University Press, 1990), 123–6.
[260] The Easter sequence *Victimae Paschali Laudes*: F. J. E. Raby (ed.), *Oxford Book of Medieval Latin Verse* (Oxford: Clarendon Press, 1959), 184–5. There is a fine setting by Guillaume Dufay (d. 1474).

than just to help with the rhythm of the dance, but it could possibly have been intended to allude to Christ as the rising sun, the light of all our expectations.[261] If so, the imagery would hark back to pre-Christian times when cosmic symbolism and the labyrinth seem to have been intimately connected.[262] Circular dances represented the paths of the sun, moon, and planets, implying an overall order to our world, however much immediate appearances may suggest otherwise.[263] It was thus a way of declaring belief in a divine order, no matter how confused our path through life at present appears to be. It is probably also into this context that dances associated with the founding of cities, such as the *Lusus Troiae,* should be set. The founding of a city would then be viewed as the imposition of an order comparable with the divine, with the enclosing circles probably also intended apotropaically, that is, as a way of warding off evil: what was within was now under the gods' protection.[264]

That tension or contrast between apparent chaos and underlying order in fact seems to have been one of the major attractions in the notion of the labyrinth, whether we turn to actual examples that have survived or consider more literary explorations of the idea. Some authorities on the subject insist that no difference should be drawn between maze and labyrinth, but, whatever the reason, it is worth observing that all surviving visual examples (whether from archaeology or in manuscripts and painting) take only one form until modern times while the literary working-out more commonly implies another.[265] The former all prove to be unicursal; that is to say, though they wind and may often turn back on themselves, there are no dead-ends and so, provided the walker does not turn back in despair, he or she will eventually reach the intended destination. By contrast, in the verbal or literary develop-

[261] The latter suggestion is, among others, that of Kern. The complexity of Doob's proposal argues against it—for her the ball represents both Christ's humanity and his divinity (*Idea of Labyrinth*, 126).

[262] Kern, *Through the Labyrinth*, 32–3.

[263] The cosmic claims of labyrinth dancing are accepted by at least one early Christian writer, namely Marius Victorinus: for a more detailed account, Doob, *Idea of Labyrinth*, 68.

[264] Kern, *Through the Labyrinth*, 77–83. The ritual described in *Aeneid* v. 545–605 may once have been associated with the founding of the *pomerium* (the ritual city boundary), discussed earlier in this chapter.

[265] Doob, though conceding the fact, denies any significance to the distinction: *Idea of Labyrinth*, 1, 40–6.

ments, the layout is multicursal; that is to say, the possibility of wrong paths turns out to be almost endless. The latter is the version with which we are most familiar in the modern world, and so that is why the term 'maze' is best reserved for it. For the apparently simpler form we may keep the term 'labyrinth', but it is as well to observe that it could of course be just as frightening. For its customary form of a series of rough, weaving circles allowed periodical sight of the eventual goal, only for the walker to be thrown back virtually to the starting point once more.

That said, we can perhaps now see why both maze and labyrinth were adopted as powerful images of what life in our world is like for those of religious faith. The labyrinth asserted that, provided perseverance and trust in God were maintained, one would, under God's guidance, eventually reach one's goal, however dark and uncertain the road may at times seem. But so too did the maze. The difference lay in the degree of responsibility thrown on us as we walk through life, for the structure of the maze suggests a burden of continual decision-making as new forks in the pathway open up, whereas the labyrinth requires but one decision on our part, the initial choice of living under divine grace and direction in the first place. Expressed thus, though, we can perhaps see why the maze is the more modern notion. It accords better with contemporary insistence that we are masters of our own destiny rather than simply in the hands of forces beyond our control. Which is the better theology it is not relevant to discuss here, except perhaps to note that the labyrinth is the version least susceptible to a secular interpretation and that is no doubt one major reason why it was for so long preferred in visual presentations, where verbal qualifications as to intended point were of course not normally available.[266] Despite all the apparent confusion, God could clearly be seen to have a plan for us. Before returning to the labyrinth it will be valuable, though, to pursue first some of the literary (and related visual) developments of the maze. For what these disclose is a rich vein of reflection on why such journeying might be valuable in its own right.

The greater range of interpretations possible in literature is well illustrated, it has been suggested, by the optimistic use of the image of the maze in Boethius and Dante as compared with what we find

---

[266] There are occasional exceptions, as in the inscription that accompanied the one at Piacenza: Kern, *Through the Labyrinth*, 158, for its wording.

in Vergil and Chaucer.[267] To some degree, of course, literary pessimism was encouraged by the notion's most obvious mythical precedents in earlier literature in the story of Daedalus and his maze in Crete. It had, after all, been made to contain something evil, the Minotaur, and so its complexity was something that the classical tradition had very much stressed. That is no doubt why we find Augustine protesting in the face of Vergil's 'inescapable maze' that the whole thing is a ridiculous fable, and Gregory Nazianzus that God's artistry was in any case very much greater, as could be seen from the work of the bee and spider.[268] But the fact that the myth had a happy ending with Theseus successfully extricating himself, thanks to Ariadne's thread, did allow other possibilities, and indeed it was not long before Christianity was comparing Theseus to Christ.[269] If the analogy initially sounds implausible, it becomes less so if one thinks of the harrowing of hell, where delivery from something negative is also envisaged. Again, where immediate application to this world was sought, an interesting parallel was available in the intricacies of the wanderings of the people of God through threatening and hostile environment, as recounted in the book of Exodus. It was a later Old Testament incident, though, that was thought to make the appropriation of the legend most apposite, and that was the help afforded by Rahab the harlot in the capture of Jericho. Not unlike Ariadne, her story makes use of flax, rope, and a scarlet cord, while it is by being encircled seven times that Jericho is eventually captured by Joshua (the Hebrew for Jesus).[270]

Dante is a particularly interesting example to pursue in trying to comprehend more fully how such imagery was used. *The Divine Comedy* as a whole opens with the lines:

> Nel mezzo del cammin di nostra vita
> mi ritrovai per una selva oscura
> che la diritta via era smarrita.[271]

---

[267] Doob, *Idea of Labyrinth*, 227–339. The literary is in any case Doob's primary interest. For Vergil, it is suggested, order is known only in retrospect even for the gods: 249. Chaucer's *House of Fame* is used to culminate her whole discussion.

[268] Augustine, *City of God*, 18. 13 (Vergil has *inextricabilis error*—*Aeneid* VI. 27); Gregory Nazianzus, *Theological Orations*, 11. 28. 25.

[269] For an early implicit comparison, Jerome, *Commentary on Ezekiel*: PL 25. 447–9, where the same phrase from Vergil is also quoted.

[270] Josh. chs. 2, 6. For the parallels between Rahab and Ariadne, 2: 6, 15, 18.

[271] *Inferno*, I. 1. 3. 'In the middle of my path through life I found myself in a dark wood where the straight way had become confused' (my trans.).

Life itself has thus become a journey through a complex maze, and, as we learn from the poem, it is only divine grace that can disentangle it for us. In marked contrast to Vergil who had placed Theseus in Hell (presumably because of his failed attempt to carry off Persephone), for Dante he becomes almost a Christ figure.[272] Perhaps more surprisingly, Rahab is actually made to replace Adam as the first to be rescued in Christ's harrowing of Hell.[273] Although the poem's journey is a metaphorical one, one feature that is particularly intriguing is the way in which each stage of Dante's path through the other world corresponds to a particular estimate of this one. Thus, although Hell initially appears to have a clear shape as an inverted cone, there is in fact no obvious path through it at all and so Dante's guide, Vergil, has to resort to various ingenious strategies instead in order to make their way, while the inmates advance only to recede once more. In hell the maze is thus truly inescapable. By contrast, while the way up the mountain that is Purgatory may be steep and circuitous, it is at least clear, and when the goal of Paradise is reached, we are left in no doubt, as directional movement is replaced by circling, dancing spheres.

Such contrasts have been well taken by some of the artists who have illustrated the *Comedy* over the centuries. Sadly, Botticelli's version, begun in the 1480s, was never finished. Yet his inventiveness and deep sympathy for Dante's project shines through. The intractability of Hell is shown, for example, in the boulders of the spendthrifts and hoarders endlessly colliding with one another, the blasphemers vainly attempting to escape the flames in 'a dance of wretched hands', or the sodomites living in a world where all things are askew.[274] But the contrast with Purgatory is perhaps made most effectively with his final illustration for the *Inferno* where readers are forced to turn their page through 180 degrees in order to see how the narrative will continue, with Dante and Vergil now 'converted', as it were: orientated in a quite new direction.[275]

---

[272] In defeating the evils of the Minotaur by a thread: *Inferno*, 12. 10–17.

[273] *Aeneid* VI. 618–19: 'sedet aeternumque sedebit | infelix Theseus'. This seems somewhat inconsistent, though with l. 122: 'Thesea magnum'. For Rahab, *Paradiso*, 9. 115–26, esp. 119–20: 'pria ch' altra' alma | del triunfo di Cristo fu assunta'.

[274] H.-T. Schulze Altcappenberg (ed.), *Sandro Botticelli: The Drawings for Dante's Divine Comedy* (London: Royal Academy of Arts, 2001), 52–3, 72–3, 74–5. The quotation is from *Inferno*, 14, 40–1: 'la tresca | delle misere mani.'

[275] Ibid. 130–3; 'convert' comes from a Latin root meaning 'to turn'.

Again, if a single encompassing circle is repeatedly used to represent the perfection of Paradise, the way in which from our perspective it is still a goal to be reached is well indicated by the modifications Botticelli makes to Dante's text. The way in which the flames that represent individual souls are made to move in sympathy with the overarching circle powerfully conveys how the twists and turns of this life can become the joyful dance of the next, while angel robes made to billow upwards reminds us of the distance yet to be traversed.[276]

Three hundred years or so later, William Blake was to respond to the same commission, in his case towards the end of his life in the 1820s. Although also unfinished, his illustrations are very much more nearly so. Yet the drafts that remain unfinished do have one compensating advantage. Through Blake's practice of writing on them, they offer considerable insight into comprehending his objectives and understanding, not least the fact that he shared neither Dante's belief in a literal Hell nor his sympathy for the classical world.[277] None the less, he does offer us some powerful images of the effects of an evil life, of passion as a whirlwind, for example, or anger as self-division, or of the infinite consequences of wrong doing as a series of receding arches.[278] Heaven as a dancing circle he also produces to great effect,[279] but it is only, I think, if we turn to his Purgatory that one might claim that he outdoes Dante. For the steepness and tortuousness of the ascent is conveyed in a way that at once challenges and promises in one illustration after another.[280] Such richness of allusion is in marked contrast to modern times where we find mazes usually built only for pleasure.

Our own day has seen a significant revival of interest in labyrinths. Here the motivation remains largely religious. In noting this, though, one must guard against supposing that labyrinths have a

[276] For illus: ibid. 230–1, 280–1.

[277] D. Bindman (ed.), *The Divine Comedy of William Blake* (Paris: Bibliothèque de l'Image, 2000), 13, 32–3.

[278] Ibid. 38–9, 50–1, 102–3. The second example departs furthest from Dante's text.

[279] Particularly in the appearances of Peter, James, and John to Dante and Beatrice: ibid. 212–17.

[280] Ibid. 170–5, 178–97 (in fact, the great majority of the Purgatory illustrations).

purity of history that mazes lack.[281] Even so, it is fascinating to observe how many cathedrals have introduced, or reintroduced them. In the United States in particular there also exists a active movement that seeks to explore their significance.[282] This could be classed as part of a more general antirationalist revolt against oppressive technological features in current society. If so, it may well have parallels in a surprising quarter, among contemporary writers of science fiction. For some analysts find one of the main motivations for such writers' versions of space travel not in the exploration of the consequences of scientific discovery, but rather in romantic engagement with the last frontier.[283] Travel should for them be both difficult and have a goal. Others, looking at more scientifically minded travellers such as Richard Burton and Claude Lévi-Strauss, have also noted the same nostalgia, but suggested that we now live in a world of two competing paradigms for travel, the scientific and open-ended, and goal-directed pilgrimage, the latter now lost for ever but still viewed with longing.[284]

But Dante and the transformation he underwent with Blake suggest to me another way of looking at our present situation. Dante opens up the possibility that an imaginary journey could be no less effective than a real one, while Blake demonstrates that the transforming power of the envisaged journey could still remain even as details of interpretation change. So, while pilgrimage can no longer be pursued in precisely the same way as it once was, the religious need for the journey (real or imaginary) remains. The notion of our world as a labyrinth with both direction and goal has

---

[281] In the Reims labyrinth, for example (Kern, *Through the Labyrinth*, 160–1), praise of the architects was a central concern, while even as devout a person as Bach probably intended by his *Kleines Harmonisches Labyrinth* of 1705 nothing more than a harmless bit of musical fun.

[282] Ely is an early example from 1870; more recently Cologne and Evry have followed suit, as has Grace Cathedral in San Francisco: Kern, ibid. 4, 154, 155, 313. Lauren Artress has been particularly influential: note her book, *Walking a Sacred Path: Rediscovering the Labyrinth as a Spiritual Tool* (New York: Riverhead, 1995).

[283] E. James, 'Per Ardua ad Astra: Authorial Choice and the Narrative of Interstellar Travel', in J. Elsner and J.-P. Rubiés (eds.), *Voyages & Visions* (London: Reaktion, 1999), 252–71. In support, the author observes how frequently existing scientific assumptions are flouted e.g. in respect of travelling at the speed of light (258–9). For the last frontier: 252, 270.

[284] Elsner and Rubiés in their Introduction to the above, 1–56. For Burton and Lévi-Strauss: 1, 4, 6. The longing would come from the fact of a clear goal.

had a remarkably persistent idea across history, continents, and cultures.[285] What it may witness to is a deep-seated human intuition that present placedness only becomes fully worthwhile and intelligible if it is set in an larger context, and for that to happen a spiritual journey is necessary, with the journey itself an indispensable part of the learning process. The goal is thus not the sole aim; travelling is as much part of the pilgrimage, and just as integral as the final objective. For what the journeying seeks to achieve, like the symbolic geography I discussed earlier, is strong links between start and finish, with both places given a deeper value but also effectively transformed in the process.

That last point might help make better sense of the occasional practice of dressing the goal of pilgrimage as though it also were on a journey. So, for instance, St James the Great (of Compostela fame) came himself often to be dressed as a pilgrim.[286] Rather more, I suggest, was at stake than his alleged missionary journeys; the claim in effect was being made that, however pursued, he too, like those at his shrine, had had to make a journey (whether real or metaphorical), in order to reach the same goal. If that is the point, it becomes intriguing to observe that this thought is applied even to Christ himself. For in the Vulgate Christ is called a pilgrim as he proceeds on his way to Emmaus, and he is occasionally so represented in art.[287] The Latin word *peregrinus* literally means a wanderer, and it is precisely as wanderer that some have been canonized, for they never reached their goal. One such person is the patron saint of Trani, St Nicholas the Pilgrim.[288] From Phocis in Greece, his destination had been Rome, but he died while meandering round southern Italy, frequently beaten (often on the orders of the clergy) for the way in which he intoned over and over

[285] Although denied by Kern, *Through the Labyrinth*, (e.g. 26–7), his proposed method of dissemination from India to Hopi North American Indians (298–9) seems hard to credit, while the posthumous edition concedes even wider distribution, in the discovery of recent parallels from South America as well (302).

[286] From at least the early 14th c. The literary tradition, though, is earlier. In the *Codex Calixtinus* he is called 'peregrinus notissimus'.

[287] Luke 24: 18. There is a famous 12th-c. example of Christ wearing the insignia of the pilgrim at the monastery of Santo Domingo de Silos.

[288] Not to be confused with the patron saint of nearby Bari, also called Nicholas, the future Santa Claus.

again, *Kyrie eleison*. For him the journeying had in itself become sufficient to create identification with Christ.[289]

This is sometimes presented as the most characteristic feature of Celtic pilgrimage; its so-called 'white martyrdom' is viewed as a commitment not only to abandon home but also to wander without any explicit goal. Certainly, some extreme examples of this are found. The Anglo-Saxon Chronicle for 891, for instance, records three pilgrims arriving at the court of King Alfred in a boat from Ireland, upon which they had embarked without any oars, knowing not where the current might take them.[290] Those who have pursued the subject in detail, though, note that, if they ever happened, the origins of such stories probably lie in the Irish criminal code and not with pilgrimage as such.[291] Much more typical was a complicated dynamic under which insecurity and goal were simultaneously pursued. Thus Celtic monasteries tended to be founded on the boundary between 'desert' and habitation, with their plans often intended deliberately to locate them in relation to the universe as a whole.[292] Romance about remote locations therefore needs to be carefully nuanced.[293] In any case, once the monastery was established, for most the pilgrimage would become a purely imaginary one under the guidance of an *ammchara* or soulmate.[294] So I doubt whether we should ever talk, except very rarely, of goalless pilgrimage.

The idea that cathedral labyrinths were used as substitutes for more distant destinations by the old and infirm has been described

[289] For an excellent accout of his life and significance, published to commemorate the ninth anniversary of his death, G. Cioffari, *S. Nicola Pellegrino: Patrono di Trani* (Bari: Centro Studi Nicolaiani, 1994). The complexity of motives for the canonization is faced: 68–71.

[290] Elsner and Rubiés, *Voyages & Visions*, 19.

[291] So P. Sheldrake, *Living between Worlds: Place and Journey in Celtic Spirituality* (London: Darton, Longman & Todd, 1995), 64.

[292] For boundaries, ibid. 30; note also the symbolic role of 'desert' in Celtic place-names such as Dysart, 22–5. For circular sites replicating the cosmos, 34–5.

[293] Iona was on a major sea route; Lindisfarne, near the ancient Bernician capital at Bambrough.

[294] The Gaelic literally means 'one who shares the cell', and presumably reflects a close pattern of spiritual guidance. For a fascinating analysis of the *Iliad* and *Aeneid* as spiritual journeys in which the former, despite its absence of any real journeying on the part of Achilles, is seen as embodying the metaphor no less powerfully than Aeneas with all his actual wanderings, T. Van Northwick, *Somewhere I Have Never Travelled* (New York: Oxford University Press, 1996), esp. 39–184.

as a 'tenacious fantasy'.[295] This may possibly be so, but in a cathedral such as Chartres there seems little doubt that we are offered a sermon in stone. The way in which its labyrinth stretches the full breadth of the nave as one enters means that sight of it cannot possibly be circumvented, nor indeed the contrast with the type of divine reality affirmed in the distance; divine order and presence, we are being told, are to be sought; they are not just there, easily to hand. So the reason why the labyrinth was so often chosen as an image of the journey can scarcely be in doubt. It was chosen because not only does it make the journey inevitably an experience of dislocation but also, unlike the maze, one in which God could be trusted to appear, in part precisely because of that dislocation.

None the less, there were also more specific goals; so it is to the nature of these that I must now turn. In contrast to the generality of the pattern in the labyrinth, such goals can often appear extraordinarily specific. In Chartres, for example, it was sight of Mary's veil;[296] at Amiens the labyrinth was so orientated that the sun would rise exactly on its axis on the feast of the Assumption, the cathedral feast of dedication.[297] How such particularity might build on and feed the general will therefore be one of our major concerns in what follows. Since what attracted pilgrims to the Holy Land is self-evident, pilgrimage to Jerusalem will be given only brief consideration before I deal at rather greater length with its point elsewhere, particularly at Rome.

The Goal

So far as can now be ascertained, it looks as though it was only really with the alleged rediscovery of the tomb of Christ that pilgrimage

---

[295] So Doob, *Idea of Labyrinth*, 120. This seems to me too strong. The absence of confirming evidence hardly in itself refutes the possibility, given how little has in fact survived from the Middle Ages.

[296] Now so called, but, ironically, only as a result of the French Revolution, which preserved the garment in order to prove that it could not be what it was claimed to be, the undergarment in which Mary gave birth to Jesus: *la chemise de la sainte Vierge.*

[297] The present labyrinth is a copy of the one first installed in 1611: Kern, *Through the Labyrinth*, 149.

to the Holy Land took off.[298] Although there is some evidence for pilgrimage in the second and third centuries and even of sites shared by Christian, Jew, and pagan, its precise significance is disputed.[299] The two earliest uncontested accounts from the fourth century are quite different in feel. What seems to interest the anonymous Bordeaux pilgrim is confirmation of the biblical stories, and in pursuance of that aim he exhibits an extraordinary naïve belief in the power of various artefacts to survive.[300] By contrast, Egeria shows a strong liturgical interest, and records in some detail her participation in various ceremonies at the shrines.[301] It is an interesting divergence, not least because it was to repeat itself in later history. Thus, one discussion of nineteenth-century pilgrimage observes a not dissimilar contrast between English Protestant and Russian Orthodox pilgrims.[302] The former want confirmation, the latter a variant on their normal liturgical life. Intriguingly, in both the language of sacramentality is also to be found. For the former it clearly invokes the memorial understanding of the Lord's Supper, while for the latter it has analogies to the way in which icons operate, as windows onto an eternal reality.[303] The existence of a third, and more characteristically Western attitude, though, should

[298] The transformation in Eusebius' attitudes is taken as indicative of a more general change in R. L. Wilken, *The Land Called Holy* (New Haven: Yale University Press, 1992), 81. The term 'Holy Land' is a borrowing from Judaism; cf. Zech. 2: 12; 2 Macc. 1: 7.

[299] For a strong presentation of the earlier evidence as indeed early signs of pilgrimage, D. Hunt, 'Were There Christian Pilgrims before Constantine?' in J. Stopford (ed.), *Pilgrimage Explored* (York: York Medieval Press, 1999), 25–40. For the Mamre of Gen. 18 as a shared site: 39–40.

[300] Perhaps best expressed by a comment such as the following: 'where the Temple stood . . . there is marble in front of the altar which has on it the blood of Zacharias—you would think it had only been shed today. All around you can see the marks of the hobnails of the soldiers who killed him as plainly as if they had been pressed into wax': Wilkinson, *Egeria's Travels*, 157.

[301] My contrast, though, may possibly reflect no more than the accidents of history, as the itinerary part of Egeria in relation to Jerusalem and its surroundings is missing. Another, perhaps better founded, contrast is that Egeria is far more interested in the people who inhabit the scriptural landscape (monks, bishops, etc.) than the Bordeaux pilgrim, who speaks only of places.

[302] T. Hummel, 'The Sacramentality of the Holy Land: Two Contrasting Approaches', in D. Brown and A. Loades (ed.), *The Sense of the Sacramental* (London: SPCK, 1995), 78–100.

[303] For a Protestant example of the use of the term 'sacramental' in this context, ibid. 91.

also be noted, one that comes much nearer to valuing the land in itself. An extreme example of this is to be found in Augustine's apparent endorsement of the value of bringing back soil from Palestine as a way of warding off evil.[304] Such attitudes will engage our attention shortly, but for the moment it will be enough to observe how the change illustrates the high value Christians now placed on pilgrimage, whatever the New Testament attitude had been, a change no doubt shaped in part by the three centuries of continuous Christian control of Jerusalem. If the Muslim conquest made matters more difficult, it should not be forgotten that of the three religions it was generally the most tolerant to the other two. The first Muslim conqueror, Umar, left the Church of the Holy Sepulchre untouched, and it was only the extreme Shi'ite Fatimids from Egypt who made visits and worship problematic.[305]

The extent of the influence of such reverence towards the Holy Land is perhaps best illustrated by the manner in which Christianity's third most popular shrine (after Jerusalem and Rome) grew to prominence. For it is clear that Alphonso II in encouraging the cult of St James at Compostela saw Spain as a new Holy Land to be delivered from the Moors, with even the shrine itself being treated in detail as the new Jerusalem. Thus, for example, a cordon of three miles round the shrine was created and gifted to it, clearly on the model of what the Levites had once been held to possess round Jerusalem. Again, if the legend of Constantine's dream and support for the shrine arise in part because of the confusion of a bishop's name with that of an unrelated and earlier pope, pertinent to note here is the way in which that dream was modelled on the magi being seen as kings also summoned on a pilgrimage.[306] Early arrivals at Compostela were even named Rey in honour of the legend, and the practice there of crowning pilgrims is probably also not unconnected.[307]

---

[304] Wilken, *Land Called Holy*, 125.

[305] Omar's behaviour in 634 was in marked contrast to the Sassanid Persians who had briefly conquered the city in 614, and who were given active support in their destructive frenzy by some Jews: ibid. 206–7. The second destruction occurred in 1009 under Al-Hakim.

[306] F. L. Alsina, 'Compostelle', in von Saucken, *Pèlegrinage*, 293–320, esp. 295–6, 315–16.

[307] Ibid. 90, 119; for more on Charlemagne's dream: 88.

By comparison with Jerusalem even Rome was for long regarded as a poor second-best, forced on pilgrims because they had neither the necessary time nor wealth to go all the way to Palestine, or else because the difficult domestic circumstances in that land itself precluded such a possibility.[308] That conceded, though, there remains, I believe, potentially more to learn about sacramentality from how pilgrimage functioned elsewhere than in Jerusalem, precisely because other destinations had to acquire their special status (it was not an already established fact). In the case of Rome, as we have seen, this was greatly helped by understandings of the penitential system then current. If the crude calculations can now only make us smile or weep,[309] it is as well to remember that, though greatly fostered by the papacy, popular belief also inclined the same way. Indeed, historians inform us that it was from popular pressure that the initial impetus came for the first Jubilee Year in 1300,[310] and that despite the fact the then reigning pope, Boniface VIII, was someone peculiarly conscious of his own dignity and that of his city.[311] Some estimates suggest that that year there may have been as many as two million pilgrims to the city, quite a strain on a town that by then had probably shrunk to a population of no more than thirty-five thousand from the million or so it had once enjoyed at the height of the Roman Empire.[312] Even so, pilgrimage to Rome had begun long before this, and so, given the topic of this chapter, it is to factors particularly associated with place that I want to draw attention here, for they too played their part, however dominant at times penance came to be. Three significantly different types of influence from place are worth highlighting.

First, there is what might seem initially a purely secular factor, and that is the inheritance of pagan Rome. It is not that anyone went to Rome as a pilgrim explicitly to honour the pagan past

[308] Jerusalem was captured in 1099, but lost again in 1291.

[309] Gerald of Wales, for example, succeeded in clocking up ninety-two years' worth of indulgences on a pilgrimage to Rome in 1204, while by the 14th c. promises of 12,000 years and more were on offer: for these and other examples, Birch, *Pilgrimage to Rome*, 179–80, 194–6.

[310] Ibid. 197–202.

[311] It was with Boniface that we get the papal triple tiara. He also imposed statues of himself wherever he could: R. Krautheimer, *Rome: Profile of a City, 312–1308* (Princeton: Princeton University Press, 1980), 151, 227.

[312] For number of pilgrims: ibid. 159; for changes in population: 4, 62, 65, 231.

(though guides were available, even in the Middle Ages, to the classical ruins).[313] No, it was rather that Christianity was seen as building on, and indeed surpassing, the greatest empire that the known world had hitherto ever seen. So it is, I think, no accident that the Lateran Palace, the centre of the papacy until the four-teenth century, eventually came to be fronted by a whole series of classical survivals, many of which were given a Christian interpret-ation, nor that in the churches pagan statues were sometimes adapted to Christian use.[314] That at least one Holy Roman Em-peror (Otto III) should attempt to make Rome his capital is perhaps not altogether surprising, but long before the Renaissance not dissimilar motivations are to be found in the papacy also.[315] It seems, for example, that modifications to the Lateran were deliber-ately designed to challenge the alleged new imperial capital in Constantinople. If such actions conjure up rather worldly concerns, the commonly recounted legend of the Emperor Augustus' dream implies a somewhat different overall assessment, that through divine providence ancient Rome prepared for, and now is sur-passed by, the new Christian dispensation, and there was no short-age of illustrations in art to reinforce this point.[316]

My second factor is perhaps the most obvious, and concerns the presence in Rome of the tombs of martyrs, not least Peter and Paul. Already in the second century reference is being made to the 'trophy' of Peter; so it is just possible that the present site under the Vatican dates back to the actual burial-place of Peter.[317] Veneration of Paul

[313] Such as the 12th-c. *Mirabilia Urbis Romae*; for description of contents, Birch, 117–18.

[314] For the gathering of classical works round the Lateran, Krautheimer, *Rome*, 192–7. The statue of Marcus Aurelius on horseback was interpreted as in fact Constantine, while the famous *Thornpicker* was taken to allude to the pain that was to follow Christ's entry into Jerusalem: H. L. Kessler and J. Zacharias, *Rome 1300: On the Path of the Pilgrim* (New Haven: Yale University Press, 200), 27. For Isis transformed into St Agnes, and Venus into St Helena, J. Hagar, *Pilgrimage: A Chronicle of Christianity through the Churches of Rome* (London: Weidenfeld & Nicolson, 1999), 62–3, 218.

[315] For Otto III, Krautheimer, *Rome*, 145.

[316] For the legend of the origins of the name of the church of S. Maria in Aracoeli, Hagar, *Pilgrimage*, 109–10; for Roman togas for the disciples at S. Pudenziana and for the Christchild as a young emperor at S. Maria Maggiore, Krautheimer, *Rome*, 41, 49.

[317] It has been questioned, though, whether the same attitude would have prevailed in the 1st c., especially with expectations of the end of the present

developed more slowly, and appears to have been led from the top, as an intellectual elite under Pope Damasus sought out a more appropriate hero.[318] However, there was no shortage of other models for the general populace, represented by the catacombs. Even if there is often considerable confusion over the precise relation between the person buried there or in a related church and the actual title given to the building, there seems no reason to doubt that in most cases we are dealing with actual martyrs.[319] Nor is it hard to comprehend what attracted people to their tombs. Their mortal remains and the places associated with them were believed to continue to mediate their presence. Although not himself a martyr, the inscription on St Martin's tomb at Tours expresses the issue well:

> Cuius anima in manu Dei est, sed hic totus est
> Praesens manifestus omni gratia virtutum.[320]

Nor was it only the presence of the saint that was mediated. Because the individuals had been martyrs for God, God himself could also be guaranteed to be involved. Some may be tempted to parody all of this as a magical or semi-magical belief, but on the other side note needs to be taken of the fact that even today people seldom discard all the items associated with a deceased loved one. Tangible memorials, and not just memories, are used to help keep their influence alive.

But it was not just a matter of invoking the past. It was also about establishing a relationship with someone believed still to be alive. Given the prominence assigned elsewhere to the search for miracle cures (as with Martin above), it is interesting to observe that this formed no part of the cult of Peter and Paul, nor a major motivation in visiting the catacombs. Speaking of a 'cemetery' rather than of a 'necropolis' indicates the new emphasis within Christianity. It was not a place for corpses of the 'dead', but for those who were 'asleep', and the symbolism of going into the bowels of the earth

world; cf. J. Toynbee and J. Ward-Perkins, *The Shrine of St Peter and the Vatican Excavations* (London: Longman Green, 1956), 155–6.

[318] So Krautheimer, *Rome*, 42.

[319] The *titulus* of a building seems originally to have implied ownership, not necessarily the person buried there. The church of San Clemente well illustrates confusion between a number of Clements.

[320] 'His spirit is in the hand of God, but he is here totally present, manifest with every grace of divine power' (my trans.).

to greet them must have given powerful expression to that belief. The apparent darkness belied a greater light: they were now with God in heaven, and that is what pilgrims also hoped for themselves.[321] In the symbolism of the cave Christianity had already been anticipated by the Mithraic shrines that were dotted across ancient Rome.[322] Contemporary Christians often fight shy of the parallels, as though any recognition of affinity must undermine the truth of Christianity's own distinctive claims. But some shared elements were surely to be expected, given the limited range of appropriate symbols available in the created order to any religion. Moreover, if God as creator is seen as the originator of all such symbols, their common presence, so far from undermining religious belief, can actually be used to support it.

As it is, even within Christianity's overarching unity there were significant divergences over how such imagery should be most appropriately applied. In Chapter 2 we noted how the theology of icons represents a significantly different approach to sacramentality from that pursued in Western and particularly Renaissance art. In the case of saints and their relics there occurs an interesting variant on this theme. Even as late as Gregory the Great the Roman view was still that the bones of the martyrs should be left in situ, but thereafter under Eastern influence a change came about, no doubt in part also influenced by the worsening political situation and the fact that most of the holy sites were outside the city walls.[323] The symbolism of the catacombs was maintained as the martyrs' bones were transferred to new situations. Still underground, they were interred in crypts with ambulatories, positioned beneath the high altar. But the connection with place was of course weakened, and it was weakened still further by the new iconography that came from the East. Instead of classical realism that had suggested the presence of the saints in our midst, the figures were now given shallow forms that seemed almost to dissolve them into another world.[324] The aim now appeared to be to draw

---

[321] Jerome records his own experience as a boy of entering into what seemed to him like hell: *Commentary on Ezekiel* (PL 25. 375).

[322] For some account of the various Mithraea discovered so far by archaeologists, I. della Portella, *Subterranean Rome* (Cologne: Könemann, 2000), 15–55.

[323] For Gregory's resistance, Krautheimer, *Rome*, 80; for Eastern influence, 113.

[324] Ibid. 94–7, 126–30. He contrasts the classical mosaics of the 6th c. in SS Cosma e Damiano with the Byzantine work fifty years later in S. Lorenzo fuori la mura, and in the 9th c. S. Prassede with S. Maria in Dominica.

worshippers elsewhere, rather than for them to experience God endorsing their present location. The two types of style fought it out in Roman churches for some time. Eventually, as we all know, the more Western approach triumphed. But perhaps it always had among ordinary people, since the search for tangible relics continued, not least in the practice of taking away *brandea* from the shrines. These were cloths that had touched the holy objects and that were used subsequently as tangible witnesses to the divine presence in the pilgrims' own homes and villages.[325]

But there was also a third factor, and this might well make one think that Rome was after all a poor substitute: the extent to which holy relics associated with Christ's life actually came to play a major role in pilgrimage to Rome no less than at Jerusalem. In particular note the extraordinary range of things that were to be found in the Lateran's Sancta Sanctorum: included were pebbles and earth from the Holy Land as well as Jesus' umbilical cord and foreskin.[326] Yet it is fascinating to observe that what were commonly regarded as Rome's two most important relics were in fact, like the *brandea*, at one remove, that is to say, not actual objects from the life of Jesus but, as it were, reflections or touched by him. This is true alike of the Veronica image kept at St Peter's and of the *Acheropita* preserved at St John Lateran; the former was alleged to have been created by the imprint of Christ's face on a cloth offered to him as he made his way to the cross, while the latter was held to be a portrait begun by St Luke but completed by angels (hence 'not made by human hands'). Both were exposed to public view in processions. The Veronica image went from the Vatican to the nearby San Spirito Hospital each January, while the *Acheropita* was submitted to a much more elaborate itinerary on the eve of the feast of the Assumption, a practice that lasted from the seventh to the sixteenth century.[327] It is that latter ritual with which I want to close this section, not least because I think it can tell us some profound things

[325] The practice existed from at least the time of the 6th-c. Gregory of Tours: PL 71. 729. A hole for the purpose has been found at S. Paolo; so Hagar, *Pilgrimage*, 200.

[326] For a detailed description, Kessler and Zacharias, *Rome 1300*, 38–63 esp. 53, 57.

[327] For details of the Veronica procession, ibid. 187–8; for that of the *Acheropita*, 65–157.

both about the nature of pilgrimage in particular and about the sacramentality of place in general.

The image journeyed from its home in the Lateran to Santa Maria Maggiore, but it was far from a direct route that was followed. It meandered in what one might call an almost labyrinthine course, partly so that certain other sites might be visited on the way and partly to avoid some locations, including a street that had become associated with the infamous, reputed female Pope Joan.[328] The procession stopped twice, first at the church of Santa Maria Nova where an icon of Mary was brought out to witness the pope washing the feet of this image of Christ, then finally at Santa Maria Maggiore where a famous icon of Mary (*Regina coeli*) emerged to greet the image of her Son.[329] Sadly today, partly through all that foot-washing, the *Acheropita* image is scarcely legible, but copies can still be seen in the mosaics of two churches.[330] More important, though, is for us to try to comprehend what was intended by these somewhat strange manœuvres.

The procession, I suggest, was intended to indicate the need for a similar journeying in our own lives, its circuitousness the twists and turns to which those lives are inevitably subject. If this dimension appears relatively straightforward, the washing of the icon cannot help but strike us now as very strange indeed. For, if foot washing there had to be, why not of some beggars in the Rome of the time? But then one observes that such an action would not have secured the same objective. For in this case the intention was not to emulate in dealings with others what Christ had himself once done but rather somehow for those present to participate once more in his own earthly life. So the successor of Peter does not copy Christ's example at the Last Supper and wash others' feet; instead, he behaves like Mary Magdalene and himself washes Christ's feet, perhaps also with the thought that they will now be dusty and weary with the journey, just like any other pilgrim. The painting is thus being used in a way that may for some smack of extreme or naïve realism but for others will surely immediately suggest a high doctrine of sacramentality. The transformations in discipleship that

[328] *Vicus Papissae*—'lane of the popess'; ibid. 71.

[329] Despite the name, both this one and the other Marian image at S. Maria Nova were of Virgin and Child: for illus., ibid. 96, 136.

[330] For the original, ibid., 62. For an almost identical copy in S. Maria Maggiore: 130; for a close parallel at the Lateran: 61.

had occurred in a different place and time were now being sought in this place and time. Through these means the penitent Mary Magdalene had achieved intimacy with Christ; so now once more could today's sinners. Christ had once been a pilgrim on earth; now he shares our feet-weariness.[331]

But matters did not end there. The Virgin Mary is also brought in on the act. Christ travels on Assumption eve, through the night of life as it were, to once more enthrone his mother on the dawn of the next day. Whether envisaged as taking place at Jerusalem or at Ephesus, Mary's transition from this world to the next was being celebrated, through a symbolic re-enactment, Christ once more meeting his mother. For not only does the *Acheropita* procession now carry its image into Santa Maria Maggiore, it also places it on the Gospel pulpit in the quire area known as the *schola cantorum*. Meanwhile another procession brings in the *Regina coeli* icon and places it on the Epistle pulpit opposite. Extracts from the Song of Songs were then sung, as mother and son, bride and groom, are once more reunited in heaven.[332] And, as if to confirm all this, one looks up at the apse mosaic and sees them sharing a common throne.[333] Initially, perhaps, one wants to protest that things have gone too far, for Mary sits no lower than Christ himself, and looks as though she is being treated as his equal. Yet closer attention reveals that she does after all still remain one of us, for, though the face in the mosaic appears to mimic that of *Regina coeli*, the hands emphatically do not; one is now across her breast, the other raised in supplication. There she is then, interceding for us.[334] Our earthly pilgrimage, we are in effect being told, could indeed conclude like hers, at least to this extent, that through her prayers and those of our

---

[331] Commentators uniformly assume a reference to the incident at the Last Supper, speaking, for example, of how 'this gesture re-enacts the episode . . . in which Christ washes the feet of Peter' (ibid. 96). But roles are reversed, and so this will not do.

[332] The open book that Christ holds reads: 'Come, my chosen one, and I will place you on my throne.' If the language is thought unbiblical, recall Rev. 3: 21: 'He who conquers I will grant him to sit with me on my throne' (RSV).

[333] For illus. of the mosaic, Kessler and Zacharias, *Rome 1300*, 143.

[334] One might compare a late 13th-c. cope in the *opus anglicanum* style and now in the possession of the Vatican: there the coronation is portrayed as more like a conversation between Mother and Son; for illus., P de Montebello (ed.), *The Vatican Collections* (New York: Abrams, 1982), 38–9.

fellow pilgrims we too one day may be caught up, like her, to share in the life of her Son in heaven.

Some, no doubt, will cavil at the way such a theology was once presented, but, amid all the speed to condemn, sight should not be lost of one underlying theme: the transformation of place. The places that belonged to the lives of Christ and Mary migrated into paintings that themselves migrated in turn to specific locations in Rome. But they too migrated into the lives and homes of the pilgrims, as mementoes and symbols of their visit were carried back with them. Yet none of these places were devalued in the process. Rather, Jerusalem, Rome, and home all acquired an enhanced value, for each embodied what was seen as a higher reality, the transforming presence of God mediated sacramentally to humankind.

In such mediation buildings clearly play a key role. So it is to consideration of their distinctive contribution that I next turn.

5

Competing Styles

Architectural Aims and Wider Setting

INITIALLY it might well be thought that architecture can have nothing to do with sacramentality. For, if the key element in sacramentality is understood to be God's communication through the material aspects of his own creation, clearly what is involved here is something quite different: an essentially human and not a divine artefact. None the less, across the centuries human beings have in fact thought quite otherwise, of architecture as being one of the major ways in which the sacred is conveyed, and by no means just with respect to buildings designed for an exclusively religious purpose. In any case, as previous chapters have already indicated, it is not just a matter of what the Creator has done, but also of how that work is appropriated. So, in this case: architecture can be seen as having a role, provided the intention or result still reflects something of what God is believed to be doing anyway through his presence in our world. In other words, architecture has the power to imitate or mimic God's actions elsewhere in the natural and human world; so through that imitation it can open up the possibility of God himself using such means to communicate with humankind.

We live in a very utilitarian age. Even worship is quite likely to be justified in terms of some further end beyond adoration of the being to whom one owes everything: 'building up the community of faith', 'refreshment for the week ahead', 'teaching', and so forth. It is little wonder then that many find a burden the constant build-up of doctrine and exhortation that so often characterizes modern liturgy, and prefer to sit quietly in the building instead of attending a church service. It is a practice that should not be despised. For each of the building styles that has characterized the history of Christianity has the capacity in its own right to convey something of the enchantment that consists in basking in the presence of God without any further end in view. Of course as a Christian and a priest I believe much is lost by those who fail to participate fully in the Church's liturgy. But I do want to protest against the implication so often drawn that this means that architecture must always be assessed in terms of a subordinate, serving role. Liturgy and architecture will each have their own distinctive message, and the question is thus not which is subordinate to which, but rather whether the overall message is a coherent one, and achieved by repetition, complementarity, or contrast. So in the survey of architectural styles that follows I shall pay as much attention to the wider setting as to the aims implicit in the architecture on its own.

The Temple and Sites of Divine Presence

So deeply secular have Western attitudes become that it comes as a great shock to most people to discover that once upon a time all building was envisaged in essentially religious terms. Divine sanction was required not because the divine initiative was thereby usurped (though sometimes no doubt such thoughts played their part), but principally because building was seen as mirroring what God had already achieved in creation, in making this world our home. It is an image that one finds in the earliest piece of Christian Anglo-Saxon poetry, in these words of Caedmon:

> Now must we praise the Lord,
> The warden of heaven's realm,
>   ...
> How for the sons of men
> He shaped heaven as their roof
> And afterwards prepared the middle world,
> The earth, for their habitation.[1]

Even so, the response of some to such attempts to make human architecture echo divine may well be that such notions smack more of arrogance or of magic than of grace: that it is a case of human assertiveness or else of human beings trying to manipulate a guar-

---

[1] Caedmon (d. 680) was a labourer at the monastery at Whitby. I have quoted the most commonly used modernized version. His poem survived as an appendix to the Moore MS of Bede. For a modern poet entering into his experience in essentially sacramental terms, Denise Levertov's *Caedmon* in *The Stream and the Sapphire* (New York: New Directions, 1997), 41–2.

antee of divine presence rather than waiting on the free initiative of divine grace. But on the other side might be set the way in which so much of the consequent symbolism is in fact parasitic on natural symbols, and so it could be argued that the related structures and patterns in human architecture are in fact loyally, humbly, and perhaps even prayerfully, following their greater antecedent model in the architecture of the universe. In the previous chapter I noted how this was sought in home and city; here I want to focus on religious buildings as such and their antecedents, in particular the Jerusalem Temple, so formative as it undoubtedly was for most Christian thinking on the matter until relatively modern times.

Perhaps the best way to explore how temples were once conceived is to pursue some actual examples. Although in some early forms of religious belief, the home of the divine was given a specific location within this world (as with Mount Olympus among the Greeks), the more common pattern was to identify the divine with the heavens and so use what could be seen to link heaven and earth as the most appropriate way of founding a connection between divine and human in the built environment. Thus it turns out to be no accident that many temples were built either on a mountain or else in the form of a mountain. Think, for instance, of how the Parthenon dominates the Acropolis, or buildings on the flat such as Aztec and Maya temples or the Buddhist temple at Borobodur in Java acquired their precise shape and location, as in effect artificial mountains.[2]

In these cases we are already dealing with fairly advanced societies. But however far back we go the same principles will be found to apply. Take the allusion to sacred trees and pillars in the patriarchal narratives and elsewhere.[3] Surely more is intended than simply a marker for a significant religious site. Rather, the thrusting heavenward of tree or rock suggested an interchange, a highway

---

[2] For the Middle-East context it is illuminating to note that the term 'ziggurat' actually derives from a Babylonian word for 'mountain peak'.

[3] Pillars are used e.g. to indicate where a covenant with, or before, God was made (e.g. Gen. 31: 43–50; Exod. 24: 3–4), while Jachin and Boaz, the two bronze pillars before the Temple (1 Kgs. 7: 15–22; Jer. 52: 17–23), as well as pointing heavenwards, may well have been intended to indicate that God had passed between them, to dwell with his people. For an example of pillar and tree combined: Josh. 24: 26–7.

between heaven and earth, and indeed the point could not be better
made than in the story of Jacob's ladder which ends, significantly,
with Jacob erecting a pillar.[4] Bath Abbey provides an interesting
variant on this theme; in a church that lacks a spire, the ladder with
its pillar is represented twice on its west front.[5] For continuity in
Jewish thought one might turn to the twentieth century and Frank
Lloyd Wright's design for the synagogue of Beth Sholom in suburban Philadelphia, modelled as it is on Mount Sinai.[6] But of course,
as already hinted, Hebrew thought is in this by no means unique.
Whether one takes the ancient totem pole or the Gothic spire, so
familiar in the northern European landscape from the twelfth
century onwards, the intention and the prayer is the same, that
here heaven and earth are linked, made sacramentally one by
realization of the divine presence here on earth. In response to
any inclined to object that this would make modern skyscrapers
essentially religious, at least one key difference may be noted, that
trees and spires strain towards a point, and indeed even sacred
towers are often designed with the same aim in mind.[7] Minarets,
for instance, even where they are of the same size throughout their
length, usually have increasingly smaller compartmental divisions in
the brickwork as they rise, precisely in order to pull the eye
heavenwards.

Significant points of contact were also made astronomically. To
mention but one recurring feature, the light of the sun is commonly
utilized, either in its light striking at some key moment in the day or
year or else, more commonly, through the orientation of the
building towards the east or west: that way either the worshippers
or the god's statue received the light and warmth of the sun's first
morning rays. Although in practice little is now made of this,
Christian churches are still orientated towards the east, while new
Hindu temples remain subject to elaborate astronomical calcula-

[4] Gen. 28: 10–22. Note also the name given to the place: Bethel, or 'house of
God'.

[5] For the mixture of motives, secular and sacred, in this unique 16th-c.
creation, J. M. Luxford, 'In Dreams: The Sculptural Iconography of the West
Front of Bath Abbey Reassessed', *Religion and the Arts* 4 (2000), 314–36.

[6] Illustrated in C. Humphrey and P. Vitebsky, *Sacred Architecture* (Boston: Little,
Brown, 1997), 110–11.

[7] For a religious critique of skyscrapers, R. Sardello, *Facing the World with Soul*
(Hudson, NY: Lindisfarne, 1992).

tions before ever they can be built.[8] Light is of course an obvious natural symbol for the divine, and so whether this is experienced in the effect of light inside the building or only as one views its exterior, the message remains essentially the same: God inhabits this space. Occasionally, one finds the claim explicitly made for us, as in a fifteenth-century painting by Crivelli where Jerome actually points to divine light emanating from a consecrated building.[9] More commonly, the tactic used to stress such presence is to represent an appropriate divine or heavenly figure disproportionately large and so in effect filling the entire building; once again, the phenomenon occurs indifferently across religions, in, for example, Christianity and Hinduism alike.[10]

A typical Protestant response might be to insist that such attitudes are essentially post-biblical. That sacramental attitudes to buildings are indeed absent from the New Testament and from the earlier history of the Church must, I think, be conceded. But increasingly Old Testament scholars are acknowledging that matters were quite otherwise in earlier Jewish history. The symbolism associated with the Temple, although sometimes distinctive, also shared many key elements with other religions. Either way, though, both alike reflect this sense of the building as embodying the Creator's presence. Not that all were agreed on this, as we shall see, but that the weight of the evidence can now be seen to point differently from the way matters have commonly been interpreted in the past needs stressing. Jews naturally wanted to see some continuity with the synagogue while Christians sought to focus on those elements that anticipated the Christian dispensation, and so on the way in which the sacrificial system acted as a type or anticipation of Christ's atoning work. Such implicit bias can be detected not only in

[8] For the rules, see J. M. Malville, 'Cosmogonic Motifs in Indian Temples', in E. Lyle (ed.), *Sacred Architecture in the Traditions of India, China, Judaism and Islam* (Edinburgh: Edinburgh University Press, 1992), 25–39.

[9] Part of the great altarpiece in the cathedral of Sant' Emidio at Ascoli and commissioned in 1492. The building Jerome holds was apparently modelled on the cathedral's baptistery. For illus. and commentary, A. Bovero, *L'opera completa del Crivelli* (Milan: Rizzoli, 1974), illus. XXB and 90–1.

[10] For two examples set helpfully opposite each other, J. M. Lundquist, *The Temple: Meeting Place of Heaven and Earth* (London: Thames & Hudson, 1993), 48–9. One is an 1810 manuscript painting by Sajanu of Durga filling her temple and the other from 1499 by Christian de Hondt of Virgin and Child similarly placed within a Christian church and filling it.

standard nineteenth-century textbooks but also late into the twentieth century. Even among some of our most outstanding biblical
scholars there has been surprising resistance to reading the surviving
texts and evidence in the most obvious way.[11]

Yet perceptions cannot help but change as soon as we ask not so
much what was done as what was the context in which it was done.
Herod's Temple was by any standard an impressive building. Although set on a hill only 2,460 feet above sea level, it was higher than
where most of the population lived,[12] while the expanse it covered
amounted to no less than thirty-five acres, or about twelve soccer
fields.[13] Admittedly, most of this space was taken up with a series of
open-air courts, and it was only in its innermost that sacrificial
offerings were made on its huge altar.[14] That worship out of doors,
however, paralleled the practices of paganism, as indeed did the way
in which the building itself was seen as confined to the god's own
use.[15] Herod's version of the Temple differed in some ways from its
predecessors, but in essence the symbolism remained basically unchanged.[16] Not only was the sacredness of the inner sanctum stressed

[11] For a 19th-c. example, first published in 1874, A. Edersheim, *The Temple*, ed.
J. M. Bimson (Aylesbury: Candle Books, 1997). For more recent examples,
E. P. Sanders, *Judaism: Practice and Belief 63BCE–66CE* (London: SCM, 1992),
47–118, and, perhaps more surprisingly because of his Catholicism, R. De Vaux,
Ancient Israel, 2nd edn. (London: Darton, Longman & Todd, 1965), 312–517 esp.
328–30 where he speaks of 'feeble support' (328) for the sort of ideas I am about to
endorse.

[12] On the Ophel hill to the south. The Mount of Olives across the Kidron
valley to the east is about 200 ft. higher.

[13] So Sanders, *Judaism*, who speaks of 'an extraordinary achievement' (58),
although conceding that it was surpassed by the temple of Amun at Karnak
which enclosed no less than 75 acres.

[14] Edersheim, *The Temple*, has helpful plans and reconstructions of the Temple
and its three courts (Gentiles, women, Israelites): 31, 36–7, 41, 43, 118–19. He
estimates that 200,000 could easily be accommodated: 54. The altar was 15 ft. high:
44.

[15] It is doubtful whether even the shewbread should be contrasted with pagan
rituals, since provision is made for both food and drink: Exod. 25: 29–30; 37: 16.
That might seem to undermine the value of the ritual, but as I argue in the chapter
on food in this volume's sequel, what is in fact entailed is the need to view pagan
conceptions more charitably: they were not nearly as naïve as Christians often like
to pretend.

[16] For the relation between the various courts and changes over the centuries,
Sanders, *Judaism*, 61–2; M. Barker, *The Gate of Heaven* (London: SPCK, 1991),
22–6.

by a graded approach both inside and out,[17] it is also clear that for most Jewish writers before, or contemporary with, Christ, it was viewed, like its pagan equivalents, as God's own special dwelling-place, or in other words as the location of an immanent reality. That was the promise given in Exodus with the Tent of Meeting which anticipated the Temple, and it was a theme taken up by many, though not all, subsequent writers.[18] The fact that the High Priest entered the Holy of Holies only once a year on the Day of Atonement might be taken to suggest as much, but one must add to this a wealth of detail that plays on two key related images: the Temple as the locus of the original act of creation itself and current Temple worship as a direct reflection of the angels' heavenly adoration.[19]

Reinforcing the theme of creation, a number of non-biblical authors inform us that the menorah was intended to represent the then known seven planets and the laver or large basin the sea that God had held in abeyance at the creation, a theme that we find reflected also in some of the psalms.[20] Little wonder then that Philo applies the imagery in reverse and speaks of the whole universe as 'the holy temple of God'.[21] There were also, however, a number of images drawn from the earth itself: among them palm trees, flowers, pomegranates, and a huge vine.[22] Again, the colours in the Temple

---

[17] There were, progressively, courts or specific areas for Gentiles, women, male Israelites, and priests. Our earliest reference to a 'court of priests' is 2 Chr. 4: 9. Internally, there was a larger Holy Place leading to the Holy of Holies.

[18] Cf. e.g. Exod. 29: 45: 'And I will dwell among the people of Israel', or Ps. 68: 16: 'the mount which God desired for his abode' (RSV).

[19] It is sometimes objected that much of this evidence is late. That is true, but at least it provides an explanation of why the Temple and the worship took the form it did, while there are no shortage of parallels to suggest comparable thinking in other cultures of the time.

[20] For the menorah representing sun, moon, and five planets, Philo, *Quis Heres*, 221–4; Josephus, *Jewish War*, V. 217–18. For the large basin as a primeval 'sea', 1 Kgs. 7: 23–6; although the Chronicler demythologizes its use, the terminology is retained (cf. 2 Chr. 4: 6). Not only does rabbinic thought record the earlier symbolism (for references, Barker, *Gate of Heaven*, 65–7), that symbolism also fits very nicely with the imagery of several of the psalms: e.g. 29: 10; 33: 7; 74: 13; 93: 3–4; 98: 7–8.

[21] Philo, *De specialibus legibus*, 1. 66.

[22] The walls had 'palm trees and open flowers' (1 Kgs. 6: 29), while the two bronze pillars before the Temple were carved with 200 pomegranates and 'lily work' (1 Kgs. 7: 20, 22). For the golden vine that decorated the entrance to the sanctuary, Josephus, *Jewish War*, V. 210–11; *Antiquities*, XV. 395.

curtain have been plausibly interpreted as referring to the four elements that were then believed to constitute the world, while the High Priest's robes were also viewed as exhibiting cosmic symbolism.[23] All this, when combined with Ezekiel's vision of a restored Temple with its four rivers, seems to force on us the idea that the Temple was viewed as itself the site of Eden.[24] Whereas in the past Ezekiel has been treated as an oddball within Old Testament theology, and other relevant material summarily dismissed as 'late', it is now increasingly recognized that this is a strand that runs right through Jewish history. Not only do the psalms sung in the Temple precincts with their image of the cosmic flood suggest as much, but so too does many another allusion, as, for instance, the equation of Mount Zion with the Canaanite cosmic mountain of Zaphon.[25] The last two decades or so have witnessed major changes in the interpretation of the second-century BC book of Ecclesiasticus.[26] So, when Ben Sira makes his work culminate in the High Priest as Adam redivivus we should not now be altogether surprised; indeed, so far from the innovation being Greek, it is his translator grandson that shows the greater caution.[27]

---

[23] For the Temple curtain with its 'scarlet' representing fire, its 'fine linen' earth, its 'blue' air and 'purple' water, Josephus, *Jewish War*, v. 212–13; for cosmic symbolism in the priest's breastplate, Philo, *Questions on Exodus*, II. 114. Innocent III adopted a similar scheme of interpretation in his *De sacro altaris mysterio*.

[24] In chs. 40–8 the negative image of the bride is replaced by a positive one in which 'the glory of the Lord filled the (restored) temple' (43: 5). He puts Eden to mythological use in ch. 28, while in ch. 47 the rivers flowing from the four gates cannot help but remind one of Eden. Indeed, as Gihon is the name of one of those rivers in Genesis (2: 3), it is not altogether impossible that even in Genesis there is a reference to the Temple, as Gihon was the name of the spring that supplied Jerusalem with water.

[25] The easiest way of making sense out of the nonsense that conventionally translates Ps. 48: 2 as 'Mount Zion in the far north': so L. J. Hoppe, *The Holy City* (Collegeville, Minn.: Liturgical Press, 2000), 25–7.

[26] Interpretation has moved from a Deuteronomic perspective with ch. 24 as its centre to a priestly orientation, climaxing in ch. 50: e.g. L. G. Perdue, *Wisdom and Cult* (Missoula, Mont.: Scholars Press, 1977), 188–211; B. G. Wright, 'Fear the Lord and Honour the Priest: Ben Sira as Defender of the Jerusalem Priesthood', in P. C. Beentjes (ed.), *The Book of Ben Sira in Modern Research* (Berlin: Walter de Gruyter, 1997), 189–222.

[27] Ecclus. 49: 15–50: 26. For detailed comparison between Hebrew and Greek text, and the way in which the Greek abandons the connection with the 'beauty' of Adam, C. T. R. Hayward, *The Jewish Temple: A Non-biblical Sourcebook* (London:

Running alongside this idea, though, was another type of imagery, the notion of the Temple's worship reflecting that of heaven. Such a stress is already there to be observed in Exodus, but it is pursued in great detail in a book such as *Jubilees*, and intriguingly it also seems to have been a major concern of the Qumran community.[28] Thus one of the main reasons for their separating themselves from Temple worship was not disparagement of ritual but because they believed the Temple authorities not to be taking the issue with sufficient seriousness, in following what they believed to be the wrong liturgical calendar and so forth. Indeed, its *Temple Scroll* can be seen as a variant on *Jubilees*. The author of the latter rewrote the Pentateuch in order to bring out more fully its presumed liturgical and theological implications, while the *Temple Scroll* was intended as its completion or sixth book with the precise form of the future Temple and its worship now duly decreed in some detail. Significantly, this paralleling of the worship of heaven also finds its place in the New Testament itself in the argument of the Epistle to the Hebrews which talks of the temple as 'a copy and a shadow of the heavenly sanctuary'.[29] Almost certainly such language is used there without any sacramental implications, not least because the author clearly thought that not only could the pattern be broken without loss, but also indeed with permanent gain. But many Jews of the time clearly thought quite differently, for to them the health of our world depended on keeping the pattern going: it was thus a means of securing the divine invasion and transformation of the material.

Yet pressures the other way that anticipate the New Testament do need to be acknowledged. The Book of Deuteronomy is an obvious case in point, where all that is allowed to dwell in the Temple is God's 'name', clearly intended to entail something quite different from simply a pious circumlocution for God himself.[30]

Routledge, 1996), 38–84 esp. 44–7, 77. Barker, Hayward, and Hoppe are all good examples of this wider contemporary trend.

[28] Moses is reminded to follow a 'pattern' set by God on Sinai: Exod. 25: 40; cf. 1 Chr. 28: 19. Wisdom speaks of 'a copy...which thou didst prepare from the beginning' (9: 8). For the theology of *Jubilees*, Hayward, *Jewish Temple*, 85–107. For how far the imagery may have been carried at Qumran, C. Fletcher-Louis, *All the Glory of Adam: Liturgical Anthropology in the Dead Sea Scrolls* (Leiden: Brill, 2001).

[29] Heb. 8: 5. The gain is direct access to God without a mediatorial priesthood.

[30] So G. von Rad, 'Deuteronomy's "Name" Theology and the Priestly Document's "Kabod" Theology', in *Studies in Deuteronomy* (Naperville, Ill.: Allenson, 1953), 37–46.

One notes too the implicit undermining of indwelling imagery elsewhere in this work and other related writings.[31] So the existence of two competing traditions does need to be acknowledged.[32] Yet at the same time anyone inclined to support this alternative track as incontrovertibly the legitimate trajectory of the future needs to recall that matters are not quite that simple. Deuteronomy is also where genocide against the native populations of Palestine is endorsed.[33] Of course, that does not necessarily make its views on the Temple therefore also wrong. My point is merely that arbitration on these issues is seldom straightforward. Equally, those who would like to see the Deuteronomist's attitude as an inevitable stage on a legitimate march towards secularism might like to pause to reflect.

Admittedly, our own world now sharply distinguishes between sacred and secular buildings, but it is important to note that for most of human history this has not been so. As the previous chapter observed, homes were once seen in essentially sacramental terms; so the early Christians in using their homes for worship would not necessarily have seen the act as rejecting the need for a holy site in quite so clear-cut a way as modern commentators so often suppose. Indeed, so powerful was that sense of the sacred in the past that great care needs to be exercised in interpreting the wide use to which religious buildings were sometimes put. Markets and shops, for instance, once commonly abutted onto churches, while from within, local government was sometimes administered, and specific chapels could even be the seat of law courts.[34] Likewise in Islam, we know that the earliest mosques were in fact modelled on the Prophet's own house at Medina, and used initially for a wide variety

[31] Note the form of the prayer in Deut. 26: 15: 'look down from thy holy habitation, from heaven'. Again, the Deuteronomic historian, unlike the Chronicler, places the choice of David above the choice of the Temple: contrast 1 Kgs. 8: 16 and 2 Chr. 6: 6.

[32] If Haggai, Zechariah, and the Chronicler support Ezekiel, Third Isaiah is indicative of a trend in the opposite direction while 2 Baruch goes as far as to picture angels actually helping to demolish the city's walls, with the temple itself now transferred to heaven. See further Hoppe, *The Holy City*, 111–26, 128–31, 163–7.

[33] Deut. 20: 10–18.

[34] As was the case for several centuries at Durham Cathedral in the use to which its Galilee Chapel was put. In its earlier history university lectures were also given in the Nine Altars Chapel.

of secular purposes as well as for worship. Such phenomena could easily be misread. What was demonstrated, thereby, I suggest, was not any lack of confidence in the sacred role of the building as such but perhaps too easy a conviction that almost nothing could ever undermine it. The contention may be thought especially implausible in the case of Islam, so insistent has that religion been on its ability to create a place of prayer anywhere. Why matters are not simple I shall try to demonstrate in Chapter 7. Here suffice it to note that within medieval Christianity and indeed most premodern culture the presence of the sacred was presumed everywhere. The role of church or other religious building was thus not to correct an absence but to secure a more readily intelligible and comprehensible form of presence.

Sacred architecture thus 'rationalized' the divine presence, and so allowed worshippers to experience their deity in a form that was no longer simply overwhelming or threatening but truly relational. That could then in turn inform their experience elsewhere. The contemporary Church, in accepting the modern division between sacred and secular, in effect presumes an absence that needs to be overcome. But that surely cannot be right in religious terms, for God as infinite is already present everywhere. The job of the religious building, therefore, must be not to initiate presence but to evoke it in a way that allows worshippers an experience that can then inform the rest of life. The Deuteronomist, in casting Yahweh back to heaven, thus totally misunderstood the objectives of those who spoke of the Temple as God's dwelling-place. What the latter were emphasizing and offering was a focused and not an exclusive presence, one in which cosmic symbolism was used to speak of the kind of God experienced in the Temple's worship and the depth of the Creator's concern for his people. Christian churches have sought a not unrelated conceptualization. Not that there was total uniformity across the centuries or across the religions, but there were shared aspects as well as significant differences. None of us can escape the fact that all human experience is conditioned. So, unless we shut our eyes, differences in architectural style will inevitably make some difference to the way in which we experience the divine and to the implications that we draw from such experience. That, though, is to put the matter altogether too negatively. For the point of the architecture is not to restrain but to liberate, to open up possibilities, if only we would avail ourselves of them: in other

Competing Styles

words, God made more easily manifest to us.[35] It is to an examination of this variety, its potential and pitfalls that I now turn.

The New Testament and Challenges to Romanesque

Before climbing the hill to Durham's Romanesque cathedral tourists sometimes call in on the way at the parish church in the marketplace, St Nicholas. In the days when the relations between the two institutions were more fragile and the controversial reordering of the Victorian church was still fresh in people's minds, visitors would find themselves confronted by a large banner declaring, 'it is people that matter not buildings'.[36] The attitude invoked can of course claim New Testament precedent, and indeed there seems little doubt that, whatever sense of sacramentality existed elsewhere in the primitive communities, the venues as such in which they assembled were accorded no such status. If there is an obvious reason for this, in that their meeting-places were temporary adaptations of private homes, many a critic of reverential attitudes towards buildings would want to push the argument further, and insist that something much more than mere pragmatism was at stake.[37] So I want first to consider the kind of critique that might be launched on the basis of the New Testament and possible responses. Thereafter in reviewing Romanesque architecture the issue will need to be faced once more as Cistercian criticisms are noted.

Going Beyond the New Testament

A number of prongs to a New Testament critique can be identified. It is argued that Jesus himself and his body of believers took over the

[35] Although I focus on possibilities, the deliberate exclusion of others should not be discounted. It can also be part of the role of architecture to discourage certain images of God as e.g. that he is malign, easily conceived, or subject to manipulation.

[36] The building was reordered by the future Archbishop of Canterbury, George Carey, while he was vicar (1975–82). The story is told in *The Church in the Marketplace* (Eastbourne: Kingsway, 1984).

[37] e.g. 'Aquila and Prisca, together with the church in their house': 1 Cor. 16: 19.

role once exercised by the Temple;[38] that the move towards synagogue worship in Jesus' own lifetime reflects a similar reorientation within Judaism; and that even when it became possible to have purpose-built facilities, Christianity adopted the secular basilica and not the pagan temple. Each of these contentions has a grain of truth, but the melting-pot that produced subsequent Christian attitudes is much more complex than any of these elements might suggest. Take the issue of the basilica.[39] Certainly, when Christianity became tolerated under Constantine, and still more the official state religion under Theodosius, borrowings were made from the structural plan of this rectangular or oblong building once intended for entirely secular uses. In pagan times it had been employed either for administering justice or else for purely commercial purposes; in the former case it would have had a little projecting apse for the judge's seat, and that explains its royal name, for the judge was seen as acting in the emperor's name. The Church simply substituted the bishop; the communion table placed well forward and the bishop usually celebrated facing the people.[40] But if the question is posed as to why this form of architecture was adopted in preference to pagan temples, hostility towards paganism is soon seen to constitute only part of the answer. Much more important was a practical reason: pagan temples were designed only to house the statue of the relevant god with sacrificial worship taking place outside and not within, whereas fundamental to Christianity was celebration of the eucharist, a corporate meal that required a gathered community.[41]

If the alleged parallels with Judaism once served the argument well, thanks largely to the work of archaeologists our understanding of the synagogue has been transformed over the course of the

---

[38] For Jesus as temple, e.g. Mark 14: 58; John 2: 19. For individual or community as temple, e.g. 1 Cor. 3: 16; Eph. 2: 21; 1 Pet. 2: 4–5; Rev. 3: 12.

[39] One of the finest surviving examples is at Trier. One should note, though, that it is now thought that there were two intermediate stages between house church and basilica, what one writer calls the *domus ecclesiae* (domestic rooms set apart) and the *aula ecclesiae* (a simple hall structure); so L. M. White, *The Social Origins of Christian Architecture* (Valley Forge, Pa.: Trinity Press International, 1990), i. esp. 102–39.

[40] At least in the basilicas of Rome. How widespread the practice in fact was is discussed in the next subsection.

[41] Jewish synagogues and pagan shrines also had dining facilities, but for them it was not the central act of worship: for some examples, White, *Social Origins*, 40, 41.

twentieth century. In the most recent extensive study of the subject, the growth of sacral notions in respect of the building is fully acknowledged.[42] If in its origins its function was probably once largely social, it soon attached to itself not only sacred terminology but also associated trappings,[43] so much so that the author suggests that instead of thinking of an increasingly aniconic religion we should conceive of Judaism going through various phases, the time of the post-biblical early Church being one of its least hostile.[44] Nor was it only specifically Jewish symbolism that was to be found; even pagan imagery secured its place.[45] Indeed, to this must be added the fact that at the end of the fourth century we find the famed preacher John Chrysostom worried because the synagogue has come to be seen as a more holy place than the local church.[46] Rituals of worship too enhanced that sense of sanctity, with certain key prayers being seen to substitute for the daily sacrifice in the Temple and the scrolls of the law treated with reverence (initially through a solemn procession and then by being given a special place of honour).[47]

One temptation we all have is to assume, if things change, a uniform pattern of development. But, as this Jewish story indicates, some of these moves were soon to be put in reverse, while the most notable were not necessarily the latest;[48] similarly, then, with

[42] L. Levine, *The Ancient Synagogue* (New Haven: Yale University Press, 2000). He notes the tendency, particularly in Diaspora Judaism, to substitute *proseuche* ('place of prayer') for *synagoge* (gathering) and to use a range of sacred terms for the building itself, e.g. 78–84, 597–8.

[43] Levine suggests an origin in traditional judicial functions at the city gate: ibid. 26–41. One example given of associated trappings is the manumission of slaves, which sometimes took place within a synagogue in much the same way as happened at Delphi before the god Apollo: 123.

[44] Levine suggests strongly aniconic attitudes between c.150 BC and AD 150 giving way to more favourable views, only to be displaced once more in their turn: ibid. 206–19. The tannaitic midrash on Exodus, the *Mekhilta*, sets the future pattern of total prohibition: 451–3.

[45] For some examples of early art, including Orpheus at Dura Europos and Helios at Beth Alpha, G. Sad-Rajna, *Ancient Jewish Art* (Paris: Flammarion, 1975), 33–118 esp. 68, 111.

[46] Levine, *Ancient Synagogue*, 273–5, with primary and secondary references.

[47] For *Amidah* prayer replacing daily Temple sacrifice: ibid. 184–5, 223; for procession leading to shrine: 327–32.

[48] One example of things moving in reverse is the treatment of women, who were not only not segregated at this time as they were in the Middle Ages but sometimes even given a seat of honour in the front row: ibid. 471–90 esp. 477.

Christianity. It is difficult to assess how significant the earliest Christian church to survive is, but certainly in the middle of the third century at Dura Europos we do find apotropaic images at the entrance and the internal walls of the room used as a baptistery adorned with biblical scenes that may have helped clarify the meaning of the sacrament and its accompanying procession.[49] If a little earlier Clement of Alexandria protests against too much reverence towards buildings, his successor, Origen, pulls in the opposite direction, with his image of angels themselves present at the community's worship.[50] Again, if the romance of Christians worshipping in the catacombs is now generally rejected and the relative poverty of the Church's early members argues against atriums always being available for separate liturgical functions, judging by parallels with other religious groups which also began very simply in adapted homes, even these could quickly acquire a degree of sanctity and corresponding imagery.[51] While that may appear to threaten Christianity's distinctiveness, it is also, I think, to be more realistic. Judaism is now willing to acknowledge that the form of its synagogues was eventually to be heavily influenced by the Christian basilica.[52] Does not Christianity likewise need to cease from its absolute polemic against classical paganism, and here too admit a debt? For in its desire to convey a sense of divine presence to an anxious world, what could be more natural than the adoption of some of the means already employed by the surrounding culture? If the evidence suggests a more cautious attitude towards art, the notion of the place of worship as itself holy may well have come very early, even while homes were still being adapted for the purpose. For there was after all an obvious alternative to such consecrated use, in simply having smaller gatherings.

---

[49] The apotropaic images included eyes, angels, and letters; water leading from death to life is the theme of the biblical miracles: White, *Social Origins*, ii. 20–1.

[50] Clement, *Stromateis*, 7. 5; Origen *De oratione*, 31. 5–6; text and trans. in White, *Social Origins*, ii. 52, 67–8.

[51] For *triclinium* (dining room) being more likely than the *atrium* (open courtyard, only available in larger villas), White, ibid. i. 107; for the cave and star vault imagery of the mithraeum, 47.

[52] Levine notes that synagogues eventually followed Christian basilicas in having a screened chancel, while at Beth Alpha the image of the hanging ram of Gen. 22 is almost certainly derived from a typology that wanted to make the parallel with Christ more explicit, *Ancient Synagogue*, 583–4, 585–6.

But that still leaves us with what is for many the most fundamental objection, that reverence for things undermines the New
Testament's central stress on people, and thus on Christ's presence
in their midst. At one level one might respond by observing that
such an orientation was borne out of a situation of crisis, being a
summons back to basics in the face of what was thought to be the
imminent return of Christ, before which all else mattered little.
Such apocalyptic fervour, though, scarcely marks our own world,
even among Christians, and I believe, rightly so.[53] Yet more needs
to be said, and that is that the objection presents us with false
alternatives. What is required is really 'both ... and' and not
'either ... or'. The point may be seen even if we confine ourselves
to the question of what it means to treat another human being as in
God's image or as fellow member of the body of Christ. For we
show concern mostly obviously through what we do, and not
infrequently through expressive physical action, such as embracing
or hugging someone who is anxious or troubled. Sometimes it is a
wise move; sometimes not. The very fact that the question can be
debated illustrates how quickly the issue becomes appropriate forms
of communication. Architecture then naturally fits into that frame
as one such means, with the form the building takes enabling God's
presence with others, potentially at least, to be made manifest to
them. It is surely, therefore, no accident that Christians eventually
came to declare of the buildings in which they worshipped that
they were 'heaven on earth'.[54] The sacred space valued others
through bringing them closer to God. Significantly, it is the same
merging of the two ideas that occurs in the modern Roman
Catholic liturgy for the dedication of a new church, as in the
following juxtaposition: 'May God, the Father of mercies, dwell
in this house of prayer. May the grace of the Holy Spirit cleanse us,
for we are the temple of his presence.'[55]

---

[53] The early Christians got the imminence of Christ's return wrong. What
remains is the need always to live in the light of God's imminent judgement; cf.
Luke 12: 20.

[54] The quotation is from the 8th-c. bishop Germanus; quoted in full in Levine,
Ancient Synagogue, 605.

[55] *Rites of the Catholic Church* (New York: Pueblo, 1980), ii. 220; cf. 225–6.

Romanesque and Bernard's Challenge

The splendours of the Orthodox liturgy are now more familiar in the West than they perhaps have ever been. In an earlier chapter I observed the essentially transcendent reference of icons, and so it is important to qualify this here with the way in which not only the liturgy is intended to bring heaven down among us, but also the architecture of the typical Byzantine church.[56] That liturgy has undergone some marked changes, not least between the extensive processional use of a large nave such as Justinian's Hagia Sophia and the later small monastic cross-in-dome church that now typifies Eastern worship.[57] The idea of the two parts of the church symbolizing earth and heaven and the painting programme on the walls rising progressively in the heavenly hierarchy are too familiar to require any further elaboration here.[58] What is important to note is the recurring treatment of the church as a microcosm of the world, with the dome as heaven brought, as it were, to earth. One sixth-century celebration of the cathedral at Edessa puts matters thus: 'its ceiling is stretched like the heavens . . . it is adorned with golden mosaic as the firmament is with shining stars. Its high dome is comparable to the heaven of heavens.'[59] The eighth-century patriarch, Germanos, put it even more explicitly: 'the church is a heaven on earth wherein the heavenly God dwells and walks'.[60] Much earlier, the historian Procopius had thought fit to borrow Homer to

[56] For a helpful liturgical survey, H. Wybrew, *The Orthodox Liturgy* (London: SPCK, 1989).

[57] The contrast is well drawn in R. Krautheimer, *Early Christian and Byzantine Architecture*, 4th edn. (New Haven: Yale University Press, 1986), 201–36, 285–300. It is also made central to Robert Ousterhout's understanding of later building techniques in his *Master Builders of Byzantium* (Princeton: Princeton University Press, 1999), e.g. 7–16, 112.

[58] Maximus the Confessor describes the nave as 'the sanctuary in potency', the sanctuary as 'the nave in act' in his account of the church as a whole representing both the visible and invisible worlds: *The Church's Mystagogy*, ch. 2. Symeon of Thessalonica expresses matters more simply in terms of the heavens being represented 'by the holy sanctuary, things on earth by the holy nave'. The latter passage is quoted in full in Wybrew, *Orthodox Liturgy*, 165.

[59] Full text in C. Mango (ed.), *The Art of the Byzantine Empire, 312–1453* (Toronto: University of Toronto Press, 1986), 57–60 esp. 58

[60] Ibid. 141–3. The apse (translated as 'conch' in Mango) is identified with the cave where Christ was born.

describe Hagia Sophia's dome: 'it seems not to rest upon solid masonry but to cover the space as if suspended from heaven by a golden chain'.[61] The typical small domed church of the East could scarcely justify such a comparison. So it is perhaps no surprise that after the iconoclastic controversy was over, this image was carefully supplemented by the now familiar, graded iconography of the walls and ceiling, suggesting immanence in a new way.[62]

It would thus be a serious mistake to think of an entirely other-worldly reference in the practice of Orthodoxy. Rather, a dialectic was constantly taking place between immanence and transcendence. Whether from a Western perspective the balance is quite right or still veering over much in the direction of transcendence is too large an issue to pursue now. The history of the West is my focus here. None the less, it was important to introduce Ortho-doxy, however briefly, not simply in order to acknowledge the counter-currents to the transcendence of icons, but also to note such ideas of immanence in architecture since they were also to help shape conceptions in the West.[63] Despite the gradual parting of the ways, the development of different forms of architecture in the West did not as yet indicate fundamentally different conceptions of how churches were conceived symbolically: there was still a common thought-world.[64] Eventually, however, those new forms of architecture did become codified in what we now call Roman-esque. This style is frequently dismissed as lacking the clarity of the spiritual values inherent in its successor, Gothic. But, while it is true that its meaning cannot be read immediately, it has a subtlety that undoubtedly merits further consideration. I shall do so under two heads, examining first the style in general and then the purified version adopted within the Cistercian order.

---

[61] *De aedificiis*, I. I. 46, quoting *Iliad*, 8. 19. Ironically, Procopius gives the exact opposite sense to the verse from what Homer intended: Homer's point is that even with all the gods co-operating, Zeus cannot be pulled *from* heaven.

[62] The connection is made by R. J. Mainstone, *Hagia Sophia* (London: Thames & Hudson, 1988), 240. That church's dome had originally been decorated in gold mosaics with only simple designs such as crosses.

[63] Although lacking domes, churches were still thought of as incarnating divine presence.

[64] Not surprising for so long as Constantinople was still thought of as the capital of Christendom; effectively not challenged till Charlemagne.

It was only gradually that Romanesque reached its classic form, and even then this varied both with respect to timing and precise locality. Inevitably, in northern Europe, for example, roofs sloped more steeply to cast off rain and snow, while openings (windows and doors) were broader than in the south to let in more light, and walls thicker to maintain what warmth there was.[65] But developments were far from being just a response to varying weather, or war for that matter.[66] More significant was the key role exercised by the liturgy. Greater frequency in the celebration of mass and the increasing popularity of pilgrimage both played their part.[67] The desire for more elaborate processions also entailed the need for longer naves, while the wish of the clergy to continue their liturgical cycle uninterrupted meant that means had to be provided for circulation of quire and presbytery.[68] Longer churches and transepts, though, entailed more strain on the ceiling. Tunnel vaulting had the added advantage of improving the acoustics for singing, but its successor, barrel vaulting, ensured the more practical demand of distributing the load, while groin vaulting was to lessen the pressure still further.[69]

[65] A point emphasized by D. Yarwood in her survey country by country in *The Architecture of Europe* (London: Batsford, 1974), 127–99 esp. 135, 173.

[66] The decline in the Viking threat made less fortress-like churches possible. Contrast the high windows of the Anglo-Saxon churches at Jarrow and Escomb near Durham, or Brixworth in Northamptonshire. For a photograph of England's earliest complete church (7th c.) at Escomb, S. Jenkins, *England's Thousand Best Churches* (Harmondsworth: Penguin, 1999), 171.

[67] In reacting against historians who had spoken of purely local and formal developments, Pierre Francastel stresses both factors, and in particular the key role played by the liturgy at Cluny and developments at pilgrimage churches: *L'Humanisme roman: critique des théories sur l'art du XIe siècle* (Paris: Mouton, 1970), 90–8, pls. III–V.

[68] K. J. Conant, *Carolingian and Romanesque Architecture, 800–1200*, 3rd edn. (Harmondsworth: Penguin, 1973), 117; X. B. Altet, *The Romanesque: Towns, Cathedrals and Monasteries* (Cologne: Taschen, 2001), 68. Even when the focus of worship was in the crossing, special passages known as *bérrichons* were created: so M. D. Costen and C. Oakes, *Romanesque Churches of the Loire and Western France* (Stroud: Tempus, 2000), 74.

[69] For the effect of tunnel vaulting on singing, Conant, *Carolingian and Romanesque*, 108–9; for developments in vaulting, Costen and Oakes, *Romanesque Churches*, 79–81. Some textbooks wrongly conflate tunnel- and barrel-vaulting (the latter has periodic reinforcements that the former lacks).

We are so used to thinking of the focus of churches being in their east end that it is as well to remember that for the laity much of their activity was at the west, and this may be one reason why so much attention was given to the portals of Romanesque churches.[70] Still, that said, there was now greater focus on the east end not least because pilgrimage to the relics stored there began to become more popular and also because high mass was now almost always celebrated facing east. It used to be thought that in earlier times celebrants had invariably faced the people and that it was only towards the turn of the millennium that change came about.[71] There was after all the precedent set by Constantine's churches in Rome, including St Peter's where the president has always faced the people.[72] But it is now widely acknowledged that different parts of Christendom offered different models, and that the early Syrian practice of congregation and priest alike facing east may well have spread much more quickly than was once thought.[73] Unfortunately, assessment of the limited historical evidence is complicated by the passions aroused on both sides in favour and against modern liturgical practice and its perceived implications.[74] The symbolism of an eastern orientation no doubt played some part in producing uniformity, but increasing stress on a sacrificial understanding of the eucharist is likely in the end to have been more decisive.[75]

[70] Among other aspects, Costen and Oakes mention the cult of relics, altars in the tribune, burials, and the beginning of the Easter liturgy: ibid. 106–7.

[71] For the earlier emphasis, R. C. D. Jasper, *The Position of the Celebrant at the Eucharist*, Alcuin Club Pamphlet 16 (London: Alcuin Club, 1959), esp. 12–13, 17. Jasper places the major change in the 9th c. thanks to changing attitudes to sacrifice, relics, and sacrament houses: 14–18.

[72] But explicable in alternative terms, as indicative that the celebrant when praying on behalf of the people was expected to face east, since these churches were orientated differently with their apse at the west end. Christ was the Christian's 'sun of righteousness', with his glory once more to come from the east: e.g. Ezek. 43: 1; Rev. 21: 23.

[73] M. J. Moreton, 'Orientation as a Liturgical Principle', *Studia Patristica* 17 (Oxford: Pergamon Press, 1982), pt. 2, 575–90. The position of the entrance to the *confessio* (*martyrium*) is used to argue that in Syria eastward-facing celebration was the norm, while in Africa, at least initially, the example of the Constantine basilicas was followed.

[74] For a rather intemperate expression of hostility to change, laced with some telling points on the way, K. Gamber, *The Reform of the Roman Liturgy: Its Problems and Background* (San Juan Capistrano, Calif.: Una Voce Press, 1993), 23–40, 117–83.

[75] Moreton 'Orientation', stresses the former, arguing for continuity with the Temple in the desire to face east: Christ had come from the east and would do so

If so, there would have been pressures on builders to help orientate the congregation in a more eastward direction, as that way their eyes would be encouraged to focus on the offering now being made through the priest to God. Certainly, at Vézelay the structure of the pillars and the designs on them and on the roof was thus all part of a single programme to draw the perceptions of the worshippers in one single direction, eastwards, and this is no less true at Durham, where variations in the pattern of the pillars are deliberately used to draw the eye eastwards.[76] In both cases as well as the altar reflecting the pull eastwards, also relevant was the fact that both were pilgrimage churches, with the bones of the relevant saint held beyond the high altar at the east end of the church.[77]

The sense of harmonic balance (rather than vertical thrust) that one finds internally in Romanesque churches is also repeated externally. The usual pattern became twin towers encasing one, two, or three portals with tympana above, themselves a Romanesque invention.[78] Sadly, the most famous Romanesque church of all, the Benedictine abbey at Cluny, is no more, and many, of course, have been much altered since.[79] A further difficulty is that little survives of direct theological reflection on their form. Indeed, even when clergy did address their attention to such matters, often it seems that their real concern was with theoretical principles rather than with the churches as they actually were being constructed about them. Indeed, if one may put the point more controversially, a not implausible parallel may be drawn with what still sometimes happens in theology today, when a predetermined theological or biblical grid is simply imposed upon the world without regard to how empirical realities might require modification of that grid. During the high Middle Ages one sees the result in works such as

---

again (583). For the two considerations united, J. Ratzinger, *The Spirit of the Liturgy* (San Francisco: Ignatius, 2000), 74–84.

[76] Although mainly concerned with the sculptural programme, a book that has also some fine views of the architecture is V. R. Mouilleron, *Vézelay* (New York: Abrams, 1999), 107.

[77] In Durham's case, Cuthbert, in that of Vézelay, Mary Magdalene.

[78] For some illustrations of such harmony, Altet, *The Romanesque*, 15 (Jumièges), 43 (Sankt Pantaleon, Cologne), 135 (Notre-Dame-la-Grande, Poitiers).

[79] Conant, *Carolingian and Romanesque*, devotes a whole chapter to Cluny: 107–25. The building was destroyed during the French Revolution.

those of the contemporary Honorius of Autun or much later Durandus of Mende.[80] The detail of alleged parallels overwhelms, but it is hard to believe anyone ever quite thought like this in practice when entering a church for worship. So, for example, piers are supposed to remind us of bishops, watchtowers of preachers, and cement of how the sand of our temporal acts needs to be energized by the waters of baptism and lime of charity.[81]

From there it might seem a simple step to question any deep engagement with symbolism at all during the Romanesque period. Certainly, English scholars still tend to show much more reticence on the subject than their French counterparts.[82] One problem is the relative paucity of written sources; another the ambiguities inherent in the buildings themselves. What does seem agreed is the wide resort to precedent, though significant details were often thought enough rather than point by point imitation.[83] Inevitably, this meant that churches such as old St Peter's, Holy Sepulchre, and Aachen played a large role.[84] Separate round baptisteries may have had their origin in Roman sepulchral monuments such as Santa. Costanza.[85] But the eventual wide range of baptismal symbolism demonstrates how expansions might occur from relatively simple beginnings.[86] Again, St Peter's had used various ways of highlighting its altar and accompanying shrine, and several of these features seem to have been adopted elsewhere, among them spiral pillars

[80] Honorius (d. *c.*1135?), *De gemma animae*; Durandus (d. 1296), *Rationale divinorum officiorum*. In both cases, it is the first book in each work that is crucial.

[81] Durandus, I. I. 10; I. I. 21–2; I. I. 27. This is not to deny the possibility of a more sympathetic evaluation if one focuses instead on his account of the liturgy: cf. J. White, 'Durandus and the Interpretation of Christian Worship', *Worship* (1974), 41–52.

[82] For an excellent (and popular) French study, M. M. Davy, *Initiation à la symbolique romane* (Paris: Flammarion, 1977). Contrast the rarity today of a book such as Ernest Short's *The House of God: A History of Religious Architecture and Symbolism* (London: Philip Alan, 1925) where the two themes in the title (and liturgy) are closely interrelated.

[83] Stressed by R. Krautheimer, 'Introduction to an Iconography of Medieval Architecture', *Journal of Warburg & Courtauld Institutes* 5 (1942), 1–33 esp. 2–20.

[84] Aachen for royal connections; cf. R. Gem, 'Towards an Iconography of Anglo-Saxon Architecture', *Journal of Warburg & Courtauld Institutes* 46 (1983), 1–18 esp. 7–12.

[85] Krautheimer's suggestion: 'Introduction to an Iconography', 2–33 esp. 26.

[86] Explored in J. G. Davies, *The Architectural Setting of Baptism* (London: Barrie & Rockliff, 1962); for illus. of some early examples: 32–3.

and distinctive vaulting.[87] But even without these features the large ciborium or baldachino that characterized the earlier history of altars, would undoubtedly have added to the sense of a housed presence.[88]

In addition, however, the great weight and solidity of Romanesque churches could, in my view, not help but speak of an earthed presence. The sheer bulk of the pillars were like great oaks, but oaks that will never rot.[89] The language of the rite of dedication spoke of the building being made sacramentally the house of God,[90] and as such this must inevitably have reinforced the literal tendency of the age.[91] The east end of Cluny culminated in a Christ in majesty,[92] but unlike Gothic there was little to pull the eye upwards without drawing it down again, and it is that drawing *into* sacred space rather than upwards that I think we should use as our clue to the meaning of this style.[93] In an innovating work Calvin Kendall has examined over six hundred verse inscriptions on Romanesque portals. What he underlines is the extent to which they reflect a

---

[87] For Durham as an illus. of the former, E. Fernie 'The Spiral Piers of Durham Cathedral', in *Romanesque Architecture: Design, Meaning and Metrology* (London: Pindar Press, 1995), 270–9; for vaults used to effect a contrast, E. Fernie, *The Architecture of Norman England* (Oxford: Oxford University Press, 2000), 135–7, 266–7.

[88] For that earlier history, C. E. Pocknee, *The Christian Altar* (London: Mowbray, 1963), 55–63.

[89] Durham's massive pillars often evoke in people the sense of a great oak forest, echoing the divine creation in nature.

[90] Familiar to many who have never attended a consecration, thanks to Bruckner's popular anthem, *Locus iste*: locus iste a Deo facto est inaestimabile sacramentum: irreprehensibilis est ('this place has been made by God a sacrament beyond price; it is without reproach').

[91] One illustration of this would be the first doctrinal monograph on the eucharist with its extreme literalism, which came from Paschasius Radbertus (d. 860). Though attacked by Ratramnus and later by Berengar of Tours, his were the views that elicited most sympathy.

[92] A contemporary of the Cluny Christ is still to be found at neighbouring Berze-le-Ville, and is thought to give a good idea of its larger neighbour, though obviously on a much smaller scale.

[93] This was a vast fresco with angels looking down from the choir vault: Conant, *Carolingian and Romanesque*, 118. This is not to deny that compared with Carolingian architecture Romanesque already exhibits some degree of movement away from the horizontal and towards the vertical (cf. Francastel, *L'Humanisme roman*, 109: 'lignes horizontales . . . piles verticales'), but this is still relatively subdued.

realist theology of the church building as itself a heavenly reality.[94] Taking their lead from classical inscriptions on public monuments and still more so from earlier Christian practice such as on the Ruthwell Cross where the cross is personified, sculptors not only carved marvellous works of art on these portals but also added inscriptions that directly address the worshippers in the name of Christ himself.[95] If at Conques this determines the portal through which one should enter and at Le Puy someone else indicates the door as Christ, elsewhere the equation is totally unqualified, with Christ himself made to declare that he is in fact the door through which the believer must enter: 'I am the eternal door; pass through me.'[96] Again at Autun Christ not only speaks but even declares that Gislibertus is the sculptor.[97] The use of Latin and indeed of written script itself (whatever the language) alike militated against comprehension on the part of the ordinary believer. Even so, they do bear witness to a common way of thinking: the physical door like the church as a whole embodied the divine presence. Not that such realism was to last. Among other factors the personal ambitions of artists themselves contributed to bringing the practice to an end.[98] But there were also more profound changes afoot. As Kendall observes, the realism of Bede gives way to the Platonism of Gothic.[99]

[94] C. B. Kendall, *The Allegory of the Church: Romanesque portals and their Verse Inscriptions* (Toronto: University of Toronto Press, 1998). Six hundred and seven in fact: 73. For the nature of the poetry (dactylic hexameters): 69–79.

[95] This 8th-c. artefact has a runic poem on it, an early version of the *Dream of the Rood*, in which the cross speaks in its own person.

[96] The quotation is from Santa Cruz de la Serós: 'Ianua sum perpes; per me transite, fideles.' For this and other examples, Kendall, *Allegory*, 93, 109–21 esp. 112, 122.

[97] So Kendall argues from the substitution of *hoc* for the more usual *me* in 'Gislibertus fecit hoc': ibid. 88–91. If so, it could provide an objection against one recent attempt to argue the sculptor out of existence, in favour of 'Gislibertus' being the patron's name: so L Seidel, *Legends in Limestone: Lazarus, Gislibertus and the Cathedral at Autun* (Chicago: Univeristy of Chicago Press, 1999), 12–26, 63–71. Another is that the more usual Latin for such a claim is *fieri fecit* ('caused to be made').

[98] Niccolò's work at Ferrara and Verona provide two conspicuous examples, the latter declaring that 'the people coming to visit forever praise him': Kendall, *Allegory*, 176, 180.

[99] Ibid. 194. Cf. Bede, *De schematibus et tropis*, 2. 12, and Kendall's discussion, *Allegory*, 9–13.

Yet it was not just Gothic or artistic arrogance that put an end to such ideas. There was also the reforming movement within Romanesque's own ranks, typified by St Bernard's famous attack on ornament and on the strange animals sculpted in monastic cloisters.[100] Once again, though, there are hermeneutical problems in interpreting the limited evidence. For, apart from those familiar comments and his well-trodden attacks on luxury, Bernard offers us little direct guidance on what he thought his rules and those of his order were attempting to achieve. One could of course conclude that little more was at stake than a rather unthinking form of puritanism, and some of the injunctions do seem to fall into this category.[101] Yet, though it lasted in its pristine purity only a short time and only a few examples have survived to this day, even so the Cistercian style does exhibit such an extraordinary beauty that it is hard not to believe that there is some deeper aesthetics behind it.[102] It is therefore a relief to find at least two modern writers prepared to search for that deeper rationale, one through the rhetorical style of Bernard's own writings, the other through meditation on direct observation set against the wider assumptions of the day.

In the former case (M. B. Pranger) the suggestion is made that the rhetoric and style of Bernard's sermons and other writings belie his proclaimed lack of interest in art. His biographer may have declared that Bernard failed to notice, but his attention to cloister decorations implies otherwise, as does his extraordinary rich play of language.[103] Today only those exceedingly well versed in the Scriptures can hope to tap fully Bernard's rich vein of allusion, one in which, for example, he moves in a few moments from fountain to wound to Joseph's brothers' money-bags to crucifixion to the value of the nativity.[104]

---

[100] In his letter or *Apologia* to William, Abbot of St Thierry. For a translation and early precedents in Jerome, C. Davis-Weyer (ed.), *Early Medieval Art 300–1150* (Toronto: University of Toronto Press, 1986), 38–40, 168–70.

[101] Sculpture was forbidden in 1124, tall towers and belfries in 1157, while any existing coloured glass was ordered to be removed in 1182: so Conant, *Carolingian and Romanesque*, 128.

[102] Fontenay and Sénanque are two particularly fine surviving examples. Illustrated in J. F. Leroux-Dhuys, *Cistercian Abbeys: History and Architecture* (Cologne: Könemann, 1998), 188–95, 334–48. Ironically, Bernard's own Clairvaux has ended up as a prison: ibid. 174–9.

[103] M. B. Pranger, *Bernard of Clairvaux and the Shape of Monastic Thought* (Leiden: Brill, 1994), 209–74.

[104] Ibid. 255–7.

'Money' through the supposed liquidity of gems could conjure up the notion of valued 'wounds',[105] and so it looks as though Bernard was protesting that Christians had already available in the potential of words enough to feed them and draw them into a rich web of imagination and memory. Architectural elaboration was thus redundant, while to this must be added the fact that in any case God is ultimately conceivable only in the simplest of geometric analogies.[106] Bernard was thus, as it were, a Mondrian before his time, with simple imagery seen as best because it can most easily draw us beyond into a world of ideas that needs no imagery at all.[107]

The approach of Georges Duby of the Académie française is rather different, though the conclusions reached are not all that dissimilar. Bernard is presented as sharing far more with one of his theological opponents (Abelard) than he ever realized, inasmuch as for them both alike intention and interiority are absolutely central.[108] Cistercian monks, unlike Benedictine, did not accept child oblates. It was adult conversion that mattered, and likewise there were no serfs among the lay groups that supported them. Cistercian abbeys, once established, were also required to be self-supporting. Their deliberate location in remote countryside encouraged that aim. It also, of course, discouraged visitors. Meditation was to be their mainstay. But architecture could support this. A simpler cloister as enclosed garden could recall the soul to Eden, while the fountain in its midst spoke of baptism and of Mary.[109] Again circle and line alike contained simple messages, while the experience of new light each day could draw the monk anew to that first and original Light of all.[110]

Such a brief summary scarcely does justice to Duby's argument, not least because so much depends on the illustrations to his text. Like Pranger he is insistent that Bernard was not motivated by the

[105] Gems were commonly believed to be crystalized liquids. Compare the way in which *sphragis* can mean both seal and plaster: ibid. 257 n. 2.

[106] 'length without extension', and so forth: ibid. 247–8.

[107] Pranger draws a parallel between the simplicity of the earlier Mondrian (e.g. *The Tower at Domburg*) and his later abstract compositions: ibid. 249. For a discussion of Mondrian, see my Ch. 3.

[108] G. Duby, *L'Art cistercien* (Paris: Flammarion, 1998), 58–9, 70.

[109] Ibid. 100, 115, 122. In one of his most famous sermons Bernard compares Mary to an aqueduct.

[110] Ibid. 130, 156–7. 'La droite, trajectoire d'une flèche, dardée vers la perfection, et le cercle des mouvements éternels où tout changement se résorbe' (130).

denial of matter, but rather by the recognition that its power is at its most effective when we view it at its simplest. Some, though, have tried to push the argument further and suggest that the architectural environment simply acts as 'a kind of screen against which one can metaphorically project one's mental processes'.[111] Ironically, though, that particular writer's own text pulls in a different direction, for she admits not only the continuing presence of images in early Cistercianism but also key symbolic roles for some of its more abstract patterns.[112] But whatever the degree of interiority and its independence or otherwise of the surrounding architecture, there still remains something deeply problematic with the whole approach. Bernard was clearly gifted with a rich imagination and so even with so simple a fare he could still easily flourish. But, significantly, even his own order was eventually to turn its back on such ideals.[113] The play of light, circle, and line were just not enough.[114] In part no doubt this was due to the corrupting influence of new-found wealth,[115] but there seems to me something deeper also at stake. In a nutshell, it demands too much of the ordinary human being. There were just not enough visual stimuli, and that is why it worked and continues to work for most of us only in some moods, and even then principally by way of contrast.

Earlier I described Romanesque as evoking, as it were, a sense of earthed presence. As such it seems to have much in common with the principal, though not sole, way in which the Jerusalem Temple was once conceived. Some may wish to talk of a naïve realism. Realism there certainly was, but to call it naïve would seem to me grossly unfair. For, if it spoke of presence, it also refused to be exclusive, and indeed much of its art pointed in a quite different

---

[111] T. N. Kinder, *Cistercian Europe: Architecture of Contemplation* (Grand Rapids, Mich.: Eerdmans, 2002), 385; cf. 143 (on glass).

[112] For the images of Christ and Mary: ibid. 172, 217; for continuing acceptance of gold chalices and fistulas: 172; for the meaning of rosettes: 218.

[113] Well illustrated by one of England's finest ruins at Fountains. Not only did their 13th-c. Nine Altars Chapel set the precedent for Durham but also a 172-ft. tower was added on the eve of the Reformation.

[114] For illus. of the play of light and circular oculi, Duby, *L'Art cistercien*, 136, 137; for Fontenay's attempt to deal with the circular astragal of the column meeting the rectangular abacus of the capitals, once bearers of the strange animals against which Bernard had protested so vehemently: 152–3 (gentle, leaf-like curves instead).

[115] The efficiency of Cistercian sheep-farming is legendary.

direction. If Bernard took exception to the apparent realism of the strange creatures that so often inhabit Romanesque cloisters, that realism was fully counterbalanced by the elongated, other-worldly figures that so often appeared elsewhere. One need only think of the Christ of Autun to appreciate that this was no narrow confining of deity to our world. Indeed, even the creatures to which Bernard took such exception could be defended as also other-worldly, inasmuch as so many of them are exotic and far from being conventional inhabitants of this world. One way of reading them is thus to think of them evoking the universality of God's sway, not its diminution or narrow confinement: nothing, we are being told, is beyond God's concern. Bernard, though, supposed otherwise. For him a proper spiritual interiority could only be achieved in the context of a supporting architectural summons to transcendence. If, as shall see, in one sense Gothic represents the complete triumph of his argument (in its architecture), in another (its art) matters were quite otherwise. What this suggests is that churches can be fully appreciated only when they each treated as what the Germans call a *Gesamtkunstwerk*, a total work of art. The rounded experience comes from their effect in its totality. But before noting that counter-trend in its art, the architecture needs first to be addressed in its own right.

Gothic Transcendence and its Limitations

Because of Abbot Suger of Saint-Denis's various positive connections with Bernard, not least their reconciliation and friendship at the time of Suger's death, it is sometimes suggested that Bernard intended only to legislate for his own order, and that he would have thought nothing wrong with the elaborate building programme on which Suger (d. 1151) embarked, and which is traditionally deemed to mark the beginning of Gothic.[116] That I find hard to credit, despite what I said above. A more moderate version of the claim, however, is to be found in one classic discussion of the origins of the Gothic cathedral that postulates two complementary intellec-

---

[116] L. Grant, *Abbot Suger of St-Denis* (London: Longman, 1998), 25–6. For the touching story of Suger wishing to see Bernard's 'angelic face' once more and the latter's gift of a handkerchief: 293.

tual streams of influence, the Platonic school of Chartres and Bernard.[117] If more recent scholarship fights shy of any notion of a school,[118] it is true that a number of connecting strands can be detected in the twelfth century that might help provide an underlying rationale for the new form of architecture that takes place first, quite hesitantly, at Saint-Denis and then, more confidently, at Chartres. If some were primarily intellectual in orientation, the Victorines provide a parallel with Bernard's more spiritual and mystical concerns.[119] Yet, it still seems to me to be going too far to postulate major direct influence from Bernard except in this sense, that, as we have seen, he already marks a revolt against the realism of Romanesque thought. Although Bernard can be placed in the Gothic world in so far as he too sees the church building as concerned essentially to point beyond itself, the complexity of Gothic forms would not, I think, have given him any great pleasure, far less the richness of its sculptural programmes.[120]

The general character of Gothic architecture is presumably too familiar to require any detailed characterization here. Perhaps most obvious is its use of the angle to point heavenwards, first in windows and then in spires. To reinforce this effect the frame of

[117] O. von Simson, *The Gothic Cathedral*, 3rd edn. (Princeton: Princeton University Press, 1988). For the Chartres school, 25–39, 188–97; for the influence of Bernard: 25–6, 39–48, 188.

[118] There is no evidence of a continuing 'school' in the 12th c. Bernard of Chartres certainly taught there, but has left us only poetry. His more distinguished younger, brother, Thierry of Chartres (d. 1155), seems to have been mainly based elsewhere, including Paris. William of Conches was a pupil but his interest was mainly natural philosophy. Even Gilbert de la Porée, who was also a pupil and succeeded Bernard as chancellor (1126–37), studied under Anselm of Laon as well and also eventually moved to Paris. For greater willingness to talk of a 'school', E. Gilson, *History of Christian Philosophy in the Middle Ages* (London: Sheed & Ward, 1980 edn.), 139–53. Contrast R. W. Southern, *Scholastic Humanism and the Unification of Europe* (Oxford: Blackwell, 1995), i. 58–101. Significantly, the section is subtitled, 'A romantic misconception'; it also includes a response to Peter Dronke's more moderate version of the thesis.

[119] The Abbey of Saint-Victor was founded near Paris by William of Champeaux in 1113. While there was some influence in their practices from St Bernard, it was a house of canons regular, and not Cistercian. Also there are some marked differences within the house on theological approach: Adam in particular should be contrasted with Hugh and Richard.

[120] Architecturally, both share an essentially transcendent reference, but only Bernard found this in a move towards interiority.

the building was made to look as light as possible, the clear object-ive in view being to draw the worshipper heavenwards. Nowhere does this find a more conspicuous application than in stained glass, for here minimal stone support and light flooding through the glass are used, working in unison, to imply a building, as it were, taking flight, with the scenes in the glass now caught up into a new and ethereal world, where lightness of stone and light in the glass are alike used to convey the transcendent overcoming of this world's limitations. Ironically in some ways it is Gothic's failures that are the highest tribute to what the style was trying to achieve. For, if Beauvais's nave collapsed, its soaring quire still provides a marvel-lous witness to what it was that its architect was seeking to express. The more common loss of many a Gothic spire bears witness to precisely the same point.[121]

Suger left us with two works that help explain his intentions.[122] Notoriously, the distinguished art historian, Erwin Panofsky, wanted to turn Suger into a great intellectual who anticipated the thought of the Renaissance, and as part of that agenda transformed him into a thinker thoroughly imbued with the ideas of Neoplatonism particu-larly as mediated through the works of the pseudonymous writer after whom his abbey was named.[123] A number of subsequent writers have challenged that status, and indeed some even have doubted the influence of Denys at all, but to my mind that is to go too far.[124] It is

---

[121] Marvellously evoked by William Golding in his 1964 novel *The Spire*, where there is the added ambiguity of whether the dean is truly motivated by human ambition, the desire to glorify God, or a mixture of both. Cf. also John Updike's poem 'Beauvais' in *Americana and Other Poems* (London: Penguin, 2001), 55.

[122] *De rebus in administratione sua gestis*; *Libellus alter de consecratione ecclesiae sancti Dionysii*. A translation and commentary of relevant sections are available in E. Panofsky, *Abbot Suger on the Abbey Church of St-Denis and its Arts Treasures* (Princeton: Princeton University Press, 1976).

[123] Strictly speaking the abbey was dedicated to a former bishop of Paris of that name martyred under Diocletian, but in the 9th c. he had come to be equated with the anonymous writer called Dionysius the Areopagite (*c.*500) in virtue of another false identification, this time the individual who sat at the feet of Paul (Acts 17: 34). Abelard was driven from the monastery by Suger's predecessor for calling this identification into question.

[124] P. Kidson, 'Panofsky, Suger and St-Denis', *Journal of the Warburg and Courtauld Institutes* 50 (1987), 1–17; followed by Grant, *Abbot Suger*, 3–6, 23–4. Kidson overstates his case, perversely interpreting the type of language quoted in my main text as implying for Suger's architecture that 'instead of conducting the soul to heaven, it brings heaven down to earth' (7).

hard to believe that such a cultivated man would not have read Denys on numerous occasions if only because of pride in his own abbey.[125] Admittedly, there are no direct quotations from Denys, nor can his works even be said to be replete with allusions in the manner of his contemporaries at the nearby monastery of Saint-Victor, Hugh and Richard.[126] Yet it would be unwise to rely on such arguments alone, as there are other forms of linguistic evidence that do suggest knowledge of, and influence from, Denys.[127]

Indeed, with appropriate qualification we may speak of the same spirit animating what Suger says and all reflecting a fundamentally transcendent orientation.[128] So, in contrast with the Romanesque portal inscriptions that I discussed earlier, Suger had placed above the main door to the abbey the following prayer: 'May this nobly bright work illumine minds so that they may go through its true lights to the true light, where Christ is the true door ... The dull mind rises to the truth through material things ... '[129] Clearly Suger has moved from realism to a system of symbolic pointers, and that is confirmed by many of his comments elsewhere. So, even if the rhetorical conclusion of his *De consecratione* seems to place material and immaterial on the same level with heaven and earth made one, this is very far from being the normal dynamic of his writing.[130]

---

[125] He wrote not only about the building of the abbey but also about his political career, serving under Louis VI. His biographer reports his ability to quote large chunks of Horace from memory; A. Lecoy de la Marche, *Œuvres Complètes de Suger* (Paris, 1865), 381.

[126] Hugh (d. 1142) wrote a commentary on Denys's *Celestial Hierarchies*. For the extent of Denys's influence on the mystical writings of Richard (d. 1173): C. Kirchenberger (ed.), *Richard of St-Victor: Selected Writings on Contemplation* (London: Faber & Faber, 1957), 47–56.

[127] Despite his commentary, Hugh's other works have no quotations from Denys, while two key phrases in Suger can be traced to earlier translations of Denys: (*speciositas*; *de materialibus* AD *immaterialia*); so D. Poirel, 'Symbolice et anagogice: l'école de Saint-Victor et la naissance du style gothique' in id. (ed.), *L'Abbé Suger, le manifeste gothique de Saint-Denis et la pensée victorine* (Turnhout: Brepols, 2001), 141–70 esp. 157–64.

[128] Note e.g. the type of quotations from Denys used by T. Burckhardt to illustrate his *Chartres and the Birth of the Cathedral* (Ipswich: Golgonooza, 1995 trans.), 40–1. The qualification is the more positive estimate of the material world.

[129] My trans.; quoted in *De administratione*, 27; Panofksy, *Abbot Suger*, 46–9.

[130] *De consecratione*, 7; Panofsky, *Abbot suger*, 120. Yet even here he may have the same movement in mind, for, though he speaks of a 'single state' (*una respublica*), it is significant that it is a matter of joining the material to the immaterial and not the other way round, and even then only when the former is suitably restored.

Images are there to 'rouse us from the material to the immaterial' and the bodies of the saints to 'snatch us, praying, after them'.[131] Again, reflection on the beauty of the jewels he has employed in the decoration of the church enables him by moving 'from the material to the immaterial' to envisage himself 'translated by divine grace from an inferior to a higher world to dwell in some strange region of the earth, which is neither wholly in the earth's slime nor in heaven's purity'.[132]

If 'slime' is a rare example in Suger of purely negative imagery for this world, that sense of a fundamentally transcendent orientation did lead some of his contemporaries who are more explicitly Platonist than he is to speak in much less positive terms. Thierry of Chartres, for instance, chose to stress the inferior character of the enmattered form in language very much reflecting the attitudes and terminology of classical Platonism.[133] It could, of course, be argued that such conflicts and tensions are inherent within Platonism and perhaps inescapable, but the extent of the pull the medieval world felt in Thierry's direction could also be used to explain why there is also a powerful counter-movement, with at least sometimes that very materiality fully affirmed. For it is striking that as churches pull more and more heavenwards, there is also an equally powerful downward thrust, most obviously in more conspicuous celebrations of the divine presence in the eucharist. For it is to the period of Gothic architecture that we must also date both the elevation of the host as a sign of that presence and genuflection as the indicator of its significance.[134] Even Suger himself at the dedication of his church prays for Christ to come down.[135] That contrary trend is also fully reflected in the new naturalism of Gothic sculptures. The incarnation is fully proclaimed, indeed so much so that some already find in some sculpture at Chartres a loss of transcendence

[131] *De adminstratione*, 34 (de materialibus AD immaterialia excitans): 21 (qui post se rapiant nos orantes).

[132] Ibid. 33; Panofsky, *Abbot Suger*, 64–5.

[133] Cf. the quotation in Burckhardt, *Chartres*, 72. For a more detailed study, J. M. Parent, *La Doctrine de la création dans L'École de Chartres* (Paris: Librarie philosophique de J. Vrin, 1938), e.g. 198.

[134] Burckhardt *Chartres*, 78, connects genuflection with the ceremony of allegiance of a vassal to his lord, but more important was the way in which genuflection was really a natural development out of the ceremonial elevation of the host (first formally recognized by the bishop of Paris in 1210).

[135] For relevant quotations: ibid. 56–8.

that was to make the increasing naturalism of the period in due course also deeply problematic.[136]

All seem agreed that Saint-Denis is an essentially transitional building that owes much to it predecessors. Its façade, for example, remains essentially Romanesque.[137] But with the building having suffered so much in subsequent centuries, it is important that the denigration of Suger and his workmen should not go too far.[138] Even Gothic Chartres was to suffer a dreadful fire as it was being built (in 1194), but fortunately for posterity the fact that the new west front was not yet linked directly to the old building meant that the new portal survived intact, and after the thirteenth century there was little further change; so of all the French cathedrals it is our best-preserved example of early Gothic. The naturalism of the drapery on those portals finds echoes in earlier Burgundian Romanesque, and it has even been suggested that Gislibertus from Autun was master-mason here as well, his style made more naturalistic to conform with the demands of the Chartres school.[139] That is a contentious claim, and difficult to evaluate. What, though, we can assert with more confidence is the way in which the cathedral's architecture as a whole conforms to a cosmic symbolism that is seen to point beyond itself to another spiritual world. One example of this is the now fashionable rose window that is used to speak at one and the same time both of heavenly spheres and even of God himself.[140] The conclusion of Dante's *Divine Comedy* is familiar, but two centuries earlier and contemporary with these

[136] As in the contrast between the majestic Christ of the royal portal and the teaching Saviour on the south doorway: for illus.: ibid. 87, 121.

[137] Its essentially transitional style is well illustrated by reconstructions of how it might once have looked: Simson, *The Gothic Cathedral*, pl. 19.

[138] For a surprisingly favourable assessment of how much has survived, P. Z. Blum, *Early Gothic Saint-Denis* (Berkeley: University of California Press, 1992). Yet even she speaks of the way in which the sculptures, though 'looking to the future' still exhibit 'the persistence of *retardataire* elements and Romanesque traditions and conventions' (121).

[139] W. S. Stoddard argued for Burgundian influence in his *Sculptors of the West Portals of Chartres Cathedral* (New York: Norton 1952), esp. 52–3. He has since supplemented this argument with his claim about Gislibertus in a greatly expanded 2nd edn. (1987), esp. 200–9; for the influence of the Chartres school in a more naturalist (incarnational) direction: 209.

[140] Cf. Simson, *The Gothic Cathedral*, 220. He attributes the first rose to Suger: 110.

building works, Hildegard of Bingen was also declaring that the divine most resembles an all-enclosing circle.[141] Another intriguing example is the building's marvellous stained glass. For, however naturalistic the imagery becomes, Gothic seems to provide two powerful counterweights, first in all that great access of light that the new building techniques now make possible and secondly in colour taking preference over line and thus harmonic balance over mere representation.[142]

Order and proportion as a sign of God's creativity were thus now being made more explicit, as human creativity sought to reflect its divine model. Frequently quoted as a precedent were God's instructions to Solomon for the construction of the temple in Jerusalem, as it was a building of carefully balanced proportions.[143] Scholars have detected a similar concern with proportions at Chartres.[144] It may well be, though, that Gothic actually witnessed a lessening of such concerns as new, more explicit forms of symbolism became available. Certainly, there is a long tradition in the West of thinking that the divine can be identified through number and proportion. If Pythagoras and Plato can be seen as the founts for such a way of thinking, much was made within Christianity of the book of Wisdom's declaration that 'You have ordered all things in measure, number and weight.'[145] So Augustine observes that 'reason is nothing else than number', while Basil talks of God 'making an harmonious symphony'.[146] Thanks to translation of Plato's *Timaeus* by Chalcidius and Macrobius' commentary on Cicero's *Somnium Scipionis* those ideas could also be claimed to have the endorsement of Plato himself.[147] But it may well be that

---

[141] Asserted by Hildegard in e.g. her *De operatione Dei*, but also indicated by some of the drawings used to illustrate her visions: cf. C. Hart and J. Bishop, *Hildegard of Bingen: Scivas* (New York: Paulist Press, 1990), 137, 159, 307. For Dante, *Paradiso* XXIII, 106–45.

[142] For an excellent guide to the glass, M. Miller, *Chartres Cathedral*, 2nd edn. (London: Pitkin, 1996), 30–81. For colour as a higher value than literal accuracy, H. Adams, 'The Twelfth Century Glass', in R. Branner (ed.), *Chartres Cathedral* (New York: Norton, 1969), 234–74 esp. 242–3.

[143] The measurements are given in 1 Kgs. 6.

[144] Simson, *The Gothic Cathedral*, 207–12; for Suger and Solomon: 95–6.

[145] Wis. 11: 20.

[146] Augustine, *De ordine*, 11. 18. 48; Basil, *Hexaemeron*, 1. 7.

[147] Although the *Somnium* is part of Cicero's *De republica*, Macrobius makes heavy use of Porphyry's commentary on the *Timaeus*.

master-masons maintained earlier traditions and continued to apply some of the ideas inherent in the plans of classical buildings; if so, how much reliance had to be placed on a more abstract intellectual underpinning from the clergy is unclear.[148] However that may be, what is fascinating about one recent investigation of the proportions in twenty-seven major early medieval buildings is that their ground plans can be seen to be based on relatively simple applications of Platonic geometry.[149] The author wishes to explain an apparent decline in applying such ideas to the lessening influence of Platonism, but, as more recent studies of Aquinas have stressed, it was much more a case of Plato and Aristotle being made to interact rather than the complete abandonment of the former.[150] My own suspicion is that, if this decline is in fact confirmed, the reason for the change should probably be sought elsewhere: in retreat from the Romanesque model of the church building as in some sense God's actual dwelling-place and its substitution by the notion of architecture's task now being primarily to point to the existence of that reality elsewhere.

Yet, as I have already mentioned, the pressure on Gothic in the opposite direction was never very far distant. Eucharistic presence was now a much more focused and celebrated reality. Elevation of the host and genuflection of the knee reiterated what doctrine also affirmed, the full presence of Christ in our midst. Equally, the elongated figures of Romanesque yielded place to a new naturalism that extended even to angels. The angelic smile at Rheims, once seen, is surely never forgotten, but it remains an essentially human smile. That naturalism in art was also supplemented by numerous church rituals suggestive of immanence.[151] More significantly,

---

[148] N. Hiscock, *The Wise Master Builder* (Aldershot: Ashgate, 2000), 97–101, 186–7. There is no need to go with Hiscock's notion of a 'secret' tradition; if unrecorded, that would suffice.

[149] Hiscock provides fourteen detailed plans. Although apparently complex, he points out that their starting point is relatively simple in basic geometric figures: ibid. 262.

[150] Ibid. 290–1; even the application to the later Chartres is problematic: 247. The undoubted influence of Aristotle on Aquinas was moderated by the extent to which he quotes both Augustine and Denys.

[151] For the exploration of late-medieval and early-Reformation experience in England, particularly helpful is Eamon Duffy's *The Stripping of the Altars* (New Haven: Yale University Press, 1992) and his more recent *The Voices of Morebath* (New Haven: Yale University Press, 2001).

however, counterbalancing immanence was also eventually sought in the architecture itself. Although it is hard to assess the tangled web of historical causation, it is not inconceivable that such moves were one key element in Gothic's eventual demise, for in and of itself, in effect, Gothic was now already hinting at alternative architectural approaches. The complexities of the issue can be usefully illustrated from the developments that succeeded Pointed or Early English Gothic, the so-called Decorated style.

This is the name commonly given to the period that lies midway between Pointed and Perpendicular and that lasted roughly from the mid-point of Henry III's reign to the mid-point of that of Edward III (roughly 1250–1350). As the name implies, there was great stress on decoration such as in window tracery. Examples that come to mind of the style writ large might include Westminster Abbey, the Angel Choir at Lincoln, and the Lady Chapel at Ely. One side of the coin was continuing attempts to render buildings even more insubstantial, as at York where window frames were deliberately placed on the inside of the walls to make the latter look even thinner. But balanced against this was the movement the other way, represented by the accumulation of detail everywhere. The twists and turns given to stone made it look sometimes almost as though it were precious metal, and so in effect very earthy indeed.[152] There was also significant interchange between secular and religious architecture. So, for instance, quite irrelevant to questions of security, towers at Caernarvon Castle were given octagonal shapes, while statues were added to battlements at Chepstow, and placed on top of the town gates at York.[153] Equally, in the other direction one finds heraldic devices decorating church pinnacles, cornices, and string courses, and indeed even in some key church symbols such as that for the Trinity the Shield of Faith, and for Christ's suffering the *Arma Christi*.[154] None of this need be read as an early form of secularism. Rather, what it reflects is dynamic interchange between church and society, with the knight seen in

---

[152] A 'metallic quality... designed to resemble more precious metals' is observed in both Ely and Lincoln (and elsewhere) by N. Coldstream, *The Decorated Style* (London: British Museum, 1994), 23. For York, 35–6.

[153] Ibid. 39, 45.

[154] Ibid. 106, 112. The *Arma Christi* represents the various instruments of Christ's Passion, while the Shield of Faith portrays the meaning of the doctrine of the Trinity within a heraldic shield.

essentially religious terms, and thus of course religion itself incarnated no less in the military world than in the cloister.[155] Even so, such trends did inevitably pull the interpretation of Gothic architecture in a much more immanent or even purely human direction, and so stored up trouble for the future. England at least avoided the excesses of the French Flamboyant style. Its own final style, the Perpendicular, had the undoubted merit of clarity: the unambiguous upward thrust of Pointed once more returned. Under Decorated English church walls and windows had everywhere been adorned with the sensuous S, known to architectural historians as the ogee.[156] It is often forgotten that despite the soaring quality of Perpendicular it too showed a love of ornament for ornament's sake. Nowadays, when churches have lost so much of their original art, it is easy to think the meaning of the architecture quite clear enough. But one wonders whether in churches crowded with colour and with artefacts the architecture would really have been able to fulfil adequately its transcendent role, once it also sought to offer immanent messages as well. Whether so or not, Gothic was now succeeded in public esteem by two markedly different approaches, first Classicism and then Baroque. To an evaluation of their quite different aims, I now turn.

Renaissance Rationalism and Baroque Exuberance

A nice reminder of how there is seldom a precise cut-off point between the cessation of one style and the beginning of another is provided by the fact that not just in England did Gothic continue well into the seventeenth century, but also, even in the country where Renaissance classicism has its roots, one of the outstanding Gothic cathedrals was still being built in Milan at precisely the same time as Brunelleschi was completing his great classical dome over the cathedral in Florence, not far distant.[157] As its name implies, the

[155] In her Epilogue Coldstream argues passionately that the style is no mere courtly external form but essentially, 'the expression of religious devotion': 186–92 esp. 192.

[156] For a fine example of ogee, see the frontispiece illustration of the Percy Tomb at Beverley Minster (*c.*1340), ibid. Coldstream rightly observes that Perpendicular was scarcely more structurally based than Decorated (58–9).

[157] Early 17th-c. Oxford provides good examples of the former point, as in several of its colleges and quadrangles (e.g. the front quad of Oriel), and also in the

Renaissance marked a rebirth of classical learning, in this case the discovery and publication of Vitruvius' great work, *The Ten Books of Architecture*, almost certainly written at the very beginning of the Christian era under the emperor Augustus.[158] Its architecture is often portrayed as marking a decline in religious values, and so as a move towards more purely human concerns. That seems to me quite unfair. Its long-term consequences may well have had this effect, but that was very far from being the intention among early exponents, as we shall see. Before any limitations are trumpeted, the more positive side to its rationalist values does therefore need to be acknowledged. It was in any case supplanted for a while by a style more concerned with mystery than with reason; so in considering in tandem Baroque on the Continent and in England there will be an opportunity to assess what happens when the attempt is made to take the worshipper beyond the purely rational.

Renaissance and Divine Order

Nowadays many popular accounts of the period stress the way in which Vitruvius' use of human proportions in architecture was picked up at the Renaissance in the oft-repeated diagram of the naked human frame enclosed in circle and square, and the conclusion often drawn from this is that the Renaissance therefore marked a move away from the divine to the centrality of the human. But this is altogether too simple an analysis. In fact, Vitruvius leaves us in no doubt that temples should be regarded as the most important buildings in any city,[159] while the human body was highlighted in this way at the Renaissance precisely in order to make a theological point, that the order and proportionality to be found in the body reflect that of the universe as a whole and thereby the nature of

new porch given to the University church of St Mary the Virgin. Milan Cathedral (capable of holding 40,000) was begun only in 1386. Brunelleschi finished his dome in Florence in 1436; the two cities are about 150 miles apart.

[158] The manuscript was discovered in the library of St Gall in 1415, and disseminated by the papal secretary, G. F. Poggio; a printed edition first appeared in 1487.

[159] Temples are treated first 'as due order requires' in Bk. III after the Preliminaries of Books I and II; so M. H. Morgan (trans.), *Vitruvius: The Ten Books of Architecture* (New York: Dover, 1960), 65. For the analogy with the human body: III. 1, pp. 72–5.

divine creation.[160] The use of classical architecture was thus intended to facilitate experience of the divine through its form no less than was the case with the other types of architecture hitherto considered. The difference lay in the specific type of experience sought and not in its general character as such.

The body's containment within circle and square provides us with a useful clue. Using the circle and/or sphere as an image for the divine has a long pedigree. Certainly the image is already there in Plato, who uses it as a way of expounding the notion of a divine World Soul immanent in our world: 'the shape the creator gave was suitable to its nature . . . a rounded spherical shape . . . a figure that has the greatest degree of completeness and uniformity . . . a blessed god'.[161] Cardinal Nicholas of Cusa in his *De Docta Ignorantia* of 1440 also spoke of the circle as 'a perfect figure of unity and simplicity which in its infinite form could provide a perfect analogy for God, so much so indeed that one might even say that "all theology is circular and lies within a circle"'.[162] It was also an image taken up in Florence itself by another Platonist, Marsilio Ficino, but its relevance to architecture is perhaps expressed most clearly by Palladio who observes that 'every part being equally distant from the centre such a building demonstrates extremely well the unity, the infinite essence, the uniformity and the justice of God'.[163]

The dome as a hemisphere is of course related to the circle. It appears that in earlier times the most common understanding of its role was as a metaphor for the vault of heaven.[164] Given the philosophical background to the Renaissance, however, the dome in Brunelleschi's cathedral at Florence or in Bramante's Tempietto and Michelangelo's St Peter's at Rome all need to be read rather

---

[160] For quotations and references making the connections explicit, R. Wittkower, *Architectural Principles in the Age of Humanism*, 5th edn. (Chichester: Academy, 1998), 23–5.

[161] My trans.; for the passage in full, *Timaeus*, 33–4.

[162] His point is that at infinity, centre, diameter, and circumference are all one and the same; so all distinctions are overcome in God, and he is perfect unity: trans. G. Heron, *Of Learned Ignorance* (London: Routledge & Kegan Paul, 1954), I. xxi. 46–8.

[163] Palladio, *Four Books of Architecture* (Cambridge, Mass.: MIT Press, 1997), IV. 2.

[164] Wittkower, *Architectural Principles*, 19 esp. n. 37. It is a pre-Christian notion, borrowed from the classical world: so K. Lehmann, 'The Dome of Heaven', *Art Bulletin* 27 (1945), 1–27.

differently. Nor were they just experimentation with a new style,[165] any more than was the imposition of round interiors in, among other examples, both the Roman churches just mentioned.[166] The symbolism of a world ordered by a single, unified source is clearly there. But there was also the question of precedent. Christianity's most holy site, the church of the Holy Sepulchre in Jerusalem, was circular, as was Rome's most celebrated surviving ancient temple, the Pantheon.[167] Even so, the Church was eventually to rebel, and demand more elongated structures, as at St Peter's. Fortunately, classical precedent could still be quoted, with reference to the Basilica of Maxentius in the Forum, then believed to have been originally a Temple of Peace.[168] At least that is the way Alberti argues, drawing attention also to the religious dimension of basilicas where justice had once been administered.[169] Circular structures were in the end to be more visible in paintings than in practice.[170]

Yet, if Renaissance ideals were not to achieve conspicuous success in that direction, matters were quite otherwise in respect of façades. An early example was Alberti's own adaptation of the Gothic church of Santa Maria Novella in Florence, where the different height of aisles and nave is concealed behind an essentially horizontal and well-proportioned façade concluding in impressive

---

[165] The innovative character of Brunelleschi's work is described in R. King, *Brunelleschi's Dome* (London: Pimlico, 2001). At 143 ft. its span was larger than St Peter's, the largest since the Pantheon and unsurpassed until the 20th c.: 9, 30, 163–4.

[166] The Tempietto ('small temple') was built on the supposed site of Peter's martyrdom in 1502. Michelangelo was inspired by Bramante's designs, but the dome was not finally erected until after his death, while his centralized plan was later altered by Maderno through the addition of a long nave to the church.

[167] Baptisteries were also often built as octagons, to represent new life (the eighth day), while that in Florence was itself thought to have been built on the site of a pagan temple to Mars of similar shape.

[168] For the application of such arguments to Alberti's S. Andrea in Mantua, A. Bruschi, 'Religious Architecture in Renaissance Italy from Brunelleschi to Michelangelo', in H. A. Millon (ed.), *Italian Renaissance Architecture* (London: Thames & Hudson, 1996 edn.), 131–2, 142–5.

[169] Cf. Alberti, *Ten Books of Architecture* (1755 Leoni edn., New York: Dover, 1986), VII. 1, p. 133; VII. 4, p. 139.

[170] As e.g. in Raphael's Stanze della Segnatura frescoes in the Vatican, no doubt under the influence of Bramante. Alberti in any case undersells his case by not mentioning the use of the circle as a metaphor for the divine but instead only appealing to it being the most common form in nature: VII. 4, p. 138.

scrolls at each side.[171] That lack of upward thrust is a recurring characteristic of the classical style. Even pediments, where they occur, seem to mark the appropriate terminus of an ensemble rather than provide an invitation for further exploration. Even so, it would be a mistake to assume therefore a purely human reference. Vitruvius demonstrates not only interest in the practical demands of religious observance but also that a sense of divine presence should be conveyed.[172] Likewise, Alberti wants his buildings to 'attract' and so 'stir up piety',[173] and there seems little doubt that in this desire he was entirely sincere.[174]

For both Vitruvius and Alberti such thoughts were engendered by a sense of proportion or harmony, and indeed the musical parallel was widely drawn.[175] In the following century the astronomer Kepler was even to entitle one of his books *Harmonia Mundi*, while Dryden could write:

> From harmony, from heav'nly harmony
> This universal frame began;
> From harmony to harmony
> Thro' all the compass of the notes it ran,
> The diapason closing full in man.[176]

So it is far from being the case that this emerged as a non- or anti-religious form of architecture. Rather, the difference from Gothic consists in this, that the world is now viewed much more positively, with God fully immanent within it. Nowhere is the difference perhaps more marked than in attitudes to the crucifixion. The focus is now much less on the pain God had to endure to set things

[171] Illustrated in R. Toman (ed.), *Die Kunst der italiensichen Renaissance* (Cologne: Könemann, 1994), 108, 110–11. Work was begun in 1458.

[172] For examples of the former (wide processions and protection from rain), Alberti, III. 3, pp. 80, 82; for the latter, IV. 5, p. 116. In the latter case he wants temples to face west so that to worshippers the statue of the god will 'appear to be coming forth from the east to look upon them as they pray and sacrifice'.

[173] Ibid. V. 6, p. 59 ('entice those who are absent to come and see'); VI. 2, pp. 112–13 ('beauty is what most attracts us to God'); VII. 3, p. 136 ('stirring up men to piety, by filling their minds with delight').

[174] A recent biography not only takes his profession of Christianity seriously but also suggests that apparent pagan influences (such as his use of the triumphal arch in churches) may have had an underlying Christian rationale: A. Grafton, *Alberti* (London: Penguin, 2001), 37, 325–30.

[175] Discussed in detail in Wittkower, *Architectural Principles*, 104–37.

[176] *Song for St Cecilia's Day*, lines 11–15.

right, and much more on the restoration of cosmic harmony that has now been achieved.[177]

It may be that sense of harmony that led Palladio to extend the use of the classical church façade to his country villas. Certainly, the move cannot be attributed to secularism as such, for Palladio was himself devout.[178] More probably, therefore, we should think of the way in which his country villas were viewed, as themselves embodying a religious dimension. One of his clients, for instance, did not hesitate to talk about 'sacred agriculture', while Palladio himself draws the connection between leisure and reflection, inspired in part by the views that the situation of such villas made possible.[179] This is not, of course, to claim that such motivation continued to play any significant part among his followers. What religious views Inigo Jones held we do not know, but we do know that he quite happily adapted religious plans to secular and vice versa.[180] Palladio himself, though, was quite another matter. Although himself still favouring round churches, he succeeded in coming up with the compromise of an ample nave culminating internally in a domed circular area, while externally the façade was given a double pediment to integrate with what now lay behind. In Venice the two churches of Il Redentore and San Giorgio Maggiore are striking applications of this design.[181] There is order and proportion but also a brilliant use of light that draws one along the nave and towards the high altar.[182]

One commentator speaks of a 'transcendent' impact that is at one and the same time 'rational' and 'sensual'.[183] Those words provide a

[177] A good example of this is Raphael's portrayal of the crucifixion in the National Gallery in London. Not only is the beauty of Christ's body maintained, but also sun and moon look benignly on, indicating that cosmic significance.

[178] J. S. Ackerman, *Palladio* (London: Penguin, 1966), 35.

[179] P. Holberton, *Palladio's Villas* (London: John Murray, 1990), 86–9, 133–4. Palladio also appeals to the likelihood that its use in houses came first: 117–18.

[180] His Banqueting House was based on a basilica plan, while the Queen's Chapel in St James's Palace borrows from the Prince's Lodging at Newmarket: J. Summerson, *Inigo Jones* (New Haven: Yale University Press, 2000 edn.), 42, 54–7. There is no firm evidence that he was a Roman Catholic: 108.

[181] For discussion and illus., Ackerman, *Palladio*, 126–59 esp. 128, 133, 135, 143, 150–2.

[182] Contrast Alberti's recommendation of high windows and 'solemn gloom' as a way of 'raising our veneration': VII. 12, pp. 151–2.

[183] Ackerman, *Palladio*, 156, 184–5.

useful warning of the danger of presenting classicism as a narrowly or wholly rational phenomenon. So, for example, though taken up by the Renaissance, Vitruvius' sexual classification of the various styles of column is now more likely than not merely to draw from us a wry smile.[184] Again, the degree of deference to the past can only strike us as quite extraordinary, especially when it leads someone like Alberti to frame his discussion of church architecture entirely by reference to ancient precedents.[185] To give one last example, if some recent research is true, the classicism of the United States' capital city may well also have running through it quite a different current, the secret symbolism of the Masons.[186] Yet it is as well to remember that the Enlightenment image of the Greeks as wholly rational has in any case long since been exploded.[187] If one recent work draws attention to the way in which the various parts of temple architecture may in fact allude to the rather grisly details of bloody sacrifice,[188] another suggests that the setting of the temples was once deliberately aligned with features in the surrounding landscape to suggest various kinds of immanent but not always wholly welcome presences.[189]

But, however much or little such counter-trends may lurk just beneath the surface, Classicism has proved an extraordinarily resilient style. If mention must be made of some defeats in the sixteenth century that culminate in the new style of Baroque in the seventeenth, it emerged with new vigour in the Neoclassicism of the following century and in the Greek Revival of the early nineteenth.

---

[184] IV. I, pp. 102–4. Doric resembles a man, Ionic a woman, and Corinthian a young maiden.

[185] The language of 'temple' is used throughout, and not a single church mentioned by name.

[186] D. Ovason, *The Secret Architecture of our Nation's Capital* (London: HarperCollins, 1999). He seems, though, to want to give the larger role for this to Ellicott rather than to L'Enfant himself: 332.

[187] If Nietzsche set the trend, the classic academic discussion remains E. R. Dodds, *The Greeks and the Irrational* (Berkeley: University of California Press, 1968).

[188] G. Hersey, *The Lost Meaning of Classical Architecture* (Cambridge, Mass.: MIT Press, 1988). The capital, for instance, is taken to allude to the victim's head, the triglyphs to its thigh bones, and the tympanum to sacrificial tables: 23, 30–1, 38.

[189] V. Scully, *The Earth, The Temple and the Gods: Greek Sacred Architecture* (New Haven: Yale University Press, 1979 edn.). For an example of a threatening side, see his remarks on Artemis, 80. Although supported by numerous photographs, his final words are extraordinarily reductionist and rationalistic: 'those recognitions of the facts of existence which are the gods' (213).

Undoubtedly, part of the explanation lies in its capacity to reinvent itself, to demonstrate itself a living and developing tradition, and significantly this is one feature of which both nineteenth and twentieth century advocates make much.[190] Important too is the fact that it can continue to speak of the intelligibility of our world and of humanity's legitimate place within it. In theory, the believer should have the greater confidence in endorsing this view, but in practice religion has in modern times often fought shy of reason, and so where the option was available frequently moved in a quite different direction when trying to give architectural expression to faith.[191]

That fear of reason, however, does seem to me a serious mistake. Rationality and rationalism are far from being exactly the same thing. Of course, endless demands for 'proof' are likely to be destructive of religion, as also the refusal ever to step beyond what is justified solely on the basis of the 'evidence'. But that is quite different from seeing in the world and what we do with it as an intelligible reflection of a divine mind expressing itself. The providential order which Poussin celebrates in so many of his paintings is scarcely reductionist. Yet those marvellous canvases spring from the same sort of notions as once inspired Renaissance religious belief. It should also not be forgotten that they also provided the *raison d'être* for the building style later adopted in many a Nonconformist chapel in England and also quite widely in the United States.[192] In effect, the earlier 'meeting house' was replaced by a more sacramental understanding, with 'sanctity in the place where God chooses to reveal himself'.[193] So the

---

[190] For a 19th-c. example, A. Potts, 'Schinkel's Architectural Theory', in M. Snodin (ed.), *Karl Friedrich Schinkel: A Universal Man* (New Haven: Yale University Press, 1991), 47–55 esp. 51, 54. For a contemporary example, D. Porphyrios, *Classical Architecture* (Windsor: Papadakis, 1998), 69–100 esp. 82, 85.

[191] Schinkel's own uncertainties are instructive. Contrast his original design for Berlin's cathedral with what he eventually built: Snodin, *Schinkel*, 4, 66.

[192] For a good survey of competing American styles, P. W. Williams, *Houses of God: Region, Religion & Architecture in the United States* (Chicago: University of Illinois Press, 1997). Classicism is perhaps more prominent than in any other country, though unusually with the addition of a steeple or bell-tower.

[193] The quotation comes from an 1818 Congregationalist dedication sermon in Connecticut. For a tracking of the changes in sensibility, G. T. Buggeln, 'Elegance and Sensibility in the Calvinist Tradition: The First Congregational Church of Hartford, Connecticut', in P. C. Finney (ed.), *Seeing Beyond the Word: Visual Arts and the Calvinist Tradition* (Grand Rapids: Eerdmans, 1999), 429–53 esp. 447.

theologian who summarily dismisses the style does so at his or her peril.

Yet, that said, Classicism did have its limitations. It is largely an architecture of immanence, and so was ideally suited to act as a complement in Protestantism so long as the latter held to a strong sense of the transcendence of the divine Word in Scripture: the sermon could thus balance the style. No doubt that was one reason why it became so popular in churches otherwise lacking a sacramental focus in their worship.[194] Once different attitudes to the Bible began to emerge, though, the style was in trouble. Music could perhaps fulfil some elements in the transcendent role once exercised by Scripture itself, but the problem was that Classicism was in effect under assault from both ends.[195] For in a less secure age its own rationalism also seemed to exhibit too much confidence and certainty, and so to leave insufficient room either for faith's struggles or for its conviction that God is so much greater than any of our reasoning capacities. Baroque at least remedied some of those defects and, although vastly more popular among Roman Catholics, it too was to have an impact within Protestantism.

Baroque Theatre and English Practicality

The new trend is already evident in what is described as the Mannerism or idiosyncratic individualism of some sixteenth-century architects. An early example would be Michelangelo's placing of columns in the recesses of the walls of his Laurentian Library, thus depriving them of their conventional supporting role, even if their expressive power is thereby increased.[196] Another, and drawing us much closer to Baroque, is Vignola's famous Jesuit church in Rome, the Gesù, where the façade seems deliberately to flout rules in order to provide an intriguing play of

[194] The danger in equating 'sacramental' with frequent celebration of the eucharist is well illustrated by the fact that Reformation churches sought a more exclusively sacred use for their buildings than had been the case in the Middle Ages. This is a central argument in J. G. Davies, *The Secular Use of Church Buildings* (London: SCM, 1968).

[195] It is intriguing to observe the way in which music and art have come to play larger roles within Protestantism, often precisely in proportion as belief in the infallibility and absolute transcendence of Scripture has declined.

[196] J. Summerson, *The Classical Language of Architecture* (London: Thames & Hudson, 1980 edn.), 47–8, illus. 54.

light and shade.[197] As noted in an earlier chapter, Michelangelo was profoundly influenced by the Counter-Reformation. One way of viewing some of his highly personal contributions is to relate them to a new restlessness in faith, the conviction that life is pilgrimage and struggle, not simply the passive endorsement of an already established order. One writer puts it well when he speaks of the move from the Tempietto as 'the symbol of an harmoniously disposed macro-order' to the Gesù as 'an allegory of pilgrimage'.[198]

Of course, it was by no means all struggle. It was all leading somewhere, and this was emphasized in decoration and architecture alike. Thus, in the case of the Gesù one looked up to an illusionist ceiling made to resemble a dome in which the delights of heaven were already anticipated.[199] Baroque's most famous architect, Bernini, effected much the same result in many of his works. So, for example, at Sant' Andrea al Quirinale the crucifixion of St Andrew may encounter us at the high altar but above we see in sculpture the saint already ascending to heaven, with angels there to greet him. Bernini was also responsible for organizing many spectacles and acts of theatre in the Rome of the time, and what therefore emerges particularly from his churches is the way in which he uses the totality of human art, sculpture, and painting as well as architecture, to create his overall effect.[200] Sometimes a reference to theatre is made quite explicit, as in his Cornaro Chapel with its monument to St Teresa of Avila where the family look on from sculptured balconies alongside. However, as detailed consideration is given to Bernini in this volume's sequel (in the chapter on body), let me here take his great rival as my example, not least because Borromini tries to achieve the same purpose through the use of architecture alone.[201]

[197] Ibid. 64–5, illus. 72.

[198] W. Jung, 'Architektur der Hochrenaissance und des Manierismus in Rom und Mittelitalien', in Toman (ed.), *Die Kunst*, 130–55 esp. 152. 'Symbol eines noch harmonisch gefügten Makrokosmos . . . zur Allegorie des Weges, welche die Menschheit hin zur Errettung gehen muß.'

[199] Added later by Baciccio.

[200] One of the most memorable apparently was the reception he organized for the arrival in Rome of Queen Christina of Sweden.

[201] 'Rival' is perhaps too strong a word, as the shyness and social awkwardness of Borromini meant that he was never really in the running, apart from during the pontificate of Innocent X, who commissioned him to reorder the interior of St John Lateran: A. Blunt, *Borromini* (Cambridge, Mass.: Harvard University Press, 1979), 22, 133–4.

Borromini's two most impressive works are two small oval churches, one commissioned for Rome's University (the Sapienzia) and dedicated to S. Ivo, the other officially called San Carlo alle Quattro Fontane but often abbreviated because of its size to San Carlino. Both were difficult sites to negotiate, but Borromini achieves his effects quite brilliantly. Of course, he had one great advantage over Renaissance architects, that the Church had now changed its attitude over the appropriate form for its buildings. Gone was the insistence on long naves, and in its place (thanks to the new emphasis of Trent) had come the insistence that all worshippers should be within easy sight of what was taking place at the mass, and also at other times be encouraged to venerate the reserved sacrament, now placed centrally on the principal altar. Carlino came first (begun in 1638), a church and monastery for the Discalced Trinitarian order, to be situated at the confluence of two streets that approached one another at sharp diagonals. Both cloister and church are oval. If cherubs and palm leaves are there to remind us of the Jerusalem Temple,[202] what impresses most are the curves everywhere, in doorways, façade, balconies, and church itself, drawing the eye in towards the altar and upwards to the dome with its symbol for the Trinity at its centre.[203] But it is S. Ivo (begun in 1643) that most overwhelms. As one stands beneath its dome, it is hard to avoid the sensation of being drawn into divine infinity as the swirling movement of its relatively plain decoration gradually but inevitably pulls the eye upwards.[204] The experience is repeated in its exterior, though more gently and reflectively. For the dome ends in a spiralling ziggurat, with the image of the Tower of Babel now used not to condemn human hubris but rather to endorse the worshipper's desire to soar aloft towards union with God.[205] However, the movement of God the other way is also acknowledged in the slender metal flames at the top which speak of the descent of the Holy Spirit.[206]

[202] Ibid. 70–1. Such symbolism reappears at S. Ivo and S. John Lateran: 121, 144.

[203] Ibid. 52–84. For curves, note particularly illus. 65, 66, 72, 82.

[204] Illustrated ibid. 115.

[205] Blunt quotes as precedents an engraving by Martin van Heemskerk, and a 15th-c. painting by Butone of the 12-year-old Christ in the Temple (the latter now in the National Gallery, Edinburgh): 126. The number of precedents suggests that the reversal of meaning was probably deliberate.

[206] For illus., V. H. Minor, *Baroque and Rococo: Art and Culture* (London: Laurence King, 1999), 90.

Borromini had few direct imitators. The nearest perhaps was the Theatine priest, Guarini.[207] He too produced theatrical works, and his energies were set to use throughout Europe. However, it is two of his works in his native Turin that most capture his distinctive style. In his circular S. Lorenzo the pediments next to the altar are on a slant and so give the impression of thrusting outwards to draw us in, while as our gaze moves upwards empty oculi unnerve us, and so prepare us for the open dome above that with its skylights seems to pass easily into infinity.[208] In his Shroud Chapel the approach is so designed that pilgrims are led almost to anticipate such an experience. Leaving the main body of the cathedral, they climb a staircase to reach the shroud, but it is no ordinary staircase; it twists and curves, adding greatly to the sense of expectant mystery.[209] For Guarini inevitably the total effect was closely bound up with the holiness of the relic itself. But even for those who doubt its authenticity (and even the medieval Church did),[210] there still remains the way in which the image, however created, alludes to Christ and thus can draw us through itself and the dome above to some sense of the intended overall impact of Christ's life: caught from the transient and material into the infinite and eternal.[211]

If *meraviglia* and *spectacolo* come naturally as descriptions of the intended effect of Baroque, so do does *quadratura*, the illusionary dissolving of boundaries.[212] This can be put negatively in terms of the lack of sharp focus in Baroque. Whether it be architecture or painting one can never be quite be sure where one thing begins and another ends. Positively, however, it is a matter of total impression rather than sharpness of detail. Where this becomes pertinent to religious faith is the way in which such means can be used to give a feeling of earth dissolving into heaven, God's world merging with our own. Good examples would be Zimmermann's Wies

---

[207] Though in his many writings he in fact never mentions Borromini, and is critical of Bernini: H. A. Meek, *Guarino Guarini and his Architecture* (New Haven: Yale University Press, 1988), 7–8.

[208] Ibid. 44–60, esp. illus. 44, 47, 51, 52.

[209] Illustrated ibid. 68.

[210] The 1389 document is discussed ibid. 62.

[211] The extraordinary power of the dome is well captured in the two photographs ibid. 78–9. For his general discussion of *Santissima Sindone*: 61–77.

[212] These and related terms are defined and discussed in Minor, *Baroque and Rococo*, 20–30. *Quadratura* is another name for *trompe l'œil* or illusionistic effects, and was the preferred term when Baroque was at the height of its popularity.

pilgrimage church (completed in 1754) or the Assam brothers' St John Nepomuk in Munich (1734).[213] Also worth noting is Balthasar Neumann's Vierzehnheiligen church (completed in 1772), where 'the fourteen' saints actually take centre stage, occupying part of our space, positioned as they are on a platform in the central oval of the three that constitute this particular pilgrimage church.[214] Nowadays, contemporary religious opinion is usually quick to condemn these last illustrations as simply being 'over the top', in the riot of decoration and imagery employed. But, unfortunately, if that approach is taken from the start, we deny ourselves the possibility of an experience that could still be ours. All theatre involves temporary suspension of belief, and so, unless we make that concession also in such churches, we are never likely to depart from them with any sense, however momentary, of having been caught up into another and richer world.

England's version of Baroque is very restrained by comparison. Indeed it is a natural inclination to doubt whether Bernini, Guarini, and Wren could ever have all been in Paris at the same time.[215] One architectural historian confesses that it is only on closer inspection that one realizes that St Paul's is in fact Baroque and not Classical. The 'serene dome set around with cool, contained, closely-spaced, slim columns' outside suggests one thing (the classical), 'a swirling façade' and 'the intrepid effrontery of a Baroque massing' within, another.[216] Some of Wren's earlier designs were in fact drawn from Serlio's sixteenth-century work on architecture,[217] but St Paul's is all his own creation, even if the commission under which he was required to work forced some major modifications along the way away from his original plan for a pure Greek cross.[218] Luckily Wren

---

[213] For Zimmermann's church with its 'insubstantial boundaries . . . floating in the empyrean mists', ibid. 106–10. For the Assam brothers' work with 'the upward thrust of the facade . . . repeated endlessly in the interior by Cosmas' illusionistic paintings', R. Toman (ed.), *Baroque* (Cologne: Könemann, 1998), 233–5. Intriguingly, the latter is included in Charles Jencks's postmodernist consideration of *Ecstatic Architecture*, discussed below.

[214] Toman, *Baroque*, 214–15.

[215] But they were in 1665; Meek, *Guararo Guarini*, 33–4.

[216] So P. Nuttgens, *The Story of Architecture* (London: Phaidon, 1983), 208–10.

[217] This is true both of Pembroke Chapel, Cambridge and of the Sheldonian Theatre in Oxford, the latter being modelled on Serlio's drawing of the Theatre of Marcellus: A. Tinniswood, *His Invention So Fertile: A Life of Christopher Wren* (London: Jonathan Cape, 2001), 101, 103–4.

[218] For development of the building through four plans, ibid. 198.

lived to a great age, and so was able to see the building completed in 1708.[219] The delay, however, was scarcely surprising given that the costs were equivalent to twice the total involved for all the other fifty-six churches combined that were built consequent to the Great Fire of London in 1666 under his supervision as Surveyor-General.[220]

The most quoted passage from Wren on the subject of church architecture is a letter in which he stresses auditory requirements as the most important consideration.[221] This is often used to argue that he stands in full continuity with an essentially Protestant and unsacramental view of church buildings. His clerical father, however, had been a supporter of Andrewes and Laud, and in his own personal benefice he had seen that statues and paintings were installed.[222] Wren certainly showed interest in matters of religion;[223] it may well be that his reticence to pronounce on its relevance to architecture and liturgy was guided more by caution in a turbulent age than any firm commitments different from his father's. In his parish his father had inscribed the words: 'Dread is this place. This is noe other but the howse of God and the gate of heaven.'[224] One can see some signs of a similar motivation in two surviving churches where we know Wren to have had a more direct hand. Both St Mary, Abchurch and St Stephen, Walbrook are circular. In the former case the dome culminates in a painting of the heavenly quire with the Hebrew for God inscribed at its centre;[225] in the latter Henry Moore's modern controversial stone central altar, to my mind at least, accords well with the feel of the building, even though it means that Grinling Gibbons' carved reredos is thus sidelined.[226]

[219] By which time he was 76; he died aged 91.

[220] Tinniswood, *Invention so Fertile*, 187.

[221] C. Wren (ed.), *Parentalia* (1750), 318–21. Given in full as app. 2 in P. de la R. du Prey, *Hawksmoor's London Churches* (Chicago: University of Chicago Press, 2000), 133–7.

[222] Details in Tinniswood, *Invention so Fertile*, 8.

[223] His first lecture attempted to relate astronomy and the Bible, while his last reflections were also biblical: ibid. 57, 365.

[224] Gen. 28: 17 (original spelling).

[225] Discussed and illus. in D. Kendall, *The City of London Churches: A Pictorial Rediscovery* (London: Collins & Brown, 1998), 150–5. The author remarks how 'a seemingly weightless saucer dome creates dramatic grandeur within a small compass' (150).

[226] Ibid. 212–15. He observes: 'the central altar reinforces the auditory centrality given by the dome' (215).

If this latter church has the usual, conventional Ten Commandments, Creed, and Lord's Prayer, there is also a pelican, symbol of the
eucharist.[227] Admittedly, none of these decorations were directly
ordered by Wren; my point is simply that they accord so well with
his overall design that it is hard not to believe that Wren had much
more than just a preaching box or circle in mind.

Yet it would be a mistake in any case to suppose that a strong
contrast between preaching box and sacrament house existed at this
time, even within Roman Catholicism. As Wren would have learnt
during his four-month stay in Paris, the Counter-Reformation was
now equally insistent on audibility, as the frequency and importance of sermons had increased, not least among the new orders such
as the Jesuits and Oratorians. Historians of Anglican architecture
sometimes speak as though Gothic Revival (the next topic to
which I turn) was essentially 'un-Anglican', so marked was the
contrast with what had gone before.[228] But matters are seldom
quite so simple. Already with Wren we see a new sensitivity to
buildings: it matters not just what is said, but also the context in
which it is said. So the practice that was growing up elsewhere of
placing a pulpit in front of the communion table was clearly rejected
and the altar given a central place.[229] Wren's pupil, Hawksmoor,
continued that sensitivity but in a way that nicely illustrates how there
is seldom only one way of doing things, even where the liturgy
remains the same. Each of his six churches is unique in the way it
presents itself, sometimes quoting continuities in classical or Egyptian
precedent, and sometimes alluding to how pagan sacrifice had now
been superseded in the Christian dispensation.[230] The very variety of
his approaches means that sometimes one has to speak of Hawksmoor
as Baroque, sometimes as Classical, and sometimes even as Gothic.[231]

[227] Strictly speaking, only the Ten Commandments were required by canon
law, but the three together were by this period the norm: G. W. O. Addleshaw
and F. Etchells, *The Architectural Setting of Anglican Worship* (London: Faber &
Faber, 1948), 102–3, 160.

[228] N. Yates, *Buildings, Faith and Worship* (Oxford: Clarendon Press, 1991), 171.
Compare the dogmatism of Addleshaw and Etchells, *Architectural Setting*, 226–9.

[229] For examples of the alternative practice, Yates, *Buildings*, 87–8.

[230] For sacrificial altars on the tower of St George's-in-the-East, du Prey,
Hawksmoor's London Churches, 92–3; for the spire of Christ Church, Spitalfields
as Egyptian obelisk: 103–4; for the spire of St George's Bloomsbury as based on the
Mausoleum at Halicarnassus: 213–15.

[231] As in his last work, the towers of Westminster Abbey.

Equally, even deep Gothic chancels can be adapted to the requirements of very Protestant worship, as indeed they once were.[232] For me, therefore, the key question is not the form of the worship as such but rather whether the building aids a sacramental sense of the presence of God or inhibits it, and, either way, precisely how.

If in architects such as Wren and Hawksmoor we witness the attempt of at least some members of their profession to transcend the rather narrow focus that infected so much English religion at the time, even in them there is little of the exuberance and uninhibited theatricality that so dominated Continental Baroque. English tourists of today tend to respond to the style by finding it effete or perhaps even unchristian. In part that response is dictated less by the style's intrinsic merits or otherwise and more by ignorance, for certainly it stands in marked contrast to what the viewer is likely ever to have encountered elsewhere within a church. Nor are such reactions helped by the insensitive way in which the reforms of Vatican II have so often been applied. It is not that Baroque is necessarily incompatible with western-facing altars, but incongruity is the only possible result if simple geometrical forms are imposed.[233] Mass celebrated behind a simple square altar in such a context cannot but look completely out of place, and so inevitably raise for viewer and worshipper alike the issue of whether it is the architecture that is wrongly placed or perhaps even the mass itself. But that need not be so: curvaceous altars can function as easily facing west as east. The more substantial question is thus what Baroque was seeking to express, what kind of experience of God it was (and is) trying to evoke.

What I suggest it offers is even more of a *Gesamtkunstwerk* than medieval Gothic. Whereas in Gothic on the whole the architecture suggests transcendence and the artwork immanence, here was a style that tried fully to integrate transcendence and immanence in artwork and architecture alike. In architects such as Bernini, architecture slides into art and vice versa, and so it is impossible always to tell where one ends and the other begins, and this applies to no less a degree to the question of immanence versus transcendence. Now

---

[232] Either through the whole of the communion service taking place there, or else only its latter stages. For the offertory and the invitation ('draw near') as marking such stages, see Addleshaw and Etchells, *Architectural Setting*, 140, 150–1.

[233] St Peter's in Rome has a west-facing altar set in the context of Bernini's great baldachino.

we see the word hallowed by God's saints; now the future reality promised in heaven. But is this how things are, or how they might be? Heaven, it appears, is both here and not here but becomes progressively more and more an incarnated reality, the more we are prepared, as in the conventional theatre, to suspend belief and enter fully in that experience. But for that to happen much contemplation and imagination is required. Without such an effort the typical Baroque ceiling that portrays heaven, for instance, will inevitably seem merely over-clever and artificial. It is perhaps because the Classical could so easily appear too rationalistic and the Baroque too demanding that the nineteenth century returned to the less complex message of pure transcendence offered by Gothic.

Gothic Revival and a Forgotten Alternative

Most churches we now see about us in Britain are nineteenth-century Gothic, and as such represent a revival of the medieval style. Because of the density of their occurrence, it is very easy to fall into the trap of supposing the revival to have been motivated by purely religious considerations, but as a matter of fact many of the revival's earliest creations were secular rather than religious.[234] Conspicuous among them were Horace Walpole's still surviving Strawberry Hill of 1750–70 and the unfortunately no longer extant Wyatt and Wyatville's Fonthill Abbey of 1815. The latter, built for the eccentric millionaire William Beckford, must have been an extraordinary sight to behold: externally, it looked like some great abbey with a spire-like tower; while internally the great hall absolutely dwarfed anyone ascending its staircase.[235] Such secular

---

[234] Indeed, one might question whether the style had ever quite died out in the secular sphere. Its frequency in 17th-c. Oxford (including the porch of St Mary the Virgin) is sometimes used to suggest endorsement by Archbishop Laud, but Laud's essentially pragmatic approach is seen in his decision to ask Inigo Jones to rebuild St Paul's in Renaissance style.

[235] The tower had already collapsed by 1825. For black and white external and internal views, K. Clark, *The Gothic Revival*, 3rd edn. (London: John Murray, 1970), 85. Clark's work itself provides fascinating insights into changing estimates of Gothic. Originally written as a sustained critique, the introduction, epilogue, and footnotes tell a quite different tale, of his gradual conversion.

buildings remind us of a wider setting in the Romantic movement, with its nostalgia for the past. Fonthill Abbey also alerts us to the potential within the style for human hubris, the attempt to provide contexts for mere human beings in which they could appear to their contemporaries in the guise of demigods.[236]

The person most responsible for ensuring that Gothic became the distinctive ecclesiastical style was Augustus Welby Pugin (1812–52). The son of a humble French Huguenot immigrant and a mere five feet five inches tall, he had an influence out of all proportion either to his size or short life. It seems to have been his mother who gave him a passion for religion, but, though he converted to Rome in 1835, he did not find life in his new communion an altogether happy one.[237] This was largely because the medieval Gothic style he chose to identify as quintessentially Christian ran counter to the Continental piety then becoming fashionable. Rome itself also seemed to suggest a quite different model, not only in the alternative precedent set by St Peter's but also in the fact that the centre of that city was able to boast only one truly Gothic church.[238] Nevertheless, he was given a hand in the design of four Roman Catholic cathedrals, including St Chad's, Birmingham, but clerical interference and the ravages of time have meant that none of these provides the best example of his ideals. Today this is perhaps best seen in a parish church: in St Giles, Cheadle.[239]

The roots of a passion that extended even to identifying a new wife as the acquisition of 'a first rate Gothic woman at last' are not all that hard to detect.[240] One can see him as part of the general romanticism of the time that looked back with nostalgia to what

[236] Gothic seems to have been chosen as best suited to exhibit his pretensions, and not out of any deep commitment to the style. Certainly, when he subsequently moved to Bath, he had a house built in the Classical style (Lansdown Tower).

[237] Helpful in this context is D. Meara, 'The Catholic Context', in P. Atterbury (ed.), *A. W. N. Pugin: Master of Gothic Revival* (New Haven: Yale University Press, 1995), 45–61. His mother's religion, however, was quite different: fervent Evangelicalism. His father had wrongly claimed aristocratic origins: 36.

[238] S. Maria sopra Minerva. Begun 1280 and completed in 1370, it was restored to something like its original form in the 19th-c.

[239] For an illustration, J. S. Curl, *Victorian Churches* (London: Batsford, 1995), 97 illus. I.

[240] Quoted in Atterbury, *A. W. N. Pugin*, 225.

appeared to be an ideal age of an integrated Christian society.[241] But to leave matters there would be to give very much less than the full answer. For, as his four key writings indicate, he saw Gothic struggling towards a perfect expression that finally reached its culmination in the English Decorated style, only to decline once more in Perpendicular.[242] If the desire to soar meant that sometimes his buildings ventured too high in relation to their size, internally it was mystery and mood that he sought to create rather than openness, a 'dim religious light'.[243] The linking of heaven and earth and the sacramentality of the altar are thus both underlined. It is within such a context that his hostility to superfluous ornament should be set: 'all ornament should consist of enrichment of the essential construction of the building'.[244]

While Pugin was still a child, two hundred Anglican churches had already been built in the Gothic style (during the 1820s),[245] but more important for determining his future influence was the work of the Camden Society in Cambridge with its stress on ethics and sacramentality in church building,[246] and, still more so, the growth of the Oxford Movement from 1833 onwards. If Newman and Keble showed little interest, its later stages were decisive.[247] For the wider liturgical changes that eventually emerged out of its thinking

[241] Seen not only in the novels of Sir Walter Scott but also in historical works such as in William Cobbett's *History of the Protestant Reformation* (1824) and Robert Southey's *Sir Thomas More* (1829).

[242] The position he adopted in 1841 with his second and most important work, *True Principles of Pointed or Christian Architecture*. Adopted also by *The Ecclesiologist*, it took Burges's victory in an international competition for a new cathedral at Lille in 1856 to establish other possibilities (in his case early French Gothic).

[243] For worries about building too high, Atterbury, *A. W. N. Pugin*, 92; the quotation comes from Milton's *Il Penseroso* (l. 160) where he seems to be describing a Gothic building.

[244] From the opening page of *True Principles*.

[245] A total of 214 churches were built as a result of the Church Building Act of 1818, with 174 in the Gothic style, apparently chosen because it was seen as cheaper: Clark, *Gothic Revival*, 95–6.

[246] 'Sacramentality' is used as the key to religiously appropriate architecture by J. M. Neale and B. Webb in the introduction to their edition of Durandus: *The Symbolism of Churches and Church Ornaments*, 3rd edn. (London: Gibbings, first pub. 1842; 1906), esp. pp. xxv–viii. Ironically, the examples they choose are more illuminating than those of Durandus himself.

[247] For the attitude of Newman to Pugin, Atterbury, *A. W. N. Pugin*, 52–5, 58, 60.

ensured that it was Anglican architects and churches that pre-eminently promoted this style, and so provided the most distinctive examples of the new approach. The result is that with few exceptions any representative selection of the most successful applications tends to read like a roll-call of bastions of Anglo-Catholicism. Thus, particularly worth noting are William Butterfield's All Saints, Margaret Street and St Augustine's, Queens Gate; George Street's St James the Less, Westminster; John Pearson's St Augustine's, Kilburn; William Burges's Studley Royal; and George Bodley's St John's, Tuebruck.[248] Some of the architects, such as Butterfield and Street, were also themselves committed Anglo-Catholics.[249] Although the leaders of the Oxford Movement had been relatively uninterested in liturgical change, their new stress on the importance of the Church's sacraments did ensure that a later generation could build on that stress to argue not only for greater frequency of the eucharist, as did Newman, Pusey, and Keble, but also, unlike them, for a new context within which this would be celebrated. Gothic reinforced the logic of an eastward-facing altar and thus the belief that internal and external beauty alike should be used to augment the sense of a heavenly mystery being symbolically re-enacted here on earth: Christ's offering now in heaven to his Father of his sacrifice made once and for all on the cross. Yet there was emphatically no slavish copying of Pugin's theories. Indeed, one commentator goes so far as to observe of All Saints', Margaret Street that it 'shows not the slightest nostalgia for the Middle Ages', while another talks of Butterfield being 'like Dickens in literature . . . a realist in a romantic age'.[250] Certainly, there is an inventiveness in later Victorian Gothic that speaks of a dynamic, developing tradition prepared to use modern materials and designs, even if to talk of the deliberate adoption of ugliness in Butterfield's case as a

[248] The late 19th-c. character of these achievements is well indicated by the years in which these architects died: Butterfield (d. 1900); Street (d. 1881); Pearson (b. Durham, 1817; d. 1897); Burges (d. 1881); Bodley (d. 1907). For illustrations of All Saints', Margaret St., Curl, *Victorian Churches*, 97 illus. III, IV. For the others, C. M. Smart, *Muscular Churches: Ecclesiastical Architecture of the High Victorian Period* (Fayetteville: University of Arkansas Press, 1989), 60, 95, 139, 169, 220.

[249] Street was even churchwarden of Butterfield's great church: Smart, ibid. 76.

[250] J. Summerson, *Heavenly Mansions* (New York: Norton, 1949), 169; Smart, *Muscular Churches*, 29.

protest against the soft and the genteel, as one commentator does, is surely to go too far.[251]

The eventual adoption of Gothic by Nonconformity is some-times explained in terms of a desire for gentility and upward mobility through emulation of one's neighbours. Certainly, some kind of explanation is required, not least because one would have thought that the desire for preaching halls would have necessitated the adoption of the Classical style, which permits square buildings, galleries, and so forth. Some of course continued to be built, but the surprise is how frequently ministers and congregations alike gave preference to the new Gothic, and so to long churches with chancels, and that despite the consequent difficulties in hearing and the fact that ideologically the building was in fact better suited not so much to the proclamation of the word as to evoking a sense of the mystery enshrouding what was taking place in the dis-tance.[252] Perhaps part of the reason lies in the desire for symbolism as such. After all the Gothic spire did proudly proclaim that beneath its upward thrust lay a meeting of heaven and earth,[253] and classical buildings did not easily lend themselves to such additions. Indeed, alternative styles may have lost out simply because of their lack of any immediately obvious and appealing rationale.

But another factor worth noting is the way in which thanks to John Ruskin Gothic came eventually to be seen, paradoxically, as the quintessential Protestant style. Ruskin was virulently anti-Catholic. Although he subsequently modified his position, in his *Stones of Venice* he wrote that there was nothing worse than being 'lured into the Romanist church by the glitter of it, like larks into a trap by broken glass . . . stitched into a new creed by gold threads on priests' petticoats; jangled into a change of conscience by the

---

[251] The essence of Summerson's argument in 'William Butterfield; or the Glory of Ugliness', in *Heavenly Mansions*, 159–76.

[252] When Beresford-Hope (in his capacity as President of the Ecclesiological Society) raised the issue in respect of Anglican churches in 1864, he argued that once the preaching-house element was taken into account it would legitimate large unified spaces and even galleries. He was met with a vociferous and largely hostile response, Archdeacon Thorp of Durham notable among them: S. Crewe (ed.), *Visionary Spires* (London: Waterstone, 1986), 78.

[253] Given how many spires were built at this time, it is salutary to recall how many further proposals faltered, e.g. spires for Chester (Scott), Durham (Wyatt), and Peterborough (Pearson) cathedrals: for designs, Crewe, ibid. 9, 10, 80, 87.

chimes of the belfry'.[254] Again, in the 1848 edition of his *Seven Lamps of Architecture* he condemned Catholic Emancipation as a national crime, while for all of the fifty-two years he lived with his parents he continued in rigorous observation of the sabbath, even covering up the pictures he owned, in case they distracted him from more biblical reflections.[255] His Protestant credentials were thus impeccable, but added to these were his attack on Renaissance and Baroque styles as papist, while the earlier Gothic was presented as embodying the workers' values of co-operation and moral earnestness. Little wonder then that Protestants felt comfortable in adopting Gothic.

Yet there were some who fought back against its apparently inevitable advance. One such rare exception was the Scottish architect, Alexander 'Greek' Thomson, five years younger than Pugin and a devout member of the United Presbyterians.[256] Sadly, only recently has interest in his work revived, and so too late to save many of what must have been impressive structures.[257] He even lost the competition for the new buildings for Glasgow University (which became yet another Gothic monument), but he was successful in securing commissions for several city churches, and all these reflect his belief that the Jerusalem Temple would have been closest in structure to surviving Egyptian temples and so provides a legitimate and strikingly different model for how churches in his own day should be built. The result is great weighty structures externally which, none the less, internally are full of light and colour and, more importantly perhaps from the point of view of Presbyterian worship, so structured that all the worshippers are within easy reach of the pulpit, itself set centrally at one end. The Caledonia Road church which now survives only as a external shell helps gives some idea of the impact he intended externally, while his St Vincent Street church (also in Glasgow) is particularly interesting in illustrating his lively internal colour schemes and

---

[254] Appendix to first vol., 1851.

[255] Though in the 1880 edn. all the strongly Protestant passages were removed: Clark, *Gothic Revival*, 197.

[256] G. Stamp and S. McKinstry (eds.), *'Greek' Thomson* (Edinburgh: Edinburgh University Press, 1994), 51.

[257] Although computer model techniques have been used to reconstruct his lost masterpiece, Queens Park Church, in the Arts Council video *Nineveh on the Clyde* (1999).

patterns.[258] There seems little doubt that the intention in each case was to promote a real feeling of divine presence, though not in any way specifically associated with the eucharist. That is no doubt why he felt able to introduce the same sort of symbolism into some of the private homes he designed, where ordinary ceilings are transformed into celestial skies, as in his Maria Villa.[259]

As with Pugin and Ruskin we are fortunate to have some of Thomson's own reflections on what motivated his architecture.[260] He sees himself as called on to function as a co-creator alongside God, and justifies the use of 'pagan' styles not only because of their presumed connection with the Jerusalem Temple but also because he sees divine revelation acting through the earlier religious traditions of Egypt and Greece.[261] Ancient Rome, however, he regarded as marking a decline, not least because of the invention of the arch which he condemns as both structurally unsound and restless and busy, lacking the obvious stability of the beam.[262] The ultimate foundation of Gothic is thus squarely condemned, and it is fascinating to compare his views on glass with those of Ruskin. Both wanted light, but whereas for Ruskin the focus should be on the form of the windows that allow the light to enter, for Thomson what matters is contribution to the overall structure of the building itself.[263] It is not surprising, therefore, that when looking at his creations one observes an obvious monumentality especially when this is measured against Gothic lightness, and that impression seems confirmed by the influence on him of the painter, John Martin.[264] It is solidity that is seen as evoking a sense of awe and of the sublime.

---

[258] For the contrast between the Caledonia Road church as it was and as it is now, G. Stamp, *Alexander Greek Thomson* (London: Laurence King, 1999), 122, 134; for St Vincent Street church: 140–9 esp. 147–9.

[259] For illus., ibid. 50.

[260] Particularly in his Haldane Lectures, deposited in the Mitchell Library, Glasgow.

[261] William Wilkins was already making such connections in an influential book of 1837: Stamp and McKinstry, *'Greek' Thomson*, 56–7. For the language of co-creator and Egypt as a preparatory revelation, S. McKinstry, 'Thomson's Architectural Theory', ibid. 63–71 esp. 64.

[262] 'In its aesthetic, as in its constructive capacity, the arch never sleeps': quoted ibid. 66.

[263] G. Stamp, 'A View from the Bay Window', in Stamp and McKinstry, *'Greek' Thomson*, 228.

[264] J. Summerson, 'On Discovering "Greek" Thomson', ibid. 3–5.

Indeed, he explicitly asserts that it is the horizontal and not the vertical that has the most potential for carrying with it a sense of infinity.[265] That suggests radically different assumptions about how divine presence is conveyed, perhaps paralleled in our own age in sculpture by the sheer weight and bulk of Henry Moore's famous *Madonna and Child*.[266] What in effect we are offered is a sacramentality of majestic immanence rather than of transcendent lightness.

History never repeats itself exactly, and the revival of Gothic in the nineteenth century was no exception. As we have seen, new and suspect motives entered, among them nostalgia for an irrecoverable, romanticized past, Nonconformist aspirations to respectability, and, perhaps most surprising of all, anti-Catholic prejudice. That is why I find the work of someone like Thomson so exciting and his willingness to strike out in new directions so impressive, though there were some Gothic architects who were in their own way just as original, Butterfield among them. None of this is to deny the considerable achievements of Gothic, among other things the new confidence it gave to the Church. The tragedy was that so much attention was devoted to the architecture compared to the artwork that its churches often lacked the compensating immanence that was so deeply established in late medieval churches. The only real exception was in celebration of the liturgy, and by definition that could not be true everywhere. When its form was dramatically altered in the twentieth century, it therefore left the architecture high and dry, now a mere symbolic reminder of the divine rather than indicative of interaction between God and his world. The movement now appeared to be going all one way, with the new liturgy stressing communal identity rather than mystic immanence. In saying this my intention is not to attack modern celebrations of the liturgy. The issue is not Latin or English, high or low mass, even eucharist or non-eucharist, but rather of whether the building aids or not a sense of a more than merely human

---

[265] 'All who have studied works of art must have been struck by the mysterious power of the horizontal element in carrying the mind away into space, and into speculations upon infinity. The pictures of Turner and Roberts afford frequent examples of this': quoted by Stamp, ibid. 235.

[266] Sculpted 1943–4; in St Matthew's, Northampton: cf. Moore's own comments on the need for 'grandeur' and 'hieratic aloofness' in P. James (ed.), *Henry Moore on Sculpture* (New York: Da Capo Press, 1992), 235–9 esp. 235.

presence. For Gothic to succeed it needs appropriate counter-triggers, to suggest divine immanence as well as transcendence. These need to be as strong as its own pull heavenwards, and that, I suspect, is usually lacking where modern liturgy is set against the backdrop of such a building. Architecture and liturgy now give off messages at a tangent to one another rather than expressing two complementary claims that can be united into a single whole. Apart from changes in fashion, that then is another, perhaps largely subconscious, reason why Gothic is now seldom chosen for modern churches.

Conclusion and Anticipation

My survey of Christian architectural styles until the end of the nineteenth century is now complete. What I have sought to suggest is that, though having widely differing aims, there is yet a common overarching theme, of transcendence balancing immanence. More often than not the transcendence comes with the architecture (most conspicuously in the case of Gothic), but sometimes from elsewhere (as in the preached word in classical American preaching houses). It is almost as though the society and its architects intuited or knew that it was only through such a counterpoise that adequate aid could be given to the human desire to encounter God in this context: human creativity had to avoid tendentious, one-sided reflections of the work and nature of the divine Creator. Inevitably, in tracing this history I have tended to start from the human initiative, but I end this chapter as I began by insisting that the fact that the means are provided by human beings does nothing to undermine the possibility (and to me the fact) that God is thereby enabled to act through such buildings and thus make his presence felt. It is an experience, though, that need not come only through buildings designed with an explicitly religious purpose in view. It can also work through the apparently secular. Many more examples of this will follow in the next chapter, but by way of anticipation I would like to end with some examples from Gothic Revival itself.

The use of the same style for secular as for religious buildings was perhaps to be expected of Classicism, but the surprise is that it proved no less true for Gothic. Familiar examples would include the Houses of Parliament, the new buildings for Glasgow University, and of course numerous railway stations, often described as the cathedrals of the Victorian age. An intriguing test-case might be the elaborate exterior and fine interiors of Gilbert Scott's splendid Midland Grand Hotel that fronts St Pancras Station in London.[267] Both alike are a feast for the eye, but arguably the result could be said to be confusion of religious emotion and awe with something quite different. But, so far from decrying such crossovers of style, an alternative approach would be to regard them instead as positive contributions towards enlarging our religious and sacramental vision, with the overlaps as in turn mutually enhancing.

It is not just that the secular gains an artificial dignity by borrowing what is primarily a religious architectural form but that the transcendent is experienced as also involved in our ordinary secular world, and so that secular world can in turn have its impact on our churches. The very form of Barry's Houses of Parliament makes it a standing challenge to any purely utilitarian understanding of government, while some of the better examples of well-preserved Victorian railway stations do actually continue to invite the reflection that travel is more than just about getting to one's destination: it is also about seeing that destination as significant and so giving value to the tasks and roles that fall to one in life; or, put in more explicitly religious terms, it is all about the dignity of vocation and providential direction. That is why some analogies with the notion of pilgrimage discussed in the previous chapter seem to me not altogether inappropriate.[268] Nor indeed were such ideas entirely absent from the thought of the time. If the quality of the poetry leaves something to be desired and our own age is more likely to be amused than inspired, something important was at stake in memorial lines such as these:

> The Line to heaven by Christ was made
> With heavenly truth the Rails are laid
> From Earth to Heaven the Line extends,
> To Life eternal where it ends.[269]

[267] Illustrated in D. Cruickshank (ed.), *Architecture: The Critics' Choice* (London: Aurum, 2000), 12.

[268] Recall the original religious motivation behind Thomas Cook's 'holiday' excursions by train.

[269] The opening lines of twenty-four on a tablet in the cloister of Ely cathedral dedicated to two individuals killed in an accident in 1845, while building the line to Ely. Another good example at Bromsgrove from 1840 commemorates two engine drivers killed in an explosion on the new Birmingham–Gloucester line.

There is surely more than just an extended metaphor here. What is at stake is the sanctification of one's daily labour, and so Thomas Richman's decision to allow the ceiling of his St George's, Everton to resemble that of a railway station, so far from being outlandish in its conception, is fully defensible as an inspired and successful twist on the whole idea.[270] Likewise, 'Greek' Thomson made a wise decision in the extension of his symbolism not only into the home but also into the marketplace. His Egyptian Halls give an impressive dignity to mere warehouses, but rather more is, I think, at stake than just that. Commerce is set in a quite different context: it is offered the possibility of a religious dignity, and why not? one may ask.[271] At all events, it is in that wider 'secular' setting that the following chapter begins its discussion of the various directions in which architecture is pulling us in the contemporary world.

[270] Illustrated and discussed in Cruickshank, *Architecture*, 176–7. Rickman co-operated with a local iron-master, John Cragg, and the result was that, though the exterior was faced with stone, the internal columns, the ceilings, and the tracery for the windows were all cast in iron.

[271] For illustrations and brief discussion of his other commercial buildings, Stamp, in Stamp and McKinstry, *'Greek' Thomson*, 98–119 esp. 105, 116–17.

6

The Contemporary Context

House and Church as Mediators

HAD this book been written or published in 1900, it is quite likely that it might have had a certain conclusiveness about it that in retrospect would have been totally unjustified. Not least because I am an Anglican, I might well have concluded that Gothic was the only possible style for church architecture. Again, in respect of the home a multitude of practical signs might also have been noted that appeared to make its sacred character manifest, and which, if anything, had been gaining in popularity over the course of the Victorian era. It was not just that husband and wife each had a clear role, and a high value was assigned to family life in general, but also that these were very frequently given religious and indeed quasi-sacramental underpinning, whether it was through the prominence afforded to the family Bible, suitable pictures on the walls, or whatever.[1] An obvious example of the latter would be the huge popularity of prints of Holman Hunt's *The Light of the World*, which sold in quantities no less remarkable than the numbers who turned up in person to view the original.[2] Yet, had I written in this way, such confidence would of course have been gradually belied by the subsequent course of events. We are now in a quite different world, and not just sociologically. Due note will also have to be taken of the phenomenal rise and subsequent undermining of modernist architecture, the so-called International style.

[1] The key role of the family Bible could also be illustrated from art, e.g. in works by Rembrandt and Van Gogh, but for me it is seen at its most sacramental in Burns's poem *The Cotter's Saturday Night*, where priestly imagery is deployed to great effect. For the relevant lines and a commentary, D Brown and D. Fuller, *Signs of Grace* (London: Continuum, 2000), 122–5.

[2] The version of the painting now in St Paul's Cathedral in London attracted more than seven million visitors when it went on a world tour at the very beginning of the 20th c.; for further details, J. Maas, *Holman Hunt & the Light of the World* (Aldershot: Wildwood House, 1987). Its popularity was greatly aided by Ruskin's defence in *The Times*; quoted ibid. 61–4.

But, if that appears to suggest purely external factors, also to be reckoned with is Christianity's almost complete failure seriously to engage with the issues raised by such architecture and its underlying principles. Whereas in the nineteenth century religion was, as the last chapter observed, at the heart of much of the architectural argument, by the end of the twentieth it had almost dropped off even the margins. While this can be explained in part by the decline in religious belief in general over the century,[3] equally important in my view was the failure of the churches to engage with the new issues that were arising. With some notable exceptions in Britain Gothic had achieved such sway among practising Christians that alternative approaches were simply ignored until it was too late.[4] Nor was this entirely for respectable religious reasons. There was a nostalgia for the past that often led in England, unlike the United States, to a time-consuming preoccupation with detail that did little to advance the mission of the Christian faith.[5] Meanwhile on the Continent the issues were often clouded by nationalism. It was good that Cologne Cathedral was at last completed, but it is a moot point how much this was due to religion and how much to the new nationalism. Equally in France, the care and restoration of Gothic cathedrals came to be heavily bound up with conceptions of national identity, and garnered as a result some strange and unexpected allies.[6] Yet, though seldom acknowledged, the simplicity that Modernism demanded could very easily have been seen in essentially Christian terms,[7]

[3] Though church attendance continued to rise until the outbreak of the First World War in 1914.

[4] 'Greek' Thomson's Egyptian style has already been discussed in the previous chapter. Two other conspicuous exceptions are the Brompton Oratory and Westminster Cathedral.

[5] Contrast attitudes in the Cambridge Camden Society and its successor the Ecclesiological Society with its American equivalent, the New York Ecclesiological Society. For the former, J. F. White, *The Cambridge Movement: The Ecclesiologists and the Gothic Revival* (Cambridge: Cambridge University Press, 1962); for the latter, P. B. Stanton, *The Gothic Revival & American Church Architecture* (Baltimore: Johns Hopkins University, 1968), 159–211 esp. 180, 187, 192, 204.

[6] For a detailed study of the role of Zola, Huysmans, and Proust, E. Emery, *Romancing the Cathedral: Gothic Architecture in Fin-de-Siècle French Culture* (Albany: State University of New York Press, 2001). She also notes the significance of the fact that the formal German surrender at the end of the Second World War took place in Reims cathedral, bombarded during the First World War: 168–70.

[7] John Betjeman is a rare example of someone who saw the point, even if he subsequently changed his mind. His architectural conversion is discussed below.

while the search for a more universal symbolism that attracted the attention of quite a number of influential architects brought no answering response or engagement on the part of the Church. Before we turn to Modernism as such two architects who were already famous by 1900 may be used to illustrate some of these dilemmas and failures.

Symbolism in Gaudí and Macintosh

Architectural historians display no unanimity about Antoni Gaudí and Charles Rennie Mackintosh. In the view of some they are best seen simply as excellent exemplars of the Art Noveau movement of which they were undoubtedly part; for others their genius is such that their inclusion is easily merited among eminent precursors of Modernism; yet others make their genius more modern still, and so place them among our contemporaries as postmoderns before their time, as it were.[8] What these various assessments might mean in context will be considered in due course, but first I want to give a brief account of the significance of each in terms of the issues I have been raising.

Although from humble background, Antoni Gaudí (1852–1926) rose to a position of great public eminence in Barcelona, where most of his surviving commissions are to be found. Undoubtedly, his Catalan nationalism helped, as did his strong Catholic faith. Nowadays his architectural reputation could scarcely stand higher, while such was his piety that there are even moves afoot for his canonization.[9] None the less, the Church was in fact less the whole-hearted supporter it now likes to appear, and so one suspects that regional pride and trusting a fellow-Catholic may have played a larger role at the time than any deep sense of the worth of his extraordinarily innovative ideas.[10] These one finds reflected in both

[8] For praise for Gaudí from two modernists, Gropius and Le Corbusier, G. van Hensbergen, *Gaudí* (London: HarperCollins, 2001), pp. xxxi, 218–19. Hensbergen twice places him with the postmodernists: 97, 270. For an example of uncertainty of where to place Mackintosh, the concluding paragraph of A. Crawford, *Charles Rennie Mackintosh* (London: Thames & Hudson, 1995), 206.

[9] In 1998 the Archbishop of Barcelona, Ricard Maria Carles, began the process of appeal for his beatification.

[10] Lack of enthusiasm was, for example, displayed over his proposals for Monserrrat and the cathedral at Palma de Mallorca: Hensbergen, *Gaudí*, 127–35.

his secular and his religious commissions. One concern is that architecture should be seen to emerge naturally out of the environment, and so his buildings can appear almost as encrustations, as natural outgrowths from the land. Examples to note would include his Casa Vicens from 1888 with its palmetto leaf fencing, sunflowers everywhere, and red berries and leaves on the ceilings,[11] and the Güell Palace of the following year where the chimneys look a bit like a forest of cypress trees.[12] So unusual was his Casa Milà of 1910 that it generated a stream of uncomplimentary cartoons.[13] But, amid all the disputes, rings through the depth of his conviction, that the divine creation must help to give shape to the human, and indeed this is how he defends his wide use of polychrome: 'Nature does not present us with any object in monochrome ... not in vegetation, not in geology, not in topography, not in the animal kingdom. Always the contrast is more or less lively, and for this reason we must colour wholly or in part every architectural element.'[14] One notes too how inside some of his houses the imagery of the heavens is given to ordinary ceilings, with the message of home and church thus merged, as in the work of Greek Thomson.[15]

Gaudí used a variety of styles during his life, but it was to Gothic that he usually turned for his religious commissions.[16] But it was anything but conventional Gothic. Flying buttresses he abhorred, and so he explored the use of parabolic curves and angled pillars as an alternative.[17] In his Güell Colony Crypt the link with nature is repeated, with the entrance apparently designed to suggest a naturally formed cave. The interior, however, conveys a quite different impression. Not only is there no column the same size or shape as they veer now in one direction, now in another, but also a great heavy star of radiating stone is to be found placed above the altar.[18] The net impact is thus to suggest that it is only something

[11] For illustrations and discussion, R. Zerbst, *Gaudí* (Cologne: Taschen, 1985), 36–47; also Hensbergen, *Gaudí*, 75–80.

[12] Zerbst, *Gaudí*, 70–85 esp. 76.

[13] For the housing complex, ibid. 176–89; for five of the cartoons, Hensbergen, *Gaudí*, 176–81.

[14] Quoted from an unpublished essay, ibid. 54–5.

[15] For an example from his Güell's Palace: Zerbst, *Gaudí*, 80–1. For Greek Thomson, see the previous chapter.

[16] Casa Vicens, for example, is Moorish, Casa Calvet Baroque.

[17] Experiments are already being made in the Güell Palace; Zerbst, *Gaudí*, 82.

[18] Ibid. 108–25.

supernatural that keeps the building upright: the pillars cannot do it, and so the job must fall, as it were, to the star. If that sense of precariousness is a little less obvious in his most famous ecclesiastical building, the as yet unfinished Sagrada Familia, present too are the same principles of organic growth that appear so frequently elsewhere in what is undoubtedly now Barcelona's most famous building.[19] The spires, for instance, are quite unlike their conventional equivalents, and so even the most unobservant among us is forced to the realization that it is not simply transcendence that is being asserted, but also the integration of that transcendence with the earth itself. The church that he received as a commission when he was only just turned 30 in 1883 is still in the process of being completed sixty years after his death. But such slow progress would not have surprised or worried Gaudí, who seems to have consciously modelled himself on the long-term perspective adopted at Cologne.[20]

But unlike Cologne cathedral the church is in not in any sense conventional. Even the statues surprise, as in Gaudí's refusal to give angels the usual wings, while the spires look more like open shells than anything else. Of course the riot of ornament and colour that characterizes his work is not to everyone's taste, but it would be a mistake to assume that this derived from personal flamboyance. It did not. He himself led a very simple lifestyle, while he could design simply when he thought the occasion demanded it.[21] His aim does genuinely seem to have been to enable human beings to find God in park, house, and church alike, a truly sacramental vision, with his architecture an extension of nature as God's creation. The pity was that he had no successors, and indeed the Church in Spain retreated from such commissions even before he was dead. No doubt part of the explanation was the degree of change involved, but he did allow Gothic to grow and develop in a way that no one else did.

[19] Experiments are already being made in the Güell Palace; Zerbst, *Gaudí* 190–215. Hensbergen notes the feeling of imminent collapse here also: *Gaudí*, 251.

[20] Zerbst, *Gaudí*, notes the parallel dimensions, but also the divergence in 'an interlinking of parabolic arches and slanting columns': 204–8. Cologne, begun in 1248, was completed only in 1880.

[21] His simple lifestyle is reflected in his vegetarianism. That at times it could verge towards extreme austerity is illustrated by his Lenten fast of 1894, which almost killed him: Hensbergen, *Gaudí*, 108, 122. Note also the wonderful reflective simplicity of his Colegio Teresiano: Zerbst, *Gaudí*, 86–95 esp. 90–1; cf. Hensbergen, *Gaudí*, 105–8.

Although Mackintosh (1868–1928) did compete to build one large church, Liverpool Anglican Cathedral, for which he proposed a Gothic building composed of Durham-like towers and astonishing fin-like protuberances to replace the buttresses, unlike Gaudí he had no deep interest in building religious structures.[22] He was not even a churchgoer. Even so, it would be wrong to conclude from this a lack of spiritual interests. His only church commission displays some innovating artwork, while the interiors of his secular buildings, probably often the fruit of collaboration with his wife Margaret Macdonald who was also an artist, are rich in symbolism.[23] As with Gaudí, architectural historians are often uncertain where to place him.[24] Modernist tendencies are exhibited, for example, in huge, exposed, steel supporting roof ties in Queen's Cross church, his design of Hill House from the inside outwards, or still more clearly in his 1915 house in Northampton, sometimes described as the first modernist house in Britain.[25] But his most famous building, the Glasgow School of Art, despite its modern look, has many features that seem dictated more by compositional values than by concern with function on its own.[26] There is a balcony that is purely ornamental and a staircase that rises externally more than it does internally. Again, although the fact that half the side elevation is merely bare wall could be seen as purely a matter of function (there is no need internally at this point for windows), the overall result does make an aesthetic contribution, and that, one suspects, is what really determined Macintosh's decision.[27] In fact, on a number of occasions Mackintosh attacked modernist assumptions, arguing that iron and glass alone would deprive a building of the necessary solidity and mass that gives it its requisite dignity and importance.[28]

---

[22] For the designs, C. and P. Fiell, *Charles Rennie Mackintosh* (Cologne: Taschen, 1995), 98–9; for a more hostile estimate, Crawford, *Mackintosh*, 87–9.

[23] For an illustrated example of his work on Queen's Cross church, P. Robertson, *Charles Rennie Mackintosh: Art is the Flower* (London: Pavilion, 1995), 84. Five times repeated on the pulpit is a design featuring bird's wings sheltering stylized new plant growth.

[24] As Crawford ends by debating between modern and postmodern, so the Fiells begin in this way: *Mackintosh*, 6.

[25] Fiell, ibid. 30, 70, 142. The point about starting from the inside is that form can then be seen to be determined by function.

[26] It was built in two stages, 1897–9 and 1907–9.

[27] Cf. Crawford, *Mackintosh*, 34–6.

[28] His views are quoted in Fiell, *Mackintosh*, 24; cf. also 42.

However, it is his interiors that do the most to engage our imaginations. That was so no less when they were first created than now since the revival of interest in his work.[29] Although some modern writers have attempted to reduce his objectives to a rather narrow obsession with sexuality, critics at the time rightly detected a key spiritual dimension.[30] So, for instance, one influential German architect, Herman Muthesius, spoke of Mackintosh's aim being 'to show humanity that there is something higher in the distance which transcends everyday reality'.[31] Unfortunately, neither Charles nor Margaret give any explanation of their symbolism. But those who have explored the matter in detail try to set the couple in the context of the Symbolist movement of the time, combined as it often was with interest in the sort of universalist imagery that we have already encountered when discussing European abstract art in Chapter 2.[32] Mackintosh makes only one known reference to Rosicrucians, but the rose does feature prominently and there are quite a number of other indicators of symbolism drawn from more than one religion, including ancient Egypt.[33] If forced to use a single descriptor, one might speak of pantheism, not least because the strongest force present seems to be the love of cultivated nature that he acquired as a child.[34] Explicitly Christian

[29] Much of the renewed interest has involved re-creation of his works, as with his Willow Tea Rooms in Sauchiehall Street ('Willow Lane') and his home recreated in the Hunterian Museum (both in Glasgow). It was also that city which used the occasion of its nomination as European City of Culture in 1990 to begin the process of creating for the first time his entry for *Haus eines Kunstfreundes* (submitted for an international competition in 1901); for the story and plans, R. Bilcliffe and A. MacMillan, *House for an Art Lover* (Glasgow: Randak Design, 1996).

[30] Crawford's tendency, e.g. *Mackintosh*, 30, 44, 67. I do not deny its presence. The question is how far it is subordinate and incidental to some wider agenda.

[31] Quoted in Fiell, *Mackintosh*, 92; cf. also Olbrich's comments, ibid. 94.

[32] T. Neat, *Part Seen, Part Imagined* (Edinburgh: Canongate, 1994), esp. 20–9, 120–32, 154–68. Symbolist art lacks a precise definition, but for two helpful analyses, M. Gibson, *Symbolism* (Cologne: Taschen, 1995); I. Ehrhardt and S. Reynolds, *Kingdom of the Soul: Symbolist Art in Germany 1870–1920* (Munich: Prestel, 2000).

[33] In one of his letters quoted in Neat, *Part Seen*, 178. The details of Rosicrucian belief are less important than its inclusive symbolism, and its appeal to a wide range of intellectuals at the time. For the use of the eye of the Egyptian god Ra by both Margaret and Charles, Neat, ibid. 95, 117.

[34] His father was a keen gardener, and the children had access to one particular garden which they nicknamed 'the Garden of Eden'; so Robertson, *Mackintosh,*

references are, though, by no means absent. In a mirror of Margaret's, for instance, we find fish issuing from Christ's mouth, or again in the basement for the Willow Tea Rooms she uses symbolism based on Psalm 65.[35]

My point in introducing these Christian allusions is not that this might make him after all 'respectable' in a Christian context. Although without hostility to Christianity, he clearly ranged far more widely.[36] Rather, what seems to have concerned him was a reinvention and expansion of religious symbolism that would take his own highly materialist society onto a quite different plane. One reviewer of his room for the 1900 Secessionist Exhibition in Vienna described it as evoking 'a Christ-like mood' and one can see what he meant.[37] Colour and symbolism in his art were meant to turn house into home, but more than that. They were also intended to suggest an earthed spirituality, one's involvement in a world larger than its walls, where, as one of his close friends put it, one 'walks with God' because 'God meant life to be a quest'. So that is why, though 'art may be a religion . . . it can never be a creed or a dogma, because it only asks the questions to which each man must find his own answer'.[38] Indeed, even Mackintosh's famous chairs have this questing character, inasmuch as their 'unnatural' height was intended not just to give added privacy but also to raise deep questions. For the symbolism of sun, moon, or whatever appearing above the person seated posed the question how one's conversation partner fitted into that larger dimension evoked by the symbolism.[39]

17. Most of his surviving watercolours are in fact of landscapes or flowers, with the more mystical therefore the exception; cf. R. Billcliffe, *Mackintosh Watercolours* (London: John Murray, 1979); for three famous exceptions: 58, 68, 69.

[35] For fish mirror, Neat, *Part Seen*, 97; cf. 108 for two charming portrayals of Annunciation and Nativity. Commissioned much later than the rest in 1917, we know that in this case the mural was Margaret's design; Fiell, *Mackintosh*, 120.

[36] One sign of lack of hostility was the fact that he married in church and honeymooned on the holy island of Lindisfarne, returning on a number of subsequent occasions; for a watercolour of its castle, Robertson, *Mackintosh*, 44.

[37] Quoted from *Wiener Rundschau* in Fiell, *Mackintosh*, 76.

[38] The words of Major Chapman Houston, printed as app. 2 to Neat, *Part Seen*, 193–8 esp. 193, 194. He was closely involved with them both until their deaths.

[39] For high chairs giving privacy, Fiell, *Mackintosh*, 64; for the wider symbolic issue, Neat, *Part Seen*, 156.

The sadness is that Christianity was so convinced of its own answers that it had ceased to engage in the same questioning in what was a rapidly changing society. Not surprisingly, therefore, the net result paralleled what happened with European abstract art, discussed in Chapter 3. Questions of religious symbolism and meaning continued to be pursued, but almost wholly in the absence of any real engagement on the part of the Church and its theologians, and that even where Gaudí was concerned. Yet both Gaudí and Macintosh had offered a sacramental vision that refused to differentiate sharply between church and home but instead sought in each possibilities for encounter with the divine. The consequences were dire for the future of faith, because by the end of the century it would become natural to talk of all buildings other than churches as secular, even the home. Yet, despite this, many of the twentieth century's most famous architects continued to remain insistent upon a spiritual dimension to their work. What they now doubted was any meaningful connection with the values of organized religion. It is to the exploration of what in fact happened that I now proceed, considering first changing architectural norms for 'secular' buildings and then their impact on the design of churches. As will become clear, religious and sacramental issues in this larger sense will not go away, even if the Church has largely turned its back on them.[40]

Non-ecclesial Architecture and Its Rationale

The simplest way to characterize the twentieth century would be to speak of it as dominated by two major movements, first by Modernism and then increasingly by reaction against it, in Postmodernism. If Postmodernism is essentially eclectic, the indiscriminate use of earlier architectural styles as mood or need dictates, Modernism has a clearer foundation and rationale in a break with the past into what was seen as essentially a new approach to design, made possible no less by new materials than by revolt against past precedent. In the Bible King David is presented as enjoying the advantage of iron weapons over bronze that the Israelites had hitherto

---

[40] This is not to deny the importance of its narrower focus on liturgical change and the practical impact this might have on the design of churches.

lacked.[41] Similar huge changes were afoot in the late nineteenth century. As early as 1800 it became possible to pass iron in a plastic state between rolls to form structured patterns, but structural steel in the true sense became commercially viable only in the early 1880s. Over the centuries various advances had taken place in strengthening concrete. While the Babylonians had used clay as a reinforcing agent and the Egyptians lime and gypsum, the Roman practice of forming a cement from slaked lime and volcanic ash was to remain the norm until the discovery of Portland cement shortly after 1800. The turn of the century, however, brought a far greater change in the invention of the huge load-bearing potential of reinforced concrete, concrete with steel bars embedded within it. That in part liberated roof structures, but so too, as we have seen with Gaudí, did greater understanding of the range of possibilities for the arch.

Simplicity, Rationalism and the Environment in Modernism

Among architects themselves, rather than 'Modernism' it was often other related terms that came to hold sway, among them rationalism, functionalism, and the international style. The precise distinctions between the various terms need not detain us here.[42] Rather what is important is overlapping concerns with simplicity and the avoidance of ornament, the stress on volume rather than mass, the priority given to function over form, and the conceptualization of efficiency in the machine analogy. It is the Chicago architect, Louis Sullivan, who coined the pithy requirement that 'form follows function',[43] and so as such he is sometimes given honour as an important precursor of the movement, though in fact his most famous building—the Guaranty Building in Buffalo (1894)—still

[41] Contrast 2 Sam. 12: 31 with 1 Sam. 13: 19–22: Israelite agricultural tools are presented as requiring expensive maintenance by the Philistines, who refuse them this facility for their weapons. The patriarchs are usually placed in the Bronze Age before the development of iron. Particularly anachronistic, therefore, is the reference to the blacksmith Tubal-cain working with iron in Gen. 4: 22, though he became a common figure in medieval art.

[42] For helpful distinctions, consult the relevant entries in V. M. Lampugnani (ed.), *Dictionary of 20th Century Architecture* (London: Thames & Hudson, 1986), 111–12, 160–4, 275–8.

[43] In his 1896 essay, 'The Tall Office Building, Artistically Considered.'

retains a significant and intriguing element of decoration.[44] Perhaps the explanation lies in part in the fact that his most famous pupil was Frank Lloyd Wright, though, as we shall see, the latter also sat somewhat loose to some aspects of the modernist creed. Henry-Russell Hitchcock in an influential 1929 work did not include Wright among the 'New Pioneers', and it was Hitchcock who with Philip Johnson was to invent the term 'international style' in 1932.[45] Its image of the finished work as 'a smooth unbroken skin tightly stretched over the building's skeletal frame' seems in any case singularly inappropriate in respect of some of Wright's key creations.[46]

A better place to begin might therefore be the founding of the Bauhaus ('building house' or school) at Weimar in Germany. By the 1890s Germany had overtaken Britain in industrial production, and already before the First World War considerable interest had been fostered in how industrial design should be related to craftsmanship, in part itself cultivated by English interest in the same issue.[47] Walter Gropius, when he took on the leadership of the Bauhaus in 1919, therefore explicitly sought that building, design, and artefact should all be taught alongside fine art under a single roof.[48] The name Bauhaus probably alludes to the medieval craft

[44] For illustration and comment, D. Cruickshank (ed.), *Architecture: The Critic's Choice* (London: Aurum, 2000), 210–11.

[45] In H.-R. Hitchcock's *Modern Architecture: Romanticism and Reintegration* (New York: Da Capo, 1993 edn.) Wright is treated as part of 'the new tradition' that anticipates elements of Modernism but the title of true innovators, 'the new pioneers', is reserved for such men as Le Corbusier, Gropius, and Mies van der Rohe (e.g. ibid. 162).

[46] The phrase is borrowed from H.-U. Khan, *International Style: Modernist Architecture from 1925 to 1964* (Cologne: Taschen, 2001), 67. One powerful advocate of the style, R. Banham, though, notes the capacity of Wright to produce 'Romantic primitivism' alongside 'Machine Age' sophistication, and adduces Taliesin West and the Johnson Wax Company Buildings to prove the point: *Age of the Masters: A Personal View of Modern Architecture* (New York: Harper & Row, 1962), 103.

[47] If William Morris and the Arts and Crafts Movement tended to reject the value of industrial products, the German government was not slow to concede what Britain was achieving. In 1896 Muthesius was sent to England as a sort of industrial spy, while the Kaiser's Anglophile wife, Augusta, had founded the Berlin arts and crafts museum as early as 1871: M. Droste, *Bauhaus* (Cologne: Taschen, 1998), 10–11.

[48] Two Saxon institutions were combined into one: ibid. 16–17.

guilds, and certainly among some of its teachers there was a element of nostalgia for a vanished world of strong social solidarity and co-operation.[49] It was thus no accident that Lyonel Feininger drew an imaginary cathedral for the front cover of the inaugural manifesto.[50] If artists of the intellectual stature of Klee and Kandinsky were to be found numbered among the staff, one should nevertheless note that the primary pressure was not towards theory but to the practical realization of specific goals. In this respect the simple but elegant artefacts that the school produced, such as lamps and chairs, continue to rebound to its credit, and indeed to be endlessly copied in one way or another.[51]

It is architecture, however, that is our primary concern here. When local growth of the Nazi party forced a move away from Weimar in 1924, Gropius himself designed a new building of engaging simplicity at Dessau. Already he had made his name with an open plan house exhibited in 1923, and his new local authority quickly employed him to produce some cheap housing for the rapidly growing town.[52] If rather obviously basic, the individual houses were at least prefabricated and cheap, and so could set a precedent for working-class housing estates of the future. After a three-year interval Mies van der Rohe succeeded him in 1930, and carried on that same stress on simplicity of form in his own work, not least when, like Gropius, he had migrated to the United States. A good example of Mies's immediate post-war work is Farnsworth House (1951), where simplicity and light are the two dominant themes.[53]

---

[49] The church-masons' guilds were called *Bauhütten*.

[50] Alfred Barr, founder of MOMA in New York, described him as 'an American, who, through some time-machine miracle, has been preserved unchanged since the 1880s': quoted in R. Heller, *Lyonel Feininger: Awareness, Recollection and Nostalgia* (Chicago: David and Alfred Smart Museum of Art, 1992), 14. For a more lengthy exploration of this backward-looking side of the Bauhaus, E. Scheyer, *Lyonel Feininger: Caricature and Fantasy* (Detroit: Wayne State University Press, 1964).

[51] For chair and lamp illustrations, Droste, *Bauhaus*, 55, 81. Four principles for good chairs were also agreed: 82.

[52] For the *Haus am Horn* of 1923 built around a central living room, ibid. 105–9; for the growth of population at Dessau (by 30,000 in three years): 120; for the houses Gropius produced: 132–3.

[53] Illustrated in P. Gössel and G. Leuthäuser, *Architecture in the Twentieth Century* (Cologne: Taschen, 1991), 226.

Mies van der Rohe's approach has been described as 'ascetic', but it is worth noting that perhaps precisely for that reason there was little attempt on his part to relate what he created to the wider environment, or to take significant account of cost.[54] Indeed, one commentator speaks of an utter indifference to urban context, and his pre-war proposed skyscraper for Berlin is an obvious case in point.[55] It was thus an aesthetic rather than a moral or religious asceticism.[56] By contrast, Gropius and his school did strive for some kind of overall unity. It is fashionable now to dismiss out of hand the first teacher of the preliminary course, Johannes Itten, as simply in the grips of an absurd religious philosophy that turned him into a power-hungry guru. To some degree this is true. Mazdaznan, his religious philosophy, and its founder are now discredited.[57] But if set in the wider context of the theosophy so popular at the time and the search for a more holistic approach to religion and to life that was seen to be entailed by it, it is possible to view Itten in a more favourable light.[58] There was, for example, his demand that use be seen from the inside, so to speak, and indeed a leaner version of his assumptions still continues to guide the core of German teaching of art appreciation even to this day.[59]

[54] William Jordy's comment that 'if no modern architect has been more ascetic, none has been more influential' is quoted in Khan, *International Style*, 170. For indifference to cost, Droste, *Bauhaus*, 214–16.

[55] So J.-L. Cohen of this proposed skyscraper from 1921, in which his 20-storey prism not only bears no relation to the surrounding buildings but also has neither base nor crown, being simply sliced off at the relevant moment: *Scenes of the World to Come: European Architecture and the American Challenge* (Paris: Flammarion, 1995), 107–8.

[56] Although he justified his work by appeal to Augustine's adage that 'beauty is the splendour of truth', he never seems to have practised the Roman Catholicism into which he was baptized: P. Blake, *Master Builders* (New York: Norton, 1996 edn.), 169–70

[57] One encyclopedia entry concludes: 'Der ... Meister ... ist von Eitelkeit und Anmaßung, von Scharlatanismus und Hochstapelei nicht freizusprechen': *Die Religion in Geschichte und Gegenwart* (Tübingen: Mohr/Siebeck, 1960), s.v. Mazdaznan.

[58] Of the three contributions which Norbert Schmitz makes to J. Fieldler and P. Feierabend (eds.), *Bauhaus* (Cologne: Könemann, 1999), it is only the fourth and last on the actual teaching course that enables one truly to see the man's strengths: 120–5, 232–41, 242–3, 360–7.

[59] 'Probably the most important inspiration of West German art teaching since 1945': Schmitz, in *Bauhaus*, 362. Gymnastics and music were used to help improve representations of the body (361–2), while there was to be no portrayal even of a lemon without first renewing the taste of it (365).

Of all those who emanated from the Bauhaus, Mies van der Rohe is now the most famous and most influential. If he did indeed go on to produce skyscrapers that are at one and the same time elegant and functional, it is still worth remembering that it was at the price of betraying the fundamental principles of the Bauhaus.[60] Despite their simplicity, their cost made them monuments to American capitalism, even as his earlier houses had failed to take practicality into account as an essential element in design.[61] So a holistic vision was lost as ideas crossed the Atlantic.[62] Yet the way in which Mies behaved should not be allowed to distort our overall assessment. Architects there undoubtedly were who continued to subscribe to simplicity as their basic creed, and no one could deny that such an emphasis has at least the potential to carry with it a profoundly spiritual dimension. To my mind that dimension is present in much Bauhaus work. The simple elegance of some of its artefacts and the clarity of lines in its Dessau building, for instance, suggest submission of their users to purposes beyond mere materialism. In other words, utility is there to serve some higher function. Of course that purpose need not be explicitly religious, but at least such an orientation opens up the question.

Working independently of the Bauhaus was another key figure, the Swiss Le Corbusier (d. 1966), the very name perhaps underlining his sense of independence.[63] Already in 1923 he had produced a long manifesto, *vers une architecture*; so we may measure his subsequent designs and ideas against those initial standards. For him the world is at a decisive turning point, and architecture is here to help reorient us. Whereas religions inevitably fall into decay because of

---

[60] In Chicago he was responsible for towerblock apartments at 860 Lakeshore Drive, while in New York he built the Seagram Building, 'possibly the most expensive skyscraper, per square foot, ever built': Blake, *Master Builders*, 268.

[61] The Farmsworth house is better described as a 'pleasure pavilion' than as a 'house for family living'. Gropius is reputed to have reacted to his earlier Tugendhat house (1930) by observing that it was a 'Sunday house', i.e. for show rather than daily use. So Blake, ibid. 245, 218.

[62] For a visual history of his principal works, A. Cuito, *Mies van der Rohe* (Kempen: TeNeues, 2002).

[63] He was born Charles-Edouard Jeanneret in 1887, and did not adopt his now familiar name till 1923. Architects quickly abbreviated it to Corbu, 'the raven': Blake, *Master Builders*, 4. Occasionally, modern architectural discussion also uses this form.

their failure to change, the house can still be changed.[64] It needs now to be envisaged as a machine for living. So it is the job of the architect to 'give us the measure of an order which we feel to be in accordance with that of our world' and thus create that machine-centred universe in which we should now believe.[65] Individual houses, he suggested, could be created in as little as three days, while cities need sixty-storey high skyscrapers, with highways in the sky thus obviating the necessity for public utilities to be expensively submerged beneath the earth.[66] In justifying such an approach he observed that, just as the Parthenon once evoked awe, so now it is called forth by an ocean liner and other such products of modern technology; indeed more so, because our earlier respect for cathedrals was insecurely based, relying as it did on such buildings fighting against gravity rather than acting with it.[67]

Although his practice did largely correspond with his theory, there were some interesting developments. His most famous house, the Villa Savoye (1930), illustrates one of the most characteristic features of his style at that time, the *Pilotis* or suspension of a house on stilts.[68] In our present climate one might have thought that the aim was the obvious advantage afforded in better views of the surrounding countryside, but Le Corbusier's intention seems to have been quite otherwise. The resultant garage provision was deliberately highlighted, while the transition to the two upper floors continued the ramp principle.[69] A later house even went so far as to provide a hedging screen that could be removed or

[64] Trans. F. Etchells, *Towards a New Architecture* (Oxford: Architectural Press, 1946 edn.), 14.

[65] Ibid. 4, 1. Cf. also 73: 'Architecture is the first manifestation of man creating his own universe.'

[66] Ibid. 231, 57–60.

[67] For Parthenon: ibid. 217, 220; for cathedrals: 30, 92.

[68] Illustrated with brief description in Cruickshank, *Architecture*, 256–7; for more detailed account, Blake, *Master Builders*, 55–64.

[69] The importance of the car is well illustrated by the fact that Le Corbusier published at the time two almost identical photographs of the house, one of a car arriving, the other of it departing. The indifference to landscape is indicated by the account in *Cahiers d'art* which declared that 'the urban client for whom this construction is intended aspires to dominate the landscape rather than finding himself close to the trees and bushes': R. A. Etlin, *Frank Lloyd Wright and Le Corbusier* (Manchester: Manchester University Press, 1994), 127, 196.

returned at the flick of a switch.[70] Again, consistent with his views on the size of skyscrapers, on his first visit to New York he complained that the local versions were too small and that there was insufficient parkland between them.[71] After the Second World War Le Corbusier then adopted a style that came to be known as the 'new brutalism'. He himself saw it as a variant on simplicity, with everything now pared down to the bare minimum. Some found it refreshing precisely because it was so stridently modern, while to others it seemed too aggressive and even antirational. One example would be the Unité d'Habitation housing estate at Marseilles (1947–52), with its streets in the sky and restaurant and play areas (including an open-air cinema) on the roof.[72] However, there was a final, third phrase in his career that seemed a little gentler. In his work at Chandigarh in India significantly the roadways are now no longer elevated but rather submerged from view.[73] His pilgrimage church of Ronchamp also has a softness about it that is not evident elsewhere.[74] Numerous less original architects followed in his footsteps, and the priority given to roads and to minimalist housing schemes has been the result throughout Europe. In England Sheffield's Park Hill is a familiar example, as is the work of Denys Lasdun on a smaller scale at Saint James' Place and Bethnal Green in London.[75]

The severity of so much of Le Corbusier and his imitators provides an interesting contrast with the Modernism of the philosopher, Wittgenstein. He used his engineering experience to serve briefly as an architect during 1926–8, when he designed a house for his sister, the Kundmanngasse house in Vienna. Certainly, there is no hostility to the mechanical or functional (he even designed the radiators) but even so the aesthetics appear quite different. There is no hint of brutalism, nor is elegance sacrificed to simplicity.[76] For, though exterior and interior alike are stripped of all ornament (even

---

[70] Provided for a penthouse apartment on the Champs-Elysées: Blake, *Master Builders*, 60.

[71] Ibid. 91–3.   [72] Ibid. 117–24.   [73] Ibid. 146–51 esp. 150.

[74] Considered in the next section.

[75] For illus., Banham, *Age of the Masters*, 70–3, 140–3; Khan, *International Style*, 178.

[76] The house is given detailed consideration in P. Wijdeveld, *Ludwig Wittgenstein: Architect* (Amsterdam: Pepin Press, 1993), esp. 73–138. For designing radiators: 37.

skirting boards vanish), the net result remains simple classical proportions that with the lack of ornament create almost 'a dematerialising aspect'.[77] Thus even within the modernist movement there was no necessity to follow the machine analogy, or, if it was followed, to pursue it in precisely the same way as Le Corbusier. Renaissance architecture reminds us that Wittgenstein need not have been an isolated exception: rationalist principles can go with elegance. Again, one might question whether what is wrong with the machine analogy is not the image as such but rather the form of its application. Le Corbusier seems to have operated with a rather narrow view of what it is to be a human being. Machines are very much part of our world, and they can be beautiful. It is just that efficiency is seldom their exclusive goal. To use one of Le Corbusier's own illustrations, the success of an ocean liner depends not just on the speed with which it gets us to our ultimate destination, but also on the quality of life it offers on the way. The danger in complete rejection of the machine analogy is retreat into a world of unsustainable nostalgia for a lost, bygone era. Despite its many merits, the work of the last remaining major modernist figure I wish to consider was not wholly without such precise difficulties.

Among the modernists it is perhaps the American Frank Lloyd Wright (1869–1959) who showed the most percipience about future directions. For, although some of his buildings do appear to demonstrate a dominant concern with function and simplicity,[78] most were individual houses and each of these has a unique and distinctive character. A truly spectacular example is *Falling Water* at Bear Run, Pennsylvania, of 1939.[79] While fitting admirably into the landscape, the house also succeeds in conveying a quintessentially modern American feel. Some others are almost Art Nouveau in character, while yet others show the signs of Maya and Japanese

[77] For lack of ornament, ibid. esp. 97, 158–9; for the quotation: 160.

[78] Apart from the Johnson Wax Building already mentioned, another good example is the Guggenheim Museum in New York; it is based on a simple spiral. While Blake attacks its utility as a museum (300), its custodians (rightly in my view) give a strong defence: H. Berg, *The Solomon R. Guggenheim Museum* (New York, Guggenheim Foundation, 1980 edn.), 17.

[79] Illustrated in P. Gössel and G. Leuthäuser, *Architecture in the Twentieth Century* (Cologne: Taschen, 1991), 194–5.

influence.[80] Significantly, he expressed quite a different attitude to the machine from Le Corbusier, declaring that 'genius must dominate the work of the contrivance it has created'.[81] Perhaps that is why even his more obviously modernist interiors such as his Johnson House of 1937 still look inherently comfortable and welcoming.[82] Wright was the son of a Baptist preacher and indeed met his first wife at a church dance.[83] If in his subsequent life he was scarcely an orthodox Christian, he did demonstrate throughout concern that his houses should show sympathy with the environment, and indeed spoke of the need to draw architectural forms from it. Yet ironically it may well have been that very sympathy which produced resistance to coming to terms with the way the world now is. During his lifetime his own nation experienced more than a threefold increase in its population. Even so, his vision for the future of the city was quite different from Le Corbusier's. Everyone was to have a single dwelling with an acre of land, and the churches were to be gathered round a single temple for universal worship on certain community occasions.[84]

What this brief survey has revealed is a less united approach within Modernism than an initial cursory look might suggest. Even the machine analogy does not offer a united front.[85] Not only did Wright rebel against it, but also it is a dangerous ally: the Nazis saw its potential, while in our own day arguably the best illustration of form following function is in the dreadful beauty of some of the nuclear age's most destructive weapons.[86] There are

[80] For the Dana Art Nouveau house of 1903, T. A. Heinz, *Frank Lloyd Wright* (New York: St Martin's House, 1982), 30–3; for Maya influence: 60–5; for Japanese: 66–8.

[81] Quoted in Blake, *Master Builders*, 337 from Wright's 1901 lecture, 'The art and craft of the machine'.

[82] Heinz, *Frank Lloyd Wright*, 74–5.

[83] So Blake, *Master Builders*, 288, 302. Later in life he was much influenced by Gurdjieff's philosophy (393).

[84] Wright's 1934 ideal image of 'Broadacre City'. See further ibid. 289, 391–2.

[85] For a history of the various analogies for architecture—the biological, mechanical, gastronomic, and linguistic—and for an impressive critique of their limitations, particularly the mechanical, P. Collins, *Changing Ideals in Modern Architecture* (Montreal: McGills–Queen's University Press, 1965), 148–82 esp. 159–66.

[86] Since the early 1980s the extent to which the Nazis utilized and exploited the Bauhaus tradition (sometimes with its members' active co-operation) has been increasingly admitted: cf. Paul Betts, 'The Bauhaus and National Socialism—a Dark Chapter of Modernism', in Fiedler and Feierabend (eds.), *Bauhaus*, 34–41. For the nuclear weapons point, B. Brock, ibid. 583.

also considerably more interconnections with religion than most believers have been aware, or perhaps ever were. The tragic consequences such ignorance has had for the relevance of religion to the modern world should make us pause. So too should the way in which this reduces the opportunities for believers to find and experience God sacramentally within the ordinary built environment. So before turning to a much briefer consideration of the postmodernist reaction to Modernism, I would like to make a few more direct observations on the religious dimensions of such secular architecture.

My thoughts can be most easily crystallized by considering the debate between Sir John Betjeman and Sir Nikolaus Pevsner (knighted in the same year) on the relative value of different types of architectural style.[87] The competition between their two rival sets of guides to the counties of England is well known, but here I have in mind something rather different. In the early 1930s Betjeman was assistant editor of the influential *Architectural Review* and a strong supporter of Modernism. He seems to have felt that it chimed in well with the Quakerism that he then practised, and to some degree that perception was confirmed by architects whom he knew, among them the semi-modernist Charles Voysey who noted that he had had a number of wealthy Quaker clients.[88] In 1932 he was even writing that 'the house will show its grace of construction in steel and concrete . . . and the main road will soar straight and unbothered as a Roman road'.[89] A visit to Leeds, however, brought a change of heart, and thus the gradual birth of the Betjeman whom the English public grew to love so well in his enthusiasm for the architecture of the ordinary and the particular: typically, Victorian city centres and Edwardian suburbia.

Pevsner arrived as a refugee in England about the same time as Betjeman was carrying out his editorial work. Embarking on a career as an architectural historian, he attempted to persuade the British that Modernism was the natural culmination of their own

---

[87] They were both knighted in 1969. Unfortunately, the parallels continued, in them both dying of Parkinson's disease. Pevsner's Guides were commissioned by Penguin, Betjeman's initially by Shell in association with John Murray and then by Faber & Faber.

[88] T. Mohl, *Stylistic Cold Wars: Betjeman versus Pevsner* (London: John Murray, 2000), 16–17, 41–2.

[89] Quoted ibid. 44.

native tradition. Morris and Ruskin were both enlisted, but even Gothic was presented as naturally concerned with function; it was only the poorer nineteenth-century architects, he argued, who deflected it from this role into pure ornament and deceit.[90] Not that all the credit was given to his new homeland. While Macintosh, unlike Gaudí was assigned a central role, so too was the concern of post-impressionist painters such as Cézanne with form.[91] Although only Pevsner could properly be described as a scholar, in their 1952 confrontation Betjeman was able to make some direct and telling hits.[92] What is of particular interest here, however, is what that confrontation says about religion and sacramentality. Pevsner was some sort of 'vague deist' who clearly thought that even a religion of transcendence was now somewhat problematic.[93] Betjeman might have responded in terms of his earlier position by arguing that simplicity did after all speak of transcendence, not least because the lack of weight or mass in so many modernist buildings did introduce an immaterial dimension, as we have seen. But instead what he now offered was very much a sacramentality of immanence. One can, I think, see why. Modernism by its very universalism fails to make us secure, at home in each of our own personal and individual contexts. Instead, it seems to demand conformity, whereas Betjeman recognized that it is precisely the familiarity of the ordinary and the idiosyncratic that can most easily speak of the security that comes from an all-encompassing

[90] The classic for this argument is his *Pioneers of Modern Design*, first published in 1936. But even in his *Sources of Modern Architecture and Design* of 1968 a not dissimilar line is still being pursued. For Ruskin and Morris, *Pioneers* (London: Penguin, 1960 edn.), 19–39 esp. 39; for Gothic as functionalist but corrupted by some of its followers, *Sources* (London: Thames & Hudson, 1968), 9, 16–17.

[91] A whole chapter in *Pioneers* is devoted to post-impressionist painting (68–89). In the 1960 preface Gaudí is described as a 'freak' (17) and Le Corbusier's Rochamp is tarred with the same brush (116). There is a telling passage in *Sources* where Art Nouveau is characterized as essentially out of keeping with the typical restraint of the English character (144).

[92] Pevsner attacked one of Betjeman's favourite London churches and Betjeman replied by pointing out some of Pevsner's inaccuracies in his guide to County Durham: Mohl, *Stylistic Cold Wars*, 126–8. Elsewhere, though, Betjeman even gets the date of his own parish church wrong (120).

[93] The phrase is Mohl's, ibid. 5. Pevsner had nominally converted to his wife's Lutheranism. There is a key passage in *Pioneers* where Gothic is contrasted with Modernism, the latter being 'clear and without mystery', and so 'its expression discourages all other-worldly speculation' (216–17).

divine presence. Even humour is used by him to underline the way in which the ordinary can thus acquire a hallowed character; 'being poet of the specific' . . . 'Betjeman embraces embarrassment as a life-enhancing quality and he draws God into it deliberately.'[94]

Simplicity has been part of the Christian aesthetic at various times in its history, for example in Cistercian architecture or, centuries later, in American Classical chapels. The problem inherent in Modernism is thus not its insistence on simplicity as such but rather its tendency to make this the dominant or even the only criterion of worth. Had the earlier Bauhaus been followed rather than Le Corbusier or Mies van der Rohe, a different estimate might well have been possible. Modernism's more recent alternative shows no such obsession with simplicity. But it is also not free from problems, as we shall see.

Limitations in Postmodern Eclecticism

It is rather hard to give a simple characterization that will cover the great range of building types that have been produced since Modernism ceased to hold absolute sway. One way of doing so might be to talk of an easy acceptance of pluralism and eclecticism. Eclecticism is well illustrated by an artwork constructed by Ian Hamilton-Finlay and entitled *Adorno's Hut* (1987). Here one is confronted by an extraordinary hybrid of metal and wood in which the diversity of materials is intended to reflect the range of styles that postmodernist architects are now willing to employ. The way in which tree trunks on one side and red metal supports on the other develop into what is therefore only partially a wooden hut is supposed to make us think of how tradition is not only used but also subverted.[95] It is an example endorsed in the writings of the architect and architectural historian, Charles Jencks. It was he who in 1972 declared the death of modernist architecture, altogether too soon as it turned out.[96] If in his earlier writings links with Derrida's philosophical

[94] Mohl, *Stylish Cold Wars*, 153; cf. 151.

[95] Used as a key illustration by C. Jencks in his book, *What is Post-Modernism?* 4th edn. (London: Academy, 1996), 10. Another commonly used example is Charles Moore's Piazza d'Italia in New Orleans (1974); illus. in Gössel and Leuthäuser, *Architecture*, 270.

[96] What occasioned the comment was the dynamiting of the Pruitt-Igoe modernist estate in St Louis: Gössel and Leuthäuser, *Architecture*, 293. Tom

deconstructionism is what he is keen to stress,[97] his more recent works have sought to engage with the possible religious significance of the new trends. Thus in his *Architecture of the Jumping Universe* he argues that the complex spins and angles and strange tilts to be found in some more recent buildings reflect the move of modern physics away from either order or chaos to what he calls cosmogenesis, a self-regulating universe where order and chaos work together, with us as co-creators alongside a resacralized earth.[98] Less successful in my view is the argument of a symposium he organized on *Ecstatic Architecture* where parallels are attempted between some more recent buildings and Baroque architecture. The most persuasive reflections come from Paolo Portoghesi as he expounds his attempt to dematerialize matter in church, mosque, and spa, all of which he had designed,[99] but many of the other illustrations seem merely to expose the superficiality of what the relevant architect was supposedly trying to achieve.[100]

A powerful exception is the work of Frank Gehry at Bilbao on which there seems well-nigh universal agreement that a stunning building of great emotive power has been achieved, though even here one needs to note the heavy reliance on computer technology.[101] Such reliance, especially in the more extreme instances of buildings radically distorted out of their normal planes, makes one wonder whether in some postmodern works more is not being said

Wolfe also treats this as a key moment in his influential *From Bauhaus to our House* (London: Picador, 1993 edn.), 80–3.

[97] Key features stressed include 'from few styles to many genres', 'from purist to kaleidoscopic sensibility', and 'from exclusion to inclusion': 59–61.

[98] *The Architecture of the Jumping Universe* (London: Academy, 1997 edn.). Although the relevant physics is especially influenced by Paul Davis and by the theology of James Lovelock and his Gaia hypothesis, Jencks is also picking up on some more widely expressed reassessments of our 'post-Christian and postmodern' world (10). Among architectural examples he quotes are Eisenman's Nunotani Headquarters in Tokyo, Libeskind's Berlin Jewish Museum, and Gehry's Vitra Furniture Museum: 57, 63, 65–7.

[99] '*Ekstasis*: Dematerialism and Movement', in C. Jencks (ed.), *Ecstatic Architecture* (London: Academy, 1999), 56–65.

[100] As in the treatment of shops by Jean Nouvel and Hans Hollein, ibid. 13,15, 134–5. Even the cinema complex at Dresden is more likely to evoke giddiness than delight: 102–3.

[101] Illustrated in Jencks's *Ecstatic Architecture*, 166. The technology apparently came from work on the mirage fighter: 171.

about computer skills than about the creativity of the architect as such, still less about any deep meaning underlining their plans. However, alongside what might be described as merely cleverness for its own sake, one must also set more serious attitudes, some of which were already current even when Modernism was at its height. An obvious case in point is the desire for an intimate relation to the environment exhibited by various Scandinavian and American architects. The concerns of Wright were noted earlier, and one finds these continued in his pupil, Bruce Goff. Other architects worth mentioning in this context would include Alvar Aalto, Gunner Asplund, Richard Neutra, and Jørn Utzon.[102] Some are even prepared to use the language of religion. Aalto speaks of his admiration for Italian hill-towns in terms of them preserving the 'religious beauty in life', while Neutra described his own architecture as motivated by the desire to create a 'harbour for the soul'.[103]

The willingness to place utilities external to the building, as in the Centre Pompidou in Paris and in the Lloyds Building in London, could also be seen as part of such environmental trends, and yet as entirely modernist. The rationale of the building was thus far more clearly disclosed than when wide-flange vertical beams were placed on top of concrete-encased steel to reveal the building's now hidden structure (hidden to make it fireproof).[104] Yet the irony is that apparently the ecological motive of making the utilities more easily replaceable could not after all be fulfilled in this way.[105] Another concern that Modernism also eventually exhibited was some desire to integrate with other buildings in the area.[106] If the mixture of styles in James Sterling's Stuttgart Staatsgalerie suggests that he has gone well beyond his earlier Modernism in his attempt

---

[102] J. Farmer, *Green Shift*, 2nd edn. (Oxford: Architectural Press, 1999), 130–42, 153–60; Gössel and Leuthäuser, *Architecture*, 239–47. Farmer, though, surely goes too far in trying also to enlist the earlier Le Corbusier's pilotis: 124.

[103] Aalto quoted in Farmer, *Green Shift*, 136; Richard Neutra in Gössel and Leuthäuser, *Architecture*, 221.

[104] As in the work of Mies van der Rohe and Johnson; rightly mocked by Wolfe, *From Bauhaus*, 74–6.

[105] So Farmer, *Green Shift*, 206–7.

[106] As in some of the work of Aldo Rossi, Gössel and Leuthäuser, *Architecture*, 307–9.

to fulfil that demand,[107] Philip Johnson's 1982 AT&T Building in New York irritated many a postmodernist by showing that Modernism did not have to go very far in order to produce something that took more account of its setting: in this case still tall but classical, and so more in harmony with the low-rise buildings nearby, whether one thinks of the resultant building as Chippendale-Highboy or classical violin.[108]

Obviously in the context of this present work it is the more explicitly religious dimension that needs to be considered rather than wider environmental concerns, whether these are conceived of as modernist or postmodernist. In one classic advocacy of Modernism that otherwise fails to mention religion, there occurs the intriguing comment that 'a new religion alone, or a new relation of some existing religion to civilisation, might relatively soon make wholly new demands upon architecture that are now inconceivable'.[109] Yet it is doubtful whether any religion is quite that simple in its implications. As has gradually emerged over the course of our investigations in the previous chapter, the world has been at such crossroads before, in, for example, the severity of Cistercian monasteries as against the richness of Gothic cathedrals, or in classical Renaissance restraint as opposed to Baroque exuberance. Modernism cannot thus be summarily dismissed as so inherently antichristian or antireligious as to be in desperate need of a successor, nor the opposite automatically be claimed for Postmodernism. Indeed, some versions of Postmodernism can legitimately be accused of flippancy in their all-too-ready acceptance of a virtually infinite plurality of styles.[110] For style does matter, but context is all-important in determining what is appropriate and when. Thus the demands of a silent, interior retreat are likely to be more easily fulfilled in the relative simplicity of a Romanesque Cistercian

---

[107] Ibid. 378–9. Contrast his Leicester University Engineering Building of 1963 (296), which might now itself be contrasted with the postmodernist De Montfort University Engineering Building in the same city (Farmer, *Green Shift*, 211).

[108] For illus., Gössel and Leuthäuser, *Architecture*, 341; for quotation, Jencks, *What is Post-Modernism?* 28.

[109] Hitchcock, *Modern Architecture*, 209.

[110] Well illustrated by G. G. Galfetti, *My House, My Paradise: The Construction of the Ideal Domestic Universe* (London: Cartago, 1999). Although the author begins by noting the way in which 19th-c. novelists (such as Stendhal and Balzac) treated house arrangements as indicative of moral character (7), all the great variety of examples subsequently pursued are essentially eccentric or flippant.

monastery than amidst the distractions of the exuberant decoration of a Baroque church. Similarly, office administration is likely to prove more efficient in a modernist skyscraper than in one of Eisenman's postmodernist 'catastrophic' buildings, with their constant reminder of the potential for dissolution.[111] But that scarcely rules out the rejected alternative in all contexts.

Yet if Postmodernism's tolerant pluralism is one of it potential weaknesses, it can also at times be a strength. For if on the one hand it permits strange incongruities that puzzle rather than please (as with, to my mind, the new entrance to the Louvre),[112] on the other it also means that considerable experimentation now exists, and sometimes as a result architects get it exactly right. Ultramodern homes are sometimes the best solution, sometimes not. What matters is the extent of coherence with the wider environment, whether built or otherwise. Postmodernism at least allows the option for more traditional looking homes where this is what the context seems to require, as for example in a historic city centre. The dogmatism of Modernism has at least gone, though perhaps not entirely. If on the whole the practising architects are more open, this seems less true of postmodernist philosophers writing on the subject. Their first stance is often negative and critical rather than concerned with how to give humanity a sense of belonging.[113]

Ideas of belonging and fit with the surrounding built environment are of course not necessarily religious notions. But if, as Christians believe, human beings were planned by God for community and interdependency then it is only when such features are taken into account that buildings are likely to aid the experience of a God who encapsulates such values. However, one must still distinguish carefully between superficial fit and real fit. The danger in borrowing earlier styles is that, though the result may look good,

---

[111] His Japanese 'folded' buildings deliberately evoke this insecurity while also guarding against it so far as possible: Jencks, *Jumping Universe*, 55, 57.

[112] The main courtyard of the Louvre now has a glass prism in its middle. While this is undoubtedly a huge success in improving access through the underground entrance thus created, what is above ground still seems strangely out of kilter with the uniform style of what surrounds it, intriguingly itself added by various stages over the centuries.

[113] Compare the relevant extracts from Derrida, Lefebvre, and Lyotard in N. Leach (ed.), *Rethinking Architecture: A Reader in Cultural Theory* (London: Routledge, 1997), with those from Bachelard, Gadamer, and Heidegger.

their coded meaning in fact flies in the face of their new applications. Gothic detail on the exterior of a modern house, for example, may seem simply pretty or pretentious; a classical façade that speaks of reason and order scarcely integrates well with what lies within (such as modern art gallery exhibits), and so becomes likely to strike a somewhat comic pose. Humour has its place, of course, but, if destructive of any deep level of meaning, we are all the worse off.

Note has already also been taken of the way in which some postmodernist architects are insisting that the best new building will reflect current understandings in physics. But, apart from the volatility of developments in science, there is also this major difference from copying nature in the past: the parallels were once instantaneously visible to the naked eye, whereas now it is a highly theoretical and abstract knowledge that is being proposed. No doubt, however, such theory will gradually seep through to the general public. In advance of that happening, religious believers do therefore need to be prepared for an architecture that, in so far as it speaks of faith at all, is likely to reflect a more immanent God than what much of Christianity has hitherto preached. To consideration of what kind of God churches of the twentieth century have in fact reflected—modernist, postmodernist, or something else—I now turn.

Church Architecture in Crisis

Inevitably, religious architecture has been much influenced by what is happening in the wider cultural context. Indeed, some of the major architects mentioned in the previous section have also designed churches. Even so, the impact was slow, and only really began to take off once the influence of the liturgical movement made its own fresh demands on Christian self-understanding. The extent of those demands is best illustrated from the interior of churches, but first something needs to be said on exteriors. Although there is much that is fresh and exciting, there seems to me little clarity of vision. That, I suspect, is due in no small part to the way in which architecture has been allowed to retreat from being a matter of religious and theological concern. Churches and congregations then get the buildings they deserve: the product of as little reflection as they themselves have given to the matter.

Exteriors and the Flight from Transcendence

With exteriors what one notes immediately is how little unanimity there is on how these should be treated. On the whole, conventional forms such as spires are distrusted, whereas by contrast there is discernible a new and marked interest in ecological issues, with the external form in consequence harnessed to try somehow to suggest that the church is at one with nature and thus with God's creation. One context where one might suppose such a conviction already firmly secured is among Christian Scientists, who are required by their faith to rely on nature alone without resort to medicine. It is therefore unsurprising to observe that this is exactly what one finds in a commission given, about the same time as Gaudí was in his prime (in 1910), to Bernhard Maybeck, to build the Church of Christ Scientist at Berkeley.[114] The architect himself described the final result as 'pure Romanesque made out of modern materials', but the contemporary observer is more likely to note how both inside and out there is a very strong feeling of naturalism and the support given by organic forms. The previous year, however, marked the completion of a much more influential building, Frank Lloyd Wright's Unity Temple produced for a wealthy Unitarian liberal congregation in Oak Park, Chicago.[115] To the uninitiated the church building might well seem to have more the appearance of a library than a church, and this is confirmed by its internal decoration which, though bright and airy, appears to lack any of the obvious symbols of the Christian faith. From such initial impressions it would then be easy to move to the conclusion that the rationale for the building was entirely pragmatic, and that this reflects the Unitarian patrons' conviction that it is all up to us rather than a matter of expecting active divine involvement in our world. But such an accusation would be grossly unfair, and so it is worth

[114] T. Garnham and E. R. Bosley, *Arts and Crafts Masterpieces* (London: Phaidon, 1999), third section of book (no page nos.). The Mother Church in Boston is, however, quite different: a Classical Revival domed structure has been imposed on an original Romanesque-style building.
[115] For a detailed discussion and illustrations, J. M. Siry, *Unity Temple: Frank Lloyd Wright and Architecture for Liberal Religion* (Cambridge: Cambridge University Press, 1996).

investigating how a non-eucharistic building can still be orientated towards an assertion of God's presence within.

Although his father had been a Baptist preacher, Wright himself had in fact extensive family connections with Unitarianism, and some of his earliest commissions were to come from this source; so he understood their theology well.[116] Unity Temple actually sits in a street of churches. Some have spires, and indeed the largest, Grace Episcopal, actually conforms fully to Pugin's demands that churches should only be built in the style of English Decorated Gothic.[117] Although at the time of the commission spires were already declining in popularity, Wright added his own arguments against, suggesting that they located God in the wrong place, above rather than among us.[118] Unitarians were also during this period much interested in relations with other religions. The tendency was to postulate a primary unity that transcended the particularities of specific faiths. Wright himself expressed great admiration for Shinto shrines, and it may well be that the Temple's dual character (with worship space and activities area divided by an entrance set midway between) is modelled on a specific Japanese shrine, the Taiyu-in mausoleum at Nikko.[119] However that may be, the strong laterals can also be seen to reflect ancient temples generally, while the carefully balanced horizontals draw the eye-line down to nature, and so to the wider context of trees and flower boxes that were part of his overall design.[120] Internally, Wright deliberately required indirect access to the worship area so that its square format could be a haven of peace and symbol of unity, while geometric lines and stylized floral patterns repeated the message of the exterior, with all this recapitulated in the central pulpit.[121] When only 16, Wright had read Victor Hugo's argument that in the fifteenth century architecture had given place as the primal human expression to

---

[116] For the details, ibid. 12–50. There were a number of connections, particularly on his mother's side, among them the influential minister, Jenkin Lloyd Jones in Chicago itself.

[117] Ibid. 59–65. Grace, though, has no spire.

[118] For decline, ibid. 77–8; for relevant quotation: 75.

[119] Ibid. 88–9, 150, 203–4.

[120] For influence of ancient temples, ibid. 196, 208–16; for trees etc.: 132, 148.

[121] For indirect access, ibid. 84, 98–9; for importance of square: 97, 136; for geometric patterns: 106, 135, 167; for pulpit: 186.

the printed word.[122] Here was his answer: architecture continued to speak, and indeed spoke even as the preacher delivered his address.

If one jumps to 1954, one arrives at what is perhaps now the best-known European example of the influence of Modernism on church architecture, Le Corbusier's pilgrimage church of Notre Dame de Haut at Ronchamp, which dates from his brutalist period.[123] There is the usual simplicity and lack of ornamentation that one has come to expect of Modernism but this is combined with elements that explain the occasional accusation of antirationalism, most obviously perhaps the fact that the disposition of the windows follows no rules, either with respect to distribution or size, both being quite random. Yet even so the building has often exercised a powerful impact in religious terms, not least perhaps because of the balance between the white tower pointing heavenwards and the mushroom-like, earth-rooted main roof. The latter in particular suggests something organic, and so appears to present a building that grows out of God's world rather than being imposed on it. Indeed, the viewer is forced to think at one and the same time of transcendence and of immanence, for transcendence is to be found not only in the tower but also within the immanence of the mushroom-roofed main building, since despite its rootedness it also succeeds in giving the impression of attempting to soar aloft. The gap between its walls and the structurally distinct roof are also used very effectively, to flood the building with light, supplemented by stained glass in the small side windows. Much less successful, though, in my view, was Le Corbusier's Dominican monastery of La Tourette near Lyons, where the influential aesthete, Fr. Couturier, had given a detailed brief.[124] It was also Couturier who had recommended Le Corbusier for Ronchamp. Couturier was fully aware of Le Corbusier's lack of religious belief but argued that it was better to commission 'geniuses without faith to believers without talent', a position that he maintained against many of his fellow Catholics throughout his editorship of the influential journal, *L'art*

[122] The argument is to be found in Hugo's novel *Notre-Dame de Paris*, in the chapter (5. 2) entitled, 'Ceci tuera cela'. For Wright's reactions, Siry, *Unity Temple*, 215–17.

[123] For a good photograph of the exterior, Etlin, *Frank Lloyd Wright*, 30, Pl. 4.

[124] Although in practice Le Corbusier seems have very much followed his own preferences. So Cistercian simplicity and interiority were simply imposed on Dominican friars, with the ancient abbey of Le Thoronet taken as his model.

sacré.[125] In that I suggest he was right.[126] The problem surely lies not in unbelievers' inability to comprehend what a religious building might be trying to say but in the inadequacy of the brief given to the architect by the Church. Confusion and uncertainty on this score are among the main problems infecting Christian belief at this time.[127]

If a more conventional example of Modernism is desired, Philip Johnson's Crystal Cathedral of 1980 (in Garden Grove, California) might be an obvious case to take.[128] The natural light streams in through this mainly glass construction, and so a warm and welcoming environment is suggested, but also one open to the wider world. That could be taken to imply mission, and that impression is reinforced by its tent-like character, which makes one think of tabernacle and pilgrimage. Yet even so there is little internally that forces thoughts of divine presence, except perhaps the height of the hall, and that would, I suggest, also be true externally, were it not for the cathedral's remarkable bell-tower. Indeed, despite its superficial modernity the overall impression is surprisingly conventional, and it is thus to less well-known architects that one must turn if one wants contemporary innovations as dynamic as Le Corbusier's much earlier in the century.

One such example comes from the work produced five years before Johnson's Crystal Cathedral by the Hungarian architect Imre

[125] The remark is quoted in W. Rubin, *Modern Sacred Art and the Church of Assy* (New York: Columbia University Press, 1961), 69. He was editor of the journal from 1937 to 1954; for a collection of Marie-Alain Couturier's own writings, *Sacred Art* (Houston, Tex.: Menil Collection, 1990). For one expression of the opposing view, P. Willis, *Dom Paul Bellot: Architect and Monk* (Newcastle-upon-Tyne: Elysium 1996), esp. 14, 21–2.

[126] Although Le Corbusier had definitely abandoned the Calvinism of his upbringing, it is not true that he lacked any religious sense. His repeated talk of *espace indicible* (a certain kind of space as 'inexpressible' or mysterious) and his *Poème de l'angle droit* of 1955 both suggest the contrary. See further, F. Samuel, 'The Philosophical City of Rabelais and St Teresa—Le Corbusier and Edouard Trouin's Scheme for St Baume', *Literature and Theology* 13 (1999), 111–25.

[127] Not helped of course by the lack of prominence given to the issues. Thus Couturier does not even appear among the entries in *The Oxford Companion to Christian Art and Architecture* (1996), whilst in *The Oxford Dictionary of the Christian Church*, 3rd edn. (1997) mention is made only of his contemporary and namesake, the ecumenist Paul Couturier.

[128] For illus. and discussion, E. Heathcote and I. Spens, *Church Builders* (Chichester: Academy Editions, 1997), 114–27.

Makovecz at Siófek Lutheran church, known locally (apparently with much affection) as 'Christ's boat'.[129] One can see why. Mounds of earth prevent a view of its walls and so all one sees is a huge undulating red roof, with a spire at its centre in the form of a winged angel and apparently about to take flight. The imagery is thus strong and clear: the ark of the church is for the moment resting on the earth but none the less it has the capacity to carry us elsewhere to God's own presence. For some the imagery will seem too folksy, and so of more appeal will be another church from the same architect and from about the same time, on this occasion created for a Roman Catholic community at Paks. Here the spire is made to split into three, with a cross placed on its central axis while the other two contain symbols for sun and moon.[130] That pushes us much more towards the language of traditional symbolism. Yet, one cannot help wondering whether the less familiar is in fact the more effective, not least because it forces us to reflect before we draw the appropriate conclusion.

If Makovecz is concerned to express through the church's exterior a community that is called at one and the same time to be in harmony with the natural world as God's creation, and to realize its need to transcend that world, most other modern architects seem to fight shy of the second aspect of the message except in the symbolism they use for the church interior, and so all we have outside is a church building merging with its surroundings. Reasons both good and bad may of course be involved here. In the past transcendence could all too easily merge into a rather arrogant triumphalism, and this may be what some fear. Again, merging into the landscape can be used to suggest a church committed to service. As an example one might consider how Justus Dahinden tackled the building of Mityana Cathedral in Uganda in 1972.[131] The church was intended to commemorate three African martyrs, and so three half-spheres that recalled traditional Bantu huts are utilized to recall these martyrs, while the waterproofing of the buildings was dyed red so that their colour would imitate that of the local earth. Martyrdom thus ceases to be an accusation against the local people and their

[129] For both Siófek and Paks, ibid. 160–9.

[130] Renaissance paintings often have this combination to suggest the cosmic significance of the cross. If angel and ark on the other church seem equally conventional, their visual form suggests quite otherwise.

[131] Ibid. 86–97 esp. 91–3.

ancestors, and instead becomes a witness to their willingness to give themselves in service to the local Bantu culture. It is thus a divine presence alongside the people that is asserted rather than one that necessarily draws them away from where they now are. That may seem a modern idea, but in fact such forms of building are by no means unique to modern times. So, for instance, the Spanish colonial church of San José in New Mexico was built entirely from natural materials, with earth walls and wooden towers; hence the reason for its long projecting water-chutes.[132] The thickness of the earth walls apparently provides excellent protection against both hot summers and cold winters. Indeed, one might argue that the colonial church is the more obviously 'natural', since even bricks were not employed, as they were in Dahinden's case. But the point of course is not the naturalness of the materials as such but rather how in both cases they were used to suggest God alongside his people.

Yet the reluctance of so many modern architects to express transcendence does seem to me a quite fundamental error. Immanence alone not only makes it more difficult to conceive of what could be meant by claiming that God enjoys an other than material existence, it also deprives him of his essential otherness in a quite different respect: the capacity of his revelation to challenge and subvert what we would like him to be saying. That is why suspicion of spires needs to be balanced, it seems to me, by a search for alternative forms of expression of just such an idea. An intriguing example comes from the work of the Italian Mario Botta. While his housing can sometimes have a fortress-like quality to emphasize the theme of shelter, for him churches should speak of silence and meditation.[133] One of his most impressive interiors is the church of San Giovanni Battista with its wonderful Romanesque-style apse.[134] Externally, though, it is ultramodern, with no windows visible from a distance, and resembling nothing so much as a cone sliced off at a 45-degree angle. This was a pattern he was to repeat elsewhere, most notably in the new cathedral at Évry near Paris,

---

[132] Illus. in D. Pearson, *Earth to Spirit: In Search of Natural Architecture* (London: Gaia, 2000), 78.

[133] I. Sakellaridou, *Mario Botta: Architectural Poetics* (London: Thames & Hudson, 2001), 6, 193–7.

[134] Ibid. 100–8. One is reminded of Vézélay.

France's first truly modern cathedral.[135] Completed in 1995, and consisting of twelve storeys in all, it has a crown of lime trees on top. Apparently the intention, inspired by some accidental growth on a tower at Parma, was to emphasize the reintegration of nature into the building.[136] Sadly, though, they simply look out of place, and the cross on top is surely too small in relation to the building to compensate. None the less, from the right perspective these sliced cones do communicate human aspiration towards something higher and better than themselves. Indeed so much is Botta convinced of the viability of the concept that he has also employed it in his best-known museum design to date.[137]

Interior Unity and Liturgical Change

As noted earlier, on the whole the Church has retreated from dramatic exteriors, and so it is to the interiors that we must look if we are to find clear indicators of belief in an accompanying divine presence. For an interesting example from the beginning of the period we are considering, one might take Edward Prior's 1905 design for St Andrew's, Roker in the north-east of England.[138] If the exterior is conventional, a surprise awaits one inside. The nave has fifty-two-foot wide, enormous, single-span stone arches that give a great feeling of space that then narrows down to a focus on the chancel. Apparently, Prior wanted to suggest the way in which Gothic may have had its origins in the 'megalithic' masonry of Anglo-Saxon Britain.[139] If that suggests a historicism that looked backwards, not only does the church as a whole in actual fact have a decidedly modern feel but also Prior intended the chancel to provide a fitting and unexpected climax. Although not finished until twenty years after the rest of the building, the painting scheme

---

[135] Ibid. 108–15; also in Heathcote and Spens, *Church Builders*, 139–47. For a variation on the theme in the chapel of Santa Maria degli Angeli, Sakellaridou, *Mario Botta*, 124–9.

[136] He was captivated by a tree growing on top of an old tower in Lucca, and introduced the idea into a number of his buildings: Sakellaridou, ibid. 35.

[137] San Francisco Museum of Modern Art: ibid. 116–23.

[138] Garnham and Bosley, *Arts and Crafts Masterpieces*, first third of book (no page nos.).

[139] Itself an unusual theory, given the fact that the Saxons mostly built in wood or in recycled Roman stone.

for this part of the building was apparently part of Prior's original plan, and what it offers is some very dramatic imagery indeed of divine presence. Images of creation hover over the eastward altar, suggesting an overarching unity between the natural creation and the new creation which the eucharist promises. On the ceiling above the celebrating priest are trees that stretch towards a central sun and accompanying moon, while the hand of the Father stretches out to bless those below.

It is interesting to compare this with some typical examples of what is being attempted half a century later. The natural symbolism is still there, but instead of a substitute representation for some element already existing in nature what we now often find is nature itself being more directly employed, even with respect to the internal space itself. Some good examples come from Scandinavia. Finnish architects in particular are prominent in this field. The Siren family, for instance, at Otaniemi (1957) used the device of a white cross against a full-length, clear, east window as a way of integrating cross and creation, and this is especially dramatic when through the windows are to be observed trees covered in snow.[140] Yet so overwhelming is the view that one might well question whether the net result is not in the end too distracting for the worshippers: with the outside world in effect allowed to dominate rather than to hint at something beyond itself. By contrast, at Orivesi (1961) that same firm allowed just as much light to enter but this time from behind the worshippers. This time their gaze is directed instead towards an altar, above which stands a great white screen. Depicted on this (in wood relief) is an abstract representation of Golgotha. If the earlier church suggests nature finding its focus in the cross, the latter, through its more direct association of altar and white screen, speaks of the crucifixion expanding into a mysterious beyond. A major problem, though, is that the image of Golgotha is so abstract that the ensemble as a whole conveys little until some explanation is given. That mystic element is also present in the work of another group of Finnish architects, the Suomalainen group who designed an underground church for Temppeliaukio, not far from the centre of Helsinki.[141] Part of the blasted rock provided material not only for the external walls but also for font

---

[140] Heathcote and Spens, *Church Builders*, 74–85 esp. 81. For Orivesi: 84.
[141] Ibid. 98–107 esp. 98–103.

and altar. Water continues to seep down into channels surrounding the internal walls, gradually changing and enriching their colour, and it is against these walls that candles are lit. However, despite the undoubtedly impressive and emotive character of such a design, the question still needs to be asked whether such an identification with nature has not gone too far. One cannot help but be reminded of another Finn, the composer Jean Sibelius. There too the question arises whether the music, like such architecture, does not finally dissolve the divine into the purely immanent.

Perhaps the issue can be more sharply focused by considering the work of Tadao Ando in Japan. In the case of his open-air Church on the Water (1988) at Hokkaido the congregation faces a small lake, in front of which is placed a cross: in effect, a very similar tactic to that employed by the Siren family at Otaniemi.[142] More unusual, however, is his Church of the Light (1989) at Osaka. Here what is little more than a concrete bunker is transformed as the congregation are made to confront a blank wall, pierced only by narrow cruciform glass that resonates with symbolism as the cross lets though brilliant shafts of light. For once the transcendent implications are so obvious that any talk of reductionism can be summarily dismissed. So the question seems to be not so much the use of nature as such as the way in which it is used, and the clarity of the resultant imagery.

But nature is of course only one way in which divine immanence can be expressed. More pertinent to the liturgy would be eucharistic presence, and in terms of contemporary liturgical thinking that presence mediated through the congregation itself. Readers will be familiar with the liturgical changes initiated by the Second Vatican Council (1962–5) when less hierarchical forms of worship were introduced with the priest facing towards the people, themselves gathered about him rather than at a distance in a distinct and separate space. Less familiar will be the fact that such changes were the culmination of a much longer period of intellectual change that was to be found occurring in Protestant and Catholic theology alike. There is no need to repeat the details of that history here. Relevant to note, though, is the way in which some architects

[142] V. Hart and P. Drew, *Places of Worship* (London: Phaidon, 1999), third section of book (no page nos.).

anticipated the change, however gradually or partially.[143] An intriguing Anglican example is Sir Ninian Comper, much admired by John Betjeman. Like Betjeman he was a convinced Anglo-Catholic, fond of ritualistic services. None the less, reflection on churches in north Africa and Spain that had preserved their original ground plans persuaded him that the altar should be among the people, and this led him to design a number of churches either with a minimal chancel or else with the altar in a single space under a baldachin.[144] Indeed, so innovative was this apparent conservative that his influence has been detected even in Frederick Gibberd's layout for Liverpool's Metropolitan cathedral, which also has a central plan.[145]

A much-quoted early Roman Catholic example is Auguste Perret's Notre-Dame du Raincy, near Paris, of 1923. But, though there is a single space, the degree to which the altar is elevated rather dampens the effect. More interesting to my mind, though much nearer the time of official sanction, is the work of the Maltese architect, Peter England. A devout but restless young Catholic student, he was granted the commission for a new church at Manikata by his doting father.[146] England sought to express the ideas of dialogue and equality by utilizing the round megalithic structures on the island. Probably originally employed in the worship of an earth goddess, he made two overlap in a sort of nuptial embrace, and so nave and chancel became one.[147] At the same time more primitive imagery (stalactite lighting, for example) was given to the chancel and the better-quality flooring to the nave.[148] Ornament was thus used to qualify apparently privileged position. In a

[143] And not just professional architects. An early modern example of a westward-facing altar (from 1840–2) is in the church designed by Sarah Losh at Wreay in Cumbria. In the shape of a Roman basilica, the church has a forward-placed altar of green marble, supported by brass eagles with carvings of corn and grapes at its base.

[144] A. Symmondson, 'Unity by Inclusion: Sir Ninian Comper and the Planning of the Modern Church', *Journal of the Twentieth Century Society* 3 (1998), 19–42. For precedents: 31, 33; for some examples, including some from the 1920s and St Philip's, Cosham, from 1937: 30, 32, 33.

[145] Through Comper's proposals for St John of Jerusalem, Clerkenwell: so ibid. 37–8.

[146] C. Abel, *Manikata Church: Peter England* (London: Academy, 1995), 17.

[147] For ideals and nuptial symbolism, ibid. 24–8.

[148] Ibid. 32.

related move the font was placed next to the altar but augmented by the sound of running water nearby. If all this sounds unlikely to appeal to Christians as traditionally conservative as Maltese Catholics, apparently what won the day was the bypassing of the usual reliance on foreign styles in preference to a truly native creation.[149] England's more recent work is also dramatic, but scarcely as innovative.[150]

From the late 1960s onwards, though, open–plan churches became commonplace. That they helped in creating a sense of community, no one could deny. However, more difficult to assess is the kind of contribution they make to a greater sense of the presence of God within the building. Is the architecture as such merely a helpful adjunct to what is primarily communicated by other means (through the assembled people), or is its contribution essential? Or should the architecture be allowed its own distinctive voice? In the decade in question liturgists could at times be very dogmatic. 'The church exists to house the community, and an architect who wishes to get his basic ideas right must begin . . . with the community.'[151] A centralized altar then comes a close second, in the author's view, as symbol of Christ's sacrifice, with any other consideration a long way behind. But all this suggests a single, unifying aim in view rather than the possibility of a number of complementary messages, including the capacity of the building to speak of God in its own right.

A useful test-case with which to conclude is Sir Basil Spence's much–criticized Coventry Cathedral. Peter Hammond's book *Liturgy and Architecture* may be used as a starting point. The other two new twentieth-century Anglican cathedrals are not even mentioned, while Coventry is described as 'a building which contributes nothing to the solution of the real problems of church design and perpetuates a conception of a church which owes far more to the romantic movement than to the New Testament or authentic Christian tradition'.[152] What irritated Hammond was the failure, in

---

[149] Gothic styles suggested Britain, Baroque Italy: ibid. 35. Though the church was not completed until 1974, the design was submitted just before Vatican II.

[150] For his House of the Good Samaritan of 1992, also in Malta: Heathcote and Spens, *Church Builders*, 108–13.

[151] C. Davis, 'The Christian Altar', in W. Lockett (ed.), *The Modern Architectural Setting of the Liturgy* (London: SPCK, 1964), 13–31 esp. 26.

[152] P. Hammond, *Liturgy and Architecture* (London: Barrie & Rockcliff, 1960), 6–7. That the book struck a chord at the time is well indicated by the fact that it went through three printings in its first sixteen months: p. xi.

his view, of the design to take into account the new understandings of worship that were then slowly advancing. The Provost who inherited the completed building also took a similar line.[153] What is odd about such objections, though, is that both bishop and architect had originally agreed on a forward-placed altar, and it was opposition from the clergy and reconstruction committee that had forced them to a more conservative design.[154] More fundamentally, one can also question whether this should in any case have been seen as the all-controlling issue. Provost Williams seems to have taken the view that any building might have served his purpose almost just as well, whereas Spence saw the architecture as making its own distinctive and indispensable contribution.[155] In this my sympathies are entirely with the architect.

Thus, significantly, in his own account of how his plans reached fruition Spence speaks of the sense of awe generated by appropriate religious architecture, and of the need to stress continuity within change.[156] Those aims he very effectively achieved in the way he chose to link the war ruin with his new building, as also in the sense of mass and solidity that he gave to the latter. For his decision to give the new building little external decoration, he quoted some perhaps unexpected precedents in the cathedral at Albi and S. Apollinare Nuovo at Ravenna.[157] He may have thought the surviving tower enough to identify the structure as a religious building, or perhaps the weight of external symbolism was to be borne mainly by Epstein's St Michael, where at least this time he carried the day against widespread opposition.[158] Spence's main focus, however, was internal and here his account makes it quite clear what enormous pains he went to in order to try to achieve an integrated artistic structure. As with Couturier at Assy, he

[153] H. C. N. Williams, *The Latter Glory* (Manchester: Whitehorn Press, n.d.), 47–8, where aesthetic considerations are blamed for the conservative position of the altar.

[154] B. Spence, *Phoenix at Coventry* (London: Fontana, 1962), 55–7; L. Campbell, *Coventry Cathedral* (Oxford: Clarendon Press, 1996), 31–2, 92.

[155] Compare Williams's comment that 'whether they were Gothic or just tin shanties, the essential purpose of a cathedral could be proved in any context': quoted in Campbell, ibid. 241–2. The previous Provost, Dick Howard, had been much more sympathetic.

[156] For awe: *Phoenix*, 19; for continuity at Ely within variety of changing styles: 21.

[157] Ibid. 23–4, 40, 52.

[158] Ibid. 80–90.

succeeded in engaging the leading artists of the day, but in a way that encouraged them to make their proposals chime with the general ethos of the building. Too often in the immediate past had artistic works been approached as though they were isolated or wholly distinct commissions.[159] If some artists, such as Sutherland, found the extent of intervention irritating and some, such as Hutton, may actually have had the integrity of their own work damaged as a result, the net effect was still a powerful building that can function on a number of different levels for worshipper and visitor alike.[160]

Spence, by advocating both tradition and innovation, ended up upsetting conservative and radical alike, but his intuitions were wise. An exclusive focus on the presence of God within the human community inevitably places a difficult, if not impossible, burden upon that group. However good and supportive they are to one another, Christians are fed ultimately by something more invisible, namely Christ himself, and so there is need of foci that can carry the eye and other senses beyond the immediate human presence when required, to reinforce that conviction, especially when the going gets tough. That is one key reason why the art employed needs to be integral and not accidental. Even in Liverpool's Metropolitan Cathedral one cannot help feeling that the individual items are marginalized.[161] By contrast, Imre Makovecz's interiors are no less dramatic but more focused and integrated. So, for instance, at Siófok worship focuses on a ladder ascending to heaven that has Christ at the summit already pointing the way, while at Paks angels join Christ on three wooden posts that stream upwards to a great window of spiralling gold and white light.[162] If that suggests the eye wandering but the body remaining static, no less important is the possibility for the body to explore and lay claim to the confining but potentially liberating space. We

[159] Couturier had, among others, enrolled Chagall and Leger.

[160] For Sutherland: *Phoenix*, 72–9, Campbell, *Coventry Cathedral*, 263; for Hutton: Campbell, ibid. 122–8, 185–92, 263 esp. 124, 192, 263.

[161] In the original design little thought was given to the placing and design of *cathedra*, pulpit, and baptistery: so P. D. Walker, 'Prophetic or Premature? The Metropolitan Cathedral of Christ the King, Liverpool', *Theology* 105 (2002), 185–93 esp. 187–8. The same volume also contains assessments of the artwork in Coventry Cathedral: 175–84.

[162] Illustrated in Heathcote and Spens, *Church Builders*, 164, 168. There is a more complete illus. of Paks (1991) in Pearson, *Earth to Spirit*, 16.

explore the rooms of our homes, as different projects come to mind, and churches surely should be no different if they are to communicate. Sometimes there is need for a space to sit by oneself; sometimes it is the font that should be the corporate focus; sometimes the shrine of a particular saint, a pew where a faithful member sat for many years, or whatever. Buildings can and do communicate a mediated divine presence, but it would be a disaster were the Church to commit itself to the view that this comes in only one particular guise.[163]

Mediated Presence through Transcendence and Immanence

The opening section of the next chapter will consider some of the assumptions that underpin architectural theory in some of the other major world religions. Now that our survey of the history of architecture within the Christian world is complete, however, it is time to draw some interim conclusions. It may appear tempting to see a catastrophic decline since the triumph of Gothic in the nineteenth century. But that would, I think, be a mistake. If twentieth-century church architecture did tend to become parasitic on widespread secular assumptions about simplicity and ecology, these can be used to highlight some key, pertinent questions for faith. The desire to impose a simple order and intelligibility on the built environment could be read as a purely human aspiration, or it could be seen as saying something about ourselves made, as Christians believe, in the divine image. If the latter is accepted, what went wrong with Modernism may well have been not its cult of simplicity as such, but rather the assumption that this is all that needed to be said. Human beings are also made for delight and joy, and therein lies part of the motivation for ornament throughout most of the history of architecture, and perhaps also thus indirectly for the rise of Postmodernism. Again, integration with the natural environment can so easily be read as merely reflecting our current ecological crisis, but it could also be seen as saying something

---

[163] That is why continuing debate on the role of architecture is so important. In England the journal *Church Building* plays a key role. On the Continent as well as *L'Art sacré*, mention should also be made of *L'Art de l'église*, *Kunst und Kirche*, and *Bauen und Wohnen*.

important about our situatedness in a world of interdependency established by God. If looked at in this way then some of the examples of church design considered above cease to be quite as trendy as they may initially appear.

Even with that conceded, though, the question still remains open of how effective they really are in conveying some sense of a sacramental presence. As I have illustrated several times in the preceding discussion, my suspicion is that this, paradoxically, only becomes fully a reality when the worshipper is also taken through the material into an experience of transcendence, as, for instance, in Tadao Ando's creative use of cruciform light or in Imre Makovecz's figures pulling us heavenwards. As the previous chapter argued was proved so often the case in the past, immanence and transcendence really need to complement one another if reductionism is to be avoided in the one case and absence in the other. Liturgy and the modern mentality alike conspire in favour of immanence. That is why Christians are so singularly fortunate in having such a rich legacy of Gothic churches, to help them resist the reduction that tends to dissolve the grandeur and majesty of God into a vague pantheism. Whereas Romanesque immanence, as we saw, could be balanced by the supernatural, transcendent character of so much of its imagery and Gothic architectural transcendence was complemented in the opposite direction both by its eucharistic theory and by the humanity even of its angels, the danger for the contemporary Church is that it lacks such complementarity. The current stress on God's presence within his people, while right and proper in its place, imposes of itself an impossible burden, however good or holy particular individuals may be.

Much of the problem lies in the assumption that worship, and so with it divine presence, are always there to serve some further end (such as mission), in short the kind of instrumental rationality that Chapter 1 identified as inevitably leading to a disenchanted world. The 1988 winner of the Booker Prize, Peter Carey, sends his clerical hero on a mad adventure to build a glass church in the Australian outback. Significantly, the test of the 'practical' is denounced as 'a word dull men use when they wish to hide the poverty of their imagination'.[164] Instead, the church is to be 'a celebration of God', 'a sacrifice'. Ruskin put the latter word first

---

[164] P. Carey, *Oscar and Lucinda* (London: Faber & Faber, 1988), 390–1; cf. 388.

in his *Seven Lamps*. Of course there is much in Ruskin that is absurdly reactionary, but he too saw the importance of the 'useless' and indeed used it to define good architecture.[165] If in those introductory remarks matters are addressed primarily from the human end, later his stress is on that same useless form as a medium for the divine, and by no means only in churches: 'our God is a household God, as well as an heavenly one; he has an altar in every man's dwelling'.[166] If our own age needs to take much more seriously churches in their totality as expressive entities and not just the liturgy that occurs within them,[167] so too is there need to focus on the home once more as a place of sacramentality that can complement church in providing a sense of God's presence and care for his people.[168]

'For his people' may suggest a narrowly Christian perspective. In later life Ruskin came to see that that was wrong.[169] I agree. Hinduism and Islam are often presented as representing the two opposing poles in worship, in the temptation either towards extreme immanence or extreme transcendence, and so with Christianity having little to learn from them. Both religions, however, have in reality been much more subtle than this. To see how each has overcome its respective temptation will be the first concern addressed in the chapter that follows.

---

[165] J. Ruskin, *Seven Lamps of Architecture* (New York: Dover, 1880), 9. His attitude to the use of iron (39–40, 56–7) and railway stations (121–2) contrasts markedly with that of Pugin: *An Apology for the Revival of Christian Architecture in England* (1843); on railway stations: 10–11; on iron: 40–1.

[166] Ruskin, *Seven Lamps*, 181.

[167] For an excellent such total study (of St Agnes in Rome), M. Visser, *The Geometry of Love: Space, Time, Mystery and Meaning in an Ordinary Church* (London: Penguin, 2000).

[168] 'Complement' does not imply the same message, and indeed the greater the immanence in the home, the more there will be need for transcendence in the church.

[169] Note the correcting footnote in later editions: 89 n. 21. For the view that the later Ruskin did not abandon religion but moved to a more inclusive faith, T. Hilton, *John Ruskin: The Later Years* (New Haven: Yale University Press, 2000).

7

Widening the Perspective

Mosque and Temple, Sport and Garden

BEFORE drawing the arguments of this present volume together in an Interim Conclusion, what I propose to do in this chapter is tackle once more the various issues I have surveyed over the course of the book as a whole, but in reverse order. So I shall begin here with architecture, then proceed to nature before concluding with sport. It may initially strike the reader as somewhat perverse to go over the same ground again, but I shall in each case tackle the issues from new angles in a way that I hope will cast fresh light on my overarching theme of the sacramentality of the world. Thus by reflecting on some non-Christian forms of religious architecture, I hope to identify more clearly what it is that has the potential to make buildings sacramental and how such pressures may actually be cross-cultural. Then the various approaches to gardening across the centuries will be used to complement what I have already said through consideration of landscape art. Finally, I return to the theme of sport, to see if, after all, there might be some sense in which it might continue to be seen as sacramental. The answers given will indicate why the present discussion must continue into a further volume.

Mosque and Temple: Learning from Other Religions

In the previous two chapters I tried to indicate some of the ways in which building styles reflected—sometimes consciously, sometimes not—the way in which God was experienced over the course of Christian history. Of course, not all architects were religious, but even where they were not a particular style could still work its effect in encouraging its own characteristic perception of God's relationship to our world. Admittedly, religious and non-religious alike (though for different reasons) can resist that impact, and so, no matter how profound the symbolism, experience no deepening sense of a divine presence in their midst. That is one reason why it is not necessarily regular churchgoers who respond best to their surroundings: belief can inhibit as well as open up the individual to new possibilities. One context in which this is likely to be especially so is in buildings devoted to worship by other religions. To acknowledge a mediated divine presence from such a source might well strike the devout of another faith as irretrievably idolatrous.

That, though, would seem to me both an unfortunate and an unnecessary conclusion to draw. Not everything in Christian shrines is good and wholesome, and so to find aspects of which the same could be said in respect of the buildings or worship practices of another religion is scarcely to force the conclusion that everything therefore is. The mix in Christian churches of good and bad surely points to the potential for a similar mix in the buildings of other faiths. Tourism and the multiculturalism of the West generally mean that the question has ceased to be purely academic. Christians are now entering such buildings in increasing numbers, and the same is of course happening in reverse. So it has become a matter of no small moment to ask whether it might be legitimate or not to think of God acting sacramentally even for the Christian through Hindu temple or Muslim mosque. I take these two as my principal examples, with Buddhism and Judaism only mentioned *en passant*, because they would seem to represent best the two extremes in attitudes towards sacredness in buildings. Hinduism has retained the ancient view of the shrine as the dwelling place of deity, while Islam in theory at least insists that prayer is equally appropriate anywhere. Christianity might therefore seem to be placed firmly in the middle. Why matters are not quite that simple will emerge as our discussion proceeds. What I also hope to demonstrate is that the various religions have in fact sometimes learnt from each other in the past, and that they should therefore continue to do so in the future.[1] More can in fact be seen to be shared at the level of phenomenology than is the case once that phenomenology is conceptualized. I begin, then, with Hinduism.

---

[1] For a study that makes the influence of other religions on Hinduism central to its architectural history, C. Tadgell, *The History of Architecture in India* (London: Phaidon, 1990). First there was the impact of Buddhism, then that of Islam, as well, of course, as influences in the opposite direction.

Grace and Mystery within Hindu Temples

Sadly, among Christians Hinduism is still quite commonly parodied as merely a superstitious form of primitive polytheism. Of course, in a religion that lacks the centralizing structures and creeds of Christianity there is tremendous diversity, and sometimes no doubt, as with Christianity, there are examples of religion at its worst. But in respect of its major temples there is a coherent theology that allows us, I believe, to answer both the question of whether Hinduism itself thinks sacramentally on such matters, and the more delicate issue of whether at times such buildings might conceivably function in such a way for the Christian as well. In our exploration we need, of course, to avoid any superficial identifications across the two faiths. The days when it was possible to speak of a Hindu Trinity in the Trimurti of Brahma, Shiva, and Vishnu are long since gone.[2] Worshippers are quite likely to be exclusive in their devotion and so it is possible to speak of a form of monotheism,[3] but even in the case of the three most commonly worshipped divinities, Shiva, Vishnu, and Devi, there remain numerous aspects where conflict with Christian belief would seem inevitable and deep-seated. Yet, to repeat what I said above, that does not entail that every aspect must be seen thus, not least because Hinduism's extensive use of mythological ways of thinking means that what literally sounds totally opposed may not necessarily remain so when appropriately decoded. Such decoding is a process with which Hinduism itself has long engaged, as the myths and even the existence of once separate gods have been absorbed into the cult of one or other of the major surviving deities.[4] The temptation is to

[2] Occasionally their names are linked in temple dedications, as in a 7th-c. cave inscription at Mandagapattu: V. Dehejia, *Indian Art* (London: Phaidon, 1997), 185. But attempts such as Hegel's to make this triad the fundamental reality for Hindus fail to correspond with the facts: cf. G. W. F. Hegel, *Lectures on the Philosophy of Religion*, ed. P. C. Hodgson (Berkeley: University of California Press, 1988), 275–82 esp. 280.

[3] Often identified in Indian philosophy and in Western discussions with Brahman, but it is important to note that this all-inclusive aspect to divine reality is not normally the object of worship.

[4] For this happening to Shiva, T. R. Blurton, *Hindu Art* (London: British Museum, 1992), 33–4. Devi perhaps, though, provides a more obvious example, for Devi means simply 'goddess' and as such her followers (*Shaktas*) tend to include all other goddesses within her 'power' ('Shatki' is her other name).

assume an inflexible system of belief, whereas change has in fact been extensive in the past and presumably will continue to be so in the future. Hinduism as we now know it is, for instance, quite different from the religion we find in the Vedas,[5] and, just as Buddhism seems to have exercised a profound influence in reshaping Hinduism prior to the Christian era,[6] so encounter with other world faiths in the modern world could generate a similar impact. Pressures can also of course come from within, as with the increasing resistance shown to the brahmin or priestly caste and their claim to have the exclusive right to serve in the inner sanctum of the shrines.[7]

Vedic sacrifice seems to have been performed in the open air and, so far as we can tell, the stress was on the correct performance of ritual rather than on buildings or images. Buddhist ascetics created monastic colleges and shrines in caves, and cave temples are now our earliest surviving form of Hindu temples. Presumably the Buddhist monks began the practice of having their community halls (*viharas*) there because caves provided an obvious place of retreat. But as imagery gradually became acceptable, so images of the Buddha were placed in special shrines (*chaityas*), and it was this latter practice that Hinduism adopted.[8] The obvious parallels can be seen by comparing and contrasting the famous fifth-century AD Buddhist caves at Ajanta with their Hindu counterparts on the island of Elephanta off Bombay.[9] Although such shrines eventually migrated to become independent buildings, significantly the heart

[5] Many speak of 'the true history of Hinduism' beginning only in the 3rd or 2nd c. BC: so G. Mitchell, *The Hindu Temple* (Chicago: University of Chicago, 1988 edn.), 16–18 esp. 17. The principal gods are quite different, and animal sacrifice has gone.

[6] Just as Buddhism developed a more theistic form in Mahayana Buddhism, so that form can be seen to have had an impact on Hinduism. Shiva and the Bodhisattva of Compassion, Avolokiteshvara, for instance, share the matted, piled-up hair of an ascetic, a trident, and an antelope skin over the shoulder: Blurton, *Hindu Art*, 29–30.

[7] Mahatma Gandhi exercised considerable influence here, but one should not discount earlier challenges nor the way in which the persistence of local cults with non-brahmin priests implies an implicit protest: R. Champalakshmi, *The Hindu Temple* (New Delhi: Roli & Janssen, 2001), 10–11, 103.

[8] The apsidal shape of Buddhist *chaityas* also appears in temples totally separate from caves, as at Aihole: illus. ibid. 64–5.

[9] Dehejia, *Indian Art*, 112–29.

of the temple where the principal image of the god resides is still called a womb-chamber (*garbha griha*). Above this rises a tall tower that is clearly meant to resemble a mountain, and indeed that resemblance is sometimes made explicit in the name of the temple itself.[10] Called a *shikhara* ('a mountain peak' or 'crest'), it often rises to a great height, which is all the more impressive given the absence of knowledge of many of the building techniques known in the West.[11] Although temples seldom correspond exactly to the requirements laid down in the sacred architectural texts (the *Vastushastras*), there would seem no doubt that the attempt was being made to invoke a particular cosmological focus that could therefore speak of the realized presence of the divine in that place.[12] Indeed, the common Sanskrit words for temple indicate as much.[13]

Because of destruction during Muslim invasions, early northern temples that have survived tend to be in more remote locations. Although the pilgrimage centre of Benares, for example, has well over a thousand temples, none date to before the seventeenth century. The south was much less subject to conquest, but it did live in fear, and this explains in part the more lateral feel to southern temples, where huge defensive gates (*gopuras*) tend to dwarf the sacred precinct itself. There is also a different pattern to the *shikhara* or tower. Instead of the relatively simple, layered, convex form of the north (the *nagara* style), the latter (*dravida*) is built up by a series of pyramids, with staggered aedicules at each stage.[14] These aedicules are clearly intended to suggest the dwellings of the gods on the sacred mountain, and indeed the gods are often seen looking out

[10] The Kailasa temple at Ellora is named after one of Hinduism's sacred mountains (the other being Mt. Meru). Although now an independent structure, it has actually been carved out of a mountain. The name of Shiva's consort, Parvati, actually means 'daughter of the mountain'.

[11] A height of 80–100 ft. is quite common, and almost 200 ft. not unknown. Post and beam is the basic technique without mortar or arch. Although concrete is now used, the knowledge brought by Muslim invasions failed to bring innovation in building techniques.

[12] For the sacred diagrams (mandalas) that are involved, and the placing of a symbolic cosmic man in the pinnacle of the *shihkara*, Champalakshmi, *Hindu Temple*, 12–19. For the complexity of the rules failing to produce 'a perfectly coherent system', H. Stierlin, *Hindu India* (Cologne: Taschen, 1998), 63–7 esp. 66.

[13] *Prasada* (seat or platform of God), *devagriham*, *devalaya* (house of God), *mandiram* (abiding place); so Mitchell, *Hindu Temple*, 61–2.

[14] For an illustration of the contrast, Dehejia, *Indian Art*, 147.

from their homes.[15] They are also to be found on the *gopuras*, and indeed in some ways in the south it is these gateways that have themselves become symbols of the holy mountain with numerous divine or semi-divine figures welcoming the worshipper.[16]

To the uninitiated Hindu temples can seem confusing places, not least because, though the shrine is usually aligned with the main entrance, not only are there often several courtyards (*mandapas*) first (some open and some covered), but also the normal practice for the worshipper is to approach indirectly through a process of clockwise circumambulation known as *pradakshina*.[17] This enables the believer to absorb the imagery on the exterior first before worship culminates in the plain, dark inner-shrine with symbolic gifts to the deity. The final image is seldom the most artistically impressive in the temple, but it is held to be the most profound, as the temple is seen as a progressive unfolding of divine presence with the lowest in the hierarchy of emanation being pressed furthest forward and so at the temple's outer limits.[18] The ultimate aim is described as *darshan*, which means not merely seeing the imagery but being seen by the god. While such a notion makes crystal-clear the characteristic Hindu approach to sacramentality of presence, the danger is that as it is developed the Christian will too readily jump to the conclusion that it is mere superstition. Where the image is anthropomorphic or zoological, artistic convention dictates that the last element to be added is the eyes and this is held to be what gives the image life, and that may seem to clinch the point. But the aim is not that the god is now there to be manipulated but rather to be available. Grace is thus the primary category, as the divine, as it were, undergoes progressive manifestation, from the indefinite mystery of Brahman to the specifics of one particular god to the

[15] For an illustration of such a *kudu*, Stierlin, *Hindu India*, 25. The fact that such windows are blank walls and do not admit light is interpreted as a symbol of light coming from the gods to the worshipper: so S. Kramrisch, *The Hindu Temple* (Calcutta: University of Calcutta, 1946), 318–21 cf. 303.

[16] For Thanjavur illustrating the *dravida* style, Stierlin, *Hindu India*, 91–9 esp. 94; for Bhubaneshwar illustrating the *nagara*: 105–17 esp. 117. For *gopuras* as the new mountains: 205–7, 216.

[17] For an excellent description of how a visit might be experienced, Blurton, *Hindu Art*, 59–74.

[18] For a helpful exposition, A. Hardy, 'Form, Transformation and Meaning in Indian Temple Architecture', in G. H. R. Tillotson, *Paradigms of Indian Architecture* (London: Curzon, 1998), 107–35 esp. 109–10.

image now before the worshipper.[19] So it is perhaps not surprising that intense devotion to the deity is a common result. A graced receptivity is in any case underlined by the way in which the worshipper not only offers simple gifts but also receives blessing through being anointed by light at the shrine, as also by some of the liquid that has been poured on the deity's image.[20]

The parallels with some forms of Christianity are surely also not all that distant. In some understandings of the eucharist, Christ is seen as vouchsafing his presence as in these sculptures in a uniquely material way, while processions that lead to discovery of the mystery of the divine in darkness and gloom recall some patterns of Christian pilgrimage, which involved descent to a saint's shrine deliberately placed beneath the earth.[21] Indeed, where the temple concerned is dedicated to Shiva the final image is at one and the same time profoundly mysterious and deeply educative, for what is most commonly encountered is the aniconic *linga*, a phallic-like stone used to symbolize divine power which also reminds the believer to move beyond all specific forms of representation as inadequate to the divine reality. But even where encounter is with an icon, realism can scarcely be the primary point since such images are often so bedecked with flowers that they are difficult to see, and their faces badly worn by repeated applications of *ghee* (clarified butter).[22] The intention does thus seem more one of focus than of supposing the divine narrowly or exclusively so confined, and indeed classical texts state as much: 'Without a form how can God be meditated upon? Where will the mind fix itself?'[23]

But if the ultimate image is thus a simple one set in a simple context, the riot of images that precedes it, it may be said, admits of no such defence. I am not so sure. No doubt some worshippers read them quite literally. But it may be questioned whether the sheer quantity does not encourage the worshipper to go beyond any particular item, and so perhaps prepare for the revelation in the *garbha griha*. Other deities, for example, often appear, only to be

[19] 'Grace' is actually the term employed by Dehijia, *Indian Art*, 137.

[20] For such ceremonies, which can include ingestation and taking items home, Blurton, *Hindu Art*, 73–4.

[21] As at Whithorn and Hexham, discussed in Ch. 4.

[22] Even where this is not so, mystery rather than naïve realism can still be the result, as in the Vishnu shrine at Bhubaneshwar; Stierlin, *Hindu India*, 137.

[23] *Vishnu Samhita* 29, 55–7; quoted in Dehejia, *Indian Art*, 137.

subordinated to the temple's principal god, while the mythological dimension is often so obvious as to demand a deeper reading. Multiple limbs and heads can scarcely be meant literally, while the taut bodies of the gods suggest not merely certain canons of physical beauty but also the power that lies within. 'Resilient with the sap of life', 'weightless in appearance', 'always in movement even when they appear to stand still', and with 'a silent radiance' is how one commentator describes their impact.[24]

It is the highly erotic imagery in some of the northern temples, though, that usually gives Western religious sentiment most offence.[25] Probably there is no single explanation for it. Perhaps in origin they were apotropaic signs of divine energy,[26] but almost inevitably their orgiastic extremes now force a different reading, and interpretations that speak of them as symbols of union with the divine have become quite common.[27] One of the *Upanishads* declares: 'Just as a man closely entwined with the woman he desires no longer distinguishes the outside from the inside, so the man who embraces the divine no longer distinguishes between outside and inside.'[28] Quoting this text, one Western commentator observes that such iconography can serve a dual function: in drawing into worship those not otherwise inclined and in challenging the priorities of those already there.[29] In saying this my point is not to defend all the imagery involved in major Hindu temples or its associated practices but to advocate a more sympathetic reading, one in which the Christian goes beyond the initial strangeness and acknowledges

[24] So Kramrisch, *Hindu Temple*, 306–8. She suggests that the lightness and energy of a 16-year-old is deliberately chosen to suggest ageless, other-worldly powers.

[25] The most famous are at Khajuraho.

[26] Mitchell speaks of 'ornamentation imbued with magical powers' as 'the only convincing explanation': *Hindu Temple*, 76.

[27] Cf. Dehejia, *Indian Art*, 166. Erotic imagery (as well as imagery of drunkenness) is also quite common among Muslim Sufi mystics, while within Christianity the case of Teresa of Avila's famous vision is of course also well known, not to mention more directly parallel medieval statuary. For one attempt to wrestle with the significance of the latter in 11th- and 12th-c. France, C. Bougoux, *Petite grammaire de l'obscène: églises du Duché d'Aquitaine* (Bordeaux: Bellus éditions, 1992).

[28] *Brihadaranyaka Upanishad*, 4. 3. 21.

[29] A. Daniélou, *The Hindu Temple: Deification of Eroticism* (Rochester, Vt.: Inner Traditions, 2001), 74–121 esp. 86, 119–21.

a divine generosity that is likely, sometimes at least, to make itself known through such material means.

It is one of those strange coincidences of history that Hinduism and Buddhism were moving towards a more iconic form of religious practice just as the Judaeo-Christian tradition was doing likewise.[30] It is thus quite untrue that imagistic ways of thinking about the divine are necessarily more primitive. Indeed, on the Indian subcontinent there were those who wished to reverse the argument, and speak of a need to move beyond words into the contemplation of images.[31] Despite its incarnational doctrine, Christianity has often strongly resisted that way of thinking, but in part that seems to me because it has sometimes operated with a rather naïve understanding of word. For, if images can, of course, at times be idolatrous, so too can a religion's treatment of its sacred words. Indeed, if the problem with the image is that it can be subject to manipulation because it appears to say too little, words contain the opposite temptation, to control the divine by supposing that all that it has to say is now within one's grasp, and indeed the imposition of creed or morality, however well motivated, points to just such a difficulty. That is an issue I want to pursue in more detail in this volume's sequel, when I shall consider the sacramentality of word. In so far as Western theologians engage with the East, the tendency still is to treat primarily of its intellectual debates, such as that between rival understandings of divinity in Shankara at the turn of the eighth century and Ramanuja in the twelfth.[32] Such an approach, however, merely reinforces Christianity's apparent logocentrism, So what I would like to stress here once more is that notion of *darshan*, of being seen by, as well as seeing, the divine.

[30] The problem of evidence means that this claim can be meant only very roughly—within a couple centuries or so. Buddha was certainly not depicted in early Buddhist art: R. C. Craven, *Indian Art* (London: Thames & Hudson, 1976), 40. Increasingly it looks as though Judaism also went through a more imagist period—at least to judge by the synagogue at Dura Europos (3rd c. AD) and the floors of synagogues from within Israel itself (discussed briefly in Ch. 5).

[31] As in the writings of the 9th-c. poet-saint, Manikkavacakar. For the contrast with Aquinas, R. H. Davis, *Lives of Indian Images* (Princeton: Princeton University Press, 1997), 32–3.

[32] The latter supported something approaching Western monotheism, the former a form of monism. Some scholars place Shankara a century later: 788–820 CE.

Even those unwilling to enter Hindu temples can appreciate something of the beauty of Hindu images in modern Western museums, but it is important to stress that such an aesthetic appreciation is still at a considerable remove from anything like the religious experience that was once intended to be mediated through them. Aesthetic perception is still altogether too active, and has nothing really of the receptivity that enables the seeker after the divine to experience the image as translucent, as bringer of a graced presence.[33] This is not to say that the image will necessarily function like this. Inevitably, many images have been abused, sometimes in ways not unlike their nearest Christian counterparts, as when they have become instruments of political power or, in more modern times, of nationalism.[34] But the more spiritual possibility remains even in such circumstances.

Islam's Indirect Pursuit of Connectedness

Islam, it has been suggested, only developed a more hostile attitude to images once it had come face to face with the alluring possibilities that Christianity offered.[35] Certainly, in more recent times Protestantism has retreated from its more extreme suspicions, in part because it has finally seen the Reformation's response to Catholic imagery to have been an absurd overreaction. Yet the suspicions remain. In turning, therefore, now to Muslim architecture what I want to explore is the extent to which (again, despite parodies in the West) Islam was in fact less extreme than much of the Reformation, and indeed, though not ever opening itself up significantly to representation in art,[36] none the less allowed the

[33] For an excellent analysis of the contrast between the two types of experience, ibid. 15–50.

[34] In his later chapters Davis offers some examples of images being treated not unlike relics in the medieval West (51–87 esp. 59–62) and a fascinating account of the Indian government's attempt to recover a stolen image of Shiva only in its turn to lock it away (222–59).

[35] O. Grabar, *The Formation of Islamic Art* (New Haven: Yale University Press, 1987 edn.), 72–98 esp. 92–5.

[36] Though even here it did so more widely than is commonly appreciated. See further, T. W. Arnold, *Painting in Islam* (Oxford: Clarendon Press, 1928), esp. 1–40, 91–116 (his illus. include representations of Muhammad's life). For a sympathetic analysis from a practising Muslim, Mahnaz Shayesteh Far, *Shi'ah Artistic Elements in the Timurid and the Early Safavid Periods* (London: Book Extra, 1999).

possibility of God speaking through the design of its mosques, and that at a very deep level. Indeed, I want to suggest that in its architecture Islam became a sacramental religion almost despite itself.

Admittedly, some introductions to the study of the mosque continue to insist on a fundamental contrast with religions such as Catholic Christianity or Hinduism.[37] Just as Islamic law (*shariʿah*) covers all of life and makes no distinction between sacred and secular, so a mosque, we are told, is simply a building of convenience, with ritual washing an act of purification not a preparation to enter something holy. In favour of such a view is the Qurʾan's own insistence that one can pray anywhere, as also the fact that Muhammad adapted his house at Medina as the first mosque.[38] Armies on the move were entitled to mark out in the sand a mosque for the day, so to speak,[39] while, if later mosques were permanent, it was still that 'secular' pattern from Medina that was followed, with an open-air courtyard and adjoining hypostyle hall suitably adapted. Islam is, of course, a religion without sacraments or priesthood. Yet there remains much that can be said on the other side. In a moment I want to come to the crunch issue of ornament, but first some more general remarks on the nature of the mosque itself would seem appropriate.

In the Qurʾan there are only three uses of the word 'mosque' (*masjid*) applied to specific buildings, two of which refer to what at the time were sacred locations under the control of other faiths, the Temple mount in Jerusalem (under Christian control) and the Kaʿba (the principal polytheistic shrine of Muhammad's own tribe, the Qaraysh).[40] Once emptied of its cult objects, the Kaʿba was to become Islam's holiest shrine, and intriguingly veneration on the hajj consists in its circumambulation much as the

[37] Cf. M. Frishman, 'Islam and the Form of the Mosque', in M. Frishman and Hasan Uddin Khan (eds.), *The Mosque* (London: Thames & Hudson, 1994), 17–41 esp. 30–2.

[38] The notion, though, that its role as a house remained primary has been challenged: e.g. by R. Hillenbrand, *Islamic Architecture* (Edinburgh: Edinburgh University Press, 1994), 39–42 esp. 40. Note also his rejection of the notion that mosques are not regarded as sacred: 32.

[39] For the practice, G. Michell (ed.), *Architecture of the Islamic World* (London: Thames & Hudson, 1978), 33.

[40] So D. Kuban in Frishman and Khan, *The Mosque*, 77.

Hindu would do, though of course without any images to focus one's attention. Muhammad decreed that all mosques must be orientated towards the Ka'ba and so this is indicated by one wall (the *qibla*) being marked out as facing that direction, with an alcove arch (the *mihrab*) as its centre. To its right in larger mosques is the *minbar* or pulpit from which the Friday sermon (the *khutba*) is delivered.[41] Nearby, in the most important, will be found the *maqsura* or enclosed space for the ruling sultan or governor, while a little distant will be the *dikka* or raised platform for a cantor to direct the responses to the prayers that the iman leads from the mihrab. If these are the only obvious elements inside, outside in the large courtyard (*sahn*) there will be a fountain or pool for ablutions, while leading off this courtyard there may well be other halls (*iwans*) and buildings.[42] Among the principal purposes of such complexes in the past have been education and medicine, though often long before modernity these had migrated to become entirely separate buildings.[43]

In the case of Sinan, the Ottoman empire's most famous archi-tect, the exterior of the building makes as much of an impression as does the interior.[44] But partly because of the narrow streets of the Arab world many mosques make an impact only once one is within their enclosure.[45] The major exception is, of course, the minaret, which can be seen from afar. The minaret is itself an interesting test-case of whether purely practical considerations do really govern the building and functioning of the typical mosque. A voice calling to prayer from any tower over fifty feet is likely to be inaudible, and yet some minarets stretch a couple of hundred feet or more into the

[41] Such larger mosques are known as Friday mosques or *jami*.

[42] One of the distinguishing features of Yemeni mosques is their large pools, forbidden to some Muslims because of the absence of running water: Frishman and Kahn, *The Mosque*, 99.

[43] As in *madrasas* or educational institutions and the *khanqahs* or monasteries for Sufis, usually modelled on military *ribats* or hostels: R. Yeomans, *The Story of Islamic Architecture* (New York: New York University Press, 1999), 22–3.

[44] Tourists in Istanbul these days are usually most familiar with the Blue Mosque, near Hagia Sophia. But the work of Sinan (d. 1587) at Süleymaniye mosque in Istanbul and at the Selmiye mosque in Edirne is really more impressive. Sinan was a Janissary, and so born a Christian.

[45] E. J. Grube opens his article on, 'What is Islamic Architecture?' by speaking of its 'main and dominant form' as 'hidden architecture': see Michell, *Architecture of the Islamic World*, 11–14 esp. 11.

sky.[46] Significantly, of the three words in common use, only one directs attention to the call to prayer, and there seems little doubt that the minaret's primary value has been as a symbol, if not of dominance over other religions, at least as a challenging presence.[47] But such symbolic weight scarcely amounts to the same thing as sacramentality, and so it is to the interior of the building that we must turn if more is to be said on this matter. It has been suggested that early ornamentation at the *qibla* end of the mosque stemmed largely from the desire to stress princely power. The central arched aisle would enhance the arrival of the ruler, while a dome over the mihrab would stress his presence in the vicinity.[48] That may well be true, but, whatever their origins, different explanations eventually prevailed, and the regal connection was forgotten. Cordoba provides an early example of a sort of chapel being formed from the mihrab, while in Iranian four-*iwan* mosques a domed shrine is the norm.[49] So it is important to speak of development, though of course periodically reforming movements arise that seek a return to a perceived earlier simplicity. The resultant exclusive stress on divine transcendence, though, must inevitably also threaten many other aspects of later Islam: much of the poetry of Sufi mystics, for instance, or the elaborate mausolea that now exist over so much of the Muslim world and celebrate a continuing role for the dead.[50]

Such adornment could be interpreted as merely incidental aesthetics, and it is true that no records survive, as with Christianity or Hinduism, of texts that suggest a deeper motivation on the part of

[46] The tallest minaret in Cairo is that belonging to the Sultan Hasan mosque at 280 ft.

[47] Two more common words have as their root the notions of light and cell: Hillenbrand, *Islamic Architecture*, 132–3. The philosopher/theologian al Ghazal in fact retreated to a minaret, while the reference to light probably alludes to the role of the minaret as a witness to the faith.

[48] Ibid. 14–16. Hillenbrand himself draws attention to the move in the opposite direction with the mihrab 'as a shrine for divine illumination': 17; cf. 26, 128.

[49] For plan of the mosque at Cordoba, Frishman and Khan, *The Mosque*, 104; for a plan of the famous Friday mosque at Isfahan, Yeomans, *The Story*, 142.

[50] Hadith record Muhammad's reluctance to have his grave marked in any special way. Although many mausolea witness to the self-vanity of rulers, their role in invoking the *baraka* or blessing of Muslim saints should not be forgotten, and thus the intention to evoke a sense of divine immanence. Although characteristically Shi'i, they are also found in Sunni Islam, as in Saladin's Shafi'i tomb. See further, Yeomans, *The Story*, 116; for Sultan Hasan's possibly blasphemous tomb: 126–8.

Muslim architects. Yet the more we investigate, the more I suggest we come close to notions of the sacramental. This is perhaps clearest on Islam's margins. In sub-Saharan Africa, for instance, the approach to mosques alludes to the presence of the ancestors, and indeed the measurements of one is actually based on the Ka'ba, suggesting that the mosque itself functions as a kind of *axis mundi*.[51] Similar notions are also to be found in Java, where the three-layered roofs of mosques clearly refer back to traditional beliefs about shrines linking heaven and earth.[52] This all might be dismissed as syncretism on the margins, were it not that such cultures are taking up in their own distinctive way currents that already run deep in mainline Islam. The presence of the Prophet, for example, is acknowledged in the convention that the iman must never stand on the top step of the minbar, while the ornament of the mihrab frequently alludes to the presence of God himself.

In the case of the minbar some hadith traditions imply that Muhammad at times sat to deliver his address, and so it is usual for the iman to place himself on the third step, and remain standing throughout his sermon. Among the finest early minbars to survive is one from Marrakesh that was made in Cordoba in the twelfth century. Despite the marked differences in theology between the Almoravid and Almohad dynasties, the latter preserved this fine piece of work that had been commissioned under their predecessors, although the decision was taken to destroy the rest of the mosque.[53] So some continuities remained. Inscribed on the minbar is the Throne verse from the Qur'an.[54] A natural inference to draw from this would be that the sermon links the congregation with the divine throne,[55] but also present may well be the notion that the ruler when he ascends the minbar himself mediates the divine will.

[51] L. Prussin, 'Sub-Saharan West Africa' in Frishman and Kahn, *The Mosque*, 181–93 esp. 183–6.

[52] H. O'Neill, 'South-East Asia', in Frishman and Kahn, ibid. 225–40 esp. 227–9. The exterior influence is Hindu.

[53] Almoravids had al-Ghazali's works burnt on the grounds that he failed to treat the Qur'an literally enough, whereas the Almohads were encouraged by his views: J. M. Bloom et al., *The Minbar from the Kutubiyya Mosque* (New York: Metropolitan Museum, 1998), 33–6, 48.

[54] And also the two subsequent verses: ibid. 19; Qur'an 2. 255–7. The key assertion in the verse is that Allah's 'throne extends over the heavens and the earth, and he feels no fatigue in guarding and preserving them'.

[55] One hadith speaks of angels listening to the sermon: Bloom, *The Minbar*, 62.

Certainly, the first Almohad ruler styled himself a Madhi or 'God's agent'.[56] Consisting of over six hundred units, the minbar's complex design can be read in a number of different ways, but overall it is suggestive of infinite complexity or richness yielding to an overall unity, and that might well be how a Muslim might wish to think of God, given the popularity of the Qur'an verse that gives Allah ninety-nine names.[57]

It is, however, the mihrab that most commonly suggests a divine agency or presence. When I turn later in the chapter to the question of gardens, I shall devote some attention to the long Muslim tradition of using the garden as an image of the believer's future destiny in Paradise. The notion is reflected across the Muslim world in places as different as the Court of Lions at the Alhambra and the wider setting of Shah Jahan's Taj Majal, but it is also sometimes the principal theme of the mihrab.[58] This is especially so where the image is transferred to prayer-rugs where stylized flowers interacting with the arch point to the believer's ultimate destiny.[59] More commonly, though, divine light is the dominant metaphor, and indeed the Light verse from the Qur'an is commonly quoted, as also sometimes on the lamps that hang before it.[60] More dramatic still, the Ka'ba is of course now empty of images, but lamps burn continuously within as a sign of divine presence.[61] Some have suggested that it is the image of Paradise that is intended in al-Walid's mosaics on his Damascus mosque, whereas for others

[56] Or, more literally, 'guided by Allah': ibid. 35.

[57] For alternative detectable patterns: ibid. 25, 90, 92; for overall unity: 54; for a richness that could not be fully absorbed in the time available (it was only brought out for the sermon): 27.

[58] For the Court of Lions, D. Clévenot, *Ornament and Decoration in Islamic Architecture* (London: Thames & Hudson, 200), 32, 36. The arch of the mihrab could easily suggest a garden gate, and hence the reason why in some prayer rugs it is surrounded by floral designs: S. S. Blair and J. M. Bloom (eds.), *Images of Paradise in Islamic Art* (Hanover, NH: Hood Museum of Art, 1991), 37, 77.

[59] For an excellent exposition from a practising Muslim, R. Yücel, *Allahs Kleine Wiese: Anatolische Teppiche und ihre Geschichten* (Munich: Südwest Verlag, 1987), esp. 22, 32 (with spring); 42 (with divine blue); 46, 56 (fly legend); 64, 66, 70, 112 (steps to heaven); 122 (battle with evil, cf. 60).

[60] Qur'an 24. 35, with its central metaphor of God as like a lamp burning olive oil.

[61] Its outer covering, the *kiswa*, has the *Shahada* (the Muslim confession of faith) inscribed on it: J. Vrieze (ed.), *Heavenly Art, Earthly Beauty: Art of Islam* (London: Lund Humphries, 2000), 77, 84.

they merely represent existing cities in harmony with Muslim rule.[62] Whatever the truth of the matter, the still more famous Dome of the Rock of his predecessor, al-Malik, does seem to suggest a gradual linkage with heaven as the white of the base of the exterior yields to blue and finally to the gold of the dome.[63] Likewise, the four minarets surrounding Sinan's Edirne mosque seem so slender that they must have been deliberately intended to evoke a lightness that pulls heaven and earth that little bit closer.

However, given the overwhelming orientation of mosques towards their interiors, it is to the interior that we must return to discover the full potential of Muslim religious architecture. What is most likely to strike the Western viewer is the way in which structure is constantly subverted or concealed. This can, of course, happen in the West also, but on the whole where load-bearing occurs it is clear, and indeed Modernism made it a principle that it should always be shown.[64] Yet nothing could be further from the mind of the typical Muslim architect. Domes internally, for example, are frequently lightened by *muqarna*s, a series of stalactites that seem to dissolve the structure into numerous small constituents.[65] There is also the constant distraction of pattern.[66] This can be in the building materials themselves: stone alternating with brick, or rows of bricks differently aligned, or some receded to create variety of light and shade.[67] Again, it may be a matter of more elaborate patterns based on geometric figures, calligraphy, or arabesque. Some have advocated purely psychological explanations such as the desire for a contrast to the desert, the reassurance of harmony in crowded and potentially tense living conditions, or else

---

[62] So R. Ettinghausen, *Arab Painting* (New York: Skira), 28.

[63] Until a recent donation by Jordan the dome was copper. Clévenot, though, thinks that the distinction between earth, sky, and the divine still holds, and talks of 'solid nature . . . visually transcended': 26.

[64] In Western medieval architecture buttresses were sometimes concealed, as at Durham. Often, though, part of the impressiveness of a cathedral can come from their exposure, as e.g. with Notre Dame in Paris.

[65] For some illustrations, Frishman and Kahn, *The Mosque*, 68–9; Clévenot, *Ornament and Decoration*, 196–201. The latter includes a secular borrowing for the Kashan bazaar.

[66] Distraction, that is, from structure. My argument, though, would be that overall such distraction enhances a sense of presence.

[67] Clévenot, *Ornament and Decoration*, 91–7. The Persian word for ornamental brickwork talks of a 'thousand weavings': *hazar baf.*

a natural Arab tendency to exaggerate.[68] Others have suggested that
the aim is to evoke the insubstantiality of the world, and so the
piercing of a veil, as it were.[69] That might well be one way to view
it. Another is to observe how the geometric patterns are built up
from relatively simple units, or in the case of the arabesque often
from stylized forms of nature, and so both might say something
about the Qur'an's own delight in the beauty of the world as a
divine creation.[70] One notes too that since God is for the Muslim
pre-eminently in his word, calligraphy can itself be a way of
asserting divine presence. The beauty of the script adds to the
sense of something vital being conveyed, a point powerfully
conveyed in the modern artwork of Ahmed Moustafa, whether
or not one subscribes to his particular theories of the underlying
geometric proportions of Arabic script.[71] Indeed, so strongly is the
power of the word felt to exist in its own right that, just as images in
medieval churches are sometimes found in places where they could
never have been viewed properly, so the same is true of some
calligraphy in mosques. It is almost as though to make the connection is enough on its own. That perhaps explains too why there can
be delight in apparently meaningless repetition. So, whereas in
Judaism God's name was never to be uttered, Islam can sometimes
produce designs in which the name 'Allah' recurs almost, as it were,
to infinity.[72]

[68] The alternatives given by R. Ettinghausen, 'The Taming of the Horror
Vacui in Islamic Art', *Proceedings of the American Philosophical Society* 123 (1979),
15–28 esp. 18–19. Despite adopting the third to explain pattern, E. Baer has no
difficulty acknowledging religious implications in the use of less abstract imagery:
Islamic Ornament (Edinburgh: Edinburgh University Press, 1998), 89–124, 126.

[69] Although rejecting Massignon's theory that such practice reflects Muslim
theories about the instability of the world, Clévenot does endorse the idea of the
image pointing to something more substantial beyond: *Ornament and Decoration*,
148, 208.

[70] For a detailed analysis of how complexity can be built out of simple
geometric forms (circle, triangle, square, and hexagon), K. Critchlow, *Islamic
Patterns* (London: Thames & Hudson, 1976). For the world reflecting God in
the Qur'an, e.g. 3. 190; 59. 1.

[71] He adopts the views of a 10th-c. geometrician, Ibn Muqla. Particularly impressive is his *Attributes of Divine Perfection* (1987), one of the principal exhibits at the St
Mungo Museum of Religious Art in Glasgow. For a discussion and examples of his
work, J. Theophilus, *An Alchemy of Letters* (Prestbury: Artizana, 1993).

[72] For an example in an 18th-c. silk textile from north Africa, Vrieze, *Heavenly
Art*, 95.

None of this is intended to suggest that Islam is as sacramental as Catholic Christianity or Hinduism, but it is to insist that it is considerably more so than some of the extremes that eventually emerged within Protestantism.[73] The mosque is usually seen as considerably more than just a convenient building. It can help mediate a sense of divine presence, and it does so, I think, in ways that could also be appreciated by the Christian. For, despite the common contention that Islam is essentially a transcendent religion, immanence is certainly also there, not only in the garden and the dance (treated in a subsequent volume) but also in those endlessly repeated patterns that speak of the richness of a God who can come as close as the nape of one's neck though without in any sense compromising his transcendence.[74] Perhaps the failure to see this arises because Islamic scholarship in the past has tended, as with Hinduism, to concentrate on its intellectual forms rather than on its phenomenology, but, as one recent study of the latter emphasizes, the notion of the sacred does indeed run deep in Islam, and not least in its attitude to nature and to the mosque.[75]

Despite its competing trends, modern Islam does, I suggest, implicitly acknowledge as much. If the design of today's mosques does at times appear simply to reflect the desire for the reassuringly familiar or even the attempt to reduce everything to a single pan-Islamic style,[76] there remain plenty of examples where symbolism is seriously considered and worked out in new ways. One can, for example, find the mihrab as a open Qur'an or even in the form of a window looking out onto a pool, or again water surrounding the

[73] There is even a limited parallel for Hindu attitudes to sexuality in the use within Islam of the image of drunkenness to explicate closeness to the divine: Blair and Bloom, *Images of Paradise*, 40, 60, 94.

[74] The nearest equivalent to the transcendent/immanent contrast within Christianity is *tanzi/tashhi*—God without comparison/the making of comparisons, both of which can be justified from the Qur'an. For the nape of the neck verse in the Qur'an, 50. 16; cf. 56. 85.

[75] Annemarie Schimmel's 1992 Gifford Lectures published as *Deciphering the Signs of God* (Edinburgh: Edinburgh University Press, 1994), 1–66. Among the most interesting are the treatment of thresholds and the use by calligraphers of soot from mosque lamps for their *beraka* (blessing): 50, 52.

[76] A major theme in R. Holod and H.-U Khan, *The Contemporary Mosque* (New York: Rizzoli, 1997), e.g. 13–14. Cf. comments on the Islamic Center in Washington in I. Serageldin and J. Steele, *Architecture of the Contemporary Mosque* (London: Academy Editions, 1996), 149.

mosque to suggest the presence of God as at creation, while minarets are invariably symbolic rather than practical.[77] Even movements in the opposite direction have met their match in strong countercurrents seeking some expression of the sacred in the people's midst. An obvious case in point is the Wahhabi movement in Saudi Arabia. Founded in the eighteenth century, it adopted an exclusivist interpretation of the doctrine of divine unity or *tawhid*,[78] and insisted upon a return to fundamentals that was seen as requiring opposition to funereal monuments, music, and minarets. But even in Saudi Arabia itself music is now regularly heard on the radio, Muhammad's burial-place at Medina has been enhanced, and minarets adorn (sometimes spectacularly) the mosques currently being built.[79] In nearby Kuwait, in rebuilding districts mosques were preserved as sacred buildings, even though sometimes there was now no one to use them.[80] Very occasionally Muslim scholars do themselves talk of the sacramental;[81] in such circumstances that seems to me exactly right.

One last thought is worth considering before we turn to gardens, and that is how the other obviously heavily transcendent religion, namely Judaism, measures up by comparison. In earlier chapters I have already indicated sacramental attitudes to the land and the Temple, though neither went unchallenged. As with Islam, the most plausible candidate, at least within Orthodox Judaism, might seem to be the divine words themselves and their mystic involvement with creation as perceived in the Kabbalah, a matter to which I will devote some attention on another occasion.[82] Here, though,

---

[77] For the open Qur'an at Islamabad, Holod and Khan, *Contemporary Mosque*, 79; for the window in the Parliamentary mosque at Istanbul: 101–3; for the use of water to refer to Sura 11. 7 at Casablanca and Khartoum: 55–6, 125.

[78] The shahada ('There is no god except Allah') can be read inclusively when the stress then falls on 'Allah' and the fact that nothing excludes his presence, or (with the Wahhabis) as focusing on 'no god' and so the danger of idolatry unless a distant transcendence is emphasized.

[79] The mosque at Medina now has numerous minarets as well as a modern, retractable roof: Serageldin and Steele, *Architecture of the Contemporary Mosque*, 25–37 esp. 25, 29.

[80] Frishman and Khan, *The Mosque*, 245. The practice is criticized by Oleg Grabar, but it would seem revealing about underlying attitudes.

[81] C. E. Padwick, *Muslim Devotions: A Study of Prayer Manuals in Common Use* (Oxford: Oneworld, 1996), 'the sacramental tendency': pp. xxiv–v.

[82] In the chapter on word in this volume's sequel.

I want simply to make a direct comparison with Islam and so consider briefly how synagogues have been treated as compared with mosques. Two recent books on the history of synagogue building, both written by Jews, may be used to illustrate some of the tensions that now exist within that particular tradition.

One from France laments the extent to which Judaism has allowed itself to be so heavily shaped by the history of the dominant Christian tradition of religious building.[83] Thus the author views with regret the way in which Gothic and Renaissance forms were so easily adopted. Even premodern attempts to create an independent tradition are criticized since these should really be seen in his view as no more than the imposition of alien forms, as with the adoption of the *Rundbogenstil* (or Romanesque) in the early nineteenth century, or the later advocacy of a Moorish style as though Judaism were essentially an oriental religion.[84] For him only the Temple has ever been truly sacred, and so it is only with the simplicity of Modernism that Judaism has at last managed to break free from a false aping of Christianity.[85] By contrast an English Jew sees 'symbiosis' as inevitable between religions in any culture.[86] So the Temple is itself acknowledged as dependent on its surrounding pagan neighbours, while the later history of borrowings is still seen as producing something distinctive and characteristically Jewish. Synagogues have two potential foci, the ark where the scrolls are stored (*aron hakodech*) and the *bimah* or preaching platform. Particularly in the Sephardic tradition the latter was centralized and sometimes given symbolic meaning as a result, but it is the former, as with the Muslim mihrab, to which most attention had been

---

[83] D. Jarrassé, *Synagogues* (Paris: Vilo International, 2001).

[84] *Rundbogenstil* was seen as less closely tied to Christianity, though some Jews did defend Gothic as the obviously religious form of architecture: ibid. 145–62 esp. 160; despite the beauty of some of the Moorish synagogues (170–204), Jarrassé blames the influence of the Masons and see the style as an implicit encouragement to racism: 168, 176.

[85] Ibid. 19, 268.

[86] H. A. Meek, *The Synagogue* (London: Phaidon, 1995). He talks of an 'Islamic symbiosis' in his discussion of synagogues in medieval Spain (100–19), while earlier he had acknowledged numerous pagan borrowings for the Temple both in building style and forms of worship (34, 41, 61–2). Even the customary Muslim way of referring to Muhammad is adopted (53).

devoted.[87] Sometimes the architectural form has been such that for the Christian the most immediate point of comparison may well be an elaborate reredos standing behind some familiar altar. Far, though, from invalidating the practice, what this suggests is a comparable strategy to suggest something subtly different, a strong sense of divine presence mediated through God's word.[88] Very occasionally, the symbolism of divine presence becomes wholly explicit, as in the synagogue at Rome where the *shekinah* is represented in the roof vault.[89] But as synagogues increasingly become adapted to wider community uses, particularly in the United States,[90] it does look as though Judaism is moving in the opposite direction from Islam, and that, ironically despite their two histories, it is now Islam that approaches more closely the traditional Christian attitude to the sacredness of its buildings.[91]

No doubt the factors explaining this change are manifold, not least perhaps the Holocaust and the resultant creation of the state of Israel, with the new emphasis this brought on the land as focus for so many Jewish hopes. But any attempt to assert complete independence of other faiths, while understandable, does seem to me to fly in the face of all the facts. As I noted earlier, in the East Hinduism turns out, surprisingly perhaps, to be in part a creation of the Buddhist revolt against the earlier Vedic religion with which modern Hinduism yet supposes itself more naturally allied. In a similar way in the West interactions and interdependency are there throughout history, not just for Judaism but for Islam and Christianity as well. So, for example, if some of the finest expressions of Muslim piety come from Iran, there seems little doubt that its architecture there owes something to the Zoroastrian building

[87] Maimonides was among those who found symbolic meaning in a centralized *bimah*: ibid. 154–5. For Muslim mihrab prayer rugs producing Jewish equivalents: 118–19.

[88] For some illus., ibid. 135 (Vittorio Veneto); 143 (Bevis Marks, London); 185 (Rome); 187 (Vienna).

[89] For illus. ibid. 170–1. Contrast Jarrassé's hesitant, almost embarrassed tone, *Synagogues*, 175.

[90] Welcomed by Jarrassé, ibid. 222–4.

[91] Khan stresses the move to a more exclusively sacred understanding in Islam, contrasting this with wider uses for the churches of today: Frishman and Khan, *The Mosque*, 267.

practices that preceded it.[92] Again, in India and further east the mosque took on many of the aspects of the native Hinduism, despite Islam's attempt to extirpate it. Indeed, some of the finest mosques come from syncretistic rulers.[93] Even the mihrab itself may have been borrowed from the Christian Copts.[94]

In all of this it would be all too easy for Christianity to see itself as providentially immune from such patterns, but its first full-scale churches were of course based on pagan basilicas, and, as we saw in an earlier chapter, there were many attempts to imitate the Jerusalem Temple, whether directly or in its now Muslim form as the Dome of the Rock. Even if it were possible, though, to speak more generally of a wholly independent standing, that would, I suggest, be a sign of weakness and not of strength. For, if to return one last time to the theme of Muslim ornament, whereas images in Christian churches put an almost exclusive stress on the presence of God in the higher elements of creation, Islam at least maintained fully and without qualification the insight that every aspect of creation, however humble or simple, can reflect the divine reality. In this respect at least, Islam thus preserved a richer stream of sacramentality than Christianity itself.

Besides architecture, another way in which Islam manifested those same views was in its treatment of gardens, and it is to gardens that I next turn. Though definitive evidence is lacking, here too, as we shall see, Christianity's debt to Islam is almost certain.

Gardens of Revelation

Here also there is something, I believe, to learn from other religions. For, if in a Christian context the attachment of religious significance to gardens is somewhat subdued, the same cannot be said for attitudes within Islam or Zen Buddhism. Islam's influence

---

[92] For extensive use of domes as one such candidate, see O'Kane in Frishman and Kahn, ibid. 119–21; for wider debts and continuities, A. U. Pope, *Persian Architecture* (London: Thames & Hudson, 1965), esp. 9–10, 78, 134–6.

[93] Some have portrayed the famous Mughal rulers, Akbar (d. 1605) and Shah Jahan (d. 1657, builder of the Taj Mahal) as highly unorthodox. For an example, see B. M. Alfieri, *Islamic Architecture of the Indian Subcontinent* (London: Laurence King, 2000), 203–25, 241–63 esp. 213–15, 252.

[94] Suggested by James Dickie in Mitchell, *Hindu Temple*, 33.

now lies almost wholly in the past, with the role it once exercised in encouraging the development of the *hortus conclusus* tradition in late-medieval Christianity. The impact of Zen, however, has been felt only relatively recently. It is one obvious sign of contemporary longing for affirmation that gardens do indeed express spiritual values.[95] That such values are at times also viewed in sacramental terms would seem confirmed by the popularity of D. F. Gurney's poem *God's Garden*.

> The kiss of the sun for pardon,
> The song of the birds for mirth,
> One is nearer God's heart in a garden
> Than anywhere else on earth.[96]

Although the last two lines are often quoted as an excuse for not coming to church, the first two given here do indicate that something rather more is at stake. In *Greenfingers*, a recent film based on a true incident, appeal is made to a related thought from George Bernard Shaw, but Gurney's 'kiss of the sun' as 'pardon' is none the less well illustrated.[97] A resentful and hardened criminal is initially softened by being asked to care for his dying cell-mate's pot plant, and then transformed as he acquires a small plot to care for in the open prison to which he is transferred. Cast indifferently on the ground, a packet of seeds from the dying man blossoms under the sun's rays. The result is that the violent assault that had led to his brother's death is not allowed to have the last word. There is in fact more in the Western tradition to justify such attitudes than may initially appear. But before exploring afresh such possibilities, I want first to look at where there can be no doubt, in Islam and Zen.

Islam like Christianity inherited from Judaism the image of Eden for human origins but, unlike Christianity, it was to retain that

[95] Echoed also in contemporary music such as Steve Millington's CD, *Zen Garden*. The mood is markedly differently from the exotic 1929 classic, 'In a Chinese Temple Garden', though another popular composition of Albert Ketèlbey's comes close, his 1930s 'In a Monastery Garden'.

[96] Dorothy Frances Gurney died in 1932. This is the penultimate verse of a five-stanza poem that begins with the Garden of Eden, 'The Lord God planted a garden . . . ' Full text at www.theotherpages.org/poems/gurneyol.html, accessed 30 Jan. 2004.

[97] A British film starring Clive Owen and Helen Mirren (2000). The prison governor justifies allowing gardening with the following quotation: 'the best place to seek for God is in a garden; you can dig for him there'.

image also for humanity's ultimate destiny.[98] For, although there are some continuing allusions in the Book of Revelation, the primary metaphor has clearly switched to the city, and that is reflected in all those hymns that speak of a heavenly Jerusalem.[99] By contrast, repeatedly in the Qur'an that future promise is spoken of in terms of a garden. Not surprisingly in the baking heat of Arabia, water too is a key element. Sometimes the image is of a fountain, and that has been used to give additional symbolic resonance to fountains in the courtyards of mosques.[100] More commonly, though, the talk is of rivers, occasionally flowing underground but also depicted running above ground.[101] As with Eden, sometimes it is also clear that four are envisaged, and indeed there is a particularly fine passage that identifies each with its own distinctive taste and pleasure (water, milk, wine, and honey).[102] Subsequent tradition went on to isolate various terms from other passages to create four corresponding names: Kafur, al-Kawthar, Salsabil, and Tasnim.

Although the Persian word from which we get the English 'Paradise' is found only occasionally in the Qur'an,[103] the frequency with which the Qur'an uses the image of gardens to convey ultimate human destiny meant that such an allusion would never be far distant when actual gardens were being created in the Muslim world. Once widely distributed in their classic form, they are now most easily accessible for Westerners in southern Spain. If there is some dispute about the purity of the design in Seville, there seems little doubt about the two examples to be found in Granada.[104] In

---

[98] That may explain why some Muslim commentators are prepared to speak of the first Eden as also an other than earthly reality: A. Y. Ali (ed.), *The Holy Qur'an* (Leicester: Islamic Foundation, 1975), 25 n. 50

[99] For continuing garden elements: Rev. 2: 7; 22: 1–2; cf. Luke 23: 43; 2 Cor. 12: 3.

[100] e.g. Qur'an 15. 45.

[101] For beneath ground: ibid. 4. 57; 9. 72; 22. 23. It has been suggested that the imagery may be derived from the aquafers running in small quantities deep beneath the Arabian peninsula: C. Glassé, *Concise Encyclopaedia of Islam*, 2nd edn. (London: Stacey International, 1991), 206–7.

[102] Qur'an 47. 15.

[103] The main word used is al-Janna. Persian, though, did exert another sort of influence, in the word that came commonly to be used for gardens divided into four parts: *shahar-bagh.*

[104] For illus. and discussions of the gardens at Granada, E. Kluckert, *European Garden Design* (Cologne: Könemann, 2000), 32–9. For his critique of Seville: 39.

the Alhambra's Court of Myrtles a great pool of water dominates with passages only round the side and the garden as whole surrounded by a hedge of myrtles. More common is the pattern (as in the Court of Lions and at the Generalife) where streams of water in effect take over from paths in dividing the garden into its various components. The purest reference to Paradise, though, would be where the garden is divided by such streams into four equal quadrants.[105] Although now a normal thoroughfare, to this day the main street of Isfahan is known as Chahar Bagh, reflecting the fact that it was originally laid out as a watercourse with four gardens.[106] It is also a tradition that was carried to Muslim India under Moghul rule, and indeed it was there that the most famous surviving example was to be created, the Taj Mahal.[107] Shah Jahan's work in honouring his wife continued a practice that had begun at Kabul with his distant ancestor, the Emperor Babur.[108]

What happened much earlier in the Christian kingdom of Sicily suggests borrowings from Islam that were to produce their impact on the medieval cloister but, intriguingly, already here water is less central, as fountains replace streams and indeed are often placed off-centre.[109] There is still the division into four, but the allusion now seems to be to the cross rather than to Paradise. The monk was thus assigned a less life-affirming message; indeed, he was exhorted to follow a hard path of self-discipline and suffering. Put at its starkest, paths of feet-weary toil now replace refreshing streams as the central image of divine involvement with humanity.[110] I have already had occasion in this chapter to challenge the image of Islam as a wholly transcendent religion. Here too, something quite different seems indicated, not only in the actual creation of

[105] As in the 12th-c. Crucero at Seville, ibid. 34; or in a 16th-c. Mogul painting, F. Pizzoni, *The Garden: A History in Landscape and Art* (New York: Rizzoli, 1997), 13.

[106] The work of Shah Abbas I in 1596–7. For further details, http://isfahan.anglia.ac.uk, accessed 30 Jan. 2004.

[107] P. Hobhouse, *Plants in Garden History* (London: Pavilion, 1992), 41–67 esp. 45, 65, 66. For a late pagan example of the same division, the 7th-c. Persian Spring Carpet of Chosroes, ibid. 20.

[108] Jahan's wife died in 1631. Babur's work at Kabul dates from the beginning of the 16th c., but was preserved in the illustrated *Baburnama* or 'Book of Babur'.

[109] Pizzoni, *The Garden*, 11, 18–19.

[110] 'Rivers of Paradise' replaced by 'paths of an instrument of torture': so A. Maurières and E. Ossart, *Paradise Gardens* (Paris: éditions du Chêne, 2000), 15.

gardens but also in the imagery that was to accrue from them. Particularly in the Sufi tradition a lively sense of God being reflected in nature was to be the result. The Persian poet Jami (d. 1492), for instance, declares that 'a beautiful creature is merely a single blossom from the vast garden of God',[111] while in Attar's tale known as *The Conference of the Birds* the duck is made to heap such rich praise on the meaning and value of water that it seems entirely natural that he should declare: 'Every hour I perform the customary ablutions, and then spread up the water the carpet of prayer.'[112] Little wonder, then, that attempts have been made of late to appropriate this rich symbolic potential for the West.[113] Rightly, though, it is not done in a way that simply copies the past. Although the quadrants are still found, new plants and ideas have been introduced, but still with the aim of evoking spiritual values.

Change is also evident in the long evolution of Japanese gardens. Japan has been profoundly influenced by its larger neighbour to the west, and this is seen in significantly different types of impact from China at some key moments in this development.[114] Shintoism, Japan's native religion, seems in origin to have been a form of animism, perhaps inevitable in a land of such sharp contrasts of mountains, valleys, and lakes. Some have drawn parallels with the standing stones of places such as Callanish in the Western Isles,[115] but the idea of rocks as alive with spirits was to be supplemented by Chinese geomancy, and so gardens were created to reflect on a smaller scale (and so influence) the surrounding patterns of the landscape on which the people's livelihood depended.[116] Pure Land Buddhism is different again. Here the thought is that one's ultimate destiny can be trusted to the Lord Buddha, Amida, who reigns over an ideal island kingdom in the west where the dead can

[111] J. Fadiman and R. Frager (eds.), *Essential Sufism* (San Francisco: Harper-Collins, 1997), 74.

[112] F. U. Attar, *The Conference of the Birds* (London: Continuum, 2000 edn.), 31. Also Persian, Attar died in 1229.

[113] As in Maurières and Ossart's *Paradise Gardens*, where three types for contemporary imitation are proposed (*bustan*, *gulistan*, and *riyad*—roughly, orchard, pleasure, and courtyard). For a strict copying: 16–17; for why change is inevitable, with so many different plants now available: e.g. 45, 98, 121.

[114] For an excellent overall history, G. Nitschke, *Japanese Gardens* (Cologne: Taschen, 1999).

[115] P. Cave, *Creating Japanese Gardens* (London: Aurum Press, 1993), 92–3.

[116] Nitschke, *Japanese Gardens*, 19, 32–7.

be brought once more to life. The role of water and islands is thus used to evoke trust in that promise, however uncertain the present may seem.[117] There was also much later influence from Confucianism in the creation of the tea ceremony and its accompanying gardens.[118] It is however the influence of Zen that is best known and which had originated several centuries earlier.

Zen likes to trace its origins to Bodhidharma, an Indian Buddhist monk of the sixth century AD, but, historically, we can only be absolutely sure of much later developments, and in particular its division into two schools, the Rinzai dating from the twelfth century and the Soto from the thirteenth, which then migrated from China to Japan.[119] Rinzai tends to place most emphasis on *koans* (paradoxical stories explored with the help of a master), while for Soto what matters is meditative techniques.[120] It is the meditative element in the latter that connects most naturally with the role of gardens. Ironically, the precise meaning of Japan's most famous surviving example (Ryoan-ji) is now no longer clear, and one adapted from the Pure Lands tradition (Saiho-ji) is thought easier to comprehend.[121] But the general aim of Zen's pattern of dry gardens is not hard to understand: it is to enable the mind to reduce itself to essentials, an objective that can also be seen in the way in which houses are treated. If rocks suggest the permanency of the landscape, ripples in the sand evoke movement of lake and sea, as also do dry steams or waterfalls created out of pebbles.[122] For the

[117] Ibid. 46–8; Cave, *Creating Japanese Gardens*, 34–45.

[118] Although reflecting the influence of Confucianism, it was actually a Zen monk, Murata Shuko (d. 1502), who bought the practice from China: Nitschke, *Japanese Gardens*, 115–17, 146–55.

[119] Zen is in fact how its Chinese name of Ch'an is pronounced. Some, though, suggest mediation through Korea.

[120] Rinzai also speaks of 'sudden' enlightenment, whereas Soto sees the process as gradual.

[121] S. Addiss, *How to Look at Japanese Art* (New York, Abrams, 1996), 119–23. The latter (also known as the Moss Temple) is now introduced by monks encouraging visitors to participate in preparatory mantras. For Ryoan-ji, illustrations, and uncertainties about its meaning, K. Seike, M. Kudo, and D. H. Engel, *A Japanese Touch for Your Garden* (Tokyo: Kodansha International, 1980), 26, 42; Cave, *Creating Japanese Gardens*, 54–5.

[122] For some good examples of dry waterfalls, Nitschke, *Japanese Gardens*, 112, 134. Note that 'sand gardens' are common shorthand, not for the use of sand as such but rather crushed granite or gravel: Cave, *Creating Japanese Gardens*, 106–7: Seike, Kudo, and Engel, *Japanese Touch*, 47.

Western mind impermanence and eternity are seen as opposed, whereas in these gardens everything becomes interrelated, with the contemplative mind itself seen as part of this flow, a 'no-self' in this nothingness that is reality.

To begin with, Western gardeners showed more interest in the delicate plants that might be suitable for such rock gardens rather than in more austere layouts.[123] That is perhaps scarcely surprising given how different the metaphysics is from Western thought. Any detailed discussion of that metaphysics is precluded here. Two related issues, though, do demand consideration: the implications of such practices and the compatibility or otherwise with theistic, sacramental religion. What I mean by the former is the need to correct a common misunderstanding in the West, which presumes that talk of a no-self and so forth must entail an undervaluing of present reality. Nothing, it seems to me, could be further from the truth. Indeed, in some ways the net result is an increase in value for the immediate moment, since such gardens inevitably require constant re-creation, not least because of the havoc wind wreaks with the patterns in the sand. Rather, what is undermined is possessiveness. An intriguing example of the contrast with Western attitudes comes in how Japan's most famous painting has been read in the West, and its most probable actual meaning. A wave that seems almost alive in its fury has been interpreted as an expression of human desire for power, whereas the artist, Hokusai, almost certainly meant it to entail acceptance of our own place in the scheme of things, even if this should mean our elimination.[124] Painting and gardening have in fact strongly influenced one another.[125] What one notices in both is a strong focus on simplicity, something seen as an appropriate aim in home no less than in garden. Indeed, what one perhaps notices the most is the attempt to integrate both into a

[123] An interesting case is point is Reginald Farrer, the great expert on alpines who converted to Buddhism in 1907. For an unfavourable estimate of the extent of his commitment to his new religion, N. Shulman, *A Rage for Rock Gardening* (London: Short Books, 2002), 35–7, 83–5.

[124] For Herbert Read's interpretation of this 19th-c. painting contrasted with the artist's own likely views, Addiss, *How to Look*, 103–4. For humility before nature in Japan's other major 19th-c. artist (where human figures are used to reinforce the theme), I. Oka, *Hiroshige: Japan's Great Landscape Artist* (Tokyo: Kodansha International, 1992), esp. 12–13, 16–17, 36–7, 75.

[125] Sesshu (b. 1420) is an important early example of a painter who uses landscape to explore Zen themes: Nitschke, *Japanese Gardens*, 98–100.

single whole.[126] So, the use of light dividers and open-plan layouts means that any sharp distinction between house and garden tends to be dissolved, while one key feature of the home is the *tokonoma*, an alcove where a simple floral or twig arrangement, perhaps accompanied by a landscape or poem, becomes the main focus of the room. The Japanese convention, like that of Muslims and Hindus, of removing shoes before entering a home is rather more than a matter of mere cleanliness. 'Clean' and 'beautiful' are the same word in Japanese,[127] and so reverence for aesthetic simplicity seems to slide naturally into an expression of religious values.

The first Chinese Zen patriarch is alleged to have declared that what meditation discloses is 'a vast emptiness and nothing holy in it'.[128] That may well seem inimical to any notion of sacramentality, and this receive confirmation in Zen demotion of the value of images. Certainly, one needs to be cautious of attempts to reconcile Christianity and Zen.[129] If the aseity and independence of God are to be maintained over against all other forms of existence, then Zen's claim that ultimate reality lies beyond all such oppositions cannot be endorsed. Yet, that said, Zen gardens need not necessarily be experienced as such a dissolution. Indeed, perhaps more frequently, they suggest the oppositions and contradictions of this world losing some of their force in the face of a greater, all-encompassing reality. That more limited claim could surely not only be endorsed by Christians but also actually be encouraged as part of their own experience. Of course, Zen, unlike Pure Land Buddhism, would still want to resist the term 'sacramental' for such experience, precisely because like comparable terms such as 'holy' and 'sacred' it appears to exalt the merely provisional. Even so, Zen monks do find the provisional helpful, and are as worried by the secularization of their practices as would be proponents of a more

---

[126] For application to the home, D. Scott, *Easy-To-Use Zen* (London: Vega, 2002), 81–105 esp. 96.

[127] *Kirei* in Japanese, which can also apparently mean 'neat' and 'in good order': ibid. 102.

[128] Bodhidharma in the 6th c. AD; quoted in D. T. Suzuki, *An Introduction to Zen Buddhism* (London: Random House, 1991 edn.), 50. For the famous story of the patriarch Joshu's attitude to images: 53.

[129] For a valiant attempt, T. Merton, *Zen and the Birds of Appetite* (New York; New Directions, 1968). Suzuki, thinks, though, that Merton did not go far enough: *Introduction to Zen*, 133.

obviously sacramental religion.[130] So, if metaphysics defies agreement, it is not clear that practice does to the same degree.

In the case of Christianity gardens too have exercised a significant role throughout its history, but on the whole this has been more subdued than was the case with either Islam or Zen. Yet things might have been otherwise, given not only the presence of the Garden of Eden in the opening chapters of the Bible but also the prominence given to gardens in the last stages of Jesus' life: he is betrayed in a garden and because he is buried in another that becomes the site of his resurrection.[131] In and of itself that might have been enough to generate a rich representational tradition, but, though sermons benefited, there was little effect on gardening as such.[132] As I have already noted, the meaning of the cloister remained somewhat ambivalent, while in monastic rules it tended to be the practical utility of gardens that was stressed.[133] Perhaps the image of Eden was itself partly to blame. At any rate, to judge by Augustine, it encouraged an ideal of the 'gentleman gardener' rather than the joy of the challenge of cultivation for its own sake.[134] Still, there was the allusion to 'Paradise' at the west end of the church, and this did sometimes explicitly take the form of a worked garden.[135]

---

[130] For the importance of temple rituals, Suzuki, ibid. 118–32; for a critique of the adoption of Zen gardens by business concerns, Nitschke, *Japanese Gardens*, 226–33.

[131] Only John mentions the latter garden: 19: 41; 20: 15. The meaning could of course be primarily symbolic, whereas the Garden of Gethsemane appears in all four Gospels, and is, if anything, almost an anti-garden.

[132] For a fine example of such a sermon, cf. Lancelot Andrewes' for Easter Day, 1620; e.g. in M. Dorman (ed.), *The Sermons of Lancelot Andrewes* (Edinburgh: Pentland Press, 1993), ii. 145–56 esp. 152, 155.

[133] As in Pachomius' rule and in the expanded version of Benedict's used in the Middle Ages: M.-T. Haudebourg, *Les Jardins du moyen âge* (Paris: Perrin, 2001), 31. Cassiodorus has no hesitation in comparing an enclosed monastery to a desert: *Institutiones*, 28.

[134] Cf. C. Harrison, 'Augustine and the Art of Gardening', in R. N. Swanson (ed.), *The Use and Abuse of Time in Christian History* (London: Boydell, 2002), 13–33 esp. 14–15. It was the Fall that brought the weeds.

[135] As in French *parvis*, now used to refer to the church porch but originally a courtyard outside, as in the famous 9th-c. St Gall monastic plan, where it is labelled *paradisiacum* and almost certainly had flowers or plants in it: Kluckert, *European Garden Design*, 22.

Although seldom given practical application, the one major area of growth in Christianity's earlier history was in the notion of the *hortus conclusus*. Taking up the Song of Solomon, the Virgin Mary becomes presented as a garden that bears rich fruit:

> Hortus conclusus soror mea, sponsa,
> Hortus conclusus, fons signatus.
> Emissiones tuae paradisus malorum punicorum
> Cum pomorum fructibus, cypri cum nardo.[136]

Although the imagery is very much older than the corresponding secular imagery, it does seem likely it grew in importance as the latter flourished, with its own distinctive notion of the garden as a place of courtly love. The way in which Mary, for example, acquires the new name of Our Lady from about 1220 onwards suggests as much. The experience of Muslim gardens in Spain and during the Crusades also probably played its part.[137]

It would be quite wrong, however, to suppose that gardens ceased to be religiously significant with the arrival of Renaissance and Reformation. Of course, there was now increasing opportunity for self-glorification as gardens became more complex. That trend reached its apogee in the Baroque gardens of Versailles, but even there it is worth noting that Louis XIV chose to borrow religious imagery in order to make his point (that he was the glorious Sun-King), for the garden culminates in a marvellous sculptured fountain that takes the god Apollo as its theme.[138] Similarly, although the imposition of highly ordered structures at the Renaissance could be seen as purely strategic exercises in human control, in fact, as we saw in an earlier chapter with the closely paralleling patterns of architecture, such gardens were often interpreted as reflecting, or bringing out more clearly, the divine

---

[136] Song of Songs 4: 12–13 (Vulgate): 'A garden enclosed is my sister, my bride; a garden enclosed, a clear fountain. Your produce is a paradise of pomegranates with tree fruits and cypress fragrant oil' (my trans.).

[137] Haudebourg, *Les Jardins*, 56–62, 144–8; Kluckert, *European Garden Design*, 27–31. The latter is more hesitant, seeing the 13th-c. *Roman de la rose* as more of an interaction, and it is certainly true that categories would be less sharply contrasted than in our day.

[138] The famous *Apollo's Bath* by François Girardon. He and other gods also appear many times elsewhere: Kluckert, *European Garden Design*, 186–208 esp. 197–8.

order in creation.[139] Pope Julius II's more worldly motivation is thus less typical than may initially appear,[140] and indeed there are some fascinating examples of other major figures in the Church pursuing carefully articulated schemes of religious symbolism, especially once Mannerism and Baroque allowed a wider range of reference. Two conspicuous examples would be the Mannerist pilgrimage garden of Sacro Bosso at Bomarzo and the Baroque evocation of heaven in Cardinal Aldobrandini's Villa at Frascati.[141]

One part of Europe where Renaissance-style gardens became particularly popular was the Netherlands. In the Protestant north, in effect gardens became a major alternative to the discarded image. That influence came directly to England with William and Mary, but in fact was already established much earlier.[142] If Charles I's queen, Henrietta Maria, tried to revive Marian imagery through the masques of Inigo Jones, it was the king's opponent, Prynne, who spoke for most when he found the garden a substitute for the offensive imagery, conveying scriptural truth in a 'more sweete and lively wise | Then all the Pictures Papists can devise'. Moreover, since Christ 'here on earth did Gardens highly grace . . .

> Each Garden then we see, should still present
> Christ to our sight, mind, thoughts, with sweete content.

Admittedly, those words on their own could be taken to imply no more than that the garden acts as a reminder of the culminating events of Christ's life. But elsewhere Prynne leaves us in no doubt that what he has in mind is what I would call a sacramental intention, the bonding of heaven and earth. He speaks of:

---

[139] The most influential work of the time was by a Dominican friar, Francesco Colonna. In his *Hypnerotomachia* or *Dream of Poliphilus* the garden becomes an allegory of divine harmony: Pizzoni, *The Garden*, 35–6.

[140] In his creation of the Belvedere Gardens; so M. Woods, *Visions of Arcadia: European Gardens from Renaissance to Rococo* (London: Aurum, 1996), 24–5. But even with Julius one must not rush too quickly to judgement. Despite his conduct, he was apparently sincere in his religious beliefs: so C. Shaw, *Julius II: The Warrior Pope* (Oxford: Blackwell, 1993), 314–15.

[141] For the former, Pizzoni, *The Garden*, 70–1; Woods, *Visions*, 33; for the latter, Kluckert, *European Garden Design*, 154–6; Pizzoni, *The Garden*, 108–10, Woods, *Visions*, 58–62. The latter case well illustrates problems of interpretation. Kluckert makes the motivation unqualifiedly spiritual, Pizzoni essentially ecclesiastical, while Woods simply keeps to the practical.

[142] Pizzoni, *The Garden*, 122–7. The joint sovereigns had Hampton Court redesigned in the Dutch style.

> Sweete, heavenly Meditations which doe spring
> From Gardens, able to rap and inspire
> The coldest Muse, with coelestiall fire;
> You melt the flintiest Heart, and it advance
> Above the Spheares in a delightfull Trance.[143]

Nor was he by any means alone in his time. The more moderate Joseph Hall, Bishop of Exeter and then of Norwich, had warmly commended the use of gardens in his devotional works, while even the cynical Bacon had opened a famous essay by declaring that 'God Almighty first planted a garden . . . and a man shall ever see that when ages grow to civility and elegancy, men come to build stately sooner than to garden finely; as if gardening were the greater perfection.'[144] If, though, for him the fashionable knot gardens were 'but toys (you may see as good sights many times in tarts),' for others they were taken to have a clear religious meaning. Just as maze and labyrinth were assumed to offer two different accounts of the nature of our dependence on divine grace, so the intricate and apparently never-ending interlacing of the knot appeared to hint at our need for such grace in the first place.[145]

For some as yet unexplained reason the imagery of gardens disappeared from English art for over a century from 1640 to 1740.[146] When it returns, it is clearly with a new sort of garden in mind. Some see the eighteenth century as marking the decisive move away from detecting divine significance in the garden to using it as a means of reflecting on processes in the human mind, but, though no doubt partly true, more spiritual perspectives were certainly not in full-scale retreat.[147] An earlier chapter has already sought to highlight why the political and moral debate over land-scape gardening had an essentially religious character: different notions of providence and what that entailed were at stake. The

[143] Quoted in S. Stewart, *The Enclosed Garden: The Tradition and the Image in Seventeenth Century Poetry* (Madison: Wisconsin University Press, 1966), 116, 127.

[144] F. Bacon, *Essays* (London: Everyman, 1994), 118–22 esp. 118, 120.

[145] R. Jay, *Gardens of the Spirit* (Alresford: Godsfield, 1999), 105–19, esp. 108. The different theologies of maze and labyrinth are discussed in Ch. 4 above.

[146] R. Strong, *The Artist and the Garden* (New Haven: Yale University Press, 2000), 56, 246.

[147] For such an argument, J. D. Hunt, *The Figure in the Landscape: Poetry, Painting and Gardening during the Eighteenth Century* (Baltimore: Johns Hopkins University Press, 1976). To maintain its full force, though, he must sometimes deny the obvious meaning of texts, e.g. 102–3 (on Pope), 135 (on Thomson).

issues, though, can be illustrated as much from details as from general theory. Although advocates of the new style spoke of integration of estate and wider environment, clearly in some cases what took place was simply the subjugation of the latter by the former.[148] This one finds reflected not just in what happens to the contours of the landscape but also equally in any accompanying religious imagery. One might contrast, for example, the artificiality of hermitages (with 'hermits' sometimes employed for effect) with Renaissance Parnassus mounts where at least the owner was also expected to reflect as he surveyed the scene.[149] Again, it is from this period that there dates the portraiture convention that represents children as little gardeners, a practice that continued as late as the twentieth century with Rex Whistler's 1939 portrait of the present queen.[150] The irony is that the allusion was not to participation in any such activity but rather to the family's overall direction of garden and landscape plans. Contrast this with the earlier monastic tradition where often it is work itself that is valued (precisely because of its violation of class rules) rather than anything that comes from it, as a famous story related by Sulpicius Severus well indicates. The hermit Paul cultivated a vegetable garden, only each year to consign it to the flames before it could bear fruit.[151]

More recent theory has tried to return the garden to a more natural style, as in the work and writing of William Robinson and Gertrude Jekyll.[152] While the renewed interest in herbs and cottage gardens indicates some success in this direction, in some ways there is no going back. Whether through import or by breeding, there is

[148] Chatsworth was less extreme than Versailles; Studley Royal more accommodating than Chatsworth. For relevant illustrations, Pizzoni, *The Garden*, 131, 154–5.

[149] For an example of a hermitage from Stowe, ibid. 170. Parnassus mounts reflected the need to see better the divine order in the Renaissance garden; for further details, Woods, *Visions*, 76–81, cf. 71.

[150] For the influence of Rousseau on the practice and an illus. from Reynolds, Strong, *The Artist*, 82–3. For Queen Elizabeth so portrayed as a child, J. Brown, *The Pursuit of Paradise: A Social History of Gardens and Gardening* (London: Harper-Collins, 2000), 303.

[151] The story is used to good effect by Haudebourg, *Les Jardins*, 72–3. The point is that monks tended to come from the 'better' social classes, and so manual labour was a way of engendering humility.

[152] Robinson influenced Olmsted in his layout for Central Park, New York: Hobhouse, *Plants*, 286–7.

now a huge variety of plants easily accessible that were not available in earlier ages.[153] Here too religion has played its part. If returning Crusaders represent one form of contribution, the fact that the bishopric of London for a time extended to Virginia is another. Nor was even religious imagery constant in all of this. As Fra Angelico's *Annunciation* well illustrates, new plants could often quickly acquire relevant symbolic meaning.[154] Amid such change, the temptation is to try to catch hold of some certainties, but it is dangerous, I believe, to suppose one style more naturally religious than another. Rather, what matters is how they are applied. If Pope can give religious grounds why Renaissance formality is not acceptable, Constable can equally protest that what succeeds it is no better.[155] Newman goes one stage further and worries whether garden and nature alike may not sometimes function as a seductress. Of a visit to Devon he remarked, 'really I think that I should dissolve into essence of roses, or be attenuated into an echo, if lived here'.[156] But that is merely to acknowledge that all forms of religious experience can go wrong, including reflection on the Bible itself. The solution is rather to note underlying intentions, and these will, I believe, disclose a far more widely disseminated desire to use gardens to aid sacramental encounters than is currently recognized.

One reason for thinking this is the fact that serious academic interest in the history of gardens is in fact a very recent phenomenon.[157] The sadness is that this has not coincided with any major interest from theologians or the wider Church. If some major

---

[153] A repeated theme in Hobhouse, *Plants:* e.g., tulips from Turkey and tagetes from Mexico in the 16th c. (96–8, 104), and magnolia and box elder from North America in the 17th thanks to the ministrations of Henry Compton, Bishop of London (134).

[154] For the inclusion of carnations and a banana tree, ibid. 136, Haudebourg, *Les Jardins*, 105.

[155] For Pope, Hobhouse, *Plants*, 192; Strong, *The Artist*, 208. For Constable, Brown, *Pursuit of Paradise*, 220; Strong, *The Artist*, 273–4.

[156] *Letters and Diaries of John Henry Newman* (Oxford: Clarendon Press, 1979), ii. 342. Later in the same letter (7 July 1831) he goes even further: 'The exuberance of the grass and the foliage is oppressive, as if one had not room to breathe' (343). For a critique, Brown, *Pursuit of Paradise*, 78.

[157] Considerable impetus was given by the founding of the Garden Historical Society in 1965 and a major exhibition in 1979: Brown, *Pursuit of Paradise* 9–26; Strong, *The Artist*, 12.

modern figures (such as Jekyll) have been inspired by religious belief, many contemporary commentators speak of Christianity's own self-imposed irrelevance.[158] That jibe is not altogether unfair, for the issues are seldom discussed within the Church, far less academic theology. Yet they remain, not just as questions of historical interpretation but also pertinent to today's world. I want, therefore, to end this section by considering two contrasting approaches to the contemporary garden both of which have the potential to be sacramental and also the exact opposite. They well illustrate the need for the assessment of theory and application to go hand in hand. Without in any way discounting the importance of the ethical in what follows, my main focus here remains on the experiential, on the discovery of God in the garden.[159]

Given the present extensive popularity of the work of the French impressionists, a garden such as Giverny is likely to be the ideal for many. Although Monet was not himself a Christian, it is not hard to see how his approach might by adapted sacramentally, the richness of the garden being used to suggest the generosity of God, its careful balance of colours the interdependence of all creation. But there is another side. One cannot fail to note the firmly middle-class character of those set within the gardens and scenes Monet paints. Indeed, the novelist Émile Zola observes of one of the parks painted by him that 'the ladies on foot trailed their skirts languorously, as though they had not lifted a foot from the carpets of their drawing rooms'.[160] It all comes dangerously close to the desire for a garden plot as a status symbol rather than for what is inherent in nature itself.[161] Among the Impressionists it is perhaps only Pisarro who was entirely free from such attitudes in his love of the countryside

[158] For Jekyll's religious views, R. Bisgrove, 'Gertrude Jekyll: A Gardener Ahead of Her Time', in M. Tooley and P. Arnander (eds.), *Gertrude Jekyll* (London: Michaelmas, 1995), 146–52 esp. 150–2. For self-imposed irrelevance, e.g. Brown, *Pursuit of Paradise*, 80–1, 307 (contrasted with Zen).

[159] To say that the issues are purely ethical would be an example of the type of reductionism I have been resisting throughout this work. For an interesting attempt to produce a general ethics founded on the practice of gardening, M. Pollan, *Second Nature* (London: Bloomsbury, 1997), esp. 206–13.

[160] The *Parc Monceau* (1878); illustrated in J. Bumpus, *Impressionist Gardens* (London: Phaidon, 1990), no. 42 (cf. 16). The remarks come in Zola's *La Curée* (*The Quarry* of 1874).

[161] For similar worries about current English attitudes, Brown, *Pursuit of Paradise*, 266–7.

and more old-fashioned values. Indeed, despite his Jewish back
ground, it is he among the Impressionists who provides the neares
to a sacramental image: trees forming a Gothic arch are used to
endow the country garden before him with transcendent value.[16]

Quite different from Monet are the kinds of garden created by
some on the edges of modern society. So far from representing
social aspiration, it can sometimes be a way of asserting value and
identity over against an alienating environment, an assertion that i
often pursed in frankly religious terms. If building a boat from cast
off material in burnt-out Newark or trying to give colour to run
down Detroit in a gathered arrangement of its trash are scarcely
gardens in any orthodox sense, the declaration of trust in God
which they affirm parallels the bottle garden of a widow struggling
to look after two dying adult children in Simi Valley, California o
the creation of an alternative Chartres in broken plates and glas
near its more famous rival.[163] More conventional grottoes have
sometimes had a similar motivation.[164] Occasionally the local
church has been supportive; more commonly indifferent or even
hostile.[165] Yet the Church surely ignores such expressions at it
peril. It goes without saying that God is omnipresent but that doe
not mean that his presence can therefore be felt everywhere equally
As I have sought to argue throughout this book, foci help and, i
conventional gardens in all their variety are one such aid, the
discovery of value in the world's detritus is surely another. Indeed
a religion that has its central affirmation in the valuing of the
despised and neglected could scarcely say otherwise.[166] Here surely
is an exciting and vibrant possibility compared with the pseudo-
science of Feng Shui, to which I alluded in Chapter 1 and which

[162] In his *Wheelbarrow* of 1881: illus. in Bumpus, *Impresionist Gartens* no. 35 (cf
20).

[163] All these examples together with others are discussed in J. Beardsley, *Garden
of Revelation: Environments by Visionary Artists* (New York: Abbeyville, 1995). For
the four cases mentioned in my text: 174–9, 184–8, 154–61, 44–8. The last, known
as Picassiette ('Plate stealer') was acquired by the town of Chartres as a museum in
1981. Apart from Chartres many other things are represented, including Jerusalem

[164] Beardsley finds this in his chapter on grottoes: ibid. 101–31 e.g. 102–3.

[165] The ark venture is a rare exception. It was supported by the local Baptis
church despite strong opposition from the city council.

[166] As Raymond Isidore observed, 'hard work can turn into beauty ... I took
the things that other people throw away' (*Picassiette: Visitors' Guide*, 11).

unfortunately, seems, despite its shallowness, to tempt so many of our contemporaries.

Sport as Religious Metaphor

With its heavy commercialization modern sport might seem at the other extreme from gardens, and in many ways of course it is. But, like gardens, it operates within a bounded space or place (the venue), and, like gardens, it was, as we noticed in Chapter 1, once seen in essentially religious terms. Most of that ambience is probably now irrecoverable. None the less, I want to end this chapter by drawing attention to one feature that does suggest some continuities, not least because it opens up issues that I intend to explore further in the volume subsequent to this one. This is the role of sport as a religious metaphor in the modern cinema. As we shall see, whereas in ancient Greece sport reflected an immanent movement on the part of the divine, the focus is now in the main on transcendence. How that works out in practice is explored by considering a number of sports in turn.

I begin, however, with one sport where the spirituality is still largely immanent, perhaps not surprisingly so given its largely unchanged character across the centuries. Pick up any instruction book on the martial arts, and you are quite likely to find stress on how physical success is not achievable except where corresponding weight is also given to acquiring the right spiritual attitudes.[167] Of course, in part this equates with emphasis on the right mental attitudes, such as patience and spontaneity, but often this easily slides into a more explicitly religious dimension, not least because of the origins of such practices.[168] Zen Buddhists like to find a common source for all variants in Bodhidharma and his work at the Shaolin Temple in the sixth century AD. Whether transposed from

---

[167] Seen clearly in some of the traditional stories connected with the art: cf. P. Lewis (ed.), *Myths and Legends of the Martial Arts* (London: Prion, 1998), e.g. 5–8, 55–7, 95–8. The last (avoiding unnecessary conflict) reappears in the film *Enter the Dragon*.

[168] For an example, Wong Kiew Kit, *The Art of Shaolin Kung Fu* (London: Vermilion, 1996). Emphasis in earlier chapters on physical expertise yields to a discussion of mental attitudes (168–780) which in turn gives place to its deepest realization in appropriate religious perceptions (179–200).

this source to China's native religion of Taoism or having an independent origin, certainly now there are also distinctive variants that find their ultimate origins in the Taoist temple on Wudang Mountain.[169] These are essentially defensive systems and are widely practised in modern China. The Zen version migrated to Japan, and there it was to have a profound influence on the culture. So used is the West to defining Japanese militarism in terms of a ruthless and unquestioning obedience to the state that the more complex reality is usually ignored. Zen interacted extensively with Samurai behaviour, and produced in effect a new code known as Bushido. Although it did place an extraordinarily high value on obligation to social superiors, this did include notions of forgiveness and restraint in relation to equals and inferiors.[170] Indeed religious asceticism and warrior action sometimes went hand in hand, though more commonly perhaps the latter would eventually have given place to the former as the practitioner entered a new phase of life.[171] Where the link was not sequential was in the notion of grace. Grace in manners and deportment were seen as the clue to appropriate action in combat since 'gracefulness means economy of force'.[172] One Japanese commentator is even prepared to speak of the whole system as a *preparatio evangelica* that the Church in its mission unwisely ignored; the inevitable result was few converts.[173]

Whether matters are quite that simple is questionable, but it is intriguing to note that modern Japan has thrown up a version known as Aikido where there is no doubt that we must speak of a thoroughly spiritualized version of martial arts. The founder, Morihei Ueshiba, is treated by its practitioners as something of a saint. More relevant to note here is that Morihei did see the sport as a way of integrating with a spiritual world. His daily prayer and martial

---

[169] Explored in P. Brecher, *The Way of the Spiritual Warrior: Soft Style Martial Arts for Body, Mind & Spirit* (New York: Godsfield, 1998). Soft style places less emphasis on muscular tension than do karate and kung fu. Its most popular variant is Taijiquan (41–59). For the distinctive contribution of Taoism: 11–39.

[170] I. Nitobe, *Bushido: The Soul of Japan* (Boston: Tuttle, 1969), 77–8. For Old Testament treatment of Isaac compared with Samurai attitudes to benefactors: 84–8.

[171] For them operating together, note the 17th-c. classic by Miyamoto Musashi, *The Book of Five Rings* (Boston: Shambhala, 1993), pp. xvi–vii. He stresses the importance of an open mind (18) and the need to act slowly (41–2), as well as insisting that dance is an appropriate parallel for the warrior's rhythm (15).

[172] Nitobe, *Bushido*, 50–60 esp. 55–7.   [173] Ibid. pp. xiv, 179–81.

practice were alike concerned to align himself with, and deepen his experience of, the immanent variegated divine reality that constitutes Shinto belief, so much so in fact that one Western follower describes the martial techniques involved as 'really sacraments' while another talks of 'the martial art of prayer'.[174] Nor are such attitudes merely confined to distinctively or uniquely Japanese sports. Archery, for example is approached in such a different way that one commentator describes it as 'a religious ritual' that when pursued correctly gives access to 'the bottomless ground of Being' and an experience of 'being breathed' through as one performs the art.[175]

However, undoubtedly the version best known in the West is Chinese kung-fu, particularly as this has been popularized in the films of Bruce Lee and more recently Jackie Chan. Lee was already highly successful as a film star in his native Hong Kong even before *Fist of Fury, Enter the Dragon,* and *Way of the Dragon* introduced his own talents and the visual potential of martial arts generally to Western audiences.[176] Despite attempts to give him almost semi-divine status, his early death at 33 revealed a rather more complex and flawed individual.[177] One commentator, though, while conceding his arrogance, none the less powerfully highlights the source of his success. He could stand for all physically weak individuals who nevertheless have the potential to overcome apparently impossible odds.[178] Lee's most successful film, *Enter the Dragon,*

[174] J. Stevens, *The Secrets of Aikido* (Boston: Shambhala, 1997), 29, 121; the latter description comes from a Japanese follower, the former from Stevens himself. The comparison is more than merely superficial: water exercises a similar role (62–3), sound is treated in a manner not unlike the divine Word (17–19, 36, 45) and reverence towards an immanent divine presence is maintained throughout (28–9, 70–1, 88), with even the sword itself treated as a sacred element (74–5).

[175] E. Herringel, *Zen in the Art of Archery* (London: Penguin, 1985), esp. 14, 17, 36. The aim is a 'purposeless and egoless' activity (96).

[176] The first from 1972, the others from 1973. Though brought up in Hong Kong, he was actually born in San Francisco.

[177] Although in theory he died from what should have been a harmless headache cure, earlier drug abuse may also have been a factor: D. Miller, *The Tao of Bruce Lee* (London: Vintage, 200), 134–5, 137. The 1978 biopic *Bruce Lee: The Man, the Myth,* while conceding various criminal connections, ends by alluding to legends that he would reappear once more ten years after his 'supposed' death in 1973.

[178] The central point made by Miller who speaks of Lee's impact on 'millions of tiny twits like me' (157; cf. 15). He ends, though, by identifying Lee's unwillingness to admit limitations as the cause of his own downfall: 175.

makes only one passing allusion to Shaolin.[179] Although Chan's more recent films have been given conventional American settings, some have featured the Shaolin temple as their main focus.[180] In addition, some other recent box office successes have also placed monks at the centre of the story.[181]

More intriguing still, the Shaolin monks themselves have attempted to place Buddhism once more at the heart of this art.[182] A group recently embarked on a highly successful world tour which told the story of the monastery and also exhibited some of the more awe-inspiring results of their physical training, all performed with a statue of the Buddha in the background.[183] I have already mentioned the ability of the art to encapsulate the struggle of weaker against stronger and of good versus evil, but at their best what elements in the practice of the art and in films alike suggest is the integration of the individual into a more inclusive reality. Without exception the Shaolin monks, young and old, saw themselves as part of a wider co-operative project.[184] Zen speaks of ultimate reality as Buddha-nature. If film characters seldom get very far along this track, they are generally portrayed as less self-centred by the end of the film than they were at the beginning, concerned with more than purely personal values. Grace of movement is thus made to reflect a more widely graced world, and there despite so

[179] As he attacks the villain Han, he declares that he does so because Han has dishonoured 'his family and the Shaolin temple'.

[180] Enlivened by some good comic touches, a good example is *Spiritual Kung Fu* (1978) in which Chan plays a temple layabout who matures over the course of the film. An additional twist is provided when in the final scene it is disclosed that the most deep-seated corruption is to be found in the Abbot himself. More recent titles have included *Police Story* (series of 3), *Rumble in the Bronx*, and *Rush Hour* (series of 2).

[181] The popular *Crouching Tiger, Hidden Dragon* (2000) explored various conflicts, among them a warrior wishing to retire and torn between monastic meditation and marriage.

[182] The monastery now has about eighty monks, and twenty special schools in its neighbourhood, as well as two to three million visitors a year.

[183] In London the show was staged at the Apollo, Hammersmith, and the choreography directed by Darshan Singh Buller of the London Contemporary Dance Theatre. The results can be seen on video and DVD in *Shaolin: Wheel of Life*; this includes interviews with the cast.

[184] Sammo Hung's 1983 *Iron Fisted Monk* is a good example. Set against the historical conflict between the Shaolin Temple and the Manchu dynasty, it traces the tortuous road of a one young man to social and spiritual maturity.

many other contrasts one finds after all a connection with the values of the ancient Olympics that I considered in Chapter 1. Indeed, one writer does not hesitate to draw the ultimate aim closer to Christianity as well, when, despite the huge differences from Christian theology, he none the less speaks of a desire to 'dissolve myself in the infinite grace of God'.[185]

Boxing was an ancient sport and so it will be interesting to consider this case next, not least to see whether anything at all survives of ancient Western attitudes. Rome produced a more brutal version, but even this did not satisfy the circus crowds.[186] Thereafter boxing's fortunes fluctuated until, ironically, it was those returning from the Grand Tour who re-established its popularity in seventeenth-century England and thus led eventually to the formation of the Queensberry Rules in 1867 and so to the present most common form of the sport (though others continue to exist).[187] In the twentieth century black boxers tended to dominate the world scene. This fact is highly pertinent to understanding the sport's wider cultural significance, for there seems little doubt that the United States' internal racial conflicts have been writ large in boxing's recent history. The black underclass could see success in this area as a foretaste of a new world to come, while whites often saw black success as threatening their own position in society at large.[188] Thus while church going could just about make a black boxer acceptable, the sporting press often quite openly presented others who appeared less conformist as the enemy to be defeated.[189] This reached its height in the conflicts over Cassius Clay, especially after his conversion to Islam and the adoption of his new name of

[185] Wong Kiew Kit, *Art of Shaolin Kurg Fu*, 184.

[186] The Greeks wore leather thongs (*himantes*) round wrists and knuckles but this was to limit rather than increase the severity of the impact of the blow (the face was the main target). By contrast the Romans used the *caestus*, a glove weighed with iron and with metal spikes on the knuckles. Even this amount of brutality, though, failed to raise boxing very high in the popularity stakes.

[187] So P. Kühnst, *Sports: A Cultural History* (Dresden: Verlag der Kunst, 1996), 123–6. It was the Venice tournaments that made an impression: cf. 67.

[188] This is a central theme of M. Marqusee's *Redemption Song* (London: Verso, 1999), esp. 11–45.

[189] The more positive treatment of Floyd Patterson is a case in point. Sadly, Patterson himself adopted the rhetoric, declaring when Ali first defeated Liston that 'as a Catholic' it was now his duty to 'reclaim the title for America': Marqusee, ibid. 140.

Muhammad Ali. Clay's words were often themselves provocative but the response to his refusal to fight in Vietnam clearly had larger issues in sight than just that question in itself.[190] The irony, therefore, is that by 1996 not only was he chosen to light the flame at the Olympic Games in Atlanta, but also he had in effect become one of the most popular sporting figures in the United States. Of course by now he was suffering from a debilitating disease, and had himself mellowed considerably. So too, though, had the American public, a fact nicely encapsulated by the film *Rocky* (1976) which now allowed the white to be presented as the inarticulate underdog and the black as dominant. Yet from the point of view of our immediate concerns here, more interesting is Ali's change in religious perspective: there is a charity, self-perception, and religious depth that was not there before.[191]

We know from surviving works of art that the faces in particular of Greek boxers were often badly marked by the contests in which they engaged, and that is still often true today. So grace of body is scarcely relevant. What is surprising, however, about the modern cinema is that grace of movement is also seldom taken up as a theme, except in kick-boxing movies where of course we move much nearer to the conventions of the martial arts in any case.[192] Instead, conventional boxing is commonly used as a vehicle for exploring the moral issue of violence. The aim, though, is not normally to condemn boxing as such but rather, more often than not, to celebrate the boxer as someone who precisely because he has learnt to contain violence within rules knows that there are limits beyond which one should not go. From within the British context a good example of this tactic is the starkly named *The Boxer* (1998), starring Daniel Day Lewis. Lewis plays a recently released IRA activist who decides to work within his old area but now for peace. He does so by organizing an ecumenical boxing

---

[190] Ali was deprived of his title and kept out of the ring for three years: 1967–70.

[191] For some examples, D. Miller, *The Tao of Ali* (London: Vintage, 1997), 154, 218, 220, 237.

[192] For two interesting examples, *Deadly Bet* (1993) and *Savate* (2001). The former features a petty gambler and criminal growing to some kind of maturity; the latter a more conventional battle between good and evil. *Savate* could be read on different levels, though, as it contains elements parodying the genre: evil is made to look evil, for example, with 'evil' glances only just emerging from beneath caps, and so forth.

training-ring for teenagers at the local Holy Family Community Centre. It is a gritty story that includes assassination and murder as well as love and fear. A key moment comes in the movie when 'Danny' decides to flee to London where he is engaged to fight. Significantly, he withdraws from the tournament when he is required to give a knock-out blow to someone who is already defeated. Although nothing is explicitly stated, clearly a parallel is being drawn with what is wrong in the Northern Ireland of the time, and Danny returns to Ireland to fight for better social 'rules'. The film ends on a hopeful note, and this is reflected in the concluding shot which has the camera zoom up a church spire to present a view of Belfast as a whole. Almost fifty years earlier John Wayne had starred with Maureen O'Hara in another boxing movie set in Ireland that is an intriguing reversal of what happens in *The Boxer*. This time it is the boxer himself who has violated the rules (through a loss of control resulting in the death of his opponent), and he goes to rural Ireland to escape. Falling in love with a local girl, he refuses to fight her brother when the brother denies her her dowry. Thanks to the local Anglican minister, however, he slowly works his way towards a fight, but one in which the rules and limits can once more be obeyed.[193]

In recent years the film that has probably engaged most with boxing's actual tortured history is *The Hurricane* (1999), starring Denzel Washington.[194] It tells the true story of Rubin 'Hurricane' Carter, a black from a poor neighbourhood who is consistently subjected to white prejudice both as child and adult when he is denied (by white judges) a major boxing title that should rightfully have been his. All this culminates in imprisonment for a murder he did not commit. His fortunes, though, begin to change in prison when a young and deprived black youth persuades some (white) Canadian lawyers to take an interest in his case, and he is eventually released. It is a fine piece of drama and deeply moving. Particularly

---

[193] *The Quiet Man* (1952). Although incidental to the main plot, another recent movie that uses to good effect the contrast between a boxer's insistence on rules and society's perversion of rule would be the crime movie *Snatch* (2000). Brad Pitt gives a powerful performance as a knuckle boxer and gypsy prepared to fight in illegal bouts but not to rig the game.

[194] Bob Dylan wrote a famous protest song based on what happened. His music has subsequently been used by the choreographer, Christopher Bruce, to produce a solo dance work, staged recently and produced by Ballet Rambert.

intriguing is the extent to which religious metaphor and imagery are utilized. In order not to be defeated by the prison system, Carter had made himself as independent as possible of it. This he encapsulates in the formula: 'it is very important to transcend the place that holds us'. However, the boy's concern transforms its meaning into a subsequent declaration that 'hate put me in prison; love is going to burst me out'. Again Carter combines the biblical setting of his own name (Rubin) with that of the boy (Lesra, or Lazarus) to announce his new status: 'behold a son who is raised from the dead'.[195] Transcendence and resurrection have thus come to him not through self-containment but rather from exposure to love and all the possibilities of failure and disappointment he once so feared.

What the two previous paragraphs on boxing films offer is two rather different types of transcendence. Both speak of transcendence of context, in the one case by adhering to the rules of boxing where these are threatened (*The Boxer*), in the other through the boxer transcending his own self-imposed rules (*Hurricane*). The most explicit references to religion are in the earliest of the three films, John Wayne's *The Quiet Man*. But that does not mean that religion has become 'mere metaphor' in the other two. For, whatever the intentions of the directors, it is the argument of this book that it is openness to precisely such experiences of transcendence that can pull us out beyond the purely moral or aesthetic and into the realm of the divine itself, and that is why it is no mere accident that religious imagery is used. In *The Boxer* we learn how by keeping to the rules it is possible to transcend one's environment; in *Hurricane* how one must sometimes break one's own self-imposed rules in order to achieve that transcendence. Either way a new level of reality and its perception are achieved.

Nothing I have said thus far should be taken as implying that any and every sporting film that goes beyond the purely descriptive has an underlying religious dimension. There is in fact no shortage of movies that use sport to deal with issues of moral development that only tangentially, if at all, relate to religion.[196] Religion can even

[195] A combination of Gen. 29: 32 and John 11, building on the biblical Reuben and Lazarus.

[196] Two examples: *This Sporting Life* (1963), starring Richard Harris and Rachel Roberts, is a case of rugby being used to explore emotional frigidity; *Young Blood* (1986), starring Rob Lowe, a case of ice hockey being used to investigate issues connected with moral maturity.

play a central role, and yet the film not advance the kind of sacramental dimension on which I am concerned to focus here.[197] What makes the difference is where the moral issues seem to push beyond themselves into a more transcendent dimension. In what follows examples are now given in turn from baseball, basketball, and golf. Thereafter I shall attempt to draw this discussion to a conclusion with two unusual final illustrations from football and cricket.

From 1989 comes Kevin Costner's *Field of Dreams*. Acting the part of a farmer in rural and remote Iowa, he starts to hear voices in his cornfield, urging him to build a baseball field on that very site. A strange series of adventures then follow: various baseball heroes of the past return from the dead to play, with their appearances culminating in the presence of his own long-dead father. The film ends with father and son reconciled. At one level the film could be read as simply a sustained, metaphorical exploration of someone trying to come to terms with their own past, but, intriguingly, at another it does suggest a thin divide between this world and another, with sport now bearing a rather weightier meaning, of itself embodying the code of honour that could link the two worlds.[198] Unfortunately, this is accompanied by an almost gnostic romanticism about how pure sport can be.[199] In this it is markedly different from another baseball film, *Hardball* (2001), starring Keaunu Reeves. It is a gritty tale of an inveterate gambler who is persuaded to pay off his debts by coaching a team of streetwise black children living on a violent projects estate. Slowly he is won to their side, in part through dislike of corruption in the local league. The film culminates in them winning the league thanks to their youngest 9-year-old player who is killed shortly thereafter in a gang shoot-out. At the funeral Reeves is given the following words: 'In watching him raise his arms in triumph as he ran to

---

[197] As in David Puttnam's splendid *Chariots of Fire* (1981), and the issues surrounding the Presbyterian missionary Eric Liddell and the Jewish Harold Abrahams in the 1924 Olympic Games.

[198] The initial voice declares: 'if you build it, he will come', but only gradually does it becomes clear that the reference is to the principal figure's father. Indeed, the first thought of the person Costner plays is that the allusion is to Shoeless Joe Jackson, 'so graceful and agile'.

[199] One actor is even given the lines: 'The one constant through all the years has been baseball . . . it reminds us of all that was once good and will be again.'

first base, I swear that I was lifted in that moment to a better place. I swear he lifted the world in that moment.' The point of course is not the victory as such, but the way in which coach and players alike have, through their working together for this goal, been caught up beyond their existing corrupt world into a better one. It seems no accident that the language used is essentially religious.

Closer to the false romanticism of *Field of Dreams* is director Robert Redford's golf movie, *The Legend of Bagger Vance* (2000). Here Rannulph Junuh, returning from the First World War to Savannah, discovers that he has lost his golf swing, and takes to the bottle. His former girlfriend organizes a golf tournament in which he is persuaded to take part by a mysterious caddie, Bagger Vance (played by Will Smith), who suddenly appears from nowhere, saying that 'he has come from enjoying God's good earth'. The caddie releases Junuh from the horrors of his war memories and then disappears once more, as Junuh rejoices in almost Neoplatonic terms about how all things are now coming together as one. In an interview Redford has declared that his aim was a spiritual one 'in an age of increasing cynicism'.[200] The photography is lyrical, and the interdependence of all things is certainly more than hinted at. Yet there remains a similar unwillingness to face more complex realities as in the Costner movie.[201] That said, it is interesting to observe how Redford chooses to focus on experiences of immanent unity rather than of transcendence, for given the distances involved in golf shots it is one sport where such imagery might find a natural home. Certainly, the novelist, Christian, and keen golfer John Updike has no hesitation in resorting to such language. It is 'to join one's soul to the vastness that, contemplated from another angle, intimidates the spirit, and makes one feel small', based, as it is for golfers 'on a common experience of transcendence'.[202] Nor does he hesitate to make the religious connections explicit.

---

[200] The interview is attached to both video and DVD. Although the word 'spiritual' is used several times by Redford it is not altogether clear what he means by it.

[201] The film ends with the young boy of the story, now an old man, playing golf despite a heart attack, saying that it is the game that matters, not the winning.

[202] J. Updike, *Golf Dreams* (London: Penguin, 1996), 147, 125.

It is of games the most mysterious, the least earthbound, the one wherein the wall between us and the supernatural is rubbed thinnest. The exaltation of its great spaces; the eerie effortlessness of a good shot...its tranced silences; its altering perspectives...the dread of lostness; the ritual interment and resurrection of the ball at each green—such are the ingredients that make golf seem a magical mirror, and outward projection of an inner self.[203]

This could of course be read as an admission that it is all simply psychological projection, but that is not, I think, Updike's view. Rather, what he means is that the game evokes and confirms certain perceived spiritual realities.

For whatever reason basketball seems a much more earthy pursuit, and this is reflected in the film *He Got Game* (1998) in which Denzel Washington once more stars. It tells the story of Jake Shuttlesworth (Washington) and his son Jesus. Washington is secretly released from prison in order to try and persuade his son to join the state governor's preferred team. The temptations of big money sport are powerfully portrayed, as also the misuse of Jesus' name in team promotion.[204] Both principal characters are flawed; yet both are presented as growing over the course of the film and in ways not unconnected with religion: the father in extending his religious belief beyond self-ambition, the son in discovering self-control and integrity. The film ends with a reference to prayer and a shared ball but speaks of something deeper: the experience of God in the grit of life and not just in pure idealism.[205]

Modern football has plenty of grit. Stories abound of players and managers who have gone off the proper track, understandable perhaps given what huge sums are now involved.[206] Yet after churchgoing, throughout the world football stadiums continue to remain the most popular public venue. That may seem surprising when the present form of the game dates only from 1863 or later, but of course this a function of the increased leisure time now

---

[203] ibid. 151. Cf. also 51, 164, 190.

[204] As the team's 'salvation', he is even portrayed on a cross with a crown.

[205] One might contrast this film with another basketball movie, *Above the Rim* (1994), which also has moral growth but is without any obvious religious dimension. It features the rap star Tupac Shakur as the defeated villain.

[206] For some examples, N. Edworthy, *Football Stories: Bad Boys and Hard Men* (London: Channel 4 Books, 2002). Unfortunately, bad behaviour often seems to increase rather than decrease popularity: e.g. 6, 25: contrast 18.

available to all.[207] Football, though, is in actual fact very much older, and despite its absence now the connections with religion once ran deep. Ball players in Central America seem to have been the first to use a rubber ball, but the game was not played simply for relaxation.[208] On the contrary, the ball was probably taken to represent the sun, and the result was the sacrifice of one or more of the losing players. In those same early days a quite different version was developing in China. This spread under the influence of Buddhism to Japan, and there it has become a matter of graceful handling rather than of winners and losers.[209] Less formal, more rough-and-tumble versions, though, have existed throughout history.[210] If it was muscular Christianity in nineteenth-century public schools and in the old universities that first attempted some degree of codification, it was clergy going out from these same institutions that first spread the sport among their working-class congregations. It is estimated that as many as a quarter of the present teams in the English League owe their origin to the Church.[211] Missionaries also had an impact abroad.

That connection with religion has not always been to the good, but still, on the whole, it has been better than what has happened with politics.[212] In some countries football even became an

---

[207] 26 October 1863 is often treated as the definitive date, but it was only later that hacking was universally banned, and passing the ball became integral largely under the influence of the Scottish team, Queen's Park. For an excellent history of the game, see Terence Stamp's two-set DVD *History of Football: The Beautiful Game* (2002).

[208] E. M. Whittington (ed.), *The Sport of Life and Death: The Mesoamerican Ballgame* (London: Thames & Hudson, 2001). The issues involved are discussed in my second volume in the chapter on sacrifice.

[209] It is known as *kumari* and grace also extends to the type of clothes worn for the occasion.

[210] In English history it was periodically banned, e.g. under Edward II, Henry V, and Henry VIII. In Florence the version known as *calcio storico* is still played to this day. Although few details are known, in the classical world there was a version known as *harpastum* (from the Greek 'to grab').

[211] R. Jeffery, *Pictorial History of English Football* (Bath: Parragon, 1998), 20–5 esp. 22. Everton is given as a typical example, just as Arsenal is of subsequent factory involvement (through the Woolwich Arsenal).

[212] What happened in Glasgow is an obvious exception. Rangers was founded in 1873 as a Presbyterian Boys Club, and did not knowingly sign their first Roman Catholic until 1989. The resultant hostility to the Catholic club Celtic (whose policies, though, were more liberal) fuelled resentment between native Scots and Irish immigrants for over a century. For more details, S. Kuper, *Football against the Enemy* (London: Phoenix, 1994), 205–19.

instrument of national policy, as in pre-war Italy or post-war Ghana.[213] Not that football was alone in this. Prior to the First World War football failed to catch on to any significant degree in the Kaiser's Germany. That was because there gymnastics was being used to enforce a definite political creed.[214] However, it would be a mistake to jump from such examples to the postulation of purely idealistic motives in England. There were conflicts of class, as control of the sport was only very slowly yielded by public-school amateurs to a wider clientele. Again, England believed so deeply in its own effortless superiority over more recent converts in other countries that it did not even join any international organizations such as FIFA until after the Second World War, and that despite clear evidence of growing achievements elsewhere, specially under Weisl in Austria and Dozzo in Italy.

Within such a setting of nationalistic jingoism it is therefore particularly interesting to discover that the first movie ever to have been filmed entirely in Tibetan should take as its subject this 'foreign' game of football, and a young Buddhist novice's determination to see the 1998 World Cup to its conclusion. In *The Cup* (1999) he is caught stealing out at night to watch the matches in a nearby village. None the less, the abbot agrees to let the whole monastery watch the final, provided the boy can raise the rent for a television set. He persuades a new arrival from Tibet to pawn his mother's watch. However, during the course of the match he sees how desperately unhappy the new arrival is without this reassurance of home and slips out to see what he can do to redeem it back. The film is really the story of the triumph of co-operative care and effort over personal ambition, and so of football at its best rather than the so often distorted reality. If the British film *When Saturday Comes* (1995) is typically Western in being more individualistic in its themes, it still uses football to explore interpersonal relationships, with the hero working through his father's fear of failure to his own eventual success on the football field. The key role assigned to his brother's funeral and to his girlfriend's decision in the confessional illustrate how easily essentially moral themes can slide into more

---

[213] In the one case under Mussolini, in the other under Nkrumah who saw it as a way of fostering pan-African unity.

[214] Kühnst, *Sports*, 238–41. Ironically, though, the movement had begun with Romantic and egalitarian ideals: 143–7.

explicitly religious, and that would seem reflected also in how the game itself is experienced. The way in which football crowds respond as 'one huge reactive body' can make the individual more open to other forms of identification with more comprehensive wholes where individuality is also transcended, while it is often claimed for the footballers themselves that the game 'allows players to look beautiful and balletic' and 'achieve a poise and grace' that other sports do not.[215] Whatever Paul Gascoigne was like off the field, one cannot doubt the transformation on the field, particularly in the dexterity of his dummy turns.[216] The lines between moral, aesthetic, and religious may not be clear-cut in such instances, but that does not mean that religious experience is therefore playing no part.

In India one significant landmark on the road to independence was when Bengalis challenged and defeated a British football team.[217] It is only in very recent years that cricket has also begun to experience something of the ambiguities inherent in the modern game of football. It is intriguing, therefore, to find that doubtful new status also reflected in a recent Indian film, *Lagaan* (2001). Of epic length it tells the story of a tyrannous English governor who tells an Indian village that its taxes will be increased despite the absence of rain unless they can defeat the local British team. Although unused to cricket, a team is produced and trained, and it narrowly wins. In contrast to British abuse of power, the Indians demonstrate a co-operative spirit throughout, and this is really what enables them to win, with Muslims, Sikhs, and Harijans alike participating as well as the dominant Hindus.[218] Religious practice is also allowed to enter naturally into the narrative at a number of

[215] The quotations are from Nick Hornby's reflections on the game: *Fever Pitch* (London: Penguin, 2000), 68 (cf. also 178–9), 191. The book has also been made into a film of the same name (1996), starring Colin Firth and Ruth Gemmell and with the love interest correspondingly heightened.

[216] Affectionately known as Gazza, he dominated the football scene in the early 1990s, scoring some astonishing goals by the dexterity with which he was able to simulate moves that seemed to suggest to opponents that he was moving the ball in a quite different direction. Off the field and sometimes on, he was a notorious prankster.

[217] The team Mohun Bagan in 1911.

[218] 'Harijan' is anachronistic in this context, but preferable to 'untouchable'. The term was eventually coined by Gandhi to give the group some dignity as 'children of God'.

key points, in, for example, prayers for rain, the prayers that open the match, and also in the central scene of petition and ritual dancing at a local temple during the three-day interval when things are going badly wrong. In *Lagaan* sport contributes to a deepening sense of a graced world, whereas in *The Cup* sport threatens to undermine community spirit only to have it transformed into grace, as all join in watching the final scene of the game, with the watch restored and thus the young lad reconciled and included.

In the West such an explicit relationship with religion is now exceedingly rare. Even the occasional hymn-singing seems but a hangover from earlier days. Indeed, Western sociologists generally speak of sport acting not as a supplement or complement to religion but as its substitute. Even theologians tend to focus on ethical and political issues rather than on sport's potential to mediate experience of God.[219] Yet it is not at all clear that contrasts are quite so sharp. Spectators' bodies we know respond in similar ways to the players' in anticipating success, in euphoria at a goal, and so forth. Much exercise can in fact be analysed in terms of transcendence, of certain limits being surpassed. If that is so, spectator and player alike can be seen as having such an experience. Of course, this is not the same thing as a religious experience, but there are surely analogies and connections. Indeed, advertising in sport has not been slow to pick up on this fact. Advertising for the footwear company Nike, for example, has made much of this, not merely in suggesting the transcendence of physical limits but also of social and economic as well, and this has sometimes been expressed in more explicitly religious terms.[220] As things have turned out, this policy has not always been to the advantage of the firm, not least when ideal and reality have been demonstrated to be out of kilter. Economically, for example, Nike was shown to be treating its foreign workers badly, while socially it was found to have exploited racial fears and spread rumours of practices that it knew did not exist. To my mind,

[219] This is certainly true of the volume of *Concilium* dedicated to *Sport*: 205 (1989). Even where religious experience raises its head, as in the articles by Ryan and Lenk (110–30), it is Zen that provides the focus, not Christianity. A similar pattern emerges in C. E. Thomas' article on 'Sports' in D. Ness (ed.), *Spirituality and the Secular Quest* (London: SCM, 1996), 498–519.

[220] R. Goldman and S. Papson, *Nike Culture* (London: Sage, 1998). For use of language of transcendence: 19, 71, 97, 153, 174; as substitute for religion: 62, 66, 128, 146.

though, this does not call into question Nike's basic intuition.[221] What it demonstrates instead is how seldom any experience comes pure. It is not that there is some pure experience in sport that Nike has now corrupted and which religion could in any case only feed upon as a leech, as it were. Rather, the experience of transcendence in sport has already implicit in it all such potential ambiguity. The wider resonances of good and bad are already there, and so the sense of being pulled out of oneself into some more profound reality comes through the ambiguity, not contrary to it.

If that is the correct conclusion to draw, it will have important conclusions for the volume that follows this one. That volume will culminate in a treatment of the eucharist, but preceding chapters will focus on such issues as word and music, body and food. In discussing body or sacrifice then, for example, it would seem important that the goal should not be set as some quintessentially unrealizable pure realm that is conceived to be religion. Because Christianity is founded on a belief in someone who was perfect God and perfect human being, it is all too easy to be led astray at this point. Certainly Jesus was celibate, but that does not mean that the sexual body cannot also speak of God, nor indeed that sexual imagery cannot be applied to Christ himself. Again, the unqualified goodness of Jesus' self-offering should not be allowed to refuse value to all other human offerings across the centuries because motivation elsewhere was practically always mixed. Even Jesus' self-offering comes polluted at the time by acts of fickle politicians and a volatile crowd and subsequently through those of a manipulative Church. Again, to take a quite different example, words should not be seen as pure in a way that the visual is not. Even the words of revelation are bound up with the earthly and the ordinarily human, and can only communicate through them. The possibility of corruption in the visual does not therefore automatically make it idolatrous, any more than word can in and of itself protect from such a sin. Instead, Christianity's fixation with word needs to be challenged, and the impurity as well as the glory of the word–experience put on a par with experiences of God mediated in other ways.

---

[221] For mistreatment of Indonesian workers: 180; for false accusations of racial discrimination: 113.

If God comes to us in the eucharist, it has to be through matter as it is: immanent imperfection as well as transcendent otherness. The images of sport that I have discussed speak of a God who is fully engaged with a fallen world. The fact that a summons to transcendence might be received through boxing or a sense of immanent divine presence come while playing one of the martial arts hardly of itself makes these two sports unqualifiedly pure. To argue as I have done in this volume for the re-enchantment of place is thus not naïvely to suppose the influence of such expectations is always good, but it is to insist that the divine can be, and is, mediated through such ambiguity. Theology therefore ignores the issues that consequently arise at the peril of its own eventual irrelevance.

A short concluding chapter follows after the Plates on page 407.

Plates

1. Jacob van Ruisdael's *View of Egmond aan Zee* (1648)

If Calvinism played a key role in the nineteenth century in inspiring the transcendent canvases of the American Hudson River School, its influence in the Netherlands of the seventeenth century was quite different. Of course, the awesome landscape that was so readily available to Church, Cole, and Cropsey on the American continent was not present in Holland's flat terrain. But that can scarcely be the entire explanation. Dutch painters were not above taking licence with the surrounding countryside. Ruisdael himself, for example, made the setting of Bentheim Castle far more majestic than it really is, for both aesthetic and religious purposes. The truth seems to be that the troubles of the times engendered a desire to emphasize in nature primarily not divine transcendence but rather order and the putting of things to right. To judge by the beliefs of his uncle painter Salomon, Ruisdael probably came from a Mennonite family. Although not baptized into a Calvinist community until late in adulthood (in 1657), it is widely believed that he was a liefhebber ('supporter') long before this. Certainly, in this painting it is possible to detect a Calvinist reading of nature, with divine order triumphing over chaos and also thus, by implication, sin. The decaying tree on the left is linked to the church in the distance both by the road below that leads to it and by the bird centrally placed in the sky that is flying from the church towards it. While not all of Ruisdael's landscapes admit of a religious reading, many do. Sometimes nature has a purely positive meaning (in his painting of Bentheim Castle it is used to underline the transience of all human endeavour compared with divine creativity and permanence). Here, however, it seems contrasted with the preached word (the church) that restores order to the world. Dutch landscape painting is discussed on pp. 110–12, the Hudson River School on pp. 115–19.

2. John Constable's *Salisbury Cathedral from the Meadows* (1831)

It is a pity that the painting of Salisbury Cathedral with which most people are familiar is Constable's 1823 version. This was commissioned by Bishop Fisher of Salisbury, the uncle of Constable's good friend, John Fisher. In its original version the uncle did not like a dark, cloudy sky, and this appears to have been lightened especially for him. Constable was certainly irritated by the complaint, and justifiably so because the symbolism of a completely cloudless sky, if allowed, would have been altogether too trite and obvious. This is not to say that Constable was averse to symbolism. In his 1831 version, however, it is employed in such a way that such symbolism is allowed to emerge gradually, and only then after the sheer aesthetic power of the work has been fully absorbed. Constable was a High Tory and a committed Anglican, worried by where all the reforms in Church and State of the time were leading. Catholic Emancipation was passed in 1829, the Great Reform Bill in 1832, and the disestablishment of the Church in Ireland threatened, though not carried into effect until 1869. This painting expresses Constable's own private relief that the worst was over. A rainbow lies over the Cathedral as the storm behind abates, though the windswept character of the tree in front is still noticeable. If the wagon and boat are derived from his *Haywain* without obvious religious intent, the black and white dog in the centre (from *The Cornfield*) perhaps suggests a trust in the divine faithfulness that the rainbow also conveys (Gen. 9: 8-17). Some further remarks on Constable will be found on pp. 120–2.

3. Vincent Van Gogh's *The Sower* of November 1888

Van Gogh greatly admired the way in which Jean-François Millet (1814–75) sympathetically depicted peasant life and labour. After *The Angelus*, one of Millet's best-known paintings in this genre is of *The Sower*. Van Gogh had attempted a copy as early as 1881, where some 'improvements' are already detectable (for example in the leggings), or at any rate improvements on the only copy known to him (by Le Rat). Here, however, as in another painting from this same year he goes one stage further, and seeks to reflect through the painting his own immanent theology. His early belief in the specifics of Christianity is gone, but not his conviction of a caring Providence (cf. Matt. 6: 25–34). The radiant sun hints at his present pantheist conviction, while its position forming a halo round the sower speaks of divine care mediated through others. Van Gogh's work is discussed in more detail on pp. 130–3.

4. Vincent Van Gogh's *The Raising of Lazarus* of May 1890

By July 1890 Van Gogh would be dead by his own hand. In that last year he experienced extremes of mood swings. A number of paintings, however, do express his continuing religious faith. In September of the previous year he had produced variants on a *Pietà* by Delacroix and a head-and-shoulders angel by Rembrandt. Delacroix was also the source for a *Good Samaritan* canvas in May of 1890. However, like the earlier angel it is Rembrandt who inspired the more thorough modifications, as in this present scene, making it something quite independent of the original. In a letter Van Gogh complains of a fellow artist who feels it necessary to include Christ in a depiction of the Mount of Olives: cannot nature be allowed to speak for itself? So here Christ disappears. The two sisters greet the risen Lazarus, one holding the cloth that she has removed from his face. But the chief figure in the biblical narrative (John 11: 1–44) has been replaced by a radiant sun. Significantly, Van Gogh gives Lazarus his own features, and Mary and Martha those of his good friends, Mesdames Ginoux and Roulin.

5. Piet Mondrian's *New York City 1942*

Piet Mondrian 1872-1944. Oil on canvas, 119.3 x 114.2 cm © 2004 Mondrian/ Holtzman Trust c/o hcr@hcrinternational.com. This painting dates from the last stages of his career. His art from this time was greatly affected by his move to New York in 1940. Gone are the large rectangles in primary colours (often divided by black strips) that had dominated his style while he was working in Paris, and in their place has come thin yellow lines crossing thin red and blue against an off-white background. Throughout his abstract work Mondrian remained convinced that it was the painter's task to bring to the surface the underlying form and construction of reality. In some of his early work it is possible to trace through successive works how he dissolves not only nature (for instance, trees) into abstract patterns but also city streets (such as the Paris skyline). Although throughout the patterns remained open at the edges (suggesting further developments), that earlier work conjures up a rather static view of reality, whereas here enthusiasm for the American way of life seems to have brought a real change of heart. Dynamic movement (perhaps suggested by the bustle of New York's streets) is not, he now thinks, incompatible with an underlying simplicity and balance. Mondrian is treated in more detail on pp. 140–4.

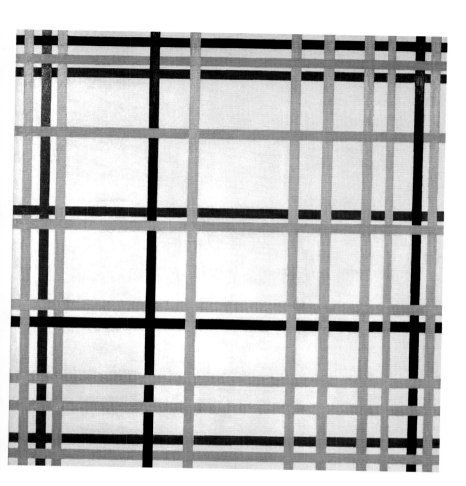

6. Vassily Kandinsky's *On Points* (1928)

This work was produced by Kandinsky while he was teaching at the Bauhaus (along with Klee) at Dessau. As such, it reflects the third period in his style, symbolist representational work and abstract colour canvases now yielding to ones where the primary focus is on the relation between various geometric figures. Here five triangular structures rest on three bars that float loose, the triangles themselves countering an 'attack' from above by some circles, sometimes aided by accompanying smaller triangles, sometimes being repulsed by them. Despite the agitated activity and the free floating base, the overall impression is none the less one of balance. It is a delicate one, however, as visual experiments in removing the square from the bottom right quickly indicate. The title of a 1930 work (*Weak Support*) that achieves a similar precarious harmony makes explicit his admiration for an ordered world that is very finely tuned: harmony is there (shown in the colours no less than the lines), but it is a delicate one with only a slight alteration threatening the whole. Although at this time all Christian symbolism had disappeared from paintings he intended for public exhibition, it is still to be seen in some work he did as a present for his wife and also in his stage designs for *Pictures at an Exhibition* (also 1928). In the latter's *Great Gate of Kiev* we find a hard-won balance, with buildings apparently teetering on the edge of collapse, yet held in place. Even so, some may wonder whether his earlier *Compositions* do not reflect reality better, where an apparent chaos of colour only slowly yields perception of an integrated and resolving pattern. Kandinsky's various positions are analysed on pp. 144–7.

7. English *Psalter World Map* (*c.*1265)

Marking its essentially religious character, the map is presided over by Christ as author and sovereign of the world. His authority is indicated by the small orb he holds in his left hand, while his right hand blesses. Angels swing thuribles of incense over his head. Jerusalem is easily identified at the world's centre, while just beneath Christ Adam and Eve look out from the Garden of Eden, as its four rivers issue from it (Gen. 2: 10–14). With the Red Sea painted literally red and the various strange creatures located in the bottom right (including cynocephali, men with dog's heads), it is easy to dismiss such work as purely mythological. But closer inspection reveals Rome down and just to the left of Jerusalem, with Greece nearer but further left and the Danube further left still. Britain, Ireland, and France too appear (at the bottom left). The distribution of these places says little for the mapmaker's accuracy, but their inclusion (as well as many others) does at least demonstrate clearly his intention, to ensure that biblical history and geography were integrated fully into his own particular world and setting. The varying degrees of accuracy and the symbolic role of medieval maps is explored in more detail on pp. 191–6.

8. The Labyrinth of Chartres Cathedral (dedicated 1260)

Although a number of former labyrinths in French cathedrals have been restored (such as that at Amiens), the best preserved from medieval times is undoubtedly that at Chartres. Although it is now questioned whether, as was once thought, these labyrinths were ever intended as surrogate forms of pilgrimage for those too infirm to travel further afield, they do still connect intimately with the notion of life as pilgrimage in the kind of theology that they sought to convey. Unlike mazes, labyrinths do not admit of the possibility of failure, provided walkers persist in their chosen course. Additionally, the goal always remains visible, no matter how often the circuitous path throws one back near to where one began. Labyrinths can thus be said to encapsulate the divine promise that, provided faith in God's future is maintained, grace will ensure the pilgrims do indeed arrive at the goal they seek. As Chartres was itself a centre for pilgrimage, the message chimes nicely with what was happening elsewhere in the building. The different symbolism behind labyrinths and mazes is investigated further on pp. 225–34.

9. Antoni Gaudí's Güell Colony Crypt (1898–1917)

The unusual title for this building comes from the fact that it was originally commissioned by Gaudí's friend, the industrialist Eusebi Güell, as a church for the new estate he was having built next to his textile factory in the south of Barcelona. Work progressed very slowly, and in the end only the crypt was completed. Even so, the extraordinary originality of Gaudí's ecclesiastical creations is fully evident in this work. Externally, the building is approached through a hall of columns that seems most to resemble a natural cave. That naturalness does nothing, though, to lessen the shock that awaits the visitor as the interior is entered. The supporting columns are of such unusual shape and set at such strange angles that they defy interpretation as human creations; yet at the same time they make the head spin with the thought of their imminent collapse. Technically, the pillars are of course an outstanding success, made possible only thanks to modern building materials and techniques. But that is not their point. The series of sunbursts in the vault is. Something after all keeps the building upright. Just as the sun encourages the growth of trees upwards, so the vaults appear to prevent the columns from toppling over. More profoundly, Christ our Sun unifies and blesses the people of faith, however unsteady their trust is. The innovative work of Gaudí in homes no less than churches is treated further on pp. 310–12.

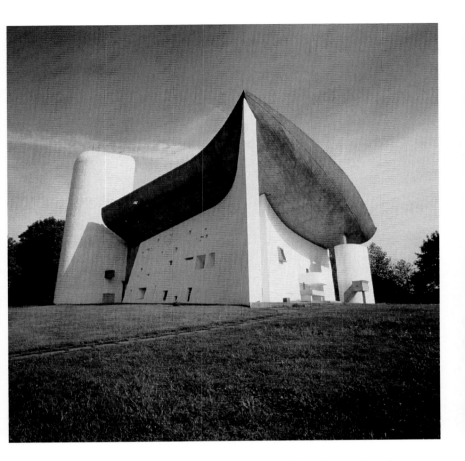

10. Le Corbusier's Notre-Dame-du-Haut at Ronchamp (1955)

Although lacking explicit religious belief, Le Corbusier was not without religious sensibilities. It is therefore intriguing to note that his only major church commission (apart from the very much less successful Dominican monastery of La Tourette) is quite unlike any of his other buildings, so typically modernist and rationalist in style as they are. In his travel journal for 1911 he records his first impressions of the Parthenon: it seemed to grow out of the rock and suggested to him *une fatalité extra-humaine* ('an other-than-human destiny'). Forty years later he insisted that this chapel was based as much on rationalist principles as any of his other buildings, including his well-known modulor system (proportions adapted from the human body). As if in confirmation, it was while Ronchamp was being built that he published his 'Poem to the Right Angle'. Yet there is more to be said. Like the Parthenon, this pilgrimage church of 'Our Lady of the Heights' was approached from below, and so can also suggest something of an organic growth. But, if there is immanence, there is also transcendence. From the outside the irregularly spaced window recesses seem to hark back to the catacombs, while internally the sliver of light entering in the gap between wall and roof has an almost magical feel. Le Corbusier's place in Modernism is discussed on pp. 321–3.

11. Tadao Ando's Church of the Light, Osaka (1989)

Tightly packed into the corner between two streets, the building has been reduced to the barest of essentials. Little more than a compact rectangle with a preaching desk at the front, even the window on the right looks out onto a blank wall. Equally, there is no ornamentation on the interior walls. All this might have resulted for the worshippers in a purely verbal experience of God, were it not for the cruciform window slits that face the people and allow light to stream through. Modern Christianity is most used to finding in the cross divine identification with human suffering. Here, however, as in first-millennium art generally, it is the joy that the cross brings that is being stressed, in victory over sin and death. Nature and revelation are thus for once allowed to speak as one. It is likely that the Japanese context of church and architect also played an important role, for the simplicity of the message and its mediation through nature has obvious parallels in Zen Buddhism. Ando is among a number of contemporary church architects discussed on pp. 333–47.

Interim Conclusion

As already indicated, a sequel to the present work will appear in due course. Its focus will be on how experience of God can be, and has been, mediated through the human body and its various activities, among them (apart from the physical body itself) dance and music, word and food, with the entire programme culminating in a discussion of the eucharist; hence its proposed title: *God and Grace of Body: Sacrament in Ordinary.* There is thus much yet to appear before my discussion can be said to be complete. However, it may be helpful to readers to have some idea of how far I hope to have carried them thus far. This I can best do, by addressing them under three different sorts of category: as religious believers or explorers, as theologians, and as philosophers of religion. Some will of course fall under more than one category.

In the modern developed world there is now, I believe, a huge mismatch between the Church and how people at large experience the divine. It is not that the latter have ceased to believe in the supernatural or only identify it in a very crude way (though this is of course sometimes so) but that, when they attend a church service, the ritual no longer seems to evoke any immediate or intuitive response. In part this is perhaps a good thing, as the Church can scarcely claim to have a distinctive gospel unless there are elements that sit ill with existing presuppositions. But the problem is that more often than not, so far from being challenged, the non-Christian simply experiences no reaction at all. The Christian and unchurched theist appear to be on quite different wavelengths. That is one reason why the exercise in natural religion upon which I have been engaged in this book seems to me of no small moment. It takes seriously the great tracts of human experience that the Church and its theologians once took seriously but now generally see as peripheral to its concerns. The natural world, the layout of a town or garden, the structure of a specific building, a basketball shot can all induce religious feelings that ought not to be summarily dismissed as though necessarily inferior to a Christian's experience of response to prayer or of worship in a church. God can be encountered in both types of experience alike as a given, the former exhibiting the same non-instrumental character that worship ought rightly to have. Inevitably, worship gets distorted when we ask for its point, for it is not there to build up the community (though it may incidentally achieve that function), nor is it there because God needs our praise. It is there simply as an expression of who we are and how we stand in relation to God. So, similarly, with the experiences I have been discussing. To ask what practical purpose a particular building style serves or to reduce gardening or sport to questions of exercise or relaxation is already to distort their potential. Their capacity for opening us to a world of divine enchantment lies precisely in resisting such pressures.

What may make some hesitate, though, is the fact that so many of the forms I have discussed have a strongly human contribution. At least with nature, it may be said, one can talk of divine creation, whereas in so many of the other areas mentioned it was a matter of human construction trying to induce certain experiences. What such an objection ignores, though, is that this is no less true of experiences in worship. Preacher and liturgist are alike concerned to establish the best conditions under which Christ can be encountered in sacrament or preached word. Of course, there is this seeming difference that the Christian believes God to have promised in the biblical revelation to vouchsafe himself under precisely those conditions. But defenders of the experiences discussed here could appeal to a not dissimilar promise for what they have in mind within nature itself. Gothic spires linking earth and heaven can appeal to mountains and standing stones performing a similar role, the regularity of patterns in ornament to the regularity of patterns in leaves or in human anatomy. Again, if something about human nature is revealed in the fact that town planning at its best provides both security and openness, it also may tell us something about God, because that is the way God has made us. So it should not therefore come as a wholly unexpected surprise that the fulfilment of those two needs is sometimes, as I argued, at its most effective in a much more explicitly religious situation, namely in the phenomenon of pilgrimage.

Much academic theology, though, is likely to remain deeply suspicious of my approach, even where it is bolstered, as here, with some account of the connections between the human contributions and the understanding of nature on which they are based. The uniqueness of the biblical revelation, it will be claimed, is inevitably undermined by any such gradualism that allows one to move from outside towards the Church's principal sacrament and its celebration of the unique significance of Christ's life, death, and resurrection, as I shall do in the second volume. But the stronger this contrast is made, the more problematic does the relevance of the biblical revelation become, for then there is little or nothing upon which God can be seen to build. Even as an answer to sin, revelation surely only makes sense if sin is found to be fundamentally a distortion of what nature already reveals of the creator God's intentions. So the eucharist is best viewed as the supreme sacrament not because it offers a complete contrast to the way the world is, but rather because it represents the culmination of how God is perceived to act elsewhere in his world, through material reality. Food, body, and sacrifice, as the second volume will try to illustrate, already have multiple symbolic resonances in natural religion, and so Jesus in instituting communion built on these, as well as in some respects challenging them. Nor did he build on these alone. If the connections are less obvious in the case of what has been discussed in this volume, that does not mean that they do not exist. So, for instance, if my analysis of pilgrimage is right, there is a tension inherent within it not unlike communion, one in which one's present locality is relativized but not trashed by being placed in the context of some more powerful alternative. Again, and more fundamentally, the dynamic of transcendence and immanence that has run through this volume can for the Christian be seen to find its appropriate culmination in a God who is willing to focus his presence in a tiny wafer yet is at the same time someone whom the heavens cannot contain. So there is simultaneously a drawing close and yet an immeasurable distance remaining.

Some of my fellow theologians may not be entirely adverse to some of these comparisons, but still object that they are, methodologically, the wrong way round. In the final analysis everything must be measured by the canon of Scripture; otherwise chaos is the inevitable result. As my two earlier volumes on the nature of revelation sought to make clear, to me this seems a quite impossible ideal. The deposit of revelation has only superficially remained the same. In practice it has been in constant process of change, as new contexts have thrown up fresh challenges that demanded that the text be read in new ways. This emphatically does not mean that the Church's understanding of revelation is simply reactive and culturally determined (the text has the power to critique, as well as respond to, context), but it does entail that it does not exist as a self-contained unit. For example, I simply cannot credit that the modern Christian belief in the equality of the sexes has been generated from the biblical text itself.[1] To acknowledge external factors does of course make criteria more difficult, but it seems to me that those who insist on purely internal ones are really engaging in a form of self-deception in supposing their own applications clear-cut. Take Hell, homosexuality, or female leadership, and it is far from clear why purely in terms of the texts themselves a different set of verses should now be prioritized over others as compared with what once the case.[2]

Such comments, though, are better put more positively. It is not that grace is something uniquely dispensed through the Christian community. God has been addressing humanity at large throughout human history both in its experience of the natural world and in the various ways in which it has expanded upon that experience in its own creativity. Theologians like to use the phrase 'scandal of particularity' affirmatively, and in this they are right, in so far as for God to be incarnate at all he had to be incarnate at a particular time and place and so with all the specificities of context. But it does become a scandal in a bad sense if this is then taken to mean that God's address to all other contexts can therefore be ignored. On the contrary, the less widely that address is found, the less plausible does God's love of his creation, and indeed his very existence, become. So, just as in my volumes on revelation I sought to rebel against conventional ways of approaching that issue and to insist on revelation continuing into the subsequent history of the Church, so here equally I want to distance myself from those who think that sacramentality can only be approached by beginning with the historical Christ.

That may seem to place me closer to those who see philosophy of religion as an essential prolegomena to doctrine, but once again I do

---

[1] For my critique and an alternative derivation, see my *Discipleship and Imagination* (Oxford: Oxford University Press, 2000), 11–31.

[2] On hell, see *Discipleship and Imagination*, 130–45, 158–60.

not find myself wholly in agreement with current approaches. Those who have followed my discussion from the beginning will have appreciated that it has more the character of what used to be known as natural religion rather than philosophical theology, that is to say, it characterizes religion in the absence of specific revelation rather than offers formal arguments for God's existence. Philosophers like to believe themselves above the vagaries of context and culture, but, just as the meaning of the biblical text is affected by such factors so too is what philosophers say. That is one reason why I explored in Chapter 2 how Platonism could be applied in two opposing directions in discussion of icons and at the Renaissance. In my view this is by no means an isolated example. The sadness is that the more philosophers insist on examining purely formal arguments and ignoring empirical and cultural realities, the less likely they are to persuade the great mass of their contemporaries. One area where this seems especially so is in analyses of religious experience. There is in my view insufficient acceptance of the fact that there is no such thing as experience of God *tout court*; it always comes mediated in some way. Of course it is not necessarily mediated through the material order, and so not necessarily sacramental. Some forms of mystical experience, for instance, are without obvious props. None the less, even here there is mediation in the types of imagery used to describe the experience, and so conditioning by one form of religious culture rather than another. So such questions simply cannot be avoided.

Very few these days find the conventional arguments for God's existence in any way convincing or persuasive. That does not mean, though, that there is nothing to be said on the matter. It is not as though there is a neutral base to human experience in terms of which religion must be convicted as an unnecessary further layering. Rather, layering inevitably occurs, in numerous ways including religious, and so the question becomes which of the many possibilities fleshes out our experience the best. If there really is a God who as creator is at the ground of all we are, then one would expect some matching between our own experience and that greater reality. Modern philosophers reflect the society in which they live (and the Church of which they may be members) in confining significant religious experience to a rather narrow range. The net result is the reduction of the relevance of God to a very small area of human life. What we need to do instead is take more seriously the great range of human experience in which God was also once found by Christians and which implicit religion continues to explore.[3]

The advantage of the types of experience that I have sought to identify here is that they are not easily exposed to the usual objection that religious experience in the final analysis collapses into moral or aesthetic. That is one reason why I have deliberately avoided, so far as possible, experience that is mediated through people (the transcendence or care can then be seen as really belonging to the human mediator). It is also why I have protested so strongly over the reduction of the experience of place to some moral or aesthetic evaluation, so commonplace now as to be virtually the norm in contemporary theological writing on the subject. Supposedly, idolatry is involved if places or buildings are valued in their own right. I could not disagree more. The enchantment of a sense of mediated divine presence came in the past (and can continue to come) precisely because buildings or places are valued in their own right, irrespective of the contribution for good or ill that they make to the wider world. So, as I argued in Chapter 4, it is one thing to offer a moral evaluation of imperial Rome under Augustus, quite another to ask what kind of religious experience might have been mediated through its layout and religious buildings. Of course, moral questions can still be asked, but the poor ought not to be deprived of the little that they have to uplift their spirits by demeaning the sense of divine presence that is mediated to them, and that despite all the evil that went into the creation of imperial or Hindu temples or even major Western cathedrals such as my own.

[3] What I am hinting at here is the need to go beyond the formal analyses that characterize the writings of Richard Swinburne and Alvin Plantinga. In the former's case, the argument from religious experience forms the linchpin of his justification of belief in God, but it is achieved by a formal strategy (the principle of credulity) not by detailed analysis. Again, Plantinga follows William Alston in using a perceptual image to explicate his use of Calvin's *sensus divinitatis*. But does 'feeling' take us very far unless we look at the specifics of what facilitates that feeling, and then might we not discover that feeling is the wrong emphasis, with more structured correlates possible? R. Swinburne, *The Existence of God* (Oxford: Clarendon Press, 1979), 244–76; W. Alston, *Perceiving God: The Epistemology of Religious Experience* (Ithaca: Cornell University Press, 1991); A. Plantinga, *Warranted Christian Belief* (New York: Oxford University Press, 2000), 172–84 esp. 180–1.

But, it may be said, even if my analysis of such experience is acceptable there is still too little in it to tell us much about God. It all depends what one is after. Certainly, there is nothing here that offers guidance about the specifics of moral conduct. Nor can the experiences in and of themselves establish the usual absolutes that are applied to God: omnipotent, omniscient, and so forth. But, if I am anywhere near right, they do something infinitely more precious, they show a God present and actively concerned throughout his world, a world in which experience of the divine was once the norm and not the exception, and can be so again. Were I writing as an analytic philosopher, I would of course have presented this material quite differently, and perhaps some day I will. In the meantime, though, I have a much more important objective, interest in the experiences themselves and their recovery to human consciousness, not just as part of an argument. For it is only by the former method that enchantment can return to our world, and it is such enchantment that I wish to pursue further in the volume that will follow this one in due course.

APPENDIX

The Internet as Visual Resource

In giving book references for all the various images I have utilized during the course of my discussion, I have tried wherever possible to make use of the most easily accessible rather than expensive, definitive editions. Even so, readers may at times have felt frustrated that the relevant book was not on their shelves or in their local library, and that my own description has failed to give them an adequate sense of what the painting or piece of architecture is about, though I have tried my best. I therefore list here some of the ways in which their computer could help. The particular image in question may not be available, but related ones by the artist will be, and so some idea conveyed. Both the address and the site name are given, as sometimes it may be easier to use a search engine. All websites were accessed on 30 January 2004.

Architecture

Ando: Tadeo Ando in Design Boom (includes illustration of Church of Light, Osaka). At http:// www.designboom.com/ eng/interview/ando.html

Botta: Mario Botta Architetto with section on sacred space. At http:/www.botta.ch/.

Cologne Cathedral: (Willkomen in Hohen Dom zu Köln). Virtual tour under Rundgang at http:// www.koelner-dom.de.

Le Corbusier: Ein kleiner Streifzug durch sein Werk with generous and unusual illustrations at http:// www.tu-harburg.de/b/ kuehn/lecorb.html.

Coventry Cathedral: Good detailed survey at http://www. exponet.co.uk/cathedral/(follow virtual tour).

Durham Cathedral: detailed historical tour at http:// www.dur. ac.uk/~dlaowww/c_tour/ cathedral.html.

Ecclesiological Society: Useful number of links for various county guides and also London churches at http://www.ecclsoc.org/.

Gaudí: Gaudí Central—very helpful at http://www.op.net/ ~jmeltzer/gaudi.html (good on specific works). Gaudi 2002— images by professional photographers, excellent, especially on details at http://www.gaudi2002.bcn.es.

Hawksmoor: Hawksmoor Church Walk—good number of photographs, though only in black and white—at http://www.dave. org.uk/cgi-bin/pics/ hawksmoor.

Hindu temples: TempleNet—good illustrations and commentary at http://www.templenet.com. Indian Temples Portal—commercial site for organized pilgrimages, but also good for illustrations—at http:// indiantemplesportal.com.

Mackintosh: Charles Rennie Mackintosh Society—virtual tour of Queen's Cross church at http:// www.crmsociety.com. Glasgow School of Art—virtual tour of the school at http://www.gsa. ac.uk.popclose.html. House for an Art Lover—virtual tour available at http:// www.houseforanartlover.co.uk/.

Mosques: Mosques and the World—world survey—at http:// www.Islamicity.com/Culture/MOSQUES. For Isfahan at http://isfahan.apu.ac.uk./ masjed/masjed.html.

Pugin: Augustus Welby Northmore Pugin—excellent range—at http://www.pugin/com. Victorian Web—also helpful, though only in black and white—at http://www.Victorianweb.org/art/ architecture/pugin/gallery2/html.

Renaissance and Baroque: stronger on classicism but plenty of illustrations at http://www.lib.virginia.edu/ dic/colls/arh102/.

Romanesque: Art et Architecture Romane et Gothique en France— plenty of examples at http:// www.romanes.com/biblio/.

St Paul's Cathedral: For some basic information about the buildings with illustrations: http:// www.stpauls.co.uk. The virtual tour panorama is currently being turned into a paying site.

Thomson: Single image of each of his works at http://www.scotcities.com/greekthomson.htm and at http://www.glasgowguide.co. uk/ images_agt_stv.html. Queen's Park Church interior— delay in images, but worth waiting for at http://www.scran.ac.uk/ dl/ale/al.htm.

Wright: Frank Lloyd Wright in Oak Park Illinois—good tour of Unity Temple at at http://www.oprf.com/ flw/.

As a general resource, try the architects index in Great Buildings on Line at http:// www.greatbuildings.com/architects.html.

Artists

Most large galleries now have their own illustrated website, but there are two disadvantages to pursuing a particular artist in this way. It varies from gallery to gallery how many of their paintings are on the web; secondly, there may in any case be very few examples of that particular artist's work in their possession. So one is likely to learn more by using one of the more general sites listed below, and then consulting the index.

Artchive: Click on Artchive after opening to get alphabetical list (small donation requested). Analysis of some paintings on offer e.g. two of Hopper's; also some rarities e.g. Tanner. At http:// www.artchive.com.

Artcyclopedia: at http:/www.artcyclopedia.com/artists/and then the artist concerned e.g. Mondrian. The one disadvantage of this site is that, although it has easily usable links to other galleries, it does not inform users in advance which specific paintings they are likely to find there.

Icons: Two good sites, one Orthodox Icons at http://www.ocf. org/OrthodoxPage/icons, the other Russian Icons at http:// www.auburn.edu/academic/liberal_arts/foreign/russian/icons/.

Olga's Gallery: at http://www.abcgallery.com/and then letter and name, e.g. P/Poussin. Biography and lots of illustrations but without commentary.

The Web Gallery of Art: at http://gallery.euroweb.hu/.Excellent range of illustrations but only for artists before 1800.

Web Museum, Paris: at http://www.ibiblio.org/ wm/paint/auth/ and then the artist concerned, followed by/. Number of illustrations varies, not necessarily in accordance with importance, e.g. Cézanne, 100; Kandinsky, 16; Mondrian, 5.

Occasionally specific artists are especially well catered for:

Van Gogh: complete catalogue at http://www.vangoghgallery. com.

Ruisdael: Netherlands Radio site that includes twelve-minute talk on artist, stressing religious input. At http://www.rnw.nl/ culture/html/ rusidaelo2073.html.

Gardens

Zen Gardens: The Japanese Garden offers excellent tours of numerous Zen gardens at http://academic.bowdoin.edu/zen/. Japanese Zen Gardens focuses on rock and sand gardens in Kyoto, but without commentary at http://phototravels.net/japan/photo-gallery/japanese-rock-gardens.html.

INDEX